To Simon —

thank you so much for all
the help & support you have given
Lorna & Me.

Allan M Hodgson.

PREACH THE WORD!

PREACH THE WORD!

The Call and Challenge
of Preaching Today

General Editor

Greg Haslam

Sovereign World

Sovereign World Limited
Ellel Grange
Ellel
Lancaster LA2 0HN

ISBN 1 85240 443 4

Transcription and editing by Sandy Waldron
Typeset by CRB Associates, Reepham, Norfolk
Cover design by Terry Dugan Design
Printed in Malta

To my three sons,
James Duncan, Andrew Alexander and Joshua Paul,
three outstanding men of God.
May they, along with many others,
become a voice for Truth to this generation.

CONTENTS

CONTENTS

FOREWORD

A story that comes from America's Deep South tells of a pastor who came up for 'recall' time. Having preached only one basic sermon during the previous year, the pastor was sure he would not receive a vote by the congregation to continue. But he got a unanimous recall. He tried to preach better the following year but he really only had one sermon. With recall time approaching, he told his wife to get packing – they were sure to be turned down this time. Lo and behold, another unanimous recall!

He worked very, very hard to improve during the third year. But the poor man wasn't really a preacher. He delivered virtually the same sermon every week. This time there was no doubt in his mind that he and his wife should prepare to leave at last. To his astonishment, he got another unanimous recall. The pastor finally got the nerve to say to the deacons, 'Now look here. You know and I know I am not much of a preacher. Yet you keep giving me unanimous recalls. Why?' The reply: 'It is very simple, Pastor, we never wanted a preacher in the first place.'

The place of preaching in the Church generally has been diminishing in ever-increasing measure for many years. This is partly owing to a preference for a particular type of liturgy, partly too because some Christians enjoy a certain style of worship far more than preaching, but also – let's face it – because of the lack of good, enjoyable and gripping preaching.

Dr Martyn Lloyd-Jones once said he was amazed that people even go to church at all these days, referring to the lack of joy in the services and the low standard of preaching in so many places. He described some preachers as being 'perfectly orthodox, perfectly useless'. When we first moved to London and I was just beginning at the Chapel, not knowing for sure how long we should stay, he surprised me by saying that a preacher – far from being merely sound not to mention colourless – should be 'a bit of a showman', a comment that many of us would not expect him to make. The best preachers in church history were, simply, enjoyable. The great Charles Spurgeon and G. Campbell Morgan are examples of this.

My brilliant successor Greg Haslam has performed a great service for the Church generally and preaching particularly by bringing together some of the best preachers in Britain – both to speak at Westminster Chapel and now to publish their sermons. This has been a remarkable feat indeed. I salute Greg – and all the preachers presented in this book for what they have done. This book should be required reading for every theological seminary and Bible college in the world, not to mention that every preacher under the sun should have this valuable volume on their shelves. But people in the pew may be the ones to be most fascinated of all by a glimpse into great preaching which they will get from this book.

The preachers Greg invited to the Chapel for his seminars are beautifully prepared, far from boring, and provide a superb example of the kind of preaching needed today. This selection provides a wide variety of preaching styles as well as diverse theological opinions under an evangelical umbrella. We are all different, we must all be utterly ourselves, and it is encouraging to me that, in all our frailty, *'we have this treasure in jars of clay to show that this all-surpassing power is from God and not from us'* (2 Corinthians 4:7).

R.T. Kendall
Key Largo, Florida
March 2006

ABOUT GREG HASLAM

The General Editor Greg Haslam was born in Liverpool, Merseyside in 1953. He became a Christian in 1967 whilst attending a television relay of a Billy Graham Crusade being held in London. Two years later, at the Keswick Convention in Cumbria, he felt called to the pastoral ministry through the preaching of John R.W. Stott on 2 Timothy – '*Guard the Gospel*'. He began preaching a year later.

In 1975 he graduated in Theology and History at Durham University, and that same year married Ruth. They have three sons, James (married to Emily), Andrew and Joshua.

After twenty-one years as Pastor of the Winchester Family Church, he was invited to become the Minister of Westminster Chapel, London, in March 2002 where he instituted the *Preach the Word!* preaching school, 'designed to raise the profile, quality and central importance of preaching in the Church's mission today'.

In addition to bringing to birth this book, Greg has written three others, and is presently working on two other titles.

He travels extensively in both the UK and internationally, and is in demand as a preacher and conference speaker among the wider Body of Christ.

DETAILS OF CONTRIBUTORS

Stuart Bell is the Senior Leader of New Life Christian Fellowship, Lincoln, a growing church of 800+. He also leads the network 'Ground Level', comprising over seventy-five church leaders from various denominations and networks who are dedicated to evangelism in the UK and Europe. Stuart's insight and revelation in Scripture, along with his humour, make him a popular speaker at conferences nationally and internationally. He is the author of three books, *In Search of Revival*, *Rebuilding the Walls* and *Sane Spirituality*.

Steve Brady is Principal of Moorlands College. He preaches with depth, clarity and, if need be, hilarity. He is a man of faith – he has to be, he's an Everton supporter!

Colin Dye is a man of great vision for revival and world mission. He is the Senior Pastor of Kensington Temple, one of the largest churches in London, and a National Team Leader in the Elim Pentecostal movement.

Michael Eaton helps lead the Chrisco Fellowship of Churches in Nairobi, Kenya – an outstanding and God-centred Bible expositor. He is the author of many fine commentaries for a wide readership.

Joel Edwards is the General Director of the Evangelical Alliance UK. Joel's vision is to see the Church become a movement together to bring biblical transformation to society.

Liam Goligher is the Senior Pastor of Duke Street Church, Richmond and is a conference speaker both in the UK and USA. He is the author of three books.

Philip Greenslade presently works with CWR as Course Director for the postgraduate programme and the church leaders' programme. He is also Consulting Editor for the new daily reading programme *Cover to Cover Every Day*. He is an insightful and popular author of several books including *A Passion for God's Story, Leadership* and *1 Peter: Living Hope*.

David Holden is based at New Community Church, S.E. London and travels internationally for the *Newfrontiers* team, particularly helping national team leaders.

J. John is regarded as one of the most creative speakers in the UK. He has an appeal that transcends gender, age, culture and occupation. His much-loved art of story-telling helps people to discover spiritual meaning in a way that makes sense of everyday life.

Jeff Lucas pastors a church in Colorado and is a leader of Spring Harvest in the UK. He is a widely respected teacher, columnist and author, blending 'seriously funny' humour and incisive comment.

David Pawson is a well-known Bible teacher and author, with a stirring voice to the Church. He has a worldwide itinerant ministry to Christian leaders and a ministry to men of all denominations.

Mike Pilavachi is founder and leader of Soul Survivor, a youth organisation seeking to reach, disciple, equip and empower young people to make a difference in their generation. He is also an author, international speaker and the pastor of Soul Survivor Watford, a congregation aiming to reach out to the young people of Watford.

Michael Ramsden is the European Director of the Zacharias Trust. He is a passionate evangelist who presents an apologetic for the gospel in a lively manner which appeals to the thinking sceptic.

Stuart Reid has an apostolic ministry based at the King's Church Amersham, serving five other churches in the Chilterns, as well as churches in Ghana and Peru.

Mark Stibbe is the Senior Leader at St Andrew's Church Chorleywood and is known internationally as a teacher and author of great clarity and sensitivity to the Holy Spirit.

John Stott is known worldwide for his outstanding Bible exposition and many New Testament commentaries that have brought the Bible alive for millions of readers.

Terry Virgo is based at the Church of Christ the King, Brighton and leads the *Newfrontiers* team, which is currently serving nearly 500 churches in over twenty-five nations. A well-known Bible teacher, Terry speaks at conferences around the world. He has written several books including *No Well-Worn Paths*, *Does the Future Have a Church?* and *God's Lavish Grace*.

Doug Williams is London Regional Superintendent for the Assemblies of God, and a highly respected motivational conference speaker and worship leader. He pastors Emmanuel Christian Centre, Walthamstow.

Chris Wright is International Ministries Director of the Langham Partnership International (LPI). LPI, founded by John Stott, is committed to strengthening Majority World churches through leadership development. Formerly Principal of All Nations Christian College, Chris is also an Anglican minister, preaches at All Souls, Langham Place, London, and is a popular lecturer and writer on Old Testament subjects.

INTRODUCTION

Back in the 1960s, American folk singer Bob Dylan sang, *'The times they are a changin''*. He was right. In the last forty years we have seen both 'the best of times' and 'the worst of times'. The Church has experienced *'times of refreshing . . . from the presence of the Lord'* (Acts 3:19 NKJV), with massive church growth in many parts of the world, a renaissance of outstanding biblical scholarship, and extraordinary seasons of Holy Spirit renewal and revival. At the same time, we have lived through some of the greatest crises in world history.

In changing times, one thing does not change: the quiet but insistent call of God to preach the gospel. Yet there has been a widespread loss of confidence in the Scriptures and growing confusion about their message. As a result, our witness has often been muted, timid and unclear.

One of the greatest casualties has been the decline of bold, authoritative and powerful popular preaching. Many critics have predicted the total demise of preaching from church life altogether, since it is increasingly seen as an outmoded relic of a former age. The result of this loss has been a widespread leakage of spiritual power, declining numbers and stunted spiritual growth in many churches.

In the autumn of 2003, at Westminster Chapel, we embarked upon a preaching school that sought to provide a remedy for this problem. It was simply called *Preach the Word!* My hope was that it would help raise the calibre, profile and effectiveness of authentic biblical preaching across every denomination and stream in the Body of Christ.

A wide range of outstanding teachers, preachers and communicators were invited to share their skills, wisdom and strongest convictions on a host of themes related to this great task, and a large number of delegates gathered each month to give them an enthusiastic hearing. The transcripts of these teaching sessions have been edited and distilled into this single volume, in an effort to reach and engage an even wider audience. These presentations will encourage renewed confidence in the importance of this ministry, and impart practical know-how in its development, both in beginners just starting out on this call as well as those considerably more experienced in the work. Men and women of all ages, who are called to this task, will benefit greatly from this extraordinary collection.

My dream is that through this book, the legacy that Westminster Chapel has long stood for, namely, the marriage of outstanding ministry of the Word of God together with strong dependence on the power of the Holy Spirit, will continue its impact and help foster the healthy marriage of Word and Spirit in the wider Body of Christ – a union that is vital if we are to bring great hope to both the Church and the world throughout the twenty-first century.

The planning and production of this work has been a labour of love for all those concerned. My special thanks to my eldest son James Haslam, who first put the idea for such a conference into my head, and regularly urged me to get on with it. Also to Sandy Waldron, for her painstaking and excellent work in transcribing and first-editing each recorded talk, and transforming it into highly readable prose.

Also to Chris Mungeam, Managing Director of Sovereign World, for his vision and constant enthusiasm for this project. This book represents his final published volume, crowning an outstanding career and legacy of over forty years in Christian publishing. And finally, my gratitude to my loyal and faithful PA, Beryl Grogan, for her intensive work in arranging the *Preach the Word!* conference and, subsequently, in connection with many behind-the-scenes tasks related to its appearance in print.

Greg Haslam
Minister
Westminster Chapel, London

Section One

PREACH THE WORD!

Preach the Word;
be prepared in season and out of season;
correct, rebuke, encourage – with great patience
and careful instruction.

(2 Timothy 4:2)

Chapter 1

PREACH THE WORD!

Greg Haslam

To set the scene for what is to follow in this chapter, allow me to take the reader on a brief 'magical mystery tour'. We are taking a day trip to a medium-sized town called 'All-is-not-well-ville' – a community of around 40,000 people boasting several Christian congregations of various stripes across the spectrum of ecclesiastical style and preference. It's Sunday, 11.30 a.m. and services in the various churches are already under way.

At St Botolph-in-the-Marsh, the vicar has just finished his six-minute homily consisting of the usual quasi-political platitudes and bland moralism – this week concerning the recent local borough council elections. Amazingly, some of the parishioners are still awake.

In a newly refurbished warehouse across town, preparations are under way for tonight's monthly 'Nine o'clock Café', featuring an experimental youth service that is participative, multi-sensory and multi-linear. It will be accompanied by smoke machines, a simulation of the quakings of Mount Sinai through sound effects, and a laser show designed to capture the awesome moment the Ten Commandments were given to Moses. The evening will conclude with poetry readings on the Commandments for Cool Christians Today.

The organ fades at a little non-conformist church in Sarcophagus Street, just in time for a short presentation on 'Kindness to Kittens', followed by an offering for the work of the Royal Society for the Prevention of Cruelty to Animals. The forty-five-minute service will be over, punctually, at twelve o'clock, or else!

Meanwhile, the 'Faithful Remnant', as they like to call themselves, at Bethesda Chapel in Straight Street settle down for some 'sound' teaching, which actually means more endless recycling of Bible truth for Bible students that no one has the least intention at all of doing anything about.

And at the fast-growing Space Cadets mega-church, in their purpose-built glass and steel cathedral on the other side of town, Pastor Robby More ('That's M-O-R-E: more for me, more for you!') is showing a twelve-minute video on 'Improving your golf swing', to be followed by an eight-minute presentation on the 'spiritual lessons to be learned by hole-in-one believers on the fairway of life'.

Here ends our day trip. If these cameos have any accuracy at all, and I believe they do, then much of the Body of Christ is being fed on a sustained, low-calorie diet of hard-tack, junk-food, cardboard and pap. Clearly, all is *not* well in All-is-not-well-ville. These various well-meaning departures from the true biblical priorities of God's people have resulted in at least seven long-term effects:

1. Both quantitative and qualitative growth in the Church of Jesus Christ has been significantly stunted in the West for decades, perhaps for a century or more.
2. Passion for Jesus Christ has almost died, even among the once faithful.
3. The Bible itself lies largely unknown by most, forgotten and neglected somewhere.
4. Faith has well-nigh faded from view in terms of its expression in vigorous prayer, in effective apologetic and interface with the world, and in terms of action that transforms lives and communities.
5. The big picture that the Bible presents, our whole world and life view, has almost totally been forgotten and is barely understood by even a minority of the Christian Church.
6. Cults and false religions have seemingly triumphed in many respects, filling the vacuum left by our abdication of responsibility and retreat from our priorities.
7. The lost have dismissed both us and our message as weightless and irrelevant – irrelevant to their lives and to the ultimate questions that are plaguing them at this time in our nation.

We have to admit that it is very difficult at the present time to preach the truth of the Word faithfully in the West. One observer of recent trends, an American writer called George Target, has said, 'Preaching is a sacred relic, a dubious thing of withered skin and dry bones, enclosed in a reliquary of fond remembrance, still encrusted with the jewels of a former glory.' That negative assessment of preaching is actually widespread today. Those who attempt to do it, therefore, are deemed to be dinosaurs – relics from a bygone era who are leading a remnant of what we could call 'Jurassic Park churches', churches full of the long-dead or dying remains of creaking old fossils. They are creatures that failed to make the transition to post-modernity and to post-evangelicalism.

Even Webster's Dictionary defines preaching as 'exhorting in an officious and tiresome manner'. If that is the case, then no wonder Madonna sang, 'Papa, don't preach'. Much preaching today actually unsettles and disturbs no one. It just fires blanks. It is too short, too trite, too boring, too empty, or too powerless to knock the wings off a gnat, let alone shake a man or woman to their boots. It is no wonder, therefore, that people are staying away from our churches Sunday by Sunday in their millions, opting instead for watching low-key breakfast shows on TV, or taking a leisurely and satisfying stroll through the Sunday newspapers, or simply lying in bed later after a busy and tiring week.

We need to remind ourselves that this has not always been the case. Someone once defined preaching as 'thirty minutes in which to wake the dead', and it was the Scottish theologian P.T. Forsyth's conviction that, 'The Church rises or falls by her preaching.'[1] I happen to believe this is true. Good preaching *shapes lives*. It renews and reforms churches to become forces to be reckoned with. It can even transform whole towns, communities, even nations, as the marvellous legacy of church history can demonstrate.

Frederick W. Robertson, the nineteenth-century preacher based in Brighton, once spoke of what he called 'the intense excitement of preaching'! Presumably he meant his own excitement and that of his hearers. Andrew Blackwood, who taught generations of seminarians how to preach, voiced the conviction that preaching should be at least as exciting as a good ball game. I would go further and say that preaching is a matter of *life or death*, and there is evidence that God Himself agrees with this. I will substantiate that claim later in this chapter, but first let me reinforce the challenge to preach the Word from the past, on through the present, and into the future.

THE POWER OF THE WORD

God Himself supremely believes in the power of the spoken word. At creation it was God who said, 'Let there be light', and then, 'Let there be an expanse to separate the waters ... Let there be water and seas ... Let there be land, dry land ... Let there be living creatures ... Let there be man.' Every time God said, 'Let there be ...' – *there was*! People have often coined the phrase 'mere words', but from the Bible's point of view there is no such thing as 'mere' words. Words are the most powerful thing that has ever proceeded from the human personality. God Himself is a speaking God, and He never uses an idle word.

In the Bible words are seen to be *powerful* and *creative*. They are what we can call 'performative utterances' – they actually effect the content of that which they describe. They make things happen. The words that God puts in our mouths have His own divine power upon them to effect the changes that God wants. They create a new reality. Preachers, especially, have to recover the confidence that this is so.

In Genesis chapter 1 we learn that words brought *something* out of *nothing*, and shaped what was *chaos* into a *cosmos*. Similarly, because we are made in His image, men and women can borrow some of God's creative force so that our words can recreate and reform a ruined world – if God ordains it – by the power of our speech. With our words, under God, we can both create and critique a new people, even bring into being a new culture, to the glory of God!

31

GOD'S VOICE IN PREACHING

One of the words we use to describe the art or science of good communication in preaching is *homiletics*. The word is derived from the Greek *homologeō*, which means 'to confess with the mouth', and etymologically can carry the idea: 'To say the same thing as, to speak in accord with, or in agreement with, something objective and outside of yourself.' Simply put, it means that through preaching we should be saying the same thing that God would say in a given situation.

Preaching, therefore, can be said to be 'prophetic' in a very real sense of the word, because true biblical preaching says what God wants to say into a specific life situation. You can hear the very voice of God in biblical preaching. The One who spoke with power to generations past is still speaking today. As the Scriptures are opened, its prophetic message unfolds from the pages and speaks to our current environment and society.

GOD ANOINTED MEN TO PREACH

The narratives that run throughout the Torah make it very clear that it was God's purpose to anoint men to preach, often in times of national crisis, for His name's sake. Jude tells us that Enoch, the seventh man from Adam, 'prophesied'.[2] We are told by Peter that Noah was a 'preacher of righteousness' for over a hundred years.[3] Israel was led from the death camps of Egypt by Moses, whom Hosea tells us was 'a prophet'.[4] All three of these outstanding figures trumpeted God's word to their generation, and were enabled by Him to change their world for the better. All biblical preaching should resound with a similar immediacy and relevance. As Jeremy Middleton said, 'The hour can ripple with the dancing currents of the Creator's voice. It is a dangerous place to be.'[5]

THE PROPHETIC VOICE OF PREACHING

Moving on, we think of the company of prophets: Isaiah, Jeremiah, Ezekiel and others. The concise brevity of the records of the ministry of these watchmen of Israel in our Bibles should not mislead us. These men were first and foremost preachers, not writers and poets. They were preachers conveying diagnostic and curative, revelatory and didactic ministry; eyeball to eyeball, face to face with their hearers, often over decades of influential ministry.

All authentic preaching is meant to do the same thing. We can still clearly detect, beneath the surface of the writings of Isaiah, Amos, Hosea, Zechariah and the rest, the kind of structure and craftsmanship, the illustration and wordplay, the rugged, direct, penetrating application, that these men of God moved in habitually, to effect the things God wanted.

Words spoken forth from the heart of God resulted in the mobilisation of thousands to His cause. Take, for example, the massive building projects that were initiated after the return from exile. The rebuilding of the temple and then the fallen city walls of Jerusalem would probably never have been completed without the ministry of contemporary prophets who spoke into these situations. Ezra chapter 5, for instance, says,

> *Now Haggai the prophet and Zechariah the prophet, a descendant of Iddo,*
> *prophesied to the Jews in Judah and Jerusalem in the name of the God of Israel, who*
> *was over them. Then Zerubbabel son of Shealtiel and Jeshua son of Jozadak set to*
> *work to rebuild the house of God in Jerusalem. And the prophets of God were with*
> *them, helping them.*
> (Ezra 5:1–2)

The result is neatly summarised in Ezra 6:14 where it says,

> *So the elders of the Jews continued to build and prosper under the preaching of*
> *Haggai the prophet and Zechariah, a descendant of Iddo.*

It is so crucial for us to understand these principles, because there is a dearth of such prophetic preaching and ministry in the Church today. No wonder then that our walls are down! No wonder that the temple of worship is so abysmally ruined! It will continue to be as long as there are no voices to declare God's heart and mind authoritatively to His people.

PREACHING IN THE ERA OF THE HOLY SPIRIT

Looking further ahead in Scripture we discover the era of the Holy Spirit – fore-shadowed by the ministry of John the Baptist, and supremely beginning with the death, resurrection and ascension of our Lord Jesus. We know that John the Baptist broke four hundred years of prophetic silence with an explosion of holy violence against the decadence of his day. His bold, earthy directness in preaching summoned the top-dogs and underdogs of his day to abandon their moral pollution and be baptised as a sign that they had done so. Even a king was on John's 'hit list' for repentance, renewal and life. John single-handedly mounted an assault, both on the corrupt occupying Roman army, and the faithless religious establishment of his day, arraigning them for their brutality, and for their formalism and empty pride. Of course, John the Baptist lost his head in the end – good preachers often do! But Christ said of him that 'no one greater than he' had been born of a woman, and added, *'yet he who is least in the kingdom of heaven is greater than he.'*[6] If John's ministry was so powerful and effective, what may we aspire to?

JESUS' COMMISSION TO PREACH

Jesus began His public ministry with the announcement that,

> 'The Spirit of the Lord is on me,
>   because he has anointed me
>   to **preach** good news to the poor.'[7]

It is interesting to note how this statement takes priority in Isaiah's prediction. Somebody put it like this, 'God had only one Son, and He made Him a preacher.' What is obvious from the gospel accounts is that preaching was Jesus' *priority*. Enthusiastic crowds would gather to Him, awestruck at what they perceived to be the authority with which He spoke. If Christ was ever promoted to 'celebrity status' for His spectacular miracles alone, and He frequently was, He would immediately move on. He would leave that healing crusade abruptly, announcing to His bemused disciples as He did in Mark 1:38,

> 'Let us go somewhere else – to the nearby villages – so I can preach there also.
> That is why I have come.'

I believe it was Jesus' top priority to preach the Word. Healing is wonderful – those who have been beneficiaries of it know this – but healing, at its best, only repairs bodies for a time. Preaching can restore souls for all eternity. So preaching was, and still is, *that* important.

Before He ascended into heaven, Christ's last order to His disciples was they should *'go into all the world and preach the good news to all creation!'* (Mark 16:15). This was the last order of our great Commander-in-Chief and it has never been rescinded. Therefore, we have no liberty to tamper with it. Christ Himself knows best how to build and prosper His Church, and we have His order as to what is best done in that connection. He also promised that for those who fulfil this faithful task, 'signs' will follow. In Mark 16:17–18 Jesus says,

> 'And these signs will accompany those who believe: In my name they will drive out
> demons; they will speak in new tongues ... when they drink deadly poison, it will
> not hurt them at all ... they will place their hands on sick people, and they will get
> well.'

Jesus is saying that supernatural attestations of both the authenticity of the messenger and the authenticity of the message we preach, will follow faithful ministry. But it is what such signs 'follow' that is highlighted as being of utmost importance here – they follow the preaching of the gospel. Therefore, preach the Word!

The first sermon of the Christian era was preached on a day of harvest festival – the Day of Pentecost.[8] It was a day that also celebrated the giving of the Law to Moses at Mount Sinai. For Moses that day had ended tragically as 3,000 drunken revellers perished amid a storm of wind and fire. Remarkably for Peter, the Day of Pentecost resulted in a similar storm of wind and fire, and 3,000 people crossed the gulf from death to life as a result of the words that were on his lips. It was truly a much more significant day to be remembered than the giving of the Torah to Moses. Now we have the gospel of our Lord and Saviour Jesus Christ to preach and the fruit will be far more spectacular.

The era of the Spirit had commenced and church growth began to snowball according to Acts 4:4. The apostles preached incessantly – so much so that the main complaint voiced against them by the authorities was that they had 'filled Jerusalem' with their teaching.[9] Oh, that the same could be said over every town and city in our nations today – that these Christians have filled the city with their teaching, the word, the message they bring.

Such effects as the apostles achieved – dramatic church growth and equally dramatic hostility as a result – were not the result of inter-faith festivals, the creative arts, jumble sales or Christian rock concerts! It was through persistent preaching, day by day in the temple courts, or visiting house to house. They never ceased proclaiming the good news that Jesus is the Christ. If we today would see the same apostolic results, then we have to emulate the same apostolic methods!

The apostle Paul did nothing more nor less than this. Indeed, he said he was always eager to preach.[10] Only one of his recorded sermons in the book of Acts was preached to believers, so far as I can tell. The rest were aimed at Jewish and Pagan unbelievers. The record of his preaching to believers is, of course, summarised for us in the epistles of the New Testament. But what Paul had every confidence in was the proclamation of the truth to *unbelievers*. As converts multiplied and churches were planted he expressed his conviction that, '*God was pleased through the foolishness of what was preached to save those who believe*'.[11] So seriously did Paul view his commission that he solemnly announced a self-imposed curse if he ever reneged on this responsibility: '*Woe to me if I do not preach the gospel!*'[12] This yields a very vital and important principle: Christianity is an enterprise that expands *primarily* through the activity of preaching. The parable of the sower, which is considered cardinal and central to all of Jesus' parables of the Kingdom, confirms that, '*A farmer went out to sow his seed ... The farmer sows the word.*'[13]

PREACHERS OF THE WORD

Church history presents a dazzling gallery of outstanding preachers for us, illuminating the darkness of an otherwise black night sky, and accelerating periods of the Church's greatest advance and progress. Thank God that He has His champions in every century.

In Chapter 3 Liam Goligher will survey the main highlights and the glorious effects of this breathtaking story, and what an inspiring story it is. But our recent contemporary history has had its own illustrious role models – those who took up the baton of faithful witness and proclamation and then passed it on to others.

Borrowing from Dickens' famous opening to his novel *A Tale of Two Cities*, the past century has seen both 'the best and the worst of times'. No century before has seen such ideological ferment, global warfare, massive cruelty, wholesale genocide and widespread devastation threatening to push us to the brink of destruction. In the Church, tragically, the cancer of theological liberalism and worldly assimilation has accelerated a massive decline, particularly in the West. Decline in the quality and quantity of preaching has led to an emptying of the churches, even threatening their total demise. But I believe that wherever the Word of God and the Spirit of God are honoured, God will always ensure there will be a 'resurrection', and sometimes phenomenal growth in His Church as well.

Among my own recent heroes of the twentieth century are Oswald Chambers, and the triumvirate of Campbell Morgan, Martyn Lloyd-Jones, and R.T. Kendall from Westminster Chapel. I am a great admirer of A.W. Tozer and W.E. Sangster; of Billy Graham, through whom I was converted; of Francis Schaeffer who taught me to relate the faith meaningfully to the culture in which I live; of John Stott, John Piper, Terry Virgo and David Pawson. Their spoken words have massively impacted their contemporaries, because they have never failed to let loose the Word of God in all of its primeval power.

THE FUTURE OF PREACHING?

So what of the present and the future of preaching in the twenty-first century? John Stott has written this: 'In preaching, God is bringing to each person's notice what holy Scripture has made publicly and permanently available, so that His timeless word comes to timely announcement, so that people believe the message and commit to the Saviour it announces.'[14] This, I am convinced, is the kind of preaching we need to see restored in the Body of Christ today – but there is a war on. There is a conflict for the minds, hearts, and welfare of humankind – particularly of the Church of Jesus Christ. We *are* at war! The Christian life is not *like* a war, it *is* a war, and Satan and his Republican Guard are out to halt our impact and progress in whatever way they can. If Satan cannot kill us directly, then he will try to starve us into weakness and disease, leading to a slow and certain death.

It brings no glory to God when His people are emaciated and weak to the point of withering. The necessity for the fullness of both the Word and the Spirit in church life is a matter for all-out spiritual warfare; something that we must constantly be prepared to fight for. Enemy propaganda has broadcast outright lies for years, telling us that preaching is passé, or that people today are 'Word-resistant'. We are led to believe that people cannot concentrate for more than seven minutes on any spoken utterance.

What we need, they say, is entertainment, dialogue, fun! Let's bring in the soft lighting and smoke machines! Let's keep the people entertained!

We don't need more entertainment though the best preaching is truly entertaining, in the highest sense of the word, but we do need more authentic preaching that changes lives. If Christianity expands primarily through preaching, then if preaching disappears we will grow pale and sicken. Whole churches will eventually disappear from the map. The world could go to hell without a single soul being alert to the fact, or even strong enough to care.

In any war we need weapons; weapons that are clean, well maintained, loaded, and fully functioning. How tragic, then, that we often appear to be firing blanks. It was said of the evangelist Charles Finney that when he opened his mouth he was aiming a gun and when he spoke the bombardment began. But we often engage in play fighting, firing corks from pop-guns, or making a noise with harmless caps and paintball repeaters. There may be a lot of smoke in connection with such activities, but there is definitely no fire!

Even within the 'best' of circles – the evangelical and Charismatic streams that once experienced such vigour and health – preaching has fallen on hard times. It is partly due to so many critics voicing their opinions about preaching, and tragically we are believing them. But mostly the problem lies with leaders themselves. A catalogue of reasons could be given for the neglect of this as a priority activity in the ministry of God's leaders in His Church, but here are some suggestions why I think preaching is ailing today:

Why Preaching is Ailing

1. Some are too busy
Our schedules are jam-packed with programmes, people, networking, and socialising, so that time in the study has become either scarce or non-existent amid our hectic lifestyles.

2. Some are too lazy
They begrudge the demanding work that good preaching entails. John Stott has said that at least one full hour of direct preparation is necessary for every five minutes of spoken utterance in the pulpit. He may well have underestimated that; he certainly hasn't overestimated it. Those who are too lazy to give that amount of time to preparation will find that their preaching suffers.

3. Some are too ambitious
It is possible to fall into the trap of climbing some imaginary ecclesiastical ladder of success which demands a lot of time spent networking with people, at the expense of direct preparation. Such people may eventually discover that the ladder they have been climbing is leaning against the wrong wall, because that isn't success as God defines it.

4. Some are too nervous

Some ministers are simply too afraid to speak the truth, the whole truth, and nothing but the truth, perhaps for fear of being disliked or alienated by their congregations.

5. Some are too polite and too politically correct

In the name of political correctness it is possible for the message to be so diluted that it leaves the congregation a sentence or two short of really hearing the truth; short of being rattled or offended at times, because the preacher feels it is too dangerous to do this. But doesn't the Bible tell us repeatedly that biblical ministry is not for the cowardly?

6. Some are too distracted

Perhaps they have many leisure pursuits, meals out, time with friends, time on the golf course, spectator sports and relaxation to timetable into their diaries. Well, they all have a place, but they are *not* our priority.

7. Some are too hard of hearing

In other words, waxy deposits have formed in their spiritual ears. In some cases they have been deafened by the booming, strident voices of men and their opinions, so that they become, in effect, stone deaf to the Spirit of God. It requires real sensitivity to hear what God would say in any situation; for some that faculty has been mislaid along the way.

8. Some are disillusioned

Under-developed preaching skills, little or no feedback of a positive nature from others, meagre results and the weariness of a constant struggle have taken their toll on many discouraged ministers, desperate for a personal renewal.

SO, WHY PREACH?

In the face of all this, one might well ask, why preach at all? Consider this: the devil would like to silence the preaching of the Word, precisely because good preaching is so effective. If the devil wants us to shut up, and he does, there must therefore be a very good reason for us to keep on speaking.

In 2 Timothy chapter 4, anticipating social conditions similar to those I have just described, the apostle Paul wrote to his apostolic protégé, Timothy. It was to be his swan-song letter, written from the place of his final imprisonment in Rome. It is Paul's lasting legacy to the Church. The context for Paul's statements was the growing battle for truth that was being waged, even in his day. Deception and lies were threatening the spiritual health of the congregations he had planted, and of others too. Paul said that such lies and deception would characterise the last days, the whole period from Christ's first to His second advent.

Paul warned us in 2 Timothy 3:1 that in the last days there will be 'terrible' times. The Greek word used here was also used of the Gadarene demoniac in the Gospels and depicts a condition of violence, of menacing, of times that are deranged and disordered that will be deadly to man. The evil one, says Paul, is going to use apostate men to drain the heart and life out of the Church of God – but thankfully there is a wonderful antidote. God has given us His Word, the holy Scriptures, and in 2 Timothy 3:15–16 he reminds Timothy of their converting power in his life:

> *from childhood you have known the Holy Scriptures, which are able to make you wise for salvation through faith which is in Christ Jesus. All Scripture is given by inspiration of God, and is profitable for doctrine, for reproof, for correction, for instruction in righteousness, that the man of God may be complete, thoroughly equipped for every good work.*
> (NKJV)

Paul speaks in glowing terms of the eternal attributes of God's written Word. He speaks of the Bible's *inspiration* in verse 16. Its origin is in God; it is God-breathed – the equivalent of God's spoken Word. What Scripture says, God says. All modern-day preachers must recover their confidence in *the potency* of God's Word. His Word is 'profitable', Paul says, to teach, to correct, to reprove, and to build one up in righteousness. The Bible possesses the divine power to change a person's life. It is capable of making damaged individuals progressively whole, over time.

Paul speaks of the *sufficiency* of God's Word in verse 17: *'that the man of God may be thoroughly equipped for every good work.'* The Bible is complete in itself and needs no supplementation by the thoughts and ideas of men to accomplish the purpose for which it was given. It is a complete tool kit containing all the resources to accomplish everything God wants us to know and to do. But in order to accomplish this, the Bible must be loosed, set free, understood, and accurately applied to whole churches and the whole lives of the people within them. Then Scripture is able to have its powerful effect. This is why the apostle issues the following charge to Timothy:

> *In the presence of God and of Christ Jesus, who will judge the living and the dead, and in view of his appearing and his kingdom, I give you this charge: Preach the Word; be prepared in season and out of season; correct, rebuke and encourage – with great patience and careful instruction. For the time will come when men will not put up with sound doctrine. Instead, to suit their own desires, they will gather around them a great number of teachers to say what their itching ears want to hear. They will turn their ears away from the truth and turn aside to myths. But you, keep your head in all situations, endure hardship, do the work of an evangelist, discharge all the duties of your ministry.*
> (2 Timothy 4:1–5)

THE APOSTLE PAUL'S CHARGE TO US

There are five things to notice about Paul's charge:

1. It is a solemn and serious charge (v. 1)

We usually pay careful attention to people's last words, especially when they come from a cell on death row, which is where Paul was incarcerated, but this adds a peculiar solemnity to what he is communicating here. Paul describes preaching as an activity that is done in the presence of no less a person than the triune God Himself. The charge to preach, therefore, is heaven-sent – it is not simply a good idea, it is a God idea! His criticism of our efforts in this regard is the only one that really matters. History is coming to a terrifying climax with the sudden appearance of history's Lord and Judge. Paul's single-minded fixation, therefore, is that we all preach the Word, while time allows.

2. It is a perpetual and timely charge (v. 2a)

So vital is it that the truth of the gospel be broadcast through human lips that Paul makes it clear that it is not merely an occasional or casual work we can do when we feel like it. Paul says we are to do it whether it is appropriate or not. There are only two times, he says, when you should preach the Word: in season and out of season – which is another way of saying, *always*. There is no closed season for preaching. It is always 'open season' on saints and sinners alike!

3. It is an all-out and manly charge (v. 2b)

Paul is using a range of exhortations that we can sum up with a few vivid adverbs:

- We are to preach the word *urgently*, or as J.B. Phillips translates it, 'Never lose your sense of urgency.'
- We are to preach the word *relevantly*. Every word we utter is to be appropriate to the audiences we address. The preacher's task is to straighten out crooked thinking. An endless barrage of propaganda has fed people's minds. Thank God there's something more powerful in the hour we address them: the Word of God. We are reproving lapsed morals and bad choices, so yes, people need rebuking! Do it lovingly, yes, but do it! We are stirring up discouraged, timid, fearful and wobbling hearts. We are setting a course for new lives and new lifestyles. We do not preach to ceilings or to seats: we preach heart to heart and eye to eye to the people before us.
- We are to preach the Word *persistently* with the patience and careful instruction that Paul enjoins here. We realise that this is slow, cumulative work, and not all the results are instant. However, we must refuse to become disillusioned,

just because things haven't changed this month. We must refuse to adopt human pressure techniques or quick-fix gimmicks which seem to be on offer at every major conference we attend. Remember, the results of this are in God's hands.

4. *It is a* comprehensive *charge (v. 3a)*

It involves the whole truth and nothing but the truth. 'The truth' is found throughout the sixty-six books of the Bible, not just in our favourite texts or pet themes. Therefore, to preach the Word means to preach the whole Bible: its narrative, its wisdom literature, its prophecy, its poetry, the Gospels, the epistles. We must preach from wherever God shows us to whomever He sends us, with the message He has given us and with the power He lends us. That was Paul's burden and it must become ours as well.

5. *It is a* strongly resisted *charge (v. 3b)*

Finally, Paul warns us solemnly that some people cannot and will not tolerate the fact that we are determined to preach the Word faithfully. They will hate both us and what we have to say, and they may be confused in their own minds as to which they really hate most. Paul knew this would be the case, because there will arise people who are intolerant of sound truth and they will sponsor false teachers to instruct them and pay them generously to do so. 'Itching ears' can always find someone to scratch them if the price is right. That's why Dr John White once said, 'Christ weeps over sheep fed on lollipops.'

There are only two reactions to good preaching: receptivity or resistance. There is no neutrality. The same sun that melts wax, hardens clay. The problem is not with the sunshine, the problem is with the substance it shines upon. It is a fact that as a preacher, you will not always be popular, and for this reason in 2 Timothy 4:5 Paul encourages us: *'Always be sober-minded, endure suffering, do the work of an evangelist, fulfil your ministry'*, as the English Standard Version puts it. Paul is saying the same thing to us today. It may be prudent for us to shut up, to tone it down, to toe the line, but we do not have that option. We have a ministry and a charge to fulfil that the triune God Himself has called us to engage in.

So this is our great task now in the twenty-first century as it was Paul's and Timothy's in the first century AD. Christ is the one who issued it. He is also the one who will fully assess our faithfulness to this task and reward it accordingly. So, whether people love you or hate you, whether they receive you or resist you, whether you see great results or very few at all, do it anyway.

William Willimon, chaplain of Duke University in Carolina, is one who has truly recovered, I believe, the sense of awe appropriate to the task God has commissioned us to do. He says,

In that moment when the congregation settles itself in the pews and all is quiet and expectant as the people look to you, you are the preacher, the essential link between them and the good news. Without you the good news is not news. No one hears or believes it. Call it a burden, call it a privilege, a duty. You know that it is worthy of your best talents, worthy of a lifetime's labour and dedication. On any Sunday you can give it your all and still know that the Word deserves more. It is no small task that the Church has set upon your shoulders. Being called to preach the gospel, you can do no more than to promise as long as you have breath, and there is someone to listen, then by God's grace you will give them the Word.[15]

Amen.

NOTES

1. P.T. Forsyth, *Positive Preaching and the Modern Mind* (Independent Press Ltd, 1964).
2. Jude 14.
3. 2 Peter 2:5.
4. Hosea 12:13.
5. *Serving the Word of God: Celebrating the Life and Ministry of James Philip*, ed. David Wright and David Stay (Mentor, 2002), p. 86.
6. Matthew 11:11.
7. Luke 4:18, my emphasis.
8. Acts 2.
9. Acts 5:28.
10. Romans 1:15.
11. 1 Corinthians 1:21.
12. 1 Corinthians 9:16.
13. See Mark 4:3, 14.
14. John Stott, *I Believe in Preaching* (Hodder and Stoughton, 1982).
15. *Preaching and Leading Worship* (The Westminster Press, 1984), pp. 88–89.

Chapter 2

THE PARADOXES OF PREACHING

John Stott

The modern world is decidedly unfriendly to preaching. Words have largely been eclipsed by images, and the book by the screen. Preaching is regarded by many as an outmoded form of communication; what one writer has called 'an echo from an abandoned past'. People today are drugged by television, hostile to authority, and suspicious of words. The consequence of this is that some preachers lose their morale and give up. Either they don't have the heart to carry on, or perhaps they transmogrify their sermons into 'sermonettes', little homilies, dialogues, or something equally unsatisfactory. Let us beg one another not to listen to that kind of propaganda, but to be re-inspired that we are called to preach the Word.

In this chapter we will deal with the *paradoxes* of preaching. I want the reader to consider that authentic Christian preaching has a number of indispensable characteristics which appear at first sight to be contradictory, but which, under close examination, complement one another in the tension of a paradox. There are five paradoxes:

1. AUTHENTIC CHRISTIAN PREACHING IS BOTH *BIBLICAL* AND *CONTEMPORARY*

On one hand, preaching is of course *biblical*, because it is an exposition of Scripture. We do not occupy the pulpit in order to preach ourselves, in order to broadcast our views, or ventilate our opinions. Our understanding of preaching is that it is essentially, in its very essence, an exposition of the Word of God. In that sense all Christian preaching is expository preaching – not in the narrow sense of that term, meaning a running commentary on a long passage of Scripture – but in the broad sense that it opens up the biblical text. Preachers are trustees of God's revelation; stewards of the Word of God; and we must be determined, above all else, to be faithful in our stewardship.

The former Archbishop of Canterbury, Donald Coggan, who died some years ago, wrote, 'The Christian preacher has a boundary set for him. When he enters the pulpit he is not an entirely free man. There is a very real sense in which it may be said of him that the Almighty has set him his bounds that he shall not pass. He is not at liberty to invent or choose his message: it has been committed to him. Moreover, it is for him to declare, expound, and commend it to his hearers.'[1] Later he wrote, 'It is a great thing to come under the magnificent tyranny of the gospel.' So, we are men and women under authority, and we are called to be faithful in our stewardship.

Yet at the same time, authentic Christian preaching is also *contemporary*, or should be. It resonates with the modern world; it wrestles with the realities of our hearers' situation. In our resolve to be biblical we must refuse to lapse into irrelevance. Instead, we should seek to relate the ancient text to the modern context. True biblical exposition goes beyond exegesis, which simply explains the *meaning* of the passage, to application – grasping the heart of the *message*.

Imagine, if you will, a flat territory that is deeply cut by a ravine or a canyon. On the one side of the ravine is the biblical world, and on the other side is the modern world. Between these two territories lies a deep gulf – two thousand years of changing culture. Evangelical people like me live in the biblical world, on one side of the divide. It's where we feel comfortable. We believe the Bible, meditate on the Bible, and love the Bible. We are essentially biblical people. But we are not so comfortable in the modern world, on the other side of the divide. If like me you're senescent, if not actually senile, then you probably feel threatened by the modern world.

Much modern preaching emanates from the biblical world. Indeed, we wouldn't dream of preaching from anywhere but the Bible. But somehow this preaching goes up in the air but fails to land on the other side of the divide. Our preaching is biblical, but not contemporary.

Those who think of themselves as liberal often make the opposite mistake. They live in the modern world. People listen to them because they seem to resonate with modernity, or post-modernity. They are not shocked or threatened by the culture of the modern world – they have built-in shock absorbers. They read modern poetry, modern philosophy, modern psychology, modern science; they are moving with the times. But in reality they have jettisoned biblical revelation. They may be contemporary, but they are decidedly un-biblical. Their preaching lands squarely in contemporary reality, but where it comes from, heaven alone knows! It does not come out of Scripture.

This very simple illustration highlights what I believe to be one of the major tragedies in the Church today. Namely, that evangelicals are biblical but not contemporary, while liberals are contemporary but not biblical, and almost nobody is building bridges and relating the biblical text to the modern context. In fact, authentic Christian preaching is a bridge-building operation. It is always struggling to relate God's ancient Word to the ever-changing world of today. Our calling is to be faithful to the biblical text and *sensitive* to the modern context. We must never sacrifice either to the other.

In order to do this, we have to study on both sides of the divide. We have to study Scripture until, in Spurgeon's well-known phrase, 'Your blood is Bibline',[2] because we have become immersed in its message and have completely absorbed the totality of God's revelation. But we don't only study Scripture, we also study the modern world. Some thirty years ago I started a reading group in London and invited about a dozen young, thoughtful, evangelical believers to join me. We met once a month and decided at the end of each meeting what book we were going to read before we met again. We would try to discover what were the 'cult' books being read by university students, and more widely by the world outside of the university. Then we would meet and we would go around the circle and each take one minute to say what we felt was the major challenge of the book we had read. After that we would go hammer and tongs in discussion, and at the very end of the evening ask ourselves the crucial question: How does the biblical gospel relate to people who think like this? All I can say is that I found it an enormous help to me. Those young people have dragged me screaming into the modern world. Many modern preachers would find such a forum useful and informative. It would compel them to read books that they probably would never have read, and it will sharpen their preaching immeasurably.

I have sometimes called this 'double listening'. Listening to the voice of God in Scripture, and listening to the voices of the modern world, with all their cries of anger, pain and despair. We don't listen to the voice of God and the voices of the modern world with the same degree of respect, of course. We listen to the voice of God in order to believe and obey Him, and we listen to the voices of the modern world simply to try to understand, so that we can relate the gospel to their situation.

2. AUTHENTIC CHRISTIAN PREACHING IS BOTH *AUTHORITATIVE* AND *TENTATIVE*

Some may be surprised that I want to argue that our preaching is *tentative*, but let's think about it. The twentieth century that we have left behind us, was an epoch of doubt. It began, it's true, with a decade of Edwardian triumphalism. While Edward VII was on the throne everything seemed stable and fixed, and immovable. But the sinking of the *Titanic* in April 1912 was an omen of worse disasters to come. The social stability that characterised the Edwardian era was shattered by the two world wars, and all the old landmarks, symbols of stability, were destroyed. Now, at the beginning of the twenty-first century, people are floundering in the swamps of relativism and uncertainty. Even the Church seems as blushingly insecure as an adolescent teenager.

Many preachers today seem to understand their task as sharing their doubts with the congregation. The parading of personal doubt belongs to the very essence of post-modernity. Bishop J.C. Ryle, Bishop of Liverpool at the end of the nineteenth century, said, 'Old and experienced Christians complain that a vast quantity of modern preaching is so foggy, and hazy, and dim, and indistinct, and hesitating, and timid, and cautious, and fenced with doubt, that the preacher does not seem to know what he believes himself.'[3] This is true of much preaching today, which consists of nothing more than a great list of uncertainties.

So, on one hand, we truly need to rediscover the voice of authority that is missing from the modern pulpit but, on the other hand, we must never presume to use formulas such as, 'Thus says the Lord...' or 'The word of the Lord came to me saying...' That was the language of the biblical prophets. These historical figures were 'organs' of direct revelation from God. Rather, our approach should be, 'The Bible says...' or, 'Listen to what Scripture says...' as we turn to it for our authority. Provided that we have done our hermeneutical homework and have been conscientious in applying proper principles of biblical interpretation to the text, then we can indicate to the congregation what these principles are, and why we have concluded that this text means this and not that. Then we can say with Paul, 'Our gospel came to you with full conviction.' Conviction and courage are essential to authentic Christian preaching.

Bishop Phillips Brooks, in his lectures on preaching given at Yale in 1877, said the following: 'Courage is the indispensable requisite of any true ministry ... If you are afraid of men and a slave to their opinions go and do something else. Go and make shoes to fit them. Go even and paint pictures which you know are bad, but which suit their bad taste. But do not keep on all your life preaching sermons which shall say not what God sent you to declare, but what men hire you to say. Be courageous. Be independent.'[4]

Clearly we need to be authoritative, but it is often right to be tentative in view of the fact that God has not been pleased to reveal *everything* to us – He has kept some things secret. Deuteronomy 29:29 says that, *'The secret things belong to the LORD our God, but the things revealed belong to us and to our children forever, that we may follow all the words of this law.'* This is why Christians combine, somewhat strangely, the elements of dogmatism on the one hand and agnosticism on the other. We should be *dogmatic* about everything that is plainly revealed in Scripture, but we should be *agnostic* about those things which have been kept secret. I believe our troubles arise when our dogmatism trespasses into the secret things, and our agnosticism into the revealed things. Let's keep them apart!

Even what God *has* revealed is not always plain. Some readers may think that statement means that I don't believe in the *perspicuity* of Scripture – but I do! The sixteenth-century reformers were affirming that Scripture had a 'perspic' (transparent or see-through) quality about it. Yet, in saying this, they did not mean that everything in Scripture was absolutely plain. They meant that the central message of the Bible – salvation by grace alone in Christ alone through faith alone – is abundantly plain. Even children, even the uneducated, can understand it. But the reformers didn't claim that everything in Scripture was equally plain.

Remember that even the apostle Peter confessed that some things in Paul's letters were hard to understand. So if one apostle couldn't always understand another, it would not be very modest for us to claim that we can! I would like to see in the pulpit today, alongside the authority that belongs to God's infallible revelation, a due humility and diffidence which belongs to the Scripture's very fallible interpreters. Calvin understood this well. I believe Calvin is the greatest expositor that God has given to the Church, and yet he often makes statements in his commentaries such as, 'I shall state my own view (as to what this text means) freely. But each of you must form his own judgment.'

Besides displaying genuine humility, I believe that if we serve up everything on a plate to our congregations, then we condemn them to perpetual immaturity. Isn't this why Jesus forbade His disciples to call anybody their father or their teacher on earth? We must never adopt any teacher in the Church as our final authority on interpreting the Bible, as if we were disciples and the teacher, our guru. There are to be no gurus in the Christian community, only pastors. And how do pastors feed their sheep? Answer: They don't! To be sure, if a new-born lamb is sickly, then the shepherd will take it into his arms and feed it with cod-liver oil or something equally delicious. But that is not the normal way by which shepherds feed their sheep! The normal way is not to spoon-feed them, but lead them into good pasture where they can feed themselves. That is what we want to encourage by our preaching – to lead people into the pastures of Scripture, encouraging them to feed themselves.

It's not easy to strike the balance between the authoritative and the tentative, between the dogmatic and the agnostic, between the infallible Word and the fallible interpreters of the Word, but we must struggle to do so. I would like to see among us more evangelical confidence in what God has plainly revealed, and more evangelical reticence regarding what He has kept secret.

3. Authentic Christian Preaching is Both *Prophetic* and *Pastoral*

So far then we've considered that authentic Christian preaching is both biblical and contemporary, both authoritative and tentative. Now, thirdly, it is both prophetic and pastoral. Indeed the whole Church is called to this double ministry. I use the word 'prophetic' in the sense that we bear witness without fear or favour to the doctrinal truths and ethical standards which God has plainly revealed. But our ministry is also to be pastoral in the sense that we deal *gently* with those who are slow to believe biblical doctrine, or fail to attain biblical standards. Some preachers have a very faithful prophetic ministry and show great courage in declaring the Word of God. They refuse to compromise it. Then they remember that it is false prophets who say, 'Peace, peace' when there is no peace. Consequently, they may often include warnings of judgement in their preaching.

But these prophetic witnesses are often pastorally very insensitive. They exhibit little of what Paul calls the 'meekness' and the 'gentleness' of Christ. They seem to enjoy seeing the congregation squirm under the lash of their teaching. They even do what Scripture says the Messiah would never do: they break bruised reeds and snuff out smouldering wicks. If they are faced with Paul's dilemma, 'Shall I come to you with a whip or in a spirit of gentleness?' they tend to opt for the whip. There are preachers, are there not, like that? God forgive us and forbid us from being that way!

That is one side of the third paradox. On the other side, there are preachers who excel in pastoral care and love. Their favourite words, indeed, are *compassion* and *tolerance*. They know the frailty and the vulnerability of human nature, and they make every allowance for it. They remember that Jesus did not condemn the woman taken in adultery, so they seek to be non-judgemental themselves, as He was. But they forget that Jesus also told the adulteress to go and sin no more. He also told the Samaritan woman to fetch her husband, and so caused her to face her sin in repentance before she could drink of the water of life. So by forgetting the holiness of God's love, and His call to repentance, their prophetic witness is blunted and their trumpet gives an uncertain sound.

Once again it is not easy to combine the two: prophetic witness and pastoral care; firmness and gentleness; discipline and compassion. It was an American Episcopal layman, Chad Walsh, who, in the 1940s, was, I think, the first person to say that, 'To preach is to disturb the comfortable and comfort the disturbed.' But we're not ready to comfort the disturbed until we have disturbed the comfortable.

4. Authentic Christian Preaching is Both *Gifted* and *Studied*

Under this heading we face the question: Who and what makes a preacher? What are the factors that equip a person to be a preacher? Does God create preachers, or do they have a share in the creative process themselves?

The answer has to be, I believe, that both are needed. On the one hand, every authentic preacher has been *called*, *equipped*, and *anointed* by God. The very concept of a self-made, self-appointed preacher is positively grotesque. Preaching is a *gift*.

The five New Testament lists of the gifts of the Spirit include pastors and teachers, those with a gift of exhortation and encouragement. I think it is highly significant that when the apostle Paul is listing the conditions of eligibility for the pastorate, nine of his ten conditions are moral and spiritual (for example, self-control and hospitality), and only one of the ten could be described as a professional gift, that is the word *didaktikos*, having a gift for teaching.

Having a gift for teaching or preaching is a necessary condition for entering the pastorate. It is therefore a great mistake to distinguish, as some scholars do, between the institutional ministry and the charismatic ministry – as if the former were appointed by the Church and the latter were appointed by God. No! The Church has no liberty to ordain those whom God has not called, equipped and gifted. On the other hand, the divine gift, call, and anointing are not enough by themselves. Every gift has to be nurtured and developed by those to whom it has been given. Timothy was exhorted not to neglect his gift (1 Timothy 4:14), but rather to fan it into flame (2 Timothy 1:6). How he was to do this Paul didn't actually tell him, but presumably it would be by disciplined study and the conscientious exercise of his gift.

I still meet preachers occasionally who are very suspicious of the exhortation to study. They think that it is incompatible with the anointing of the Holy Spirit. They imagine that if they are truly trusting in the Holy Spirit, then study will be altogether superfluous. Some even go so far as to quote, or rather misquote, Jesus when He said, 'Don't be anxious about what you shall say, or what you shall speak. It will be given you in that moment what you are to say, because it will not be you but the Holy Spirit speaking in you.'[5] That promise, however, was made to prisoners in the law courts, not to a preacher in the pulpit! So, more appropriate than that text is 2 Timothy 2:7 where Paul says to Timothy, *'Consider what I say* [use your mind, think about what I'm saying, reflect on it, turn it over and over in your mind] *and the Lord will give you understanding . . . '* (NKJV). God gives the understanding, but we have to do the studying. They are not incompatible with one another.

The need to study has long been recognised by leaders in the Church. If I may quote Calvin again, 'No one will ever be a good minister of the Word of God unless he is first of all a scholar.'[6] Spurgeon said, 'He who no longer sows in the study will no more reap in the pulpit.'[7] Phillips Brooks said, 'Learn to study for the sake of proof. Then your sermons will be like the leaping of a fountain, and not like the pumping of a pump.'[8] Dr Lloyd-Jones said, 'You will always find that the men whom God has used singularly have been those who have studied most, known their Scriptures best, and given time to preparation.'

Billy Graham, speaking to about 600 clergy in London, in 1969, said that if he had his ministry all over again he would make two changes. The atmosphere was electric. People were sitting on the edge of their seats. What? The greatest evangelist in the world needing to make two changes? 'Yes,' he said, 'I would study three times as much as I have done, for I've preached too much and studied too little.' And secondly, he said, 'I would give more time to prayer.' And, of course, you will have noticed that the ministry of the Word and prayer are exactly the apostolic priorities given in Acts chapter 6.

5. AUTHENTIC CHRISTIAN PREACHING IS BOTH *THOUGHTFUL* AND *PASSIONATE*

That is to say, in all authentic preaching, the *mind* and the *emotions* are both engaged. Clear thinking and deep feeling are combined.

Some preachers are extremely thoughtful. If you were to visit their office, you would see their desk piled high with dictionaries, commentaries, concordances and the rest. Their biblical orthodoxy is impeccable. They not only study the text, but they bring the fruits of their study into the pulpit. Every sermon is the product of painstaking exegesis and application. But their sermons are often as dry as dust and as dull as ditchwater. They would never dream of leaning over the pulpit with tears in their eyes, begging people to be reconciled to God. There's no feeling, no heart, no heat. They would never provoke a child, as Charles Simeon did, to turn to her mother and say, 'Oh mama, what is the preacher in a passion about?' But how can anybody preach the gospel of Christ crucified and remain unmoved? I would like to see more emotion as well as more study in preachers today!

There are other preachers who make the opposite mistake. They are all fire and no light. They rant and rave in the pulpit. They work themselves up into a frenzy like the prophets of Baal. Every sermon is one long, fervent, interminable appeal. But the people are often very confused as to what they are being entreated to do, because there has been no exposition, only an appeal. I think it is a safe rule to say: No exposition without an appeal, no appeal without an exposition.

The apostle Paul is the great example of this combination. He wrote: '*the love of Christ tightens its grip on us, because we are convinced . . .* '.[9] Thus his conviction about the cross led to his deep feelings about it.

Richard Baxter in his great book *The Reformed Pastor*, written in 1656, said, 'First light, then heat.' Somewhat similarly, Spurgeon wrote, 'There must be light as well as fire. Some preachers are all light and no fire, while others are all fire and no light. What we need is both fire and light.'[10]

The best quotation of all on this topic, I think, is from Dr Lloyd-Jones in his great book, *Preaching and Preachers*,[11] based on lectures he gave at Westminster Theological Seminary: 'What is preaching? Logic on fire! Eloquent reason! Are these contradictions? Of course they are not. Reason concerning this truth ought to be mightily eloquent, as you see it in the case of the apostle Paul and others. It is theology on fire. And a theology which does not take fire, I maintain, is a defective theology. Or at least the man's understanding of it is defective. Preaching is theology coming through a man who is on fire.'

SUMMARY

So, in summary: authentic Christian preaching is both *biblical* and *contemporary*, relating the ancient text to the modern context; both *authoritative* and *tentative*, distinguishing between the infallible Word and the fallible interpreter of the Word; both *prophetic* and *pastoral*, combining faithfulness with gentleness; both *gifted* and *studied*, necessitating a divine gift and human self-discipline; and both *thoughtful* and *passionate*, allowing your heart to burn when you open the Scriptures to others.

Our adversary, the devil, is the enemy of moderation and balance. One of his favourite hobbies, I'm persuaded, is tipping evangelical Christians off balance. If he cannot get us to deny Christ, then he will be happy if we distort Christ. Instead I want to encourage the reader to develop what I like to call B.B.C. – Balanced Biblical Christianity. Let us seek to combine these truths that complement one another, and let's not separate what God has united. For it is in these unresolved paradoxes that authentic Christian preaching is to be found.

Notes

1. Donald Coggan, *Stewards of Grace* (Hodder & Stoughton, 1958), pp. 46, 48.
2. Quoted by Richard Ellsworth Day in *The Shadow of the Broad Brim* (Judson Press, 1934), p. 131.
3. J.C. Ryle, *Principles for Churchmen*, 4th edn revised (1900), pp. 165–66.
4. Phillips Brooks, *Lectures on Preaching* (1877; Baker, 1969), p. 59.
5. See Mark 13:11.
6. From his commentary on Deuteronomy 5:23ff.
7. C.H. Spurgeon, *An All-round Ministry* (1900; Banner, 1960;), p. 236.
8. Brooks, *Lectures on Preaching*, pp. 159–60.
9. 2 Corinthians 5:14.
10. C.H. Spurgeon, *The Soulwinner* (Pilgrim Publications, 1978), p. 98.
11. Martyn Lloyd-Jones, *Preaching and Preachers* (Hodder & Stoughton, 1971), p. 97.

Chapter 3

THE PLACE OF PREACHING IN CHURCH HISTORY

Liam Goligher

> Preaching has in it two essential elements: Truth and personality. Preaching is the bringing of truth through personality. The truth is itself a fixed and stable element. The personality is a varying and growing element. In authentic preaching divine truth is conveyed through human personality.
> (Phillips Brooks)

Preaching is the distinctive Christian form of communication. No other world religion uses preaching in the way Christianity does. The most essential element of preaching is proclaiming the truth of God. It is telling someone else the truth that God has given to us.

Preaching has an ancient history. However, right from the outset it is important to make clear that, in talking about the history of preaching, I am not talking about the history of the pulpit. The history of preaching is primarily the history of proclaiming the Word of God in a whole variety of contexts.

PREACHING IN THE BIBLE

People have proclaimed the Word of God since the world began. We are told that both Abel and Enoch, *'the seventh from Adam'*, were prophets,[1] and Noah, in the time of the Flood, was described as a *'preacher of righteousness'*.[2] The first time the word 'prophet' is used in the Bible is in connection with Abraham.[3] These early characters in the Bible would communicate the word that God had given to them to their families – however that word had come – so they were principally preachers to their families.

By the time of that most outstanding of characters Moses, we already see the form of a sermon developing. In his addresses to the people of God, as he unfolds the covenant stipulations, he applies them and presses home their application in blessing and cursing (see e.g. Deuteronomy 5ff.). His successor Joshua, too, gathering all the children of Israel together in order to address them, reminds them of what God has said in the past and tells them what God is going to do in the future. He applies God's word directly to their lives, reaching his climax in his affirmation, *'But as for me and my household, we will serve the LORD'.*[4] There is, in preaching, always the declaration of what God has said, and the application of this word into people's lives.

As the Bible develops, so too does the preaching of God's Word. Associated with both the tabernacle and the temple we see priests and prophets. Part of the role of the priesthood was to teach the people the Word of God. One of the reasons behind God's injunction to Aaron not to partake of wine or strong drink before going to the tabernacle was surely to ensure that his head was clear so that he could teach the children of Israel all the statutes that the Lord had given them.[5] At the temple or the tabernacle the people could be gathered together so that those entrusted with ministry could teach them God's truth and point them in His way. To be deprived of these vital leadership roles was a keenly felt tragedy for the nation, as the bitter cry of the people in Lamentations 2:20 illustrates, *'Should priest and prophet be killed in the sanctuary of the Lord?'*

As the Old Testament progresses and the people of Israel are taken into exile, the temple becomes less significant and instead the synagogue becomes the place where the people gather together and the Scriptures are taught. The apostle James refers to this aspect of synagogue ministry in his address to the assembly gathered in Jerusalem:

> *'For Moses has been preached in every city from the earliest times and is read in the synagogues on every Sabbath.'*
> (Acts 15:21)

In the New Testament John the Baptist is primarily a preacher. He comes in the spirit and power of Elijah, 'heralding the news' and proclaiming his message of repentance in the wilderness of Judah. Then Jesus marches onto the scene. God has only one Son and He makes Him a preacher. He comes preaching – proclaiming the Kingdom of God wherever He goes. The Lord Jesus models ministry for us. In private He brings together a close-knit group of people whom He instructs and teaches, and in public He addresses a wider group of people, proclaiming to them the Kingdom of God and the good news of the gospel. The whole ministry of Jesus in public and private is a proclaiming ministry.

Into the post-Jesus phase in Acts, preaching continues to take place in a variety of contexts. It is a fascinating study to investigate the contexts in which the word 'proclaim' and the various words for 'preach' are used in the book of Acts. We discover that Paul 'preaches', for example, when he is in dialogue with people; when he is proclaiming the

Word to the gathered church (e.g. Acts 20:7–12); when he is interacting with the philosophers on Mars Hill (Acts 17). The proclamation of the Word of God takes place in public and private; it takes place within the church and outside the church; it takes place among Christians and towards non-Christians: it takes place in a whole variety of situations.

PREACHING IN THE POST-APOSTOLIC PERIOD

This continues into the post-apostolic period. It appears that at least as far as the early second century preaching remained quite a simple affair. In his *Apology* addressed to the Emperor, in which he defended Christianity against misrepresentation (*c.* 130 AD), Justin Martyr writes,

> On the day called Sunday all who live in the cities or in the country gather together to one place, and the memoirs of the apostles, or the writings of the prophets are read as long as time permits; then, when the reader has ceased, the president verbally instructs, and exhorts to the imitation of these good things. Then we all rise together and pray, and as we said before, when our prayer is ended, bread and wine and water are brought, and the president, in like manner, offers prayers and thanksgivings according to his ability, and the people assent, saying 'Amen'.[6]

His description is notable both for the prominence that is given to the reading and the preaching of the Scripture, and to the combination of the Word and the sacrament. It is clear that when the church met together, the Scriptures were read and an extemporary explanation of the Bible was given, starting where the text started and ending where it ended.

The preachers of the third and fourth centuries – men like Basil the Great (329–79), Gregory of Nazianzus (*c.* 325–89), Gregory of Nyssa (d. *c.* 385/6) and Augustine (354–430) – were conscious of the heavy use of traditional rhetoric by their contemporaries. People flocked to hear the rhetoricians giving their declamatory speeches – it was the entertainment of the day. However, these preachers understood very clearly the difference between what they were doing and what the rhetoricians were doing. While the latter were using the spoken word as a form of entertainment in order to impress their audiences, the Christian preachers were concerned to proclaim what God had said and apply it to the lives of their listeners. For example, in one of his writings on Christian doctrine, Augustine is at pains to distinguish between rhetoric and preaching, arguing that preaching is an entirely different means of communication. It is based on the Bible, it is applied to the heart, and it is not intended as a show or form of entertainment.

One of the great preachers of this period is John Chrysostom (*c.* 347–407), a name all Christian preachers need to know. The description 'Chrysostom', meaning 'the golden mouth', was given to him about a hundred years after he died, a telling memorial of the esteem in which he was obviously held. He had amazing oratorical gifts. Although he became archbishop, it was a responsibility he never desired, and he had to be accompanied to the church for his consecration under military escort. In 398 Constantinople was *the* great city of the Empire. The church in Constantinople had a membership of about a hundred thousand people, with a whole army of church staff to look after them – it was a mega-church indeed. John Chrysostom had a heavy preaching workload – he preached every Sunday, on saints' days, on most weekdays and on several evenings. Surveys of his preaching reveal three important aspects. First, his preaching was biblical: he preached systematically through several books of the Bible. In his sermons he quoted the Bible liberally and there are many allusions to Bible stories and events. Second, his interpretation of the Bible was straightforward and simple. He did not use allegory, which was to become very popular in the Church in later years. Third, he is known for his very practical application of the Bible and his plain speaking. His sermons give a very clear picture of what was going on in the society of his day and his tough stance on moral issues. For example, from the pulpit he confronted people who aborted their children, he condemned materialism and gambling on horse races, and he challenged the rich for their treatment of the poor.

Preaching was a subject of great interest to John Chrysostom and he made every effort to encourage good preaching in his church congregation. He was very concerned about the use of preaching as entertainment, complaining, 'Most people usually listen to a preacher for pleasure not profit, as though it were a play or a concert', and on occasion had to rebuke his congregation for their unruly behaviour, which included interrupting his sermons with applause. He was very aware of the dangers of personality cult in this type of very public ministry and warned against them. Over eight hundred of John Chrysostom's sermons have survived and in fact are still frequently preached in the Eastern Orthodox Church to this day. His was a great ministry.

PREACHING SINCE CONSTANTINE

It is at the point of Constantine's supposed conversion that things began to go seriously wrong for the Church of Jesus Christ. Up until then Rome had been the capital of the Empire. Roman society had long been multifaith but during this period an eastern religion called Mithraism dominated the city. Christianity was still a persecuted minority. For three hundred years, since the execution of Paul by beheading and Peter's execution in the circus of Nero at the foot of Vatican Hill, the Christian Church in Rome had known bouts of persecution followed by periods of toleration – so long as they kept their heads down and didn't say too much.

The small church of St Clement, a short distance away from the Coliseum in Rome, provides a simple illustration of the transition that took place when Constantine became

Emperor and Christianity was legalised. The present church building dates from the fourteenth century but beneath it lies a fourth-century church. It was probably the second or third church building *ever* in Christian history. It is quite amazing to realise that, until this church was built, there were virtually no church buildings. It was built as an ordinary 'basilica', which was a Roman public hall, not intended for any religious purpose. Beneath that fourth-century building lie the paving stones of a Roman street and the remains of a Mithraic temple, a school room and a private house with a living-room. It is known that this living-room belonged to Clement, who is mentioned in the New Testament,[7] and that for about three hundred years Christians had met there for worship and to hear the Word of God. Paul had taught in that house; Peter had taught in that house: no wonder they wanted to keep it as their place of meeting. When, then, the Emperor declared that he wanted to provide the church with a building, they asked him to build it on that same site so they could keep their connection alive with their roots. But a very interesting thing happened when the church was erected. With the Emperor now telling the people of Rome to attend their church services, the Christian community constructed within the basilica an oblong box-shaped room, with a door at each end, that was the same size as Clement's living-room, and the Christians met inside this room. Outside the box there was a lectern from which a Christian preacher would explain what the Christians were doing and what they believed. The Romans would come into the basilica and mill around, watching what was going on – if you like, it was the first seeker service. Anyone who became a Christian would be baptised and would then join the Christians meeting inside the room.

The Romans were, however, used to temples; they were used to theatre and drama. They soon became bored with watching these Christians inside their box and listening to their lectures. It was not long, therefore, before the Christian church took the decision to minimise their proclamation and maximise all their ritual until worship became a kind of dramatic show. They took the small plain table on which they used to place the bread and wine and moved it to the east end of the building, where the shrine would be placed in the pagan temple. In the first few centuries there was nothing theologically wrong with what they were doing; they were not articulating the kind of priesthood ideas that would eventually emerge in Post-reformation Catholicism. In the beginning it was a way of communicating and connecting with the largely pagan Roman population. It was an attempt to be culturally relevant. But it marked a sea change in the nature of Christian services. Slowly it became doctrine. As Christian ministers were elevated in status within Roman society, they were allowed to wear the senatorial robes of the high-powered in society, and of course this practice has stuck and such robes are still being worn in some branches of the Church to this day.

An outstanding preacher of this period was Pope Gregory the Great (*c.* 540–604). The title of 'pope' is, of course, given retrospectively, since the role did not exist in those days. From a wealthy senatorial family, through natural ability he had worked his way up to become the Prefect of Rome, a secular job, before deciding to give it all up because he believed God was calling him to serve people. He gave away all his wealth and lived in seclusion, reading the Scriptures and praying. He was later made the pastor of the Church in Rome, presumably because of his background. He became the driving force in sixth-century missionary work, urging the monks out of the monasteries, where they had gone to live holy lives of seclusion, to the far regions of the Empire to preach the gospel.

Gregory the Great's *Pastoral Rule*, written in 591, deals particularly with preaching. In it he outlines the categories of people who are liable to be in any preacher's audience and explains how the preacher is to address each category:

> You are to differently admonish the different people who are there: men and women, the poor and the rich, the joyful, the sad, the prelates, the subordinates, the servants, the masters, the wives, lovers of strife and the peacemakers. Let the joyful learn by the threatenings what they are to be afraid of, let the sad hear what joys of reward they may look forward to. Woe to you who laugh now, for you shall weep. But I will turn your heart from sadness into joy, and your joy no one will take away.

Above all he believed in the practical application of the Bible.

In the Middle Ages preaching waned in influence. There were, however, some notable exceptions to this trend. Bernard of Clairvaux (1090–1153), Francis of Assisi (*c*. 1181–1226), Anthony (1195–1231) and Thomas Aquinas (*c*. 1225–74) were all great preachers of this period. A man called Berthold of Ratisbon (*c*. 1210–72) addressed between 60,000 and 100,000 people near Glatz in Bohemia.

By the end of the Middle Ages, however, the situation was dire. By and large preaching had died out. The majority of the priests could not read Latin: they merely recited it when they led Mass. Neither could they read Greek or Hebrew, and many of them had no access to books. Their role had diminished largely to priestcraft.

It is against this background that several outstanding figures emerge: the Englishman John Wycliffe (1324–84), the Bohemian Jan Hus (1369–1415) and the Italian Girolamo Savonarola (1452–98). These men began to preach the gospel in a way we would recognise it today. They did not pull their punches as far as the Word of God was concerned, often aiming their hard-hitting messages at the ecclesiastical establishment.

A new band of travelling preachers also began to emerge both in England and across Europe. As far back as 1382, during the reign of Richard II, an Act of Parliament was passed addressing a grievance that was clearly being expressed by local priests and clergymen about the number of unlicensed preachers who were going from town to town and from house to house. In England there are a number of ancient 'Gospel Oaks' which were clearly favourite sites for such open-air preaching – for example, the oak in Addleston, Surrey, where the followers of Wycliffe used to preach the gospel (John Knox is also known to have preached there). In Europe travelling preachers proclaimed God's Word in Germany, Spain, The Netherlands and Southern France.

As we look back over church history the question raises itself, where did the Church go wrong? If we take the Church in Rome, we can conclude that it went wrong when it moved away from the proclaimed Word in an attempt to be relevant to people. It was without doubt Helena, Constantine's Christian mother, who was the driving force behind the Christianisation of the Roman Empire. It was Helena who sent soldiers to the Middle East to try and discover the remains of the cross in order to bring them to Rome. It was she who had the steps from Pilate's judgement hall transported to Rome. Her reason for doing this was because she was determined that Christianity should win over Mithraism which up until that point was still the dominant religion. She believed that this could be achieved if she could only demonstrate to the Roman population that Christianity, unlike Mithraism, had a historical basis in the life and death of Jesus. She believed that these visual aids would help to illustrate the historical reality of Christianity. But once the focus was moved away from the Word of God, once drama, in the sense of the theatre of the Mass, became the dominant thing, then the untaught (particularly in Rome) were open to wild superstition. They were used to a pantheon of gods: the martyrs and the apostles took their place. They were used to a female presence within the godhead, so they took the mother goddess, familiar in the Middle East, changed her name and put Mary there. They took away her spear and placed a baby in her arms, all with a view to relevance. In every generation the Church faces the very real danger of making microscopic moves towards relevance which over time – even hundreds of years – take it so far off course that a major shift is required to bring it back to where it should be.

Preaching Since Luther

This major shift came in the form of one man who, as he crawled on his knees up the *scala sancta* of the Church of St John Lateran in Rome (as far as we know the only person ever to do this), was convicted halfway up by the words, 'The just shall live by faith'. He got up and walked back down those stairs, thus paving the way for the Reformation to begin. This man was Martin Luther.

Martin Luther (1483–1546) was a preacher above all preachers. One of his prayers reveals his passion for the exaltation of God in His Word. He prayed, 'Dear Lord God, I want to preach so that You are glorified. I want to speak of You, praise You, praise Your name. Although I probably cannot make it turn out well, won't *You* make it turn out well?' He also said, 'If I could today become king or emperor I would not give up my office as preacher.' Martin Luther had a passion for God and His Word.

Between 1520 and 1546 Luther preached approximately three thousand sermons. He knew the burden and the pressure of weekly preaching, ministering regularly in the town church in Wittenberg. On Sundays at 5.00 a.m. he would preach from an epistle; at 10.00 a.m. he would preach from a gospel; in the afternoon he would preach from the Old Testament; on Mondays and Tuesdays he would preach from the Catechism; on

Wednesdays he would preach from the Gospel of Matthew; on Thursdays and Fridays he would preach from the epistles; and on Saturday he would preach from the Gospel of John. Such was his commitment to the preaching of the Word. Martin Luther emphasised that, when the Word is preached, it is the very Word of God Himself: it is the Word living, the Word personalised, the Word spoken through an individual. For him, the preacher embodies the Word of God. The voice used becomes the very voice of God. It is the Word of God written now living and breathed as it is proclaimed. That is the mystery of preaching.

A generation later, John Calvin's whole ministry was also one of unrelenting exposition of the Word of God, which he believed unleashed the majesty of God. His own experience had taught him that, 'The highest proof of Scripture derives in general from the fact that God in person speaks in it' and this led him to the following conclusions. Since the Scriptures are the very voice of God, since they are therefore self-authenticating in revealing the majesty of God, and since the majesty and glory of God are the reason for all existence, it followed that his life would be marked by invincible constancy in the exposition of Scripture.

When one considers the history of those who were inspired by Calvin's twenty-five-year ministry at St Peter's Church in Geneva – French Protestantism, in particular, the Huguenots – one sees people who were prepared to risk all because of their commitment to proclaiming the Word of God. These people were vibrant; they knew a dynamic certainty based upon the Word of God. The Bible came alive to them. They would preach anywhere: they weren't limited to the pulpit. They would take the Word of God wherever God gave them an opening, and they would proclaim it boldly and fearlessly. They knew that preaching the Word of God would probably mean death, but they did it all the same.

The productive Puritan era, in which there was a great passion to exalt Christ in the Word, was followed by yet another period in which the Church languished and England found itself once again in a critical state. Drunkenness was the order of the day and immorality was rife. The state of society was such that one writer has commented that England was heading at breakneck speed towards a bloody revolution that would have been worse than anything France had experienced. Society was on the verge of destruction and the Church had become perfunctory and dead. The masses attended the Church of England, where they were not exposed to the gospel at all.

This is the context in which the ministries of John Wesley (1703–91) and George Whitefield (1714–70) were raised up. The new move of God began with Wesley's realisation, recorded in a diary entry on board a ship returning from North America, that, 'I discovered as I was going out to preach to the Indians that here I was and I wasn't converted myself.' In London, he famously experienced God in a new way when he felt his heart 'strangely warmed' by the Holy Spirit while attending a meeting in Aldersgate Street. Thereafter he began to preach and, having been banished from the Anglican Church, he moved onto the street. Although, at this point in history, it was an unprecedented move, as we have seen preachers have done this throughout the centuries. In 1733 Whitefield, an orator of unbelievable skill and ability, was converted. Under this powerful work of God the British Isles were transformed by the Evangelical Awakening.

John Wesley was a man of remarkable simplicity but a man of style and force in argument. While in York in 1753 he made the following entry in his diary:

> I began preaching at seven and God applied it to the hearts of the hearers. Tears and groans were every side among the high and low. God is at work. Bowed the heavens and came down, the flame of love went up before him, the rocks were torn in pieces, the mountains flowed down with his presence. I spoke with such closeness and pungency as I cannot do but at some peculiar seasons in my life. It is the gift of God and cannot be attained by all the efforts of nature and art united. God himself made the application. Truly God preached to their hearts.

In one of his journals, George Whitefield writes of his experiences in America:

> After I had begun the sermon the Spirit of God gave me freedom until at length it came down like a mighty rushing wind and carried all before it. At night the Lord manifested his glory and after singing I gave a word of exhortation, and with what power! None can fully express but those that saw it. Oh, how did the Word fall like a hammer and like a fire. I had not discoursed long but the Holy Spirit displayed his power, and every part of the congregation somebody or other began to cry out and almost melted into tears.

God the Spirit took the Word and applied it to people's lives, resulting in a mighty spiritual awakening.

This second great Evangelical Awakening changed the shape of the nation, as men like Lord Shaftesbury and William Wilberforce rose up to work to alleviate poverty and bring such injustices as child labour and slavery to an end.

In the nineteenth century preaching again lost its way when it became an art form. The preaching of this period has been described as 'a form of literature'. Ministers preached in order that their sermons would be published. Men like Dr Joseph Parker at the City Temple in London and Dr Lyman Beacher in Boston, one of the great fashionable cities of America, would be imitated by ordinary ministers in churches up and down the country. There was a great emphasis on language, skill and drama, all the time losing out on the vital 'I–You' confrontation between preacher and listener. It is this connection that is key in preaching, setting it apart from a lecture or piece of dramatic oratory. The preacher drives home to the listener what God is saying through the text, constantly seeking to find hooks into people's experience on which to hang the truth – seeking to find an entry-point for the truth, in order to get to the heart.

Two preachers of this period stand out head and shoulders above their contemporaries: the Englishman Charles Haddon Spurgeon (1834–92) and the American D.L. Moody (1837–99). Unlike other well-known orators, their preaching hit home – it got to the heart. Spurgeon was a man of huge personality who dominated the pulpit in London. When D.L. Moody visited London, people were amazed that an unlettered American was able to speak the Word of God so directly into people's lives, making an impact in the hearts and minds of his listeners.

The Twentieth Century Until Today

The twentieth century was a century of ups and downs as far as preaching is concerned. Preachers ranged from the cool English communicator Campbell Morgan, on the one hand, to the fiery Welshman Martyn Lloyd-Jones, who said,

> What is preaching? Logic on fire! Eloquent reason! Are these contradictions? Of course they are not! Reason concerning this truth ought to be mightily eloquent, as you see it in the case of the apostle Paul and others. It is theology on fire. And a theology which does not take fire, I maintain, is a defective theology. Or at least the man's understanding of it is defective. Preaching is theology coming through a man who is on fire. True understanding and experience of the truth must lead to this. A person who can speak about these things dispassionately has no right whatsoever to be in a pulpit, and should never be allowed to enter one. What is the chief end of preaching? To give men and women a sense of God and his presence.[8]

He also said,

> I can forgive a man for a bad sermon, I can forgive the preacher almost anything if he gives me a sense of God. If he's given me something for my soul, if he gives me the sense that, though he is inadequate in himself, he is handling something which is very great and very glorious. If he gives me some glimpse of the majesty and the glory of God, the love of Christ my Saviour, and the magnificence of the gospel – if he does that I'm his debtor, and I'm profoundly grateful to him.

John Stott's contribution to preaching in the last century has been outstanding. His great book on preaching is a must-read for anybody who wants to understand the mechanics of it.[9] He reminds us that preachers stand between two worlds – the world of the Bible and the world in which their hearers live – and they must understand both: they must bridge the divide, so that contemporary hearers really hear in their circumstances and experiences the timeless, infallible, completed and sufficient written Word. Preaching is the means by which the objective written Word becomes, without changing its message one bit, the Word of God spoken to us. There must be that crisis moment, he says, in which this must happen.

The great task of preaching has caught the minds of the most outstanding people throughout history. Although I have focused to a large extent on the great figures who have influenced preaching in Europe (i.e. since the post-apostolic era) it is important for us to remember that all over the world there are many, whose names we are not familiar with, who have proclaimed Christ to great effect. Throughout history and today such preachers have witnessed masses of conversions, seen churches established and the work of God continued. We are only a small part of the global picture of what God is doing in the world, but each of us has our own part to play. Whether it is proclaiming the gospel to our families, a group of friends, a small cell group or to a larger congregation, the task of simply communicating God's Word, which has occupied the saints of God throughout history, is now our task for our day and our generation. May God help us in it for His glory's sake.

NOTES

1. Luke 11:50–51; Jude 14.
2. 2 Peter 2:5.
3. Genesis 20:7.
4. Joshua 24:15.
5. Leviticus 10:9.
6. *The First Apology of Justin*, Chapter LXVII: Weekly Worship of the Christians.
7. Philippians 4:3.
8. *Preaching and Preachers* (Hodder & Stoughton, 1971), p. 97.
9. *Between Two Worlds: The Art of Preaching in the Twentieth Century* (Eerdmans Publishing Co., 1982).

Chapter 4

INTRODUCING THE GIFT

Mark Stibbe

Teaching is one of the most neglected spiritual gifts in the Body of Christ, particularly in Charismatic circles. It is for this reason that I am passionately committed to persuade, motivate and incite Christians, and particularly pastors and leaders, to start preaching and teaching with hearts on fire – to start expounding the Bible. It is my heartfelt concern that preaching and teaching should be seen to be absolutely critical in the move of the Holy Spirit that is on its way and is already in some sense here among us. At that time preaching and teaching will not take a back seat. Some Charismatics say to me, 'When the Holy Spirit is manifestly present in the Church, and God's glory is there, we won't need to preach any more.' Such talk is, frankly, nonsense – and I usually tell them so. When people are drawn to the presence of God like moths to a light bulb we will need to preach and teach the Bible and the gospel of our Lord Jesus Christ then more than ever.

In Romans 12 Paul exhorts the members of the Body of Christ to find their gift and start using it for the glory of God and for the up-building of the Church:

> *God has given each of us the ability to do certain things well. So if God has given you the ability to prophesy, speak out when you have faith that God is speaking through you. If your gift is that of serving others, serve them well. If you are a teacher, do a good job of teaching. If your gift is to encourage others, do it! If you have money, share it generously. If God has given you leadership ability, take the responsibility seriously. And if you have a gift for showing kindness to others, do it gladly.*
> (Romans 12:6–8)[1]

Third in this list of seven gifts, which is not exhaustive, is the spiritual gift of teaching which I want to introduce. My reading of the New Testament leads me to the conclusion that in the church there were people who were anointed specifically for the task of teaching. The evidence for this can be gathered from a number of places, but principal among them is Ephesians 4:11 where Paul talks about the gifts that the Lord Jesus Christ in His ascended, glorified status has given to His Church. He writes:

> *He is the one who gave these gifts to the church: the apostles, the prophets,*
> *the evangelists, and the pastors and teachers.*
> (Ephesians 4:11)

In His earthly ministry Jesus embodied all five of these ministries, supremely and pre-eminently. He was pre-eminently an apostle sent from the Father to do a pioneering, extraordinary work here on the earth. He was pre-eminently an evangelist who came to proclaim the good news of the Kingdom of God. He was pre-eminently a prophet who brought revelation from the Father to those who were prepared to listen, and many, many people recognised Him in this role. He was also pre-eminently the pastor of pastors, the model Shepherd who lays down His life for the sheep. Lastly, he was pre-eminently a teacher sent from God, a fact which even the Pharisee Nicodemus recognised.[2] Jesus, then, exercised all five of these ministries. Since the time of His death on the cross, His resurrection and His ascension into the heavenly realms, He gives those gift ministries to people in His Body so that He may continue His work through the power of the Holy Spirit in the here and now until the second coming, whenever that may happen. There are, then, in the Body of Christ:

- *apostles* – pioneer leaders who do extraordinary things for the expansion of the Kingdom of God
- *prophets* – who hear the word of the Lord and transmit revelation to people for encouragement, strengthening and comfort (1 Corinthians 14:3)
- *evangelists* – who are anointed and equipped to preach the good news
- *pastors* – who are enabled and called to shepherd the sheep
- *teachers* – who are called to bring God's Word in a fresh way in every generation.

These are all the ministries of Jesus which He gives to His Church to continue in the here and now – the already and the not yet – between the first coming of the Kingdom and its consummation on the last day.

What is the Gift of Teaching?

I define the spiritual gift of teaching as follows: *the God-given ability to instruct believers in a biblical and a revelatory way.*

Firstly, it is a 'God-given ability'. Whenever Paul talks about the gift of teaching, he emphasises the fact that, whatever natural predisposition we have to be effective teachers and communicators of God's Word, in the end it is a gift from heaven. It is a supernatural donation or anointing from the Father, who loves to give good gifts to His children when they ask.

The man who has had the greatest impact on my life, in terms of my spiritual formation, is John Wimber. I probably owe more to John than to any other Christian, and I hold his memory in great affection. He taught and, more importantly, modelled in many aspects what I would describe as 'balanced biblical Christianity'. In 1985, while I was at theological college, three of my friends dragged me kicking and screaming to the John Wimber conference on the Kingdom of God in Sheffield because they felt that 'it would do me the world of good to go'. Half of me was petrified in case God did to me what He was doing to other people through this man and half of me was crying out to God, 'Please, God, don't miss me out.' During the conference I was really quite subversively won over both by John's emphasis on the Word of God and his Christ-centredness. My fears were disarmed and my natural theological scepticism overcome. Over the course of the conference God was powerfully releasing and anointing many people – indeed, to me it seemed to be happening to everyone but me. I felt very left out. That is, until the last morning when John taught on the five ministries listed in Ephesians 4:11. He told the conference that he believed that, as he read out the names of these five ministries and prayed, God would release them or at least call them forth, since some people already had them but were not exercising them. As he did so, the Holy Spirit started touching people all over the auditorium which held about three thousand. When he began to pray for a release of teachers, God started to touch me in a very powerful way. Bizarrely, my right hand began to shake uncontrollably – as a theologian I asked myself what the significance of this could possibly be. Then I sensed the Holy Spirit saying, not in an audible voice but more in terms of an impression, that the Father was calling me to be a teacher and writer in the things of the renewal, and that is exactly what has happened. It took about seven years before it began to come about, which is an interesting fact in itself, but this is where I find myself today.

At the same time I know that there are natural abilities that are associated with the gift of teaching. I am very interested in the whole subject of how our personality, experience, heart abilities and spiritual gifts are all woven together. I became a Christian during a revival at Winchester College in 1977 when between a third and a half of the pupils at that highly atheistic, secular, intellectual school were converted. When I arrived at the school there were only six Christians in the Christian Union; when I left there were one hundred and fifty. It was a really extraordinary time of revival. Before my conversion, all I was into was football – it was my religion; nevertheless I can remember joining the debating society. My friends all thought I was mad and asked me, 'What on earth are you doing joining the debating society?' I now believe it was a Holy Spirit set-up because in the debating society I learnt how to present a point of view passionately, even one I didn't believe in at all.

Imagine, then, how useful these techniques have proved in presenting arguments to which I hold fervently. No experience in our lives is wasted: God knows what He is doing, even before we are saved. Although our natural abilities may contribute towards us being effective communicators, I would still stress that a teaching ability is God-given. It is a gift from the Father which we don't deserve, but which He graciously bestows because He is so kind and because He wants to see His Church nourished, nurtured and growing up in God.

Secondly, the gift of teaching is given for the instruction of believers. The primary audience for the teaching gift is not non-Christians but those who are already saved and who need not just the Spirit but also the Word; not just power but also theology. I love the description of the teacher as somebody through whom 'theology comes forth on fire'. That is exactly right, and it is a crucial emphasis.

In looking at this aspect of the spiritual gift of teaching it is helpful, without over-emphasising the point, to make a distinction between *kerygma*, on the one hand, and *didachē*, on the other. In the New Testament *kerygma*, from the verb *kērusso* meaning 'to proclaim', is associated with the gospel message, with a very strong emphasis on proclamation. However, *didachē*, associated with the Greek verb *didaskō*, 'to teach', really means 'teaching' or 'doctrine'. I see these as distinct but overlapping ministries. Of course, we should not make too hard and fast a distinction between these two because the one who teaches – who engages in *didachē* – will always, hopefully, be rooted in the *kerygma*. And the one who brings the *kerygma* to not-yet Christians will hopefully be grounded in *didachē*. So, although I would not wish to force a wedge between the two, I hold that there is enough of a distinction between them to make the following point. As a teacher, my base ministry is teaching those who are already believers. As an evangelist, J. John's base ministry is preaching the gospel to those who are not yet Christians. I can go into a secular environment and do a gospel presentation, but I wouldn't say it's my base ministry. To be honest it is an environment in which I have to work very hard. J. John would say the same about the teaching gift. I am mindful of what I have heard R.T. Kendall say on more than one occasion when asked, 'What is the anointing?' He replies, 'The anointing is when it's easy.' It is very important not to misunderstand what he is saying. It is not to say that the teacher has not sweated over his preparation in his study or that the actual execution of it has not exhausted him; but it is to say that while he is teaching there is an ease about it. The teacher knows that this is what he was made for. The teacher experiences an ease in instructing believers and the evangelist experiences an ease in proclaiming the gospel. Each is exercising his base ministry.

Once again I would not want to overstress this, but the audience and purpose of each gift/ministry differs. For preaching, the audience is unbelievers, the gift/ministry is the evangelist and the purpose is salvation. For teaching, the audience is believers, the gift/ministry is the teacher, and the purpose is sanctification. Evangelists are called to bring people in, but pastors and teachers are called to bring people up and on. We need both ministries. In a church situation it is fatal if the gospel is preached but the people are never instructed and discipled. Likewise, it is fatal if the gospel is never preached and the church just provides a cosy club for those who want to become more and more knowledgeable. A church needs both.

The purpose of teaching is, I have said, sanctification. By this I mean that the teacher's role is to impart, in a relevant way, right beliefs and right behaviour. In my own church I have taken this calling seriously by running an annual doctrine course in which instruction is given on the foundational doctrines of Christian faith. The purpose is not that people should become more and more puffed up with knowledge but rather that they might be equipped to explain their faith to seekers in a more compelling way – in line with Peter's command that believers should always be able to give a reasoned defence of their beliefs (cf. 1 Peter 3:15). We link the course with the church's fundamental vision which is to reach the lost.

I am also wholly committed to helping believers in their lifestyle issues so that they know how to live the life and walk the talk. In this respect teaching is about the renewal of the mind, in learning how to look at issues from God's perspective, not just my perspective. When people catch the revelation – for example, in relation to stewardship, learning that they are not the owners but the managers of what God has given to them – their lives are revolutionised.

Thirdly, the spiritual gift of teaching is the God-given ability to instruct believers in a biblical way. I want to stress this. It is our responsibility as teachers always to be rooted in the Scriptures; always to keep the Word of God central; always to maintain the Bible's absolute authority. I can't stand it when preachers basically give their own views and then find Bible passages to support their argument. For me, God's views are paramount: my views must be shaped in relation to His. When I present His views, I am on much safer ground. I can feel totally confident. My challenge, then, is not just to expound God's view but to help each member of my congregation to apply it.

Recently I heard a sermon on marriage, divorce and remarriage, in which the teacher, who should really have known better, based his whole view on the latest report on the subject from the Anglican bishops. I was not interested in his reflections on the bishops' report; if the truth be told, neither was I interested in the bishops' report. What I want to know is what the Bible says, and whether what we as a community of faith are thinking, individually and corporately, is consistent with God's revelation in Scripture. Whether what the bishops are saying is in line with what the Bible says is a secondary issue. We must keep the Word of God central.

One of my favourite chapters in the Bible is Nehemiah 8. The city and the temple have been restored after the Exile and it is time for the Law to be re-established. We read in verse 8:

> *They read from the Book of the Law of God and clearly explained the meaning of what was being read, helping the people understand each passage.*

69

This verse expresses clearly and simply the challenge to every teacher. His task is twofold:

1. to explain the meaning of a passage in terms of historical criticism, and
2. under the guidance of the Holy Spirit, to explain its significance for now – not just for Sunday in church but for Monday in the workplace.

While the original meaning of a passage is fixed, the way it applies to today may be fluid – its application may be different today from what it would have been ten years ago. I call this 'Charismatic exegesis' – the exegesis of Scripture in the power of the Holy Spirit, bringing its meaning and its significance to life. In the Nehemiah passage the Word of God had a profound impact on its hearers, causing them to weep. They had not heard the Word of God read or explained for many years. Ezra, however, told them that this was not an occasion for sorrow but for joy and celebration. Nehemiah then sent them away to celebrate with the words: *'This is a sacred day before our Lord. Don't be dejected and sad, for the joy of the LORD is your strength!'* (Nehemiah 8:10).

The fourth and final aspect of the definition is that the gift of teaching involves bringing the Bible to life in a 'revelatory way'. The teacher imparts the prophetic significance of God's Word for now. When this happens, it is almost as if we say with the apostle Paul, *'These things were written for our sakes'* (cf. 1 Corinthians 9:10 KJV). Of course, they weren't, but when a teacher is anointed, the Bible passage comes alive and there is a sense that it could have been written *'for just such a time as this'*.[3] The actual significance of a passage is being brought to light in a revelatory way. I would say from my experience, over twenty-seven years as a Christian in evangelical circles, that we tend to be very much better at explaining the meaning in an expository way than we are at finding the prophetic significance for right now and teaching that to our people. In many ways we are fearful of this challenge but we need not be. If we apply biblical criteria to test our interpretation, then I am convinced we can be on safe ground here too. As I have been saying for years, information added to revelation brings transformation. Information – what the passage means; revelation – its prophetic significance: together they bring life-change. It is the role of the teacher not just to impart information but to teach: to be an agent of transformation for the people to whom he is speaking. The Word is radiant with light and it is quickened to our spirits and hearts, not just to our minds. There is life *in* it and life-change *from* it.

The association of prophecy with teaching always causes anxiety and debate. I believe prophecy and teaching are distinct gifts. In the Romans passage quoted earlier it is interesting that Paul makes a clear differentiation between the gifts of prophecy and teaching. The academic James Dunn talks about this issue with great lucidity in his book *Jesus and the Spirit*,[4] which was published as long ago as 1975. I keep referring back to this book, along with Gordon Fee's *God's Empowering Presence*,[5] because in it theological substance and biblical foundation are given to things which many are actually experiencing now. For James Dunn prophecy is more creative than teaching: not in the sense of receiving fresh revelation from God that is inconsistent with Scripture, but in the sense of receiving fresh revelation that is consistent with old revelation. Teaching, on the other hand, brings fresh insight, under the anointing of the Holy Spirit, to the existing Word – God's Scriptures.

Five or six years ago I was invited to teach at a conference in Holland on the subject of revival in the hope that it might stimulate some faith among the conference delegates for God to move in power again among the lost. In my preparation I had really been submerged in the subject and had studied the Scripture in depth, so I had five or six messages that I wanted to bring to that particular group of people. However, throughout the conference, which seemed on the face of it to be going well, I kept sensing and being drawn to 1 Corinthians 13. Although the worship was musically excellent, and the congregation seemed to be really entering into it, I couldn't get away from the idea that the favour of God was not upon it. The feeling persisted throughout the conference.

The last meeting of the conference was the Sunday morning church meeting. At the prayer time before the service, while everyone else seemed excited and upbeat, I felt a great sense of heaviness. I asked the senior pastor for his permission to share a word, and he gave it. I shared what the Father had laid on my heart, which concerned disunity in the church. The moment I started to speak the senior pastor's wife, who had been very ebullient up to that point, started weeping and weeping. To my surprise nobody did anything about it. The prayer meeting ended and, still wondering what it was all about, I moved with the others into the church.

Throughout the time of worship I could not shake off my feeling that something was wrong. Then my interpreter came to me and said that what I had shared in the prayer meeting had been a prophetic word from God and I should share it again in the service instead of the sermon I had prepared. I felt he was right. Asking once again for the permission of the pastor, which he gave rather tentatively, I shared with the church what I felt the Holy Spirit was saying, which could be summarised as: 'Dear children, would you please love one another.' I had only spoken about a sentence before my interpreter broke down weeping and could no longer interpret. What happened next was holy and sacred.

I had not realised that the senior pastor and his wife had only recently taken over the leadership of the church and that the former pastor and his wife, who had built up the church, were still members. This situation had given rise to extraordinary divided loyalties in the church between an 'old camp' and a 'new one'. The old pastor was a real saint and he was doing nothing wrong, but he was still there in the background and people were still relating to him. The new pastor was under such heavy stress that he was having to take medication, because he just didn't feel he had ownership or acceptance from the people. When I had finished speaking something very moving happened. The whole congregation came forward and embraced the new senior pastor and his wife and asked for their forgiveness. Then the senior pastor fell on the floor under the power of the Holy Spirit and was unable to do anything.

By then it was time for me to leave for the airport, which turned out to be excellent timing. As I walked out of the room I looked back and saw the senior pastor's wife (who had been weeping her heart out earlier), standing up to preach on Psalm 133, *'How good and pleasant it is when brothers live together in unity ... there the* LORD *bestows his blessing, even life for evermore'* (NIV). Her composure and sense of authority were evident. Later I received a letter from someone who had been in that church for all thirty-two years of its life. He wrote that he had never seen the Lord move in the way that He had on that morning.

We have to be very careful when we talk about such things as these because they are sacred, but Jesus was glorified that morning. It was Jesus who spoke and Jesus' will, I believe, that was done in that place. The essence or spirit of prophecy is the testimony of Jesus. Those of us who find ourselves in such situations must continually decrease so that the Lord Jesus can increase.

My reason for relating this story is to underline my conviction that there is a difference between prophecy and teaching. On that occasion I was prophesying. From time to time I find myself in situations into which God breaks and says: 'You could unpack the Word of God in this situation, you could expound the Scriptures – and I love it when you do because that's what I've called you to do – but just for now I want you to prophesy and bring My word, My direct word, to My people.' This is different from the spiritual gift of teaching which is my base ministry.

I long to see the gift of teaching released more and more in the Church, particularly in small-group settings where it will not always be exercised as an office. We desperately need this gift. All five of the ministries – apostles, prophets, evangelists, pastors and teachers – are vital for church health and growth. In Ephesians 4:12–14, following on from the verse quoted earlier, Paul tells us why we need them:

> *Their responsibility is to equip God's people to do his work and build up the church, the body of Christ, until we come to such unity in our faith and knowledge of God's Son that we will be mature and full grown in the Lord, measuring up to the full stature of Christ. Then we will no longer be like children, forever changing our minds about what we believe because someone has told us something different or because someone has cleverly lied to us and made the lie sound like the truth.*

Like each of the other four ministries, teaching has a four-fold purpose: equipping, building, maturing and stabilising. The Bible is very clear that in the last days there will be more and more deception, and I believe we are seeing this happening, with people running after those whose teaching scratches what their itching ears want to hear. The Church desperately needs to be rooted in the Word of God, and those of us who are teachers in the

Body of Christ need to be equipping believers – not just imparting information to them, but equipping them. Referring again to John Wimber, I loved the fact that he equipped believers by both teaching them biblical principals and showing them how to implement them. For example, in the area of healing the sick he provided a simple five-step programme which at St Andrew's Chorleywood we have found mightily effective for the last twenty-five years. He modelled and demonstrated it, and then he said to people like me who just did not believe they could do it, 'Now you do it' – in the same way that Jesus did.

Through teaching we build up the Body of Christ so that believers do not remain in perpetual spiritual adolescence but grow up in God. Mature in their faith, they know what they believe and are no longer tossed about by one wind of doctrine after another. As deceptions arise, the teacher stabilises the people by teaching bravely and compassionately from the Word of God. Whenever their focus is deflected to whatever is the current issue, he gently draws them back and reminds them of the essence of the gospel. A church is like a ship with the pulpit the crow's nest. The teacher is in the crow's nest, saying, 'This is where I believe we need to go.'

Whatever their situation teachers and preachers must faithfully persevere in their exposition of the Word of God, believing that it never returns empty but will accomplish God's purpose.[6] If they preach the Word in season and out of season, then God will come through and the Church will eventually see a day of deliverance – a day of victory.

NOTES

1. The Scriptures in this chapter are quoted from the New Living Translation.
2. See John 3:2.
3. Esther 4:14.
4. Westminster John Knox Press.
5. Henrickson Publishers, 1994.
6. Isaiah 55:11.

Chapter 5

THE BOOK THAT SPEAKS FOR ITSELF: INTERPRETING THE BIBLE

Liam Goligher

This is a transcript of an actual conversation that took place between a US naval ship and Canadian authorities off the coast of Newfoundland in October 1995:

> [*US naval ship*]: Please divert your course 15 degrees to the north to avoid a collision.
> [*Canadian authorities*]: Recommend you divert your course 15 degrees to the south to avoid a collision.
> [*US naval ship*]: This is the captain of a US navy ship. I say again, divert your course.
> [*Canadian authorities*]: No. I say again, you divert your course.
> [*US naval ship*]: This is the aircraft carrier *USS Lincoln*, the second largest ship in the United States' Atlantic fleet. We are accompanied by three destroyers, three cruisers and numerous support vehicles. I demand that you change your course 15 degrees north, that is one-five degrees north, or counter-measures will be undertaken to ensure the safety of this ship.
> [*Canadian authorities*]: This is a lighthouse. Your call!

How vital it is to contextualise! In our day-to-day dealings with people it is very important to understand the context in which words are spoken, otherwise we can very soon find ourselves getting the wrong end of the stick. This is perhaps even truer when it comes to interpreting the Bible.

In my view interpreting the Bible is not as simple a task as some people make it out to be. As soon as we begin to attempt to interpret the Bible all sorts of questions begin to raise themselves:

- *textual* questions: Do I need to be able to read it in its original languages? How do I know which version to choose from all those that are available, and how will my choice of version affect my understanding? How can I be sure that what I am reading is exactly what the author intended to write? Since there are a variety of literary genres within the Bible, how can I know whether I am reading a poem or an historical account or a word of prophecy?
- *cultural* questions: Do I interpret the Bible from my perspective in the twenty-first century, or should I try and place myself in the shoes of an ancient Hebrew or a first-century Greek? How do my own preconceptions from my particular cultural context colour the way in which I look at the text of the Bible?
- *contextual* questions: What sort of society did the people about whom I am reading live in? Was it a commercial and industrial context, or a rural one?
- *moral* questions: how is my understanding of the text affected by the fact that I am myself not morally neutral but am shaped by my behaviour, attitudes and leanings and may be carrying guilt about all sorts of areas of my life? How is my understanding of the text influenced by the fact that I live in a very individualistic society in which there is a great emphasis on the subjective self?

Our interpretation of the Bible will also be influenced significantly by the way in which we approach knowledge. One of the biggest issues in our twenty-first-century post-modern culture is whether we can 'know' anything. As has been well documented and much discussed, there has been a huge philosophical shift away from Enlightenment thinking, when it was regarded as possible to approach a text from a position of neutrality or objectivity without any outside influences affecting our judgement. Post-modernism has taught us that this is a lie and that we must recognise that when we come to a text, we bring with us all of our experiences from the past. Furthermore, in post-modern thinking nothing can be known, so we can only 'interpret' the text. This has also led to a loss of belief in the grand meta-narrative and the growth in importance of the little stories of everyday life.

For all these reasons reading the Bible is not as straightforward as it used to be. As Christians we do believe in the Big Story. We believe in 'the unfolding drama of redemption',[1] the unveiling of God's great plan of salvation, and, while we too value the little stories, we understand their contribution to the grand meta-narrative of God's plan for the world.

This is the background against which we struggle to interpret the Bible. John Stott has said, 'Sometimes, surprising though it may be, God blesses a poor exegesis of a bad translation of a doubtful reading of an obscure verse of a minor prophet.' I have certainly found that to be true many times in my own experience.

Before I begin to look in more detail at how we go about interpreting the Bible I want first to look at three assumptions which undergird our understanding of Scripture and three resources which God has provided for our task.

THREE ASSUMPTIONS

1. The authority of Scripture

As evangelicals we believe in the authority of Scripture. We believe that the Scriptures are the written record of the words which God spoke to our forefathers. As the writer of the book of Hebrews says,

> *In the past God spoke to our forefathers through the prophets at many times and in various ways...*
> (Hebrews 1:1)

All the knowledge that we have about God is the result of His initiative towards us. He is the Revealer; we are the receptors of that revelation. We follow our Lord's example in treating the Scriptures as God's voice, so that when Jesus quotes Moses He says, 'The Spirit says...' and when He quotes David He says, 'God says'. To hear Moses is to hear the Spirit. To hear David is to hear God. To listen to Paul is to listen to Jesus. When we say that we believe in the authority of Scripture we are making more than simply a theological affirmation. We are affirming that we recognise that it has authority over us both as individuals and communities. It has the ultimate authority over what we believe and over how we behave; it governs our convictions and our conduct. The Scriptures are the necessary control and corrective of all human thought about God.

2. The clarity of Scripture

We also believe in the clarity of Scripture, which in times past used to be referred to as the 'perspicuity of Scripture'. The Bible is lucid and clear. Its basic message can be grasped by everyone. Even if they cannot read it for themselves, they will be able to understand it if it is read to them. This is not to say that all the Bible is equally clear nor to ignore those parts of the Bible that are difficult to understand. I am always encouraged by the apostle Peter's frank admission that some of Paul's writings are difficult to understand:

> *His [Paul's] letters contain some things that are hard to understand, which ignorant and unstable people distort, as they do the other Scriptures, to their own destruction.*
> (2 Peter 3:16)

While Martin Luther would have agreed, he believed that what is obscure or difficult in one place is stated more clearly and simply elsewhere.

Christianity is not an esoteric religion. The Bible speaks of God in meaningful patterns of speech because God wants to communicate with His people. As Christians we wonder at the condescension of the God who stoops down to us and speaks to us in our language.

77

3. The sufficiency of Scripture

The Scriptures are our God-given guide in all matters of faith and life. This conviction sets us apart from every other expression of the Christian faith. Mediaeval Catholicism taught, for example, that those who want to know the mind and will of God on the essentials of the Christian faith should listen to the teaching of the Church and finally let tradition guide them. Subjectivists say that we should listen to the experts – the expert theologian perhaps – and finally let our own judgement guide us. All evangelicals of whatever brand believe that we should listen to Holy Scripture and finally let its teaching guide us.

Paul says that the Scriptures are sufficient:

> *All Scripture is God-breathed and is useful for teaching, rebuking, correcting and training in righteousness, so that the man of God may be thoroughly equipped for every good work.*
> (2 Timothy 3:16–17)

This does not mean that it will satisfy every idle curiosity we may have, nor does it answer all our questions. It does not tell us, for example, if there is life on other planets, so there is no point trying to argue on such subjects from the Bible. There are secret and revealed things (Deuteronomy 29:29). God tells us what we need to know – and the challenge for us as human beings is to have the wisdom to discern what we do and what we do not need to know. The purpose of God's Word is to train us to distinguish between good and evil, but we also need to know our limits. While not pretending to know everything we should, we should none the less live up to the truth that we have attained and err on the side of caution when it comes to things we are not sure about. As Martin Luther said, 'My conscience is captive to the Word of God.' *'Hier stehe ich. Ich kann nicht anders. Gott helfe mir'* ('Here I stand. I can do no other. God help me').

THREE RESOURCES

In addition to the three assumptions we make every time we interpret the Bible, we have three resources on which we are able to draw.

1. The Holy Spirit

The Bible is the Holy Spirit's book. In the upper room, on the night on which He was betrayed, Jesus promised His immediate disciples a specific anointing of the Spirit to help them in three ways:

  (i) to remind them of all that He had said
 (ii) to supplement His teaching by leading them into all truth
(iii) to tell them the things which are to come.

It is fascinating to note how these three ways in which the Holy Spirit helps us are reflected in the make-up of the New Testament:

(i) the gospels: the reminder of all that Jesus said and did
(ii) the epistles: the supplementing of Jesus' teaching (i.e. *'I have much more to say to you, more than you can now bear. But when he, the Spirit of truth, comes, he will guide you into all truth'*[2])
(iii) Revelation: the things to come.

Since the Bible is the Spirit's book, we need His help in order to interpret it.

The person who is best able to interpret a book is the author him- or herself. I have occasionally heard discussion programmes on Radio 4, in which a panel of critics discusses a book. Sometimes the author of the book is also present. In listening to such discussions I am always stunned when I hear the commentators arguing with the author about what she meant by a particular aspect of the plot or a particular sentence in the mouth of one of her characters, and telling her that she meant something other than what she is saying she meant! It is ridiculous! But we do it with God all the time! In 1 Corinthians 2:13 we read,

> *This is what we speak, not in words taught us by human wisdom but in words taught by the Spirit, expressing spiritual truths in spiritual words.*

The Spirit interprets spiritual truths to spiritual people. In order to interpret the Bible we need the Holy Spirit. Every day we need to get down on our knees and ask the Lord to give us His Spirit to enlighten our eyes, so that we may see wonderful truths in His Word.

2. A Christian mind

God wants to transform us *'by the renewing of our minds'*.[3] He wants us to be mature in our thinking. The Bible is addressed primarily, though not exclusively, to our understanding, and that means our mind. A Christian mind is, therefore, one of the resources we have at our disposal to help us in our interpretation of the Bible.

Now this emphasis on the mind sits uncomfortably with us because we are living in an age which is anti-intellectual, and this anti-intellectualism can invade the Church. But it is important to realise that by saying that we need to use our minds in interpreting the Bible, I am not talking about a cold rationalism. I am talking about a sanctified, Spirit-led, renewed mind. Paul tells us that *'We have the mind of Christ'*.[4] We have an anointing from the Holy One and we understand *'all things'*.[5] The Spirit of God renews our minds so that we are able to understand things which without Him we could never understand. This is what Paul is talking about in 1 Corinthians 2:9–10:

> 'No eye has seen,
>   no ear has heard,
> no mind has conceived
>   what God has prepared for those who love him' –

> but God has revealed it to us by his Spirit.

The natural man does not understand the things of God, they are foolishness to him. But we understand them because our minds have been renewed by the Spirit. Believers are to judge all things; we are to test the spirits.[6] We are to use our renewed minds to do the hard work of interpreting what God has said to us in the Bible.

3. The Church's witness

It is the birthright of every child of God to hear the Father speaking directly to him or her through Scripture, but we would be somewhat lacking in humility if we ignored the fact that the Holy Spirit has been speaking to people throughout the centuries of church history. In Ephesians 3:18 Paul speaks of our understanding growing *'together with all the saints'*. Christianity did not come into being in my lifetime; God did not start working in my lifetime. God has been working throughout the history of His Church, and therefore we need to avail ourselves of the resources that are available to us as a result of His work over many centuries. We dare not skip from the first century to the twenty-first century, however convenient that might seem. George Santayana said, 'Those who cannot remember the past are condemned to repeat it.' We would be fools if we ignored the whole wealth of the Church's experience. We can learn about the mistakes the Church has made and how at times it has gone off track; but we can also learn how the Church has grown and flourished as the Spirit moved through people in the past.

THREE PRINCIPLES FOR INTERPRETING THE BIBLE

1. The natural sense

Whenever we interpret the Bible we must look for the natural sense. Since God has chosen to communicate to us in human language, we must pay attention to the words of Scripture. The words are used in a straightforward way, and they should be interpreted in a straightforward way. I remember hearing of a preacher who wanted to preach against a particular evil that was occurring in his congregation. The women in his congregation were coming to church with their hair tied up in a knot on the top of their heads, and he wanted to expose this terrible misbehaviour by preaching against it. He chose as his text Matthew 24:17 ('*Let him which is on the housetop not come down...*', KJV, emphasis added)! We must not use Scripture in this way. We must handle the words in the way in which they were intended to be used.

We also need to remember that the various writers of the Bible wrote in the way that suited them. As a man who was in touch with his feminine side, King David used the medium of poetry and was very expressive. When we read Hebrew poetry, we need to be aware that much use is made of the technique of repetition, as, for example, in Isaiah 53:5,

> *But he was pierced for our transgressions,*
>   *he was crushed for our iniquities;*
> *the punishment that brought us peace was upon him,*
>   *and by his wounds we are healed.*

By repeating a truth in several different ways, it is reinforced and pressed home.

As well as taking account of the different genres of writing which the Bible contains, we need to be aware of the writing and story-telling techniques that its writers employed. Some of the language of the Bible is, for example, figurative. When we read about the 'new birth', we are not to be like Nicodemus who took Jesus' words literally, *'Surely he cannot enter a second time into his mother's womb to be born!'*[7] When we read about the 'windows of heaven', we should not be imagining literal windows, out of which God leans. By taking literally what is meant figuratively, we can land ourselves into all kinds of trouble.

It is also possible to make the opposite error of interpreting figuratively what is meant to be accepted as simply part of the detail of the story. One of the early church fathers, Origen, made the mistake of turning the parables into allegories and seeking to interpret their every detail. For example, in the parable of the Good Samaritan, the coins that were given by the good Samaritan to the innkeeper to pay for the injured man's care were interpreted as the two covenants. This is an abuse of the parable. By the time I was studying theology, the pendulum had swung in completely the opposite direction and, influenced by theologians such as A.M. Hunter, there was a great emphasis on understanding that a parable only conveyed one message. I personally was always stumped by this idea, because if you take the parable of the sower, which is one of the few for which Jesus gives the interpretation, the seed represents the word of God and the soils represent the hearts of the hearers – so, in this parable at least, there are two meanings!

Two other techniques that are used by story-tellers are hyperbole and metaphor. Hyperbole is the use of exaggeration for effect, which a great many preachers are also very good at! When, for example, Jesus describes the mustard seed as *'the smallest of seeds'*, He is not giving a scientific description, because there are in fact seeds that are smaller, but is using hyperbole to emphasise the point He wants to make. Jesus is clearly using metaphor when He makes such statements as *'I am the door'*.[8] When we are interpreting Scripture we need to look for the natural sense, just as we would if we were reading any other type of book.

Looking for the natural sense will also help us to avoid other mistakes in our interpretation of the Bible. For example, it will help us to avoid using the horoscope approach to the Bible, where we simply dip into it and look for a text that speaks into a particular situation. This was very popular at one time. Someone would come up to you and say, 'I have a word for you', and would read out a verse from the Bible taken completely out of context. I am reminded of the teacher who, looking for guidance in his life, prayed, 'Lord, I want you to guide me from the Scriptures' and then, with eyes closed, opened his Bible at a random place and put his finger in the text. Opening his eyes he read, *'Judas went and hanged himself'*. Thinking, 'That's not the kind of guidance I want', he decided to try again. This time his finger landed on the verse, *'Go and do thou likewise!'* Disappointed once again, he decided to try a final time: *'That thou doest, do quickly!'*[9]

Some people make the mistake of being over-literalistic in their interpretation of the Bible. R.W. De Haan, who was a very godly man and wrote a number of helpful books, fell into serious error with his book *The Chemistry of the Blood*. Taking the Bible's teaching on the power of the blood of Christ too literally, he attributed power to the physical blood of Jesus. He described the chemistry of the blood of Jesus in detail and believed that, after Jesus' death on the cross, God had collected up His Son's blood and had taken it to heaven in a great censor, where it will remain for all eternity. He failed to allow himself to be exposed to the traditions and the teachings of the Church throughout history. When I sit at my desk studying the Bible, I like to remind myself that I am not alone but in a great line of preachers down through the centuries, whose books are lining my shelves, and allow their experience of preaching the Word to act as a stimulus to me to be as thorough as I can in handling the words of Scripture.

2. The original sense

In theological terminology, this is the grammatical, historical method. Each of the books of the Bible was given to a specific people, at a specific time, in a specific country. For example, Psalm 2 proclaims Israel's king as the ideal son of God with a mandate to rule the earth through prayer and power. It was given to the Jewish nation in the country of Israel in pre-exilic times. It would originally have been sung by the people of God in the first temple, probably on the occasion of the coronation of a king. However, its significance extended beyond that particular people, time and place. After the exile when Israel's throne was vacant and the nation was waiting for the promised Messiah, the psalm took on a prophetic significance. Then, of course, after the coming of our Lord Jesus, the concept of the Messiah took on its fullest and clearest sense.

Charles Simeon wrote the following about the ideals of his preaching ministry: 'My endeavour is to bring out of Scripture what is there and not to thrust in what might be there. I have a great jealousy on this head never to speak more or less than I believe the mind of the Spirit is in the passage that I am expounding.'[10] He believed passionately that the Bible was the Holy Spirit's book.

Our commitment to interpreting the Bible in its original sense will cause us ask the following questions about the text which we are studying:

- who wrote it?
- to whom was it written?
- in what circumstances was it written?
- for what reason was it written?

This summer I had a fresh experience of how powerful it can be to understand the circumstances in which a text of the Bible was written when, while on holiday with my family in Rome, I visited the Marmatine Prison where both Paul and Peter were held captive for a year or so before they were executed. The Marmatine Prison is in the shape of an upturned teacup. In the base of the teacup, so to speak, there is a small hole, through which prisoners were lowered and through which food was lowered. Standing beneath the prison's curving walls on the very stones on which the two apostles would have stood, seeing the water running down the walls, feeling the claustrophobia of the place in the heat of summer and imagining the sheer cold that they must have experienced in winter, made 2 Timothy, written from that very place, come alive to me in a way that it never had before. I could understand some of the emotion behind Paul's words to Timothy,

> *Do your best to come to me quickly . . . When you come, bring the cloak that I left with Carpus at Troas . . .*
> (2 Timothy 4:9, 13)

When we see the circumstances in which the Bible was written, it comes alive to us.

Understanding to whom the words were written can sometimes explain texts which otherwise seem contradictory. For example, James and Paul seem to contradict each other in what they say about Abraham being justified by faith,[11] but when we understand that Paul was seeking to counter the argument of legalists whereas James was addressing antinomian religionists, what they are saying begins to make sense and their apparent differences disappear.

We come to the Bible with many questions and often feel frustrated that it sometimes does not provide as clear an answer as we would like it to. Take the issue of slavery, for example. We ask, is slavery wrong? We may feel frustrated that the Bible does not give a direct answer to the question. In order to find the answer, we need to dig a little deeper. If we investigate the cultural context of slavery in the first century, we discover that it was taking place against a very different background from the slavery that was occurring in America and Europe in the nineteenth century. For the most part, in the first century people sold themselves into slavery voluntarily because the life they would live as a slave would be better than the life they were previously living. We also need to bear in mind that for economic reasons most slaves were set free by the age of thirty, and stipulations within Roman law prevented serious abuse of slaves by their masters. Furthermore, in the first century it was impossible to distinguish a slave from a free man by the colour of his skin. This cultural background helps us to understand why the writers of the New Testament did not speak out unequivocally against slavery. In stark contrast, nineteenth-century slavery was unique in history because it was specifically enslavement of the black man by the white man. In order, therefore, to answer the question of whether slavery is wrong, we need to look for other biblical principles that apply. The principle that all human beings are made in the image of God means, for example, that no human being of whatever colour should be treated without dignity.

We must let the text of the Bible teach us what it wants to teach us. It cannot mean what it has not meant, and therefore it is vital that we understand what it meant to those to whom it was first written. I would love, for example, to know what 'baptism for the dead' meant to the Corinthians.[12] Since it is evident that they understood this phrase, I need to try and understand what it was they understood: this is the challenge we face over and over again in interpreting the Bible today. A phrase I sometimes use in this connection is 'climbing a ladder of abstraction'. We need to climb up the ladder to try and discover what the biblical situation was at the time the text was written and then climb back down again to allow it to speak into the situation in which we find ourselves today. For example, we may find ourselves preaching on the injunction from Exodus not to boil a kid goat in its mother's milk.[13] I first need to find out why originally this particular law was given. As we research into the customs of the time we discover that this was a pagan practice which was carried out as part of idol worship. The real issue behind the practice was then idol worship. The people of Israel were not to involve themselves with any of the practices associated with idol worship, even those which did not involve them in physically going to the idol and bowing down to it. This is a principle which we can apply in our modern context.

When we come across a difficult passage, we need both to abstract up to God and to look for what I term 'the depravity factor'. In other words, as well as saying something about God, every passage reveals something about human rebellion against God. Paul's teaching in 1 Corinthians 8 about whether it is permissible to eat meat offered to idols is a good example of this. The apostle Paul abstracts up to God by giving us a vision of God:

> yet for us there is but one God, the Father, from whom all things came and for whom we live; and there is but one Lord, Jesus Christ, through whom all things came and through whom we live.
> (1 Corinthians 8:6)

He then points to the depravity factor:

> *For if anyone with a weak conscience sees you who have this knowledge eating in an idol's temple, won't he be emboldened to eat what has been sacrificed to idols? So this weak brother, for whom Christ died, is destroyed by your knowledge. When you sin against your brothers in this way and wound their weak conscience, you sin against Christ. Therefore, if what I eat causes my brother to fall into sin, I will never eat meat again, so that I will not cause him to fall.*
> (1 Corinthians 8:10–13)

The depravity factor is the Christian's lack of care for his brother or sister in Christ.

3. The general sense

The reformers spoke about the 'analogy of Scripture' or the 'analogy of faith', by which they meant that the Bible is its own interpreter: the Bible is a unity and all the parts of the book together tell one story. If, then, there are two possible explanations of a passage and one of those explanations goes against the rest of the Bible while the other is in harmony with it, common decency dictates that we should go with the one which is in harmony with the story of the Bible. This is what we do in normal conversation with other people, so why should we not do it with the Bible? If somebody tells me something about a person I know which seems to contradict my experience of him or her, I give him or her the benefit of the doubt, and this is what we should do with the Bible. The Westminster Divines said, 'The infallible rule of interpretation of Scripture is Scripture itself, so when there is a question about the true and full sense of any Scripture, which is not many but one, it must be searched and known by the other places that speak more clearly.'[14] We must keep in mind how the whole Bible fits together.

NOTES _____

1. Graham Scroggy.
2. John 16:12–13.
3. Romans 12:2.
4. 1 Corinthians 2:16.
5. 1 Corinthians 2:15.
6. 1 John 4:1.
7. John 3:4.
8. John 10:9 KJV.
9. Matthew 27:5; Luke 10:37; John 13:27 KJV.
10. William Corus (ed.), *Memoirs of the Life of the Rev. Charles Simeon*, 2nd edn (Hatchard, 1847), p. 703.

11. Romans 3:28; 4:1–3; James 2:21–24.

12. See 1 Corinthians 15:29.

13. Exodus 23:19.

14. Westminster Confession of Faith, Chap. 1:IX in *Confession of Faith* (Free Church of Scotland, 1955), p. 6.

Chapter 6

LEARNING FROM JESUS

Mark Stibbe

It has been said that there are three types of teachers: those you listen to, those you can't listen to, and those you can't help listening to. I believe that Jesus falls into the third category: He is the kind of teacher you can't help listening to. Jesus is the greatest teacher there has ever been in the whole of human history. No one has ever surpassed or even come close to the Lord Jesus Christ in terms of the profundity and the memorability of their teaching. Jesus' teaching is just as life-changing today as it was two thousand years ago when He gave it.

I want us to imagine that we are on a Galilean hillside, spending a day in the presence of the Lord Jesus Christ listening to Him teaching. There is a Japanese proverb that says, 'Better than a thousand days of diligent study is one day with a great teacher.' I don't know whether that is true generally but I certainly believe it is true of Jesus. As we spend time in His presence, I want to reflect on ten characteristics of Jesus' teaching. This list is by no means exhaustive, but just the beginning of an exploration of important ways we can learn from Him.

1. REVELATORY IN CONTENT

I believe profoundly that the teaching of Jesus would have struck us powerfully as revelatory in content. Jesus was totally different from the teachers of His day. Although there were some formal similarities with the rabbinic style of teaching, He was totally different in the respect that He didn't get His message from books, He didn't get His message from other rabbis, He didn't get His message from other religious traditions that were proving popular at the time, but He got His message directly and immediately from the Father. I have been deeply impacted by the following verses from John's Gospel where Jesus says,

> 'For I did not speak of my own accord, but the Father who sent me commanded me what to say and how to say it. I know that his command leads to eternal life. So whatever I say is just what the Father has told me to say.'
> (John 12:49–50)

I believe these verses were the keynote of Jesus' teaching ministry and should be the keynote of every individual who wants to be a teacher like Jesus. Jesus' teaching was revelatory because He listened to the Father's voice. Everything that He did in terms of ministry emerged out of intimacy. The hallmark of Jesus' whole spirituality was intimate communion with the Father, and it should be no different for us. Of course, we are not the Son of God by nature but we are the sons and daughters of God by adoption. Adoption is one of the most precious but neglected doctrines in the Church, and if only we could recapture it, especially in the fatherless generation in which we minister today, it would be a great asset to us in our ministry both in the Church and in the world. Jesus called His Father in heaven, 'Abba'. It is the language of the Hebrew nursery; it is also the language of profound intimacy. Through adoption we are able to call God our 'Abba', our 'Daddy'. Thanks to what Jesus has done on the cross, intimacy with the Father is our legacy. Sadly, many of us live as slaves rather than as sons and daughters. We need to learn to enter into the experience of intimacy, not just the head knowledge of the doctrine of adoption, so that we too as teachers may spend many, many hours in intimacy with the Father, in personal Bible study, prayer and especially in worship. Then, when we come to the people of God on a Sunday or on any other day on which we are teaching, we bring what the Father has been speaking into our hearts, not just what cerebral study has said to our heads. Intimate communion with the Father is key.

We also need to note the fascinating insight that Jesus gave in explanation of His words *'For I did not speak of my own accord'*. He says that the Father taught him both *'what to say and how to say it'*. That means that, when Jesus was in a situation say with the Pharisees, He not only heard the content of what to say to them, but He also heard from the Father the form of that teaching and how it was to be presented. As He was speaking, He was asking the Father whether He should use a parable or a story or perhaps a pithy proverb. He was in constant dialogue with the Father. Some people may regard this as rather a sentimental view, but I believe it is closer to the truth than the model of a committee meeting being conducted in Jesus' head which is so often inferred. Jesus was in intimate dialogue with the Father.

2. Anointed by the Spirit

As well as being revelatory in both content and form Jesus' teaching was also anointed by the Spirit. In His very first sermon Jesus quoted from Isaiah 61, which says:

> 'The Spirit of the Lord is on me,
>> because he has anointed me
>> to preach good news to the poor...'
> (Luke 4:18)

In applying that scripture to His own ministry Jesus is saying many things but number one among them is that the anointing of the sovereign Lord is upon Him for preaching and its attendant ministries, including ministering healing. If we had had the privilege of spending time in His presence I think we would have been aware of two signs of the Spirit's anointing:

1. the authority of His words, and
2. the power of His works.

It is very important that we understand what I said earlier, that unlike many of us today in the Body of Christ, Jesus ministered both in word and works. Everything that He gave in terms of proclamation was backed up by demonstration. As Reformed Evangelicals I think we too quickly attribute Jesus' works to His divinity and conclude that, therefore, He could do it but we can't. But, as James Dunn rightly says in his scholarly work *Jesus and the Spirit*,[1] I honestly believe that Jesus did these things in the power of the Holy Spirit, and we can do the same. We too can speak under the anointing of the Holy Spirit with authority in a way that will cause amazement – and, can I say, not just amazement in the people who are listening but amazement in us as we speak. There have been times when I have sensed the powerful anointing of the Holy Spirit as I have been preaching and heaven has seemed to be breaking out among the people in a dynamic way. On such occasions I am so amazed at the words I am speaking, which I don't remember having prepared, that I am half thinking to myself that I must get the tape so that I can listen to my own sermon! That, I believe, is the anointing of the Holy Spirit. That is Jesus speaking, not me. And the sense of amazement lies in the fact that Jesus can use me, even me – and there is no greater joy than being used by Jesus, whether it is in evangelism, prophecy, teaching, pastoring or apostolic ministry. You are doing what you love to do and, to quote, R.T. Kendall, 'It's easy', because the anointing of the Spirit is on your life. There is nothing that brings greater joy and purpose to life.

The teacher expresses that anointing both with words of authority and works of power. The Scriptures tell us that those who heard Jesus commented that His teaching was quite unlike that of the scribes *'because he taught as one who had authority'.*[2] They were amazed because He had something the rabbis did not have: He had an authority that was immediately and directly given from the Father.

The anointing of the Spirit also results in works of power. So often in His teaching ministry Jesus would minister in power to the sick so that lives were transformed. I never cease to be amazed when I see life change occur as a result of my preaching. Last summer when I was preaching at the New Wine Christian Conference, I was aware that God was at work in the big tent in which I was preaching. Little did I know that amazing things were also happening in the caravans on site, into which the preaching was being relayed. I heard one story about a young woman in her late twenties/early thirties who had been dragged to the camp kicking and screaming. She had not been in church for about fifteen years. As I preached on spiritual warfare from the story of Jesus and Legion in Mark 5, she was listening on the radio. A few seconds before I finished, she surrendered her iron will to the Lord Jesus Christ and ran from her caravan down to the tent and, arriving just at the ministry time, came to the front and gave her life to Him. That is the sort of thing that happens when we faithfully teach under the anointing. Sometimes we get to hear about what the Holy Spirit is doing and sometimes we are totally unaware of it. The Holy Spirit wants to use us, but it is ' *"not by might nor by power, but by my Spirit," says the* LORD *Almighty'* (Zechariah 4:6). We can have all the learning in the world and we can have our reformed theology absolutely watertight, but unless we have the Holy Spirit we will never see real life change – and that is what I am after, because I think Jesus is.

3. BIBLICAL IN ITS SOURCE

Everything that Jesus taught was biblical in terms of the Old Testament Hebrew Scriptures. He constantly quoted the Old Testament, introducing what He was about to say with such words as, *'You have heard that it was said . . .'*,[3] and I love it when He says to the Pharisees, 'Haven't you ever read . . . ?'[4] He was totally Bible based the whole time, stressing at every point, in particular with the Pharisees, that God's Word is far superior to human wisdom and tradition. Jesus' commitment to Scripture is something from which we need to learn and something which we need to model. Jesus said,

> *'Don't misunderstand why I have come. I did not come to abolish the law of Moses or the writings of the prophets. No, I came to fulfill them. I assure you, until heaven and earth disappear, even the smallest detail of God's law will remain until its purpose is achieved.'*
> (Matthew 5:17–18 NLT)

Of course, the demands of the ceremonial law have all been met through the finished work of Christ on the cross but that has in no way abrogated the moral law of the Old

Testament whose principles still apply. We must keep our rootedness in the Word of God. Thomas Carlyle made this amazing statement, 'The Bible is the truest utterance that ever came by alphabetic letters from the soul of man, through which, as through a window divinely opened, all people can look into the stillness of eternity and discern in glimpses their far-distant long-forgotten home.'[5]

4. ALWAYS RELEVANT

If we had been among Jesus' listeners on a Galilean hillside I think we would have been powerfully impacted by His relevance. To the woman at the well, Jesus said, 'Let's talk about water.' To the fishermen, Jesus said, 'Let's talk about fishing: I want to make you fishers of men.' To the taxmen, He said, 'Let's talk about money.'

To whomever He was speaking, Jesus had the same basic message on His heart, which was the message of the Kingdom of God, the dynamic reign of almighty God which has broken into history in the here and now. But He unpacked that complex revelation in ways that people could readily understand. Jesus is relevant to everyone. It is we who make Him irrelevant through the language games that we play and the jargon that we use.

Recently a painter came to paint the vicarage and was with us for about ten days. On the tenth day I realised I hadn't evangelised him at all, so I thought now, just before he left, was a good time. I made him a cup of coffee and we started chatting. It is very interesting what strikes non-Christians because he started talking to me about the car park, commenting, 'Your car park is always full, not just on Sundays – every day it's packed full. A lot of people come to church, don't they?' Then he began to talk about his experience of church and how he had been forced into going as a small boy which resulted in him being put off church. At that point I said, 'Do you mind if we change the subject? You're talking about my least favourite subject.' He said, 'What's that?' I said, 'The church.' He said, 'But you're a vicar.' I said, 'I know but I hate talking about church.' He said, 'What do you like talking about?' I said, 'Jesus.' So he said, 'Tell me about Jesus then.' As I started talking to him about Jesus, his eyes began to fill with tears.

When we begin to talk about Jesus in relevant language, the power of the Holy Spirit is let loose. I could see that my words were having an effect, but one of the things God has taught me about evangelism is there is a point beyond which it is not right to go. I could see that if I went on any longer there would be a premature birth. It would be much better to give him time, and trust that God would bring another Christian along to help him make the final step. So I finished our conversation with this old story which I remembered from the collection of illustrations J. John and I have put together to help preachers find relevant stories, jokes and anecdotes for their sermons.[6]

I said, 'Have you heard about the painter who became a Christian?' 'No, I haven't', came the reply. 'Well, he became a Christian because in the middle of the night he heard God speaking to him.' And he said, 'What did he hear?' 'God said to him, repaint and thin no more.' There was a moment of stunned silence, during which he just looked at me and I looked at him, and I thought, 'He hasn't understood that', but then suddenly he fell apart not just in laughter but in total hysterics. Then I let him go, and as it was my day off I lay on the sofa watching cricket on the television. A few moments later I could hear him talking to his mate who was working on the back of the house. He said, 'Do you know what the vicar has just said? He told me all about this painter who became a Christian.' Then I heard him tell his mate the joke I had just told him. Same silence and then suddenly both of them in hysterics. The point I am trying to make is that he was a painter, so I told him a joke about painting, not about rocket science. Jesus was relevant to everyone. In my book *The Teacher's Notebook* I wrote this:

> To the artist he is the One altogether lovely. To the architect he is the Cornerstone. To the baker he is the Living Bread. To the banker he is the Hidden Treasure. To the biologist he is the Life. To the builder he is the Sure Foundation. To the carpenter he is the Door. To the doctor he is the Great Physician. To the educator he is the Great Teacher. To the farmer he is the Sower and the Lord of the Harvest. To the florist he is the Rose of Sharon and the Lily of the Valley. To the geologist he is the Rock of Ages. To the horticulturist he is the True Vine. To the jeweller he is the Pearl of Great Price. To the juror he is the True Witness. To the lawyer he is the Righteous Judge. To the oculist he is the Light of the Eyes. To the philosopher he is the Wisdom of God. To the servant he is the Good Master. To the student he is the Truth. To the theologian he is the Author and Finisher of our faith. To the worker he is the Giver of Rest. To the sinner he is the Lamb of God. And to the Christian he is the Saviour, the Son of the Living God and the Redeemer of the World.[7]

Jesus is relevant to everyone and He made His message relevant to everyone. In Matthew's Gospel alone He addresses the following subjects in His teaching: anger, sex, divorce, swearing, revenge, giving, prayer, fasting, money, anxiety, criticism, hygiene. Aren't those subjects still relevant today? Jesus is forever relevant and it is up to us as teachers and evangelists to make Him relevant.

If as preachers we are in any doubt whatsoever as to whether we are being relevant, we must connect with our people and find out. Like the contestants on *Who Wants to Be a Millionaire?*, we need to 'ask the audience'. If we want to know what subjects the members of our congregations are concerned about, we need to ask them. That is why the teacher needs to have a bit of the pastor in him and be visiting, emailing, dialoguing, telephoning his people and listening to what they are saying. I go to work with some of my people. I go and speak at meetings in their workplaces. I want to know what sort of lives the people in my congregation are living, so that I can make my preaching relevant. I have learnt a lot from Rick Warren's preaching training course called 'Preaching for Life Change'. One very practical thing I have learnt from him is always to make the headings in my sermons to my congregation applicational. So, for example, if I am preaching on 'The Heart of a Volunteer' based on Psalm 110:3, my headings might be:

(i)   Remember that the Father loves you, and
(ii) Sign up now as a volunteer.

They are things that people can do. Furthermore, in every point I make I try and structure my teaching so that it is 50 per cent exposition and 50 per cent application, because I am convinced that most preaching has been 95 per cent exposition and 5 per cent application, and the application has very often been John 3:16 and very little else.

5. COMPASSIONATE IN ITS MOTIVATION

This is another key characteristic for us as preachers. Jesus really loved the people whom He was teaching. When as preachers we stand up in front of the people that we teach, our heart needs to be filled with affection for them. When we see those who are going through extraordinary difficulties in their marriages, with their children's health, in the workplace and all the other situations that life throws up, our heart needs to be breaking for them. People do not care how much the preacher knows until they know how much he cares. We must never forget that. In a post-modern culture more than ever we as preachers have not earned the right to teach until we have learnt to pastor and care for our people. Only then will they truly listen to what we have to say. Compassion, I think, is an extraordinarily powerful force behind effective and anointed teaching: it is, in fact, its wellspring.

This is particularly true when we come to address the most difficult pastoral issues, such as the Bible's teaching on homosexual practice. I would say that I have heard two types of teaching on this subject: teaching that is full of love but almost wholly devoid of biblical truth, and teaching that is full of truth, but very lacking in compassion and love. The command of Scripture is to speak the truth in love.[8] Jesus Himself was full of grace and truth. When we are speaking on an issue like homosexuality it is simply not acceptable to stand up and rant in an angry voice and make every homosexual listening feel automatically excluded by our tone. If that is what is in our heart, it is much better that we do not speak on the subject at all. We must speak the truth with grace. I say this very seriously. Those of us who know homosexuals are well aware that the last thing they need is to be condemned. What they do need is the Father's love, and they will come into a place of repentance if they are introduced to the Father's love through the way we speak, as well as through the words we say. I make this plea because I have heard some teaching on homosexuality that was full of truth, but devoid of any semblance of love. We must get the balance right. Compassion was the wellspring of Jesus' heart. Yes, there were times when Jesus was angry but whom was He angry with? He was angry with the Pharisees who thought that they were always right.

We read in Mark 6:34:

> *A vast crowd was there as he stepped from the boat, and he had compassion on them*
> *because they were like sheep without a shepherd. So he taught them many things.*
> (NLT)

There is a cause and effect relationship between those two statements which is summed up very pivotally in the very simple word 'so'. He had compassion on them *so* He taught them. We can have everything wrapped up in the most beautiful and skilful way, we can have all the points absolutely perfect, but without compassionate love it is worthless. The eminent Victorian John Ruskin said: 'When love and skill work together, expect a masterpiece.' When these two things come together in the pulpit it is a masterpiece for the glory of God.

6. Visual in its Appeal

Jesus was constantly painting word pictures. He used indirect communication. Of course, the primary example of this is the parables which He used to bring Kingdom truths into the lives of the people. We too need to understand that in today's culture, as many people have said, it is no longer the ear that is the primary organ of receptivity in terms of communication but the eye. So, in our preaching, we need to paint more word pictures. Jesus' teaching is very like what the poet Horace said poetry should be. In his view poetry should both instruct and delight. Jesus' teaching instructed but it also delighted. Of course, it did not delight the Pharisees but it did delight the crowds, as we learn, for example, from Mark 12:37, *'The large crowd listened to him with delight.'* The Greek word translated 'with delight' is *hedeos*, which means 'gladly'. In Mark 4:33–34 we are told:

> *With many similar parables Jesus spoke the word to them, as much as they could*
> *understand. He did not say anything to them without using a parable.*

In His public teaching Jesus always used parables. In Matthew's Gospel He draws on the following imagery: salt, light, gates, roads, trees, houses, foxes and birds, brides and bridegrooms, wine, farmers, weeds, seeds, bread, treasure, fishing, plants, pits, dogs, weather, rocks, mountains, sheep, vineyards and lamps. All the time Jesus, operating with a Jewish mindset, was seeing the whole of creation as the arena of God's benediction and blessing. He did not operate with a Greek dualism, which regarded what was material and physical as evil and what was spiritual as heavenly and good. I think that this is what we need to do as well. As well as drawing from what is around us in nature and in our environment we can draw from the movies and pop music.[9] There is material being said, broadcast, sung, portrayed through the media that is a gift to us in our preaching, if we just opened our eyes and opened our ears to become aware of it. We have got to learn to connect with people. Martin Luther once said, 'People are captivated more readily by comparisons and examples than by difficult and subtle disputations. They would rather see a well-drawn picture than a well-written book.'[10] Although that was said during the Reformation, I believe it is equally true today.

7. Varied in its Approach

Jesus adapted His methodology. The Father did not just tell Him what to say but how to say it. His many teaching techniques have been well documented. He used:

- parables
- stories (e.g. the lost coin, the lost sheep, the lost son, all in one chapter in Luke 15)
- proverbs (e.g. Matthew 19:24: *'it is easier for a camel to go through the eye of a needle than for a rich man to enter the kingdom of God'*)
- pithy statements (what might be called 'words of wisdom' in Charismatic circles)
- paradoxes (e.g. Matthew 23:12: *'For whoever exalts himself will be humbled, and whoever humbles himself will be exalted'*)
- posers/riddles (e.g. Matthew 11:7: *'What did you go out into the desert to see? A reed swayed by the wind?'*)
- puns/word plays (e.g. John 3:8: *'The wind blows wherever it pleases'*, where the word translated 'wind' can also be translated 'spirit').

8. Practical in its Application

Jesus taught by doing. Just two examples are prayer and the ministry of healing. We read in Luke 11:1:

> *Once when Jesus had been out praying, one of his disciples came to him as he finished and said, 'Lord, teach us to pray, just as John taught his disciples.'*
> (NLT)

The disciples were motivated to want to pray by seeing Jesus modelling it. Jesus got the disciples involved in healing ministry by sending them out two by two to put into practice what they had witnessed Him doing (see Luke 10). As the proverb says, if you give a person a fish you feed them for a day, but if you teach them how to fish you feed them for a lifetime. We need to have the same very practical dynamic to our teaching ministry as Jesus did. It is salutary to remember that it has been proved that people retain 10 per cent of what they hear, 15 per cent of what they see, 20 per cent of what they see and hear,

40 per cent of what they discuss with others, and 80 per cent of what they experience directly (i.e. active learning).

9. Courageous in its Directness

A teacher needs to be courageous. Jesus' teaching was fearless in its delivery. Even the Pharisees, the enemies of Jesus, are recorded as saying in Matthew 22:16: *'Teacher, we know how honest you are. You teach about the way of God regardless of the consequences. You are impartial and don't play favourites'* (NLT). I am convinced that Jesus' fearlessness can be traced back to His sonship. I don't think we are truly really free to be courageous as teachers until we cease caring about what human beings are thinking and start caring only about what the Father thinks, as Jesus did. Jesus said,

> *'I do nothing on my own, but I speak what the Father taught me. And the one who sent me is with me – he has not deserted me. For I always do those things that are pleasing to him.'*
> (John 8:28–29 NLT)

As preachers we need to find out what pleases the Lord. We must not be man pleasers, but God pleasers, always remembering that our security lies not in our successes but in our sonship and our daughterhood.

10. Potent in its Impact

Jesus' preaching was life-changing – and not just two thousand years ago but it remains unbelievably powerful for the changing of lives today! It has been said that, although Socrates and Aristotle each taught for forty years and Plato taught for fifty years, while Jesus taught for only three, Jesus' influence far surpasses the combined 130 years of the teaching of these men who are acknowledged as the greatest philosophers of all antiquity. He painted no pictures, yet the finest paintings of Raphael, Michelangelo and Leonardo da Vinci receive their illumination from Him. He wrote no poetry, yet Dante, Milton and others of the world's greatest poets were inspired by Him. He composed no music, yet Haydn, Handel, Beethoven and Bach reached their highest perfection in hymns, symphonies and oratorios composed in His honour. Jesus is quite simply the greatest teacher who has ever lived.

Notes

1. SCM Press, 1975.
2. E.g. Matthew 7:29.

3. E.g. Matthew 5:21, 27.

4. E.g. Matthew 12:5.

5. Latter Day Pamphlets, 1850: no. V.

6. *A Box of Delights, A Bucket of Surprises, A Barrel of Fun*, published by Monarch Books.

7. Kingsway Communications, 2003.

8. Ephesians 4:15.

9. For more on this, see Chapter 42, 'Using Movies in Preaching'.

10. *Luther's Works*, ed. Jaroslav Pelikan, vol. 26, *Lectures on Galatians, 1535, Chapters 1–4* (Concordia Publishing House, 1963), p. 359.

Section Two

GOD MADE THEM GREAT

'As the rain and the snow come down from heaven,
and do not return to it without watering the earth . . .
so is my word that goes out from my mouth:
It will not return to me empty,
but will accomplish what I desire
and achieve the purpose for which I sent it.'

(Isaiah 55:10, 11)

Chapter 7

GOD-CENTRED PREACHING

Michael Eaton

Within minutes of being filled with the Holy Spirit on the Day of Pentecost Peter was preaching to the crowd. God never sends revival without touching the preachers first and, when it comes, their preaching is changed in both style and content. People begin to preach with a power they never had before, and, at the same time, their preaching ceases to be man-centred and focuses instead on God. Then it begins to pierce people's hearts. This is the type of preaching I want to talk about in this chapter, by asking two questions: what is preaching and what do we preach?

WHAT IS PREACHING?

This question is at the heart of our subject. We tend to take it for granted that we know what preaching is, but do we? It is all too easy to categorise everything that goes on in pulpits as preaching but sadly this is not the case. There is much that goes on in pulpits that is not preaching, and there is much true preaching that does not take place in pulpits.

I want to deal first with what many take to be preaching but is not. Preaching is not lecturing, although lecturing can become preaching. To lecture is to impart knowledge. Preaching is not lecturing on biblical themes, even if it is accompanied by exegesis or interpretation. Some preachers seem to believe they are doing 'expository preaching' when they are doing nothing of the sort. They may be giving an *exposition* of the text, but they are not *preaching*. On the other hand, there are some great preachers whose lecturing cannot be distinguished from their preaching – Luther, for example. There was no difference whatsoever between his preaching and his lecturing. When he lectured at the University of Wittenberg he was doing the same as when he preached in the parish church

101

of Wittenberg. By this I mean that Luther's lecturing was really preaching, and sometimes the power of the Holy Spirit would come down as he was lecturing to his students at the University of Wittenberg. So lecturing can become preaching, but generally speaking preaching is not lecturing.

Just as preaching is not lecturing, so also it is not oratory. In fact, the preacher may have to avoid oratory. It is instructive to remember how Paul described his coming to Corinth: *'I was with you in weakness and in fear and much trembling...'*[1] We can be certain he was not afraid of the Corinthians. He was arriving in Corinth, the second most intellectual city of the ancient world, having come from Athens, the most intellectual city. If ever he was tempted to be clever, if ever he was tempted to preach with Greek wisdom and use the kind of arguments that would appeal to the philosophers, it would be in Athens and it would be in Corinth. He had already preached on the Areopagus in Athens to one group of philosophers (see Acts 17:22); now as he arrived at the next most intellectual city in the ancient world, he made a crucial decision about the content of his preaching: *'I decided to know nothing among you except Jesus Christ and him crucified.'*[2] He also made a decision about the manner of his preaching. He resolved to come not with *'plausible words of wisdom, but in demonstration of the Spirit and of power'.*[3] He was anxious to avoid looking learned or philosophical. The preacher may have to avoid oratory in his preaching.

In addition, there are three other things which preaching is not. It is not Bible survey, it is not Bible analysis, and it is certainly not speaking about oneself, which some preachers seem to do constantly.

What, then, is preaching? We find the answer in 1 Thessalonians chapter 1. Speaking very informally Paul tells the story of what happened when he first arrived in Thessalonica. He spends three chapters getting the record straight. He wants them to have a clear picture of what happened because it is going to be a model for the future. Although at first sight he does not seem to be saying anything very important and, like many a preacher, he seems to be taking his time to get to the point, he is doing it for a reason.

Paul says, *'Our gospel came to you not only in word, but also in power and in the Holy Spirit and with full conviction'* or *'with much assurance'* (v. 5). Although the gospel Paul brought was not simply about words, it was conveyed through words. Preaching is to do with *words*. One of the secrets of preaching is to have a lot to say. Those who have nothing to say cannot preach. Great preaching – like great hymns and great worship songs – comes as a result of great material. When Charles Wesley wrote his timeless hymn 'And Can It Be?' his heart was bursting with what he wanted to say. The preacher must be the same. Paul could preach all night when he wanted to, as he did in Ephesus on the night Eutychus fell out of the window and was raised from the dead.[4] He was still preaching when daybreak came. Paul had a lot to say. He had a message in his heart which he was desperate to share with anyone who would listen. He wasn't interested in lecturing or teaching philosophy. He knew a power in his words that came from the Holy Spirit: that is preaching.

When the preacher has a message from God and shares that message in the power of the Holy Spirit, there is great *assurance*. This is another mark of preaching. Paul speaks of the message being preached to the Thessalonians 'with deep conviction', or deep assurance. Was this assurance experienced by those who heard the message or by Paul as he preached the message? I answer: both. In mighty preaching, both the preacher and the people have great assurance. The preacher knows that what he is saying is from God; he does not say, 'I suggest to you' or 'it seems to me'. He says, 'This is what God says'. There is a certainty about his message.

Likewise the people know they are hearing from God. Paul expresses this truth when he says in chapter 1 verse 6, '*You received the word . . . with the joy of the Holy Spirit*', and later on in chapter 2 verse 13, '*When you received the word of God, which you heard from us, you accepted it not as the word of men but as what it really is, the word of God . . .*'. There was assurance on both sides. This is a characteristic of true preaching.

Preaching also has about it an element of mystery. Any great preacher feels that he has hardly ever 'preached'. Dr Lloyd-Jones once made the remark, 'I have a feeling that I have only really preached twice in my life, and on both occasions I was dreaming.'[5] He also quotes James Henry Thornwell as saying, 'My own performances in this way fill me with disgust. I have never made, much less preached, a sermon in my life . . .'[6] Why is it that these great preachers who had such a baptism of power on their lives, talk as if they scarcely ever preached a good sermon? It is because they know what preaching is. They know that preaching is not just being learned or being a good orator. In true preaching there is a baptism of power. I sometimes think that the test of my preaching is what people say as they walk out of the church. If someone says to me, 'Thank you, Pastor, that was very interesting', I know I have failed. If someone says to me, 'Thank you, very nice', I know I have failed. I would rather that they did not say anything to me at all, but responded as the crowd did on the Day of Pentecost when, cut to the heart, they cried out, '*Brothers, what shall we do?*'[7] Then I know I am getting somewhere. It is not preaching until people's hearts are being touched.

I now want to highlight some characteristics of preaching that you will find in Martyn Lloyd-Jones's *Preaching and Preachers*. There are twelve of them but I will put them in my own way.

(i) Involvement

A preacher has a sense of involvement in the lives of those to whom he is preaching. He knows that it is not a small thing that he is doing but that it will have a deep effect on his hearers' lives. Depending on how they respond, they will come alive as never before or their hearts will become hardened – their eternal destiny will be affected. Paul said, '*To the one we are a fragrance from death to death; to the other a fragrance from life to life.*'[8]

That is why preachers are sometimes afraid to preach, why like Paul they come 'in fear and trembling'. They carry a sense of responsibility for the way in which they are touching into people's lives.

(ii) Authority

At the end of Matthew 7 it is said that *'the crowds were astonished at Jesus' teaching, for he was teaching them as one who had authority, and not as their scribes'* (vv. 28–29). They were amazed at this man Jesus – both at what He said and how He said it. Jesus spoke with authority, and the crowds recognised it. It distinguished Him from their own teachers of the Law, the scribes. When Jesus said, 'I say unto you', they heard the note of authority in His voice. They knew it was the voice of God. A preacher should also have this note of authority because, although he is not infallible, he knows that what he is saying is the word of God.

(iii) Freedom

If a preacher does not experience freedom, he is not preaching. It is not my intention to lay down rules and regulations as to whether or not a preacher should use notes, but what I would say is: the freer a preacher is the better! And I would also want to ask those who preach whether they could preach without any notice, as Peter did on the Day of Pentecost. Just six weeks before Peter had been afraid of a servant girl; just six weeks before he had had very little theology of the cross. But suddenly when the Holy Spirit came down upon him he saw more about the cross than he had ever seen in his life. It seems to me that any preacher who is really a preacher can preach when the Holy Spirit prompts him to, and when the revival comes for which we are earnestly praying we will be called upon to do so.

On one occasion I was speaking at a conference in South Africa on prayer and I had my messages well prepared. In a half-hour break one of the delegates went back to her room in the conference suite to have a quick bath. She was an epileptic and, tragically, while having the bath, she lost consciousness, slipped under the water and drowned. A few minutes later the next session was due to start. Everyone in the conference was shattered. There was no point at all in my attempting to preach on my planned topic. I abandoned my message, and preached instead on Jesus' words in John 11:25: *'I am the resurrection and the life'*. Surely a preacher must be able to respond to any situation with which he is faced.

Lloyd-Jones mentions the number of preachers who abandoned what they had planned to say, when in Madrid in 1859 there was an earthquake which shocked people all over Europe. The preachers had to forget their planned sermons and preach on what had just happened. I had occasion to remember Lloyd-Jones's comments in this connection when I was once in India during an earthquake. Although it took place 1,500 miles away from Mumbai where I was staying, the shock waves were powerful. People were screaming with terror in the middle of the night. I remembered what Lloyd-Jones had said: 'If there is an earthquake forget your sermon and preach on the earthquake!' On that occasion everywhere I went I preached on *'There will be earthquakes in diverse places'* (Matthew 24:7) and on the Philippian jailer who thought he knew where life was going until an earthquake gave him pause for thought (see Acts 16:23ff.). Now, whenever I go back to India – which is probably twice a year – people often come up to me and tell me that they were saved during that time of the earthquake. The preacher must grab his chance. If there is a natural disaster the congregation is going to be more attentive on Sunday morning than ever before, but the preacher can only respond to the situation if he can preach on the topic without notice.

Jesus was able to respond to the man who shouted out, *'Teacher, tell my brother to divide the inheritance with me'* (Luke 12:13). He was in the middle of his preaching but He took time to deal with what the man had said. It was unprepared. The parable of the rich fool was part of his spontaneous response. I was preaching once in Pietermaritzburg in South Africa when a young woman began to wave her hand in the middle of the sermon and started calling out that she had a question she wanted to ask. The pastor tried to silence her but I gave space for her to speak and then for five minutes answered her question before returning to my topic. It is not the preacher's task to produce model sermons. We preach into a living situation and it is far better that people respond than that they sit there impassively. Sometimes they may get angry – praise God for that. They are responding, they are reacting. I remember one occasion at Westminster Chapel when R.T. Kendall was preaching on hell. One man became so angry that he slammed his hymn-book down on the pew and marched out. But the next week he was back in a more chastened mood. Sometimes when people get angry it is because the word of God is piercing their heart.

(iv) Rapport

Dr Lloyd-Jones had his own way of expressing this next characteristic of preaching, but I refer to it as 'rapport'. The preacher establishes a rapport between himself and the people. When God is at work, the preacher knows that the people are listening to him and a closeness develops between them. People will interpolate their comments and begin to express their agreement audibly. In some congregations there can be a kind of routine in the way people say 'Hallelujah' or 'Praise the Lord' every few minutes – a practice about which Lloyd-Jones was somewhat disparaging. 'When the Holy Spirit comes down people stop saying "Hallelujah"', he used to say. But this is different from the comments that are expressed when the preacher establishes a rapport with his congregation – they are engaging with what he is saying. He might be preaching to a huge auditorium full of people, but he still feels connected to them.

There is much more we could consider. Dr Lloyd-Jones mentions: (v) seriousness, (vi) liveliness, (vii) zeal, (viii) warmth, (ix) urgency, (x) persuasiveness and (xi) 'pathos'.

By 'pathos' Lloyd-Jones means that there is a depth of emotion. Sometimes people will break down and begin to weep; sometimes there is an outbreak of joy. The preaching has touched their hearts.

(xii) *And then true preaching always has* power

In true preaching it is Jesus who is doing the preaching. This comes across very clearly in Ephesians 2:17 where Paul writes: '[Jesus] *came and preached peace to you who were far away and peace to those who were near'*. Jesus never went to Ephesus in person – but through the apostolic preaching it was as if He was there and was Himself doing the preaching. He had become the preacher and consequently the preaching had great power. Martin Luther said, 'Our Lord God Himself wishes to be the preacher as you are preaching. It has often happened that my best outline came undone. On the other hand, it sometimes happened when I was least prepared, my words flowed during the sermon.' Like many before and after him Luther had the experience of having prepared his sermon but, as he began to preach, the Holy Spirit came down upon him and gave him a different burden in his heart, causing him to wander away from his outline. Or, on other occasions when he was least prepared, his words just flowed. Luther was an invalid for much of his life and he would often feel weak and tired, but when he came to preach he would know power and he would come to life. His words would flow and he would have liberty.

Luther also said that 'the Church is not a pen-house, but a mouth-house'. By this he meant that the Word is oral and living. He said: 'At one time the gospel was hidden in the Scriptures but since the advent of Christ it has become an oral preaching. It must be preached and performed by mouth as a living voice. Christ Himself has not written anything, nor has He ordered anything to be written' (authors – myself included – take notice!). The power is in the preaching. Writing can only provide a backup to preaching. The Bible doesn't say that faith comes by reading; faith comes by hearing.[9] It is the living voice that has the power to bring change. The world needs preachers.

At the risk of being misunderstood, I want to quote from Michael Burleigh's book *The Third Reich*. Burleigh addresses the question of how a man like Hitler could have exercised so much power that a whole nation was swept along by him – a question that perplexes many young Germans still to this day. Burleigh has an explanation. He tells us that Adolf Hitler took great care about his speeches, his messages.

> Anthems, hymns and stage lighting were used to generate mass pathos and sentimentality. Hitler swept in accompanied by drums, fanfares and salutes, and then embarked upon speeches that could last for hours. The overall effect was like being whirled around inside a warm wave of unfathomable emotions. Contemporaries noticed that after low meandering beginnings, 'after about fifteen minutes something occurs which can only be described by the ancient primitive metaphor: the spirit enters into him'.[10]

These are the words of a secular historian. Notice how he uses the same word that Martyn Lloyd-Jones used – pathos. Notice, too, how he speaks of 'the spirit' entering into Hitler, which he can only describe as 'an ancient primitive metaphor'. Burleigh says Hitler had something of the revivalist about him. 'In the act of speaking he was transformed into a man with absolute convictions, expressed with total sincerity.' Hitler would sweep people away with the sheer power that was resting upon him. I would call that *demonic preaching*. I would call that preaching in the power of an evil spirit. I am quoting Burleigh because in a strange way his description of Hitler illustrates what preaching is. If Hitler had that kind of power from an evil spirit, can we not seek the clean controlled power of the *Holy* Spirit? Can we not seek to discover that God comes down upon us and we are transformed into people gripped with absolute conviction? And if Hitler could sweep a whole generation away with his lies, can we not sweep a whole generation away with the truth? That is what preaching is.[11] Even demonic preaching illustrates this matter of spiritual power.

WHAT DO WE PREACH?

This question brings us back to Paul's words to the Thessalonians which I have described as the model for the preacher. He says: *'Our gospel came to you not only in word, but also in power and in the Holy Spirit and with full conviction'* or *'with much assurance'*.[12] Here again, I want to look at the negative before looking at the positive – what did Paul not preach?

It is my view that in the preaching of contemporary churches in Britain there is a lack of the ordinary. I will explain what I mean. For the last fifty years, ever since the Charismatic Movement began in the 1960s, we have been concentrating on the extraordinary. We have been looking for signs and wonders, we have been marching around cities casting out demons, and so on. I would not wish to criticise any of this, but I have some questions: What has happened to ordinary preaching in the power of the Holy Spirit? What has happened to ordinary praying? What has happened to ordinary discipline? What has happened to all the ordinary things? When God moves extraordinary things do happen, but when the extraordinary happens the ordinary must not be forgotten.

This same trend has occurred with regard to the content of our preaching too. Nowadays people are preaching on strange topics. We must remember that it is much easier to see yesterday's heresy than it is to see today's, just as, in the words of R.T. Kendall, 'it is always easier to see yesterday's prophet than it is to see today's prophet'. As we know, Jesus castigated the Pharisees for admiring the prophets whom their forebears killed, while wanting to destroy Him. What is true of prophets is also true of heresy. My feeling is that we are failing to recognise what is the heresy of our day. In Luther's time the heresy of the day was sacramentalism, which received a deathblow in the Reformation. Two centuries or so later the heresy was modernism, with its destructive approach to the Bible. In the 1960s, when John Robinson wrote his book *Honest to God*, the Church's enemy was destructive theological liberalism. But these are all old enemies. The question is, what is today's enemy? What is the modern heresy? What is going on in pulpits today?

I am of the view that the modern heresy is the idea that God's supreme task is to make life comfortable for us. That, I believe, is the modern deviation from the gospel – and it is worldwide. If you go to certain quite lively churches in this country – and this country is not at all the worst in this respect – you will hear this message. God is a kind of sugar-daddy, as we say in Africa. But this kind of teaching is everywhere, it seems. I was in a midweek lunchtime service in an African city recently. Basing his message on Isaiah 40:1, for fifteen minutes or so the preacher preached that, whatever problems people might have in their lives, their 'warfare has now ended' and they would soon have a breakthrough out of their difficulties, whether they be financial, business, marital, health issues, or whatever. The other lines of the verse (iniquity pardoned, receiving double for sins) were not mentioned. Nor I think was the name of Jesus. The service ended with triumphant chanting, 'Our warfare is ended! Our warfare is ended! Our warfare is ended!' In the name of Jesus I say that the good news of the gospel is not a life of success, prosperity or ease. Is it conceivable that Paul would ever preach that?

In its origins the Charismatic Movement was a back-to-the-Holy-Spirit movement inspired by God. Many of the early Charismatics had a good Bible background, but that is not so true of 'Charismatics' today. I believe that in the contemporary churches the *ordinary* gospel of the Lord Jesus Christ is not much being preached – and I believe that only the preaching of the ordinary gospel can bring down the Holy Spirit upon our nation. Until then, I don't think there can be revival in this land. When the Holy Spirit comes down, He has to have something to come down upon. Isn't that true? When the temple was first built, it was furnished and prepared, but it was an empty shell until the Holy Spirit fell and consumed the sacrifice. When Elijah challenged the false priests to a contest to see whose God was greatest, he first had to build the altar and prepare the sacrifice before he could call on God to come.[13] I have a feeling that in this nation and in many European nations we are at the stage of rebuilding the altar. We have got to get back to the place where the blood was shed – the altar, the cross of Christ. We have got to get back to the gospel – the old, old gospel – and we have got to get back to teaching and preaching if we are serious about wanting the fire to fall. As Dr R.T. Kendall used to say, the Holy Spirit cannot bring back to our remembrance that which we did not know in the first place.

So what did Paul preach about? *He preached about God.* By the time he arrived at the next village on his itinerary, people already knew the message he had come to bring. It says in 1 Thessalonians 1:8–10:

> *The word of the Lord sounded forth from you in Macedonia and Achaia, but your faith in God has gone forth everywhere, so that we need not say anything. For they themselves report concerning us the kind of reception we had among you, and how*

you turned to God from idols to serve the living and true God, and to wait for his Son from heaven, whom he raised from the dead, Jesus who delivers us from the wrath to come.

The way had already been prepared for Paul to preach about God. Most of the time in our preaching we talk about people's problems and issues. We need to preach about God, as Paul did: the God of the Bible, the Holy God, the Righteous God, the Pure God, the Sin-hating God. The Bible does not discuss God's origins or put forward arguments to prove His existence. It just starts talking about Him (*'In the beginning **God** created the heavens and the earth . . .'*) and that is what we should also be doing. The Bible tells us that in their hearts people already know that God exists. They don't know everything of the gospel but they know something. The very creation speaks and reveals to them that God exists. I know what is like to go into an Indian village where they have never heard the name of Jesus or heard anything about the Bible. As soon as the fact that there is a God is mentioned, instinctively something inside people says 'Yes'. When Paul was in Athens he used the concept of the altar to the unknown God to begin to declare the truths of God. We don't need to argue for God; we need to declare Him.

■ *Paul preached about sin*

He told the people that the idols they were worshipping would never be able to do them any good. The idols would never be able to forgive their sins, bring them joy, hear their prayers, give them peace. Worshipping idols only enslaved them. Paul preached that they must turn from their idols to the living God. He is a merciful and compassionate God who loves the whole world, but He hates sin because it spoils and destroys His creation. Like any parent who loves his or her children but get angry at their disobedience, God is angry about sin and has to punish it.

■ *Paul preached about Jesus*

He told them that God had made a way out of their slavery to sin and to idols and that way was through *'his Son from heaven, whom he raised from the dead, Jesus, who delivers us from the wrath to come'.*[14] Jesus is the Rescuer. Paul does not preach that Jesus comes and helps us to rescue ourselves, nor that Jesus helps us to improve ourselves and live a better life. We cannot rescue ourselves. Jesus comes to pick us up and take us out of the kingdom of darkness and judgement, to clothe us with righteousness, and to give us the power of the Spirit. Jesus' primary purpose was not to be a great Teacher (although He was): He came as the Rescuer! That is the gospel.

■ *Paul preached about faith*

Having preached about God, having preached about sin, having preached about Jesus, Paul called upon people to respond. As Paul preached with power and authority, his hearers were pierced to the heart, they turned away from their idols and began to serve the living God. Their minds were changed (Greek *metanoia*) and their lives were turned around (Greek *epistrophe*). First comes repentance, then faith, then a total turning around, as the result of faith.

There are many important tenets of faith upon which Paul does not touch in his preaching of the gospel – the Church, the doctrine of the Holy Spirit, the Scriptures, predestination, to name but a few. These can all be 'filled out' after an individual has come to faith and is in the process of working out his or her salvation 'with fear and trembling'. Sometimes Paul doesn't even quote from the Scriptures in his preaching (e.g. Acts 17). In our preaching central to everything must be the God of the Bible, our Saviour Jesus Christ and the mighty power of the Holy Spirit.

The Thessalonians *'welcomed the message with the joy given by the Holy Spirit'*. There was a response to Paul's preaching. Not everyone responded but some did, despite severe persecution. This response made a basis for further preaching. It is the longing of many in Europe to experience the power of God in the preaching of His Word, but they struggle to find a starting point. How it is possible, they ask, to get the unsaved to listen to the preaching of the gospel? Our starting point must be the lives of those we do have listening to us – even if it is only a small number. Acts 17 tells us how long Paul had to form the church at Thessalonica. He was only there three Saturdays, and from Sunday to Friday he was busy making tents! In three short weeks there was laid the foundation of a church, which would exist for many, many years. How was this possible? It happened because there was power there. The message had such an impact upon people's lives that they found faith in Jesus and their lives overflowed with rejoicing. People who met them were so impressed that they began to ask what had happened in their lives. The answer they were given is: 'Come and hear the preacher.' There was power upon the preacher and there was power upon the people. This is what we need to see happening today. It is the preacher's task to get the people so full of joy that non-believers start asking questions. When that starts to happen, it will touch every corner of our land. Let us rebuild the altar looking for the day when the fire will fall. Let us learn again how to preach.

NOTES

1. 1 Corinthians 2:3. Scripture references in this chapter are Michael Eaton's own translation from the original Hebrew and Greek.
2. 1 Corinthians 2:2.
3. 1 Corinthians 2:4.
4. See Acts 20:7ff.
5. D.M. Lloyd-Jones, *Knowing the Times* (Banner of Truth, 1989), p. 263.
6. D.M. Lloyd-Jones, *Preaching and Preachers* (Hodder & Stoughton, 1971), p. 99.
7. Acts 2:37.

8. 2 Corinthians 2:16.
9. Romans 10:17.
10. M. Burleigh, *The Third Reich* (Macmillan, 2000; Pan Books, 2001), pp. 114–15.
11. Of course, there are other significant and wicked characteristics about Hitler's meetings, which Burleigh draws attention to, but there is no need for me to go into them here.
12. 1 Thessalonians 1:5.
13. 1 Kings 19.
14. 1 Thessalonians 1:10.

Chapter 8

THE SACRAMENT OF THE WORD

Philip Greenslade

> Preaching is the manifestation of the incarnate Word from the written Word by the spoken word.
> (Bernard Lord Manning)

Dr Martyn Lloyd-Jones was recorded at the Westminster Theological Seminary in 1960 as saying that preaching is a 'great mystery'. Because it is slightly mysterious, many have found that it eludes analysis. Fortunately for me, two years after making his statement, Dr Lloyd-Jones published a large book on the subject based on the lectures he gave in the Westminster Seminary.[1] However, I still approach the subject of preaching with some temerity, because no one should think of themselves as an 'expert' on this topic.

Throughout my formative years, until I left for university, I sat under the preaching ministry of my home town Baptist pastor, John Tugwell. John believed passionately in preaching, and practised it passionately. As he declared the gospel and preached God's Word, you were left in no doubt that preaching was *the* most important thing, or as the author Dorothy L. Sayers once put it, 'the only thing that's really ever happened to the world'.

John's preaching was logical and fervent. It was doctrinal; it shaped my mind and my thinking. But above all, as he preached to me as a young man, I was *enthralled*. I was wooed by the gospel. I was enticed by preaching to fall in love with God, with the gospel and with the crucified and risen Christ Himself. No wonder some of the early 'pulpit heroes' of the nineteenth century wrote books on preaching with titles like *The Romance of Preaching*. I became enraptured by the preaching of the gospel and I felt that this was the most glorious truth one could ever hear. Pretty soon, I wanted to be a preacher myself.

When I told my pastor of this increasing desire, he told me of the flames that had fired his own heart and passion for preaching. One of his great influences was Peter Taylor Forsyth who died in 1921, and who was probably one of the most significant British theologians of the modern era. My pastor advised me to immerse myself in Forsyth's book on preaching, *Positive Preaching and the Modern Mind*[2] based on lectures he had given at Yale in 1907. This, for me, is still the greatest book on preaching ever written, but I would not recommend it to people for general reading. Forsyth is an acquired taste and has a love of paradox as well as a great intensity and depth of thought. Don't attempt to read it if you are looking for a light snack, or a quick fix on how to preach. However, I dare you *not* to read it if you have a passionate need to plumb the depths of the whys and wherefores of preaching.

It was through reading Forsyth that I was able to understand why preaching had so radically affected me and shaped my life's direction; and from him that I gained my deepest convictions about preaching. Forsyth also helped me develop what I would call a philosophy of preaching: Why preach? And what exactly is preaching?

WHAT IS PREACHING?

Biblical preaching, empowered by the Spirit, is *performative* speech. It is speech that prolongs the gospel, prophetically envisions, confronts enemy powers, and does so in priestly service of the God we worship – all attributes that we will examine in this chapter. Simply put, it is speech that is not merely 'words', but words that perform an action.

In true preaching something is not merely *said*, something is *done*. Forsyth said in *Positive Preaching and the Modern Mind*, 'The preacher's place in the church is sacramental. It is only an age like ours that could think of preaching as something said with more or less force, instead of something *done* with more or less power.'

As a further illustration of this, Forsyth goes on to discuss the differences one would find having experienced a Protestant service of worship and a Catholic Mass. He says that as Protestants we rightly take our stand against the Mass, but that the Catholic form of worship will always have a vast advantage over the Protestant so long as people come away from its central act with the sense of something *done* in the spiritual realm. Too often people will leave a Protestant service only with a sense of something having been *said* in this physical realm, rather than *done* in the spiritual realm. Forsyth reaffirms, 'In true preaching as in a true sacrament, more is done than said.'

True biblical preaching, empowered by the Spirit, is a means of grace to us. Preaching does not merely describe God's grace, it imparts grace. Preaching does not merely talk about God, it confronts us with God. It does not merely initiate a discussion about God, it sets up an encounter with God. The content of preaching is, of course, instructive, but it is not primarily about imparting information. This is what makes preaching unlike all other forms of communication.

Modern linguistics provides interesting if oblique confirmation of the potential for words to 'do' things in what is known as 'Speech-Act theory'. It supports the performative view of preaching by pointing to the fact that certain statements have definite effects on those who hear them. Simple, obvious examples are statements such as 'I love you' spoken to another person; 'I will' declared in marriage vows. Even phrases such as 'I declare this bridge open' are words which are not merely information or description, but words that cause something to happen. The words perform a function. How much more is this true for preaching?

I believe that the practice of preaching finds its roots in the dynamic and creative way that God's word operates in the Bible. Throughout the Bible we see that God's words accomplish tasks according to His purposes:

> 'Let there be light', and there was light.
> (Genesis 1:3)

> He sent forth his word and healed them ...
> (Psalm 107:20)

> 'The Sovereign LORD says to these bones ... you will come to life.'
> (Ezekiel 37:5)

> My word ... shall not return unto me void, but it shall accomplish that ...
> whereto I sent it.
> (Isaiah 55:11 KJV)

> 'The words I have spoken to you are spirit and they are life.'
> (John 6:63)

> 'Stretch out your hand.'
> (Luke 6:10)

> 'Lazarus, come forth!'
> (John 11:43 NKJV)

The Bible is full of examples of the way in which the creative word of God accomplishes such things. Is it too much to claim that through mere human speech in preaching, God does the same? Some people think it is, but I do not think so. It may be that preaching is one step removed from such dramatic incursions as illustrated above, but it comes from the same lineage. Preaching has its roots in the creative and powerful speech of God Himself.

GOD-CENTRED PREACHING

I believe much modern preaching would improve if God more often featured in our sermons as their central theme. Some seeker-friendly Christians now disparagingly call such an approach 'vertical preaching'. Yet, in true preaching, not only is God the central topic, He is also the chief actor. Unless God's voice is somewhere, somehow, found echoing through our human speech, then it is not true preaching. God's Word should reverberate through our faltering speech to feed the hungry and raise the dead in mind and conscience. Just as the real presence of Christ does not reside in the elements of bread and wine alone, but in the whole act of taking, blessing, breaking, giving and eating in remembrance of Him with faith in the power of the Holy Spirit, so Christ the incarnate Word gives Himself to us again and again in preaching – in the taking, blessing, breaking, giving and eating of the living Word.

I share the concern of those who believe that true preaching is in decline, certainly in the western world. I believe the main reason for this is that the unique character of preaching is being corrupted. Instead of being asked to 'preach', more often we are asked to 'come and share something', or to 'give a talk'. As a result, the understanding of what is true preaching is being diluted. True preaching is also in decline because of this moving away from focusing on God as its central theme. Whilst our worship in the last twenty-five years has begun to move us more God-ward, it seems that preaching has tended to move in the opposite direction. It has become more man-ward than God-ward and is addressing only those issues that are deemed to be relevant to the immediate, felt needs of the congregation. I have fought a long-running battle with the false idol of 'relevance', to which so many preachers unthinkingly bow. If our primary goal is only to be relevant, then preaching becomes little more than therapy – or as someone once called it, 'helpful hints for hurtful habits'.

THE NEED FOR, AND EFFECT OF, PREACHING

There is a wonderful passage in Karl Barth's book *The Word of God and the Word of Man*,[3] taken from an address Barth gave to a ministers' meeting in July 1922 on 'The Need and Promise of Christian preaching'. Barth speaks from a wealth of pastoral experience of the thousand-and-one conscious reasons why people come to church, and the myriad thoughts and preoccupations that swirl through their minds as they gather for worship. Beneath everything, he says, there is a deep, silent undercurrent of expectation and longing that *something* might happen. What is that 'something'? Barth says it is that people want to find out and thoroughly understand the answer to this one question, 'Is it true – this talk of a loving and good God?' He goes on to extrapolate that thought further:

> People do not shout it out, but let us not be deceived by their silence. Behind their
> blood and tears, deepest despair and highest hope, is a passionate longing to have the
> Word spoken. The Word that promises grace in judgement, life in death and the
> beyond in the here and now – God's Word – this is what animates our churchgoers,

however lazy, bourgeois and commonplace may be the manner in which they express their needs in so-called real life.

There is no wisdom, therefore, in stopping at the next to the last and the next to the next of the last want of the people, and they will not thank us for doing so. They expect us to understand them better than they understand themselves and to take them more seriously than they take themselves. To this end the Reformers took from us the splendours of the Catholic Mass in order to give us, dare we say it, something better: the preaching of the sacrament of the Word of God. The objectively clarified preaching of the Word is the only sacrament left to us by the Reformers.

It is the habit of many people today to take notes when listening to someone preaching. Dr Martyn Lloyd-Jones for one disliked the congregation taking notes, because for him, what was crucial was the effect of the preaching upon those who were listening at the time. Lloyd-Jones quotes revivalist Jonathan Edwards to this effect, who had said, 'The main benefit obtained by preaching is by impression made upon the mind at the time, and not by an affect that arises afterwards by a remembrance of what was delivered.' Edwards maintained that the greatest benefit of preaching was the impact it had on a person at the time when they heard it, as opposed to looking back over notes in order to recall what had been said. People will most often be able to recall specific events if they have strong emotions attached to them. Likewise, when people think back to how they *felt* when someone preached a powerful word, then that message has another opportunity to work in them for transformation.

This is what distinguishes preaching from other forms of teaching and training that are more egalitarian and based around discussion or group work – both of which are valuable in their own right. I might add that for preaching to have this effect, it must take place regularly. Its effect is both cumulative and progressive.

My number one rule of thumb throughout my life, and increasingly so in the last decade, has been 'let the text speak'. We must do everything we can by whatever means, however hard we have to work, by whatever scholarship we have to employ, and by whatever imagination we have to bring, in order to let the text of Scripture *speak*. Clayton Schmidt, Associate Professor of Preaching at Fuller Theological Seminary, recently expressed the thought like this: 'God is at work in preaching, bringing power to the words that preachers use to point to what is being said in Scripture. Just let those words loose and trust their effectiveness to accomplish God's promise among God's people. Only say the word.'[4]

PREACHING PROLONGS THE GOSPEL

A key function of preaching is that it 'prolongs' the gospel. The Bible makes it clear that after a person has heard the word of the Lord and come to Christ, through the ministry of preaching, the word continues to have an ongoing effect in that person's life. This is illustrated perfectly in two statements Paul makes in his first letter to the church at Thessalonica:

> *For we know, brothers loved by God, that he has chosen you, because our gospel came to you not simply with words, but also with power, with the Holy Spirit and with deep conviction.*
> (1 Thessalonians 1:4–5)

> *We also thank God continually because, when you received the word of God, which you heard from us, you accepted it not as the word of men, but as it actually is, the word of God, which is **at work** in you who believe.*
> (1 Thessalonians 2:13, my emphasis)

Notice the phrase Paul uses when he says that the word of God is *'at work'* in the believers' lives. He has spoken of their initial conversion from idolatry to the living God under the impact of the first preaching of the gospel, and then he implies that that gospel is prolonged in their lives and continues to be at work in them as they continue to believe. The word goes on working to bring about further transformation.

Listen to Forsyth again: 'No true preaching of the Cross can be other than part of the action of the Cross in drawing men and women to the crucified Christ. The preacher, in reproducing this gospel Word of God prolongs Christ's sacramental work.'

Preaching is not normally looked at in this way, so I ask the reader to indulge me. Preaching is a Spirit-empowered reiteration of the explosive news of that once-for-all Easter event. It follows, then, that biblical preaching empowered by the Holy Spirit applies not only to evangelism, or initial conversion – preaching is the prolongation of the gospel to the church as a regular, ongoing means of grace.

There are many learned voices within evangelicalism who would strongly contradict that statement. Many current critics of preaching would urge us to discard it as an outmoded relic of the nineteenth century, or worse, as an attempt to practise the style of Greek oratorical rhetoric which Paul repudiated when writing to the Corinthians. They demand to know where such regular, expository, biblical preaching is in the New Testament. Where is it? Well, it is an argument from silence essentially, but arguments from silence can cut both ways. What in the New Testament is against preaching? And what are the gospels we have if not a *preached* record of the testimony to Christ? What are the epistles if not records of what the apostles *preached* and taught in the first churches? Paul's letter to the Romans is Paul *preaching* the gospel over again in intense detail to the church.

James Thompson, in his book *Preaching Like Paul*,[5] expresses the consensus of opinion among New Testament scholars when he says that,

> Paul's letters were a substitute for Paul's presence and communicated his apostolic authority and self-understanding to the churches. Paul's apostolic authority is transmitted to the churches from which he is apart, through his letters being read out publicly in the congregation gathered together for worship. Being absent, Paul for example is made present by the reading out of his letters. In this way his apostolic authority is brought to bear on the church as though he were there in person.

While we are arguing from silence, can anyone really imagine that when Paul's letters were read aloud in the churches to which they were sent (as they were intended to be) they were then put away in a drawer to gather dust? Isn't it much more likely that they were read and re-read, commented on, explained and interpreted to congregations eager to feast on apostolic authority and truth?

In another helpful book, this time focusing on Romans, Catherine Greib says,

> Letters as complicated as Paul's epistles would probably have required an interpreter who could not only read the letter out loud to the community, but could also explain and clarify its difficult ideas. The letter would have been read aloud in the context of the gathered community's worship, probably like a sermon. It would have been as if Paul himself was there with them proclaiming to them the gospel of God as the letter is being read.[6]

Listen to Forsyth once again:

> To be effective our preaching must be sacramental, it must be an act prolonging the great act, mediating it and conveying it. Now the consequence of this immediately arises. We lose our way, I believe, when we put our confidence in what preaching leads to rather than in what it achieves in and of itself.

We are in grave danger of doing this in our generation – believing that the real action takes place *after* the preaching. It betrays our total lack of confidence in the preaching of God's Word that we assume nothing significant occurs *during* it. This is a symptom of a larger malaise – a massive lack of confidence in the Word of God generally. We pay lip-service to biblical authority, but I suspect that many people are unsure that this Word actually works. It is easy at the point of preaching to rapidly lose our nerve. In modern evangelicalism we are under pressure to 'make something happen' after the preaching, so we call people to the front to make decisions, or we lay hands on them, or bring them out for 'carpet time', as if the significant action has not yet happened and is about to start.

Similarly, under pressure from a congregation to be practical or relevant we lapse into moralism. At the end of some people's sermons there are always three steps you must do, five keys you must get hold of, etc., and too often, however well meaning, the gospel is reduced to techniques of self-improvement. Why? Because we don't trust that simply preaching the Word is doing anything. Michael Horton said recently that the cry for more practical preaching is the call of the old Adam for more self-help. We may dress it up and call it application, but it is, in effect, moralism and legalism by any other name.

PREACHING HAS THE POWER TO ENVISION PROPHETICALLY

During the 1990s I spent five enjoyable years teaching and preaching in a small, but long-established evangelical church not far from my home. On the last Sunday I spoke there, I reminded them of the fact that, during our time together, I had never sought to make them feel bad about themselves but, rather, to make them feel good about God (for which I was rewarded with knowing looks and wide grins). That is, after all, what we are called to do, isn't it? We are called to preach in ways that glorify God in the gospel of Christ. We are called in preaching to confound the wisdom of the world with the cruciform foolishness of God. We preach to smite the disenchantment that so saps the energies of our shoulder-shrugging, post-modern weariness with the glory of the resurrection. Ask yourself this question: Does it take the message of the cross and the resurrection of Jesus to achieve the ends for which you are aiming in your preaching? If not, then you are not preaching the gospel, but offering self-improvement techniques with a Christian veneer.

Preaching is performative speech which *prophetically envisions* – in other words, true preaching opens people's eyes and enables them to see the truth. Consequently, the use of imagery and visualisation is very important in preaching. That is why the prophets in the Old Testament, and prophetic ministries everywhere, use such vivid imagery and paint such stunning pictures. The Old Testament prophets of God knew instinctively that people only learn by a re-education process. People are not changed by moral exhortation, but by having a transformed imagination.

People are not affected all that much by constant moral exhortation, but they do begin to change when their imaginations are transformed and they see things from a different perspective. People need to have their eyes opened to the truth. The great exilic prophets of Israel did just this when they painted a vision of a completely alternative scenario to the one the Babylonian pagan culture was offering. They offered people the opportunity to see themselves as the people of God, called and empowered to live and behave differently. They helped people to see God Himself differently, as the majestic and mighty One who blew the wind of truth on Babylonian propaganda so that it faded away like grass, withered by the scorching wind.

The apostle John saw a vision on Patmos and wrote it down. 'I want to tell you what I saw,' he says, 'because when you see it too, it will change everything for you.' His amazing vision of the victorious Lamb who was slain would have prophetically envisioned its first readers. 'Despite all appearances to the contrary,' John says, 'it is not the beast of imperial power and oppression that is triumphant in the end, but the slain

Lamb who is finally victorious. It is not the Babylonian whore of sexual perversion and economic seduction that is married to God's future, but the Church of the martyrs and the faithful followers of the Lamb – they are the Bride of Christ.' John opened the eyes of early believers, and continues to envision us today with his prophetic preaching.

One of my favourite Christian writers is Lewis Smedes who died recently. In one of his last books, on the subject of hope,[7] he recalled how Martin Luther King kept people's hopes alive by continually raising their sights above the abuse and degradation they were suffering, so that they could *see* and *imagine* a land where life would be decent and fair. On 28 August 1963 King gathered 250,000 people at the Lincoln Memorial in Washington to appeal to the conscience of America. The authorities apparently feared trouble and they urged King to keep his rhetoric cool. He agreed and proceeded to give a very careful speech that seemed designed to dampen down ardour and enthusiasm.

The story goes, as Smedes tells it, that the gospel singer Mahalia Jackson was sitting behind Dr King on the platform and was beginning to feel very let down by the flat tone of the speech. As he seemed to be concluding and about to turn and sit down, she shouted out to him, 'The dream, Martin, the dream – tell them about the dream ... tell them the dream!'

At that point Dr King launched into the famous words, 'I have a dream, that one day on the red hills of Georgia, sons of former slaves and the sons of former slave-owners will be able to sit down together at the table of brotherhood...'

Preachers, *whatever else you do, tell them the dream!* Open the eyes of people's hearts to the vision and the hope of God's alternative kingdom manifest by God's alternative community.

PREACHING IS A POLITICAL ACT

According to Ephesians 6, the only offensive weapon the Church possesses is the sword of the Spirit which is the Word of God. Here Paul is referring to the apostolic preaching of the gospel. As the theologian Gordon Fee puts it, 'The Word of God is the Spirit's sword, and as it is faithfully spoken forth in the gospel, in the arena of darkness, men and women hear and are delivered from Satan's grasp. Biblical preaching, empowered by the Spirit, proclaims a redemptive word that sets the church free from its captivity to the powers.'[8]

Preaching is, in the broadest sense, a political act. It operates as part of the challenge that God issues to the powers that be. True preaching must confront the powers that oppose God's Kingdom with the sovereignty of God and the Lordship of Jesus Christ; it must seek to expose the spiritual forces, the principalities and powers, that act as oppressive and dehumanising forces and seek to destroy and distort God's good creation.

I am increasingly challenged by how political the New Testament is in that sense. Jesus is not some spiritual guru who floats above contradiction and political involvement. Someone has said that Jesus quite deliberately chose preaching as a weapon of warfare in the clash of the kingdoms. It was a visible sign of what kind of kingdom He was representing. He took up not the sword of revolutionary violence, but the sword of the Spirit of God which was and is the preaching of the gospel of the Kingdom.

The apostolic preaching of the early Church was carried out as a deliberately public act which aimed to create a culturally distinctive community. The very concept of 'gospel' thrust the Church into the political arena and the bear-pit of spiritual powers. The roots of the apostolic understanding of gospel went back to the writings of Old Testament prophets such as Isaiah, who clearly expressed the social and political implications of the gospel. In that great passage of Isaiah 52:7, the prophet talks of the herald with 'beautiful feet', who announces the victory of God over Babylonian oppression. Evil has been defeated, justice, peace and salvation have now come for the people of God, and God is returning to reign as king in Zion. Having read and understood this message in its original context, the first apostles would have then read it into their contemporary context – the oppression of the Roman Empire.

At that time, Roman Emperors themselves issued regular 'gospels' proclaiming that victory and honour belonged to the Emperor in Rome, and so everyone should rejoice. So, when the apostles began to preach the gospel of Jesus Christ, it was inevitably a political activity. It was not long until they were accused in Thessalonica of turning the world upside down, because they were declaring another Lord other than Caesar. No wonder the apostles wrote from prison cells, or faced lonely martyrdoms.

THE PRIESTLY ACT OF PREACHING

All the elements of preaching that we have examined so far can be encapsulated in the truth that preaching is a *priestly act*. Read how the apostle Paul expresses this in Romans 15:16–17. He reminds the believers of the grace of God that has been given to him to be a minister of Christ Jesus to the Gentiles *'with the priestly duty of proclaiming the gospel of God'*. Preaching the gospel is a priestly act; therefore preaching has its place at the heart of Christian worship because preaching is itself an act of worship. It is a doxological activity. P.T. Forsyth put it like this: 'It is the Word of God returning in confession to God who gave it, addressed to men, but offered to God.' Here Forsyth describes the genius of true preaching. If you can attain to that, then you will be a preacher – addressing people, but as you address them, offering your words to God as worship. That is priestly preaching.

This provides us with ample reason to give our preaching a celebratory tone. We can articulate with fervour and joy what the Church believes when declaring the gospel that has been delivered to the saints. John Piper recently spoke of preaching like this: 'Christian preaching, as part of the corporate worship of Christ's Church, is an expository exhortation over the glories of God in His word, designed to lure God's people from the fleeting pleasures of sin into the sacrificial path of obedient satisfaction in Him.'[9]

The aim of preaching is to persuade others to surrender themselves as an acceptable offering to God. That is what true, biblical preaching empowered by the Spirit will achieve. True preaching casts fire from heaven on the altar of our hearts and kindles a flame of sacred love. It incites God-loving and Christ-honouring devotion. Forsyth said of the apostles that they 'sang their joy in preaching'. As you preach in this way, and rhapsodise over the majesty of God's grace that has come to us in Jesus Christ, you will lure your listeners into the obedient sacrifice of themselves to God.

When you discover a lack of faith in your congregation, don't preach another series of sermons on faith! Rather, preach Christ so that they can't help believing in Him. Preach the ethical qualities of the new life of the Kingdom not as a guilt trip laid upon people, but as a great adventure they are called to.

True biblical preaching cleanses consciences with the washing of the water of God's Word. It leads minds polluted by the lies and spin of the culture to be detoxified and renewed at the fountain of truth. It dazzles people with a vision of how God's will for their holiness is the sure and certain way to their happiness. It empowers feeble wills to go over the barricades of cultural conformity and to be risk-takers for Jesus. That is the effect of preaching.

I leave the last word to Forsyth, who said that preaching is 'the organised hallelujah of an ordered community and an intelligent faith'.

NOTES

1. *Preaching and Preachers* (Hodder and Stoughton, 1971).
2. Independent Press, 1953.
3. Hodder & Stoughton, 1928, pp. 108–9, 110, 114.
4. Clayton Schmidt, *Too Deep for Words: A Theology of Liturgical Expression* (Westminster John Knox Press, 2002), p. 58.
5. Westminster John Knox Press, 2001.
6. *The Story of Romans: A Narrative Defense of God's Righteousness* (Westminster John Knox Press, 2002).
7. *Keeping Hope Alive – for a Tomorrow We Cannot Control* (Thomas Nelson, 2000).
8. *God's Empowering Presence: The Holy Spirit in the Letters of Paul* (Hendrickson, 1994), p. 729.
9. John Piper, *God's Passion for God's Glory* (IVP, 1998), p. 39.

Chapter 9

PREACHING THROUGH A BOOK OF THE BIBLE

Michael Eaton

The great preacher C.H. Spurgeon believed it was entirely wrong ever to preach through a book of the Bible and, consequently, he never did so. In fact, he never preached a series of sermons, believing that it was impossible for a preacher to know, if he preached on a verse one week, that the Holy Spirit would lead him to preach on the next verse the following week. Although he occasionally would preach for two consecutive weeks on the same subject, he was very firmly against the idea of expounding a book of the Bible and went so far as to believe the practice grieved the Holy Spirit.

A nineteenth-century scholar called Edwin Hatch, who had a great influence on Martyn Lloyd-Jones, wrote a book entitled *The Influences of Greek Ideas and Usages upon the Christian Church*,[1] in which he argued that the very concept of a sermon was really a Greek idea. In his view, early Christian preaching was entirely prophetic. A man would stand up, not knowing what he was going to say and then prophetically, under the power of the Holy Spirit, would pour out his heart. It was only the influence of Greek thinking upon the Church, with its tidiness, structure and argumentation, that produced the sermon.

Lloyd-Jones admitted being troubled by the arguments of Edwin Hatch, who he felt had made a good case. However, he was not entirely convinced, finding structure in Peter's sermon on the Day of Pentecost and believing that the apostle knew where he was going and displayed a kind of logic in the development of his ideas. So, while very interested in this idea that early Christian preaching was highly prophetic, he answered Hatch by saying that there is indeed some kind of structure in New Testament preaching.

It is against this background and with these views very much in mind that I want to try and persuade preachers to take up the task of expounding books of the Bible. And not only that, but to try and persuade them to encourage members of their congregation to read the Bible in the same way. However, it is important for us to look very deliberately at the question 'Is it right to preach through books of the Bible?' For although I have been doing it for decades, there are some cautions and questions we must consider.

IS IT RIGHT TO PREACH THROUGH A BOOK OF THE BIBLE?

One of the most convincing arguments against the practice of expounding a book of the Bible is the fact that it is not found in the Bible. The Scriptures themselves have a doctrine about Scripture. In the same way that the doctrine of inspiration is itself a biblical doctrine, there is also a biblical hermeneutic concerning what the Bible implies about itself in connection with its application and interpretation. We do not bring hermeneutical principles to bear on the Bible from the outside; they come up out of the Scriptures. The Bible itself has its own principles of interpretation.

This argument can be taken a stage further. Just as the Bible's doctrine of Scripture is our model, and just as the Bible's hermeneutic is our model, so the Bible's model of preaching is our model. The biblical model tends to involve preaching with the use of several verses. Rarely in the New Testament does a writer expound a single text. On the Day of Pentecost Peter begins by expounding verses from Joel 2 but later goes on to speak about Psalm 16 (see Acts 2). This cannot really be described as expounding a single text. Nowhere in the Bible does Paul preach on Isaiah for a year. Nowhere does Isaiah preach on Leviticus for a year – nowhere does a later writer expound the text of an earlier writer in the manner of some lengthy sermon series that became customary in some parts of the Christian Church.

On what grounds, then, do I or anybody else argue that we should preach through books of the Bible? For me preaching through a book of the Bible falls into the same category as a church building, a church choir or a hymn-book. None of these things are to be found in the New Testament. In fact, in my own circle of churches, the Chrisco Fellowship of Churches, in Kenya, we still don't use hymn-books or an overhead projector and we scarcely have a building. Yet we don't do too badly. Buildings, hymn-books and even printed Bibles are not essential to the growth of a Christian community. For how much of the history of the Church have ordinary people had access to a copy of a printed Bible? Printing wasn't invented until the fourteenth century and for most of church history the great majority of people could never have afforded to buy one. Even today there are Christians who don't have a Bible. Surely these things are highly useful *tools*, but they are not indispensable. And it is into this same category that I put preaching through books of the Bible. It is no more indispensable than a church building or a hymn-book or a piano or guitar, but it is very useful. But, as with all highly useful tools, there is a danger of coming to trust in the tool and no longer trusting the Holy Spirit. Before a church has a building, it has to trust God week by week; but when it has a building, it is all too easy to start trusting the building. So it is with all aspects of our highly organised church life. When a church is living in persecution or revival where the situation is constantly changing, the believers have no option but to trust in God.

I believe the same is true with regard to preaching through the Bible. There are certain dangers inherent in the practice of which the preacher must be aware. I don't want to persuade anyone to expound the books of the Bible if his church ends up dead as a result. I know of churches that are not like churches at all: they are more like universities. The preacher has been preaching on Ephesians for two years and everyone takes notes. They are all experts; they are all like students in a college. But try and get those people witnessing and you have a battle on your hands. When revival comes they don't like it. For a start, it messes up the sermon series! We must beware the danger – and I cannot stress this enough – of becoming overly intellectual.

My answer to the question 'Is it right to preach through the books of the Bible?' is, then, 'Yes, it is right', but I think we should regard it as a matter of convenience. It is very useful to preach through sections of the Scripture, applying them and impressing them upon the people of God, as long as we remain aware of the dangers of intellectualism inherent in it. The term 'expository preaching' should have the emphasis on the second word not the first.

WAYS OF PREACHING THROUGH THE BIBLE

Let us consider a number of possibilities.

1. Lifelong exposition
A seventeenth-century Puritan preacher called William Gouge (1575–1653) preached on the book of Hebrews for thirty-three years. He gave his entire life to Hebrews and still today a massive folio volume of his on Hebrews is in print[2] – but they are only the notes not the sermons. His preaching became a kind of tourist attraction at his church in Blackfriars in London. Along with the Tower of London and other famous sites the tourist would attend a sermon on Hebrews at William Gouge's church. Another man, a Puritan called Joseph Caryl (1602–73), spent his life preaching on Job, and his twelve-volume work entitled *Practical Observations Upon the Book of Job* can be found in the Evangelical Library in London.

2. Many years, but not a lifetime
A less ambitious method is to spend many years (but less than a whole life) *on a few books*. This way of preaching through the Bible provides preachers with the opportunity to give themselves to very detailed exposition of the Scriptures. Lloyd-Jones, for example, covered six, almost seven, books in his lifetime: Habakkuk, Ephesians (over eight years with a year gap in the middle), Philippians, 1 Peter, 2 Peter, 1 John; in addition he got as far as Romans 14:17 after fourteen years of preaching through Romans.

In around 1534 or 1535 Martin Luther announced to his students that he would spend the rest of his life preaching on the Law. He said he would preach on Genesis and then he would die. His prophecy was fulfilled. He preached on Genesis for the next ten years,[3] delivering his last sermon on Genesis 50:20 in November or December 1545. He died a couple of months later without having preached again.

I do not think many people are called to devote themselves to such lengthy exposition of books of Scripture, and it is not a practice I would generally recommend. However, I do believe that certain situations merit it. Luther preached in the university town of Wittenberg and Lloyd-Jones served in the metropolis of London – both unique situations. In addition to serving their unique communities such men have also provided a service for the Church that will last forever. People will be reading Lloyd-Jones on Romans until the end of church history, I would imagine. A piece of work has been done for the churches that will last for generations. I think this is also true of J. Alec Motyer's Commentary on Isaiah.[4] Motyer has spent more than thirty years studying and preaching on Isaiah. Nobody – if he has sense – will ever write another book on Isaiah without making use of what has been done already. Every single word is weighed; the scholarship is outstanding. His book could never be rivalled without the author undertaking the same kind of extensive study as Motyer, and even then he or she would be forced to many of the same conclusions. His work will also last for all church history. However, this was not a sermon-series.

I believe that the Church needs some congregations which are given over to such detailed exposition of the Word. In fact, I would say that during Lloyd-Jones's time Westminster Chapel functioned as a major theological college in London. People attending the Chapel for a couple of years would have learnt as much theology as a student at Cambridge, if not more. A church functioning in this way would provide much better theological training for preachers than many of our present colleges. Surely, only preachers actively engaged in the task should be training preachers? This seems much closer to the biblical model of on-the-job training.

3. The hurried Bible survey

At the very opposite end of the spectrum stand those who attempt to preach through a major book of the Bible in a couple of weeks. To me preaching through a book like Romans in four weeks, as I have heard some preachers attempt to do, is not preaching. It is more like entertainment or watching TV. I am not a believer in this type of Bible survey, generally speaking. Such preaching does not pierce people's hearts and cause them to cry out, *'Brothers, what shall we do?'*[5] Lloyd-Jones was very critical of this type of preaching, and it was for this reason that he would never speak at meetings like the Keswick Convention with its 'Bible-readings' (unlike Campbell Morgan, his predecessor). He used to say, 'I start where other preachers stop.' By this he meant that he would spend the first five or so minutes of his sermon doing what those preachers did for their whole sermon, putting the text into its context. He believed that it is only when the preacher begins to apply the text and make it relevant to his hearers' lives that it has life-changing power.[6]

4. A middle way

The practice I would recommend lies somewhere in between the two extremes I have described. I do not believe that it is right for most people to spend their whole lives expounding one book to one congregation, nor do I believe that it is right to give biblical surveys which dash through Scripture at breakneck pace. Unlike Lloyd-Jones I do believe it can be justified at places like Keswick and in certain other situations, but not for Sunday by Sunday preaching. I recommend *taking three or four verses at a time*. Calvin went through Galatians in forty-three sermons, that is 3.4 verses per sermon. I once preached forty-four sermons on Ephesians to young people (3.5 verses per sermon). When preaching on a gospel or a history book, it makes sense to take a story per sermon, generally speaking. At that sort of pace the preacher is able to do justice to the text, without having the feeling that it will take him his whole life to finish the book. Dwelling on a passage too long can become very tedious.

PRACTICAL SUGGESTIONS FOR PREACHING THROUGH THE BIBLE

There are a number of practical suggestions which can be a real help to the preacher who embarks on preaching through a book.

First, it is sometimes a good idea to break the series down. I mentioned having preached forty-four sermons on Ephesians to teenagers in Nairobi, but I didn't do it in forty-four weeks in a stretch. I would preach for about thirteen weeks on Ephesians and then take a break and preach on something else. In a church with several pastors, one of the other pastors can preach every few weeks and so break up the series.

It is my view that a series of sermons should last no more than thirteen weeks without a break. Someone might object that Lloyd-Jones preached for fourteen years on one book, but the reality is not as cut and dried. For one thing, he would take long summer holidays and in any year he would actually preach about thirty sermons. For another, in the middle of his eight-year-long preach on Ephesians, he took a break for a year to preach on revival. In his evening evangelistic sermons he never preached a series longer than thirteen weeks, that is until his last one on Acts, which he continued to the end of his ministry. For most of his life he did not preach long series to unsaved people.

Second, it is possible for preachers who minister in many places to preach through a book for themselves. Not all preachers are in the situation where they can do this, but it is an option for those who travel or who are responsible for more than one congregation. I have done this recently with the book of Leviticus. The only person who is hearing the whole of my series on Leviticus is me! I have preached parts of it in Germany and parts in

England. The congregations who have heard my sermons have no idea that they are hearing part of a series. The great advantage of this method for the preacher is that it gives him the discipline of working through Scripture. He works through a book from beginning to end. What other way is there to read the Bible? I would find it very strange if people read a letter from me in the way many read the Bible, picking out a nice phrase here and an interesting sentence there. In truth, I would probably be offended. But that is the way many people read the Bible. Surely, as with any text, we begin at the beginning and work through to the end. I believe it is very important for preachers to be encouraging their congregations to work through books of the Bible from beginning to end and to be seeking to find any and every possible means to help them. They are not just to dash through the Bible, but should spend time pondering on the text. For example, if I find a little booklet, maybe from Selwyn Hughes or Scripture Union, that works through a book of the Bible in daily readings, I will have copies put in the church bookstore and encourage my people to use it.

Third (and here I am thinking of Spurgeon's important objection outlined at the start of the chapter), a preacher should not hesitate to interrupt a series in response to the guidance of the Holy Spirit. For example, if he is working through a series on a book when an unusual event occurs in the life of the church or the nation, he must not feel obliged to carry on regardless. Personally I never promise that what I am doing next week will be a continuation of this week. Even if I have preached week after week on one book, I do not promise that it will be the same book next week. In our preaching, as in every area of our church life, we must never quench the work of the Holy Spirit. Although we have our study, our methods, our series, we still need the Holy Spirit. If we ever let anything replace our dependence on Him, we will be in serious trouble.

There are some wonderful stories about Spurgeon in connection with his desire always to preach in response to the leading of the Holy Spirit. On one occasion he was about to preach when a verse caught his eye – it was Isaiah 50:10 about a child of light walking in darkness. He was thrown into a quandary because, although he had a message prepared, he felt a very strong compulsion to preach on this verse. Sensing that it was the Holy Spirit, he abandoned his message and started to preach. Within seconds the building was plunged into darkness and remained in darkness for the remainder of the service. Nobody could see a thing, but it made no difference to Spurgeon because he was not using his notes anyway. He preached with great power on his text about a child of light walking in darkness – and did so in the dark!

Spurgeon used to work during the week from about Wednesday onwards on his Sunday morning sermon, but his Sunday evening sermon he used to prepare on Sunday afternoons. His Thursday prayer-meeting address he generally prepared while riding in a horse and carriage to church! Sometimes he had unusual experiences when a message would 'come' to him only at the last moment. One Saturday evening he was still unprepared and unclear about his text for Sunday morning ('Never verse in the Scripture has puzzled me more than this . . . '). He was so tired that he felt he had to go to bed, so he asked his wife to wake him before dawn the next morning in order to prepare. As he was sleeping, he started talking in his sleep. When his wife suddenly realised he was preaching a sermon on Psalm 110 verse 3 in his sleep, she had no time to get a notebook but made a determined effort to remember what he was saying. She didn't wake him up until about 6 o'clock. At first he was upset that she hadn't woken him earlier but she explained what had happened. That morning he preached the sermon his wife had heard him preach while he was asleep.[7]

In connection with being led by the Holy Spirit it is also important to say – and this may seem to contradict my earlier point about the optimum length for a series of sermons being thirteen weeks – that every preacher discovers that on some occasions he does not get beyond the first verse because the Holy Spirit comes down in power and takes over. The Holy Spirit gives such liberty to preach that what the preacher had planned to say is expanded and enlarged and has a powerful impact on those who are listening.

Terry Virgo tells the story of an occasion when he was visiting Westminster Chapel and Lloyd-Jones was preaching. That night Lloyd-Jones preached in great power for about an hour and fifteen minutes, as he sometimes did in the evening services. After the service Terry asked him how he was able to minister like that. In response Lloyd-Jones asked him, 'How many points did I say I would have?' Terry thought for a moment before replying, 'Three.' Then Lloyd-Jones asked him, 'How many did I *actually* have?' As he thought about it, Terry realised Lloyd-Jones had actually not got beyond his first point. Lloyd-Jones agreed, explaining that the Holy Spirit had come upon him and from that moment all that he had said had been spontaneous. He waved his hand towards a pile of notes on his desk. 'They will do for next week,' he said.

This is why it is important for the preacher not to tie himself down by announcing in advance that he will preach on specific verses each week. There must always be room given for the Holy Spirit to come in power. The preacher *must* leave himself free to follow the leading of the Holy Spirit.

While I cannot emphasise this last point enough, it has been my experience, and the experience of many others, that as I have preached through books of the Bible I have found myself to be at the right place at the right time. This is one of the great mysteries of heaven. Although it may be many months since I decided to preach on a certain book, I often find the very text on which I am preaching on a particular Sunday speaks right into the situation the church is facing at that particular moment in time. I don't know how the Lord does it, but it is a very common experience.

Some years ago I was preaching through Isaiah, using the strategy I outlined above of preaching through the book for myself at the various churches at which I was speaking in Africa at that time. On a Tuesday evening in September I was preaching on Isaiah 10 – on how God can use one wicked nation to judge another wicked nation. '*Ah, Assyria, the rod of my anger! The staff in their hands is my fury*' (v. 5).[8] I was getting ready to say how

God can raise up anyone of His choosing – even a pagan Assyrian nation – to be the rod of His anger. The date on which I was preaching that sermon was September 11, 2001, the famous 9/11! Even if I had had a transcript of the daily newspapers for September 12 in front of me as I prepared my sermon, I could not have chosen a better text than the one I was committed to by preaching through Isaiah. All I was doing was working through Isaiah. It *is* possible (despite Spurgeon!) to remain in the Holy Spirit while preaching through a book. Again and again God uses His Word as the preacher works through a particular book to speak with incredible relevance into the current situation.

I have experienced this many, many times. On another occasion, while I was preaching through Luke's Gospel in one of our churches in Chrisco Fellowship, Nairobi, the congregation was suddenly evicted from their place of worship and forced to find another venue. On the very Sunday morning that this incident occurred I was preaching about the need to put new wine into new wineskins explaining that sometimes when God does something new, there has to be a new structure in a new place. That was exactly the experience of the church. They found themselves in a new location on the university campus with a new kind of ministry. I had not planned it, but it had just happened as I worked through the Scriptures.[9]

At other times the preacher may need to adapt what he was going to say to fit the situation in which he finds himself. The sermon he has prepared is almost right but not absolutely right. In such circumstances I believe it is perfectly acceptable to reshape it a little. It is the preacher's task not only to expound the Word of God but to speak into a situation. We believe in expository preaching – and I hold the view that it is the second word, not the first word, that is important. It is the *preaching* that matters.

I remember one occasion in South Africa when I found myself in a very strange situation because I was at a church but didn't feel that the Lord had given me a message to preach. In fact, I felt that the Lord was withholding a message. He seemed to be holding something back. I think Ezekiel had the same experience when he described himself as 'dumb'. Up to that point in my visit of South Africa I had been preaching on Galatians, and I still wanted to do that, but I didn't feel any liberty from the Lord whatsoever. I was due to preach at 10 o'clock that morning, but at breakfast time I still did not know what I should preach on.

I was struggling with my problem at the breakfast table when suddenly the pastor at whose church I was due to be speaking, asked if he could share a problem with me. As I listened to the difficulty he was facing, I knew what I should be preaching on. A short time later in the church I spoke on Galatians 4:12–20. It was a sermon with three points concerning 'Authority gained' and 'Authority regained'.[10] Then I began to apply my points to that church situation. The issue in the Galatian passage was not exactly the one that this church was facing, but it does deal with authority in the church and people having different ideas about where the church should be going. I was not misusing the text but I was adapting it to fit the situation into which I was preaching.

Expository preaching must be expository *preaching*! The preacher preaches *into* a situation. He must not be so concerned with his text that he forgets the needs of the people. He must not preach to educate himself or to enjoy himself. He must be relevant and he must sometimes address what is happening. It is not enough to produce perfect model sermons; what matters is that they meet the needs of the people.

Lloyd-Jones was a master at the art of adapting his sermon to fit the current situation. Although he might be in the middle of a series he would always find a way to address important issues – for instance, when King George VI died or when John Kennedy was assassinated. When the Prefumo scandal hit the news in 1963, Lloyd-Jones preached his evening sermon on the text that he had planned, but he made it relevant to people caught out in sin. Again he was in the right place at the right time. His text said: *'Be not deceived: neither fornicators . . . nor adulterers . . . shall inherit the kingdom . . . but ye are washed, ye are sanctified . . . '* (1 Corinthians 6:9–11 KJV). 'They might very well have been written for just this present hour,' he said.[11]

PREACHING THROUGH THE BIBLE TRANSFORMS UNDERSTANDING

It is my conviction that preaching that does *not* arise from working through Scripture (publicly or privately) leads to heresy and false teaching. If a preacher chooses a verse here or a verse there, taking them out of context, they can easily be made to fit his own understanding or particular pet theory. I think, for example, of one preacher I know who always ends up talking about money whatever text he is preaching on. One day he announced that his text was Ezekiel 33 and I thought, 'Wonderful! He is going to preach on revival or new birth or being raised to life by the Lord Jesus Christ.' In fact, he preached on money once again! 'Ezekiel's bones is your poverty,' he said. 'Preach to the bones and you will get rich!' That is what can happen when preachers select passages at random – they can easily just preach on their favourite subjects.

Preaching on a verse in its context has the power to transform our understanding of it or even to unlock our understanding if previously we had been baffled. In the former case we may be blinded by our own preconceptions. We believe we already know what the verse means. In the latter, we may simply find a verse difficult. I remember having this experience with 1 John 5:16 which speaks about the 'sin unto death'. Although I had written about 1 John 5 in my doctoral thesis, I had always found this verse difficult. However, when I began to preach through the epistle, the meaning of the verse became clear to me (as I see it!). Chapter by chapter John has been saying that sin can be forgiven. If we confess our sins, God is faithful and just and will forgive us. But alongside this there is another recurring theme. John writes about those who refuse to recognise that Jesus is the Son of God come in the flesh. Such people have no part in the gospel, and believers should not even greet such teachers or invite them to their home. Having worked through four chapters of John's letter, the expositor experiences little difficulty knowing what this 'sin unto death' is. It is not believing in the gospel! That is what John has been saying all along. Speaking in much the same vein, Luther once said that the secret to understanding Romans 8 is Romans 1–7 and R.T. Kendall admitted he felt rather nervous about interpreting James 2:14 until he began to preach through the epistle. Then he saw the verse in a completely new light.[12] Many of the questions we have arise because we are not following the thread of the author's argument and the flow of his thought. If we will put in the necessary work, our understanding will be transformed.

Preachers are often told that they should make a distinction between preparing their sermons and their own personal Bible reading. I disagree. There is no difference in my mind between preparing something for personal study and preparing a sermon. My reason is this: surely I ought not to preach anything to anybody else that I have not preached to myself first? Surely what I preach to others must first have gripped me?

I ask the question: what is the difference between the two kinds of ministry? When a preacher is preparing his sermon, without doubt he wants to know what the text means and he wants to apply it to his own life. How is this any different from his own personal times of devotion? I tell preachers, even in their own times of private devotion, to study the Bible as if they were preparing a sermon – but to prepare it for themselves. Preachers should work through the books of the Bible whether they will preach on them or not, because they need every book of the Bible. If they work their way through the books of the Bible, putting their notes in an almost sermonic form, with numbered points, then when they do come to preach on a particular text, 80 per cent of the work is done already.

Sometimes people ask me how long it took me to prepare my sermon. If I possibly can, I try to avoid the question, but if I have to answer them, I say there are two answers. One might be, 'I prepared it five minutes ago sitting on that chair just before I began to preach.' The other answer is that it has taken me many years. I have been working on it all my life. Spurgeon said, 'He who would prepare little, must prepare much.' Whether we are preachers or 'ordinary' Christians our whole lives must have a space in them in which we give ourselves to the Word of God. Then, when it comes to the time to preach, he who has prepared much will find that he need prepare little.

NOTES

1. *The Hibbert Lectures*, 1888 (published in London, Edinburgh and Oxford, 1901).
2. *A Commentary on Hebrews* (Kregel).
3. See Luther's Works, Vols. 1–8.
4. *The Prophecy of Isaiah* (InterVarsity Press, 1993).
5. Acts 2:37.
6. He did occasionally do it, however! Consider his sweeping exposition of the whole of Revelation in eight sessions of the Friday Bible School (chapters 14–21 of *The Church and the Last Things*, Hodder & Stoughton, 1997).

7. See C.H. Spurgeon, *The Early Years* (Banner of Truth, 1962), pp. 419–20. The sermon, preached on 13 April 1856, was published in *New Park Street Pulpit*, Vol. 2, Sermon 74 (repr. Banner of Truth, 1963).

8. Michael Eaton's own translation.

9. An abridged version of the sermon is found in *Preaching Through the Bible: Luke 1–11* (Sovereign World, 1999), ch. 23.

10. A reshaped version of the same sermon appears in *Preaching Through the Bible: Galatians* (Sovereign World, 2005), ch. 25, but without its particular applications to a particular situation.

11. See D.M. Lloyd-Jones, *The Kingdom of God* (Crossway, 1992), p. 137. John Profumo was a government minister who had a sexual relationship with a girl who was also involved with a Russian Military Attaché.

12. See R.T. Kendall, *'Justification By Works' – Sermons on James 1–3* (Paternoster/Spring Harvest, 2001), chapter 23, with linguistic support from M.A. Eaton, *James*, Preaching Through the Bible (Sovereign World, 2003), ch. 13.

Chapter 10

PREACHING THE BIG STORY

Philip Greenslade

In *The Lord of the Rings*, on the journey to Mordor, Sam asks Frodo, 'What sort of tale have we fallen into?' 'I wonder,' says Frodo, 'but I don't know, and that's the way of a real tale. Take any one that you are fond of, you may know or guess what kind of tale it is, happy ending or sad ending, but the people in it don't know.' A decade ago the American mainline theologian Robert Jensen wrote a notable essay, often quoted, called 'How the World Lost its Story', in which he argues that the entire Enlightenment project on which the modern western world was based was self-defeating:

> The experiment has failed. It is after the fact obvious that it had to. If there is no universal story-teller, then the universe can have no storyline. Neither you nor I, not all of us together, can so shape this world that it can make narrative sense. If God does not invent the world's story, then it has none. Then the world has no narrative that is its own. If there is no God, or if indeed there is some other God than the God of the Bible, there is no narratable world.[1]

For post-modern theorists the fact that there is no overall plotline is a cause for celebration. When pressed to simplify the post-modern condition, Jean-François Lyotard famously said in 1984, 'If I have to simplify, I would say that post-modernity has to do with incredulity to all meta-narratives.'[2] These universal accounts of the world are now apparently discredited and all we are left with is our particular domestic stories. One of the reasons, sociologists tell us, why so many people watch soap operas is a psychological need for a surrogate family that makes some sort of linear sense to them. Summarising the social consequences of the loss of meta-narrative, the Chief Rabbi of Britain, Jonathan

137

Sacks, said recently, 'Something happens when change is so rapid that nothing confers meaning ... When lives become lifestyles, commitments become experiments, relationships become provisional, careers turn into contracts, then life itself ceases to have the character of a narrative and becomes instead a series of episodes with no continuing thread.'[3]

I believe as biblical preachers of the gospel we can take our stand against post-enlightenment, post-modern despair. We can assert what post-modernity denies and we can supply what post-modernity demands. First of all, we assert what post-modernity denies: we say there is a master story which makes sense of reality and it is the story of the one Creator God told in the Bible. Next, we supply what post-modernity demands. The story of God told in the Bible is at the same time the very localised and historically conditioned story of the one Creator God's involvement with the special people Israel and their Messiah Jesus, who represents what used to be called 'the scandal of particularity'. Our preaching, then, is unavoidably and unashamedly biblical. For us the Bible is a living and dynamic book. When I plunge into what Karl Barth famously called 'the strange new world' within the Bible, I feel like J.B. Phillips did when he began to translate the New Testament into modern English some forty or fifty years ago. He said he felt 'like an electrician rewiring an old house with the live current still switched on'.[4] Absorption with this book alone will keep us God-centred, and its bracing truth and cleansing judgement will save us from the mawkish self-centredness and cloying sentimentality of so much contemporary evangelicalism. Barth said once, 'We have found in the Bible a new world: God. God's sovereignty, God's glory, God's incomprehensible love, not the history of man but the history of God.'[5]

The starting point for biblical preaching is the realisation that the Bible is essentially one Big Story. The Bible is not a pick-and-mix catalogue of religious goodies or spiritual recipes. It is not an occult code book to be deciphered by elite disciples. It is not even, as it is sometimes misused in our circles, a compendium of proof texts available for us to buttress our own predetermined doctrinal position. Under pressure to make the Bible relevant or to apply it to life, we too often trivialise its overall message, and reduce its impact to slogans or soundbites. All too frequently we drain the Bible of its colour; we squeeze the life out of it, and render it a flat book, with bland moral injunctions or passionless spiritual principles. This is not the way the Bible has come to us. The Bible has come down to us essentially as a story, a vast sprawling untidy story but a story nonetheless. Of course, not every part of the Bible is narrative in literary form, but I believe that all the parts have significance only as contributing to or reflecting the grand narrative which the Bible unfolds. Even those parts of the Bible which in a literary sense are non-narrative, its laws and songs and wisdom literature, I would argue presuppose the particular storyline of the one Creator God and His people Israel. The non-narrative parts of the Bible were treasured and preserved within a believing community, a community shaped by this story and sustained in its true identity by the memories and hope the story inspired. Eugene Peterson has gone so far as to say, 'The way the Bible is written is as important as what is written in it … this huge capacious story that pulls us into its plot and shows us our place in its development from beginning to end. It takes the whole Bible to read any part of the Bible.'[6] In other words, rambling and topsy-turvy as this long historical story is, we can detect movement and purpose and we can begin to detect that God is the chief character in the drama that unfolds. Through God's participation in the story God makes Himself known to us. In my book *A Passion for God's Story*[7] I seek to produce a hermeneutic for my interpretation of the Big Story by suggesting a model based on the five interlocking Olympic rings: the Bible may be viewed as five overlapping and interlocking stories that make up the big narrative. These five circles can serve, I think, as five lenses through which we can read the Bible and interpret it. Like lenses on a camera all of them are eventually needed to give clarity and depth of focus as we move from the long-range view of God and His world through Israel in Jesus to the close-up application to ourselves and our story. Biblical preaching, as I have argued in my book, needs to be alert to seeing the Bible through all these five lenses.

THE FIVE LENSES

1. The God lens

Fairly obviously, the Bible is God's self-revelation and God is the chief and central character of our preaching. Stanley Hauerwas and William Willimon have said: 'We are forever getting confused into thinking that Scripture is more about what we are supposed to do rather than a picture of who God is.'[8] Stanley Hauerwas has also said that there is no more fundamental way to talk about God than in a story.[9] In some ways we introduce ourselves to one another by beginning to tell our story to each other, and it's the same with God. To see the world through God's eyes is to see the world as the stage for the greatest story ever told. It is to see history as the unfolding of a great drama in which God is both the author and the chief actor. By saying that God is the author of the story, we recognise that the threads of meaning, all the covenantal connections, all the trajectories of truth, are traceable to God's own sovereign purpose. It is of course the one Creator God who initiates this story, and as He supervises His creation, steering it to its intended goal in the face of history's sin, setbacks and rebuffs, we can find out who this God really is.

Now this is an enormous challenge to us as evangelical Christians. As in many of the things we do, we are prone to bring to the Bible strong preconceived ideas about who God is and how gods are supposed to act. Many of us have imbibed, on the one hand, all kinds of Greek philosophical notions or, on the other, nineteenth-century hymnody versions of how gods behave. When we read the Bible, we try to fit it into our preconceived ideas about who God is and how God acts. But it is actually only as the story is allowed to run – and I might add, allowed to run through to the end – that we actually discover who this God really is. Our aim in preaching, then, will be to tell the gripping story of how God achieves His purpose for His creation so that our hearers discover just what kind of God He is.

Furthermore, it is equally important in preaching to show that not only is God the author of the story, but He is the chief actor in it. This is something that we as evangelicals need to note very carefully. Not only does God work out His authorial purposes from the outside, but He works them out from inside the story by becoming a character in the drama. The God we proclaim does not occupy an Olympian detachment from the achievements and struggles of His creation; rather He has fully immersed Himself in the history of His creation making Himself vulnerable to its pain and ambiguity. By working within the drama, not outside it, God exposes Himself to misunderstanding. By working within the drama God puts His reputation for holiness and omnipotence on the line. By working within the drama God risks His good name through association with some pretty shady characters. God is willing in short to become the God of Abraham, Isaac and particularly even Jacob. We find a God who is involved, a God who is intimate, a God who is wild, a God who is passionate, unpredictable, utterly faithful, vulnerable, persuadable, open; a tough and tender God who travels and travails with His people with genuine emotions. It is as if God did not think that being God was something to be exploited to His own selfish advantage, but humbled Himself to the level of His human partners, submitting to bear the cost of whatever His creation might come to.

This is the God lens through which we need to read and preach the Bible. In other words we preach theologically with a God-orientated stance seeking to demonstrate first of all who God is, what God is saying, what God is feeling, what God is doing, what God has planned to do and what God is purposing to do in the future. We preach with respect for the givenness of the Bible. We receive it and teach it as revelation from God so that we and our hearers are confronted by its truth.

2. The world lens

We need to preach the Bible with a wide-angle global lens. The Bible is not simply the story of personal salvation: it moves from first creation to new creation, from the origins of the cosmos to their final total renovation. Consequently, it will inevitably in some way address the concerns of the whole earth and of all humankind, which our preaching must also do. I have been gripped by the strong connections that are threaded through this story so that the story of Adam and the story of Israel and the story of Jesus are directly linked together, with Israel being seen if you like as that sample new humanity that God intended to bring on the earth. Although by the end of the Old Testament story, Israel has proved itself to be as much part of the problem as part of the answer, from within it comes the one true Israelite, the Messiah Jesus, who will be the obedient and voluntary covenant partner of God. With this world lens we will not limit the scope of our preaching to private, pietistic devotional exercises but we will relish the power of the Bible to speak truthfully across the whole range of human affairs from international politics and economics to social justice as well as Christian living in the world of business and the home from within the community of faith. Although the Bible will not give us ready answers to every question we might ask of it, viewing the Bible through the world lens will give us a true vantage point on reality. This creational approach, I believe, will save us from a gnostic devaluation of the material and the physical realm in favour of the spiritual realm and, hopefully, it will incite our thinking to a world view and our mission to a world mission.

3. The history lens

The history lens, which is probably regarded as the most problematic nowadays, is crucial if we are to understand our faith, and especially if we are to understand and preach the Bible. The history lens will help us pay close attention especially to the story of Israel in the Old Testament. It will keep us alert to that story of one particular people through whom the one Creator brings to fulfilment His saving plan for all people and all nations. At its most basic, Israel's story in the Old Testament is bracketed by two key events, which enable readers to understand both the Old Testament and to a large extent how the apostles viewed the New Testament gospel. These two events are the Exodus and the Exile – the Exodus from Egypt where the descendants of Abraham and Joseph had becomes slaves and, 800 hundred years later, the Exile to Babylon where they were in some measure enslaved again. The great tragedy and irony of the whole story is that the people of God ended up in Babylonia, from whence according to the beginning of the story Abraham had come.

It has been pointed out that history is usually the top-down story of conquerors, leaders and victors – the powerful, successful and influential. Such stories can be read in the victory annals of the Egyptian Pharoahs, the Assyrian potentates, and the Babylonian emperors. In contrast, the story of Israel is told from the underside. It is the story, initially at least, of the powerless and the poor. It is the story told of those who with passionate prophetic protest and innocent suffering hold out for the hope of redemption and glory.

In order to tell us the full story of Jesus, the New Testament writers consistently use typologically these two great paradigms of Exodus and Exile taken from Israel's story. The New Testament sees the salvation that comes into the world through Jesus Christ as that return from exile long awaited by the people of Israel, and it views it, as the prophets did, as a new exodus, an act of liberation and freedom. Preaching on the New Testament will look to tease out the roots of the apostolic gospel and message of Jesus, listening not just for quotations from the Old Testament but for the echoes of Scripture, as Richard Hays does, for example, in his very informative book entitled *Echoes of Scripture in Paul*.[10] In so doing we will approach these ancient texts with a respect for their history. We must acknowledge that none of these ancient texts was first addressed to us. They were spoken to another people in another time and in another place – only in the continuity of faith can we take these texts as written for us. If we are to hear those texts speak for ourselves, we need to take the trouble to find out to whom and for what purpose they were written. From within the Old Testament we can trace in our preaching the trajectories of promise that climax in Jesus and still shape our future hope. What theologians call eschatology, the study of the last things, is simply the recognition that history is not random but purpose driven, that the historic story has a beginning, a middle and will have an end.

4. The Jesus lens

We preach Christologically. Jesus is the convergence point of the story. As our preaching draws our hearers again and again into and through the biblical story, they will surely begin to experience its cumulative force. For want of a better illustration, it is like a snowball that grows in size as it moves through the snow. We evangelicals believe in revelation; indeed, we believe in progressive revelation. As the story of the Bible unfolds, it grows, it accumulates: it carries cumulative force. In its technical details, in its language and its verbal echoes, the Genesis narrative of Noah recapitulates Adam's story. Noah is a new Adam. He is given the commission to have dominion and reflect God's image. A careful examination of Israel's calling reveals that she was entrusted with the royal priestly calling that was conferred first on Adam and Eve, then on Noah and carried forward in Abraham's promised destiny, which was to be a means of blessing to all the nations on the earth. In Israel's later history the identity and the destiny of the nation was gathered together in the figure of the king. Here again, we have to use the historical lens in order to understand that kingship in the ancient world is an incorporative function. The king had a sacral function in representing God, but he also represented the people. Somewhere around 1 Samuel 8 the story stops being the story of the children of Israel and becomes the story of the kings of Israel. From that point in its history Israel's destiny and fate as a nation depends on whether the kings do well and walk faithfully in covenant or not. Unfortunately, with hardly any exceptions, it is all downhill. Again and again, sometimes in two sentences, sometimes in half a chapter, sometimes in two chapters, a king will be written off with the deadly epitaph that he did not walk in the ways of his father David.

Jesus gathers all these threads together and makes sense of them all. He successfully reruns Israel's story and, in doing so, successfully rewrites the human story as the last Adam. The story of Jesus is the climax of the longer, earlier parts of God's story, and it is the key to its unfolding in the future. Preaching the Big Story will be preaching that has Jesus at the centre.

5. The contemporary lens

The contemporary lens is where most people start, and many people stay. Through the contemporary lens we ask such questions of the text as: What does it mean – for me, for us? I want to suggest that preaching has much to do with opening the eyes of the heart –

with transforming people's imaginations. We are called to preach the Bible imaginatively so that our hearers can envisage themselves living within the world of the biblical text. In the last thirteen years when my life has been given over completely to Bible study and teaching, I have discovered that the more historical my preaching has become, the more the text leaps off the page and the more contemporary and relevant it becomes. We can re-imagine our post-modern lives as part of God's story in Christ and learn to live in the light of that story. This is surely how faith begins in the first place. Faith comes by hearing, and hearing by the preaching of the Word.[11] As we respond in faith, we trade in the dog-eared self-written scripts of our lives in order to be written in to the larger saving script of God's Big Story.

As members of Abraham's faith family, our roots go back 4,000 years. We follow in his footsteps. When Abraham, surrounded by what was by those standards a fairly advanced civilisation in Babylonia, heard the voice of God and, according to the first Christian martyr Stephen, glimpsed 'the glory of God',[12] he became disenchanted with the glories of the Babylonian culture around him. But he did not say, 'Wonderful, now I can have God in my life.' Abraham did not try to get God into his story: what happened was that God got Abraham out of his cosy retirement into His Big Story. How much of our evangelicalism is trying to get God or Jesus into our already existing and pre-set lifestyles? How much of it takes us out of that life into God's Big Story? Because that is what biblical preaching of the Big Story should do. By faith we are joined to the one community of faith that stretches back 4,000 years, and we gain a new history and we gain a new future. To this strange new world of the Bible we come, as David Wells has put it, to 'take meaning'. We come to give up the narrative of our own lives with its parables of self-constructed meaning in order to find the truth that God has given in His own narrative. As the Church we become new chapters written by the Spirit into the script of the ongoing story. Or as William Willimon puts it, 'The Bible seeks to catch us up into a grand narrative, a great saga of God's dealings with humanity, a saga begun in God's journey with Israel, continued in the call of God even unto Gentiles. The Church is the product of that story.'

Biblical preaching will seek to immerse our listeners in this Big Story, and thereby enable them to encounter the real God. As in preaching we relive God's story with Him, we find ourselves saved and shaped by it. As we follow the flow of God's self-disclosure, we learn to appreciate the great unity of Scripture, while we enjoy its fascinating diversity. As we preach the Bible in this way we are drawn into its action finding ourselves caught up in the saving movement of God. Stories have this power. By preaching the Bible in this way as a great narrative we train our people, as the late Lesslie Newbigin used to put it, to indwell the story, to indwell the Bible, and so enable them to look out on the contemporary world through more biblical eyes. Our task as preachers, I venture to say, is to stop trying to make the Bible relevant to modern people, and to hold fast to our truer ambition of making people relevant to the Bible.

THREE IMPLICATIONS OF PREACHING THE BIG STORY

Preaching the Big Story will, first of all, have an impact on how we preach about *Bible characters*. As preachers we need to behave responsibly in our preaching on Bible characters. How often I have heard wonderful, eloquent series of sermons on Bible characters in which these individuals have been held up as moral and spiritual exemplars and heroes. But to draw moral or psychological or spiritual lessons from the lives of biblical characters is hazardous. It is often preaching on the cheap. It is the soft option, because these characters should never ever be isolated from their context, as preachers are so prone to do. Bible characters find their meaning and significance only in their contribution and connection with the big drama of redemption: often the story that is being told is about how even such an unlikely person can by grace be grafted onto God's redemptive story.

Ruth is a shining exception to the dubious examples, but even her charming story is included in the canon in a special place for a special purpose. Placed between the terrible chapters at the end of the book of Judges and before the rise of kingship in 1 Samuel, it highlights the darkness of the days of the Judges and forges a link with the future King David, as chapter 1 verse 1 and chapter 4 verses 13–22 alert us. In short, Ruth serves to offset the terrible trilogy of stories at the end of the book of Judges all of which are connected to a place called Bethlehem, and her story anticipates both the model Davidic king and the Messianic Davidic king who will share that very same birthplace. So when we preach on biblical characters we need to connect them all the time to the biblical narrative and to see them as unlikely characters caught up by grace in God's Big Story.

Second, there will be an implication for our preaching on the *books of the Bible*. As I said right at the beginning, not all parts of Scripture are narrative, but all, I believe, are narrative based. The Old Testament is the unfolding story of God's often emotional resolve to *be with* Abraham and the sons of Jacob, the Chosen People Israel – a presence with them which is turned into a partnership by God's covenantal commitment. The story of the one God is told through the story of His people Israel. The historical books, for example, tell how the post-Deuteronomy generation fared, re-evaluating the story of their life in the Promised Land from the perspective of the Babylonian exile. Oversimplified in a nutshell, 1 and 2 Kings look back on Israel's long history and ask, 'How on earth did we get into this mess?' while 1 and 2 Chronicles ask, 'Is there any hope for the future?' They go over the same history but draw slightly different lessons. Yet, all four books are interacting with that one story. For their part, the prophets are surely recalling the kings and the people back to the nation's vocation – to the heart of their story – and the singers and psalmists are singing the story, because liturgy exists to tell the old, old story of Yahweh and His love.

When it comes to the New Testament, the gospel is the decisive account of God's action in and through the life, death and resurrection of Jesus. While each evangelist has a distinctive angle, they all follow the same basic outline of the Jesus story, especially marking the intensity of action leading up to the cross. The book of Acts tells the story of how the gospel has already gone out to the Graeco-Roman world and the letters written by the apostles, sometimes regarded as purely conceptual and propositional, are in fact always working with this storyline in mind.[13] Everything that Paul does comes out of what Ben Witherington has called 'Paul's Jewish narrative thought world'.[14] He is thinking about how the gospel fits in with the long story from Abraham right up to his own people. It is clear from the letter to the Galatians that even the actual chronology matters to Paul as he follows through his argument about where circumcision comes in the sequence of covenants with God and Abraham. Richard Hays has shrewdly suggested that the problems that Paul addresses have arisen because the church, or groups within it, have lost the plot and placed themselves in a wrong part of the storyline. Isn't that what the Corinthians had done? There were people among them who had gone so overboard on the charismatic experience of the Holy Spirit that they thought they had jumped ahead to the end of the story: they were pre-empting something that was not theirs to pre-empt. Paul has to pull them back into the here and now reality of life that is still lived in the mode of bearing the cross. The Galatians, on the other hand, were acting as if they were living *before* the time of the coming of faith and the coming of Jesus. In all his letters Paul, in one form or another, recasts the old, old story of Israel and her God to show how Jesus embodies the destiny of one and reincarnates the destiny of the other.

Third, our preaching of the Big Story will affect how we preach *for ethical change*. I believe the vision of human life portrayed in the New Testament is narrative shaped: everything we do as believers makes sense because everything is connected with the Big Story of who God is, who we are in Christ, and what we are here for, which is to 'image forth' that story. Think of Ephesians. I was brought up on the idea that Ephesians was a book of two halves, with chapters 1 to 3 comprising worship and prayer and 4 to 6 containing ethics. Forget all that. Actually, it is out of the worship and prayer that the picture of the life we have in Christ flows. In Christ everything we do is meaningful because it is connected to the Big Story.

Let us consider as an example the ethical question, why get married? For Paul, Christian marriage is a vital sign of the greater mystery of the story of Christ and His Church. I do not believe that he is just using marriage as an illustration or an analogy, but that the reason we get married is to live out that story. The Church's vision should not be defined by an agenda set by a dysfunctional society. As Christians we ought to be asking the bigger question. The final answer of the New Testament to the question why we get married will, I suggest, be something like this: we get married because marriage enshrines the great mystery: it tells the world something about the Big Story that we believe in. To vow to be faithful and to keep covenant unto death or desertion breaks that covenant, is to tell the story of the one Creator God who promised never to disown His creation until His redemptive purposes were complete. It is to illustrate the narrative of a God who made covenant with Israel and remained, as Hosea did, obstinately determined to redeem His love, even if it cost Him the life of His only Son on the cross. That's the reason for getting married and for having children, it seems to me. Living in and living out the bigger narrative of our God is the Christian rationale for every action and relationship.

If we take the question, why work, we answer: because God is a working God who made the world in six days and pours out His life to maintain it and blesses us with fantastic creativity as He does so, not because He has to but because that is the kind of God He is. Why do we forgive? We forgive because God in Christ forgave us. That is not just an incentive, or a means of exerting pressure, it is a way of living out the story. We have been caught up in the forgiveness story, and now we live it out. We know we are a part of the Big Story; we know what we are here for.

Let me finish with this story recounted by the playwright David Lodge. The day is 22 November 1963. He is in a playhouse watching one of his creations being performed on stage. There is a scene in the middle of the play where a character, according to the script and the demands of the plot, turns on a transistor radio and tunes into a local station. On this day the theatre is full. The actors are caught up in the drama of their performance – the scripted lines, the choreographed movements, the contrived emotions. The audience is spellbound, pulled into the world wonderfully conjured up before them, when along comes this scene. The character takes the radio and flicks it on: there is a crackle and hiss of static. He dials the tuner, a jumble of noise, voices surge and fade, music blares and stutters and then, stark and urgent, a voice breaks through, 'Today in Dallas, Texas President John F. Kennedy was shot and killed.' The actor quickly switches off the radio but it is too late. The reality of the real world has with just a few plain words burst in upon the closeted self-created world of a play being staged, and the play is over. That is what preaching will do. Preaching the Big Story of God's redemptive plan that centres in Jesus Christ and is about the renewal eventually of His whole cosmos will at some point, by the power of the Spirit, break in upon the unreal drama that people are being sold by the devil as the best one they are going to get. This is a divine drama: it is the Trinity drama of the Father, the Son and the Spirit into which we are drawn – and what a breathtaking mystery it is. As Chesterton once said, 'This story answers the yearning for romance because it is a love story and answers the needs of philosophy because it is a true story.' Go and preach it.

NOTES

1. Robert Jensen, 'How the World Lost its Story' in *First Things*, vol. 36 (1993), p. 3.
2. Jean-François Lyotard, *The Postmodern Condition* (University of Minnesota Press, 1984), pp. xxiii–iv.
3. Jonathan Sacks, *The Dignity of Difference* (Continuum, 2003), p. 75.
4. J.B. Phillips, *Letters to Young Churches* (Collins, 1947), Introduction.

5. Karl Barth, 'The Strange New World Within the Bible' in *The Word of God and the Word of Man* (Hodder & Stoughton, 1928), p. 45.

6. Eugene Peterson, 'Eat This Book: The Holy Communion at the Table of Holy Scripture' in *Theology Today*, 56:1 (April 1999), pp. 13–14.

7. Paternoster Press, 2002.

8. *Resident Aliens* (Abingdon, 1993), p. 85.

9. Stanley Hauerwas, *The Peaceable Kingdom* (SCM Press, 1984), p. 25.

10. Yale University Press, 1994.

11. Romans 10:14ff.

12. Acts 7:2.

13. See, for example, Paul's summary of the gospel in 1 Corinthians 15, which is a compressed account of the Jesus story.

14. Ben Witherington, *Paul's Narrative Thought World* (Westminster John Knox Press, 1994).

Chapter 11

ESSENTIAL INGREDIENTS OF POPULAR PREACHING

Greg Haslam

What makes a good sermon? This is a question that I believe we as preachers should be constantly asking ourselves. Over the course of a lifetime we will listen to hundreds and possibly thousands of sermons, but I wonder how carefully we do, in fact, listen. In order to be able to preach well, I believe that we have first to learn to listen well. Good speaking requires good listening.

Few of us, I think, have ever really learnt to listen to sermons properly. We probably make that complaint about our hearers, but we too have a responsibility to listen to sermons with some degree of acute analysis and constructive criticism. If we desire to grow and mature in the skill of preaching, we should regularly ask such questions as:

- Why did I like that message?
- What arrested my attention in the first place, and held it from that point onwards?
- What made me laugh? What made me cry and touched me in the depths of my emotions?
- Why is it now so clear to me what I'm meant to do, and why do I feel motivated to do so? Why is that not true of some sermons I have heard?
- Why do I like this preacher so much, both as a preacher and as a person?
- What was there in this sermon that made me feel so close to God?

Preachers must first be listeners themselves. In effect, preaching is passing on a word that has been overheard by the preacher.

The preacher, of course, has heard many things; he has been listening to many voices. It is very important not to confine this listening to one or two narrow aspects. The preacher has listened carefully to the text of Scripture itself and to God speaking through it. He has listened to the scholarly and pastoral insights of others who have commented and written upon this text. Furthermore, he has listened to the dealings of God and the devil both with himself, and also with the people in the congregation to whom he preaches. He has listened to the direct voice of the Holy Spirit as he addresses the angry misunderstandings, the confused questions, the silent pains and the moral dilemmas of those he is in contact with week after week. A great deal of listening is going on. David Schlatter said, 'Effective sermons are much more listened for, than they are written or "done" or worked up.' We must listen before we can speak.

The words we utter as preachers may not simply *lead to* the transformation of the life of another: they may transform it there and then. Some words are powerful, for example: 'This meeting is adjourned', 'I now pronounce you husband and wife', 'You have just won £500,000', as the cheque is handed over on the TV quiz show. They carry the inherent power to make a difference in people's lives from that moment onwards. They are what philosophers call 'performative utterances',[1] i.e. they actually convey what they say and they effect the very things that they describe, and they often do so there and then. Preaching is one of those performative activities. We as preachers are not merely reporters, where people can take or leave what we say; we are in a very real sense creators, albeit in a secondary sense to the way God is. Nevertheless, God has brought us to a ministry that has the power both to create and critique a people. Both individuals and whole communities can be transformed by the activity of preaching. God has ordained that preaching will bring about realities that did not exist before. Preaching, then, is an event. It is an encounter with the living God Himself – and, if it is not, then it is nothing at all. Part of the reason why preaching has fallen into such disrepute is that it has become, for the most part, a non-event. Samuel Proctor said, 'The sermon is very different from other staged events because it seeks to tilt life Godwards and to encourage us to answer as we are addressed by God.'

Donald Coggan, former Archbishop of Canterbury, wrote a small book on preaching which he called *Preaching: The Sacrament of the Word*.[2] Now a sacrament is a physical action that is designed by God to convey a spiritual blessing to people. In the Protestant tradition we are wary of the word 'sacrament' and probably have less faith for what the ordained effects of these ordinances of Christ can actually convey to people's lives. I am thinking particularly of the bread and wine of communion and water baptism, but the definition can also be extended to the act of preaching. Preaching is also a physical action that conveys spiritual effects, and is therefore a creative extension of God's Word of life to His people. Preaching achieves what it symbolically announces.

What Makes a Good Sermon?

There are, of course, a number of possible answers to this question. One person might respond that the preacher told such excellent stories. Another might say that she felt that

150

the message spoke to her personally, so that it was as if she was the only person in the auditorium and the preacher was having a personal conversation with her. A third person might appreciate the fact that the preacher's approach was plain and uncomplicated, arising clearly from the passage and enabling him to make sense of it. While still a teenager, I was introduced by a friend to the sermons of C.H. Spurgeon, and despite the fact that he was a Victorian preacher, I was literally captivated by the wealth of illustration and humour they contained, and this paved the way for me to hear the theological truth that came in such richness from him. Good communication is made up of elements like these, motivating even reluctant hearers to be arrested by what is happening and to begin to think and to live differently.

As I explore the whole question of what makes good preaching, I want to divide my answer into two headings:

1. some essential ingredients of best preaching, and
2. some essential ingredients of the best preachers you have heard.

1. Some Essential Ingredients of Best Preaching You Have Heard

In the past, the mnemonic TULIP was used in the Calvinist tradition to provide a succinct summary of its distinctive doctrines but I want to borrow it and use it in an entirely different way to illustrate the ingredients which I believe are common to good preaching.

T: Therapeutic

All preaching that is God-centred and leads to encounter with God will inevitably be therapeutic, or healing in its effects. A key text is Proverbs 4:20–22, where in the context of commending the Word of God, the sage says:

> My son, pay attention to what I say;
>   listen closely to my words.
> Do not let them out of your sight,
>   keep them within your heart;
> for they are life to those who find them
>   and health to a man's whole body.

There are healing effects to the Word of God, and especially if we broaden the term 'healing' to describe the wholeness that God wants to bring to all of the parts of humanity: body, soul and spirit. The Word of God brings healing to the lives of those who hear it well. It improves their condition in every way: mentally, emotionally, spiritually, psychologically, and even physically. Good preaching has penetrative power to touch every part of their redeemed humanity, cumulatively and progressively. It has power to remove ignorance and move the emotions. It has power to direct their life choices, and so affect their wills. It does people good.

In 2 Timothy 3:16 we learn that all Scripture is *'God-breathed'*: it is God's expelled breath. What Scripture says God says. We learn also that Scripture is profitable for teaching, for reproof, for correction and for training in righteousness. God's Word will affect us cognitively, emotionally and behaviourally. It will undo bad habits in our lives. It will set us on a course of progressive sanctification. It will do all those things and more. Calvin Miller puts it like this, 'Preaching has much to do. We dare not reduce it to mere entertainment.'[3] People will get bitter or they will get better under preaching, but they will never remain the same person who came in. Preaching divides people. To some we are the savour of death, to others the savour of life.[4]

U: Unconventional

Within good preaching there is an element of surprise, so that it often startles and, dare I say, even shocks the hearer. It has this ingredient in common with a good film, for it is said that moviegoers are looking for an element of surprise in every movie they watch. Going to church on Sunday should have something in common with the experience of climbing the summit of a live volcano. There is smoke; there are slight tremors underfoot; there is ash falling all around; and the lingering smell of something slightly ominous, even dangerous in the air. You never know if and when that volcano is going to erupt. Auguste Lecerf said, 'When you preach, you do not know what you do; you wield lightning.' The only difference is that they say lightning never strikes twice in the same place, but, of course, in preaching it does so very regularly indeed! No one within reach of it is ever really safe.

On the principle that it is often easier to obtain forgiveness than it is permission, I would say that if, in the course of preaching, a preacher thinks, 'I probably shouldn't say this', he should say it anyway. We need to take some risks in our preaching. We need to become bolder, particularly in the realm of application. We need to be graphic, and intrusive, and sometimes even rude, like Jesus and His apostles were. For example, He addressed the Pharisees and scribes as *'whitewashed tombs'*[5] or as *'blind guides'*.[6] I wonder how the apostle Paul might have fared in an interview to become a church pastor. On occasions his language certainly fell into the category of 'graphic' as he expressed the hope that his Judaizing opponents in Galatia would go the whole hog and cut off all their private parts, or when he compared his righteousness as a devout Jew to human excrement, although the word he actually uses is much less polite.[7]

It is even right to be unbalanced in our teaching from time to time, because biblical balance is rarely the tight-rope walk of hanging precariously in the middle somewhere. Biblical balance is rather attempting to hold both biblical extremes in tension together, for both are equally true, even if we as human beings find them difficult to reconcile. As preachers of the whole counsel of God we have to learn to live with paradox and unresolved mystery.

152

As preachers we also need to be earthy in our links and associations. Jesus lived in the real world, and it should be obvious that the preacher does too. We often look and sound as if we have stepped out of the nineteenth century! Yet we have been called to minister in the twenty-first century, and this should be reflected in our language, our manner and our style. When Jesus spoke about the issue of spiritual uncleanness, He made reference to the movements of the digestive system and the bowels; when He thought about the end of the world, He spoke of a woman in childbirth and the agony and screams of labour; when He wanted to castigate the hypocrisy of religious leaders, He talked about dirty unwashed eating bowls full of decayed left-overs. He spoke of 'bent' magistrates, blind people toppling into ditches, and pushy intruders seated at top tables. He compared a desperate Syro-Phoenician woman to a dog, to her face. He even compared God to a completely undignified, aged but running father, complete with knobbly knees on display, as he lifted his robes and ran to meet the returning prodigal son. No wonder Jesus often earned the frowns and censures of the staid and religious. Good preaching is unconventional.

L: Lucid

A sermon is both a spiritual and an intellectual exercise. It will make demands on the intellect and should engage it completely. Learn to work, then, with how God has designed the human mind. Some preachers boast about the fact that they spend no time in preparation but rely on the Holy Spirit to help them as they stand to preach. Thus, the Holy Spirit is blamed for what often amounts to a sustained outpouring of disconnected and disjointed gibberish, repetition, trivia, trite comments and contentless drivel – *for which God is given all the glory!* Not only is such preaching dishonouring to God but it can be very confusing to the people. There are no handles or pegs on which people can hang their thoughts. There is often no clear structure, no clear path to follow, and no obvious end in sight. If the preacher does not know where he is going with his message, then neither he nor his people are ever likely to get there. If, on the other hand, he knows the destination, he can safely make detours and follow the promptings of the Holy Spirit, secure in the knowledge that he will be able to come back to the original route, without anyone getting lost.

Let there be substantial amounts of information and exposition in what we say, throwing light upon the difficult concepts of Scripture. Let there be corroborative quotations from some of the very best writers on the theme on which we are speaking. All this, of course, requires a great deal of preparation. Marion Le Fever said, 'Becoming an effective preacher is simple: you just prepare and prepare until drops of blood appear on your forehead.'[8]

Despite all the post-modern criticism that we hear, people need a good introduction to draw them into a sermon. They need clear headings and good, memorable points and subdivisions, but, of course, not too many. Some sermons resemble the tragedy of a famine victim: all skeletal bones and protruding joints, but little or no flesh on them. This is ugly and unattractive. We need to make sure that there is a clear linear progression in presenting our ideas. We need to be sufficiently free from our notes that we are able to make eye contact with people. We need to include rhetorical questions that will demand thought from our hearers as we progress. If, once he has prepared his message, a preacher can't sum it up in a single sentence, and a short one at that, then he is probably preaching more than one sermon, perhaps two or three. We need to apply our teaching in down-to-earth ways, not just telling our people *what* they are to do but *how* they are to do it.

I: Illustrated

I would go so far as to say that without illustrations it is probably not possible to teach or preach from the Bible very well. Of course, everyone's approach to illustrations is different, and we all need to use our own God-given imaginations. We need increasingly to think pictorially, and to read widely and mark what we read for easy retrieval. For years I have been in the habit of reading a book with a pencil or a red pen in my hand. In my view it is well worth the price of a book to mark it heavily. I also make a brief marginal note of why I have marked it so that I can easily find any illustration or quotation I want to use. I believe this is good stewardship. Some might say that we run the danger of plagiarism but all good preaching is, in effect, plagiarism. I heard the American preacher C.J. Mahaney, who is one of the most effective preachers I have ever heard, say that he did not think he had ever had an original thought in the whole of his life. Although he may be overly modest in this assertion, he is acknowledging his indebtedness to others.

We can compile our own collection of illustrations and stories, drawing them both from books, including a judicious use of books of illustrations and quotations, and from our daily lives. All of life illustrates biblical truth: our journeys; personal meetings; dangers we have encountered; sickness; trouble; our children (though we do need to be careful since they are under scrutiny enough as it is); our work; our world; our garden; movies; novels; fabulous facts we have come across; celebrities and their antics; news stories. It was the great C.H. Spurgeon who said, 'If you never quote anybody, then you probably never will be quoted.'[9] He was alluding to the fact that we learn the art of crafting words by watching how others have done it before us. Our objective in using illustrations is to turn people's ears into eyes, so that they see as well as hear what we are saying.

P: Passionate

Our preaching must contain emotion and also evoke emotion in our hearers. It should be full of pathos, energy and enthusiasm. In the West we urgently need to reconnect the broken circuits between our heads and our hearts. In Luke 19:41 we read that Jesus wept over the city. In our culture it is not considered manly, and certainly not macho, for a grown man to weep. However, Christ must set the standard for true manliness. Jesus

Christ is the only authentic man who has ever lived. The apostle Paul could remind the elders at Ephesus of his many tears when he was among them.[10]

We are not automatons, we are not shop-window dummies, who are merely cold observers and reporters of what is going on around us. Quite the contrary. We feel passionate convictions and make heartfelt appeals. We vigorously argue against nonsense and demolish strongholds, taking captive every thought to Jesus Christ. Furthermore, we are fathers and mothers when we speak to others. Our loving care will be heard in our voices. Emotion affects the voice. Dull monotonous voices are actually an indicator of a dull monotonous heart. Regular tears are indicative that we care. John Stott said, 'What is needed today then is the same synthesis of reason and emotion, exposition and exultation, as was achieved by Paul.' Paul's emotions run through every line he wrote: it is what Dr Lloyd-Jones called 'logic on fire'.[11]

Something will be lost in our preaching if the appropriate emotions are not there. Wesley put it like this, 'Get on fire for God and men and women will come to watch you burn.'

2. Some Essential Ingredients of the Best Preachers You Have Heard

A compelling call from God

In my view the number one reason why there is so much bad preaching today is because our pulpits are often occupied by preachers who do not have a divine mandate to be there. To echo Paul's words, there is no necessity laid upon them by God.[12] Calvin Miller said, 'Knowing what we would die for gives us the primary clue as to what we should live for.' In the heart of every preacher there should be a sense that this is a task that he would be prepared to die for, and, therefore, that he is prepared to live for. The preacher needs to know without a shadow of a doubt that he has been sent from God, so that, as Richard Bolles put it, 'Earth might become more like Heaven and that human lives might become more like God's.' I do not believe that such a calling needs to be written in the skies – which is what many of us are looking for – but is, rather, something that has been written into the very fibre of our beings, perhaps from our earliest years, and that we are unable to shake off. We have the sense that this is what we were born to do. I love the way that the writer Frederick Buechner expresses it: 'The kind of work God usually calls you to is the kind of work that (a) you most need to do, and (b) the world most needs to have done.' The vocation of each individual Christian is the place where that individual's deep gladness and the world's deep hunger meets. For this very reason, I believe that not just preachers but *every* Christian ought to have a sense of calling and vocation about what he or she does.

Tony Benn, the veteran Labour Party MP, recommended that every politician should be asked the following three questions:

155

1. Who put you there?
2. Who keeps you there?
3. Who can get rid of you?

I believe that every preacher should ask himself the same three questions, and if the answer to all three questions is not 'God', he will probably find himself in trouble sooner or later.

A growing, varied and fresh life with God

Jesus said,

> 'For out of the overflow of the heart the mouth speaks.'
> (Matthew 12:34)

We can think of preaching as the run-off or surplus of all that wells up in the life of the preacher. But, sadly, many preachers are running on empty much of the time. They have allowed other things to crowd out their time with God. They have people to see, places to go, conferences to attend, administrative tasks to fulfil. The busyness of our lives militates against preachers being filled to the brim with all that God wants us to convey to His people.

As preachers, our experience of God needs to be deepening and expanding all of the time. We are to be those who have really listened to God's Word and to the direct dealings of the Holy Spirit both with our own lives and the lives of others. We need to listen both to the cries and needs of the world around us, and to the great minds and great thinkers of the past by disciplined reading. Such preachers will always have something worthwhile and striking to say.

The best preachers have also proved God in many circumstances. Their words have a ring of truth about them because of their proof of God through times of trial and testing. In 2 Corinthians 6:3–10 and 7:5–7, Paul lists a whole catalogue of experiences – good and bad – through which he had proved God's faithfulness. Many of these trials the apostle would not have volunteered for, but they had been arranged for him by God. We will all need to come to a point in our lives when we know what it is to enjoy success, and failure. We need to know what it is to pass through elation and depression, popularity and vicious opposition, prosperity and deprivation, immense reward and bitter disappointment. In *all* of those experiences God is with us and He will tailor them to make better preachers of us. He will take us through the whole gamut of God-ordained experiences, and not just for our sake, but for our people's sake as well.

Happy with their own identity, both as a person and as a preacher

My plea to all preachers is: be the genuine article. I remember hearing R.T. Kendall talk about the Southern Baptist theological seminary where he once studied. In the homiletics course students were taught how to preach and then sent out to various churches to preach. In the feedback reports from those churches, one question was consistently asked as to why the young preachers all had the same mannerism: during the course of the sermon every one of them would put their hand to their brow and flick, as though pushing their hair back. They all did this, including one young man who was bald. Kendall explained that the homiletics professor was a man who had unusually long hair for a Southern Baptist and, when he got worked up in his lectures or preaching, a great forelock of hair would drop over his eyes, obscuring his view, so he had a habit of flicking it back over his head. All of his students had picked up this mannerism, probably unconsciously in most cases. They aspired to be 'clones' of the great man.

We do not need clones of great preachers like Dr Lloyd-Jones or Billy Graham. Since preaching is, as Brooks defines it, 'truth coming through human personality',[13] God surely wants us to be free to be ourselves. He wants us to be secure in the person He made, free from slavish imitation of the style or personalities of others. The Scriptures encourage us to be confident in our distinctiveness and uniqueness. They model a great variety of preaching excellence, as does church history. The only comparison that can be made between the writings of such worthies as Moses, Amos, Zechariah, Haggai, Paul and Peter is that they knew the same God and taught the same truths, but they did so in entirely different ways and styles. And this has remained true through the centuries of Christian history, with such great preachers as Augustine of Hippo, John Calvin, Martin Luther, George Whitefield, John Wesley, Oswald Chambers and Martyn Lloyd-Jones. All of these people were simply themselves and, for that reason, God was able to use them significantly. He takes the natural and adds the supernatural.

Increasingly liberated from the fear of man

In order to be faithful to God, we have to become comparatively indifferent to men's resistance, criticism or opposition to us, as well as to their flattery or ridicule. In Proverbs 29:25 we are told, *'Fear of man will prove to be snare'*. We will never be a free person if we are afraid of human reaction. In 2 Corinthians 2:17 Paul says,

> *Unlike so many, we do not peddle the word of God for profit.*

It is a picture reminiscent of the illegal street traders on Oxford Street, selling 'designer' goods in all the right packaging, but they are not the real thing. Instead, as preachers we need to speak with sincerity and remember that we are sent by God. Paul also said that those who have been given a trust must prove faithful. He adds,

> *I care very little if I am judged by you or by any human court; indeed I do not even judge myself . . . It is the Lord who judges me.*
> (1 Corinthians 4:3–4)

Like Paul, we must make it our aim to please the Lord, and not man. Carol Wimber, the wife of the late John Wimber, said, 'You'll never understand my husband's ministry if you do not realise that from the day of his conversion, he conducted his whole life for an audience of one.' Early on in my own ministry I promised the Lord that I would say and do what the Lord asked me to, regardless of the consequences, and I would commend such a commitment to all preachers.

A genuine love for the people

We think immediately of Paul's famous words in 1 Corinthians 13:1:

> *If I speak in the tongues of men and of angels, but have not love, I am only a resounding gong or clanging symbol.*

If it is true that fear drives out love, thank God it is also true that love will drive out fear. It is love alone that makes us truly consistent and pastoral in our concern. Love helps the preacher to prove faithful. Love motivates him to ensure complete comprehensibility, so that no one is in any doubt at all about what he said and what he meant. Love forces adequate preparation on him, in terms of clear structure, rich nourishing food, clear searching application, riveting interest, simplicity and down-to-earth application. Love ensures that he does not abuse the pulpit by getting something off his chest with respect to someone present with whom he has had an argument that week. Everything the preacher says should be accessible to even the simplest of minds. In all of his teaching and preaching Martin Luther aimed for the eight-year-olds in his congregation, on the ground that if they understood him, the adults most certainly would as well.

Love also helps the preacher to cultivate a penetrating directness in his speech. I find it very irritating listening to a preacher who looks at the ceiling while he is talking or to the light fittings, or four inches above the heads of the people. Look people directly in the eyes and to the owners of them. Use the second-person pronoun 'you' rather than 'we', 'one', or 'some people'.

A conscious dependence on the Holy Spirit

While a 'can-do' mentality might be appropriate on a platform at the Conservative or Labour party conference, where image is everything, it is an alien concept in the Christian pulpit. As preachers we always need to be aware of our true source of power and we need to tell God how much we depend upon His Holy Spirit. Be prepared to follow the Holy Spirit's promptings, His applications into people's lives and His prophetic utterances. In fact, they are often the best moments in the sermon and people will often tell you so. Spurgeon would mount the curved steps to the high platform of the pulpit of the Metropolitan Tabernacle twice every Sunday to preach to capacity crowds of 6,000 or 7,000 people, and I am told that on each step he would repeat these words, 'I believe in the Holy Ghost.' Dependence on the Holy Spirit was the secret of his great success. It will perhaps yet prove to be the secret of any success we enjoy as well. Donald Coggan put it like this,

> When true preaching takes place, the main actor is not the preacher nor the congregation, but the Holy Spirit. It is essential that we grasp the fact that when an act of real preaching takes place, the most active part, the most vital part of the enterprise is taken by the third person of the Trinity. Without him and his creative and re-creative activity there can be words, there can be essays, there can be the reading of a paper, but there can be *no* real preaching.[14]

Infectious in zeal and enthusiasm

Watch any long-standing performer, such as Shirley Bassey, Luciano Pavarotti, Mick Jagger and Tom Jones, and it becomes immediately obvious that they put their whole heart and soul into what they are doing. This is how good preachers are to be as well. Absorbed in what they have to say, they will absorb the attention of others. Often, even the most casual and indifferent hearer realises something important is taking place. If the truth of the message does not grab you, how can it be expected to grab anybody else? One Sunday morning in the 1880s a horse-drawn cab driver picked up a London tourist who wanted to go over the river to the Elephant and Castle to hear C.H. Spurgeon. The driver asked his passenger, 'You don't believe everything *he* says, do you?' He received the simple reply, 'No, no, *but he most certainly does.*'

Since the emotions of the soul are often accompanied by movement of the body, let there be action and movement. Whether we shake with laughter, clap with gladness, run with excitement, collapse in awe or jump with joy, movement is always more interesting than immobility. Let us not put out the Spirit's fire when we are preaching. Don't be tied to a manuscript. That will be there next week, the Holy Spirit may not be.

Preaching is a unique form of communication, a communal event. It is unpredictable and it is amazing. It is, in fact, a dance with divinity, because when it is done properly it carries the very authority of God Himself into that living situation. Let a man or woman taste this reality in their preaching, and they will be ruined for anything else. Let a congregation experience this in hearing preaching and they will be ruined for anything else. The best preaching requires, however, a definitive call for the task. The purpose of our gifts is not self-promotion or celebrity status, it is stewardship of heavenly mysteries. Our gifts are ultimately God's; we are but stewards of them. Os Guinness puts it like this,

> God is not like some divine employment agency, just wondering, 'Now where shall I see best to put her?' No, the truth is that God is not finding us a place for our gifts but that God has created us and our gifts for a place of his choosing, and we will only ever be ourselves when we finally get there.[15]

NOTES

1. See also Chapter 8 by Philip Greenslade.
2. HarperCollins, 1987.
3. *The Sermon Maker* (Zondervan, 2002).
4. 2 Corinthians 2:15–16.
5. Matthew 23:27.
6. E.g. Matthew 23:16.
7. Galatians 5:12; Philippians 3:8.
8. Quoted in Miller, *The Sermon Maker*.
9. C.H. Spurgeon, *Lectures to My Students* (Zondervan, 1980).
10. Acts 20:19, 31.
11. D.M. Lloyd-Jones, *Preaching and Preachers* (Hodder & Stoughton, 1971).
12. 1 Corinthians 9:16.
13. Phillips Brooks, *Lectures on Preaching* (1877; Banner, 1969).
14. *Preaching: The Sacrament of the Word.*
15. *The Call* (Spring Harvest Publications), p. 47.

Chapter 12

EXPOSITORY PREACHING

Michael Eaton

In this chapter I want to look, very practically, at how a preacher develops an expository preaching ministry.

DISCERNING OUR MINISTRY

For anyone embarking upon Christian ministry the first step is to ask, 'What kind of ministry do I have?' and to structure his or her day accordingly. The preacher, having answered this first question, must then ask a second question: 'What sort of a preacher is God calling me to be?'

In order to answer this question, the individual must think very carefully about who he is as a person. Am I the kind of person who could happily sit at a desk for two or three hours a day, or does the thought fill me with horror? Or am I much more the type of person who loves being with people, pastoring and counselling them, and serving them in their day-to-day needs? We are all different with different God-given gifts. While we need to be careful that our gifts do not become weaknesses (for every gift if used lopsidedly becomes a weakness), yet I believe we have to follow our gifts. I have never known two pastors that are alike. I have never known two men with an apostolic ministry that are alike. I have never known two people with any kind of a prophetic ministry that are alike. Every single one of us is different, and we are each at our best when we are being ourselves.

I don't think every pastor has to be a great Bible expositor. Some people are not made for it. We each have to decide what sort of person we are, what our gifts are and what our desires are – since the Lord gives us the desires of our heart. Our answers to these questions will help us to decide how much time per day and per week we ought to be giving to preparation for preaching, and it will be different for each one of us. For myself there is scarcely ever a day when I don't preach and therefore I have to give myself plenty of time to be involved in the Word of God. My rule of thumb is to be at my desk from 8.00 a.m. until 12.30 or 1 o'clock, and I won't allow many things to interrupt my daily routine. This is the way that God calls me, and it may or may not be the way God calls somebody else. But we each have to decide how much time we are going to give to our preparation. It will vary from person to person.

We also need to consider what is a realistic level for us in our preaching. Not every one is an original thinker who wants to spend hours delving into the Scriptures. Some people are content to rely on material that others have presented, and there is nothing wrong with that. Sometimes when I visit a remote village in Kenya or Malaysia, for example, I find someone preaching one of my sermons. The preacher may feel a bit embarrassed and explain that he is drawing on material from one of my 'Preaching Through the Bible' series. But that is the very reason I wrote the series in the first place – I want to put material into people's hands. The first step for every preacher, then, is to consider his gifting and decide how much time he is going to spend in the Word each day.

STUDYING GOD'S WORD

In our study of Scripture a sharp distinction needs to be drawn between exegesis and exposition. Exegesis is the basic interpretation of any written text, word by word, sentence by sentence, paragraph by paragraph. It is interpreting the bare bones of the text. In exposition I would say we go beyond the bare bones of what the text says to ask about its significance. What is it teaching? What doctrine can we learn from it? What does it mean for me? We draw out the wider ramifications of what we are reading.

Now I know that philosophers will say that what I am proposing is unsound. They will say that the meaning of something is the same as the use to which it is put; that it is only as we use it that we know what it means. I know that philosophically and linguistically it is true that there is really no difference between exegesis and exposition. The two are interwoven and cannot be separated. But still this distinction has to be made, because when the preacher steps into his pulpit on Sunday morning, he is not going to be giving a textual analysis – or at least I hope not. He is going to be expounding what God is saying through the text. As preachers we have to get from the basic interpretation of the text to what it means for the people to whom we are preaching.

However, before we get to the point of preaching our sermon from the pulpit there is another very important step that has to take place. Before the preacher can preach the text to anybody else, he must first of all preach it to himself.[1] I need to know what it means for me. How must I repent? What thing have I not seen in Scripture that I see now? What needs modifying in my life? Maybe I am not doing the very thing which I am about to preach that others should do. I read in the text that I must forgive all those who sin against me. Suddenly

I start thinking of all the people I haven't forgiven. How can I preach on forgiveness when I know there are people that I myself have not forgiven? So I need to repent and seek the Lord in my own life. Surely this is what we have to do as a part of our study. How can we preach something to somebody else that we haven't preached to ourselves?

As far as I am concerned there is no difference between what might be called devotional Bible study and preparing for preaching. Surely we preach what we have learned for ourselves and surely what we have learned for ourselves we want to preach! They are one and the same. We should not be drawing a distinction between preparing for ourselves and preparing for others. No, throughout our study we want to be gripped by what God is saying to us. Then we want to go and preach to others what we have learned. The one distinction that has to be made, as far as I am concerned, is, for practical purposes, to draw a line between the technical side of preaching and the expository side, and for this we will need two types of resources.

MAKING USE OF THE RESOURCES AVAILABLE

As a third-world man I am very conscious that the vast majority of the world can hardly afford to buy a Bible let alone resources for Bible study. In Nairobi City Hall I have a system whereby, before I publish a book, I sell it to people five pages at a time at a cost of about 20p, because that is the only way many people can afford to buy it. So I am very aware that not everyone can afford to buy books. But, to the extent to which we can afford it and to the extent to which God is leading our ministry towards in-depth study, I want to suggest that the resources that we need fall into two categories.

The technical side

The first kind of books we need are those that will help us to understand the technical data in the text. At the moment I personally am preaching through Leviticus. As I explain in Chapter 9, wherever I go in the world at the moment I preach on Leviticus, and every day I am studying Leviticus. Leviticus is full of technical information, containing details of what the priests wore, what offerings were to be brought, and so on. If we are to make any sense of it we will need to do our homework by referring to the various commentators and dictionaries. One of the writers to whom I refer in my study of Leviticus is Jacob Milgrom.[2] This Jewish scholar is the world's leading expert on the Mosaic Law. Although his commentary is not spiritual in any way and the name of Jesus is not mentioned in it, it helps me along in finding information I need in order to understand what the text is saying. For this aspect of my study it does not matter to me whether the man is saved or not, as long as he can tell me all about Leviticus. I do draw the line at people whose sole aim is to tear the Bible to shreds, because, since they do not believe it, they will inevitably end up twisting the data. But any writers who basically have a positive attitude to Scripture, even if they are not evangelical Christians, will be a help to us.

Milgrom, for example, helps me to explore what it means when Leviticus speaks about somebody being 'cut off', which is a crucial piece of information for anyone studying the book. Does it mean that the individual will face execution, or will be banished from Israel, or that he will not go to heaven, or that he won't have any children? What does it mean? Is it something done by the magistrates or judges, or is it something God does? I had better look up every reference to being 'cut off' and read everything I can on the subject in order to make sure I find out what it means.

One of the surprising nuggets of information I came across in Milgrom, is that from the day of the high priest's ordination he had to give a whole burnt offering every day of his life. I did not know that. It is a little bit difficult to get to the bottom of the matter, because the high priest appears to have had so many things to do on the day of his ordination that it seems impossible for him to have fitted them all in. But according to Milgrom the word usually translated 'in' can also mean 'from', if the verb carries a sense of motion – anyone who knows their Hebrew will tell you he is right. So with reference to the burnt offering, the text could either mean that he was required to present it *on* the day of his ordination or on every day from that day onwards. Now this is information I cannot *exactly* preach on a Sunday morning. The Sunday congregation do not want to know about such details. However, unless I have a thorough understanding of the text, I will not be able to preach to my congregation on what it means for them. So, for this kind of information, I turn to people like Jacob Milgrom. Milgrom argues that, every day of his life from the day on which he was ordained until he died, the high priest offered a whole burnt offering on his own behalf, in addition to the daily and evening sacrifices. What convinces me in Milgrom's argument is that he refers to Josephus, who in his writings includes the information that the high priest offered a whole burnt offering consecrating himself to God morning and evening every day of his life. Vital as this kind of knowledge is to our understanding of the text, we must not preach it – it makes the congregation fall asleep. And although it may make us too fall asleep over our books, we do need to know it. We transform it into something more direct and practical for our people.

Thus, for the technical side of our study we need dictionaries, translations and commentaries.[3] They may sometimes be very boring and they might not bless our soul at all, but they provide us with the information we need.

The expository side

Once we have gathered the information, we need to start asking questions about its significance. For instance, what is the significance of the information which I have gained about the high priest making a daily sacrifice of a whole burnt offering? Fairly obviously it speaks of Jesus' daily offering of Himself as the High Priest to the Father in heaven on our behalf, continually interceding for us. In this way we move from exegesis to exposition. Now the preacher begins to find the kind of material that will not only bless his own soul, but which he will be able to preach on Sunday morning, or whenever.

At this stage of his preparation, the preacher has to start asking expository questions, not just informational questions. In our gathering of information and in our asking of expository questions we need to be putting down notes on paper. The exegetical information and the answers to our expository questions must not be kept on the same page; they must be kept on separate pieces of paper. Here are some of the questions the preacher needs to be asking about the passage he is studying:

- what is it teaching?
- what is its significance?
- what does this mean to me?
- if it is in the Law, how is it fulfilled in Jesus?
- since I am not under the Law, how do I walk in the Spirit and fulfil what I am discovering?

As we find answers to these questions and as we meditate on the information we are gathering, we list what we are discovering in points: point 1, point 2, point 3, etc. *Herein lies the great secret of preparing for expository preaching.* One day these points will become the points of a sermon – in fact, it is almost a sermon already. The work has been done. Sometimes, even at this stage, the points of a sermon almost leap out from the notes, demanding to be preached.

For this second stage of preparation the preacher needs a different type of resource. He thinks and prays for himself but he will also now value any commentary which will help him to draw out the significance of the text, and these are few and far between. Such a commentary can only be written by someone with spiritual insight. Many commentaries do not even make the distinction that I am drawing. Nine times out of ten, even a book called *The Message of Leviticus*, although it purports to be about the message of the text, will in actual fact be about the technicalities. My favourite commentary on Leviticus of this more expository type is by Basil Atkinson, who was once the Under-Librarian of Cambridge University and often used to preach at St Paul's, Cambridge. Anywhere you open it, you will find him talking about Jesus. He was an eccentric guy and had some funny ideas, but that, as far as I am concerned, is not always such a bad thing. The important thing is that he had a heart for Jesus and he saw Jesus all over the book of Leviticus. Anyone who is serious about being an expository preacher should keep their eyes open for writers who have a heart for both the accuracy of Scripture and its message. Years ago Alec Motyer wrote some notes on Jeremiah for Scripture Union, which are worth more than a hundred commentaries: they are like gold dust. Selwyn Hughes, too, has the extraordinary ability of finding practical truth even in some of the most obscure books of the Bible. If there is something to get out of it, he will find it.[4] As expository preachers we need to be collecting anything we can to help us in our task. In the same way, if we hear of a pastor in our locality preaching through a book of the Bible, we need if possible to go and hear him. When R.T. Kendall was preaching on Galatians at Westminster Chapel, I used to come to hear him as often as I could. Such preaching is extremely rare. We need to grab it wherever we can. Our very life as preachers depends on finding people who will help us to discover the significance of the text.

We go from exegesis to exposition. We go from Jacob Milgrom to Basil Atkinson. The exegesis might make us fall asleep; the exposition wakes us up again, as we begin to find the Word of God speaking to us. It rouses us; it stirs us. We are not bothering about preparing sermons. We ponder; we meditate; we work it out for ourselves. This is where our own spirituality comes in. This is where the anointing of the Spirit comes. We do not need the anointing of the Spirit to understand Hebrew grammar, but we do need it to search out the *significance* of the Scriptures. And for this we need to be on our knees. George Whitefield said, 'I never read my Bible except upon my knees.' Even if we do not do this literally, we should do it in spirit. On our knees before God we ask Him to speak to us from His Word. We are not preparing sermons, but we do note down various points as we begin to see the significance of the text. Then, if suddenly someone asks us to preach at short notice because, for example, the scheduled preacher cannot come, we have got something ready to say immediately. People may ask us how long it took us to prepare our sermon, and we may say, 'I prepared it in ten minutes sitting on that chair before I spoke.' We may not tell them that we have been spending a month on it, spending some hours every day with Milgrom and a few others, and a pile of Hebrew dictionaries and grammars. Our whole lives are spent preparing for preaching in this way.

GETTING FROM EXEGESIS TO EXPOSITION

I want now to illustrate how to get from exegesis to exposition by looking at Leviticus 8, in which the items of clothing worn by the high priest are explained. We see that there are four pieces of clothing that every priest would wear and a further four that the high priest uniquely would wear. Both priest and high priest wore:

   (i) undershorts
  (ii) an undershirt
 (iii) some sort of hat or cap
  (iv) a belt.

In addition, the high priest wore:

   (v) a long blue robe with bells and pomegranates at the hem
  (vi) an ephod
 (vii) a breastpiece
(viii) a turban with the words 'holiness to the Lord' embroidered into it.

166

On certain days, such as the Day of Atonement, the high priest was not permitted to wear the more glamorous multicoloured clothes, but had to wear very humble white ones. This is the first stage of our preparation: digging out the information. It may sometimes be hard to find, but we need to root around to find it. In the case of Leviticus, if the information I am looking for is not in Milgrom I may find it in the Puritan John Owen who has seven volumes on Hebrews. On occasions he has what are called 'dissertations' in which he digresses into related subjects, and in these he does talk about the garments worn by the high priest.

Having completed stage one, we now move on to stage two, to ask what the information we have gathered from the text means. We discover, very importantly, that before the high priest could embark upon the ministry he was being given, certain things had to happen. As we look at these things in more detail, we begin to see immediately that these are points we should expound practically in our preaching. Before the high priest could begin his work,

1. he had to be washed;
2. he had to be clothed;
3. he had to be anointed;
4. his ministry was put into his hands.

Looking at just two of these points, we discover that, if we want to be in ministry:

1. We need to be washed

No priest could come anywhere near the temple in order to carry out his ministry unless he had been washed. Right outside the tabernacle complex by the front gate was the laver, the great bowl provided so that those who were appointed to enter the tabernacle could wash. The priest could do nothing unless he was washed and clean, and neither can any servant of God. Remember the conversation that Jesus had with Peter on the subject of spiritual 'washing'.

> Peter said to him, 'You shall never wash my feet.' Jesus answered him, 'If I do not wash you, you have no share with me.' Simon Peter said to him, 'Lord, not my feet only but also my hands and my head!' Jesus said to him, 'The one who has bathed does not need to wash, except for his feet, but is completely clean. And you are clean, but not every one of you.'
> (John 13:8–10)[5]

Before we come into priestly ministry we need to be washed!

2. We need to be clothed

Every item of the clothing which the high priest and the priests wore says something to us.

167

We ask ourselves the question, 'It meant something for the people of God, what does it mean for me?'

On the day that Moses clothed the priests in preparation for their ordination only seven of the eight are mentioned: the undershorts are not mentioned, which may cause us to wonder why. If we do our homework, we will discover that when the pagan priests of the ancient world carried out their extremely vile practices they often did so naked. But no Jewish priest was allowed to function in that way. There was no need for the undershorts to be mentioned because the priests and high priests were already wearing them. The shorts therefore speak about the need for God's servants to protect their modesty.

Second, there was the linen undershirt which was gleaming white. Revelation 19:8 tells us that fine linen stands for the righteous deeds of the saints. Such gleaming white garments will be worn by those who hold on to faith through great tribulation; they are those who have washed their robes in the blood of the Lamb. The writer of Revelation draws on the symbolism of Leviticus. Leviticus explains Revelation; Revelation explains Leviticus.

Third, the high priest and the priests wore a girdle to hold their long robes in place and stop them getting in the way. There are a number of verses which use the imagery of the girdle, such as Luke 12:35: *'Let your loins be girded about.'* Ephesians 6:14 speaks of *'having your waist girded with truth'*. In 1 Peter 1:13 we read: *'Gird up the loins of your mind.'* The girdle speaks of being ready to move for God so that we can work for Him in His holy temple.

Fourth, the robe speaks of office. A person could not volunteer for the job of being high priest; he had to be chosen by God. Only one man in the whole of Israel was allowed to wear that blue robe: it was the mark of his office. Anyone who saw him knew he was God's high priest with God's call upon his life. For us, the blue robe speaks of our certain knowledge that we are appointed by God to be in the position we hold. We are where we ought to be.

Fifth, the ephod which the high priest wore had stones stitched into the shoulders engraved with the names of Israel's twelve tribes. Therefore, whenever the high priest went into the presence of God, he was bearing Israel upon his shoulders. He was the intercessor, and if we are in any kind of ministry, we too will have to be something of an intercessor. Without the ephod we are hardly ready to serve in God's temple.

Sixth, the breastpiece with the Urim and Thummin set into it, speaks of guidance. If somebody needed guidance he or she would go to the high priest and ask for help. The high priest would take out the stones, which were like dice. They could give three answers. The first answer they could give was 'Yes'. The second answer was 'No'. So a king would go to the high priest and ask for himself if he should advance in battle against an enemy and he might receive the answer yes or no. But there was a third possible response, which was 'I'm not telling you'. We remember how Saul tried in vain to find guidance from God, becoming so desperate that he even tried to consult the dead Samuel, but as a result of his disobedience God had refused to speak to him either by prophecy, or by the Urim and Thummin.[6] The Scriptures give us a warning: *'Today, if you hear His voice, do not harden your hearts.'*[7] However, there is also another reason why God might not give us the guidance we desire. Sometimes it is because He wants us to search for Him a bit harder, to spend time waiting upon Him and seeking His face. The breastpiece tells us that, if we go to God, He will guide us. We have a great High Priest in heaven who is wearing the breastpiece. He might say yes, He might say no, or He might say, 'Seek Me a bit more', but He will guide. We have a certain promise.

> *Whether you turn to the right or to the left, your ears will hear a word behind you, saying, 'This is the way; walk in it.'*
> (Isaiah 30:21)

Our Lord Jesus Christ will guide us: guidance is His job, much more than it is our job.

Seventh, there was the turban (Leviticus 8:9). It spoke of discipline (Leviticus 10:6: *'Do not let the hair of your heads hang loose . . .'*); and it spoke of suitability for service in the tabernacle (conversely the leprous person had to let the hair of his head hang loose – Leviticus 13:45). Leviticus 21:10 demanded that the high priest shall not let the hair of his head hang loose in the manner of undisciplined people.

Eighth, there was one last item: the golden ornament, the holy crown (8:9). This spoke of the purpose of the entire sacrificial procedure. It was a kind of label on the entire work of the priesthood. Its purpose was to promote holiness and purity in the service of God. Titus 2:14 is perhaps its New Testament equivalent. Jesus, our great High Priest, *'gave himself for us that he might redeem us from all iniquity and purify for himself a people of his own who are zealous for good deeds.'*

In this way we get from exegesis to exposition. We take the information we have gathered and ponder and meditate upon it until we discover its significance. If a preacher follows the method that I have outlined, I promise that he will always have plenty to preach. In fact, he will be looking for opportunities to preach all that he has upon his heart. This is the call upon the preacher's life – and anyone who does not have this passion in his heart must seriously question his calling. Like Jeremiah he might say, *'I will not mention him, or speak any more in his name.'* But he will not be able to do that. He will have to go on to say, *'But there is in my heart as it were a burning fire shut up in my bones, and I am weary with holding it in, and I cannot.'*[8] The Word begins to burn like fire in his bones so that he has to preach it. The preacher who learns to read the Scripture and to lay it out in points in the way I have described will always have plenty to say. The Word of God will always be at his fingertips, and there will be fire in his bones.

NOTES

1. See also Chapter 9.
2. See his *Leviticus* in three volumes in the Anchor Bible series (published by Doubleday).

3. The best commentaries on Leviticus are by Gordon Wenham in the New International Commentary series and by J.B. Hartley in the Word Commentary series. Andrew Bonar's *Leviticus* (reprinted from the edition of 1861) is of great value. S.H. Kellogg's *Leviticus* (1899) is excellent. In a class all of its own is *Leviticus as Literature* by the anthropologist Mary Douglas. It is very thought-provoking and some of its ideas are useful to the Christian expositor.

4. Selwyn Hughes died on 9 January 2006.

5. Scripture passages quoted in this chapter are Michael Eaton's own translation from the Hebrew and Greek.

6. 1 Samuel 28.

7. Hebrews 3:7–8.

8. Jeremiah 20:9.

Section Three

RIGHTLY HANDLING THE WORD OF GOD

Do your best to present yourself to God as one approved,
a workman who does not need to be ashamed
and who correctly handles the word of truth.

(2 Timothy 2:15)

Chapter 13

PRESENTING THE WORD:
A PREACHER'S JOURNEY

David Pawson

My definition of preaching is: declaring the whole truth to the whole person. In two sessions we will consider 'the whole truth' and 'the whole person'. In the first session we will look at the content of preaching – how my message developed – and in the second at communication – how my method developed.

In this first session my message is in six parts because my preaching has gone through six phases, each quite different from the previous one. My approach will be auto-biographical because I do not feel it is my job to tell preachers how to preach.[1] Since preaching is truth through personality, preaching will be as different as every individual. A preacher must not copy or imitate anyone, but should pick up from other preachers what is relevant to him as an individual. I have found that so often people discover their calling in resonating with somebody who is already exercising it, and they know it is what they too ought to be doing.

My own story is a unique story because I am unique, as is each individual. My first attempt to preach was a failure. The congregation numbered three, and I was aged ten. For some reason which I cannot recall, my father was away and we couldn't get to church, so my mother said, 'We're going to have a service here at home and you, David, will preach.' She and my two sisters were the congregation. Turning an armchair around and using the back of it for my pulpit, I remember expounding the parable of the labourers in the vineyard, first of all reading through Matthew 20, next retelling the story of how the vineyard owner went out at the third, sixth and ninth hours to find workers, and then going through the story a third time to draw a message from each part of it. It was at that point that my elder sister in a tone of exasperation said, 'Isn't that vineyard full yet?', and the service came to an untimely and unseemly end. As far as I recall, the experiment was never repeated. That was proof to me that heredity and environment do not make a preacher, because if anybody had a preaching heredity and a preaching environment, I did.

In my possession I have three books which relate to ancestors of mine who were preachers. The first is a fascinating book called *The Letters of John Pawson*. John Pawson, a Wakefield farmer, was one of Wesley's first twelve preachers. The second is entitled *Harvesting for God* and tells the story of my grandfather who was a Methodist minister but, as the title suggests, was more of an evangelist. There pictured in the book is my granddad with the same little beard as I have, copied quite unconsciously. My father was neither a minister nor an evangelist: he was Professor of Agriculture at Newcastle University, but at weekends he was a Methodist local preacher, and he always preached for a verdict. In fact, he kept a book in which he wrote down the name and address of every person who responded to his appeals. When he died and the book came into my possession, I discovered that it contained 12,000 names. There are many full-time evangelists who could not match that! His mentor was a man called Samuel Chadwick, Principal of Cliff College, so you could say that Chadwick was my spiritual grandfather. With all that heredity, preaching should be in my blood, but that did not lead me to preach.

What about environment? I had the most extraordinary boyhood in Newcastle upon Tyne because our home was called 'The Preachers' Inn', and any well-known preacher who came to preach on Tyneside stayed with us. I have jotted down some of the names of the preachers I met at that time: from Scotland James Black, James S. Stewart, William Barclay; from England William Wallace, Norman Dunning, John Broadbelt, S.W. Hughes, Campbell Morgan, Townley Lord, Martyn Lloyd-Jones, and the three Methodist preachers, W.E. Sangster, L. Weatherhead and D. Soper – of whom it was said that Sangster loved the Lord, Weatherhead loved people and Soper loved an argument. From overseas came saints like Toyohiko Kagawa from Japan, and Martin Niemöller from Germany. All these preachers and many, many more stayed in our home. Yet I never heard any of them preach. Perhaps it is because I saw them out of the pulpit that I didn't get any desire to preach from them. My mother was an amateur photographer, always into the latest thing, and she made movie films of all these preachers, a series she called 'Preachers out of the Pulpit'. At home I have a suitcase packed with old 9.5mm and 16mm films of all these preachers off duty. So I was born with a silver spoon in my mouth as far as preaching was concerned but had no ambition or desire to be a preacher myself. Isn't that extraordinary? But it just goes to show that environment is not the real factor either.

In the late 1940s, after the Second World War, there was a widespread desire in England to build a new society and start afresh. Many evangelists took advantage of this desire to hold crusades, and some were held in Newcastle. It was at these that I began to listen to and study preaching. The first preacher who made an impression on me was the best-known rugby player in the North-east – the Johnny Wilkinson of his day – a great big giant of a man called Alan Redpath. Next came a rather thin, lanky young American representing Youth for Christ, whose name we were later to become very familiar with:

Billy Graham. Then followed my cousin, Tom Rees, who used to joke that he had a little mission hall in Kensington called the Royal Albert Hall, which he packed month after month after month in those days. He also ran Hildenborough Hall in Kent, a conference centre for young people, which I visited in 1947. After a week there, I realised it was high time that I lived on my own faith and not on my parents' faith. Returning to the farm where I was working, I found myself singing choruses to the cows at four o'clock in the morning – the first to discover that music in the cowshed increased milk yield. Bursting to tell the world about Jesus, I began to preach not in churches but in the open air, alongside cinema queues, down at the beach at Whitley Bay, anywhere there were people. My pulpit was an ex US Army Jeep, which I would park in strategic locations. Very soon there were seventy or eighty young people joining me, and we learned how to preach in pubs and working men's clubs, and down the coal mines in County Durham and Northumberland, anywhere that people would give us a hearing. Looking back I am grateful that I began there. It taught me a great deal without my realising it.

I want to go on from that time to show how the Lord has led me through six different phases in my preaching.

1. TESTIMONY PREACHING

The first phase began when I went to tea one Sunday with a converted bookmaker, with whom I was very friendly. That evening he was preaching in a place called Spennymor and I accompanied him on the bus. I asked him, 'Jack, what are you going to preach on tonight?' He replied, 'I'm not preaching tonight. You are.' And that was my first introduction to preaching from a pulpit in a church. I got through my whole testimony, quoted every text I could remember and shared every bit of doctrine I knew – all in seven to eight minutes flat, a feat I have never been able to repeat. So now I was preaching in Methodist churches and chapels. This first phase of preaching I call 'testimony preaching'. It was highly subjective, focusing largely on my testimony and experience. For the matter in my sermons I drew on scriptures that meant something to me, or scriptures that I had discovered, or scriptures through which God had spoken to me. It was not a bad place to begin, but it was not a good place to stay. There was no eschatology and no pneumatology. I never preached about heaven and hell. I never talked about the Holy Spirit because I had no conscious relationship with Him at that stage. I wasn't preaching the whole truth by any manner of means, but a highly subjective selection of the Word of God. Happily that phase passed, and I went into my second phase.

2. TEXT PREACHING

The second phase was text preaching. I picked this method up from the Methodist preachers of that time. It was their habit to begin their sermons with 'My text this morning is . . . ', and then they would quote one verse from the Bible, which they would expound. Looking back it was often a case of a text out of context being a pretext: just one verse to hang some thoughts on. That, of course, was again highly subjective and highly selective. Which texts did I choose? The ones I wanted to preach on, or the ones that I thought other people might be interested in. It was still not the whole truth by a very long way. In fact, for a preacher on the Methodist circuit there was no opportunity for pastoral teaching. As part of a circuit of up to thirty churches, the preacher only really needed four or five sermons a year, which could be trailed round from one place to another. Again, I was preaching nowhere near the whole truth, but was still only touching a tiny percentage of God's Word.

3. TOPIC PREACHING

I then moved into what I would call 'topic preaching'. I bought myself a big, fat book called *Nave's Topical Bible*. I thought it was a wonderful book. Why hadn't God thought of doing it this way? Every verse in the Bible was listed under a heading. If you wanted to preach on the topic of humility, for example, all you needed to do was turn up the relevant page and the information you needed was there. Once again, this method suffers from being subjective. Which topic are you going to choose? One that scratches where your congregation is itching, or perhaps one which enables you to set them right on a particular issue? Topic preaching meant at least that I was getting multiple texts from all over the Bible and not just taking one solitary verse as the base for my preaching. The problem was that every one was taken out of context and was only selected because it related to the overall topic.

It was while I was still in my topical phase that I was called by the Methodist Church into the Royal Air Force, which is a story in itself. This move meant switching from lifeboat congregations – that is, women and children first – to congregations in which there were hundreds of men. Little did I realise that the pocketful of sermons that I had preached on the Methodist circuit would go down like a lead balloon with a bunch of men. I discovered that men want a very different kind of preaching to that which I had unconsciously adopted. Men want it straight from the shoulder – even if they disagree and come up and argue with you afterwards. They don't want to be pussyfooting around, as they put it to me. Faced with a congregation of up to 200 men, at first I despaired of ever finding out how to reach them. As I sought the Lord about it, something happened which was to change the course of my life, as well as my preaching. I felt the Lord say, 'I want you to preach My whole Word.'

'What do you mean, Lord?'

'Well, the Bible.'

'All of it?'

'Yes.'

'From Genesis to Revelation, the whole lot?'

'Yes.'

As a result of this conversation with God, I announced to the men in the Royal Air Force – I was by now out in Arabia – that I was going to take them through the whole Bible in a few months. So we galloped through the entire Bible with spikes in our shoes over about eight months. I was totally surprised by the result. These men for the first time were seeing and grasping the whole purpose of God. They were getting a big view, not snippets, or little pep talks, or little bits of moral advice. They got more and more excited and even now, many decades later, wherever I go in the country I usually meet somebody who came to Christ through that systematic biblical teaching while he was in the RAF. My life was now on a very different course.

4. PASSAGE PREACHING

When I had finished my time in the RAF I did not want to go back into Methodist circuit life because there would be no opportunity whatever to give the kind of teaching that God had revealed to me, Sunday by Sunday. That was one reason, but there was also another reason why I came to part from the Church of my fathers. Now that I was teaching the whole Bible, I could not avoid certain passages or certain subjects, which I had either been blind to before, or had avoided tackling because they were somehow disturbing. One in particular was the theme of baptism. However, I found myself so convinced by what I was studying in the Word that I had to say to the Methodist Conference that I could no longer baptise babies. Bless them, they were so keen to keep me that they offered me a full-time deaconess to do all the babies, but knowing that would be dishonest I refused, adding that in any case I would in the future be preaching a different kind of baptism. Those two things put together meant I had to resign from the Methodist ministry, with no future. I remember saying to my wife that I was going to lose my job, my pension, and our house. Her reply was that she wanted to be married to a man who obeyed God. In an amazing way, within a week, I found myself pastor of Gold Hill Baptist Church in Buckinghamshire. I discovered then that the Lord is the best employer. I discovered also that He doesn't ever call anybody to a denominational post. By that I mean I realised that He hadn't called me to be a Methodist preacher, or a Baptist preacher, but to be a preacher in His Body, and that He would move me around as necessary. Now, for the first time I had the same pulpit every week, and I was able to take that very brief survey of the whole of the Bible which I had taught in the Royal Air Force, and begin to do it in depth. My target was to take a congregation right through the Bible every ten years. That involved one chapter from the New Testament or two to three chapters from longer books in the Old Testament each service. Thus I gave myself to the fourth phase, which I call 'passage preaching'.

For the first time I was wrestling with context, and was discovering that, if you are really going to preach the Word of God, you have to spend one hour in the study for five minutes in the pulpit. I know of no short cut. Ninety per cent perspiration and ten per cent inspiration. I felt it was so important to be able to feed my people that I gave priority to my preparation, and did not allow other things to steal the time that I needed to get to grips with the Word of God. My aim was fourfold. First, I wanted to make my preaching *real*, which meant going back into the past and reliving it with my people; with imagination and information taking them back into the Bible days so that they could live in it and, above all, feel the Word of God and not just think it. My second aim was to make the Scriptures *relevant*: to come back from the past into today and ask how the Word relates to our present situation. Here again there is no short cut. It is necessary first to go back into the past, because every Scripture has what the Germans call a *Sitz im Leben* – a situation in life. God did not give us a topical Bible. Everything He said was spoken in the context of a life situation. Real people in a real situation, with His revelation coming through the story. Third, I wanted my preaching to be *reliable*. As regards my actual method, I would sit with my Bible and a pile of plain paper and I would study the passage, filling page after page after page with what I could get out of it. Many times I would translate the Bible into my own language to make sure that I had understood it. I wanted to be absolutely reliable in terms of being true to that Scripture. That was probably what took most of the time in my preparation. I would only look at commentaries and other writers – not other preachers, I refused to read what other preachers said – when I had enough material of my own, in order to check out what I had found with what others had found. It didn't always agree. In that case I had to wrestle with the text to see whether perhaps I had misunderstood it, or they had. But that was all part of being a reliable expositor. Fourth, I wanted to be *refreshing*. This is what I call putting the gravy on the meat. Making it tasty, making it interesting, making it lively – interesting to the mind. The unforgivable sin in a preacher is, in my view, to be boring.

During that period I found my gifting and my calling. I was a teacher. I know it comes fifth in the list of 'ascension' gifts in Ephesians 4 but that doesn't worry me at all. I have long since discovered that it is freedom to live within your gifting, and not try to be what you are not. It is freedom to discover what you are, and it is freedom to discover what you are not. I have always endeavoured to stay within my gifting.

As I began this expository ministry, I soon found that it was an 'open sesame' to evangelical conventions. I began to receive invitations to teach the Bible all over the country – and then I had to go and ruin it all by becoming Charismatic! Soon all the doors that had opened so readily shut again. But God had other plans.

There was a man in the church who had an old-fashioned tape recorder with spools. He was a man with most unusual views and he didn't agree with much of my preaching, but he was a delightful and kind individual. One day he approached me with the suggestion that he would like to tape my sermons for the sick and the elderly in the congregation, so that they wouldn't have to miss them. I immediately gave him the go-ahead, little dreaming what that would mean. Ultimately it would mean being a missionary in 120 countries without any of the hassle, but we didn't know it at the time. Even with the old spools the ministry grew and grew. But, praise God, then came the invention of the audio cassette, which is used in the same form worldwide. We immediately seized on it, because by then the tapes were beginning to circulate everywhere. As I asked the Lord about this, I felt He was saying something like: 'David, now I can use your preaching on a wider scale. I couldn't use your testimony preaching or your text preaching or your topic preaching, but your passage preaching I can use, and I am going to use it on a very wide scale.' That was, of course, very encouraging. I felt I had touched something I was made for.

The big advantage, of course, of systematic passage preaching is that the preacher has to deal with the subjects he would rather avoid. And he can do so, without getting at members of the congregation – because it is there in the text and he has to preach it. Systematic preaching sets the preacher free to preach the whole counsel of God. I loved it.

One of the things I did, which proved very successful, was that I decided to get together on a Thursday evening all the Bible school teachers who would miss the main teaching in the Sunday morning service and give them the study, so that they weren't robbed of being taught. Not only did that have a profound effect on their Sunday school teaching, but it helped me enormously by having a 'dry run' before the Sunday morning.

My passage preaching phase went on right through my ministry at the Millmead Centre in Guildford. I still don't think I have covered every chapter in the Bible but I have covered a great deal, and there is now a library of some 1,100 tapes from that era. In 1979, I was praying about the future of the church. I could see very clearly the way the church should go and what God's plans for the next decade were, but I couldn't see my place in it. Finding that quite disturbing, I went to what was called a Prayer and Bible Week at Ashburnham Place in Sussex, with the express purpose of discovering from the Lord during that week whether I was to be part of the church's future or not. I needed to know. By the way, this incident provides a small insight into the way I seek guidance from the Lord. He is the Boss. It is not my job to try and read His mind: it is His job to tell me. If an employee goes to an office or factory on Monday morning, the boss doesn't come to him and say, 'Try and guess what I want you to do this week.' Yet, that is how we treat God. Years and years ago I made a solemn promise to the Lord, 'Lord, if You speak to me clearly, I promise to obey, whatever the cost or consequence.' I just say simply that it has worked. He has kept His part and I by His grace have kept mine. In fact, to go back to the very beginning when I was working on the farm, I was torn between farming and preaching, because I was still doing both. I could have gone on doing both, but I felt it was going to be a case of either/or. One morning I said to the Lord, 'Lord, if You will tell me by midday today which it's to be in Your will, I will do it.' At 10.30 I was having a cup of coffee with another farm worker, when he looked me straight in the eye and said, 'David, you won't finish up behind a plough, you'll finish up in a pulpit.' I said, 'That's not clear enough, Lord.' Soon after leaving him – and to this day I know exactly the spot where this incident occurred – I bumped into a retired Methodist minister whom I hadn't seen for years. I said, 'How are you, Mr Scott? Nice to see you again.' His reply was, 'David, why are you not in the ministry?' I said to God, 'That's clear enough.'

One of the main speakers at the Prayer and Bible Week in 1979 was Alex Buchanan. When he had finished giving one of his talks, he said, 'I have a word from the Lord for four men here. I don't know who they are, but you will know.' I cannot recall anything of what he said in the first three words he gave, but the fourth I can recite word for word: 'My son, you have ministered to the extent of your gift in the place where I certainly put you. I set you free from that place and I set the land before you, but one thing I require of you, that you surrender into My hands all that remains to be done in that place, for it is My church and My congregation. And I want you to go out and so serve Me that one day you will look into My face and say, "Lord, we did it."' I took a recording of the prophecy back to the elders of the church – I would not do anything until they had weighed and judged it – and they said, 'We have got to let you go.' At that time the Lord set the land before me, and within two years I had been in two hundred towns and cities in this country.

5. Burden Preaching

However, what a change it made to my preaching. No longer could I work through passage after passage. Being in a place for one, two or at most three days was a very different matter and I found that I returned to a form of topic preaching. As I travelled from place to place I found that burdens would come heavily on my heart: burdens for the Church as God's people. I began to live on a wide canvas. How easy it is to assume that the whole Church is a mirror of one's own little patch. But now I was seeing the wider picture, and I began to 'burden preach', as I have come to call it. As I picked the burden up, it became heavy in my heart. As I began to share it in various meetings it would get bigger and bigger. Feeling that there must be a more efficient way of dealing with these burdens than going from place to place and speaking about them, I asked the Lord what I could do. Opening my Bible in Jeremiah, who is the Bible character I most identify with, my eyes alighted on the passage, *'Write in a book all the words I have spoken to you'* (30:2). In previous years publishers had often asked me for books but I had always steadfastly resisted, believing that I was not a writer and that it was not my calling. But now God said, 'When you get a burden, I want you to share it around the country and get feedback, and then write a book.' As I did that, and the book was written, the burden lifted. So it was burden preaching that became burden writing. And thus far it has been about twenty burdens. The first came into being because I found that many Christians are badly birthed: they did not have a good midwife when they were born again. So I wrote *The Normal Christian Birth*.[2] Then I discovered that the eschatological dimension of the Christian life had been exchanged for an existential one, so that a gospel of good news for the future had become preoccupied with the present. So I wrote *When Jesus Returns*.[3] Then I discovered that many people, including evangelical Bible teachers, no longer believed in the eternal torment of hell. So I had to write a book called *The Road to Hell*.[4]

My books have been widely misunderstood. When *The Normal Christian Birth* went to the British Library to be categorised, it was placed under 'gynaecology', and it appears in the public libraries in the medical section! When I wrote the book *The Road to Hell*, it was advertised in a national Christian magazine under the heading 'Read David Pawson's autobiography'. More recently I found myself deeply burdened about the feminizing of the Church and its increasingly effeminate character, which led to my writing *Leadership is Male*.[5] One Christian bookshop handed it out in plain brown paper bags from under the counter, as if it were pornographic! Outside another, which was displaying it in the window, there was a feminist demonstration! *Leadership is Male* was probably the best-known and the least-read book of 1998, but I have a file stacked full of letters of thanks, every one from a woman and saying, 'Thank God this has been said'. It was not putting women down, it was trying to put men where they should be.

My most recent burden concerns Islam. About fifteen months ago I had what I came to believe was a revelation of the Lord that Islam will become the dominant religion in this country, and that God is allowing its rise to purify His Church. For six months I lived with the burden, not even talking to my wife about it. Then I began to share it and people said, 'David, you're just the person to say this.' Never have I had so many volunteering to stick my neck out! The week before a planned day's recording for video and tape with an invited audience at Waverley Abbey I had a stroke which robbed me of my speech and, although I had every test imaginable, the doctors could find no physical cause. It only affected my throat, my lips and my tongue. But hundreds prayed and, when the day came, I was able to speak for five and a half hours, though I finished standing on one leg, because my left-side had lost all control. That material has also been put into a book entitled *The Challenge of Islam to Christians*.[6]

And so I have been burden preaching for the last twenty years. People ask me, 'What are you now, David?' I say, 'I'm still a teacher, but where I was a pastoral teacher, I am now a prophetic teacher.' The noun hasn't changed but the adjective has – and I believe that can happen to every gifting. Most of us have a noun and an adjective. Apparently someone said to Martyn Lloyd-Jones in his later years, 'Is there any such thing as a prophetic preacher today?' In reply I am told he said, 'I can name two', and one was my name. Unfortunately, I didn't hear about this until after he had died, so I was never able to find out what he understood by prophetic preaching, but I understand it to be a preacher receiving a burden from the Lord and applying it to the situation in which he is preaching, using relevant scriptures.

6. BOOK PREACHING

The Lord had one more surprise for me. A group of churches up in the Thames Valley invited me to go and get their people back into the Bible. This is another burden I have, because I find that even some evangelicals no longer study the Bible for themselves, and the reason is because we preachers don't give them the appetite and help them. I agreed to come once a month for four months, for three hours on a Sunday evening, and speak about one book in the Bible on each occasion. My aim was twofold. First, I wanted to give them such an appetite for the book that they couldn't wait to read it for themselves and, second, I wanted to give them enough information and analysis to help them to understand it when they did read it. At the end of those four months the pastors asked if they could book me for the next six years. I laughed and said I might be in heaven by then. But I did it actually, and over six years we went into every book in the Bible.[7]

At this stage God's pathway took another unexpected turn. Having introduced me to tapes and audio cassettes when I was passage preaching and to books when I was burden preaching, God now opened radio and television wide to me. I am on Sky television twice a week, teaching the Bible. It is an unnerving experience to be stopped in the street by a complete stranger and told, 'I saw you on TV last night', but many tell me what an effect the teaching is having on their Bible study. With over a hundred radio stations in Australia also transmitting the recording, I have never had such a huge congregation in my life. As I look back I see that the Lord has had His hand on passage preaching, on burden preaching, and now on book preaching.

As I finish, I just want to make one comment on a type of preaching I have never got into: I call it gospel preaching. I have literally never been able to preach a gospel sermon, for example on John 3:16 or Revelation 3:20. I have been asked to many times, but I find I am quite incapable of doing it. One of the reasons is, I believe, because I have stayed within my gifting as a teacher. It is the evangelist who preaches the gospel to the unbeliever. But that does not mean that I have not seen evangelistic results. Glory to God alone, but we rarely had a Sunday when people were not converted, though I never once made an appeal and yet, as a result, we had to have baptisms every single month. I found that when the Word is preached totally, sometimes the most surprising Word, it convicts of sin, righteousness and judgement. But I also believe it is because I have never been able to accept what is called a 'simple gospel'. My gospel is much bigger than 'Christ died for you'. My gospel includes the resurrection and the ascension and His return. I have never been able to condense it into a simple gospel talk. That's a confession. Others have been able to but I cannot.

These then are the six phases of preaching, through which the Lord has led me. I don't know what He has yet in store for me. I've asked Him if I can serve Him till I'm eighty, and then we will reconsider it! I just thank the Lord that preaching is something I love to do: feeding hungry people is so satisfying. Like a meal it may take hours to prepare, and it's eaten in minutes, but it is worth it when you see people grow and mature. There is a desperate need worldwide for the presentation of the whole truth, the whole Bible, the whole Word of God.

NOTES

1. David Pawson offers further insights on his preaching method in his autobiography *Not as Bad as the Truth* (Hodder & Stoughton, 2006).
2. Hodder & Stoughton, 1989.
3. Hodder & Stoughton, 1995.
4. Hodder & Stoughton, 1996.
5. Highland Books, 1998.
6. Hodder & Stoughton, 2003.
7. The material from this series was further developed to become the *Unlocking the Bible Omnibus* (Collins, 2003).

Chapter 14

CHRIST'S ASCENSION GIFTS

Terry Virgo

To each one of us grace was given according to the measure of Christ's gift.
Therefore it says,
> *'When He ascended on high,*
> *He led captive a host of captives,*
> *And He gave gifts to men.'*
... And He gave some as apostles, and some as prophets, and some as evangelists,
and some as pastors and teachers, for the equipping of the saints for the work of
service, to the building up of the body of Christ; until we all attain to the unity
of the faith, and of the knowledge of the Son of God, to a mature man, to the
measure of the stature which belongs to the fullness of Christ.
(Ephesians 4:7–8, 11–13)[1]

Ephesians 4 is the classic passage on the ascension gifts. The risen and ascended Christ, now reigning from His throne in heaven, *'gave gifts to men'*, which interestingly is a re-interpretation by Paul of verse 18 of Psalm 68, where it says, *'You have received gifts among men'*. Jesus sends forth His Spirit in and through His Church, both in a broad outpouring and by equipping His Church through diverse gifts: gifts of gifted people among the Body.

The giving of gifted people is, in a sense, not a new concept: God has always led His people through anointed, gifted people. The Old Testament prophets, for example, were people whose lives were interrupted by God's call and by God Himself coming to them, anointing and equipping them so that their words came from heaven. Then there were the men and women anointed as judges, many of whom were ill equipped to lead until they were gifted from on high. When the Spirit came upon the fearful Gideon, for example, he received a powerful anointing for leadership. The kings, too, were anointed. Unlike other nations which were influenced by philosophers, such as the Greeks by Aristotle and Plato, the people of God had always been led by individuals who had a heavenly anointing on them. When there was a particularly gifted leader, such as King David, the people knew times of extraordinary blessing. David himself was always aware that he was raised up and established, not for his personal glory, but so that the nation as a whole could be blessed. The raising up of gifted leaders has always been God's way. God is not a God of committee; He is a God of anointing. He is a God who comes upon people and gifts them with skills for leadership.

However, while there is continuity with the past, there is also discontinuity. It is a new age. The gifts still come from heaven, but now they come from the ascended Christ. In Ephesians 1:20–23 we read:

> *He raised Him from the dead and seated Him at His right hand in the heavenly places, far above all rule and authority and power and dominion, and every name that is named, not only in this age but also in the one to come. And He put all things in subjection under His feet, and gave Him as head over all things to the church, which is His body, the fullness of Him who fills all in all.*

The cosmic Christ reigns from His throne. The Jewish Messiah is now established as King of the nations and gives to His Body those who can equip it to come to maturity. There is an end goal in view. God, with His magnificent perspective, is looking for a many-membered Body spanning the nations, in which every tribe and every tongue is represented. He is looking for a multiplicity of people who together are the Body of Christ. The Head is in the heavens; the Body is here on the earth. We might say that where once Jesus of Nazareth was the body of Christ, we are now the Body of Christ, made up of individual members. The task of this Body is to represent Christ to the nations, but, in order to achieve God's glorious vision, it must attain the fullness of the stature of God. To this end Jesus has sent forth apostles, prophets, evangelists, pastors and teachers to equip His Church. It is good for us to remember the reason why these gifted individual are given to the Church: they are to bring it to maturity so that the people of God can fulfil their God-ordained destiny.

It is perhaps helpful to remember that prior to the Reformation there was a clear divide in the church at local level between the priest and the people, with the priest seen as a mediator for the people. He was clergy; they were laity. He was the holy man; the people knew God from a distance, as it were. Come the Reformation, there was a wonderful rediscovery of the biblical truth of the priesthood of all believers. Since Jesus Christ has gone through the heavens for us, He is the only Mediator we now need – although we can quite correctly confess our sins to one another and find great benefit from one another in the Body of Christ. Thus, with the Reformation came a huge release as regards the understanding of the gospel and how it should affect church life.

Sadly, however, as the years have unfolded, in many churches there is still the pre-Reformation scenario of a man and the people, although he would now not so often be seen as a priest or a mediator. Now we might call him pastor, or we might give him some other title, but sadly he is still regarded as the man who does whatever needs to be done: he does the preaching; he does the praying; he does everything really. We sit and listen to him. Tragically the Church has almost lost the breadth of the diversity of the giftings that God has given. In various places around the world, however, there has been a great recovery of God's plan for the Church and I hope that, as we look afresh at the Scriptures, we too will receive fresh vision.

I want now to focus on the two most controversial ascension gifts, the apostle and prophet, before concluding with a brief word on the gift of evangelist.

APOSTLE

Great Bible teachers down through the ages have questioned whether each of the five gifts is given to the Church for the whole period of its history. The traditional evangelical view has been that some of them were short term, but the line has been drawn in different places. Dr Martyn Lloyd-Jones, one of my great heroes, takes the following view in his commentary on Ephesians 4: 'In the first group, the extraordinary and temporary, we have apostles and prophets and evangelists. In the second, permanent group we have pastors and teachers.'[2] He believed that apostles, prophets and evangelists were temporary gifts intended for the beginning of the Church's life, with only the gifts of pastor and teacher ongoing. Furthermore, in order for a person to be considered an apostle, in Lloyd-Jones's view he must have fulfilled the following five criteria:

1. he must have seen the risen Lord;
2. he must have been called and commissioned to do his work by the risen Lord Himself in person;
3. he must have been given a supernatural revelation of the truth;
4. he must have been given power to speak not only with authority but infallibility;
5. he must have been given power to work miracles.

Although there would have been some variation, this would broadly speaking have been the commonly accepted position. The respected biblical commentator Leon Morris takes a different view:

> Apostle does not apply solely to the Twelve. Paul frequently claimed the title for
> himself and sometimes in such a way as to show he saw it as important. But while I

think it is clear that it does not refer solely to the original Twelve, it is not clear exactly who could claim the title nor how apostles were chosen. Barnabas is called an apostle along with Paul in Acts 14:14 and, reasoning from the 'we' of 1 Thessalonians 2:7, we probably could include Silvanus.

In other words, not everyone would wish to limit apostles and prophets to the Twelve.

At the other end of the spectrum to those who hold that there were only ever twelve apostles and that is the end of the story, are those who take it for granted that there are apostles today. One such is the church observer and commentator Peter Wagner, who is the author of a number of books, including *The New Apostolic Churches*.[3] In his book *Look Out! The Pentecostals Are Coming*,[4] in which he charts the phenomenal growth of the Church in South America, he writes:

> The new apostolic reformation is an extraordinary work of God at the close of the twentieth century, which is to a significant extent changing the shape of Protestant Christianity around the world. In virtually every region of the world these new apostolic churches constitute the fastest-growing segment of Christianity. This is the day of the most radical change in the way of doing church since the Protestant Reformation.

While he describes the common features of churches that are enjoying wide influence and success and attributes this in part to travelling apostolic gifts and ministry, he does not actually point out what is apostolic about them. Although it must be said that Wagner is not seeking to write a theological work, but is simply observing the terrific growth of the Church in the Third World, I am worried by what seems to be a growing trend of using the word 'apostles' without being very clear about what we mean by it. We need to have a biblical perspective on the gift of apostles to the Church and I believe that it is as we understand the uniqueness of the Twelve that we will begin to unlock the question of whether there are still apostles in the Church today.

We need to understand, first of all, that the New Testament teaches there are different categories of apostle. In the first category there is the Lord Jesus Himself, who is described as *'the Apostle'* in Hebrews 3:1. He is set forth as the unique 'sent one', which, as is often explained, is the original meaning of the word 'apostle'. Jesus is the unique apostle and obviously unrepeatable in His uniqueness.

In the second category of apostle come the Twelve, who in my view should also be regarded as unique. As Revelation 21:14 makes clear, they laid the foundations of the universal Church:

> *And the wall of the city had twelve foundation stones, and on them were the twelve names of the twelve apostles of the Lamb.*

Just as there were twelve tribes of Israel, so now we have twelve apostles in the foundations of the new community of God. The twelve apostles gave definition and identity to the new people of God. When Jesus came, He came to Israel uniquely. Although He allowed some Gentiles to press through to find healing, and He commended their faith, essentially He came to Israel, but sadly *those who were His own did not receive Him*.[5] But to those who did receive Him, He gave a new identity. They became branches in the True Vine: they became a unique people in the earth now related to the Messiah personally and intimately, whether they had Abraham's blood in their veins or not. They had a relationship with God through the Messiah.

When, however, we come to the Day of Pentecost – the day on which the Church was born – what was the identity of the three thousand that were gloriously saved? Although called by some the Nazarene sect,[6] they were, in fact, added to the apostles (and, if you like, to the 120 as well), and they devoted themselves to the apostles' doctrine.[7] In other words, there was a new community on the earth that had never existed before, whose identity was given to them through their relationship with the apostles. Its members no longer went to the synagogue; they no longer observed the Sabbath; they were no longer circumcised; they no longer followed the dietary regulations. They stepped out from their identity of the past, and now had to learn a new identity; they had to learn how to display and demonstrate who they were without reference to the historical demarcation points. I believe that the primary role of the apostles was to give identity to this new community.

Having recognised this primary role of the apostles as the foundation of the universal Church it is important to see that their ministry developed on from there. In this regard it is very instructive to see what happened in the days of the Acts of the Apostles when the Church was growing in extraordinary ways. In Acts 8 when, as a result of the work of the evangelist Philip, people were saved in Samaria, the apostles did not just applaud another evangelistic breakthrough and then leave the fledgling church to establish itself. On the contrary, their response was to send Peter and John down to Samaria, where they laid hands on the new believers so that they received the Holy Spirit. Such apostolic involvement indicates, I believe, that not only did the apostles lay the foundation for the universal Church, but they needed to lay a foundation for the new communities of believers that were coming into being. On another occasion, when the gospel spontaneously arrived in Antioch as a result of evangelism by scattered, persecuted believers and a church was formed, the apostles in Jerusalem delegated Barnabas, who was not called an apostle at that time, to make a visit to them. His task, no doubt, was to make sure that foundational teachings were established in this new community.[8]

It is also very interesting to notice when the term 'apostle' is first applied to Barnabas and Paul. At the beginning of Acts 13 Luke includes the two men in a list of prophets and teachers. Then in the following chapter they are named as apostles (14:14). This leads me to presume that up until the time when the Holy Spirit instructed that these two men should be separated out for the work He was calling them to do, they would have been regarded as either prophets or teachers. But after they had been commissioned by the Holy Spirit their role changed to that of apostle. From that time on, they were constantly on the move, planting churches and laying good foundations.

So often the chief reason that is given as to why there can no longer be apostles in the Church today is that the Scriptures are complete, and the fear is that anyone named an apostle would wish to add to the Scriptures. The apostles are associated with the writing of Scripture, and since the Scriptures are now complete, there can be no more apostles. This is the view that most good evangelical biblical scholars take. In his recent paperback on leadership, which I found very helpful, John Stott makes this very point.[9] I would say that the root of this way of thinking goes right back to the Reformers who were opposed to apostolic succession out of the heavily authoritarian Roman Church of that time. Although it is motivated by a proper desire to keep the doctrine true and pure, to my mind it fails to look at the whole picture. It concentrates solely on the authority of Scripture, and fails to take the role of the apostle into account. Since not all the New Testament apostles wrote Scripture and since not all the authors of the Bible were apostles, it is a mistake to associate the two so closely. Just as in the Old Testament there were many different types of prophets – some such as Isaiah and Jeremiah who wrote their prophecies down, and some such as Elijah and Elisha who did not – so there are different types of apostle. It is totally inappropriate to tie the role of the apostle in with the writing of the Bible.

We need to expand our thinking on the work of the apostle. In 1 Corinthians 3:10 Paul writes, 'According to the grace of God which was given to me, like a wise master builder I laid a foundation'. We tend to think from Ephesians 2 that the laying of foundations for the Church is a process that was carried out for the universal Church and is now complete. Although there is a sense in which that is true, we must also remember that when an apostle set out on a missionary journey his primary preoccupation was not to set up a hospital or a school or to undertake agricultural work – all of which are excellent in themselves – but to plant churches. His purpose was to extend the New Testament community – that miraculous new creation community. The apostles literally laid a foundation in each of the places to which they were sent by the Holy Spirit. Yes, the apostles laid the foundations of the universal Church at the beginning, but the work goes on. The dynamic ongoing ministry of apostles is to lay foundations. On another occasion Paul makes the comment that he does not want to build on another man's foundations.[10] This implies, I think, that it is possible for another man to lay a foundation. It was a gift and ministry that was recognised by the early Church.

Since it is evident that both Paul and Barnabas laid foundations, it was clearly not just a function of the Twelve. Some Bible expositors have taught that Paul took Judas Iscariot's place among the Twelve, making everything neat and tidy once again, and that the eleven remaining disciples were hasty in the steps they took to fill the gap in their ranks. There is, however, nothing in the Bible to suggest that that is the case. It is clear from Paul's words in 1 Corinthians 15:5–8 that he does not regard himself as one of the Twelve. Furthermore, James, the brother of Christ, who was not one of the twelve disciples, is seen in Acts 15 clearly functioning as an apostle, even the leading apostle, at the Council of Jerusalem. So although the Twelve must be regarded as unique, the fact that there were other apostles laying foundations, including Paul, Barnabas and James, must lead us to conclude that it is not the end of the story. And once you break apostleship open from the Twelve, you are forced to take a fresh look at the whole subject. Restricting apostleship to the Twelve locks it up, but widening the concept breaks it wide open.

Some would seek to counter this argument by saying that the Bible's apostles are replaced by today's missionaries. However, many modern missionaries may serve in a number of different capacities, as mentioned earlier. As well as church planters, they may work as doctors, nurses, agriculturalists, development workers, etc. Few modern missionaries would be comfortable with the title 'apostle', and it is evident that modern missionary work is very different from apostolic work as described in the New Testament. We also need to note the statement made by Paul in Ephesians 4 that *'He gave some as apostles . . . until we all attain to the unity of the faith, and of the knowledge of the Son of God, to a mature man, to the measure of the stature which belongs to the fullness of Christ'*. I believe his use of the word 'until' suggests that apostle is an ongoing gift.

A very interesting point to notice is that once Paul had laid a foundation in a church community, he was happy to move on. He didn't see it as his duty to stay in that church. I am not saying therefore that every church should have in residence an apostle, an evangelist, a prophet, a pastor and a teacher. Paul saw, from his apostolic perspective, that once the foundation had been laid, once the life had taken root and was secure, it would now give life of itself. He was happy to appoint elders and move on, because his ministry was essentially to lay the foundation. The Church needs to rediscover this ministry. If we are concerned about world mission, we know that we have to set about planting churches all round the world. It is the role of apostles to lay foundations. For the sake of world mission it is vital that we must rediscover the biblical place of apostles.

PROPHET

God's people have always been prophetic. Right from the time of Abraham, who was called a prophet,[11] God's people have always represented God in the earth. The people of God are essentially a prophetic community. While we are also a pastoral community and the flock of God does need to be shepherded, we are not essentially to be a shepherding community. We must not forget that our *raison d'être* is to be God's voice to the world.

All sorts of problems arise when the church forgets its identity as a prophetic community. When we emphasise the shepherding aspect over and above the prophetic aspect, the people very soon start thinking that the purpose of the community is to meet their needs. They start to focus on such issues as whether they are being fed and their needs met, whether their children are being well catered for or whether another church might perhaps meet their needs better than the one they currently attend. Of course, it is the shepherd's responsibility to care for the flock and God will judge those shepherds who fail in their task. But it can become dangerous if we emphasise this aspect of ministry over the prophetic dimension of the church's calling. Some churches become very adept at meeting people's needs and come to be regarded as very successful. However, even though they may become very good at being a pastoral community, they may not be succeeding in being a prophetic community and fulfilling their mandate of speaking God's words to the end of the earth. We must not forget that the church is built upon the foundations of the apostles and the *prophets*. Martin Robinson has said, 'If the church doesn't rediscover its *raison d'être*, it will continue to die in the West.'[12] The church will die if it does not understand that it is meant to be a community on the move reaching the world. We are to be a prophetic apostolic community.

It is not just missionaries who have to be serious about following Jesus. We need to change the whole ethos of our churches so that we regard ourselves as a community on the move. We need more men and women like those who have personally told me that they have given up a possible job promotion because they were committed to service within the local church. That is what the church needs. It needs ordinary church members flooded with prophetic vision about the vital role of the church of God in the modern world, apostolically inspired, prophetically envisioned, grabbed and captivated by their understanding of what the church of God is. They do their job to put bread on the table, but they have a vision to see the church advance and bring God's prophetic word to the world.

It takes apostolic and prophetic ministry to release people from regarding the church as a static pastoral community and to transform it into those who understand that the church is charged with world mission.

When I talk about 'church' I am, of course, not talking about church meetings at 11.00 a.m. on a Sunday morning. I am talking about a vibrant, vital community which shines God's light into the world. I am talking about churches like the ones we are working alongside in Meru, Kenya, led by an amazing man called Edward Buria. When he set out to plant a church in a certain region, the authorities warned him against it because it was such an evil place. Undeterred, he has done an amazing work, with many being saved, a thriving church established and over a hundred churches planted in the region, as well as all sorts of micro industries being set up to create employment. Now, whenever men and women are saved, he asks them whether they have any history with the police. If they say yes, he phones the police to tell them that he is in contact with a certain individual and they say, 'Well, you keep him. You'll do better with him than we can.'

The New Testament does not give us any further definition concerning the gift of prophet beyond what we learn from the Old Testament. It picks up, as it were, from where the Old Testament leaves off, and so we see the prophet Agabus acting in a very similar way to the prophet Elisha. On one occasion he prophesies famine and on another he ties his belt around Paul's hands and feet and prophesies that Paul is going to be arrested.[13]

The prophet is not beyond Scripture or indifferent to Scripture. Often, it is as the prophet is studying Scripture, that God brings further revelation. It was, for example, while Daniel, one of the greatest Old Testament prophets, was praying and meditating on Jeremiah, that God spoke to him. In other cases the revelation comes to the prophet directly. Furthermore, they range from those, like Daniel and Ezekiel, who saw phenomenal and mysterious things, very broad in their range and difficult to understand, to those, like Nathan, who spoke a specific word into a specific situation. *'You are the man!'* says Nathan to David, bringing God's word of judgement to him after his adulterous affair with Bathsheba and his murder of her husband.[14] While Zechariah saw apocalyptic visions in the heavens, Haggai challenged the people of God about why they were giving more priority to their own concerns than to God's concerns. In the same way that there were many different kinds of prophets in the Old Testament, we need different kinds of prophets to build up the Church of God today.

EVANGELIST

'He gave ... some as evangelists ...' We need to understand that the role of evangelist is a separate gift in its own right. It is so important that we understand that there is an anointing to reap. I recently read an article about Billy Graham in which he is quoted as saying, 'When I say to people, I want you to get up out of your seats and come, I feel the power of God on me.' The gift of the evangelist is in operation.

Of course, since most churches nowadays only have one leader, who is usually the pastor, it is very difficult for the evangelist to find his rightful place within the Body of Christ. Sometimes a man whose gift really is evangelism has to call himself pastor because that is all that is available to him in our current church set-up, leaving him and some-times his people frustrated. Such a man can sometimes become a one-message preacher. His message is 'Come to Jesus' – and people do come, because there is a gift upon him. Other evangelists work in para-church organisations such as societies that specialise in evangelism as a way of using their gifting and put a lot of effort in trying to organise events to serve the Body of Christ.

It shouldn't be like this. In our churches we need to make room for all the ascension gifts. Of course, most churches would not be able to support and fully utilise an evangelist on their own, but groups of churches could work together in a region to release an evangelist. Then he could have a home base where he, his wife and children are loved and cared for, where he is not alone in his ministry but part of a body of God's people, and where he can work with the churches, equipping the saints for evangelism and reaping a harvest for the Kingdom. Not only is the evangelist a reaper in his own right, but when he is part of a community of God's people, others rally to him and are stirred themselves to be evangelists. In such groups there can be accountability and mutual encouragement. In his commentary on Ephesians John Eadie says this:

> In one sense apostles and prophets were evangelists for they all preached the same holy evangel, but this official title implies something special in their function in as much as they are distinguished also from teachers. These gospelers may have been auxiliaries of the apostles not endowed as they were but furnished with clear perceptions of saving truth and possessed of wondrous power in recommending it to others, passing from place to place with the wondrous story of salvation and the cross they pressed Christ on men's acceptance, their hands being freed all the while from matters of detail in reference, ritual and discipline.[15]

We too need to see people released from eldership and pastoral responsibility so that they can concentrate on proclaiming the message of the gospel and seeing people won for Jesus.

Notes

1. Scripture quotations in this chapter are taken from the New American Standard Bible.
2. D.M. Lloyd-Jones, *Christian Unity* (Banner of Truth Trust, 2004).
3. Gospel Light Publications.
4. Coverdale House, 1974.
5. John 1:11.
6. Acts 24:5.
7. Acts 2:42.
8. Acts 11:22ff.
9. *Basic Christian Leadership* (InterVarsity Press, 2002).
10. Romans 15:20.
11. E.g. Genesis 20:7.
12. Martin Robinson and Dwight Smith, *Invading Secular Space: Strategies for Tomorrow's Church* (Monarch, 2003).
13. Acts 11:28; Acts 21:10ff.
14. 2 Samuel 12:7.
15. John Eadie DD LLD, *Greek Text Commentaries. 'Ephesians'* (1883, reprinted Baker Book House, 1979).

Chapter 15

PRESENTING THE WORD: TO THE WHOLE PERSON

David Pawson

In my preaching I have learned far more from people in the pew than from people in the pulpit, but the two from the pulpit to whom I owe most are my father and Bob Morley, a fellow pastor in the Shetland Islands when I began my ministry in 1950, looking after five churches and travelling between them in a motorboat. Bob Morley, who has gone to glory now, will never be famous and he never made a great splash in his ministry, but I wanted to be a preacher like him. He was so honest with Scripture: he didn't try and fit Scripture into what he believed. Bob taught me to be totally honest, to face the problem passages head on. I have found that being honest with Scripture is not the way to be a popular preacher, because even the most evangelical people are creatures of tradition and their own traditional interpretation. I have tried constantly to say, 'Lord, I will preach what I believe Your Word says, whether I agree with it or not, whether it fits my ideas or not.' I want to be absolutely true to Scripture.

But I've learned far more from the pew. The whole time I'm preaching I watch people in the congregation and I get feedback from their faces. When I make a video I cannot preach to a video camera, I have to have a live audience. That is because preaching is a two-way process. I know exactly when people haven't understood what I have said and I need to stop and explain it more fully, and I know that when they start shaking their watch and holding it to their heads, I have lost them! I have made it a practice to stop preaching as soon as people stop listening, which is an important principle – I will explain later how to keep them listening. That is why I have never in my life written out a sermon. It means my eyes are free most of the time to roam over the congregation. I try to make it a principle to look at everyone in the congregation at some point in a sermon, so that everyone feels I have had a personal contact with them. Eye contact is a vital part of communication, but it is prevented if the preacher has his eyes down on his paper for three-quarters of the time he is preaching. I make pages of very full notes. Before I preach I read and reread them, and while I am preaching they are there as a safety net in case I get lost. I try to be independent of my notes because I want to be in communication with the people in front of me. This brings me to my first subject, which may come as a surprise:

How to Involve the Body

All communication is through bodies. This may sound an obvious statement to make, but why then do we not think about our physicality when we preach? Preaching is body to body communication. Looking first at the use of the preacher's body in communication, it may again sound very obvious but God has given us a voice. The voice is the most skilled musical instrument anyone will ever handle: it can communicate almost any mood, tone, feeling and thought. Yet most preachers do nothing about their voice, which I think is a tragedy. Years ago I had some training from a voice production teacher, who taught me how to use my voice as a musical instrument. For example, the very simple technique of speaking from the front of the mouth rather than the back trebles a preacher's communication ability. I would recommend all preachers to have a few sessions with a voice production coach if they possibly can. It will help them to avoid the mistakes that make communication more difficult.

Voice production specialists often say, 'By your consonants you will be heard; by your vowels people will know where you come from.' If I speak my native dialect, most people can't understand me. I am afraid that, in conquering it, I have finished up with what I call an 'Azores accent', a mid-Atlantic accent, but I still have the short 'as' of Newcastle, and that's how people can tell where I am from. It is not whether or not a preacher has an accent that is important, but the clarity and musicality of his speech. A voice that people find pleasant and easy to listen to is a very great asset, while an awkward or irritating voice is going to be a barrier.

The other major asset a preacher has is his face. Many preachers do not realise that, while two-thirds of the message that people receive comes through their ears, a third comes through their eyes. Most people lip-read without realising it. This was proved by an experiment conducted by Surrey University. A television set placed in Guildford High Street showed a man saying continuously, 'Pop, pop, pop...', but out of the speaker came the words, 'Dad, dad, dad...' Passers-by were asked to stand in front of the TV for one minute and then write down what the man was saying. Nine out of ten people wrote 'Pop'. A congregation reads the preacher's face. It is the best visual aid he has. I totally disapprove of the practice of putting the text of the sermon up on a screen behind the preacher. In so doing a warm face is transformed into cold print. And at the same time the people are distracted from the preacher's face. It is just as important for people to see the preacher as to hear the preacher – which is something we rarely think about. To ensure optimum communication, the preacher first needs to be in front of a plain background with no banners, no texts, no flowers, no choir behind him: nothing that takes the eye away from the preacher. Even the vertical line of a column will distract the eye, causing it to travel up and down its length. Second, a preacher must be within two metres of his background. This is because the human eye looks beyond the object of focus, and it is important to stop it. In order to look at anything nearer than two metres, the muscles of the eye have to pull the eye back which gets very tiring, so the eye rests on whatever is two metres beyond. This is very practical teaching, but it has very important implications, since a congregation with relaxed eyes can listen comfortably for a couple of hours.

This fact also means that the people at the back of an auditorium have to be able to see the preacher as well as the people at the front. In my spare time I design churches, really just to save churches money, and in order to overcome this problem I usually try to have a half-height platform and a sloping floor so that the people sitting at the back can have a totally uninterrupted view of the preacher's face. In traditional churches where there is poor visibility I often use the pulpit, simply so that people at the back feel as much in touch with me as people at the front. Today, not only is there a reaction against preaching but there is also a reaction against pulpits, but the pulpit is purely for the preacher's benefit. He likes to feel he is near the people. By coming down from the pulpit in an effort to get nearer the congregation, a preacher is favouring the people at the front and causing those at the back to feel they are spectators. Wherever possible, we need to try to adapt the buildings in which we preach to make the best use of them, in order to ensure this direct continuity with the congregation. One solution in large gatherings is to have a giant TV screen blowing up the preacher's face, which is what many of the big evangelists do.

What then about the congregation's bodies? I have already referred to the fact that they need to be able to hear well and nowadays, of course, most churches have good amplification systems so the preacher has no excuse. However, it must be added that most of the amplification in use is designed for music and not for speech and, therefore, the voice booms out from big base speakers at the front, which is the worst possible arrangement for preaching, since it sounds threatening. A system designed for speaking will have small speakers placed all around the meeting room. When I design a church, I advise that two systems be installed, one for music and one for speaking.

Even the chairs on which the congregation sit are important. Some new chairs are so uncomfortable that people are constantly changing position. The pew I designed for the Millmead Centre, Guildford, holds the backbone absolutely still and upright, if people sit on it properly – if they lounge or sit sideways, it becomes very uncomfortable. It is patented as the Guildford Pew. We adjusted and adjusted it until we got a seat on which people could sit for a couple of hours in real comfort. It is important that people are comfortable – but not too comfortable – so that they can relax and listen without constantly shuffling in their seats to find a new position for their tired muscles. Physical communication is important because people are in the flesh. We are communicating from one body to other bodies, so we need to take all these factors into consideration.

How to Interest the Mind

As I have already said in 'Presenting the Word: A Preacher's Journey', the unforgivable sin in a preacher is to be boring. When we've got such exciting things to say and such amazing announcements to make, to say it in a lifeless voice really is unforgivable. The first sentence of a sermon is, of course, crucial: if you don't strike oil in two minutes, stop boring. When I was at Cambridge there was a very dry professor who could dive deeper into the truth and come up drier than anyone else we knew. However, on one occasion he began his sermon by saying, 'I suppose the priesthood of all believers means that the Pope is sometimes right.' There was dead silence, and from that moment he had the ears of everybody present, who were asking themselves where he would go from there. An arresting beginning is worth working at. Nevertheless, I believe the preacher should get straight into the subject and not waste time trying to get people interested. If the subject is interesting, get into it as early as possible. But maintaining interest is not the same as gaining interest, and I want now to give some pointers on how to maintain interest.

1. Use the right language

Very few preachers are aware that there are two kinds of English: there is Anglo-Saxon English and Latin English. Latin English is the language of the university, and many preachers having come out of university use Latin English, but it does not communicate well. Anglo-Saxon English, which is the language of the street, the 'vulgar' language, does. Even in New Testament days there were two kinds of Greek. There was the classical Greek of the university and there was the *koine* Greek of the backstreet: the New Testament is written in backstreet Greek. In English, the Anglo-Saxon word will often be crude, even vulgar, but it will conjure up a picture in people's minds, which the Latin word won't. Latin words are usually multi-syllable and abstract, for example: justification, sanctification, glorification. They do not evoke much of an emotional response. When the translators of the Bible into New Guinean Pidgin English wanted to convey the sense of the word 'justification' they used the phrase 'God, 'e say 'im alright'. That communicates a feeling and evokes an emotional response! And this is what Anglo-Saxon English does: it communicates feelings as well as creates a picture. When Winston Churchill wrote books, he used Latin English and employed a vocabulary of 25,000 words, but when he spoke on the radio to the people of Britain to boost morale, he only used Anglo-Saxon words and limited his vocabulary to some 5,000 words. It is clear from the extracts of his speeches that are often quoted that he uses very short, sharp words, 'Never was so much owed by so many to so few', or 'I have nothing to offer you but blood, tears, toil and sweat'. Now he could have said, 'I have nothing to offer you but sacrifice, labour and perspiration.' 'Perspiration' is the Latin word for Anglo-Saxon 'sweat'. But it is clear which has the most power to touch feelings and evoke a gut reaction. I am often criticised for saying what I am now about to say, but I am happy to be. Paul, writing to the Philippians, says about his self-righteousness: 'I count it but [he used a very crude Greek backstreet word, the Anglo-Saxon equivalent of which is] shit.'[1] That is what he thought of his self-righteousness. Like a little boy holding up his potty and saying, 'Look what I've done.' The King James Version was written in Anglo-Saxon English because it was based on William Tyndale's translation (that is not an argument for using it today because the Anglo-Saxon words have changed meaning so radically that we cannot use it), but that is why it was so popular and spoke to so many people. *'A city set on a hill cannot be hid'*:[2] simple short words, everybody gets the message.

My plea to preachers is: use Anglo-Saxon words. Years and years ago I made up my mind that I would try and keep away from Latin English because I wanted to reach ordinary people, and the result is that my tapes can go right around the world to countries where anybody has basic English, whereas Latin English would never have opened that opportunity up to me. Kill long, abstract words dead. The use of simple Anglo-Saxon English helps to maintain interest enormously.

2. Keep up a good pace

Another factor in maintaining interest that I have discovered from watching congregations and gauging how they responded is that it is most important to maintain pace. Notice, I didn't use the word 'speed'. By pace I do not mean how quickly the preacher speaks, but how rapidly he moves from one idea on to the next. A sermon will hold interest if the preacher maintains a good pace and is constantly moving on to a new thought. I have heard sermons that only had one thought in them, which was spun out for twenty minutes, and it seemed like an eternity. People will stay with the preacher if he keeps moving: a brisk walk is more stimulating than a leisurely stroll. But if the preacher starts slowing down, so does the congregation. It is not that they need to remember everything the preacher has said. Somebody once analysed my sermons and discovered that in an average fifty-minute sermon I had seventy different ideas, more than one a minute. It didn't bother me that people didn't remember them all – far from it – but at some point everybody in the congregation heard from God and went away with that one truth uppermost in their minds.

I believe we have a duty to interest people, and that means including information they have never heard before. It also means provoking thinking by making stimulating statements. Here is an example. If I am preaching on the book of Jonah, the first thing I want to tell my congregation is that it contains eight nature miracles – not just one.[3] Furthermore, the whale is not the biggest miracle: the worm is. I say that because I have met people who have trained whales, but I have never met anybody who has trained a worm! It takes God to tell a worm what to do. Immediately, people begin to become interested.

Then I ask whether it is possible for a man to live inside a whale. In 1921 James Bartlett was lost overboard from a whaler near the Falkland Islands. The next day the ship's crew caught a whale, hauled it up on deck and were cutting it up with big knives when they saw something moving in the whale's stomach. Quickly cutting the stomach open they found James Bartlett, deeply unconscious but alive! Two days later he regained consciousness. However, the skin of his body that had been exposed to the whale's digestive juices remained bleached white, whereas the clothed parts of his body retained their normal colour, and so for the rest of his life James Bartlett was pointed out because of the extraordinary appearance of his skin. This story cannot fail but to grab the congregation's interest.

 Then I tell them something that will make them think even more, namely that Jonah was not alive in the belly of the whale: he was dead. Read the story carefully.[4]

I am amazed how many people have missed the fact that Jonah drowned. When the sailors threw him overboard, he sank to the bed of the ocean and lay among the seaweed at the roots of the mountains. He recalls that, as he went down, the waters gushed into his throat. It only takes a minute and a half to drown but much longer to reach the bottom of the Mediterranean. Jonah was dead. When you read his prayer carefully, you understand that he is praying from Sheol, which is the Hebrew word for the abode of the dead. Many Christians believe that Jonah was alive in the belly of the whale and do not consider that the whale might have picked him up dead from the ocean bed. This possibility only occurred to me when I saw a film shot by a friend of mine who trains killer whales in Marineland, Florida. One particular whale shared its pool with a dolphin. One day the dolphin died, and my friend was intrigued to see the whale pushing the body of the dolphin to the surface to try and get it to breathe. A dolphin is about the size of a small man.

The fact that Jonah was resurrected means that his life was a remarkable foretelling, a foreshadowing, of Jesus' resurrection, which Jesus Himself recognised.[5] Furthermore, Jonah died an atoning death. The sailors put him to death in order to turn away the wrath of God, and it worked. So here is a prophet who died an atoning death, had a bodily resurrection three days and three nights later, and incidentally, since he came from the town next door to Nazareth, was the local hero in Jesus' boyhood days. This is how I get my congregation interested.

The next huge question a preacher must tackle is, why did Jonah ever run away? Not to address this question is to miss the point of the book of Jonah. And it has a most unusual answer. Jonah ran away because he believed that God would let the Ninevites off. Back in his own country Jonah had been sent as a prophet to one of the wicked kings of Israel to tell him that God would bless him, would enlarge his borders and give him more land than his father ever had (2 Kings 14:23–25). You would have thought that the king would be so grateful for this blessing that he would have turned over a new leaf, but far from it. He did just the opposite. He took advantage of God's mercy and became worse than ever. Jonah is saying, 'I am not going through all that again, Lord. You let people off.' And so, after he had preached to all of Nineveh, he went and sat on the hill overlooking the city in a temper, watching to see what would happen. Jonah suspected that the people of Nineveh would revert to their old ways, and he was right. A hundred and fifty years later, God had to send the prophet Nahum with the message that Nineveh was finished.[6] So Jonah was absolutely right, but he was wrong in God's timing. He wasn't as patient as God.

All this brings a prophet alive. He is a real person in a real situation. It is the preacher's task to make Scripture fascinating but it means he has got to do his homework first. He must find out as much as he can about that Scripture with an open mind and not just come to it with a closed mind full of what he has heard other people say.

3. Touch people's hearts

The third way in which the preacher maintains interest is by touching the heart. It is interesting that most prophecy in the Scripture is poetic. Poetry touches the heart; prose appeals to the head. The reason why God gave His prophets mostly poetry is because He wanted to touch the hearts of His people. Unfortunately a lot of biblical preaching is for the head only. It is cerebral. It is little different from a lesson at school. Hebrew is a very emotional language. I once heard a lecture from an Old Testament scholar who described Kenneth Taylor's *Living Bible* paraphrase as by far and away the best translation when it came to conveying the emotions of Hebrew. That is why we chose it at Millmead when we read the Bible right through nonstop, which took about eighty-two hours. We began Sunday night and finished Thursday morning at breakfast time. One of the people who had signed up to read was unable to make it on the day, so she sent her non-Christian husband who happened to be a council official. He asked me what he had to do. I explained that he just needed to read on from where the last person had finished. When his turn came, it was Proverbs 31, and he read about the ideal wife who gets up at dawn and looks after her family. Then he read this, *'Her husband is well known, for he sits in the council chambers with the other civic leaders.'* When he staggered back to his seat, he whispered to me, 'I've just read about myself in the Bible.' I said, 'That's what most people find.' We chose *The Living Bible* not because it is the best translation, because I don't think it is, but because it touches people's hearts in a way that no other translation can.

I have always made it my ambition to help people to *feel* the Word of God because that is the fuel that gets the will going. They do not just think the right thoughts but feel the right feelings, whether of joy or sorrow. Let me give you a down-to-earth example. There is one verse that always sends me into giggles whenever I hear it: *'And it came to pass, in the morning, behold, it was Leah.'*[7] Here is Jacob on the first morning of his honeymoon. After a great wedding feast, it was late at night by the time they went to bed so all was in darkness. He wakes up in the morning to discover that he has got the ugly sister. Now we

201

would laugh if this happened to our best friend but not if it happened to us! When people feel the emotion of that verse, when they feel the humour, they will never forget the truth that the preacher draws from it, and it will touch their hearts. This is the man who cheated everybody. This is the man who deceived his own blind father, and now the biter is bit. The Bible says very clearly, '*A man reaps what he sows.*'[8] When I am preparing the Word, I find that if I can't *feel* it, there is not much point in me continuing. If I don't feel it, I say, 'Lord, why? What is wrong with me?' Because I know that if it touches my heart, I'll be able to touch other people's. I am a bit peculiar in my emotions – tears are as much an expression of joy for me as sorrow. A church member once said to me, 'David, you have never preached without tears in your eyes.' Get people to feel the Word. Touch their hearts. But the preacher needs to feel it first.

4. Tell people what they need to do

A preacher should never finish his sermon without telling people what they need to do about what he has said. One of the most frequent, and most neglected, words in the Bible is the little two-letter word 'do'. We teach that Christian discipleship is a matter of faith, but it is actually a matter of doing faith. The apostle James said: '*Show me your faith without deeds, and I will show you my faith by what I do.*'[9] Jesus said,

> '*Go and make disciples of all nations, baptising them in the name of the Father and of the Son and of the Holy Spirit, and teaching them to obey everything I have commanded you.*'
> (Matthew 28:19–20)

Teach them to observe, to obey, to *do* . . . Repentance and faith are both things to *do*. All too often we teach people things to say when we should be teaching them things to do. Repentance is something a person does. Paul said,

> I was not disobedient to the vision from heaven. First to those in Damascus, then to those in Jerusalem and in all Judea, and to the Gentiles also, I preached that they should repent and turn to God and prove their repentance by their deeds.
> (Acts 26:19–20)

Today we ask people to say the sinner's prayer, 'I'm sorry for all my sins', but that is not repentance. It hasn't named a single sin, and confession in the Bible is always specific. I remember a young motorbiker with all the leathers coming to see me. I opened my front door to find him standing there. I asked, 'What is it, Paul?' 'I wanna talk,' he said. I invited him in, and he came in and squirmed into our settee which still bears the marks of his brass studs. Our conversation went:

'What do you want to talk about?'

'I wanna be baptised.'

'Well, Paul, do you know how we baptise people here?'

'Yeh, you duck 'em.'

'So you wanna be ducked?'

'Yes.'

'Paul, do you know what the word "repent" means?'

'No.'

'Now, listen carefully. Go home and ask Jesus this question: is there anything in my life You don't like? Cut it out and then come back. That's what "repent" means.'

He didn't come back for two weeks. As I opened the door to him a second time, he showed me his fingernails and said, 'I've stopped biting my nails.' I said, 'Right, I'll baptise you now, Paul.' Many people are baptised without even having to produce that much repentance. But Paul talks about those converting to Christ proving *their repentance by their deeds*'. The gospel is not something to be accepted, but something to be obeyed, which includes repentance and baptism, and faith is not something you think or say: it's something you *do*. Therefore, in our preaching we do need to make it quite clear to people that the response to every word of God is something to be *done*, and it is helpful to suggest what that something might be. Though we are justified by faith, we shall be judged by works.

HOW TO INSPIRE THE SPIRIT

For many years I never preached about the Holy Spirit because I didn't know Him. Feeling very guilty about this I decided to preach a series of sermons about everything the Bible says about the Holy Spirit, so I prepared ten sermons. I got on quite well with the Old Testament, but things began to get a bit sticky when I reached John, and I was very aware that Acts 2 was looming. I didn't have a clue about what happened in Acts 2, and I was dreading getting to it. At that time we had a very awkward deacon in the church. There is always one! Whatever I suggested at a church meeting, this awkward deacon would either say, 'We've never done that and we're not going to try', or 'We've done it before and it didn't work'. My wife would say, 'Forget about him: he is the only one opposing you', but I found it very difficult. Every year this man was laid low with a sort of very serious hay fever for six weeks at a time. How I enjoyed that – for six weeks we were free of this man! Anyway, as I was preaching my way through the sermons on the Holy Spirit, this man kept coming to mind and I knew I should go and visit him. So one day I went and, all the way there, perhaps because his name was James, I kept thinking 'James 5'. Pondering what was in James 5, I remembered the command to anoint the sick with oil and pray for them. I thought I couldn't do that for Jimmy, I'm glad he's sick! However, the first thing he said when I arrived was, 'What do you think about James 5?' and I replied, 'Well, I have been thinking about it, Jimmy.' He then told me that he was due to go on a business trip to Switzerland on Thursday and asked me if I would anoint him with oil on Wednesday evening. I agreed to pray about it.

I went home and prayed, 'Lord, give me a good reason why I shouldn't do this.' But He didn't, so I went into the chapel and knelt in the pulpit, and tried to pray for him. But I couldn't. 'Lord,' I said, 'You'll have to help me to pray for him.' Suddenly I began to pray in fluent Chinese – I had never done that before. I prayed for about an hour, and I knew I was praying for this brother. I was amazed. Then I thought, I wonder if I can do that again. I opened my mouth and this time I prayed in a totally different language. I thought, 'This is Acts 2!' Before I went to his house on the Wednesday evening, I bought a big bottle of olive oil at Boots the Chemist. Going into his bedroom and kneeling around the bed, we went through James 5 as if it were a car servicing manual. *'Confess your sins...'* Oh well, better do that first. So I said, 'Well, James, I have never liked you.' He said, 'That's mutual.' Having dealt with that, I took the top off the bottle of the oil and I poured it all over his head and, guess what happened, absolutely nothing! I got up and ran for the bedroom door. I couldn't face it. I thought, how did I ever get into this mess? But somehow the Holy Spirit stopped me at the door and I turned back and said, 'Have you still got your ticket for tomorrow?' He said, 'Of course.' I said, 'I'll pick you up and take you to the airport.' Then I ran. The next morning I didn't dare to contact him. I didn't want to know. I was thinking, 'Oh what a mess to get into with the most awkward member of the church.' But he rang me and said, 'Can you pick me up at 10.30?' I said, 'Are you all right, James?' He said, 'Fine.' I asked, 'Have you been to the doctor?' 'Yes. Doctor says I am all right.' Then he added, 'I have been to get my hair cut, but the barber said, "I'm afraid I'm going to have to shampoo you first. I have never seen such a greasy head of hair in all my life."' Praise God, that man never suffered from that recurring problem again and he became my best friend! The next Sunday, after I had preached on the Holy Spirit, a young man came up to me and said, 'What's happened to you this week?' I said, 'Why do you say that?' He said, 'You know what you are talking about this week!'

We need to preach in the Spirit and rely on the Spirit, realising that we will never convict anyone of sin or righteousness and judgement, unless He does it with our words. When we preach in the Spirit, the gift of the Spirit called *parrhēsia* in Greek, which is holy boldness, becomes ours. And that, I believe, is one of the most desperate needs in our preaching today: people who will preach with boldness, with no intimidation from the congregation, with no fear of man or woman, but with fear of God. Then, we will preach as Jesus did: *'as one having authority'*. As one of the old preachers in America used to say, 'I thinks myself clear, I prays myself hot, and then I just lets go.'

Notes

1. Philippians 3:8.
2. Matthew 5:14.

3. The storm; the casting of lots; the calming of the sea; the whale swallowing Jonah's body; the whale vomiting Jonah's body onto dry land; the vine that sprang up over night; the worm that killed it by eating its roots; the hot, scorching desert wind.
4. See Jonah 2.
5. Matthew 12:40.
6. See book of Nahum.
7. Genesis 29:25 KJV.
8. Galatians 6:7.
9. James 2:18.

Chapter 16

APOSTOLIC PREACHING

Terry Virgo

For this reason I, Paul, the prisoner of Christ Jesus for the sake of you Gentiles –
if indeed you have heard of the stewardship of God's grace which was given to me
for you; that by revelation there was made known to me the mystery, as I wrote
before in brief. By referring to this, when you read you can understand my insight
into the mystery of Christ, which in other generations was not made known to the
sons of men, as it has now been revealed to His holy apostles and prophets in the
Spirit; to be specific, that the Gentiles are fellow heirs and fellow members of the
body, and fellow partakers of the promise in Christ Jesus through the gospel, of
which I was made a minister, according to the gift of God's grace which was given
to me according to the working of His power. To me, the very least of all saints, this
grace was given, to preach to the Gentiles the unfathomable riches of Christ, and
to bring to light what is the administration of the mystery which for ages has been
hidden in God who created all things; so that the manifold wisdom of God might
now be made known through the church to the rulers and the authorities in the
heavenly places.
(Ephesians 3:1–10) [1]

I want to look at apostolic preaching in the light of Paul's understanding expressed in
Ephesians 3:1–10 that truths that had previously been hidden were now being revealed to
God's holy apostles and prophets. Although we believe that all Scripture is God-breathed,
we also believe in growing revelation. What is often obscure in the Old Testament
becomes clear in the New. Our understanding of the Servant of the Lord is advanced,
for example, through Isaiah's magnificent portrayal of Him, and then, of course, in the

opening pages of the New Testament, we see His arrival in person, and through Him the revelation of the gospel of grace:

> For the Law was given through Moses; grace and truth were realized through Jesus Christ.
> (John 1:17)

The revelation grows and grows as the Scripture unfolds.

It is interesting to notice that throughout Jesus' ministry there were seasons during which people were unable to comprehend what He was saying. When, for example, He proclaimed,

> 'Truly, truly, I say to you, unless you eat the flesh of the Son of Man and drink His blood, you have no life in yourselves,'
> (John 6:53)

we read,

> As a result of this many of His disciples withdrew and were not walking with Him anymore.
> (John 6:66)

Many drew back because they could not comprehend what He was saying.

Just before He was to face the cross, Jesus said to His disciples gathered in the upper room:

> 'I have many more things to say to you, but you cannot bear them now. But when He, the Spirit of truth, comes, He will guide you into all the truth; for He will not speak on His own initiative, but whatever He hears, He will speak; and He will disclose to you what is to come.'
> (John 16:12–13)

Jesus told them that they would be given further revelation. When, on the Day of Pentecost, the Holy Spirit came to the apostles, that promise was fulfilled so that what had previously been difficult for them to comprehend, now became open and clear to them. The Holy Spirit revealed to them the extraordinary truth and reality not only about who Jesus of Nazareth was and what He had accomplished on the cross and through His resurrection and ascension, but also how mystically and marvellously we as His followers were crucified with Him, were buried with Him, were raised with Him and are now seated with Him in the heavenly places. It was the apostles who received this previously hidden revelation. It was the apostles who had the privilege of proclaiming these hitherto unknown truths. Apostolic preaching is, then, the proclamation of mysteries that were previously unknown; it is the announcement of truths that surpass anything that was previously expected.

THE LORDSHIP OF CHRIST

When Jesus asked His disciples the question, *'Who do people say that the Son of Man is?'* the disciples reported that some people believed that He was Elijah while others believed He was John the Baptist come back to life. When pressed to say who they considered Him to be, Peter made his declaration: *'You are the Christ, the Son of the living God.'*[2] But what was the people of Jesus' day's expectation of their Messiah and, perhaps more pertinently, what was the disciples' expectation?

It is evident from a study of Old Testament and other literature that they were expecting someone very like King David. David came at a time when Israel was at a very low ebb with Saul as king. The Philistines were overwhelming the nation, but by virtue of the anointing of God that was upon his life, David not only overcame Goliath but eventually replaced Saul and became the most successful king that Israel had ever known.

In addition, Jesus' contemporaries also knew the Old Testament prophecies concerning the Messiah, just one example of which is Isaiah 9:6 and 7:

> *For to us a child is born,*
> *to us a son is given,*
> *and the government will be on his shoulders . . .*
> *Of the increase of his government and peace*
> *there will be no end.*
> (NIV)

They were, therefore, expecting that the Messiah would reign over a kingdom that surpassed anything that had previously been known. He would reign in righteousness (cf. Isaiah 32:1) and would bring peace and justice. Furthermore, they believed He would reign internationally. These lines from a psalm written in 40 BC give us a good idea of contemporary longings:

> Raise up, O Lord, the King, the Son of David and gird him with strength
> To shatter unrighteous rulers and purge Jerusalem from the Gentiles.
> (The Seventeenth Psalm of Solomon)

The Jews were awaiting a Messiah who would liberate them from Roman subjugation.

It is onto this scene that Jesus walks – and the Jews don't know what to make of Him. Even soldiers sent to arrest Him return empty-handed, and when questioned, their response is: *'Never has a man spoken the way this man speaks.'*[3] Lepers are cleansed; the lame leap; the blind see; the deaf hear; five thousand are fed with a few loaves. Suddenly one greater than Moses is here, and in John 6, interestingly at the time of Passover – the celebration of Israel's liberation from Egyptian subjugation under the leadership of Moses – we read that they tried to force the issue and make Jesus king. In the same way that David had suddenly turned up one day, bringing food for his brothers in the army, could this Jesus be the one who would realise all their expectations? When Simon Peter had uttered his declaration, *'You are the Christ, the Son of the living God',* Jesus had responded:

> *'Blessed are you, Simon Barjona, because flesh and blood did not reveal this to you, but My Father who is in heaven.'*

Subsequent conversations, however, reveal that even the disciples' understanding of the coming Kingdom was very different from Jesus' vision. We remember how the mother of James and John asked, *'Command that in Your kingdom these two sons of mine may sit one on Your right and one on Your left',*[4] and how those same two disciples wanted to call down fire from heaven on a Samaritan village which did not welcome Jesus.[5] Jesus, on the other hand, commands them to love their enemies, to turn the other cheek in the face of assault by an enemy and to carry his cloak not just one mile but two … All this did not fit with their concept of a Messiah who would liberate them from their enemies. It is following Simon Peter's confession of Jesus' true identity that we are told:

> *From that time Jesus began to show His disciples that He must go to Jerusalem, and suffer many things from the elders and chief priests and scribes, and be killed, and be raised up on the third day.*
> (Matthew 16:21)

Everything within Peter cries out that this must not be so, but he and the other disciples must learn that it is not as they thought: they need to revise their expectations of who the Messiah is and what He has come to do. Almost every modern endeavour to dramatise the story of Jesus, such as the musical *Jesus Christ Superstar*, portrays Him as a man who bursts vibrantly onto the scene but then loses His way and finally disappears in obscurity. But Jesus did not lose His way. Jesus never took His eyes off the Kingdom. Jesus knows that He is going sit on David's throne, but first He must face the cross.

On the Day of Pentecost Peter proclaims:

> *'Men of Israel, listen to these words: Jesus the Nazarene, a man attested to you by God with miracles and wonders and signs which God performed through Him in*

your midst, just as you yourselves know – this Man, delivered over by the
predetermined plan and foreknowledge of God, you nailed to a cross by the hands of
godless men and put Him to death.'
(Acts 2:22–23)

He then quotes from Psalm 110, which is the most quoted Old Testament verse in the
New Testament:

'*The Lord said to my Lord:*
"*Sit at My right hand,*
Until I make Your enemies a footstool for Your feet."'
(Acts 2:34–35)

Now Peter knows who Jesus is – He is the Lord, who sits enthroned at the Father's right
hand in heaven. This is apostolic preaching. Apostolic preaching proclaims the Lordship
of Christ.

Having declared that '*God has made Him both Lord and Christ – this Jesus whom you*
crucified', Peter then tells the listening crowds that they need to repent. Very often we
personalise repentance, and perhaps there is nothing wrong with that, but I believe that
when Peter spoke about repentance in Acts 2 he had something very specific in mind. The
Jews needed to change their thinking about who the man they had crucified actually was.
They had been wrong about Jesus Christ. He is the King of Glory and is now seated on a
throne. Apostolic preaching is centred in who Jesus Christ is. We may have many relevant
and helpful things to say about the personal needs of those to whom we are preaching, but
apostolic preaching focuses on the necessity for people to change their mind about who
Jesus Christ is. The big issue for each one of us – which is as relevant today as it was then –
is: who is Jesus Christ? Interestingly, the apostles were proclaiming the gospel in a world
in which the current world leader, Augustus Caesar, was calling himself, among other
things, 'the saviour of the world' and the 'son of god'. They went out proclaiming that
Jesus is the Saviour of the world; He is the Son of God; He is the Lord. He had not fulfilled
the Old Testament prophecies in the way that had been expected by sitting on a tangible
throne in the city of Jerusalem, but nevertheless He *had* fulfilled them. He had gone
through the heavens and is now seated on a much bigger throne. If we want to be a truly
apostolic Church, we must preach and declare what the first apostles preached and
declared.

Look at the opening verses of Romans 1:

Paul, a bond-servant of Christ Jesus, called as an apostle, set apart for the gospel of
God, which He promised beforehand through His prophets in the holy Scriptures,
concerning His Son, who was born of a descendant of David according to the flesh,

211

who was declared the Son of God with power by the resurrection from the dead, according to the Spirit of holiness, Jesus Christ our Lord, through whom we have received grace and apostleship to bring about the obedience of faith among all the Gentiles for His name's sake, among whom you also are the called of Jesus Christ...
(Romans 1:1–6)

So often in the past I have jumped straight down to Romans 1:16 where Paul declares, *'For I am not ashamed of the gospel, because it is the power of God for the salvation of everyone who believes'*, and failed to grasp the important truths that he is expressing in these opening verses. Note that he says: *'the gospel of God, which He promised beforehand through His prophets in the holy Scriptures, **concerning His Son**'*.[6] The first apostles preached about what had been prophesied in the Old Testament. They preached about the enthronement of the Messiah. With our historic Anglican Church seeming to be on the verge of disappearing into oblivion, so often nowadays the question is being asked, 'Has the future got a Church?' But I believe the question we need to be asking is, how was the Church born? And that had nothing to do with Henry VIII! The Church was born on the Day of Pentecost. Peter tells us that it came about as a result of what was promised by the prophets. It came about as a result of what God said would happen. Like Peter, Paul makes immediate reference to David's throne. Jesus is the one descended from David and, although on earth He was the Son of God in weakness – He was beaten and crucified and died in weakness – now He is *'Son of God with power'* by the resurrection from the dead (and some have said this phrase could almost be hyphenated 'the-Son-of-God-with-power'). In Psalm 2 the Messiah is called *'My Son'* (v. 7). He is the appointed King; He is the reigning King promised by God. Whether we are talking about Acts 2, the first time the apostles ever preached, or about Romans 1, apostolic preaching concerns Jesus. The testimony of the Church is that we are witnesses to His resurrection. We are here to tell the world that Jesus is alive. The coming of the Holy Spirit in power proves that Jesus is alive because a dead Messiah could not give the Holy Spirit to anyone.

THE OBEDIENCE OF FAITH

In Romans 1 Paul continues his opening statement by declaring that *'we have received grace and apostleship to bring about the obedience of faith among all the Gentiles for His name's sake'*. The goal of apostolic preaching is to bring about the obedience of faith. Apparently the song most requested at funerals is Frank Sinatra's 'I Did It My Way'. These five short words encapsulate the root of all sin. Adam could have sung it as he was thrown out of the Garden. The world is disobedient; we are children of disobedience. But God wants to call us back to obedience rooted in faith.

When Satan tempted Adam, he undermined his faith by saying,

> *'You surely will not die! For God knows that in the day you eat from it your eyes*
> *will be opened, and you will be like God, knowing good and evil.'*
> (Genesis 3:4–5)

Adam and Eve became disobedient because they did not believe that God wanted the best for them. Satan undermined their confidence in God's love by suggesting that He was withholding something from them, since they had the potential to be like gods, making their own decisions and doing things their own way. The problem of the human race is not so much 'sins' (plural) as 'sin' – wanting to do things our way, to make our own choices, thinking we know best, not trusting that our heavenly Father desires the best for us. In short, our problem is unbelief. Paul declares that the call and grace of apostleship is to turn people around: to bring about the obedience that is rooted in faith. It is no longer about imposing laws, about saying, 'You must not do this': it is about setting people free to choose God's way for themselves. Grace teaches people to say no. It sets them free to believe that God knows what is best. And that is what we want in our churches: we want people who are obedient because of faith.

God does not want people to do what is right because they are not allowed to do a certain thing, sleep around for example, all the while believing in their hearts that they are missing out. That is obedience rooted in the rule 'You are not allowed to . . .'. God wants obedience that is based on faith – that is based on believing that God knows best and wants what is best for me. He wants people who will say, 'God, I really believe You know what You are talking about. I believe that You are utterly right.' The gospel of grace sets people free to make choices from the inside. It is a thorough revolution.

This is especially true when such obedience is demonstrated not just by isolated Christians but by a community of believers who, knowing they have been snatched out from a rebellious world and made new from the inside, choose to obey by faith. Truly apostolic ministry will raise up grace-filled churches that want God's way because they are persuaded it is the best way. Apostolic ministry says that the letter kills but the Spirit gives life.[7] We are not under law, we are under grace. Thus, apostolic preaching has to do with releasing people from bondage to rule-keeping as a way of relating to God. Just imposing rules on people does not bring about a community of faith that celebrates freedom. Apostolic preaching brings about a community of faith that *wants* to be obedient because we trust that God knows best. It comes from an understanding of His inner working within us. Paul says that he has received *'grace and apostleship to bring about the obedience of faith among the Gentiles'*. He knows he is anointed and gifted to do it. He believes it will take place through his ministry.

'CHRIST IN YOU, THE HOPE OF GLORY'[8]

The expectation of the Jews was that material structures, such as the temple, and physical places, such as Jerusalem, had a central and fundamental role to play in their worship. The temple was one of the great wonders of the ancient world. It was a holy place to which the Jews came to worship. But one day, when the disciples draw Jesus' attention to its magnificence, He replies:

> *'Do you see these great buildings? Not one stone will be left upon another which will not be torn down.'*
> (Mark 13:2)

In his conversation with the woman at the well, in the context of a discussion about whether people should worship at Jerusalem or Samaria, Jesus says:

> *'Woman, believe Me, an hour is coming when neither in this mountain nor in Jerusalem will you worship the Father.'*
> (John 4:21)

Both are extraordinary answers. Any one of us who had been a bystander at that conversation by the well would have been sure we knew what Jesus would say next. With all our knowledge of the Old Testament we would be convinced that He would answer 'Jerusalem'. But neither the temple nor Jerusalem is relevant any more. God has moved on. Paul says, *'you are a temple of God'*.[9] What was previously hidden has now been revealed. This is Holy Spirit-inspired apostolic teaching. Jerusalem was no longer a holy place, any more than Sinai was a holy place. Sinai was called the holy mountain when God was there, when His fire was on it, but God moved on. Now God has moved on from Jerusalem. He has moved on from the temple. Where is He then? He is in each one of us. We are a temple of the Holy Spirit.

The writer of Hebrews says,

> *For here have we no continuing city, but we seek one to come.*
> (Hebrews 13:14 KJV)

This is the reason why members of the early Church sold off their land. They knew it wasn't about a piece of land, but about an eternal city. They sold off their land so that they were in a better position to obey Jesus' command to go into all the earth and preach the gospel.[10] They understood that God wants a people from every tribe, every tongue, every nation and every people. This is apostolic teaching.

214

A Supernatural Community

Let us imagine for a moment what the dynamics must have been in those early churches which were coming into being as a result of Paul's preaching. Both Jews and Gentiles were being saved and together they were working out their godliness. The Jews had always known that it was their destiny to be a blessing to all the nations of the earth and for centuries proselytes had become Jews, but it had always been people coming to the God of Abraham, of Isaac and of Jacob. The Jews thought they knew what God liked: He liked the Sabbath kept, He liked certain foods to be eaten, He liked people to worship at the temple. Gentiles who came to faith needed to learn what God liked. But apostolic preaching blew all this apart. Paul declares:

> *There is neither Jew nor Greek, there is neither slave nor free man, there is neither*
> *male nor female; for you are all one in Christ Jesus.*
> (Galatians 3:28)

This is radical; it is revolutionary – both from the perspective of the Old Testament and that of the world in which the first believers lived. One day is no longer above any other; there is no longer any need to be circumcised; all foods are permissible. People no longer come into Israel: they come into the very family of God. We think we have difficult issues to overcome in our churches, but imagine the huge differences between converted Jews and converted Gentiles coming together to worship God. Apostolic preaching says we are all one together in a supernatural community.

The Church is breathtakingly wonderful. It is a new community such as has never before existed on the earth, made up of Jew and Gentile; male and female; Greek and Jew; slave and free: knit together in love, full of the presence of the Holy Spirit – a new creation in the earth. That, Paul preaches, is what the Church of God is.

Nearly all the ethical teaching in the New Testament is about how the people of God should act towards one another. The New Testament does not simply say, 'Be loving': it says: 'Love one another'. It does not say: 'Be gentle': it says, 'Be gentle to one another'. In fact it contains over forty 'one anothers'. There is a lifestyle appropriate to the supernatural nature of this new community. It corporately is a temple of the Holy Spirit. God is among us and together we can be a city set on a hill that cannot be hid. Now, of course, outside of the house of God we will also be kind and gentle, but the burden of New Testament ethics is that the church is a community with a totally new lifestyle. We are kind to one another; we forgive one another; we pray for one another; we confess our faults to one another; we don't devour one another; we don't lie to one another; we speak the truth in love to one another; we build one another up in our most holy faith. Why? Because we are a special holy people; we are a royal priesthood, a holy nation; we are God's own people.

Apostolic preaching builds community. We have got to help our fragmented society build people into community. Family life is so broken. We have a housing problem in this country but the population is going down, not up. We have a problem because marriages are splitting up and children no longer want to live with their parents. But the Church knows how to gather. Forgive one another, love one another, have mercy on one another, become part of the community.

It is instructive to notice how Luke describes the large numbers converted on the Day of Pentecost. He says, *'and that day there were **added** about three thousand souls'*.[11] He does not say that three thousand people asked Jesus into their hearts – no, they were added to the community of believers. When I got saved, I gave up all my friends because all we did together was sin – that was our lifestyle. I went to the local Baptist church, which was a very good church, but at the end of the service they would say, 'See you next Sunday.' That was no good to me – I had just lost my life. I needed a community. The church has got to be a community. We have got to know one another, be in and out of one another's homes, have fellowship together, share our lives together, meet one another's material needs: we need to be an alternative society that people can join. On the Day of Pentecost, Peter preached, 'Leave this wicked generation and be added to our community.' As a result of his preaching three thousand people were added and learned the values of the community.

There is quite a lot of talk these days about the need to preach a complete gospel, and the inadequacy of some preaching is being challenged. Although I am sure that those behind this campaign are motivated by the highest of motives, namely that people should get properly saved, I feel the premise on which it is based is wrong in as much as people get saved by fragments of truth. For example, they may just pick up a crumpled tract or watch something on television and get saved. I ask myself, how much of the gospel did I hear on the day I got saved, and the truth is I don't remember. The fact of the matter is that I was blind, but now I see. The truth was preached and suddenly I saw the light. I believe that what makes Christians properly whole is the health of the body to which they belong. We take on the family likeness; as Paul said, *'You became imitators of us'*.[12] The crucial question is, is the church to which we belong worth imitating? More important than guaranteeing that the gospel we preach contains every detail in it, is ensuring that the community we are building, the church, has such a life quality about it that it is provocative. Its difference strikes those who come into it. They say, 'Oh, I see you don't gossip here. Oh, I see you walk in the fear of God ... You pay your bills ... You are loyal to one another ...' They begin to learn the family values. It is not all learnt in a day, but over time as the life of the community is lived together. Of course, we want to be as thorough as we can in our preaching of the gospel but the biblical emphasis is the community.

Many of the biblical commands we take to be addressed to us as individuals are in fact in the plural in the Greek and as such are addressed to the community of the church.

English is confusing in this regard, as 'you' can be both singular and plural. I was told by a Scandinavian man, to whom I was talking about this, that their Bible makes this corporate aspect much clearer. Thus, a command like 'Be filled with the Spirit', which I have always taken to be my personal responsibility, is actually in the plural form addressed to the community. We are to be a Spirit-filled community. Our life together is to be flooded, energised, by the Holy Spirit. The Church is the heart and hub of apostolic preaching. It is the passion of apostolic preaching. We work out our godliness within the community of the church.

THE BIG STORY

Apostolic preaching understands that world history is in the hands of the people of God. This is so important for us because today there is no longer any meta-narrative. We are the post-modern generation. We no longer believe that the human race is getting better. We have given up on the big stories of the past such as evolution and progress. We no longer believe there is a purpose, a meaning: nothing really matters any more. People should do whatever they like.

But, beloved, as believers we have not just found out how to get right with Jesus: we have discovered the Big Story. We know there is a purpose, a plan, behind the world. We know that it began when God promised Abraham,

> '*I will multiply your descendants as the stars of heaven, and will give your*
> *descendants all these lands; and by your descendants all the nations of the earth*
> *shall be blessed . . .*'
> (Genesis 26:4)

It progressed through the great kingdom manifestation of glory during the reign of David until eventually another David came in fulfilment of the Old Testament prophecies, and now He is enthroned on high. This is the great story of history. It is very important that faith does not become just 'Jesus and me'. Apostolic doctrine blows the thing wide open and says there is a great, great plan. God is on the move and the Church is at the heart of history.

It will soon be impossible for people to reduce Christianity down to a 'western religion'. A breathtaking recent statistic reveals that there are now more churches in India than there are in America. The centre of gravity of the Church in the world today is in the southern hemisphere where thousands of churches are coming to birth. Moreover, in the not-too-distant future we may see hundreds of thousands of missionaries pouring out of China so that no longer will Christianity be able to be equated with western imperialism. God's rule is increasing.

The apostles preached a huge message. Their preaching caught the churches up in world mission. They reminded the churches of their identity as the light of the world.

217

They freed them from becoming domesticated, from being shut in. They reminded them that we are here to change the nations; that we are here to bring in the Kingdom.

It has been said that the Bible is the tale of two cities. On the one hand, there is Babylon, that great and arrogant city which says, 'We will build without God.' Babylon is the personification of worldliness and it will one day be judged for its rebellion and indifference to God. On the other hand, there is the holy city of Jerusalem that will come down out of heaven like a bride. The book of Joel speaks about *'multitudes in the valley of decision'*.[13] Being a Christian is not just a question of inviting Jesus to live 'in my 'heart', it is about deciding which city I want to live my life in. The early Church lived in the church and went out each day into the world. We tend to live in the world, and occasionally go to church. We must build up the wonder of the church. We must build a wonderful community based on Jesus as Lord and flood it with the Spirit, so that we live in the knowledge that we are not under law but under grace, so that we obey from the heart by faith, really knowing that God is for me, comprehending grace not law. To such a city the people of our world will be attracted.

NOTES

1. Unless otherwise stated, Scriptures in this chapter are taken from the New American Standard Bible.
2. See Matthew 16:13ff.
3. John 7:46.
4. Matthew 20:20ff.
5. Luke 9:51ff.
6. My emphasis.
7. 2 Corinthians 3:6.
8. Colossians 1:27.
9. 1 Corinthians 3:16.
10. E.g. Barnabas, Acts 4:36–37.
11. Acts 2:41, my emphasis.
12. 1 Thessalonians 1:6.
13. Joel 3:14.

Chapter 17

GIVING OURSELVES TO THE WORD AND PRAYER

Terry Virgo

ACTS 2–13

The New Testament Church was characterised by a strong emphasis on prayer. Reading through the pages of the book of Acts it is impossible to come to any other conclusion. The centrality of prayer is unavoidable. In Acts chapter 2 we read that the fellowship of believers devoted themselves to, among other things, *prayer*. Prayer was central to their life together as a community:

> *They devoted themselves to the apostles' teaching and to the fellowship, to the*
> *breaking of bread and to prayer.*
> (Acts 2:42)

Some people no doubt take the view that prayer meetings are boring places to be. Leaders often struggle to gather people together to pray for this very reason. But prayer meetings in the early Church do not appear to have been boring at all. In fact, the book of Acts reveals that their prayer gatherings were always connected with action and were dynamic events, rather than boring ones.

Acts shows us that the first believers were *constantly* in prayer. Whenever a challenge or crisis presented itself, they prayed until God gave them a breakthrough.[1] On the Day of Pentecost the disciples gathered in an upper room to pray and were visited by the Holy Spirit. Not long after that momentous day the disciples were told they could no longer freely go about preaching about Jesus (Acts 4). The elders and teachers of the Law in Jerusalem had discussed among themselves what the disciples were doing and had come to the decision, *'to stop this thing from spreading any further among the people, we must warn these men to speak no longer in this* [Jesus'] *name.'*[2]

The disciples' response to this was not one of despair, but *prayer*. They gathered together and started to pray, beginning with the words, *'Sovereign Lord . . .'*.[3] The word translated 'sovereign' is *despotēs* in the original Greek, from which we get the English word 'despot', denoting one in complete authority. Faced with apparently impenetrable opposition and hostility, the disciples appealed immediately to a 'higher' authority.

The centrality of prayer is something that must also characterise our modern churches. Our own church in Brighton has seen how important it is to engage in prayer to receive a breakthrough. At one point our church wanted to take over some industrial premises, but we were told we couldn't do it. We decided that we needed to appeal to a higher authority – to ask God, and to pray and pray and pray until we saw that decision reversed. God is the same today as He was in the disciples' day – He hears the prayers of His people and is well able to change circumstances on our behalf.

THE DISCIPLES' COMMITMENT TO THE WORD AND PRAYER

In Acts 6 we notice an interesting verse. The disciples were coming under criticism because others expected them to be more 'hands on' in their ministry to the poor. But the disciples responded by saying, *'It would not be right for us to neglect the ministry of the word of God in order to wait on tables'* (v. 2). Instead they appointed seven other Spirit-filled believers saying, *'We will turn this responsibility over to them and will give our attention to prayer and the ministry of the word'* (vv. 3–4).

It was part of the fruit of their incredible success that they were seeing thousands saved. Among those being added to the church were many poor and needy people. It is quite possible that there were many younger new believers who had been disowned by their Jewish parents for claiming Jesus as the Messiah, and who were now homeless as a result. There were also widows, and numerous other needy people within the community. Yet amid these new challenges and social concerns, the disciples were very clear about their calling. They could not afford to be personally involved with all of these needs – primarily, they had to be devoted to the Word of God and to prayer.

This presents a huge challenge to those who are in ministry. The needs and demands of others so often compete to shape our lives. More often than not, these needs seem perfectly valid. As a leader you think to yourself, 'These are good people; I want to serve them; these people are the fruit of my ministry – the people that I am responsible for.' But the apostles did not allow others to dictate how their time would be spent. 'We can't allow that,' they said. 'We will appoint others to look after these good people.' The apostles chose Stephen, Philip and five others, all of whom were said to be full of the Holy Spirit and wisdom, whilst they themselves focused on their number one priority: prayer and the Word of God. It was their apostolic priority.

The centrality of prayer presents a challenge for every one of us – not just those who are leaders. Often we see prayer as a preliminary matter – something that we do *before* we get on with the 'real thing'. But to the apostles, prayer *was* the real thing, the main focus. Throughout the ensuing pages of Acts, prayer is constant:

- In Acts 7 when Stephen is martyred, he is praying and the Bible says, *'his face became like the face of an angel'.*
- In Acts 9 when God tells Ananias to go and visit Paul, Ananias is very reluctant to go – until, that is, the Lord says that Paul is praying. Samuel Chadwick said that, 'Prayer is the privilege of sons, the mark of sonship.' This persuades Ananias to go to Paul.
- In Acts 10 the breakthrough for Gentiles comes when Peter is praying, falls into a trance, and has an encounter with God in the context of prayer. The Gentile household of Cornelius is saved as a result and this is the beginning of the gospel advancing into the Gentile world.
- In Acts 12 Peter is in prison. The church reacts by gathering together to pray. They didn't protest outside the prison with placards: 'Release Peter now!' or 'Killing Stephen was enough!' – their first thought was *to pray*. Would that be our immediate response? Do we have that much confidence in prayer?
- In Acts 13 the believers are praying, fasting and ministering to the Lord. That is one of the ways in which they proceeded – they set times aside to fast and pray over specific issues. Out of those times came results like Paul and Barnabas being released into apostolic ministry.

JESUS MODELLED A LIFE OF PRAYER

How did the disciples learn the importance of the place of prayer in ministry? Simply because the Twelve had spent three years with Jesus. They had watched Jesus, they saw His emphases, they lived around Him and watched His style; they became His *disciples*, and the whole point of being a disciple is that you become increasingly like the person who disciples you. Jesus' life was characterised by prayer and the disciples' lives would develop this same characteristic.

Mark 1:35 says,

> *Very early in the morning, while it was still dark, Jesus got up, left the house and went off to a solitary place, where he prayed.*

Before anyone else in the house was up, Jesus was already in prayer. At His baptism, Jesus was praying.[4] While He was doing so, the heavens opened and the Holy Spirit descended upon Him. There are numerous other examples that Jesus was a man who prayed constantly. I will cite just a few here:

In Luke 5 great crowds had gathered, but Jesus withdrew to pray. Here we see Jesus modelling the behaviour that the disciples mirrored in Acts 6. Though there were vast crowds demanding His attention, Jesus did not allow them to dictate His actions or affect His lifestyle. Rather than do what was popular, He obeyed His Father and quietly withdrew.

In Luke 6:12 we read that Jesus prayed all night. It was the night before He chose the twelve apostles who would remain closest to Him throughout His ministry. One might think, 'Why did He need to pray about that so much – He is divine, isn't He?' This is the mystery of Christ's humanity and His deity. All we know is that He decided to pray all night.

In Luke 9 we see Jesus praying again. Verse 18 is unusual because it says that Jesus was praying in private – yet His disciples were with Him. After some time praying, He asked them, '*Who do you say I am?*', to which Peter replies, '*The Christ of God*' (v. 20). From this we can draw the conclusion that Jesus must have been praying *for* the disciples, because in the context of His prayers, they received *revelation*. Once again Jesus presents an excellent model for those who are pastors. Like the apostle Paul we should be able to assure the people under our care that we are praying for them continually.[5] Jesus was praying earnestly for His followers. When they saw and understood that He was the Christ, He must have prayed, 'Thank You, Father, You have revealed it to them.' God broke through in the disciples' lives because Jesus was praying.

Later in Luke 9 we read of Jesus' transfiguration before Peter, John and James, again in the context of prayer. This highlights the potential of prayer to have the power to transform us. In 2 Corinthians 3 Paul tells us that as we behold Jesus, we ourselves are being transformed – changed into His likeness from one degree of glory to another by the power of the Holy Spirit. Effectively we are *transfigured* – it is the same Greek word that is used to describe both experiences. So, for us praying should never simply be a matter of going through lists of requests: 'Dear God, please help this person; please help that person . . .'. Prayer is not *worrying aloud!* Prayer is about beholding the glory of God, and at the same time being *transformed* by His glory.

In Luke 11 we see that eventually the disciples approached Jesus and asked, 'Teach us to pray.' It should be our personal goal so to exemplify a life of prayer that people will approach us and say, 'Could you teach me to pray like that?' The disciples saw the incredible fruit that was produced by Jesus' prayer life and they wanted to know how He did it. As always, He provided them with a simple yet incredibly effective model to imitate.

There are so many examples of Jesus modelling prayer for our benefit. In Gethsemane He cried out loudly and prayed with tears. Jesus was battling. He knew that prayer was powerful and not merely a duty. We too must be persuaded that it is powerful and effective.

Jesus said in Luke 18:1 that men '*should always pray and not give up*'! I love that last phrase. It is so simple. It answers every question. Even if you find prayer difficult, *don't give up!* Jesus said, '*Ask and it will be given to you; seek and you will find; knock and the door will be opened to you. For everyone who asks, receives*'.[6] Jesus is giving us helpful inspirational teaching, telling us the important place of prayer.

THE IMPORTANCE OF PRAYER IN PREACHING

Reading through his various epistles, one notices that the apostle Paul's regular method of communication is to set out the details of a doctrine, then to pray for his readers, and finally to urge them to respond. We need to be like that also. When we are called to preach, we should not just be praying that we will be able to deliver our message well, but also that the people listening will receive revelation from God concerning the message. Rather than simply delivering a 'good' sermon, we want God to change people inwardly and affect their lives by His Spirit. It is important that in our praying we shift the focus away from ourselves and on to others.

I remember an incident that occurred years ago when David Pawson was the minister of Guildford Baptist Church at Millmead. At that time he was probably the most prominent preacher in this country, phenomenally well thought of and with a magnificent Bible teaching ministry. I was asked to go and speak at Millmead, and I was scared out of my life! As I drove to the church, I was thinking, 'Oh God, help me ... save me ... let me live!' I went on like this for some time until I felt God say to me, 'Get off the road!' I pulled over and continued to pray, when I felt God say to me, 'What about the people?' I thought, 'Well, what about the people? Just get me through this God!' But the Lord said to me, 'Do you care about the people?' I thought, 'If I'm honest, not a lot, no.' I really hadn't thought about them at all. God said to me, 'Pray for the people.' So in that lay-by I started praying and stayed there for about fifteen minutes, just praying for the people of David's church. When I had finished I felt calm in my spirit. I realised that I didn't need to be overawed or taken up with myself and how I would perform, I just needed to care for the people and about what God was wanting to do for them.

Jesus showed us that divine intervention in some mysterious manner is conditioned on believing prayer. It is for this reason that prayer is set forth as the chief task of the believer. What an amazing thing! How much more important, then, is it for those of us who are servants of God in the context of ministry? Martin Luther said, 'As it is the business of tailors to make clothes, and of cobblers to mend shoes, so it is the business of Christians to pray.' That is our calling. That is what we are meant to be doing.

OVERCOMING HINDRANCES TO OUR PRAYER LIFE

Since prayer surrounding our ministry in the Word is so vital, we need regularly to examine whether we are as devoted to prayer as we should be. If our prayer life is flagging, it can be for a number of reasons:

A lack of a sense of purpose

It may be due to the lack of a sense of purpose. Sometimes in our praying we don't see the big picture: we are not gripped and captivated by the relevance of what God has done for us in Christ and our own calling to bring in the Kingdom. Whatever we are passionate about will thrill us and grip us. If prayer is not captivating us in this way, we need to ask God to help us, so that we will grow in our understanding of His promise regarding prayer – that the fervent, effectual prayer of a righteous man avails much. When we truly grasp the immense power and potential of prayer, then we will devote ourselves to it.

A lack of discipline

It can be a simple lack of discipline. We live in a very undisciplined society – an 'instant' generation where at the press of a button or two we can access everything we could ever want or need. It all comes so easily to us that it causes us to become undisciplined in spiritual matters as well. I believe God wants us to be disciplined in our approach to prayer. Spurgeon said, 'I must take care above all that I cultivate communion with Christ. Although that can never be the basis of my peace [*mark that, it is a very good statement*], nevertheless it shall be the channel of it.' We must never become legalistic in our prayers. As Spurgeon is saying here, our peace with God doesn't arise from the quality of our prayer life. We have peace with God because we are justified by faith in Christ. Focusing on anything other than faith in Christ for the basis of our right-standing before God leads to guilt and condemnation, and the erroneous idea that if we are 'good enough' God will be pleased with us. But we must not confuse legalism with godly discipline. As 1 Timothy 4:7 says, '*discipline yourself for the purpose of godliness*' (NASB).

Some people like to go for 'prayer walks' in order to spend time talking to God. Whilst I don't wish to discourage anyone from doing this – because it is wonderful to walk and talk with God – I believe that there is something very important in the instructions that Jesus gave about prayer. Jesus says, when you want to talk to the Father, go into a room and speak with Him in secret. To me that is a crucial part of praying. To prayer-walk is great, but seeking out a private space to spend time alone with God helps us to cultivate a prayer-discipline.

A lack of planning

John Piper says that one of the main reasons so many of God's children do not have a significant life of prayer is not so much because they don't want one, but because they don't plan for one. They do not have a specific time which they set aside for prayer. Each of us needs to be diligent about our routine of prayer according to the rhythm of our lives. Some people are 'morning' people, whilst others are 'evening' people. Those of us who know that they are useless in the mornings should plan to pray in the evening. We need to understand how we function best and work accordingly. During my life I have moved from one end of the spectrum to the other. I used to be more awake at night, but now I am much more alert in the mornings.

When I was at Bible College I had to share a room with another student. At the beginning of each new term the first thing I did was to look and see when he would be out of the room in a lecture, and when that coincided with me being free. I wanted to find out when our room was going to be empty. I was diligent about it, because I wanted to make sure that I had time for prayer planned in advance. This is something that we all need to work on – diligently to plan time for prayer. It isn't legalism. Legalism is doing something to try to impress God, to earn points. Spiritual discipline is entirely different.

A lack of clear objectives

In our prayer lives it is helpful to be clear on the things that God wants us to pray about. These could be simple things or seemingly unreachable targets. Part of the discipline of prayer is learning to develop 'prayer muscle'. There are times when sustained and persistent prayer is necessary until we feel as if we have pushed through some invisible barrier and gained some ground in faith. We will not be able to learn lessons like this without being disciplined and having objectives. Sometimes we need big targets to motivate us and to get us really praying.

We must 'work' at prayer to develop its discipline, and at the same time learn to depend on the Spirit. Sometimes it is difficult to find the energy for prayer. Some mornings we feel as though our soul is still in bed! Maintaining the discipline of regular prayer helps us to overcome those times. And when we persist with our praying, even though we don't feel like it, the Holy Spirit can use the time to re-energise us. Some people say they don't pray because they can't sense God's presence. But, instead of yielding to that sense we should choose to believe what God's Word says and thank the Lord for His presence with us anyway. God has promised never to leave us or forsake us – so, we can thank Him for that and choose to align ourselves with that truth. As we persist with this kind of praying we will find that God will strengthen our prayer life, and increasingly we will be praying with more faith, reliant upon God and His promises. A by-product of this will be that our view of the greatness of God will be expanded. We will see that God actually wants to answer our prayers.

STIMULATING THE FAITH OF OTHERS

One of the most important responsibilities of a leader is to stimulate the faith of others. It is one of the great callings of a preacher. But in order to stimulate the faith of others, our own faith must be genuine. We must have our own walk with God and our own experience of God – then we will be able to communicate to others the expectation that God will answer their prayers. Otherwise, we are just placing a *burden* of prayer on them. It is possible to hand out guilt to people, making them feel bad because we say they ought to pray more. But if we can say, 'I am enjoying the benefits of this and you can too', then we will be passing on a *blessing* instead of a *burden*.

As a young Christian I read A.W. Pink's book *The Sovereignty of God*. I felt it was a magnificent book, but having read it, I felt I couldn't pray for weeks afterwards. It presented such a big view of God's sovereignty that it blew me away. I thought, 'Well, if God is running the whole thing, then what can I really pray about?' It gave me a really big view of God, yet somehow undermined my prayer life. Not long afterwards someone said to me, 'You should have read Pink's *Elijah* too, because that would have got you praying again.'

It was actually another book that eventually got me praying again, namely the story of 'Praying Hyde'. It didn't answer my theological difficulties about sovereignty, but it helped me realise again that, although God is sovereign, somehow He has interwoven His purposes with our prayers. One of the most helpful books I've ever read on this topic is D.A. Carson's *A Call to Spiritual Reformation*,[7] which is his treatment of the prayers of Paul found in the epistles. Carson shows how Paul celebrates God's sovereignty, and then his prayer life somehow just locks into that. I found it very helpful as a practical guide to developing in prayer, in connection with the Word of God.

PRIORITISING PRAYER IN OUR CHURCHES

Paul says in 2 Corinthians 1:11,

> *as you help us by your prayers. Then many will give thanks on our behalf for the gracious favour granted us in answer to the prayers of many.*

Philip Hughes in his commentary on 2 Corinthians says, 'prayer is stressed over and over again in the New Testament as a vital prerequisite for the release and experience of God's power.'[8] If that is so, and I believe it is, then we must make prayer the number one priority, not only in our personal lives, but in the life of the church. As leaders of churches we need to encourage the saints to give themselves to prayer, both corporately and individually.

In his book *Destined for the Throne* Paul Billheimer simply comments that, 'Prayer is where the action is.'[9] He goes on to say that, 'Any church without a well-organised and systematic prayer program is simply operating a religious treadmill.' None of us wants that, either in our own lives or in the churches for which we are responsible.

Jim Cymbala, pastor of the Brooklyn Tabernacle in New York, commented that his church's prayer meetings were the spiritual 'barometer' of the church and the gauge by which God blessed them.[10] The story of what God has done at the Brooklyn Tabernacle as a result of their emphasis on prayer is both fascinating and challenging. How many of us would like God to evaluate our church by the quality of our prayer meetings? We *must* make prayer our priority!

Allow me finally to suggest some things that will help you to give prayer the pre-eminence it deserves:

▨ *Read books on prayer*

Reading about the experiences and perspectives of others can be both helpful and encouraging. There are so many books on prayer, but a few I would highly recommend are *Prayer: Key to Revival* by Paul Yongi Cho (Paternoster, 1985); *The Path of Prayer* by Samuel Chadwick (Cliff College Publishing, 1995); and *With Christ in the School of Prayer* by Andrew Murray (Whitaker House, 1985). It can also be stimulating to read the biographies of praying people like Hudson Taylor and George Müller – praying men and women who have proved God through prayer.

▨ *Read books on revival*

Because prayer is one of the most difficult disciplines of the whole Christian life, we need all the help we can get to fuel that fire. Personally, reading books on revival stirs me and motivates me afresh.

▨ *Find someone to pray with*

I thank God that I met a praying guy soon after I gave my life to Christ. He encouraged me by praying and inviting me to pray with him. It was so helpful to me early on in my Christian walk to pray regularly with another person. Find somebody who prays, who really believes in prayer, and get alongside them.

▨ *Persist through setbacks and difficulties*

Whatever happens, don't give up on prayer. Press through the difficult times. The difficult times are inevitable, but we must pursue prayer and not lose our confidence.

▨ *Remember the grace of God and the help of the Holy Spirit*

Recently I met with a small group of trainee leaders in my home and someone said, 'If there was just one thing you could say to us, what would it be?' Without hesitating I said straightaway, 'Keep yourself in the love of God.' I feel this is the most important thing for pastors to remember. We need to keep ourselves in the love of God and keep enjoying His favour towards us, because the demands of ministry are huge. The challenges of living in the modern world, and the kind of pastoral pain and problems we deal with are immense. Unless we learn to keep ourselves in the love of God, then we will find ourselves being shaped by other people's pain and problems – their disappointments, fears, frustrations and anger. Rather we must be shaped by the love of God, which happens as we spend time in His presence, enjoying His love and worshipping Him. For this reason it is vital that in our prayer we should give a good deal of time to worship – in praise and adoration, recognising how big, good and loving He is. We need to focus on God, His greatness, His attributes, His wonder and His majesty. When we receive a revelation of His love, faith grows. It is not so hard to ask big things when we have a big God. The more we are enjoying Him in our own experience, the easier it is to ask big things of Him. Let us give ourselves to the Word and prayer. Let our insights into Scripture come as a result of prayer; let Him enrich our comprehension of Scripture through prayer; let our preaching of the Word be bathed in prayer; and let the Word motivate our praying because the Word itself stirs our faith as we pray.

NOTES

1. Acts 1:14.
2. Acts 4:17.
3. Acts 4:24.
4. Luke 3:21.
5. E.g. Colossians 1:9.
6. Matthew 7:7–8.
7. D.A. Carson, *A Call to Spiritual Reformation: Priorities from Paul and His Prayers* (IVP, 1992).
8. Philip Edgcumbe Hughes, *II Corinthians* (Marshall, 1962).
9. Bethany House, 1996.
10. Jim Cymbala with Dean Merrill, *Fresh Wind, Fresh Fire* (Zondervan, 1997).

Chapter 18

PREACHING THE PROPHETS

David Pawson

The Bible is the record of the God who both acts and speaks within time and space through nature and nations. His words sometimes come in direct speech, in which He amazingly moves the air in such a way that people hear words, often described as thunder, but most of His words in the Bible come indirectly through spokesmen and women, through prophets and prophetesses.

The prophets of God were not just people who spoke for God but they were those who first of all heard from God. They received the message in one of two forms, either verbally in words or visually in pictures. When the message was delivered, sometimes it was simply spoken, sometimes it was written, and sometimes it was acted, as when Ezekiel buried his underwear, or Isaiah ran naked through the streets of Jerusalem, or Jeremiah wore a yoke. They spoke it, they acted it, they lived it and they wrote it. In order to be prophets these individuals needed two things: one was the word of God, giving them the knowledge of what God wanted to say, and the other was the Spirit of God, giving them the courage to speak, because it requires considerable courage to give a prophecy especially if it is going to be unpopular. The Bible distinguishes between true prophets and false ones. True prophets challenge people; false prophets comfort them. False prophets say, 'Peace, peace' when there is no peace, and this is one of the easiest ways of distinguishing between a true prophet and a false one.

However, as we preach the prophets, the most important truth we must understand is that they were part of history. The prophets were located in a particular time and at a particular place, and their message cannot be understood apart from that time and place. Their history, the history of the Jewish people, was 'His-story', and Bible history is really the story of what God did and what He said about what He did. He spoke in advance of

His deeds to tell His people what was to happen, and He spoke after His deeds to tell them why they had happened, so the words explain the deeds, and they belong together.

In looking at how the prophets were related to the history of Israel, I will divide the history of Israel into its rise and its fall. It took a thousand years for the people of Israel to rise from a tribe and a family to become an empire under David, but it took them only five hundred years to lose everything – and that is the tragic story of the Old Testament. At every point of that rise and fall there were prophets engaged in its drama. The Old Testament is, in fact, made up of a series of journeys: journeys into the Promised Land and journeys out of it again. The journeys began when Abraham went from Ur to Canaan, and the prophets of that crucial historical event were Abraham, Isaac and Jacob. They are called prophets in the Bible, but it is important to notice carefully that Joseph was not called a prophet: he was an interpreter of dreams. The next journey was of course from Egypt to Canaan, and the leading prophet of this period was Moses. At every point on those journeys, whether God was bringing them from Ur to Canaan or from Eygpt to Canaan, there were prophets to explain what God was doing.

Then we have two journeys out of Canaan. The first of these involved the ten Northern tribes under the name of Israel, who went out from Canaan to Assyria and were lost, and the prophets who spoke into their situation included Elijah, Amos and Hosea. Later, the two Southern tribes of Judah and Benjamin were taken off to Babylon, and here again there were a number of prophets who explained to the people why this was happening. The books known as 'the Prophets' contain the writings of the prophets associated with this exile from the Promised Land, speaking either before, during or after it. When I was given the subject 'Preaching the Prophets' it was of these prophets that I immediately thought. There are sixteen of them in our Bibles, or seventeen if Daniel is included. Unlike the compilers of our Scriptures, the compilers of the Hebrew Canon of Scripture did not consider Daniel to be a prophet, but rather an interpreter of dreams like Joseph. Thus, when we talk about 'the Prophets' we are talking about three major prophets (Isaiah, Jeremiah, Ezekiel) and Daniel and twelve minor prophets, all connected with the exile to Babylon.

THE PROPHETS' MESSAGE

The chart on the next page summarises the messages which the prophets brought. The prophets are sometimes called 'seers', because they had remarkable sight. They had hindsight about the past, insight about the present, and foresight about the future. This remarkable hindsight, insight and foresight gave meaning to the history of Israel. Most of their prophecies were about one Jewish nation – the descendants from Isaac, the child of Promise – and the Promised Land – the nation of promise. But they also had prophecies for other nations, principally the small nations lying around Israel and two large ones further away. The left-hand column of the chart contains information regarding the *time* and the *theme* of each of the prophets. The prophets appealed to the past, constantly

Chart summarising the prophets' messages

Time and theme	One 'Jewish' nation (promise)	Other 'Gentile' nations (proximity)
Appeal to the *past* **Recollection**	**Special redemption** *Appeal to:* Exodus from Egypt (Passover) Covenant at Sinai (Pentecost) Wandering in wilderness (Tabernacles) *Major themes:* Divine faithfulness Human faithlessness	**General revelation** *Appeal to:* Creation Conscience
Analysis of the *present* **Recrimination**	*Criticisms:* Idolatry (adultery) Immorality Injustice *Major themes:* Failure to love God Failure to love neighbours	*Criticisms:* Inhumanity (particularly to God's people) Failure to respect humanity
Anticipation of the *future* **Retribution**	*Near future:* Nature: droughts, locusts, earthquakes, etc. Nations: invasion, occupation, deportation	*Part 1:* Vengeance on Gentiles Vindication of Jews
Restoration	*Distant future:* Survival in exile Return to land Independence under king Government over nations	*Part 2:* Incorporation (into God's people)

recalling the people to what God had done for them: this I term **recollection**. In fact, the prophets talk as much about the past as about the future. I have given the name **recrimination** to what they had to say about the present: they were always criticising God's people for the state they were in, in the light of all that God had done for them in the past. They wanted the nation to understand how far they had fallen. When they anticipate the future and move into foresight, there are two almost contradictory themes: one is **retribution** – the bad news – and the other is **restoration** – the good news.

The prophets' appeal to the past, the recollection, is always based on the People of Israel's Exodus from Egypt (their escape from slavery), the covenant that God made with them at Sinai, and the wandering in the wilderness that followed. These three vital events from their past were enshrined in the three major feasts of the year: the Feast of Passover, the Feast of Pentecost and the Feast of Tabernacles. The two themes that the prophets kept reiterating as they appealed to the past were God's faithfulness and the people's faithlessness, their dreadful response to all that He had done for them through those long years of wandering bringing them at last to the Promised Land.

When they come to recrimination – their analysis of the present – the prophets major on three ways in which the people of God were at fault: their idolatry, which is always said to be adultery, their immorality, and their injustice to their own people. Amos in particular majored on injustice. Behind these charges the prophets were really saying that the people had failed to love God and had failed to love their neighbour – according to Jesus the two most important commands.

When the prophets anticipated the future, they looked first at the immediate future and then at the ultimate future. The immediate future was always bad news. They promised droughts, locusts, earthquakes and all kinds of natural disasters, and then, as the state of the nation worsened, they foretold that nations would come against them, invading and occupying the Promised Land, and deporting the people to distant lands as their slaves. This threat is found in almost every one of the prophets. Although their first anticipation of the immediate future was always disasters in nature and destruction caused by other nations, beyond that they consistently pointed forward to a time when there would be a restoration of Israel because God would never break His covenant. The people might break it, but God would never ever let them go. In every one of the prophets, even Jeremiah, there are these rays of sunlight piercing the clouds with the promise that one day national security and autonomy would be restored in their own Promised Land. Thus, the prophets anticipate a near future view which is generally bad news and a distant view of the future which is very good news.

As we have already seen, many of the prophets preached to their Gentile neighbours, and in fact some prophets like Obadiah and Nahum only preached to non-Jews. On these occasions the prophets did not appeal to a special redemption from Egypt, but rather they appealed to the God who had created them and had given them a conscience. In other words, God's prophets never blamed people for what they did not know. Instead of rebuking them for idolatry and immorality, the prophets criticised the other nations for their inhumanity, especially when cruel treatment was meted out to the children of God. For example, God through His prophets criticises the Assyrians for their sheer barbaric cruelty. God assumes that everybody knows better than to be unnecessarily cruel. Cruelty directed at God's people particularly hurt Him and that is because Israel was the apple of God's eye.[1] That is not a reference to a Cox's Orange Pippin, but to the grey iris of the eye, which looks just like an apple on end with the stalk in the middle and is the most sensitive part of the body. When anything – even a tiny speck of dust – touches that part of the eye, the eyelid clamps down to protect it. The word for 'eyelid' in Hebrew is usually translated in our Bibles as 'keeper'. *'The LORD is your keeper'*, for example, means 'The Lord is your eyelid'.[2] Anyone who touches the Lord's people touches the most sensitive part of Him, and He will protect His people.

In anticipating the future of Gentile nations, the prophets' message had two parts. First that God would take vengeance on the Gentile nations for their cruelty. This is a very relevant word for today. There will come a day when all cruelty, including terrorism, will be answerable to God. God also promised that there would be a public vindication of His people, the Jews. One day God will acknowledge publicly that the Jews are His Chosen People, and then the nations will know that they have been terribly mistaken in what they have done. I have stood in the cremation ovens of Auschwitz and seen the marks of human nails on the concrete walls as they tried to scratch their way out, when the poison gas was fed through the shower heads. I have been in the ghettos of Warsaw and in Treblinka where it was impossible not to walk on the three-feet-deep remains of thousands of Jews. One day God will vindicate His people. But the prophets also had some good news for the nations, namely that it was God's plan to incorporate the Gentiles into His Chosen People, and that one day there would actually be more Gentiles among their number than Jews.[3]

Having given a summary of the message of the prophets, and how it related to what was happening historically at the time, I now want to turn to what I consider the crux issue in preaching the prophets:

HOW DO WE APPLY THE PROPHETS' MESSAGE TODAY?

The prophecies of the Old Testament were given to Jews, not Christians; they were given to Israel, not the Church. So how do we preach them today?

My answer is that we cannot preach the prophets today without translating their message for a Christian audience. We need to think very carefully before we take a prophecy and preach that it applies to Christians today. To take just one aspect, when the prophets spoke of 'other nations', they were talking about pagan nations. Although Britain is now no longer a Christian nation in any real sense, it has a long Christian heritage. How do we take the prophecies given to Israel or the pagan nations and apply them to Britain? One glaring example is the frequent application of 2 Chronicles 7:14 to the British context:

> *'if my people, who are called by my name, will humble themselves and pray and seek my face and turn from their wicked ways, then will I hear from heaven and will forgive their sin and will heal their land.'*

Despite the fact that 'their land' is the Promised Land given by God to the Jewish people, this is the most popular verse today for prayer for our nation. It was, however, never intended for the United Kingdom. I use this as an illustration of how easily we pick up a word from the Old Testament and apply it to Britain or to the Church, without even thinking about what we are doing and without considering whether God intends us to do so. The prophets spoke to Jews not Christians; they spoke to Israel not the Church; and they spoke to pagan nations, not to Christendom.

The key issue for all preaching of the Old Testament is to understand what the real relationship is between the Old and the New Testaments. And unusual though it may seem, a fundamental part of the answer to the big question I have posed centres on how many covenants there are in the Bible. Through history and still today Christians have taken four different views on this matter.

There are those who say that there is one covenant running right through the Old and New Testaments, which they refer to as 'the Covenant of Grace'. This phrase actually never occurs in Scripture, but is a theological construct for the idea that from the beginning of time to its end there has only been and will only ever be one covenant between God and the human race. The strength of this position is that it establishes a strong sense of continuity between the Old and the New Testaments, as if a straight line runs through from Israel to the Church. This approach stresses, for example, the continuity between circumcision and infant baptism, and between the Jewish Sabbath and the Christian Sunday. In other words, there have been slight changes, but in essence it is the same covenant, and therefore the Old and the New Testaments are one continuous story.

At the opposite end of the spectrum are the 'dispensationalists'. This term has spread around the world through books like *The Late Great Planet Earth* by Hal Lindsay, and through the Scofield Bible. It is very common among Brethren and Pentecostals. One of its key ideas is that the Church will be raptured secretly years before Jesus returns. Dispensationalists believe that there are seven different 'covenants' in Scripture, or ways in which grace is dispensed.[4] Under each covenant the human race relates to God on an entirely different basis. Consequently, there is extreme discontinuity in the way the Old and the New Testaments are treated.

Most ordinary Christians believe there are two covenants. They simply know the terms 'Old' and 'New' Covenant without defining them in any particular way. They may think it means the Old Testament and the New Testament without troubling to examine the concept any further, and they would stress some continuity and some discontinuity – for example, they would put the Ten Commandments up on the church wall, but not the six hundred and three others.

My study of Scripture has led me to the conclusion that there are five covenants, and it is this understanding that enables me to discern where there is continuity between the Old and the New Covenant and where there is discontinuity. The first of the five covenants is

God's covenant with Noah, the Noahic Covenant, which was made with all the nations of the earth, that while the earth remains, seedtime and harvest, summer and winter will not cease.[5] God put a rainbow in the sky to remind not us but Him of His promise/covenant with Noah, and He has kept His promise to keep the human race alive. Then He made three covenants with the Jews, the first with Abraham, the second with the people of Israel through Moses, and the third with King David, that there would always be a king from his line on the throne of Israel. The fifth covenant in the Old Testament is the Messianic or the New Covenant set down in Jeremiah 31:

> 'This is the covenant I will make with the house of Israel
>   after that time,' declares the LORD.
> 'I will put my law in their minds
>   and write it on their hearts.
> I will be their God,
>   and they will be my people.'
> (Jeremiah 31:33)

So the New Covenant is a Messianic covenant, first for the Jews and then for Gentiles. We Gentiles have now come into that New Covenant, and for us it is commemorated not in Passover, Pentecost and Tabernacles but in the Lord's Supper. The acceptance of five covenants in the Old Testament leads to continuity because it gives us a way of reinterpreting the prophets' message for the Church today. Let us look again at the prophets' message in the terms I indicated earlier:

1. Recollection

The Messianic New Covenant excludes the Mosaic Old Covenant: that is why Christians are not under the Law of Moses. I am not under the Ten Commandments: I am under nine of them, because nine of them are repeated in the Law of Christ in the New Testament, but the Sabbath law is not. It is so important for us to realise that as Christians we are under a different covenant, for otherwise, if we are not careful, we can so easily fall again under the Law. I remember a young preacher who was at least consistent. In a sermon on tithing, he first taught all the blessings that God has attached to tithing, and then he went on to point out all the curses that will befall all those who do not tithe. As he did so, a hush came over the congregation. Explaining that the families of those who do not fulfil their obligation to tithe will be cursed to the third and fourth generation, he challenged his congregation, 'If you don't tithe, your great-grandchildren will suffer. Do you want that?' Afterwards I went up to him and said, 'That was wicked preaching. That was not Christian preaching.' I am constantly amazed at how many preachers lift prophetic words about tithing and Sabbath-keeping out of their context and apply them to Christians today, and thereby succeed in putting Christians under the Law again, a

Law which carries both blessings and curses. Malachi 3:10 is a classic example of a verse that is frequently taken out of context. We must be honest with Scripture. Personally, I can never teach tithing. I teach giving – sacrificial, proportionate, cheerful giving. I tell Christians that God doesn't want their money unless they *want* to give it. Therefore, if we are going to preach the prophets today, we must take their basic message and retranslate it for Christians and for the Church. Where the prophets' recollection of the past focused on the Exodus, our recollection of the past must focus on the death of Jesus. When Jesus appeared with Moses and Elijah on the Mount of Transfiguration we are told they discussed the exodus which He was about to accomplish in Jerusalem.[6] Our prophetic appeal must not be to the Sinai covenant but to the New Covenant in Jesus' blood and the exodus which He accomplished at Calvary.

2. Recrimination

When we, as we should, offer recrimination for betraying that covenant, we must not use the prophecies of the Old Testament to do so, but we must show people how they have betrayed the New Covenant – and that will involve very different sins from the ones we might otherwise point out to people. We are under a new law: the law of Christ, the law of the Spirit, the law of liberty in Christ Jesus; and it is that law that we must challenge Christians to keep, not the Mosaic Law.

3. Retribution

When we come to retribution, we have to ask: are all the curses to be left with Israel? It is very interesting to notice the paragraph headings inserted in the books of the Prophets in the King James Version. Where the prophets promise a curse, the heading says 'A curse on Israel'. Where they promise blessing, it says 'A blessing on the Church'. To my mind it seems terrible prejudice to take all the blessings from Israel and appropriate them for the Church, while apportioning all the curses to Israel. As preachers we must ask ourselves: how far do the sanctions of the Old Covenant apply to people in the New Covenant? Let me here grasp a nettle. The ultimate sanction for breaking the Old Covenant was to be removed from the people of God, and thus to be cut off from their God. God would discipline in many ways first but the ultimate threat was to be cast out and, although God always kept His covenant with the people as a whole, many individuals lost their place among His people. Can we apply that thinking to Christians? I believe we not only can, but should. It is striking that sanctions against Israel are repeated in the New Testament again and again. Take one example: two million people left Egypt, but only two entered Canaan; the rest perished in the wilderness. Paul, Jude and the writer of the letter to the Hebrews use that fact as a warning for Christians: Christians too may set off but never arrive; they may begin the Christian life but never finish. Paul could not be clearer in Romans 11 where, in the context of speaking about individual Jewish branches being broken off from the olive tree which is Israel, he says that the Gentiles have been grafted into the tree in their place, replacing some of the Jewish branches but not all of them. But then he goes on to urge against arrogance or complacency with these words:

> *But they were broken off because of unbelief, and you stand by faith. Do not be arrogant, but be afraid. For if God did not spare the natural branches, he will not spare you either. Consider therefore the kindness and sternness of God: sternness to those who fell, but kindness to you, provided that you continue in his kindness. Otherwise, you also will be cut off.*
> (Romans 11:20–22)

Paul's language is unequivocal. For me there is no way around the fact that a Christian can suffer in the same way that a Jew could and be cut off from God's people. The Jews were cut off because of their continued unbelief and the solemn warning to Christians is that they can be too. Frankly, in the light of that Scripture I cannot believe in 'once saved always saved'. Here is a sanction that should cause Christians to fear the Lord and fear breaking the New Covenant He has made with us in Christ.[7]

4. Restoration

As far as ultimate restitution or restoration is concerned, the Church has, as we have seen, regarded itself as the new Israel and has therefore appropriated to itself all the promises of blessing given to Israel in the Old Testament. But how does this 'replacement theology', as it is known, deal with all the many promises that God has given to the Jewish people, namely to bring them back finally to their own land, to give them their own kingdom under their own king again, to make them the head and not the tail of the nations, and to govern the nations from Jerusalem? There are five possibilities:

The first is deliberately to ignore these promises, and many preachers do just that on the grounds that they are all irrelevant. The fact that Israel has returned to her land, for example, is regarded simply as a political accident.

The second possibility is to say that these promises of ultimate restoration to Israel were conditional and have therefore been forfeited. Having broken the covenant and having lost her place as God's people, Israel has lost her right to the land, and her right to any future restoration.

Third, some say that all the promises of restoration were fulfilled when the nation of Israel returned from exile in Babylon. In fact, many of the promises of ultimate return to the land and restoration were made after this period and therefore are clearly yet to be fulfilled.

A fourth option is that all the promises of blessing were transferred under the New Covenant to the Church. However, those who hold this position are then forced to allegorise or spiritualise the promises. It is no longer possible to talk about a literal land, but only about vague spiritual blessing for the Church.

The fifth possibility is that the Old Testament promises will one day in the future be fulfilled, as indeed has already begun to happen. In this view, the return of Israel to her own land is regarded as a prophetic fulfilment of the promise of restoration. Although I recognise that this is a minority position today, it is the only one that seems to me to make sense of all the references. I believe that God is fulfilling these promises in our day and before our very eyes. I believe that one day we shall see Israel totally vindicated and that once again the King of Israel's Son of David will rule the nations. That is my hope for the future.

This possibility commits me to the belief that God has two peoples on the earth today: not just the Church, but also Israel.[8] Israel is still God's Chosen People. Romans 11 makes it very clear that God has a future for His people. One day He intends to save the Jewish people as a whole, and that will be like a resurrection. However, in Christ these two peoples become one new man, one new humanity.

One of the most exciting things that is happening in the world today is that more Jews are becoming believers in their own Messiah than ever before in history. There are now about fifty indigenous Israeli churches in the land of Israel. Last year, while my wife and I were in Jerusalem, we went out for a walk, and a taxi driver pulled up. Since there are now no tourists in Israel, the taxis are getting no business whatsoever. The taxi-driver asked hopefully, 'Can I take you somewhere?' I said, 'No, we are just going out for a walk.' But we decided to chat and in the course of our conversation, I said, 'You're a believer.' And he was. He took us to see where his fellowship met, which was in a kibbutz on the south side of Jerusalem. As he showed us the large public hall, he told us that 500 Israelis meet there to worship Jesus. This exciting development is not happening as a result of missionary work, but is occurring spontaneously. God has not finished with the Jewish people. It is God's intention to save them through their Messiah.

My belief in God's future purpose for Israel means that, when I come to the promises which speak of Israel's future, I don't just lift them out and say, 'This is a spiritual blessing for the Church', I say, 'This is our future': the future of the Christian and the Jew are interlocked. Jesus said, *'I have other sheep that are not of this sheep pen. I must bring them also.'*[9] There will be one flock, Jew and Gentile together, all saved by the blood of the New Covenant, and there will be one shepherd over them all. This knowledge makes Old Testament prophecy exciting for me.

I will finish with this: I was in New York with a few hours to spare, so I got a Yellow Taxi Cab to take me round and show me the sights. I asked him to let me off at the United Nations Building on the banks of the Brooklyn River. First I looked at something I wanted to see outside the front door. In the grass there is a huge granite rock, with inscribed upon it half a verse of Scripture which is the hope of the United Nations:

> *And they shall beat their swords into ploughshares, and their spears into pruning hooks; nation will not lift up sword against nation, neither shall they learn war any more.*

Then I joined a tour and was led around the building by a young woman in a blue uniform. It was very interesting but by the end of the tour I had not seen the thing I had come to see. I asked the guide to be allowed access to the room I wanted to see, which was not in her power to provide but, after much perseverance, she advised me to approach the security guard in the foyer. Again a long conversation ensued, but eventually he agreed to let me into the room for two minutes. Inside, I saw the god of the United Nations. I had heard about it but I had not been able to believe what I had heard. Now I could see it with my own eyes. The room was very dark but I could just see a circle of prayer stools and prayer mats, and in the middle the god of the United Nations. It is a big black block of iron, the size and shape of a coffin, on a pedestal. When I asked how it had come to be there I was told that when the United Nations' building first opened, the then Secretary General had questioned the absence of a prayer room, so one had hastily been installed. But then came the big debate about what to put in it. Not being able to reach agreement, they finally asked a sculptor to model something that would represent all the gods in the world. He modelled this big black block, painted with a matt finish so that it doesn't reflect anything: the individual is supposed to kneel down in front of it, look into its blackness and imagine his or her god in there. That is the god they pray to in the United Nations. I didn't know whether to weep or laugh. I thought of the half a verse of Scripture quoted outside the building and remembered that the beginning of the verse says,

> *When the Lord reigns in Zion, he will settle the disputes among the nations, and he will settle them with justice, and they shall beat their swords into ploughshares...*

Multilateral disarmament will follow the return of Christ. We are looking forward to a world of peace; a world where money is no longer spent on bombs and landmines, but spent on food and clothes; a world where wars have ceased; a world where peace is based on absolute justice for all. This is the world promised by the Old Testament prophets. God meant what He said and His words will one day come true.

NOTES

1. Zechariah 2:8.
2. Psalm 121:5 NKJV.
3. See, for example, Romans 9, where Paul quotes Hosea.
4. (1) *Innocence* – Adam to Fall; (2) *Conscience* – Adam to Noah; (3) *Promise* – Abraham to Moses; (4) *Law* – Moses to Christ; (5) *Kingdom* – David to Christ; (6) *Grace* – Pentecost to the Millennium; (7) *Kingdom* restored – Millennium to Eternal State.
5. Genesis 8:21–22.
6. Luke 9:31 (Greek *exodus*, literally 'out-way' or 'way out').

7. For more on this see *Once Saved Always Saved: A Study in Perseverance and Inheritance* (Hodder & Stoughton, 1996).

8. By 'Israel' I do not just mean the State of Israel or the people who live there but Jews the world over.

9. John 10:16.

Section Four

THE ANOINTING TO PREACH

. . . our gospel came to you not simply with words,
but also with power, with the Holy Spirit
and with deep conviction.

(1 Thessalonians 1:5)

Chapter 19

AUTHORITY IN PREACHING

Greg Haslam

Authority has little to do with our appearance, our background, our breeding, or even our age, but it has everything to do with our message, our confidence in God, our authenticity in lifestyle, the consistency with which we live, and, above all, our reliance on the Holy Spirit who brought us to this task. Throughout his ministry the great nineteenth-century Baptist preacher C.H. Spurgeon preached to crowds of thousands. However, there was one occasion when, at the age of eighteen, he preached to a handful of people at Isleham Ferry in Cambridge. In anticipation of huge numbers the deacons of the church had borrowed a large building but only seven came. Nevertheless, Spurgeon preached one of his very best sermons. By the evening there was no standing room in the place. I also remember reading about Peter Cartwright, the great circuit rider evangelist in the early 1800s in America, who went to conduct an evangelistic mission somewhere in the Mid-west. On the first night only one person – a one-eyed Presbyterian elder – turned up, but Cartwright preached his best for forty-five minutes. That elder went and told everyone in the district that it was the best sermon he had ever heard, and the next night the hall was overflowing. It was the beginning of a revival. There is something about such men of God. It may be indefinable, it may be intangible, but they are carriers of something which means that, no matter what adversity or discouragement they face, things change. Their preaching carries authority.

Once, while filling in a form for an insurance life policy, I was required to answer the question, 'What is your job?', to which I answered 'Christian minister'. There then followed the supplementary question, 'Is your job dangerous?' Of course, I wrote, 'No', but in answering in the negative I was lying! The Christian ministry can be very dangerous – very dangerous indeed! All hell is opposed to what we are doing. Although it is probably not wise to dwell on this matter too often, there is a contract out on all of our lives, if we did but realise it. However, whether our ministry actually is dangerous is determined by the issue of upon whose authority we are relying to do it. If it is only weak and human authority, then most probably it will be harmless; but if it is divine, and therefore disturbing authority, then our job will be very dangerous indeed. The business of preaching is to tell the church and the world what neither of them wants to hear. And that can get a person into deep trouble.

THE NATURE OF AUTHORITY

Authority has been defined as 'the power and the right to command change'. It is the right to command change in both belief and behaviour in the lives of those whom we are privileged to lead, in line with the will of God. Bernard Ramm expands on this definition by saying that authority is 'the right or power to command action or compliance, or to determine belief or custom, expecting obedience from those under authority and, in turn, giving responsible account for the claim to that right or power'. Such language is strange to us in the twenty-first century. One of the reactionary causes of suspicion towards, and resistance to, preaching in our day is that we live in a climate that is deeply suspicious, even rebellious, towards authority of any kind. As we are all well aware, autonomy, independence, self-will, self-direction, self-assertion and self-fulfilment are all highly prized within western culture today. Consequently, there has been incalculable loss of authority in every sphere, including, of course, the Church of Jesus Christ. Many leaders no longer know what it is to really lead God's people. Anyone who dares to exercise some degree of command or influence is often faced with such questions as, 'Who do you think you are talking to me like that?' or 'Where are you coming from here?' It is not so much 'Who says?' any longer, but rather the even more sassy, *'Says who?'*

Where authority has been merely traditional because it has been handed down through bishops and through a succession of leaders, or where it has been sentimental, so that we have had 'gooey' feelings about people in pulpits, or merely from historical precedent, it is understandable, and in fact good, that it should be questioned. However, if we are to see the effects we desire to take place in God's people through the ministries we exercise and through godly leadership, particularly through the agency of the preached Word, then it is imperative that we see a recovery of truly God-given authority in our ministry. The Greek words used in the New Testament for 'authority' (*exŏusia*) and 'power' (*dunamis*, from which we derive words like 'dynamic'), are in Scripture closely related in practice. Power is the ability to effect change, both in the circumstances around us and in the people who are connected with us. Authority is the permission or authorisation to use that power; it is a responsibility that has been delegated to an individual. In order to fulfil any ministry successfully, we need both power and authority. Yet we can be missing out on either one or the other, or even both. Authority without power is like a policeman confronting a gang of armed robbers outside a bank in the high street with a badge but no gun. Power without authority is like the hit man in that gang of robbers with a gun but no badge – highly dangerous. Both a badge and a gun are required. The idea and the ideal is that we have both a badge *and* a gun. We need authority *and* power in order to serve Jesus Christ effectively. The responsibility is given along with the enabling to back it up and make things happen.

As Christian ministers our authority implies that we have been given responsibility to a particular delegated sphere of God's concern, including the lives of the people in it and the geographic area in which they are placed. We are given a stewardship and we are accountable for how we perform that stewardship. We are accountable, in some senses, to other human authorities around us; we are not lone agents, we are not mavericks, we are not the Lone Ranger – 'Who was that masked man?'! However, in God's work our supreme accountability is to Him. It is an awesome thing to be given responsibility to have input into other people's lives with the most powerful weapon in the universe: words. We need to know that we have permission and authorisation to do so. Too many people are impertinent enough to step up into leadership, and even into a pulpit, without proper preparation or even the gifting to do so. Their words and spoken utterances lack power to effect the needed change and impact that God wants – and which such activities are supposed to see happen. 'Who sent you?' is a vital question to be asked of any preacher. We also need to ask: 'Why are you here?', 'Who or what is backing you up?', 'Who is owning what you say?' As I hope to show, the preacher's authority is a complex of several ingredients, all of which must be in place if he is to expect to see the appropriate power of God flowing upon him and through his ministry.

Erasmus, the sixteenth-century Dutch Renaissance scholar, who in many ways anticipated the Reformation, said, 'If it is possible to train elephants to dance and lions to play and leopards to hunt, it ought to be possible to teach preachers to preach.' Nevertheless, there is no mechanical art to learn which will enable us to preach with the authority for which we long. We can learn to communicate more clearly and assemble our material in such a way that we will hold attention from beginning to end, but the greatest teacher and trainer of all is the Holy Spirit Himself who illuminates the minds and hearts of men and women of God and authorises them to pass on what they have received to other people.

I want now to look more closely at the multifaceted nature of the authority we are meant to carry as preachers.

THE NATURE OF THE PREACHER'S AUTHORITY

1. The authority of Holy Scripture

The preacher's authority stems, first of all, from the authority of the Scriptures. It is not so much the authority of our ideas, but the authority of the Scriptures that we serve and represent. As we know, we live in a deeply sceptical world that seriously questions whether or not objective truth can ever be found or known. We see the loss of objective standards everywhere; the loss of absolutes; the loss of all certainty about any assertion that is made. And this uncertainty leads to a withdrawal and, particularly in the West, into a kind of trust in existential experience and feelings to give us meaning and purpose in life. We have turned to non-rational categories of sensation, so that what we *feel* becomes the only criterion of significance. Even among Christians the emotional category is substituted for the phrases involving the mind that we once used so confidently – phrases like 'I think', 'I believe', 'I maintain that this is true'. I, however, hold fervently to those phrases, for behind them lies the verbal, propositional and inspired authority of the Bible itself. Large sectors of the Church have even abandoned the Bible as their infallible guide to belief and to practice. They are at sea on an ocean of subjectivity, clinging to the flimsy lifeboat of sometimes majority but even minority opinions. Emil Brunner said, 'The fate of the Bible is the fate of Christianity itself.' A dishonoured and neglected Bible will ultimately lead to a dishonoured and neglected Church, and has done so in our nation on an incalculable scale in the last century. But if the Bible is honoured, we can dare to believe that it will hold increasing sway in the lives of formerly rebellious people and that, then, the Church's fortunes will similarly be on the ascendancy again.

As preachers it is vital that we have clear and settled in our mind the fact that God has spoken, that we have a word from above that has come to us from outside ourselves. It is a word that has been accurately transmitted and relayed to us. People have questioned this, denied it, argued with it. They have attempted to twist the Bible, abridge it or burn it. But God has insured it against all loss by the personal presence of His Holy Spirit and it is still intact today. If we are to have authority in our preaching we have to be clear about the nature of the Scriptures. Reject them and we will become flaccid, flabby, and, dare I say it, flatulent in our preaching. That is why there is often such a stink in our churches. Paul put it this way, *'If the trumpet gives an uncertain sound, who will prepare himself to battle?'*[1]

What we have in the Bible, according to the critics, is a kind of *Readers' Digest* anthology of wit and wisdom, of myths, of fantasy and often the disturbed or deranged reminiscences of pious men from the ancient world; a scrapbook of dated experiences and encounters of the long dead who lived in another time and in another place. In the modern world, they say, we can only really read this book for our entertainment and in order to learn about the past. On this presupposition, the preacher is seen as awkwardly straddling two utterly different worlds that are far removed from each other. On the one hand, there is the ancient world of this old yellow text of the Bible. On the other hand, there is the modern world of information technology, microchips, computers and telecommunication satellites. Bridging that gulf, philosophically and intellectually, has become an increasingly tall order. The gap is too great. Thus, our task has been conceived as trying in some way to 'make the Bible relevant' to the modern world – but this is not the whole truth. Those who grasp hold of the issue of the preacher's biblical authority will conceive of their task very differently indeed.

The preacher's task is no less than one of *making the modern world relevant to the Bible*. It is our modern world that is antiquated and out of joint, ill-conceived, twisted and erroneous. Not the Bible. It is our modern world that is shot through with ancient error and pagan thinking, that is out of accord with reality and living in a fantasy, that is insane with its love of error. The Bible was not only true then: it is true now. Indeed, it is the way ahead for all of us. It doesn't need to adjust to us; we need to adjust to it. The alternative, if we neglect this book, is for us all to cease to be relevant at all. Everything but the Bible is doomed to become effete and passé. Bible in hand we are here to debunk modern humanity's inflated sense of its own self-importance and, therefore, we stand as ambassadors: ambassadors of another world and another world-view. We are here to turn the world upside-down, as it says in the book of Acts, or better still perhaps 'the right way up'.

The modern attack on the Bible is really a conspiracy on everybody's behalf to maintain the status quo. It is a conspiracy to relativise all perspectives so that they are counted equally true and valid and, therefore, equally untrue and invalid. It is to condone a policy of pluralism and easy tolerance of ideas and ultimately of a syncretism between alien gods and alien world-views so that we can all 'pick and mix' what we want to believe. People say, 'There are always two sides to a question, you know.' There are also two sides to a strip of fly-paper, but it makes all the difference in the world to a fly, which side it lands on! Bible-believing Christians actually refuse to play ball with this nonsense. Like Jesus we will not settle down to become inmates of one vast concentration camp, who have been promised a reasonably good life if they remain on their best behaviour and don't rock the boat. We are here to cause trouble. We are here to say, 'No, no, there is another world beyond the barbed wire.' We are here to unsettle people's comfort-zone with a reality that should horrify them. We are here to destabilise the situation and do so as often and as menacingly as we possibly can. We are here to beckon people out of their drunken stupor, to shatter the false world-views that they take for granted. We are announcing the end of this present order. We are saying that a liberation army is on its way. We are saying that the gates are going to swing open and that freedom can be enjoyed now. Bible in hand we can't help being subversives for Christ.

We don't come to people saying, 'You know, I feel this . . .' No, we come with another tone altogether: we say, 'Look, this is the case. These are the facts of the matter.' There are times when, becoming more urgent and even quite bolshy, we say things like, 'Do you agree with this?', 'Are you convinced?', 'Will you transfer allegiance?'

As a young preacher, having been exposed to liberal perspectives, Billy Graham was for a while plagued with doubts about the Scriptures. In an often told personal story he relates how one day he knelt before God with his Bible open and prayed this prayer,

Lord, many things in this book I do not understand, but you have said, 'The just shall live by faith.' All I have received from you I have taken by faith, so here and now I accept the Bible as your Word. I take it all without reservation. And where there are things I cannot understand I will reserve judgement until I receive more light. If this pleases you, give me authority as I proclaim your Word and through that authority convict men and women of sin and turn sinners to the Saviour.[2]

Many will know that one of the most characteristic phrases of Billy Graham's preaching is 'The Bible says'. Billy Graham would daily acknowledge a borrowed authority: the authority of the Bible itself.

In Athens, where there were idols on every corner and relativism in truth and, above all, scepticism in theology, for they had erected an altar to 'the unknown god', the apostle Paul declared that *what you worship as something unknown I am going to proclaim to you*.[3] 'The God you call unknown, I will declare to you.' Commenting on this William Willimon says,

> The God whom Paul proclaimed in Athens is not just another option for human devotion, not a pluralistic God content to be one among many. The God who sent the Christ is still the Holy One of Israel, a jealous deity without rivals, an exclusive lover who tolerates no competition, not from money, or sex, or philosophical ideals or institutions, who fiercely judges all idols made by human hands or minds: Christian speakers do not just massage the world as we find it, we create a new world.[4]

Furthermore, as Hebrews 1:2 clearly states, *'in these last days he has spoken to us by his Son, whom he appointed heir of all things, and through whom he made the universe'*. God has spoken now fully and finally in His Son Jesus Christ. We are here to preach Jesus and His resurrection. The King is now on the throne and His restored honour and rule and order are emanating from that throne, advancing relentlessly through the world, capturing scores of thousands of lives every day. Now this is not my personal opinion. This is fact, and facts are facts. In truth, facts are stubborn things: run against facts and you could do damage to yourself. Jesus does not fit into any polytheistic pantheon of exotic gods. He is Lord of heaven and earth. Truth is reality as God defines it to be, and we know how He defines reality because He has told us. God has spoken, and the fact that God has spoken gives us also the right to speak.

2. The authority of the Holy Spirit

The confidence we have in the Bible ought always to be accompanied by another confidence that is meant to run alongside it: confidence in the Holy Spirit who gave us the Bible in the first place. We are to be consciously dependent on the Spirit every time we open this book. Each time C.H. Spurgeon mounted the steps to the pulpit at the Metropolitan Tabernacle, where he regularly preached to between 6,500 and 7,000 people, he would say quietly under his breath, 'I believe in the Holy Ghost. I believe in the Holy Ghost.' We, in our generation, dare not forget or neglect this factor. We will be nothing without it.

In the second volume of his wonderful biography of Dr Martyn Lloyd-Jones, Iain Murray tells how the Doctor finished his ministry at Westminster Chapel. On 1 March 1968 he preached his final message in his thirteen-year-long series on Romans which took place on Friday nights. His text, which he had already preached on for two weeks, was 'The kingdom of God is not a matter of eating and drinking, but of righteousness, peace and joy in the Holy Spirit' (14:17). He ended his sermon on peace that night, and never came back to his text. He was already suffering the serious symptoms of cancer, for which he then received treatment. During his six-month convalescence, he resigned the pastorate of Westminster Chapel. Speaking later about the experience of finishing the text halfway through, he explained that he had felt diffident to go on because he was not sure that either he or the church were experiencing the joy of which the text speaks. He said, 'I knew something, but not enough about it.' Later he challenged the ministers of the Westminster Fellowship, many of whose churches he visited during his convalescence, looking for a word from God, saying quite frankly, 'I heard great exegesis and fine homiletics but I did not hear anything for my own needy soul.' He went on,

> My general impression is that most of our services are terribly depressing. I'm amazed that people still go to church. Most who go are female and over the age of forty. The note missing is this joy in the Holy Ghost. There is nothing in these services to make a stranger feel he is missing something by not being there.
>
> The main trouble with evangelicalism today is its lack of power. What do our people know of joy in the Holy Ghost? Without this joy in the Holy Ghost the situation in this country is hopeless.[5]

I think he would say the same today. What Dr Lloyd-Jones was looking for is what I sometimes call the 'wow-factor' in church life. Even unbelievers know the very first time they encounter it. They go out saying something to the effect of, 'Wow, I've never experienced church like that. When do you meet again?' Such an experience of church can never be simply explained away. It was A. W. Tozer who said, 'The greatest tragedy of the Church in the twentieth century is that she has been explained – the surest evidence of her fall.'[6] Explained sociologically, explained historically, explained socially and psychologically, explained traditionally. The church should not be able to be explained! John Murray said, 'If Pentecost is not repeated, neither has it been rescinded. This is the era of the Holy Ghost.' There are too many unholy spirits contesting what we say and what we are for us to be confident of any other enabling or confirming power than that of the Holy Spirit in what we are doing. Demons oppose us relentlessly; silly and foolish people oppose us regularly, and our own fears and inhibitions undermine us in the carrying out of our ministry. Society has happily abandoned all norms and does not even notice the disintegration that is occurring in every sphere of life. How are we to win in the fight against such overwhelming odds without the Spirit of God? If the fight is to be won, there will need to be more than the preacher in the pulpit. And if he is not to buckle and blow with the wind, he will need another wind altogether, blowing over his heart and mind into the lives of sometimes hostile listeners. Their enormous need is to be dismantled by this Bible and detoxified in the process, to be reborn and be remade – and this is all the work of the Holy Spirit. Flesh cannot do it. Words alone cannot do it: clever arguments are easily refused and refuted. We need God to come upon us. Older preachers used to call it 'unction' or 'anointing'. We may not be able to define what it is exactly, but both we and our hearers know when it is there, and when it is not.

One of the best definitions of anointing that I have ever come across is: 'Anointing is God on human flesh doing what only God can do.' We could also put it like this, 'The Holy Spirit makes dull people bright and bright people brilliant.' As preachers we need to covet this power of the Holy Spirit because no conventional speech-making can do what we are called to do. Preaching has been called 'thirty minutes to raise the dead'. Who can produce a resurrection? Only the Holy Spirit can, and we desperately need Him!

If God's Word is to be properly heard it has to be attended with power. A Red Indian who lived on an Indian reservation was invited to visit a mega-church in the United States of America to hear an outstanding, white-suited pastor with a gold medallion. At the end of the meeting his friends asked him what he thought. He paused in silence for a few moments with his arms folded across his chest and then he said, 'Hmmm, big wind, loud thunder, no rain.' Many of us would echo the lament of the Anglican bishop who bemoaned the fact that wherever the apostle Paul went, there was either a riot or a revival, but wherever he went, they simply served cucumber sandwiches and tea! We need God the Holy Spirit working on human flesh to do what only He can do.

The night before He was crucified, Jesus assured His disciples that His departure would be to their advantage, because, unless He went away, the Advocate, the Helper, the Comforter would not come. He said,

'but if I go, I will send him to you. When he comes, he will convict the world of guilt in regard to sin and righteousness and judgment: in regard to sin, because men do not believe in me; in regard to righteousness, because I am going to the Father, where you can see me no longer; and in regard to judgment, because the prince of this world now stands condemned.'
(John 16:7–11)

This promise of the enabling of the Holy Spirit in our task adds weight to everything we say, but I would like to suggest that there are four specific aspects that He will bring to our ministry.

(i) It is the Spirit who convicts

The Holy Spirit makes clear that people's lives are out of joint with God and with ultimate reality, producing fear, apprehension and alarm in them so they know that they are not 'safe' anymore. The Holy Spirit turns preachers from frightened rabbits into ferocious ferrets, who will fearlessly go down every nook and cranny for their prey, not concerned in any way what they will confront there or what the repercussions might be. In short, He puts boldness into us.

(ii) It is the Spirit who convinces

The Holy Spirit convinces people that the words of this ancient yellow text are the only real and true thing in a world full of the lies and threadbare rags with which people have covered themselves. I am often asked why I am a Christian, and one of my favourite replies is, 'Because it's true!' I became convinced it was true when I was a fourteen-year-old teenager and I have never had reason to change my mind since. The Holy Spirit persuades people that they cannot live without this God or His word in their lives.

(iii) It is the Spirit who confirms the Word with signs following

This is how Mark 16 puts it. Nowadays we are confidently told that verses 9 to 20 of this chapter did not belong in the original text and many commentaries on Mark's Gospel do not even touch on them. I think there are very good reasons why this passage might have been excised since it tells us that 'these signs' will follow those who go about the fulfilment of our Lord's last command. It assures us that the Holy Spirit will come to substantiate our truth claims in a climate where they are difficult to substantiate; He will affect people's bodies, minds, spirits, and even their tongues as we speak; He will cause them to speak with new languages which they have never learned; He will give us new gifts of access to God in prayer; He will empower us to evict demons and grant us immunity from both demonic and human murderous assault. And they are only a representative display of what is possible when the Holy Spirit is on us and in us. When He empowers us, the watching world will eventually conclude, 'These people are dangerous. They are threatening. We had better make peace with them and their God because we will not be able to make war with them successfully.'

(iv) It is the Spirit who conforms

The Holy Spirit changes people from the inside out, metamorphosing them and bringing about the realignment of their whole inner life: their psyche or mental life, their spiritual life, their somatic life, their physical life. It is a gospel that can be heard as well as seen, seen as well as heard, and that touches the whole of redeemed reality. Dynamic change happens through the agency of authorised preachers because they are here constantly to critique and create a new people for God.

Bruce Horner says, 'The best way to revive a church is to light a fire in the pulpit.'

Oswald Chambers writes, 'If we honestly ask God to baptise us in his Holy Spirit and fire, then anything that happens is his answer. And some appalling things may happen.' Writing to reassure nervous preachers, William Willimon says, in effect, that we are here to preach what we have been told, and adds:

> We make clear our authority. This is great grace for us preachers. Then when they say they don't like something we've said, we can say, 'Don't tell me. It's not *my* book. I didn't call you here to listen to me, I called you forth to listen. Don't complain to me.'[7]

He also says to preachers everywhere, 'If you're a coward by nature and if boldness does not come to you naturally, then get down behind the text. You can peek out from behind the text and say, "It's not me that's saying this. It's in the text!"'[8]

3. The authority of the call to preach

There is, however, a third and last element to the preacher's authority: the authority of his call to preach. Since conflict and confrontation are the inevitable environment of his task, every preacher needs to know that he is called. Like Jeremiah he needs to know that God is putting His words in his mouth:

> *'Now, I have put my words in your mouth. See, today I appoint you over nations and kingdoms to uproot and to tear down, to destroy and overthrow, to build and to plant.'*
> (Jeremiah 1:9–10)

Like Moses he needs to know that it is the Lord who is sending him:

> *'So now, go. I am sending you to Pharaoh to bring my people the Israelites out of Egypt.'*
> (Exodus 3:10)

If he is to bring lasting change from slavery to sin and demonic oppression, he needs a call to do this.

Isaiah heard the voice of the Lord saying, *'Whom shall I send and who will go for us?',*[9] and what a gospel ministry unfolded from that! The apostle Paul recalled how the Lord had appeared to him on the Damascus Road and said to him,

> *'I am Jesus, whom you are persecuting ... Now get up and stand on your feet. I have appeared to you to appoint you as a servant and as a witness of what you have seen of me and what I will show you.'*
> (Acts 26:15, 16)

The call of God is essential. For the preacher it is the *sine qua non*. Without it the preacher is nothing. There will be seasons in Christian ministry and service where emotions of depression, fear, discouragement, desertion, loneliness and even self-criticism will be relentless, to the point of being overwhelming. At such times the only thing that will keep the Christian minister going will be the burning, or still smouldering but not-yet-snuffed-out recollection that 'God called me to do this'. To be called is to be summoned. To be called is to be wooed by the warm voice of the One who knows us and has something very special for us to do, and who has no one else in mind to do this specific task.

Frederick Buechner, an American Presbyterian pastor and beautiful writer, said, 'The place God calls you is the place where your deep gladness and the world's deep hunger meet.'[10] In this connection Os Guinness wrote, 'The truth is not that God is finding us a place for our gifts, but that God has created both us and our gifts for a place, a place of his choosing, and we will only ever be ourselves when we finally get there.'[11] When Paul went to Philippi, having responded to the vision of the Macedonian man to come over and help them, his visit ended in an earthquake, jail, flogging and beating. Eventually the city's magistrates sent their officials to ask him to leave quietly, but he responded,

> *'They beat us publicly without a trial, even though we are Roman citizens, and threw us into prison. And now do they want to get rid of us quietly? No! Let them come themselves and escort us out.'*
> (Acts 16:37)

Here was a man who knew he was supposed to be there. The preacher needs to know that he is in the place of God's choosing, the place for which God has created both him and his gifts. It is in this place that he will know that God has authorised him to preach His Word. My plea to all preachers is that they would truly begin to live as if they have God's Word and His Spirit and enter into their true calling of being servants and witnesses of what they have seen of God and what He has shown them.

These components are the essential factors of any legitimate authority we possess to help change God's world and the lives of men and women, children and young people within it. Without them, what on earth could we possibly accomplish?

Notes

1. 1 Corinthians 14:8 KJV.
2. See, for example, *Billy Graham* by John Pollock (McGraw-Hill, 1966), pp. 51–53.
3. Acts 17:23.
4. *Peculiar Speech* (William B. Eerdmans Publishing Co., 1992), p. 86.
5. Iain Murray, *The Fight of Faith* Vol. 2 (Banner of Truth Trust, 1990), pp. 603–4.
6. A.W. Tozer, *Paths to Power* (Oliphant Ltd, 1964).

7. Willimon, *Peculiar Speech*.

8. *Ibid*.

9. Isaiah 6:8.

10. Frederick Buechner, *Wishful Thinking* (Mowbray, 1994), p. 119.

11. Os Guinness, *The Call* (Paternoster/Spring Harvest, 2001).

Chapter 20

NOT IN WORD ONLY: THE WORK OF THE HOLY SPIRIT IN PREACHING

Colin Dye

A proclamation of the gospel through words only is not enough. There must be another form of communication that is Word and Spirit – Word that is charged with the Holy Spirit's power and influence. In 1 Thessalonians 1:5 Paul says,

> *For our gospel did not come to you in word only, but also in power, and in the Holy Spirit and in much assurance, as you know what kind of men we were among you for your sake.*[1]

This verse has led many people to draw a distinction between the Word and the Spirit. They say that the Word has to do with doctrine, the Spirit with experience; that the Word has to do with people coming to hear, the Spirit with people coming to see and observe; that the Word has to do with mere talk, the Spirit with manifestation; that the Word has to do with exposition, the Spirit with demonstration. To a point this may be a helpful distinction but we must not exaggerate it or overemphasise it. There is, in my opinion, no dichotomy between the Word and the Spirit. It is a marriage made in heaven, and what God has joined together let no man put asunder. The Spirit and the Word belong together. Genesis 1:2 speaks of the Spirit of God hovering over the face of the waters. The Hebrew word used is indicative of a bird brooding over a nest or hovering on the wing. Driving along a motorway it is often possible to see a sparrow hawk hovering in the wind: suddenly it leaps into action, folding its wings and diving to take its prey on the ground. That is the image here. The Holy Spirit is hovering, waiting in preparation. The next verse says, *'God said'*. God's word is released, and then the Spirit leaps into action. It is my understanding that it is an impossibility to have the Word without the Spirit or the Spirit without the Word. In 2 Timothy 3:16, speaking about the inspiration of Scripture, Paul describes the Word as *'God-breathed'* and therefore profitable for doctrine, reproof, correction and instruction. 'God-breathed' means that, in the very same way that I use breath to speak my words, so God's Word comes to us by His breath. The parallelism in Psalm 33:6 makes this clear:

> *By the word of the LORD the heavens were made,*
> *And all the host of them by the breath of His mouth.*

The Word of the Lord is the breath of His mouth; it is His Spirit-produced Word. The Word carries the Spirit; the Spirit is integral to the Word. The apostle Paul sees the Word of Christ and the Spirit of Christ working in much the same way in our hearts as believers, producing the same effects in our lives. If Ephesians 5:18–20 is juxtaposed with Colossians 3:16, it is evident that they are almost parallel passages:

> *be filled with the Spirit, speaking to one another in psalms and hymns and*
> *spiritual songs, singing and making melody in your heart to the Lord, giving*
> *thanks always for all things to God the Father in the name of our Lord Jesus*
> *Christ...*
> (Ephesians 5:18–20)

> *Let the word of Christ dwell in you richly in all wisdom, teaching and*
> *admonishing one another in psalms and hymns and spiritual songs, singing*
> *with grace in your hearts to the Lord.*
> (Colossians 3:16)

So far as Paul is concerned, there is no functional difference between the Spirit of God taking control of a person's life, heart and experience and the Word of God doing so. A dichotomy between the Word and the Spirit is unbiblical.

Where, then, does this unbiblical division come from? I believe it has three roots, all stemming from false philosophy. The first root is the familiar teaching of rationalism that truth is a matter of the intellect. This is the emphasis of the 'Word only' camp. Despite the fact that we are living in a post-modern generation, it is surprising how dominant rationalism still is, as I have seen very clearly in some recent philosophical publications I have read. The second is the romanticism of popular culture which has given rise to an unbiblical distinction between the head and the heart, in which the head has to do with logic or the intellect and the heart with the emotions. As far as Scripture is concerned, the heart is not just the centre of the emotions but of the totality of the human personality: the mind, emotions and will. Thus, when speaking about the head and the heart, we have to be careful not to fall into the trap of false romantic language. Proverbs 4:23 says,

> *Keep your heart with all diligence,*
> *For out of it spring the issues of life.*

The heart is the motivational centre: it is not merely the emotional centre. The third root is the teaching of relativism, in which there can be no objective knowing but only subjective experience and perception of truth. I believe that these three influences, which have come together in our culture, have one thing in common: they pit the mind or the intellect against subjective experience. Their influence has permeated into the Church, with the result that we have a so-called evangelical–charismatic divide. Evangelicals are characterised by charismatics as 'dry as dust and devoid of the anointing', and charismatics are likened by evangelicals to 'public swimming baths where most of the noise comes from the shallow end'. And it's all true! Yet it is becoming increasingly clear as we mature in these issues that both charismatics and evangelicals have a like passion for the Word and the Spirit. Charismatics, many of whom are evangelicals, are great consumers of the Word and, likewise, evangelicals are by no means seeking to under-estimate their need of the presence and activity of the Spirit in their lives and churches. In my view there is a far greater continuity than we realise.

Preaching is and must be a Trinitarian activity. The truth that the Living God acts and speaks through His Son by the Holy Spirit must impact our preaching. Preaching is the means by which people hear the gospel, come to faith in Christ, and are developed in their Christian discipleship. Therefore we must see it as God's way of intervening in people's lives through Christ by the power of the Holy Spirit. We are living in the era of the physical absence of Christ, awaiting His physical bodily return to this earth. In the meantime we enjoy His presence, His power and His activity mediated through the person of the Holy Spirit. All that we know of Christ, all that we know of God the Father, comes to us through the revelation of the Spirit. In John 16:5–15 Jesus speaks a great deal about the role of the Holy Spirit. He says that it is to the disciples' advantage that He should go away because then He will send the Holy Spirit, whose presence would more than compensate for His physical absence. In fact, the Holy Spirit's presence would mediate to us the very presence and person of Jesus Christ Himself. The Holy Spirit would begin to do what we could not do. He would bring full conviction concerning sin, righteousness and judgement. He would continue the declaration of Christ concerning the Father by illuminating the truth of God's Word to our hearts. Of course, in the first instance He would ensure that there would be a full, sufficient and infallible record of what Christ taught and what God said to humanity and, then, when the last word of Scripture had been penned under His inspiration, He would illuminate that Word and make it a living reality in people's experience. Ephesians 1:16–17 says:

> [I] *do not cease to give thanks for you, making mention of you in my prayers: that the God of our Lord Jesus Christ, the Father of glory, may give to you the spirit of wisdom and revelation in the knowledge of Him . . .*

Our preaching should have a Trinitarian framework. We preach the gospel of God concerning His Son in the power and demonstration of the Holy Spirit. So, if we encounter Jesus Christ in the proclamation of the gospel through the Holy Spirit and if it is the Holy Spirit who brings the revelation of the reality of who God is, what implication does this have for us in preaching?

The Work of the Holy Spirit in Preaching

We know that the Holy Spirit uses preaching to bring people to Christ and to shape them into the image of the Saviour. Paul speaks about this process in 2 Corinthians 3:18: '[we] *are being transformed into the same image from glory to glory, just as by the Spirit of the Lord.'* This means that we should preach in conscious dependence upon the Holy Spirit, for His help, for His enabling and for His illumination. Practically speaking, this begins in our preparation and we should ensure first of all that in our study – the hard exegetical work that lies at the root of our exposition – we line up our message with the Holy Spirit's purpose concerning the passage or the theme of Scripture. In his excellent book *Preaching with Purpose*,[2] Dr Jay Adams speaks about the need to discover the *telos* of the passage on which we are preparing to preach. The *telos* of the passage is the Holy Spirit's purpose in causing it to be written and recorded in Scripture.[3] The preacher must ask the key question: what was the Spirit's purpose in including this passage in the Word of God? It is important to recognise that the Spirit's purpose may be broader than the purpose of the human author. But what we can say is that the Bible speaks, that the Spirit of God speaks.

There are numerous references in Scripture that make it very clear that every word of Scripture is God speaking: it is not just Paul or John or Moses. The Holy Spirit has brought together not just a library of many books written by multiple authors over many centuries, but in truth the Bible is one volume: the unity of the Word of God. This understanding is fundamental to our theology as evangelicals. Although it is a highly complex matter, we know that when we turn to the Word of God we can say, 'The Spirit of God says . . . '. If that is the case, we must also ask, why did the Holy Spirit include this passage? What is its purpose? In many Old Testament passages the *telos* of the Spirit was far beyond the understanding or purpose historically in the minds of their authors. In 1 Corinthians 10:11 Paul writes,

> *Now all these things happened to them as examples, and they were written for our admonition, upon whom the ends of the ages have come.*

The authors of the Old Testament passages to which Paul is referring, cannot have had any idea of the meaning or purpose of what they were writing for the twenty-first-century Church, or indeed for the first-century Church, as it developed under the worthy leadership of the apostles. They must sometimes have puzzled over the things they were being inspired to write, as the Spirit caused passages to be written for purposes way beyond their historical value. Peter speaks about this in his letter:

> *Of this salvation the prophets have inquired and searched carefully, who prophesied of the grace that would come to you, searching what, or what manner of time, the Spirit of Christ who was in them was indicating when He testified beforehand the sufferings of Christ and the glories that would follow. To them it was revealed that, not to themselves, but to us they were ministering the things which now have been reported to you through those who have preached the gospel to you by the Holy Spirit sent from heaven – things which angels desire to look into.*
> (1 Peter 1:10–12)

As we are preparing to preach, we must remember that we are handling a precious, holy word from God that was recorded for a purpose way beyond the understanding of the original author. This is a significant truth for us because the Holy Spirit's power is much more likely to be released through our preaching if we line up with His purpose for the passage or theme we are presenting. In our sermon preparation we must develop a keen and heightened sensitivity to the Holy Spirit to enable us to discern the message that He wants specifically to be brought and applied to our hearers. We need to align our purpose in preaching the message with the Holy Spirit's purpose, understanding that He knows the needs of every single person who will hear it.

To this end we need to ask the Holy Spirit to speak to us, lead us and guide us through all the processes. I am not talking here about an exaggerated dependence on what might be called charismatic inspiration. It might come through good old-fashioned, hard-earned evangelical perspiration. But however it comes, let it come. We must be totally open to the Holy Spirit. We must give Him full access to our hearts, our minds and our spirits during sermon preparation, constantly asking, on our knees, 'What does the Holy Spirit want me to say to these people? How does He want me to minister to them?' All of this is a learned skill of listening to the Holy Spirit in sermon preparation, and of course in personal preparation as we ensure that we are totally surrendered to His influence. This conscious surrender to and dependence upon the Holy Spirit is a major key in effective preaching. If the marriage between the Word and the Spirit mentioned earlier is a correct analogy, then it is impossible to overestimate the need for us as preachers to depend on the Holy Spirit throughout the whole preaching process. We offer ourselves to be used by the Spirit to reveal Christ and influence our hearers towards Him. There is no arrogance here. There is no self-reliance; there is no reliance on the mere soundness of the message; there is no reliance on intellectual ability or clever argument; there is no reliance on communication skills or past experience. It is total reliance on the Spirit. It is to preach under the anointing of God or remain ineffective.

We move on in the preaching process to the delivery of the message. This is when we as preachers will reap the benefit of having cultivated a living relationship with the Spirit. However, if we want to experience the reality of the Spirit's activity in and through our preaching we also have to develop a relationship with Him in which we are sensitive to His leadings and open to His direction *while* we are preaching. If we merely follow our notes and deliver our message without this inner dependence on the Spirit, it is almost as if we are saying, 'Thank you, Holy Spirit. I have my message. You can sit down and join the congregation.' No matter how diligent our sermon preparation may have been it is not until we stand up that our thoughts clarify and crystallise. Sensitivity to the Spirit during preaching gives us a clear indication of the very things that often turn the sermon into something living and effective. Somebody once said, 'If you want your sermons to bear fruit, prune them.' As preachers we develop a sense of what to expand and what to contract; what to add and what to leave out. In my case, it is often what I leave out that makes the impact. We sense that this is a point upon which the Holy Spirit wants us to dwell and take further – it seems to have the touch of God upon it – applying it in a direction that had not previously occurred to us. Or that this is a point, which, although during sermon preparation it seemed significant, does not seem to resonate, and so we move rapidly on to the next one.

In studying the life of Charles Spurgeon it becomes clear that it was not uncommon for him to add illustrations in his sermon which we, in our understanding of the Holy Spirit's work and as practitioners of charismatic gifts, would term words of wisdom or knowledge. He might say, for example, 'There is someone here today who has stolen such and such. God would have you repent.' And there would indeed be such a person there, who would ask himself how the preacher could possibly know about him. One of the things I have found most humbling as a preacher is to be complimented for something I did not say! Members of the congregation have thanked me for my 'wonderful message' and, when pressed a little more, they have described how what I said has spoken directly into a situation they were facing. I am left with no idea how they could possibly have got what they did from the message I had given, but profoundly grateful for the work of the Holy Spirit. There is an element in the preaching process that is totally supernatural: the dry bones cannot live without the breath of God. Only the Spirit can bring conviction, only the Spirit can apply the Word to the hearts of our hearers.

This dependence on the part of preachers should be to the point of desperation: for without Him we can do *nothing*. My favourite prayer is: 'God, do what only You can do.' Elijah carefully prepared the sacrifice under the direction of the Holy Spirit. When he had done exactly what God wanted him to do, he handed the situation over to God. Then, in that little bit of extra-biblical revelation that we Pentecostals are so famous for, he stepped back. Why? Because he expected the fire to come. He had learnt the art that every preacher needs to learn: *the art of getting out of the way* because the fire is going to fall.

We must make room in our preaching for the spontaneity of the Spirit: we can never be quite sure how He will move. This can catch us both ways. Sometimes we expect a great deal and we receive very little. At other times God seems to take over and He makes a great deal of very little. And it is His sovereign prerogative so to do. When we read some of the sermons of the great preachers in times of awakening and revival, we see that there is some substance to them, but they don't strike us as particularly out of the ordinary (and I don't think that this is just a cultural perception). We compare those sermons with our own and wonder why God does not use them more. It may be that we have not learned how to make room for Him. During our preaching we need to be exhorting our hearers to open up to the Spirit's work in their hearts. Or we need to pause for the Spirit's help as we preach, being willing to hand over to Him if He comes in an overwhelming way. Peter never did finish his sermon to Cornelius and his household. Maybe as a preacher he was frustrated, but our sermons do not matter. That is, they do not matter if God comes. If there is an overwhelming sense of the presence of God and He intervenes in such a way that the very point and purpose of our preaching – the answer to our prayer – comes in the middle of our sermon as the Holy Spirit moves, thank God. I am not talking about the sort of behaviour of one would-be charismatic preacher, who is reported to have allowed the worship to extend on and on, because 'the Spirit's so strong here, I just can't preach'. The only operative word, according to an observer, was the last phrase, he 'can't preach'.

The person in the wilderness praying for rain does not say when the rain comes, 'Not now, Lord. I haven't finished praying.' Unless we are ready to get out of the way of the Holy Spirit when He begins to move, we are putting our sermon in place of Him. Preaching is not an end in itself. We are not about preaching fine sermons: we are about shaping people's lives. I personally believe it matters more what the preacher does when he gets down from the pulpit than what he has said in it. Our preaching is not just about words: it is about action and it is about implementation of the truth that is being preached.

An old Pentecostal preacher said to a young man learning to preach, 'Remember, son, when you are done preaching, you are not done.' In other words, the end of the sermon is not the end. *'Our gospel did not come to you in word only, but also in power, and in the Holy Spirit and in much assurance, as you know what kind of men we were among you for your sake.'* What kind of men were they? They were anointed men, mighty in word and in deed. Here Paul is referring to powerful preaching of the gospel, that is in words, yes, carrying the full conviction of the Holy Spirit in hearer and preacher alike, but the verse also strongly implies that the preaching was accompanied by active demonstrations of the Spirit's power through signs and wonders.

In his comprehensive work *God's Empowering Presence*, the Pentecostal theologian Gordon Fee, who is one of the world's foremost authorities on Pauline pneumatology,

261

says about 1 Thessalonians 1:5: 'Even though the primary reference in the phrase "with power", that is with the Holy Spirit and full conviction, is to Paul's Spirit-empowered proclamation of Christ, such passages as 2 Corinthians 12:11–13 and especially Romans 15:17–19 indicate that his Spirit-empowered Word was regularly accompanied by Spirit-empowered miracles as well.'[4] He goes on to build the case, through study of Paul's use of the words *dynamis* and *pneuma*, that when the two are put together it is characteristically not just an experience with the empowering Spirit, not just the presenting of powerful words, but also manifestation of the power of the Spirit through signs and wonders. Signs and wonders ought, therefore, to be part of our expectation and practice. Passages, such as Mark 16:20 which says,

> *And they went out and preached everywhere, the Lord working with them and*
> *confirming the word through the accompanying signs,*

are then an embarrassment to us as preachers, because we are very good at speaking but we have cut out what should come alongside and accompany it. Earlier in Mark chapter 16 (see v. 17), when something similar is said, a slightly different word is used which conveys the sense of the signs coming alongside the preaching or the believing[5] and now in verse 20 we have signs following very closely behind.[6] Either way there is a connection here. In his Gospel genius Mark is continuing to present his unique portrait of Christ, the Servant of the Lord, because even in His exaltation and ascension He is still working: He is still serving, *'the Lord working with them'*. I can't imagine anything more significant, anything more wonderful, anything more desirable than to have the Lord working with me. What an incredible statement! What an incredible trust that we can be representatives of His Body!

The height of New Testament ecclesiology is that the Church is the Body of Christ, His agent in the world. We must never rest until that ecclesiology is seen and demonstrated; until the hotchpotch collection of people that make up the Church of Jesus Christ have in reality become an integrated Body, with many wonderful individual expressions but each and every one of them striving to be and indeed becoming His agent and doing what Jesus did. The Servant of the Lord still works with us in signs and wonders and miracles.

I remember an occasion when I was preaching in another nation which is not subject to the kinds of spiritual restraints and restrictions that limit us in this country. I simply preached the Word of God as best I could and in a wonderful way God began to move in signs and wonders. God was working spontaneously and the most amazing creative miracles were occurring. People were stepping out of wheelchairs; flesh was being restored to human bodies; blind eyes were opening; people who were unable to walk were instantly walking. Everyone was amazed and astonished. After the preaching my role was simply to be there and to help direct things, in terms of managing the movement of people who were waiting to receive prayer, and so on. I also had the privilege of interviewing people who were coming up onto the platform to give their thrilling testimonies of healing. In the midst of all this I became aware of a distinct sense of the presence of the Lord and at that moment I remembered why I am in the ministry, or at least why I had responded to God's call. It was because of God's promise that when we are about the Father's business Jesus works with us.

Whether that is in the spectacular signs and wonders which are all too rare – and please don't ask me to explain any more than that because I haven't a clue about how to explain how God chooses to work in His sovereignty and it is a very complex issue, but I do believe we need to be desperate for it to happen – or whether it is in our personal witnessing and we sense His presence. We experience joy as we know the Holy Spirit is at work. As we learn to co-operate with the Holy Spirit and submit to Him I believe we will experience this more and more. Our responsibility as leaders and preachers is to believe for these signs and wonders and miracles and to be open to them. We must not look directly for the spectacular: we must only look for Jesus and His presence with a desperation that drives us to our knees and causes us never to get up from that place of prayer and that attitude of desperation until He comes with power in our lives and our ministries. I would rather say five words with power and sit down than say five thousand words devoid of any sense of Holy Ghost conviction.

The pattern is set for us. In the opening words of his book of the Acts of the Apostles Luke writes, *'The former account I made, O Theophilus, of all that Jesus began both to do and teach'*. He puts the doing before the teaching. It is obvious that Jesus could move so easily between the two, but Luke is emphasising the fact that Jesus continues to 'do' as well as to teach. That was not just true for the inscripturated and authoritative accounts and oracles of the book of Acts but the same Holy Spirit is bearing witness to the same Jesus today all over the world, and not just in the far corners of Africa, Asia and South America, but in our nation as well. God is alive and at work. I do not believe that signs and wonders in any way replace faith in God's sovereign ways of dealing with us. Neither do I believe that they replace the Word of God. Signs and wonders underline and confirm what God says; they are means by which He arrests people's attention. They vindicate Jesus' identity and authority.

In preaching we need to have this very clear dimension of the Holy Spirit's activity throughout the whole preaching process: from preparation through to proclamation, and finally ending in demonstration of the works of God. There are many different ways of working this out, and it is important that we each find the way that takes into account who we each are and how God wants to use each one of us. But whoever we are and whatever model of ministry we choose, the Holy Spirit must also be there and we therefore must develop a desperation and a hunger and a thirst that will only be satisfied when God comes upon our preaching and uses us in something like or even approaching New Testament proportions. Our gospel is to come 'not in word only'.

NOTES

1. The Scriptures in this chapter are taken from the New King James Version.
2. *Preaching with Purpose: The Urgent Task of Homiletics* (Zondervan, 1986).
3. See also Chapter 21, 'Preaching for a Verdict and a Response' in which I develop this theme.
4. Hendrickson Pub. Inc, 1994; see pp. 43–45.
5. Greek *parakoloutheo*.
6. Greek *epakolouthe*.

PREACHING FOR A VERDICT AND RESPONSE

Colin Dye

Many sermons are impeccable in respect of their understanding and interpretation of Scripture but they miss the mark in enlightening the mind, touching people's emotions and shaping the will. As preachers we must become as Jesus was, for He was the Master of human nature. We are the students, but we certainly must become, as He was, those who understand human nature, who understand what is happening in the hearts of men and women, and what it is going to take to bring them to a verdict and a response concerning the truthfulness and relevance of the preaching in their lives. There are no short cuts to this, no gimmicks – I am not just talking about six clever ways to make an appeal. We need to go right back to the Scriptures to understand that they have a very significant and often specific purpose. In our interpretation of Scripture we must go beyond the normal patterns and principles of hermeneutics to include what God wants to achieve through those particular Scripture passages, and that is how we will preach for a verdict and a response. That is how we will be effective in applying the truths of Scripture adequately, accurately and relevantly to the hearts and minds of our hearers.

Part of the work of Scripture interpretation is to determine the purpose of the passage, which Dr Jay E. Adams calls 'the *telos* of the passage'.[1] Thus, in one sense there is, if not a new hermeneutical principle, at least a new hermeneutical dimension that has to be mastered. I believe that the purpose of the passage will be elicited through the normal processes of hermeneutics. So, as a first step we seek to discover through the tools of historical, grammatical and theological analysis what was the purpose in the mind of the author when he wrote a particular passage of Scripture. But the *telos* of the passage goes further than this because it answers the question: what was the Holy Spirit's purpose in causing this passage to be written? As the ultimate Author of Scripture the Spirit had a purpose in mind for every passage. God does nothing without purpose, and often that purpose of Scripture is broader than that which was in the minds of the human authors. In the same way we as preachers, though not with infallible ability, take the Scripture and interpret and apply it to people in line with the Holy Spirit's purpose.

Let us think for a moment about the purpose of the Holy Bible. What is the *telos* of Scripture? The apostle Paul comes close to describing this for us in 2 Timothy 3:15–17:

> *from infancy you have known the holy Scriptures, which are able to make you wise for salvation through faith in Christ Jesus. All Scripture is God-breathed and is useful for teaching, rebuking, correcting and training in righteousness, so that the man of God may be thoroughly equipped for every good work.*[2]

From this we see that Scripture has one overarching telic purpose, which is to provide wisdom for salvation through faith in Christ. So the whole of the Bible from cover to cover is written that we might have the understanding of how to be saved, and I am sure the word 'salvation' here is in the fullest sense, not just of a ticket to heaven but of bringing God's rich salvation, lifestyle and experience, including sanctification as well as justification. That in itself is very helpful. In our preaching we ask the question: What is there in this Scripture that is going to bring people to salvation in the fullest sense? Our goal is then to take the Scripture and preach so as to shape people's lives according to God's salvation purpose for them. I believe that if that purpose alone were introduced to all preaching in Britain, we would have the subversive revolution that Greg Haslam has spoken about.[3] So often preachers do not preach with this purpose in mind. They dip into the Word of God for a thought here and a thought there and forget its real purpose and its real intent. If we understand that the Word of God is given to bring people to faith in Christ, to bring them to salvation and to perfect them in that salvation from here until they go to heaven, then we will be preaching with a purpose in mind to shape people's lives, to challenge them, to bring them to conviction, to bring them to decision. I am not saying that all preaching must be crisis preaching – there is a lot of evidence in Scripture that the sheer joy of meditating on the truth of God's Word and the appreciation of who God is has in itself a very salutary and saving effect upon the human soul and human personality. But the general purpose of Scripture, the overarching *telos* of Scripture, is to bring God's rich salvation.

Paul breaks down this overarching *telos* into four main subpurposes that follow on from it. He says all Scripture is *'useful for teaching, rebuking, correcting and training in righteousness'*. By 'useful' he means 'of practical use'. It is a practical tool. God intends preaching to be practical. There are then four great sub-*tele*.

1. Teaching

We teach the truth that shapes people's lives. This truth should not be tampered with or apologised for, but proclaimed and communicated as it really is. However, I do believe that there are some post-modern considerations we have to make in terms of our communication: not in changing the message but in understanding that people will best receive it in an atmosphere which is accepting and in which they are personally valued. We have to be careful before we simply go down the confrontational route, standing up and saying, 'Thus says the Lord . . . like it or leave it.' We have to get back to an approach that says, 'Thus says the Lord to you where you are in your situation of human need.' After all God did not lean out of heaven and use the divine equivalent of a megaphone to say, 'What's the matter with you lot down there? You had better listen to what I have to say.' He came down as the Living Word made flesh and He showed us that He highly valued us. The truth He proclaimed cost Him everything He had because on the cross Jesus Christ paid the price to bring its reality into our lives. If we as preachers haven't listened to our church members they are not going to listen to us. Having listened to people we proclaim our message in the way that they can best receive it and hear it as being relevant to their lives.

2. Rebuking

This is a very necessary activity of preaching. The word translated 'rebuking' here means 'bringing to full conviction'. It does not mean standing in front of people and telling them that they have got it all wrong. It is communicating in such a way that people come to a conviction about where they are out of line. This sense of conviction is one of the single greatest omissions in people's experience of God and of Jesus Christ in our churches today, let alone our society. There is very little sense of real conviction as to why we are so out of line. We are telling people to shape up before they have understood exactly what it means to be under the Spirit's conviction.

3. Correcting

The Word of God is so practical. It tells people how to deal with the fault or the problem. Jesus was very good at this practical instruction – just one example is the way He taught His disciples how to pray and how not to pray. The practical instruction that comes out of the Word of God is amazing: there are practical how-tos about every area of life that can be deduced and applied into people's lives. The self-help shelves in our bookshops should be empty: there is more than enough divine aid coming from the Scriptures to help us deal with our marriages, sort out our lives and discover all that God has for us as human beings.

4. Training

Our preaching should help people develop a disciplined lifestyle. Their lives and characters are shaped and moulded by the truth of the Word of God, so that real change is internalised in a person's life and developed into their thought and behaviour practices.

THE PARABLE OF THE LOST SHEEP, THE LOST COIN AND THE LOST SON

Having looked at the overarching purpose of Scripture and its four main subpurposes I would like now to illustrate how we should constantly be seeking to discover the *telos* of a passage through exegesis on a very familiar parable, the parable of the prodigal son in Luke 15. I find this parable one of the most challenging and the most fruitful of passages for fresh understanding of who God is and how His Kingdom operates in our lives. It is, of course, the parable that Jesus told in the light of the scribes and Pharisees' criticism concerning His attitude towards sinners. When they preach on Luke 15, many preachers focus on the so-called prodigal son and often wrest the story from its true *telos*, losing its full meaning and application. In so doing, their preaching is weakened and the opportunity that the Spirit has given in inspiring the story in the first place, or at least inspiring it to be written and recorded for us, is lost.

As we know, the passage breaks the parable up into three stories. It is not three parables; it is one parable, but it is in three sections: the lost sheep, the lost coin and the lost son. The key is in the introduction. Jay Adams speaks about looking for telic cues – clues in the text that point in the direction of the purpose. Here we have Holy Spirit recording for us exactly why this passage is in Scripture: it says in verse 1, *'The tax collectors and the sinners drew near to Him to hear Him.'* That's amazing. We need to stop and experience a sense of wonder at that. Here is Jesus Christ, the Holiest One who has ever lived, the spotless Son of God, the second person of the Trinity incarnate, and sinners are flocking to Him. Show me a preacher like that. Show me a preacher that the people will flock to. Jesus has something so special about Him that He draws sinners to Him. Whatever else it is, it is His intense love for sinners – yes, *for sinners*. Not just for churchgoers, the pious, the pompous. But for the ordinary people in the street. One of the biggest revolutions that has to come is that we have to give birth to a Church that cares for the lost and for sinners like Jesus did. Frankly, we don't care that much. But Jesus did. He cared so much that the Pharisees and scribes complained, *'This man receives sinners and eats with them.'* He receives sinners. He accepts them. He welcomes them. And He eats with them. Even in British hospitality but more particularly in Middle Eastern hospitality, to eat with somebody is extremely relevant and significant. It means that the guest is being received by the host and the host by the guest. By eating with sinners, Jesus was accepting them. In verse 3 Luke says, *'So He spoke this parable to them.'* The purpose of the parable is then to address this situation. The Holy Spirit is, therefore, investing the passage with very significant telic intent. It is to expose us to the heart of the Father so that we understand His love and His grace towards sinners and so that we would similarly receive sinners and proclaim to them His free, unconditional and total acceptance of them in Christ.

Jesus is the Master Story-teller. How does He grab people's attention so effectively? First of all there is a lost sheep which is found, and there is rejoicing. Then there is a lost coin which is found, and there is rejoicing. Finally, there is a lost son who is found, and there is complaining. Suddenly we ask, what's this all about? It catches our attention. It grates with us. We are drawn into the story, but soon we are confronted by the elder brother's attitude, and our understanding of the gospel is tested. Even in a congregation of preachers I can guarantee that understanding of the gospel is tested by this story. We see that the son is of greater value than a silly sheep that has gone wandering over the mountain, or of greater value than a coin, albeit probably part of the woman's dowry and therefore very precious to her. As the son is found, who is of much more value than sheep and coins, there should be even greater rejoicing.

The lost sheep was found by the shepherd, the lost coin was found by the woman, and the lost son was found by the father. This lost son did not find himself. He did not come to his senses and repent in a foreign land. He repented in the father's arms. He was found by the father. This tests our understanding of the gospel because virtually every sermon that I have heard on the parable of the prodigal son, as they call it – which is a misnomer because it is the parable of three lost things including the lost son – speaks of him repenting in a foreign land. He *did not* repent there. He found a way to get back from there. This was not a repentant son: this was a hungry son, this was a son who was broke, this was a son coming home for mum to do his washing and for dad to give him a meal. He knew that the only way back into the house was to rehearse the kind of speech that would get him in. At the very best his sincerity was nevertheless misplaced and misjudged for he had no idea or understanding of the kind of father he really had. He thought he could negotiate and say, 'Accept me back. I will work, I will do this, I will do that, I will do the other.' My feeling is he was hoping to pay off his debt so that he could get the old man off his back again. But in the meantime he was hungry.

To some extent he might have been genuine in his understanding that he had done wrong, as the scribes and Pharisees were probably genuine in their understanding that they were far from God and had a debt towards Him. But the scribes and Pharisees' totally false understanding of the gospel is exhibited in the fact that they thought they could work off that debt and they thought that acceptance before God was totally dependent on behaviour. This is the opposite of the gospel. We are saved by faith and by faith alone. What else does evangelical Protestantism stand upon if it is not the divine rediscovery of Martin Luther that we do not first repent and clean up our lives and become acceptable to God? We are found as sinners in the arms of a loving Father, and we live for God and do good works not in order to be saved but *because* we are saved.

What Jesus is saying here is an absolute revolution of thinking and understanding. 'If you knew the love of God and the way that is open to you, you would not be criticising Me for receiving sinners. You would change your attitude yourself and enter into relationship with the Father.' We understand that the real lost son is the elder brother.

He remains lost. Even at the end of the parable he remains lost for he has no relationship with the father. Yet in his own mind and understanding he had always done everything that the father wanted. He had always served the father. His legalistic righteousness, to draw the parallel theologically, was flawless but, like the apostle Paul until he found Christ, he had no relationship with God whatsoever.

This shows us the poverty of religion in any shape or form, whether it is the Christian religion, the Buddhist religion, or the Islamic religion. Religion does not cut it when it comes to relationship with God. As preachers we have to preach such a free and unconditional gospel. We have to preach the love of God so strongly that it will hit people between the eyes as they understand that the Christian message is entirely different from any other philosophy, ideology, or so-called theology of any other religious belief, including false theology emanating out of the so-called Christian Church down through the years. Nothing short of a new revolution, a new reformation of understanding of the power of the gospel of Jesus Christ, is going to make any difference in Great Britain. That is why this is a very relevant passage for us today. The Holy Spirit recorded this story so that we might be drawn into Jesus' teaching. As we are confronted by this elder brother's attitude, we see that the real heart of the father is in embracing his son, no matter what his son had done and conferring upon him unconditional love and acceptance. The repentance of the son did not precede his experience with the father: it came out of his experience of the father. I think many of those who are seeking to preach the gospel of Jesus Christ in evangelical circles today have virtually rewritten Scripture. Have we forgotten what the gospel is?

John's Gospel records the story of a woman caught in the very act of adultery, no doubt dragged in by her hair and thrown at the feet of Jesus (see John 8:1–11). The Pharisees and teachers of the Law confront Jesus with a trick question. Jesus would have been condemned whichever way He had answered. If He had said, 'No, don't allow her to be stoned', He would have been going against Moses and would Himself have been stoned as a false prophet. If, however, He had said, 'Yes, go ahead and do it', He would have been playing fast and loose with Jewish authority that had no entitlement to pronounce such a death sentence under Roman occupation. Or, more to the point, He would have gone right against His own purpose and mission for He Himself had said,

> *'For God did not send His Son into the world to condemn the world, but that the world through Him might be saved.'*
> (John 3:17)

Jesus is not fazed: He says,

> *'He who is without sin among you, let him throw a stone at her first.'*
> (John 8:7)

This is a great statement. Out of it flow such Pauline statements as, *'all have sinned and fall short of the glory of God'*.[4] Paul and Jesus say the same thing; there is no contradiction here. One by one, under conviction, everyone leaves.

When Jesus is left alone with the woman, He asks her, *'Woman, where are those accusers of yours? Has no one condemned you?'* *'No one, Lord,'* she replies. And Jesus says to her, *'Neither do I condemn you; go and sin no more.'* There are actually two parts to that sentence. The first part is in the indicative mood; it is a statement of fact: 'I do not condemn you.' It is given freely, unconditionally, before Jesus in any way measures her response, save for one thing which I will come back to. The second part of the statement is in the imperative mood: it is a command, 'go and sin no more'. As evangelicals we often preach the gospel as if Jesus said, 'I do not condemn you if you go and sin no more.' He did not say that. We have confused justification and sanctification. One of the greatest theological issues preachers need to be grappling with today is just exactly what justification is, just exactly what sanctification is and how they are related – because they are related. For the same Jesus who said, 'I do not condemn you' also said, 'go and sin no more.' We cannot accept the one and reject the other. Both hold true in our lives. But God's unconditional acceptance of us does not depend on anything we have ever done, on anything we are doing or on anything we shall ever do. It depends on this one thing alone: on our believing in the gospel. That is what Martin Luther taught: justification by faith alone.

So how was it possible for Jesus to make this wonderful statement lifting the condemnation off this woman, 'Neither do I condemn you'? Jesus knew that in not many days He would mount the steps of Calvary and become the substitutionary sacrifice for the sins of the world, bearing not only this woman's condemnation but indeed all humanity's: this is why He can speak these words. Moreover, He is the ultimate Judge, and now the Judge of all the earth has spoken: He declares her righteous. But, on the basis of that, He then says, 'go and sin no more.' This is a command of Jesus upon every one of our lives: not to tolerate even one single sin in our lives and to be totally committed to ensure that we grow in holiness and in sanctification. As believers sin has absolutely no place in our lives.

The scribes and Pharisees taught the people that in order to be saved they had to live in a certain way. Jesus teaches, 'No. Salvation isn't found that way.' There is nobody who will ever be able to keep any standard – either before they are saved or after they are saved – that would qualify them for heaven. The only qualification for heaven is the free pardoning of God's grace received by faith, and by faith alone, in Christ Jesus. Earlier I said I would return to a point in connection with the woman's response. There was something about this woman that gave Jesus a reason to say, 'I don't condemn you.' It wasn't her behaviour; it wasn't that she had proved herself through a set of discipleship principles or through water baptism; it wasn't that she had achieved a certain level of sanctification. It was because she simply looked to Jesus and saw something about Him which she recognised as the answer for her need. It was simple faith. Because of her simple faith she was freely declared totally and completely righteous by the grace of God.

Returning to the story of the lost son as part of this parable of three stories, the *telos* of this passage is, then, that we should receive sinners in the same way God does by virtue of the fact that He has received us as unconditionally as the father received his younger son. The path to acceptance and intimacy with the Father is through grace not law, through relationship with God, not rules. The gospel is God's means of reconciliation. It speaks of relationship with Him and with each other. It also speaks of the reproduction of His nature in us. All of this is contained within the telic intent and purpose of the passage, and its power is discovered when we preach it according to its true purpose, which is to shape people's attitudes and actions through the gospel of grace. Knowing we have been forgiven and accepted unconditionally, we live in this same way in relation to others. If that simple change came upon the Church of Jesus Christ in this generation we would have a real revolution.

PREACHING WITH A PURPOSE

There are three basic categories of the telic intentions of Scripture. While most passages will have one or two of these elements, they will usually have one as a main feature. There are passages of Scripture which are almost sheer *information*. These are passages through which God wants to inform us about something, such as when Paul says, 'I would not have you ignorant ...'.[5] Then there are passages whose purpose is *persuasion*. Before we can believe something that God would have us believe, we have to 'unbelieve' a whole lot of other things. Repentance and changing our mind and our mindset means rejecting false notions and accepting the truth of Jesus Christ. Then there is a *motivation* element, as the Word of God seeks to motivate us to do something or not to do something.

As preachers we must grasp the *telos* of the passage and keep it as the dominant theme throughout our message. This helps us to become much more targeted, for everything from beginning to end is based on the passage's purpose. The purpose of the passage is the purpose of the message. In the introduction we raise the purpose of our message to arouse interest and to establish relevance. We need to do that in the opening seconds before people switch off. In the exposition we develop our theme in line with the purpose. In the conclusion, hopefully, we arrive at the destination we set out to reach. In our application we drive the point home so that it achieves the response that we desire. If it is effectively an information message, there is a revelation from God's Word that we want to be received and understood by the people. If it is a persuasion message, there is a truth to be embraced or an error to be rejected. If it is a motivation message, there is an action to be taken.

Now when I speak about application, I do not wish to give the impression that the application comes at the end of the sermon. The message must be applied all the way through. In some homiletical schemes the preacher is taught to put the application at the end. That is too late – it is three points too late, or five points too late. I so exaggerate this that I say I begin with my application. We must not leave our application to the last point in our message when we ask the question, 'Now what has all this got to do with us?' The congregation has been asking this very question for the past forty-five minutes! We must keep applying our message, and in doing so we must ensure that our application is in line with our purpose.

One of the best ways of doing this is through the illustrations and stories that we use. Probably in my own preaching illustration is one of the weakest aspects, which I am aware I have to work at. I know that some preachers don't even prepare their illustrations; they just rely on what occurs to them at the time. We have all listened to those preachers! Unless a preacher is very experienced or has a very special instinct, it is not good enough. Our sermons must not become all stories and no substance, neither must they be all substance and no stories. Jesus was the greatest story-teller. He had an amazing ability to take the details of this life and the world which people know and to draw parallels to the Kingdom of God which were so memorable that people carried them home in their hearts and minds. Skilful selection of stories and illustrations enables the preacher to take the purpose of the Spirit of God that is upon the message he is preaching further and further to its goal of changed lives.

It is also important to touch every area of the personality. An old preacher said to me once, 'In every sermon there should be an element of wonder, an element of wooing and an element of warning.' We should be aiming to be complete in our preaching, and with this in mind there are a number of checks we can put in place. For example, we can ask: Is my preaching really relevant to where people are? Does my preaching really cover all of life? Does it cover people at every stage of life? Does it cover every kind of profession? We want people to feel included in the message. Most of all I seek to ensure that my preaching touches the three aspects of human personality. I include something that will speak directly into the mind. I do this, not so that people will think I am more clever than they, as someone once advised me I should do, but so that their understanding is enlightened. Preaching must enlighten the mind.

I include something that will impact the emotions. I'm not talking about emotionalism or playing on the emotions, but about touching the emotions. Jesus' three-part parable does this. Who can fail but be moved at the sight of this rather dignified Middle-Eastern patriarch picking up his robes and running in a very undignified fashion to embrace his son who had insulted him in a way that meant he should have been banished forever? At the sight of this son trying to get his speech out but never getting past the first few words because he has been interrupted by the father and he might have still been talking but nobody heard him because his father had him in a full nelson of love and affection? Preaching must impact the emotions. The Holy Spirit will often use the preaching of God's Word to stir up such emotions as joy, holy fear, sorrow, or sometimes a sense of complete wonder, and that is good and healthy.

I include something that will touch the will because, ultimately, the human will must bend itself to God. Each of us is as holy today as we have chosen to be. Preaching must move the will. That is how we bring people to a verdict.

Of course, our success in hitting our target depends solely on the Holy Spirit who alone can truly apply the message. We can be as strong or even as crass as we like in seeking to apply the message, but without the Holy Spirit's work the people are not going to hear. We call for the public response in any way that seems appropriate, whether it is an appeal, an invitation, a prayer, a song of response, a silence or some form of specific action, but it is God who brings conviction to people's heart. Depending on His divine action we preach for a response.

NOTES

1. See also Chapter 20, in which I introduce this concept. I am indebted to the work of Dr Jay Adams for his whole understanding of the telic intent of Scripture, which is explained in his book *Preaching with Purpose: The Urgent Task of Homiletics* (Zondervan, 1986).
2. NIV. Other Scriptures in this chapter are taken from the New King James Version.
3. See Chapter 19.
4. Romans 3:23.
5. See e.g. Romans 11:25; 1 Corinthians 10:1; 12:1; 2 Corinthians 1:8.

Chapter 22

IN DEMONSTRATION OF
THE SPIRIT'S POWER

David Holden

*For I resolved to know nothing while I was with you except Jesus Christ and him
crucified. I came to you in weakness and fear and with much trembling. My
message and my preaching were not with wise and persuasive words but with a
demonstration of the Spirit's power, so that your faith might not rest on men's
wisdom, but on God's power.*
(1 Corinthians 2:2–5)

Effective preaching must be more than words. In 1 Corinthians 2:2–5 the apostle Paul
makes it clear that he wants his listeners to know that their faith is not based on words,
but on God's power, and to that end he has a deep concern that his preaching should
always incorporate a demonstration of the Spirit's power. If we look at Acts 8, which
gives an account of the days following the outpouring of the Holy Spirit when the early
Church was scattered all over the Roman empire, we see the outworking of this same
emphasis. We read that preachers went out proclaiming Christ – and the inference is that
the people listened to their preaching. However, verse 6 says:

*When the crowds heard Philip and saw the miraculous signs he did, they all paid
close attention to what he said.*

The people heard some words which grabbed their attention, but they then experienced a
demonstration of the Spirit which grabbed their attention even more. The society in
which we live traffics in nothing but 'words, words, words', and in our preaching we can

also easily fall into the trap of just speaking words, but, if our preaching is to make an impact, words will not be enough. Of course, we must preach 'Christ and him crucified', but it must be with the belief that in, through and as a result of our preaching we will see a demonstration of the power of the Spirit of God.

It is interesting that, while Paul clearly states the importance of a demonstration of the Spirit's power in and through his preaching, he does not tell us what that demonstration is in this context. We do know that people came to the Lord and that their faith was built on the power of God and not word alone, but we do not know whether the demonstration of the Spirit's power occurred while he was preaching, or after he preached as 'signs following'. All that we know is that, for Paul, preaching went beyond words.

In our preaching we need both the Word and the Spirit. We must see that these two supposed enemies are friends. Biblically they are joined together at every point because they both need each another. I believe that today we desperately need churches that are full of men and women who are as passionate for the Word as they are for the things of the Spirit. In my mind it is churches that have the combination of the Spirit and the Word together which will change the nation; not churches which have one without the other, but those which are passionate about both together. We need our preaching to be an amalgam of Word and Spirit; we need our meetings to be absorbed in Word and Spirit. I cannot think of one thing that we do in the life of our churches that should not have this combination of Word and Spirit together.

As we consider the issue of preaching, this amalgamation is extremely important. All too often in our churches people still view the worship as the realm of the Spirit's activity and there is no expectation that the Spirit wants to work through the Word. There is little understanding of our need for the help of the Holy Spirit both for the preacher as he preaches and the congregation as they listen, and this is, I believe, a fundamental mistake. As much as my preaching needs to be truth, it needs the anointing of the Holy Spirit. Neither the Word without the Spirit nor worship without truth will actually feed the people of God. I have been in meetings where, despite much spiritual activity in worship, I have left the meeting very disappointed and dissatisfied, and I have asked myself why. Nearly every time it is because I haven't been fed. There was a lack of truth in what was going on. There was a lack of contributions that were rooted in the Word of God. It is this reservoir of truth that builds us up, which is why the songs we sing must also be worship in Spirit and in truth. Spirit and Word are joined together. We desperately need both to be in harmony with one another.

IMPARTATION

In my preaching I am passionately and increasingly concerned that there should be a process of impartation. By the time I have finished preaching I want to make sure that I have really communicated with my listeners. And the only way I can be sure of this is if I have help in the process of impartation from the Holy Spirit. A well-shaped sermon is not enough. Visual aids and other techniques, although helpful, are not enough. The only true guarantee of communication is 'impartation' by the Holy Spirit, which I believe was Paul's understanding in 2 Corinthians 2:2–5. Preaching is beyond words alone. Something needs to be imparted to the people who are listening which words alone cannot achieve. Preaching is not lecturing; preaching is not a political speech: preaching essentially is giving something away. The preacher gives of himself, but more than that, he gives something from the heart of God. Anointed preaching leaves a deposit with people that will last beyond that one particular sermon.

Sometimes when I finish preaching a sermon I feel totally drained, totally exhausted. Why should this be when I have only been speaking for forty-five or fifty minutes? It is because I have imparted something. When we are preaching, the Holy Spirit is at work, and He is wanting this preached word to really communicate with the people. And that is why, as we preach, we sometimes sense opposition. It is because preaching is more than words being spoken: something is being imparted.

In Romans 1:11–12, speaking about his desire to visit the Roman church, Paul makes this statement:

> *I long to see you so that I may impart to you some spiritual gift to make you strong –*
> *that is, that you and I may be mutually encouraged by each other's faith.*

Again he doesn't tell us what that spiritual gift is, but what is clear is that his concept of visiting a church was not just to leave them with some sermons but to impart something, so that when he was no longer there, these people could continue to live out their faith. The hint is that there would be an impartation of faith which would result in mutual encouragement. Paul wanted to leave something with people. In preaching we should be conveying something tangible to those who are listening. This is what I believe is meant by 'a demonstration of the Spirit's power'.

For example, I can preach a word of faith. I have done so in fact many, many times. But while I am speaking, I need the Holy Spirit to impart something. I want the people listening to me to begin to experience faith. We all know that one of the greatest weaknesses of the western Church is unbelief and cynicism. We need a huge dose of faith. Now that faith doesn't come just by seeing miracles. That faith comes by hearing the Word of God: it is the preaching that must impart faith. But words on their own cannot achieve this. It is very interesting to note what it says in Hebrews 4:2:

> *For we also have had the gospel preached to us, just as they did; but the message they*
> *heard was of no value to them, because those who heard did not combine it with*
> *faith.*

The people need to be instructed that, when they are listening to the Word of God, they need to mix what they are hearing with faith so that they will actually absorb faith and become men and women of faith. I don't just want to teach sermons on faith. My aim is to impart something so that the lives of the people listening change and make an impact in their workplace or in their college or school, in their family and in the street in which they live. That is a demonstration of the Spirit's power to do something which I cannot do.

True communication occurs when our preaching is dependent upon the Holy Spirit. He is the Communicator; He is the Imparter; He is the One who anoints what I say. The implication of this truth is that the antidote to boring preaching may not be the addition of gadgets and gimmicks and technology; the antidote to boring preaching may not be shorter sermons because people cannot listen for as long as they used to in the past; the antidote to boring preaching is impartation, which comes from the person of the Holy Spirit. I therefore expect the Holy Spirit to be totally involved not only in my preparation of a sermon, but also in the proclamation of it, and in the demonstration that follows it.

I want to ask three questions about the involvement of the Holy Spirit in our preaching which I hope will encourage us as preachers to have a greater expectation of a demonstration of His power as we preach the Word of God.

What is the Holy Spirit Doing While I am Preaching?

While I am preaching I believe the Holy Spirit is at work in a number of ways:

1. He is anointing me as a person and the words that I speak

In some circles the impression is given that the preacher is the channel which God uses for the proclamation of the message and that, somehow, the individual himself is bypassed. In my view this is neither true biblically, nor in terms of actual application. The Holy Spirit uses me. While I am preaching He wants to have a relationship with me and He wants to use and anoint my words. Sometimes I am very aware that the Holy Spirit is using me, while at other times I am not aware of it at all. On occasions nothing seems to be happening, but that does not mean that the Holy Spirit is not at work. This is not a matter of feelings but of faith.

I actually believe that the Lord wants to use the personalities of those He calls to preach. Sometimes I preach from pulpits which have engraved in them the words 'Sir, we would see Jesus'. The inference is that it is the task of the preacher to disappear from sight so that the congregation can just see the Lord. One of these days, when I am preaching in one of those pulpits, I am going to announce my text and then disappear behind the pulpit! In all sincerity I do want to lift up Jesus, I do want people to see Jesus, but I believe that in the process He wants to use me. Sometimes people say that what we need is a 'nameless' or 'faceless' generation. That is never going to happen. The Bible is full of names and faces – men and women used by God to fulfil His purposes. God uses the preacher. He uses the experiences we have had over the past week; He uses our personalities; He doesn't bypass us; He uses us to glorify His name. Some years ago a friend of mine was so blessed in a worship time by the fantastic skill of the pianist that he went over to her at the end of the service to express his appreciation. She replied, 'It wasn't me, it was the Lord.' He replied, 'Then who played the duff note?' The Lord uses real people. We need to expect the Holy Spirit to use us.

2. He is bringing understanding to people

As I am preaching, the Holy Spirit is helping people to understand the truth that I am seeking to impart. The Holy Spirit is the Spirit of truth and He comes and explains the Scriptures to people in ways that they can understand. In my own church more and more people are being saved out of a completely non-Christian background: they will only come to an understanding of the Word that is being preached if the Holy Spirit helps them.

3. He is bringing revelation

And how people need revelation! Even Christians who have been around for years and years still need revelation – and such revelation is beyond words. Take the doctrine of the grace of God, for example. I may preach a sermon on grace and people may hear my words, but they will never grasp the reality of grace unless there is illumination from the Holy Spirit. Some preachers who proclaim the doctrine of grace from the pulpit are in their day-to-day lives the most miserable people imaginable. They do not know God's grace for themselves. We can preach the grace of God with all our heart, but only the Holy Spirit can bring revelation so that our hearers do not just receive intellectual understanding but so that the truth practically impacts the way they live their lives. In the course of our preaching some of those listening to us begin to get very excited – they are the ones upon whom the truth is beginning to dawn; they are receiving revelation.

I believe that 2 Timothy 4:2 is a very timely and important scripture for the Church in this country at the present time. All the while hoping for people to receive revelation, all the while hoping for impartation, all the while hoping for communication and understanding, we are enjoined,

> Preach the Word; be prepared in season and out of season; correct, rebuke and encourage – with great patience and careful instruction.

Whether or not we see what we long to see, we are to keep preaching, carefully and patiently applying the truth knowing and believing that the Holy Spirit is gradually bringing revelation to people. I have seen churches transformed by the constant preaching of truth week by week, month by month, year by year. It can cleanse a church; it can take it on a journey. If we teach everything that we would love our churches to move into, they will come into it through revelation. It is not a case of persuading people or hitting them over the head with the truth, it is a case of convincing people through the Word of God, with the help of the Holy Spirit who brings revelation.

4. He is bringing conviction
John 16:8 says,

> 'When he comes, he will convict the world of guilt in regard to sin and righteousness and judgment...'

The Holy Spirit convicts unbelievers of sin but, wider than that, during the preaching of the Word He is constantly convicting Christians of issues that are relevant to their lives also. There is so much more going on than the preacher can know or identify. As preachers we must never gauge what is happening by the faces of the people who are listening. So many times I have felt terrible when I have looked at people's faces: everybody seems totally switched off and I have tried to hit them harder with the words I am speaking. Later, I may discover that I have totally misread the situation. The Holy Spirit is at work even when we are not aware of it. He never condemns, of course, but He is convicting people of issues that need to be dealt with in their lives. We need to ask the Holy Spirit to anoint the words that we have prepared so that this application can take place.

5. He is communing with me as I preach
As I preach, the Holy Spirit gives me guidance on what is really living in the material I have prepared, and how I can best apply it. Therefore, as I preach I am constantly desiring to submit myself to Him. Many times after I have preached a sermon, I have asked myself why I spent so long on one point. The answer is often because the Holy Spirit was compelling me to do so. He was powerfully anointing certain aspects of the Word that I had prepared. While we are preaching, we need to listen very carefully to the Holy Spirit.

A friend of mine tells a very interesting story about something that happened to him one time, back in the 1960s, when he was undergoing a period of great turmoil in his life and he came to hear Martyn Lloyd-Jones speaking at Westminster Chapel. He was disturbed by teaching which he had been hearing about the Holy Spirit and was convinced that our churches needed the power of the Spirit of God. At the end of the service, he grabbed Martyn Lloyd-Jones as he was making his way out, and asked if he could have a quick word with him. Explaining that he was in great turmoil, he spoke of his passion to see the Spirit and the Word come together in the Church. Dr Lloyd-Jones's reply really surprised him. He had expected a reply along the lines, 'Well, you have got to be grounded in truth', but in fact Dr Lloyd-Jones said, 'I just happened to notice something about my sermon tonight. How many points did I say that I would make at the beginning of this sermon?' My friend replied, 'Three.' 'How many points did I actually make?' continued Dr Lloyd-Jones. Thinking it might be a trick question, my friend replied tentatively, 'One.' 'Exactly,' came the reply. 'I only made one point of the three I had announced and the reason for that is that the Spirit of God compelled me not to move on to the next point I had announced.' This is an experience that many preachers are familiar with. The Holy Spirit longs to commune with us as we preach.

6. He is planting seeds into the hearts of men and women that will later be watered by Him

It is very important for preachers to understand this aspect of the Holy Spirit's activity. Sometimes after having preached, I have felt that it was a complete waste of time – it had achieved nothing. I couldn't get away quickly enough. But, whatever the reaction to our sermons, we can have no idea what has been sown into people's hearts, which may bear fruit in a week's time, or two weeks' time, or a month's time, or even longer. The Holy Spirit ensures that God's Word will not return to heaven empty and void. God's Word is never preached without purpose, as Isaiah makes clear: 'It will not return to me empty, but will accomplish what I desire and achieve the purpose for which I sent it' (55:11). It is not my responsibility to ensure that it achieves the purpose for which it was sent; it is the Holy Spirit's responsibility. As I am preaching, I don't know what is proving effective, but the Holy Spirit does. He will plant the seed and water it. It will not return to Him empty. We, as preachers, are not good judges of how our sermons were received. Sometimes I have preached a storm without any response; at other times I have preached what seemed to me to be a complete dud of a sermon and I couldn't wait to get out, but people have come up to me afterwards, and spoken about the impact it has had upon them.

Can we really embark on the adventure of becoming a preacher without the Holy Spirit? A true understanding of all that the Holy Spirit is doing while we are preaching drives us to the realisation that we cannot do this successfully without Him. Jesus said, 'apart from me you can do nothing'[1] – and this statement applies also to preaching. Some of us are good preachers. We can actually preach out of our own ability, but not if we want to impart something; not if we want to communicate; not if we want our listeners to be still working out our sermon in a week's time. That is the work of the Holy Spirit.

HOW DOES THE INVOLVEMENT OF THE HOLY SPIRIT AFFECT MY PREACHING?

1. I must therefore be a man of the Spirit

I not only need to prepare what I am about to proclaim, I must also prepare myself. I must see how impoverished I am without Him. He is my Helper, the Paraclete, the One who comes alongside to enable me to do this task. I don't ever want to preach again without being dependent on the person of the Holy Spirit and without myself being a man of the Spirit. Being totally dependent on the Holy Spirit personally in our own lives is the key to everything we do as preachers.

2. My sermon preparation must include the Holy Spirit's involvement

I have already mentioned this but it is an important point which I want to emphasise. Beyond my study of the Word and my reading of commentaries and other theological works I must also involve the Holy Spirit in my preparation. I must be submitted to Him. He helps us in our weakness (cf. Romans 8:26, spoken in the context of prayer). While being very serious and thorough in our sermon preparation, at the same time we need to be asking the Holy Spirit to come and help us as we engage in this work. We must believe that as we take our pen, or work at our computer, *'we have the mind of Christ'*.[2] What does the Holy Spirit want to emphasise? What is my goal through this sermon? What is His goal? All the time in my preparation, I am asking the Holy Spirit to help me to take the basic theological truths that I discover in the Word and apply them, so that the people who are listening to me might really grasp them in their lives and might bear much fruit. We need to pray over our preparation and invite the Holy Spirit to come and help us, as He has promised to do.

3. While I am preaching I need to be in submission to the Holy Spirit

As I give room to the Holy Spirit to give me direction and emphasis and even to interrupt what I am saying, power is released. I have to be honest and admit that I am not sure I know a lot about a demonstration of the Holy Spirit's power actually while I am preaching but I am full of expectation to see it more and more. I fully understand and endorse the expectation that there should be a demonstration of His power after I have preached, but I have a feeling that we are meant to see it happening actually while we are preaching. When I recall that the Word of God's own description of itself is that it is *'sharper than a double-edged sword'*,[3] I have a feeling that there should be a greater demonstration of this power as I am actually speaking. I already understand that while I am preaching people are being set free and transformed, faith is being rekindled, and minds are being renewed, but I also want to see people being healed and delivered, as happens in many other parts of the world, often in very dramatic and disturbing ways. The truth is that, wherever we are in the world, the Word of God has the potential to do all these things while we are actually preaching. Perhaps one day we will even be overcome by the need to stop preaching, because there is so much Holy Spirit activity. We must be open to such things happening. When we read between the lines of the accounts of the great historical preachers whom we all love, such as Whitefield and Wesley, it is clear that they faced interruption in their preaching because the power of God was at work. It can't have been easy to handle what was happening. All the time, as we are preaching, we need to be in submission to what the Holy Spirit is doing among us.

4. I need to be asking how the anointing of the Spirit is to be applied

This is something that recently I have tried to be more and more disciplined in doing: while I am preparing a word I am asking myself, how will this be applied? Many preachers think that their task ends with their closing prayer and final amen, but I think we need to push the application of the word a bit further. Obviously there are a number of practical considerations that constrain us – although we *could* make our sermons a bit shorter – but we need to be asking how the Holy Spirit wants to apply what we have preached. We need to ask, 'Holy Spirit, is there something else?' Perhaps the application of the word will require a time of ministry, or perhaps it is a word which can only really be worked out in the workplace or in the home. Since we are talking about a demonstration of the Spirit's power, perhaps the application of gifts of the Spirit, which in Charismatic circles seem traditionally to operate during worship, should start operating after the preaching of the Word. I just throw that out as a suggestion, because it seems to me that the truth has then built a safe context for such ministry. The preacher may have stopped preaching, but the Holy Spirit has not stopped working.

DOES THE HOLY SPIRIT EVER BACK OFF MY PREACHING?

Although this is rather an unusual question, I think it is an important one to consider. Surprisingly and soberingly, I think the answer is yes. I believe the Holy Spirit may withdraw for the following reasons:

1. If I am preaching from wrong motives

This is easier to do than we may think. Perhaps I want to get my own back on my congregation, or a particular individual, for something that has happened. Or there may be a truth that I believe an individual or couple needs to hear, so I use my sermon to make sure they hear it. Or, less dramatically, I may just use my sermon to preach on my own pet subjects or out of my own particular bias. In any of these situations I believe the Holy Spirit may withdraw because I am not actually speaking the truth that He owns.

2. If I ignore or avoid the Holy Spirit

Scripture warns us not to grieve or quench the Holy Spirit. I think that sometimes I can ignore the Holy Spirit in my preparation when He wants to come alongside me to help me, or I can ignore Him in my preaching by not being dependent on Him. In such a situation I believe the Holy Spirit will take a step back from me.

3. If I am not preaching His Word

The Holy Spirit loves to anoint the Word, but if what I am preaching is not the Word, I believe He may withdraw from me. Instead of preaching the Word, as preachers we may be tempted to preach the latest ideas, the latest theories or some good thoughts – but if we do that, in the end our church will just die. One of the reasons why exegetical preaching is so wonderful is because it stops us preaching our pet subject, or the latest idea or theory, and it also stops us trying to avoid the difficult passages. The Holy Spirit loves to anoint the truth that we are proclaiming, and He loves to anoint the difficult passages. We saw from 2 Timothy 4:2 that the Word is to be preached *'in season and out of season'*. If this is not a word for today's Church I don't know what is. Verse 3 continues:

> *For the time will come when men will not put up with sound doctrine. Instead, to suit their own desires, they will gather around them a great number of teachers to say what their itching ears want to hear.*

The Holy Spirit does not anoint sermons that are only geared to what people want to hear.

4. If I compromise the Word of God

There are all kinds of situations in which I can be tempted to do this. For example, I may compromise the Word of God if it contradicts my church tradition. It is very important that if there is a conflict between our Church's tradition and the Word of God, we should preach the Word of God. Or perhaps the Word of God may contradict my culture. A year or two ago I was preaching through Malachi and reached chapter 2 verse 16 where the Lord says, *'I hate divorce'*. This posed a dilemma for me since in my congregation there are a number people who, for all kinds of different reasons, have gone through a divorce, and that would be quite typical in a large congregation of people nowadays. I decided to speak to some of the divorcees in the congregation, tell them that the topic was coming up and explain that I didn't want to offend them. The people to whom I spoke all told me that I must go ahead and preach the Word of God, which is what I did, proclaiming the truth that God hates divorce but in no way does He hate the person who has been divorced. We must not allow cultural difficulties to throw us off track.

As far as the example of church in-house rules and laws is concerned, I had a terrible experience of this a couple of years ago when I was invited to speak at a leaders' conference overseas, which was attended by about eighty people. I was actually asked to speak on the subject of grace, not knowing that the group to which I was speaking was extremely legalistic. Over the course of the conference I would preach for an hour, and then we would spend the next hour arguing about what I had said. I never once departed from Scripture, I just defended everything I was saying from the Word of God, while their arguments were all based on pragmatism and cultural considerations. In the end, I realised that the only way to win the argument was by joining them and so I used the example of smoking. Having explained the facts about how bad smoking is for a person's health, and how nasty a habit it is, I asked the question: 'But does God love you any the less if you still smoke?' By now everyone had become really quiet, and I couldn't work out what was going on, so I asked my interpreter to explain. It turned out that no one was allowed to join the church unless they gave up smoking. Then these words just came out of my mouth, 'Are fat people allowed to join your church?' – noticing that there were a number of portly pastors sitting on the front row. I continued, 'I think the Bible has got a little bit more to say about greed and gluttony than it has about smoking.' Once again it went very quiet. We must faithfully preach the Word of God even if in the process we offend people.

5. If I preach out of my lack of experience
I need to preach the Word of God as it is, even if I personally have not experienced the truth which it contains. Some people find this very difficult. For example, some people have never experienced God's healing power today, so they try desperately to explain that God no longer heals people, which is quite a difficult exercise biblically. What they are really doing is defending their position from their tradition or their lack of experience, i.e. 'I have not been healed', or 'I have prayed for people and they have not been healed'. They come to the Word of God with their agenda, and that is very, very shaky ground. Whether or not we have experienced the truth which the Word of God contains, we must preach it as it stands.

In conclusion, I want to say that surely what our land and the Church in the UK needs today is a restoration of Word-based preaching that is powerfully anointed by the Holy Spirit. When, week by week, there is a mixture of Word and Spirit in everything that we do and when there is an impartation taking place in the preaching so that there is a demonstration of the Holy Spirit's power, then we will see men and women's lives changed and transformed. Instead of being switched off by the preaching of the Word, people will be full of expectation that the Spirit of God will come and change lives.

NOTES

1. John 15:5.
2. 1 Corinthians 2:16.
3. Hebrews 4:12.

Chapter 23

VISION, FAITH AND EXPECTATION IN PREACHING

Colin Dye

I would like to begin by saying as strongly as I may that preaching is not an end in itself, but rather a means to an end. There is more to preaching than learning the art of sermon making. There is more to preaching than achieving a perfect, flawless message. While we should learn all we can – and as the years go by I wish I had learnt more – we must always remember that preaching is not the end, but the means to the end. The end of preaching is to form in people the character of Christ and to enable them to meet with God. Astonishing as it may sound, our words can be so used by the Holy Spirit that people experience God! In the same way that we can learn the laws of aerodynamics but still believe it is a miracle that an aeroplane is in the sky, so we can learn the principles of teaching and preaching and still ever marvel that something supernatural takes place. It seems there is a synergy that occurs, so that the effect exceeds the sum of the individual parts. All this is unashamedly the language of experience. The question is, then, how do we preach with a realistic expectation that God will act through our preaching, in other words that people will genuinely experience and meet Him?

Some will say that all we need to do is 'faithfully preach the Word, brother'. We just need to preach and then wait for God to act. There is some truth in this approach. If God doesn't do it, certainly we can't. There can be no form of manipulative underhanded technique by which we can demonstrate that the Spirit of God is present. We know all too well that there is a stylised way in which we fall into that error, whatever our tradition – whether it is the Pentecostal 'pout', the Charismatic 'cluck', the evangelical raised eyebrow, or the fearsome look over the rim of the glasses which says, 'The preacher has arrived and it is now time for you to listen up.' We know that none of this is God, but merely the expression of our humanity. Although without doubt the Word carries the power, I believe there is more to effective preaching than being merely a mouthpiece. I believe that the preacher must walk in concert with God, so that he is in the best possible place to be used of Him if He so chooses, and his prayer must me, 'Choose me more often, Lord, as an instrument in Your hand.'

It is my thesis that preaching is a tool in the hand of God. Just as students sitting an exam must believe that the examiner is on their side and is looking for the opportunity to give the pass mark, and therefore they must try to make his or her job easier, so the preacher must preach in such a way that God can bless the message and make it powerful and effective. Preaching is a process, not the product. It is possible to have fine-looking tools hanging in the tool cabinet but nothing will get done unless they are used. The more a workman focuses on the tool rather than on its purpose, the less gets done; the more he focuses on the purpose, the more he will want to use the tool and perfect his skill so that the tool will achieve the desired end result. Fine preaching is not the goal, but being used by God is. Through God-ordained means God-ordained results will come, but there is an element of human responsibility. Consequently, as preachers we need to ask ourselves repeatedly, what are our sermons producing? Monday morning, after a tiring Sunday, is probably not the best time for any preacher to ask himself this question but, when he is feeling refreshed, it is good for him to take an objective look at what his sermons are producing.

'In Demonstration of the Spirit and of Power'

The New Testament advocates preaching in the power and demonstration of the Holy Spirit. Such preaching powerfully affects the preacher first of all. Paul wrote to the Thessalonians that the *gospel did not come to you in word only, but also in power, and in the Holy Spirit and in much assurance*,[1,2] the word 'assurance' reinforcing and endorsing the ministry of the Holy Spirit. There must be conviction in the pulpit, as the Holy Spirit brings the preacher the assurance that what he is preaching is a word from God – not just because he is reciting Bible texts but because he has heard from God. As preachers we dare not mount the pulpit and stand before men and women until we have been on our faces before the Lord.

The demonstration lies, second, in the convicting power of the Holy Spirit. The preaching convinces where human argument cannot. In 1 Corinthians 2:1–4 Paul writes,

> *And I, brethren, when I came to you, did not come with excellence of speech or of wisdom declaring to you the testimony of God. For I determined not to know anything among you except Jesus Christ and Him crucified. I was with you in weakness, in fear, and in much trembling. And my speech and my preaching were not with persuasive words of human wisdom, but in demonstration of the Spirit and of power...*

Here the 'demonstration of the Spirit and of power' is not primarily the signs and wonders we see in other contexts, although as I will argue later it is a very important part of the demonstration, but the convicting power of the Holy Spirit, so that a person's faith does not rest on human argument, but on the power of God operating in his or her heart and mind. In other words, preaching is not effective because the preacher has a better argument than any other religionist in town but because the Holy Spirit has taken the word and 'argumented' it into people's lives. What a wonderful thing it is for a preacher to know that he can preach with the conviction that the word will be received and will achieve far more than human argument can.

Third, there is a demonstration of power despite persecution and human weakness. In 2 Corinthians 12:12 Paul writes,

> *Truly the signs of an apostle were accomplished among you with all perseverance,*
> *in signs and wonders and mighty deeds.*

This is not just a proof text for signs and wonders. Paul is saying that those who are moving in power will encounter persecution, which will be manifested in weakness. One of the true 'signs of an apostle' is that he is able to accomplish his ministry *'with all perseverance'* in the face of incredible opposition. Certainly, there were signs and wonders as well, but moving in power meant something more. He speaks in similar terms in Romans 15:18–19 where the power comes in 'word and deed' with 'signs and wonders'. I am deliberating setting the matter of power in preaching in different kinds of contexts because I do not believe that the issue of the miraculous is going to be settled just by focusing on the need for signs and wonders. In fact, there is great limitation in that attitude which can lead to the reductionist approach of thinking that, if only we had signs and wonders, then everybody would believe. The sad truth is that they didn't in Jesus' time. When He had done the signs and wonders tour of Galilee, He came back and pronounced woe on all the cities He had visited – cities such as Chorazin, Bethsaida and Capernaum – for

> 'if the mighty works which were done in you had been done in Sodom, it would have
> remained until this day. But I say to you that it shall be more tolerable for the land of
> Sodom in the day of judgment than for you.'
> (Matthew 11:23–24)

There is a story told of one of our former ministers at Kensington Temple who felt one Sunday greatly impressed to be open to the unexpected in a morning service. To his disappointment the whole service passed uneventfully and, as he was pronouncing the benediction, he was saying in his heart, 'Well, Lord, nothing unexpected happened today.' Just at that moment a woman who had been brought in a wheelchair, leapt up and ran excitedly around the building. Everybody went wild in a way that only Pentecostals are entitled to. They honestly thought that revival had broken out. But it hadn't – the evening service was the same as it always was. We must not have the romantic view that if only we could empty hospitals, people would come to faith – which is a total fiction anyway in terms of biblical understanding. It just didn't happen that way. I remember a time when we were in contact with a very famous musician, who was being nursed through the last stages of a terminal illness by a member of our church. The church prayed as earnestly as we could for the healing of this woman. As we pleaded with God that He would be pleased to do a miracle, the argument we frequently used was, 'Lord, if only You would heal her, then the whole nation would know.' As an argument that seemed to make sense to me but it was not enough to persuade the Lord and she died. Feeling puzzled that God had not answered our petition, I went to prayer, and the words of Jesus I have just quoted came to mind. I wonder if sometimes there is a withholding not just in judgement but also in mercy because, when God begins to move so openly and unambiguously, people who out of hardness of heart would reject even that level of His manifestation bring a greater judgement and condemnation on themselves. I think that could be a factor. Does this mean that God is never going to move in signs and wonders? Of course not. But it does mean there is a ripening of His purposes in a nation, and there is a season. There is no other way I can explain it. Whatever reasons I or anyone else put forward, none of them comes near to the full story. I have been in situations where over a matter of days absolutely everybody with whatever sickness they had who came into contact with the preaching or the preacher was instantly and totally healed. But I have also been through seasons when you could yell and scream and jump up and down, but still nothing happened – if God's not doing it, it can't be done. We must understand above all that God works through many ways, and it is as powerful and as dynamic to see somebody come to faith as it is to see a miracle of healing, for example. The greatest miracle is always to see somebody come to faith in Christ! It takes power to bring that level of convincing in any generation but particularly in the backslidden, secular, humanistic society in which we live.

We can believe that God does want to use us in signs and wonders, and we can base this belief on the life and ministry of the apostle Paul. There are, of course, people who claim that Paul's experience and that of the other apostles was exceptional precisely because they were apostles. There is a definite unique purpose of miracles which belong to a unique season, they argue. These were eye-witnesses of the resurrection. They were to become instruments of infallible inspiration, so therefore it is quite understandable that they should become strong examples of workers of signs and wonders. But that does not mean it died with them. The ongoing manifestation of God through signs and wonders has happened throughout the history of the Christian Church and is continuing today. I am not saying that it has always been equally present everywhere and continuously, but I am saying that the evidence of God stepping in miraculously is well attested in history and in current experience across the world, through people's lives and bodies being transformed by Christ. There have even been times when New Testament experience has been surpassed. I am thinking, for example, of the extraordinary things that are happening in Africa at the present time. Not so long ago, as part of a group, I visited a church in a region of Africa which has seen God move in phenomenal power. As visitors we were asked to preach but in some ways I would have loved to sit in the pew and hear the minister himself preach. Over lunch I tried to find out a bit more about what was going on in the church and I questioned our host closely. Although he was rather reticent, I eventually managed to tease out of him the subject of his last Sunday sermon. He was preaching through one of the Gospels and his topic that day had been 'When not to raise the dead'. Astounded, I pressed him to tell me what he meant, and he told me that they had had a problem with some overenthusiastic young people who had been going into the villages and raising elderly believers from the dead! His message to these young people was, 'Listen, if they are old and they are believers, don't disturb them. Let them go.' What a contrast with our paucity in this area! We have so much theology but so little power and influence.

IN DEPENDENCE ON GOD'S POWER

Paul made it clear that the proclamation is in word and deed:

> *For I will not dare to speak of any of those things which Christ has not accomplished through me, in word and deed, to make the Gentiles obedient – in mighty signs and wonders, by the power of the Spirit of God, so that from Jerusalem and round about to Illyricum I have fully preached the gospel of Christ.*
> (Romans 15:18–19)

Paul is testifying here that it is more than powerful preaching that brings conviction: it is the supernatural ability to work mighty signs and wonders by the enabling power of the Holy Spirit. For such preaching we need to be 'baptised in the Holy Spirit'. I have put the phrase in inverted commas because there are so many different models of understanding of what the New Testament means by this. Whatever our theology, it is enough simply to grasp that God has not left us alone and never intended to send the early Church out into the field of battle and conquest naked: they were to stay in Jerusalem until they were clothed with power from on high. Personally, after going through prolonged periods of doubt concerning my theology in this area, I have come to a model of understanding that satisfies me. It may not satisfy others, but I am not too worried about that – so long as they are not satisfied despite the lack of what they say they have. I believe that both for Pentecostals and non-Pentecostals the important thing is to have a doctrine that says that the empowering of the Holy Spirit follows faith and is linked to the preaching of the gospel. I am thankful that there appears to be a consensus emerging today and, if we dialogue responsibly in a rather less confrontational way and learn to listen to each other's different views, we will probably find there is much more consensus than we realised. For the purpose of our present topic, all that interests me is: *are we moving in power?* There is hardly a preacher around who, when really pushed to it, would not say that he needs more of God and, whatever our particular stance is, we all need an ongoing conscious interaction with the Holy Spirit and His power in our lives. There is also a fairly strong consensus emerging that the gifts of the Holy Spirit were not just for an apostolic bygone age but are for today. Across the spectrum of the Christian Church there is a much greater openness and a much greater expectation that God will do surprising and supernatural things, whether it is a model resting in the sovereignty of the first person of the Trinity, God the Father – who can do what He likes when He likes how He likes, without permission from us; or whether it is more of a faith-school approach focusing on Jesus Christ and what He achieved through His atonement on the cross; or whether in relation to signs and wonders it is the more Pentecostal model of anointing by the Holy Spirit. Whatever it is, we need God to give us the ability to produce the proof that He is alive. Preaching is a supernatural experience; it must be in dependence on God's power. Of course, as I have already emphasised, the greatest effect that our preaching can have is that people believe – this in itself is a miracle. However, I would suggest that one of the greatest needs of the hour is the desperation which drives us to our knees and drives us to pray: 'Lord, thank You for fine preaching but if fine preaching could do it, it would have been done by now.' We need more: we need His power. So the question is, how do we minister in this realistic expectation that we have obtained the power? In Luke 24:49 Jesus promises that His disciples will be *'endued* [or clothed] *with power from on high'*. In other words power is not something that we can manufacture but only something that we can receive and submit to and co-operate with. Acts 1:8 says,

> *'But you shall receive power when the Holy Spirit has come upon you; and you shall be witnesses to Me in Jerusalem, and in all Judea and Samaria, and to the end of the earth.'*

The true answer to the question, then, is, that we receive power, in Greek *dunamis*, when the Spirit comes. Often I hear preachers in my circles go from *dunamis* to 'dynamite' and the idea of a massive explosion. I understand what they mean, but I don't believe it is always a very helpful way of conveying the sense of what Jesus was saying. A more helpful understanding of *dunamis* is gained from the alternative meaning 'ability'. It might be quiet ability or explosive pyrotechnical ability, but it is always supernatural ability.

Why then are we given this supernatural ability? What did Jesus mean when He said, *'you shall be witnesses to Me . . .'?* Amongst other things, a witness is a producer of evidence or even proof. If you are in the witness box in a court of law, whether you are a witness for the prosecution or for the defence, all that you can bring to court is evidence – evidence which is being used as proof in an argument for or against the accused. There was a highly significant period of history when Jesus Christ Himself was His own witness to His own resurrection, i.e. in the six-week period between His resurrection and His ascension. Luke begins the second part of his story by saying in Acts 1:

> *The former account I made, O Theophilus, of all that Jesus began both to do and teach, until the day in which He was taken up, after He through the Holy Spirit had given commandments to the apostles whom He had chosen, to whom He also presented Himself alive after His suffering* **by many infallible proofs**, *being seen by them during forty days and speaking of the things pertaining to the kingdom of God.* (Acts 1:1–3, my emphasis)

Jesus was producing proof that He was alive. By revealing Himself to His disciples and to the believers, He was His own witness. Then after six weeks He went away, leaving His followers with the commission that it was now their turn to produce the proof – to witness to Him and to His resurrection. This immediately poses the question, how? People say, 'Prove it – prove that what you are saying is true.' They want unambiguous proof of the existence of God that can be demonstrated by rational empirical means. As we know such an expectation is unrealistic. Even when Jesus appeared to His disciples as a witness to His resurrection, we are told that *'some doubted'*.[3] This indicates how hard it is to penetrate the human mind and understanding. Even when there is medical evidence which nobody can refute people will still not believe. I have been in situations where there has been irrefutable evidence that a miracle has taken place and still the medical profession has refused to accept it. A humble doctor may say that something medically unexplainable has taken place, but others simply insist that, while an unexplained phenomenon has occurred, given enough time and medical advance an explanation will emerge. What is there in people's minds that is so resistant to God? It is a mistake to believe that, even if the dead were raised in front of the British press, faith would follow. I have heard accounts of outstanding miracles taking place in the presence of newspaper reporters who still refused to publish the story. The BBC has admitted that stored in its achives there is footage of miracles they could not explain, which will not be screened until some rational explanation is available.[4] Despite the fact that we don't get a fair deal in terms of exposure, God has a way of demonstrating who He is. Jesus promised that when the Spirit came, He would give us the ability to produce proof that He is alive.

How, then, do we carry the anointing? There is no technique to this. It is not possible to manufacture the anointing. In fact, in Old Testament priestly ministry it was forbidden so to do. The recipe for the anointing oil was secret and sacrosanct. The oil could only be made for the purpose of priestly ministry.[5] When it comes to the New Testament understanding of anointing we know that it cannot be manufactured at all. The only way to carry the anointing is by surrendering completely to Christ through the Holy Spirit, submitting to His initiative in all things and submerging our personality to His empowering presence.

The sad truth is that the Church no longer knows how to say,

> *'Silver and gold I do not have, but what I do have I give you: In the name of Jesus Christ of Nazareth, rise up and walk.'*
> (Acts 3:6)

In my experience it is not an issue of coming before God with a blueprint or even with a proof text. It seems to me the height of all insults to remind God of His Word, as if He had forgotten it – He knows what He has promised. Nor is it just a matter of saying, 'God, now it is over to You. We have done our bit.' Have we done our bit? Do we make room for God to work in miraculous ways? This is not a subject that can be lectured upon, with a model for how to produce miracles. It doesn't happen that way – we all know that. If it did, we would all be putting it into practice already.

For many years I was involved in helping to shape and lead a congregation in another nation, which has now exploded all over that nation. They used to have an open-air crusade, to which I used to take a team of people as a way of mentoring them. One year I had a couple of fearsome Swedish young men with me. When I met them I understood why the Vikings were so successful all those years ago. One evening, before the mission meeting, as I was seeking God and preparing for the preaching, they were in the adjacent room praying for me. I could hear them using every ounce of energy they had praying for me, yelling and shouting and screaming. When they started to pray about the passage I had in front of me, it was a fantastic confirmation of God's word for that evening. The more they prayed, the clearer the message became: it cut my preparation time in half. It was wonderful. But when I had finished preparing my message, I was still not ready. I then moved into the second phase of my preparation before the Lord, and began to seek His face, asking Him to come and revive His wondrous works in our generation, to give us as a team the ability to produce the proof that Jesus is alive.

While I was praying in this way, they were still being Pentecostal next door. Whereas before they were helping me, now they were hindering me. So I decided that I would bring them into the secret. I went and joined them and said, 'Thank you very much for all your praying. You have done a fantastic job, with the result that I have finished my preparation of the Word, and it's in front of me here. Now I need to have the assurance that God is with us and that outstanding things are going to happen. I need the anointing that brings miracles' – I expressed it in the way that they as Pentecostals would understand. Explaining to them that this level of supernatural operation is not released by yelling and shouting, I said, 'Let me show you how.' As we joined hands in a little circle, I began to lift us all up to the Lord. As we waited on the Holy Spirit in this way His presence filled the room, and after a while I received the assurance in my heart that God was going to be with us that night in that place, and that we could go with the confidence and expectation that God would do amazing things.

That night every single one of us went back to the hotel with outstanding stories to share of instant visible demonstrations of God's healing power. Of course, there is much that happens that cannot be measured and all that appears to be happening ultimately isn't happening and much that appears not to be happening ultimately is happening. But I know from subsequent visits that amazing things were taking place that night. And although I stood there with the rather presumptuous words, 'Let me show you how', from that day to this I don't know how. I have no idea. I just know it is something to do with God. I just know it is something to do with being desperate for Him. It is something to do with our being totally incapable in our own ability to produce the proof that Jesus is alive.

We live in a spiritual Nazareth in so many ways. I believe that we need to get back to our prayer closets and to our prayer meetings, back to our heart searching and crying out to God, to plead that He would renew His works in our day and generation. We need to cry out to God: 'Where are the mighty wonders that we heard about from our fathers? "O God, our hope in ages past, our hope for years to come", yes, but what about today, O God? What about now? What about here? What about today? What about in this place? What about in this city? What about in this nation?'

I believe we need to come before God with this level of desperation. It is not just a matter of faith technique. It is not just a matter of saying, 'I believe it, therefore it's going to happen.' It is not just a matter of working ourselves up to try and make it happen. It is being in the position with God whereby He can take our life and so energise it in some supernatural way, which is still a mystery to me, that supernatural effectiveness is imparted. Is this not a crucial part of the vision, faith and expectation we need to cultivate in our preaching?

NOTES

1. 1 Thessalonians 1:5. See also Chapter 20.
2. Scriptures in this chapter are taken from the New King James Version.
3. Matthew 28:17.
4. For example, a BBC news item in the late 1990s linked a spontaneous remission of cancer reported by the medical profession to healing meetings where people apparently experienced unexplained cures from their diseases.
5. Exodus 30:22–33.

Chapter 24

Preaching to Change a Nation

David Holden

Very few preachers are obviously in contexts where what they preach on a Sunday morning has the ability to change a nation. Even if the Prime Minister were sitting in the congregation, most probably do not feel their sermon would have this potential. However, I want to explain why every single person whom God has called to be involved in the preaching ministry can preach to change a nation. The reason I am convinced this is true is because we have the privilege of being involved in a ministry that changes people one by one. Our nation actually will not be changed by a political manifesto or a law that is passed, or even by gathering thousands and thousands of people to some kind of Christian convention, although I am sure these things can help. Our nation will be changed one by one.

Years ago someone who was not a Christian asked me very antagonistically, 'What do you people think you are doing for our society anyway?' The answer I gave was this: 'Well, if we are changing people one by one and they really are transformed, so that their lives are different and they have an immediate effect on the people around them, then I believe we are changing society.' When the Spirit of God is anointing the Word of God that is being proclaimed, lives can be changed.

Sometimes as preachers we can have high hopes of the congregation to which we are preaching. Perhaps it is a gathering of students, and it is easy to believe that we have before us the future nation-changers. But that is not always our experience. One of the first times I ever preached was at a large Baptist church in Chesham which seated a thousand people and there were fifteen in the congregation, three of whom were college students of mine who had come along to support me. I had been given a programme to follow, and halfway through the service it said, 'The choir will now sing.' Looking around trying to think where the choir might be, I made the required announcement, at which point eight people got up and sang to the three that were still in the congregation. At moments like these it is hard to hold onto the truth that our preaching has the potential to change a nation.

This truth is not only an important one for preachers to get hold of. What would the impact be if every member of our congregations understood that, by outworking the truths they are hearing in the preaching, they each have the potential to change the nation? The parable that Jesus told about the foolish man who built his house on the sand and the wise man who built his house on the rock is so important for preaching (Matthew 7:25–27). Somehow we have come to believe that this parable is about Christians and non-Christians, but it is not. The parable distinguishes between those who hear and those who hear *and do*. My congregation could be full of people building their lives on sand, if all they do is hear what is being said. It is those who are hearers and doers that are building their lives upon the rock – in other words, when the sermon is over and people start to apply what they have heard in their daily lives. It is ordinary men and women whose lives are being impacted by the Word of God anointed by the Holy Spirit who will change this nation. Therefore our preaching must be equipping people. Our preaching must increasingly be equipping people to be effective in the market-place where they work; to be effective in the community in which they live; to be effective in the places in which they spend the vast majority of their time and expend most of their energy. Our preaching should not be tested in terms of the fruit it bears on Sunday mornings but in terms of how it affects people's lives throughout the rest of the week. Therefore preaching to change a nation is very practical. It must be relevant to everyday life. It must cause people's faith in God to grow for themselves. It must cause people to become genuinely more Christlike and equip them to become salt and light in their community. It must give people their own personal vision and give them a corporate vision of the life of the Church. It must give people a sense of calling and destiny, which will often be worked out beyond our corporate life together. It must feed people, not just make them fat Sunday by Sunday: by this I mean that our feeding of their lives must enable them to go and do something with what we are giving to them. Our preaching must not even be aimed at making people feel happy, at meeting their felt needs, at making them feel more comfortable about themselves. Our preaching must equip people to make a difference in the world in which we live. It is a means to this end. I am convinced that if we believe we are preaching to change a nation one by one, it will surely affect the way we preach, it will surely affect the way we prepare our sermons and it will surely affect the way we make our sermons applicable to people's lives.

THE CHALLENGE

As those who preach to change the nation of the United Kingdom we face a huge challenge which I believe it is very important for us to acknowledge. The challenge that we face is that we preach essentially to a very static prevailing view of Christianity. The effect of this is that it dulls both the preacher and those who are listening. The same is not true of many, many parts of the world today where there is a very dynamic and mobile view of Christianity and where people often naturally work out what they hear. Neither was this true of the New Testament where the company of people listening to the apostles' teaching were consumed with the concept of mobility: they were a 'going' people. These were people who knew they could be suddenly scattered either by persecution or by apostolic commission – it was happening all the time. These were people with a mission-minded view of church and the words of Jesus still ringing in their ears, *'Go into all the world and preach the good news'*.[1] They also had the words ringing in their ears that they should wait until the Holy Spirit had come upon them and then they should go to Jerusalem, Judaea, Samaria and the ends of the earth. They knew they were being 'fed' in order to make a difference to their nation. Preaching to this mobilised company of people must have been very exciting. Whether or not they were moving somewhere geographically, they were moving on in God. They were discipling others, giving away what they heard. They were wanting to hear and *'devoted themselves to the apostles' teaching and to the fellowship'*.[2] They were people who were being prepared for leadership, for taking responsibility, who wanted to learn about servanthood, who were potentially church planters and preachers: people who did what they saw their leaders doing. Paul says to Timothy,

> *And the things you have heard me say in the presence of many witnesses entrust*
> *to reliable men who will also be qualified to teach others.*
> (2 Timothy 2:2)

It was a dynamic view of the church.

As I have said, in many parts of the world today the modern Church is becoming equally mobilised. Not so long ago I was preaching at a very lively church in Dubai in the Middle East. In common with many parts of the Middle East, Dubai has had a huge influx of people from all over the world, so that currently 80 per cent of its population is non-Arab, a diversity that is reflected in the Church. Anyone who preaches at the church I visited in Dubai is aware that they are preaching to people from all walks of life and different parts of the world. It is also a mobile congregation and many of its members will move on to other locations. These people drink in what they hear the preacher saying because they are aware they may need it in the future when they move to other nations. The church has already planted churches into Oman, Kuwait, Pakistan, Sri Lanka and Egypt, and some of its members are now going to Canada to do the same there. They do not just talk about changing a nation but changing *nations*. For me it is like heaven on earth preaching there. It is exciting because these people are making the most of what the preacher is saying – they are aware that they might be on their own somewhere one day not knowing what to do, and they might need what they are being taught that very day. There is a dynamism because they are a mobile people.

Compare this with the Church in the United Kingdom and you will often find a very static view of Christianity and very parochial thinking. The people in our churches on a Sunday morning do not expect to do very much with what they hear and very often do not even sense a need to do anything about it. They do not expect to be asked, 'What difference has the sermon made to your life? How are you going to work out what you have heard?' So few people have an awareness of function or ability or gift even in the local church. Few people see themselves as being changed for what is next, or being trained for their workplace on Monday morning, or being changed to be effective at their college or at their school or in their family.

The huge challenge of static Christianity is compounded by twenty-first-century lifestyles. Confronted with increasing work demands, combined with the pressures of raising a family and the general busyness of many people's lives, mission and mobility come low down on their list of priorities. Our preaching needs to address these issues. There needs to be a kind of revolution amongst the people in our churches so that we turn from a static view of Christianity to something far more mobile, radical, flexible and fluid; something which will cause our people to want to work out everything they are hearing Sunday by Sunday in the places where they live and work. This increasingly is my passion: to raise up a church full of people who are following Jesus, whether this means that one day they move geographically or whether, in staying where they are, they are always moving on in the purposes of God. We need to see a church raised up in which Christians are equipped for every day of their lives.

This is the huge challenge facing the British Church. It needs to change, and our preaching needs to change. The question I now want to address is: How do I preach to change a nation?

How Do I Preach to Change a Nation?

1. I need to preach the big picture

Every time I speak I make it my aim to fill everybody's horizon with truth. I do not begin with pragmatics: I begin with the big themes of truth. This is very important if we want our people to make a difference in the world in which we live. It is very tempting in our modern context to preach sermons on 'how to' live our Christian lives – how to pray; how to tell your neighbour about Christ, etc. But if as preachers we do not teach people the truths of Scripture before we get to the 'how tos', we will find ourselves in all sorts of problems. We must give people a reason for their faith; we must preach about who God is and the great things He has done. And not only must we be continually pointing people to who God is, but we must be continually reminding them of who they are in Christ. In this day and age when Christianity is constantly under attack and people are being battered by one philosophy after another, we need to be lifting up people's heads through our preaching. Truth lifts people. Let us fill their horizons with truth.

I must also paint the big picture of history. I want people to know as they go into their workplace on Monday morning that they are part of a chain of people which stretches back through generations and generations. I want people to know their roots. I want them to be established and to be absolutely firm and secure in who they are in the purposes of God.

I need, furthermore, to paint the big picture of what God is doing in the world. Hearing what God is doing around the world also lifts people and encourages them amid the mundane issues they are so often facing. As preachers we need to keep ourselves informed about what God is doing around the world, and with the Internet and other resources this is now easier to do than ever before. In the United Kingdom our thinking can easily become focused on what is happening here, but God is doing mighty, mighty things around the world that can thrill and inspire us. We have got so much to learn from other Christians around the world which can help us to become the people God wants us to be. We desperately need to get hold of God's view of the Church. We need to tell our people about the Church that Jesus is building right across the world.

2. I need to apply what I call the 'therefore' factor

In his epistles Paul always begins by painting the big picture. He always begins by proclaiming doctrine – the wonderful truths about what God has done and who we as Christians are in Christ. However, there often comes a point when Paul says, 'Therefore': 'Therefore, in the light of all this truth, here is how you should live.' He never begins his epistles with 'therefore'. He never launches straight into the solutions to whatever problems a church might be having. The book of Romans is a classic example. Christians everywhere love to quote verse 1 of chapter 8, *'Therefore, there is now no condemnation for those who are in Christ Jesus.'* But what is the 'Therefore' there for? It obviously refers back to chapters 1 to 8. However, since so few Christians know what these chapters say, many people's lives are dogged by condemnation. Yet, for seven chapters Paul has been proclaiming justification by faith, and the 'Therefore' in chapter 8 verse 1 signifies the outworking of this. While revelling in the glorious doctrines of biblical truth, there must also be practical application for people's lives. Our preaching should be relevant on a Monday morning to the bank clerk and to the single mum with four kids whose husband is in and out of prison. With our increasingly diverse congregations it is impossible to address every issue that affects every individual, but we can preach doctrine and then explain its application for everyday lives. Whenever we are preparing a sermon we must be thinking of how it can be applied. In my preparation I always try to keep three things in mind: the goal; the content, which is the truth (the bulk of the sermon); and the 'Therefore', the application into people's lives. As we submit ourselves to the Holy Spirit, this is how we can preach to change a nation.

3. I need to preach truths that people can relate to

If my preaching is not relevant to ordinary life or does not equip people for work on Monday mornings, then something is missing. This means the illustrations that I give must be ones that people can relate to. I am convinced more and more that preaching should be earthed. It must not be mystical. It must not be gnostic. It should not produce the comment, 'That was a great sermon, but I have no idea what it was about.' When my friends saw the film *The Matrix*, they all raved about it and used it in their sermons to explain the gospel. However, by the time the third film in the series came out, they all began to go very quiet because no one had the foggiest idea what it was all about. Sometimes our preaching can be very mystical, very spiritual, but it is not earthed. Of course, some Scriptures are very complicated – like Hebrews 2 which I recently preached on at my church as part of a series on Hebrews. My first point from the text was that everything has been made subject to Him: there is nothing in heaven or earth that is not subject to Him. But my second point was: we do not see all things subject to Him. Thank God, my third point was, 'But we see Jesus highly exalted . . . ' I had to take my people on a journey through this passage to show them how seemingly contradictory statements could be true. The truth is that, although Jesus is now seated at the Father's right hand where He rules, we do not yet see everything subject to Him; we live in the 'now and not yet'. The enemy knows he is defeated, but as his final end approaches, he thrashes around more and more to cause as much havoc and destruction as he can. The way I applied this passage was by teaching people how to see Jesus, even in the difficult circumstances of their lives. Our circumstances don't necessarily change but, as we look up, our whole perspective changes. In order to make our preaching relevant to people's lives, it must be full of illustrations that are earthed into people's existence.

In the early days of my preaching I used to quote a lot of Greek because I had studied it at Bible College, and I used to think it really enhanced my sermons. I still think it is good to study Greek and it can be very helpful to know what the original words say, but sometimes I know I was using it in an attempt to impress and to make my sermons sound a bit mystical. Nowadays, it is far more important to me that people should be able to relate to what is being said.

Our preaching should be full of humanity. Not everyone would agree, but I have found over the years that if I share some of my own personal struggles people always find it helpful. Someone always comes up to me afterwards and thanks me for sharing my experience. It helps people to know that others face the same struggles that they do.

4. I need to make my preaching very practical

If my preaching is to change a nation, it must go beyond the pulpit and I must find a context in which my people can learn *to apply* what is being taught in their lives. In Colossians 1:28 Paul declares:

We proclaim him, admonishing and teaching everyone with all wisdom, so that we may present everyone perfect in Christ.

In order that we *'may present everyone perfect in Christ'* we need to ensure that our preaching is being applied. In my own particular church context small groups meet during the week and discuss questions which apply the sermon from the previous Sunday. More and more as I travel around the United Kingdom, I am asked to supply questions beforehand which can be distributed for discussion in small groups. As people ask one another, 'What did you think about what he said on Sunday?' 'Did you agree with it?' 'How does that apply to your life?' they are fulfilling an important aspect of church life. The little phrase 'one another' occurs fifty-eight times in the New Testament demonstrating that mutual accountability and discipleship are key. It can also happen in groups of men meeting to discuss together, or groups of women. When people are working out in their lives what is being proclaimed in our churches, our nation will really begin to be affected.

This goes back to the static view of Christianity about which I spoke earlier and the huge challenge that is before the British Church. People can be listening to tremendous preaching, and yet remain very passive. We need to raise up a teachable people. People need to understand how vital the Word of God is to their daily lives, and they also need to comprehend – and this is very sobering but we need to preach it – that people will one day be required to give an account for all that they have heard. Jesus Himself said, *'For everyone to whom much is given, from him much will be required.'*[3] People need to realise that the more they hear, the more God requires of them. Going back to the parable about the foolish man and the wise man, we need to be raising up a people who not only hear but do. So often we preach about the sovereignty of God on a Sunday but by Wednesday half of those who heard the sermon have been knocked sideways by something that has happened in their everyday lives. What happened to the sermon on the sovereignty of God? What happened was that people heard it but they did not apply it. The seed did not fall upon good soil. People must be taught to be teachable. If we are going to change a nation, people must have good soil in their hearts, so that when the word comes it actually goes deep and it produces *'a crop ... some thirtyfold, some sixty, and some a hundred'.*[4]

I sometimes wonder, too, if we over-teach people. In other words, if we move onto the next subject before they have had time to work out what we have just been preaching about. This is why exegetical expository teaching is good. As we preach through a book of the Bible, we can expand and consolidate the themes with which it deals. It takes time for people to grasp what is being said. Before we rush onto the next topic, let's make sure our congregation is in the good of what we have already been teaching.

5. I need to build faith through my preaching

In the United Kingdom something is going very wrong because our preaching is not producing dynamic faith. Dynamic faith is the crying need of the Church in the western world. It is full of unbelief and cynicism, which is at least in part the reason why we sometimes do not see much happen. It is not faith in a formula; it is not faith in faith. It is faith in an unchanging God and faith in His unchanging promises, a faith that works in everyday situations. In our preaching we must look to God to produce faith in people so that when they are in the market-place they are able to work out what they are hearing. Hebrews 4:2 says,

> For we also have had the gospel preached to us, just as they did; but the message they heard was of no value to them, because those who heard did not combine it with faith.

There must be faith in the preacher who believes that what he is preaching is really going to affect people, and there must be faith in the congregation who believe that, as they apply God's word to their lives, it really will make a difference.

6. I need to preach mission

Jesus taught His disciples, *'where I am, there you may be also.'*[5] Wherever He is, we go. If that means I live in the same town for the rest of my life because I am following Jesus, praise God. If it means I go somewhere else, even another nation, because I am following Jesus, praise God. We need to teach our people that whether they stay or whether they go, they must keep moving. I do believe that in this country we have got beyond the concept of the missionary as someone who goes overseas to tell people about Jesus. We have grasped as Christians that we are all missionaries and, particularly in our paganised nation, that everyone needs to regard themselves in this way. Too often in the past people have allowed the knowledge that others have gone to absolve them from any sense of responsibility to go themselves. We need constantly to be reminding people that we are all called to be missionaries. We need to mobilise the Church for mission and mobility.

Nothing really has changed since New Testament days. Every time we preach we are still preaching to potential nation-changers. We are still preaching to future leaders, people who will take responsibility, people who will go to other nations, people who will plant churches whether it is down the road or across the world. We are still preaching to people who, though they may stay for years and years in our congregations, never stop moving – people who will change their street or their college or their business. I have had the privilege of raising four children. I have not raised them to survive in the world but to make an impact upon it. In the same way in our preaching we are influencing a people who will make a difference in the society in which they live. What we preach now will affect the nation.

In conclusion, I want to give an illustration of a church in a very difficult part of the world that I have never visited but I know a lot about. It is the River of Life Church in

Harare, Zimbabwe. It was begun about seven or eight years ago by a white couple, both of whom as children had gone out to Zimbabwe from England with their parents. Their parents have since left but they have stayed. They were both working as teachers until God called them to go to Harare and begin a church. That church, which has a mainly black congregation, has grown and grown and grown. It is well known that Zimbabwe as a nation is currently facing terrible problems. As I read reports from this church and have personal contact with its leaders, the thing that impresses me most is that, as they have now grown from the original dozen to about 1,500 people, they have trained a company of people not just to do church, but beyond that to make a difference to the nation. They have raised up leaders that are both gifted and are on fire for God, who are now planting churches throughout the Harare area. Many of their young people have obtained key jobs so that they will be in the right position one day to be able to bring a godly proclamation and lifestyle into every walk of life, whether it is education, medicine, law or government. They have raised up a generation which will make a difference in their nation. When you meet people from this church, there are filled with a passion for God and His Kingdom. They know their nation is in trouble and they are desperate for the Word of God. What God has done in Harare, Zimbabwe, He can do here, if every time we preach, we do so knowing that we are preaching to change this nation.

Notes

1. Mark 16:15.
2. Acts 2:42.
3. Luke 12:48 NKJV.
4. Mark 4:8 NKJV.
5. John 14:3 NKJV.

Section Five

The Nuts and Bolts

By the grace God has given me,
I laid a foundation as an expert builder,
and someone else is building on it.
But each one should be careful how he builds.
For no-one can lay any foundation
other than the one already laid,
which is Jesus Christ.

(1 Corinthians 3:10–11)

Chapter 25

STARTING FROM SCRATCH

Chris Wright

Whenever we start anything from scratch we need good models. I want to look at two biblical models of the preaching of the Word, the first provided by the church builder Paul and the second by the community builder Ezra. Then I will move on to look at how we as 'body builders' can build our sermons from the Word of God.

PAUL, THE CHURCH BUILDER

In looking at the model of the apostle Paul I particularly want to consider what he has to say about his own preaching and teaching ministry in Acts 20. Here Paul is reminding the elders of the church in Ephesus of his almost three years of ministry among them, which was in fact the longest of any period of ministry in his career.

In Acts 20 he makes two interesting comments about his ministry, which he introduces with the same phrase '*I have not hesitated*':

> *You know that I have not hesitated to preach anything that would be helpful to you* [or to preach what is needful to you] *but have taught you publicly and from house to house.*
> (Acts 20:20)

> *For I have not hesitated to proclaim to you the whole will* [or whole counsel] *of God.*
> (Acts 20:27)

I am fascinated by the fact that Paul seems to have a double focus to his preaching/ teaching ministry. It is his aim to preach (1) on 'what is needful to you' and (2) on 'the whole counsel of God'. His double focus reflects the very familiar double affirmation that is made about the Word of God in 2 Timothy 3:16,

> *All Scripture is God-breathed and is useful for teaching, rebuking, correcting and training in righteousness, so that the man of God may be thoroughly equipped for every good work.*

1. 'What is needful to you'

By this I understand that Paul is seeking to respond to the local context. First-century Ephesian society was very similar to the society in which we live today. It was cosmopolitan, multifaith with all kinds of idolatry and worship of other gods, and immoral. In seeking to live out their faith in that society, the believers would have faced many different issues, and it is to these issues that Paul seeks to respond in his preaching. His practice indicates that it is legitimate for biblical preaching sometimes to take as its starting point dealing with the issues raised by living in society. However, I am quite sure that, in doing so, Paul would constantly go back to the Scriptures to provide a biblical rationale for his arguments.

2. 'The whole counsel of God'

This must refer to Paul's practice of teaching systematically through the Scriptures. Day by day, as most people rested from their work during the hottest part of the day, Paul would be in the lecture hall of Tyrannus, preaching and teaching the whole counsel of God, the scriptural basis of the faith.[1]

Aiming to preach the 'whole counsel of God' is an excellent goal for any preacher. Even those just starting out on a preaching ministry can make it their long-term aim to take the whole Bible as their textbook, not just the New Testament and not just their favourite texts. I believe that one of the greatest lacks among western Christians today is a biblical world-view, which can be attributed to the fact that the majority of Christians are only taught little snippets of the Bible, if they are ever taught the Bible at all, and are not taught to read the Bible for themselves in a systematic way. As preachers it is our duty to seek to provide our congregations with a biblical world-view by following Paul's example and taking the Bible as a whole.

In my view building a biblical world-view means at least three things. First, it means taking from the Bible the reality of who God is. Many people today claim that they believe in God, but is it the biblical God they believe in? Very probably not. And in the case of those who say they don't believe in God, it is very likely that it is not the biblical God they don't believe in – if you see what I mean. The only way to confront people with the reality of God's true identity is through the Bible. They need to be taught the story of God: His character, His ways, His purpose, His actions, His dealings with people, and His plan and purpose for human history. We need to preach the Bible so that people come to know the living, personal, communicating God whose story it tells. In the Ephesian context, in which people would have come to faith from the worship of other gods, knowing God's true identity was very important. This is equally true in our society in which there is enormous ignorance of who God is. Knowing the identity of God is not something that happens in a moment of conversion, but takes a lifetime of discovery.

Second, a biblical world-view incorporates the story of God and the world. It is only through our knowledge of the grand narrative of the Bible that we are able to find answers to the four key existential questions which all religions and philosophies seek to answer. These four fundamental questions at the core of every world-view are:

- what is the nature of the universe?
- what does it mean to be human?
- what has gone wrong with the world?
- what is the solution to our problem?

Of course, these four basic questions of human existence can be phrased in any number of ways. Whether consciously or unconsciously every single member of our churches is required to answer these questions during the course of their lives. The question that we as preachers and teachers need to ask is, whether it is the Bible that is giving them their fundamental understanding of the nature of the world, the identity of humanity, the reality of sin, and the solution that God offers through the cross and resurrection and the new creation that He will bring, or whether it is some other world-view. We need to preach the Bible so that people have a coherent understanding of the world and of where they fit into the great scheme of things.

Third, we need a biblical world-view that tells people not only about the identity of God and about His story, but also about who we are – not just as human beings, but as the Church. What does it mean to be the people of God – created by God, called through Abraham, descended from the Old Testament people of Israel, redeemed through the Lord Jesus, now one in the Messiah with our brothers and sisters all over the world and destined for God's mission, which is to bring the nations to Himself? People need to have a biblical perspective on what it means to be the people of God.

Paul's model is an excellent one for us to follow. In our preaching we should have this double focus of addressing the needs of the people together with the whole counsel of God. We need both relevance and faithfulness. We do not preach in such a way as to be relevant without using the Scripture and we do not preach the Scripture in such a way that we are never relevant to people's needs.

This double focus requires a 'double listening':[2] we need to be listening to our people and the world, and we need to be listening to our God and His Word. We listen to God in order that we can submit to Him and obey Him. We listen to the world not because we submit to it and obey it, but because we want to understand it and know where people are coming from. Preaching the whole Bible will put the whole God at the centre of our whole lives.

EZRA, THE COMMUNITY BUILDER

Ezra is well known for his role in building a community of God's people after the Exile, a task in which he worked closely with Nehemiah. I want to look briefly at two texts, one of which highlights the example of his personal life and the other the example of his public life.

The first of these two texts is Ezra 7:10 which I would offer as a very appropriate motto for anyone starting out as a preacher. In a fairly literal translation the verse reads:

> *Ezra set his heart to study and to do and to teach the Word* [or the law] *of the LORD His God.*

The New International Version translation, *'For Ezra had devoted himself to the study and observance of the Law of the LORD'*, with its use of the abstract nouns 'study' and 'observance', seems to me to lack the sense of activity and purpose which the Hebrew gives. It is a wonderful verse and a wonderful objective to have. I personally would be very happy to have Ezra 7:10 as my epitaph.

Despite being a leader, a scribe and a political figure – in short a very busy man – Ezra remained a student of God's Word throughout his life. We too need to be lifelong learners. But as well as studying, Ezra was putting what he was learning into practice and teaching it to others. Those who are starting out on the task of preaching would do well to learn from Ezra's personal example. We must always remember that we can't teach or preach what we haven't studied, and we shouldn't teach or preach what we personally are not putting into practice in our lives. It seems to me that Jesus had much to say to His disciples on this subject.

As well as Ezra's personal example, I also want to draw attention to his public example by looking at Nehemiah 8, which is the occasion of the reading of the Book of the Law after many, many years. The city wall had been rebuilt by Nehemiah, but the people needed more than physical security: they needed foundations; they needed to be consolidated as a community of God's people based upon God's Word. Knowing he was not the man for that task, Nehemiah summoned Ezra who set about establishing these foundations in a well-planned and well-managed way. In some ways Nehemiah 8 is the first example of theological education by extension, and I think it provides us with a number of insights about what it is to be a teacher or a preacher of God's Word.

Notice, first of all, that where Paul's preaching had a double focus on the context and the Word of God, here in Nehemiah 8 there is a double origin of Scripture. The book from which Ezra read is described both as 'the Book of the Law of Moses'[3] and 'the Book of the

Law of God'.[4] The phrase 'the Book of the Law of Moses' expresses the human authorship of what Ezra was reading, and 'the Book of the Law of God' expresses the divine authorship. There is a double reality here, which gives us two different perspectives on our preaching task. Knowing that we are handling the Word of God makes us approach it with a proper sense of awe. We accord the Word of God the respect it is due. Peter writes, referring presumably to the context of Christian worship, *'If anyone speaks, he should do it as one speaking the very words of God.'*[5] I do not take this to mean that the preacher can say 'Thus saith the Lord' when he is preaching; rather that he should be very aware that he has the Word of God on his lips. Later, in his second letter, Peter admits that some of Paul's letters contain matters which are *'hard to understand'* (3:16)! We need to recognise that there is a human authorship to Scripture which requires study and hard work in order to find out what the original writer meant to say, and a humility which acknowledges that our interpretation may not always be right.

In Nehemiah 8 it is clear that, because it was the Word of God that was being read to them, both the preacher and the people responded to it with reverence and worship. In verses 5 and 6, we see, for example, that when Ezra opened the Book of the Law in the sight of the people and praised the Lord, the great God, all the people lifted up their hands and responded, 'Amen, amen' before bowing down in worship. It was not the book they were worshipping. When the book was opened they knew that God was going to speak, and it was therefore important for them to have an attitude of reverence and worship before Him. As preachers it is important for us to model this same attitude and also ask our congregations to approach the Word of God with profound humility. Sadly, humility is not always associated with preaching but, as John Stott has said, our preaching must be both authoritative because it is from the Word of God, and characterised by the humility that says that I as the preacher am just as much under this Word as you the people are: together we bow before the God who gave it to us.[6]

Second, because it was the Word of God, there was also a response of the heart and the emotions. In verses 9–12 we read that the people were so distraught as a result of what they heard that the priests and the scribes had to spend time comforting them. Presumably they were grieving because the Word which was being read was touching their consciences. In other words they were recognising how far short they had fallen of the Law of God. The Word of God was not only affecting their ears and their minds but it was also touching their consciences and hearts, convicting them of their failure and their disobedience. It is important for us to notice how Nehemiah responded to this outbreak of emotion. He did not try to stifle it in true British 'stiff-upper-lip' style. Instead he urged the people to transform their weeping into rejoicing. The people needed to learn that this God whose law they knew they had broken, was also the gracious saving Lord who had redeemed them and brought them back from exile. They needed to learn that the joy of the Lord was their strength.[7] They needed to learn that, when they broke God's Law, they needed to go back to the Lord Himself. And of course we as Christians need to know that we find joy in forgiveness at the foot of the cross. Teaching God's people about repentance, it seems to me, is part of the authentic task of preaching God's Word.

Third, because it was the Word of God, there was also the response of practical obedience (vv. 14–18). The Word which had entered their ears and focused their attention, and then had entered their hearts and affected their emotions, was now also going to touch their hands and generate their obedience. We read in verse 13 that the heads of families and priests and Levites gathered around Ezra to give further study to the Word of God. As they did so, they discovered the instructions given concerning the Feast of Tabernacles[8] and, realising that it was the very time of year when the festival was due to be held, they set about putting God's Word into practice. The significance of this for us is not so much in the precise action they took but in the fact that they were determined to obey the Word of God. Ezra and the priests were preaching for obedience. They were teaching the Law not only so that people could understand it but also so that they could do something about it.

However, in addition to it being the Word of God, it was also the Law of Moses: it was also a human word. And because it was a human word, it needed quite literally to be physically read and heard. The Word had to touch the ears of the people so that they could focus their attention on it. In verses 1–6 of Nehemiah 8 we see how Ezra paid attention to simple practical details that actually are not unimportant. For example, he built a platform so that he could be seen and heard. In some of the places where I go to preach, they don't seem to have thought about the preacher at all – there is a flimsy music stand instead of a lectern or the microphone hums and buzzes. Often there is all the technology in the world for the worship, which is good, but no one seems to have thought about making sure that the preaching can be heard. Don't they want to know what the Scripture says? I don't think there is anything unspiritual about caring about the physical aspects of preaching God's Word such as the lighting and the sound. They are important. Ezra made sure that people could see him and hear him, so that he could be sure that the Law was being understood.

But secondly, because it was the Word of Moses, it also needed to be translated and explained (vv. 7–8). There was nothing magical about the words themselves; it was not enough for the text to sound beautiful and somehow appeal to their ascetic sense of balance and beauty. What was important was that people should understand what God had said to them. For this reason Ezra organises the Levites and sends them out among the people to explain what was being read to them. We must not forget that the task of the priests was first and foremost to educate the people in the Law of God. We tend to think they were just there to carry out the sacrifices, but they were in fact professional teachers, as Leviticus 10:11 makes clear:

> 'you must teach the Israelites all the decrees the LORD has given them through Moses.'[9]

As the Levites were moving among the people of God, they were helping the people to understand the Word of God in two ways. Firstly, they were translating it (v. 8a). Although the New International Version does not actually say this in the text, it does have a footnote to this effect, and other translations interpret the verse in this way. Almost certainly, by this time the post-exilic people in Judah were speaking a common form of Aramaic or some mixture of Hebrew and Aramaic. Since, of course, the Torah was in Hebrew, their experience of listening to it being read would be a bit like us listening to Chaucer. We would know vaguely it was English but we would probably not understand what it was all about. This is then the first example not only of theological education but also of Bible translation. Preaching, too, is a form of translation. The preacher is, in effect, interpreting the ancient text into the language of ordinary people so that they can understand it and connect what is being said to their world.

In addition to translating the text, the Levites were also explaining it (v. 8b). They were telling the people what it meant. This is the task of exegesis: explaining what the text says so that people can understand it. Another well-known example of this would, of course, be Philip and the Ethiopian eunuch.[10] The eunuch's response to Philip's question about whether he could understand what he is reading, *'How can I unless somebody explains it to me?'*, is a cry from the heart which all of us who are preachers would do well to remember. This is the fundamental core of what biblical preaching is: it is teaching what the text says. That is presumably what the Levites were doing: they were making the text clear so that the people understood what God was saying to them through the Book of Moses.

In addition to translating and explaining the Book of the Law, there was also a further aspect to what the Levites were doing: they were also training others to do the same. In Nehemiah 8:13 we are told that all the heads of families – that is the senior figures in each household, probably the father or the grandfather – gathered around with the priests and the Levites in order to give attention to the words of the Law. So we see that Ezra was teaching the Levites, the Levites were teaching the heads of the families and the heads of the families were teaching their own families. There was an organised programme of systematic Bible teaching, aiming to ensure that the whole community understood the words that were being read to them.

BODY BUILDERS

In this final section I want to look at our task as preachers by using a model which I owe to Ramesh Richard, who is an Indian Christian leader with a ministry working among Indians and other Asians both in the Indian subcontinent and in America. In his brilliantly titled book *Scripture Sculpture*,[11] Ramesh Richards uses the metaphor of a body to illustrate how a sermon can be built out of the body of a text, which is why I have chosen to call this section 'Body builders'.

A body has, of course, many parts, but Ramesh Richards focuses on three in particular: the flesh (including muscle, etc.); the bones (skeleton); and the heart. If all our bodies had was flesh and muscle, we would of course be reduced to an amorphous mass on the floor. It is the skeleton which gives our bodies shape and recognisability. Then inside the rib cage is perhaps the most important organ of the body: the heart. If the heart is not beating and pumping blood around the body, then it is no longer a body but a corpse. Without a heartbeat there is no life at all. Ramesh Richard explains how these three aspects of the human body can help us in our exegesis of a biblical text.

Having chosen the text on which he is going to preach, the first thing the preacher needs to do is to *chew through the meat of the text*. This is the process of study. He studies the background and context, asking such questions as:

- who is the author of the text?
- to whom was the text written?
- for what reason was it written?
- at what period of biblical history was it written?
- what is the historical, social, literary background of the text?
- what kind of writing is it?

These questions are fundamental to the interpretation of any biblical text. The preacher chews his way through the words, the paragraphs, the sentences, asking constantly what they mean. I liken this to having a telephone conversation with the author of the text. For example, if anyone reading my commentary on Deuteronomy, comes across a passage or a section they do not understand, they could telephone or email me and ask me to clarify, and I would be happy to explain what I meant. This is what we are trying to do in the task of exegesis: we are trying to come up with an explanation of the text with which we feel the original author would agree. It takes work; it takes effort; it takes study. But no one ever suggested that biblical preaching should not take those things. I believe that the Holy Spirit is just as involved in the study and preparation of a sermon as He is when it is being preached from the pulpit.

In the work that the Langham Partnership undertakes to encourage excellent preaching we sometimes still come up against resistance to the idea that preaching requires preparation. Some people think that such preparation is unspiritual, often justifying their view from Jesus' injunction not to worry about what we will say, because the words will be given to us.[12] What they forget, of course, is that Jesus' promise is addressed to prisoners in court, not to preachers in a pulpit. Applying it in this context is a very bad misuse of the text. As preachers, we need the Holy Spirit's help and guidance as we chew through the meat of the text.

The second stage of the process is *outlining the bones of the text*. This is rather like taking an X-ray of the text so that we can see the skeleton. We do this by going through all the notes we have made on the text as a result of our personal study and our reading of commentaries, etc., and trying to work out what the key points are. We should aim to get down to between four and six main points which are the 'bones' of the text. Any more than that, and it will probably be too much to try and tackle in one sermon. We need to get those key points onto a single sheet of paper, or better still a single piece of card which we can carry around in our pocket. We are aiming to arrive at a mental X-ray of the passage. Then, if anyone were to ask us to summarise the passage we had been studying, we could give a simple explanation of the bones of the passage. These bones are the key points on which everything else depends.

The Bible itself gives us examples of the skeletons of the text. For example, in Deuteronomy 10, the question is posed: '*And now, O Israel, what does the* LORD *your God ask of you...?*' The answer might be given that there are 613 laws which God requires His people to obey (i.e. all the flesh of the Torah). But in reply Moses actually gives a very straightforward skeleton of what the Law is about, which comprises five bones:

> *...to fear the* LORD *your God, to walk in all his ways, to love him, to serve the* LORD *your God with all your heart and with all your soul, and to observe the* LORD*'s commands and decrees that I am giving you today for your own good...*
> (Deuteronomy 10:12–13)

There is great deal of flesh around that skeleton but that is it. Of course, Jesus reduced it even further to two bones.[13]

The third stage of the process is to *feel the heartbeat of the text*, and only when we reach this point are we able to preach a sermon on it. To get to the heartbeat of the text, we have to be able to reduce it even further so that we could summarise its message in one sentence. This will then become the thrust of the sermon we will preach. When we have identified the heartbeat of the sermon, we are ready to begin to build our sermon, which is the aim and objective of exegesis. We do this by going in reverse order through the same procedure, building outwards from the heart to the bones and then the flesh.

Thus, the first and most important question the preacher needs to ask himself as he prepares his sermon is: *what will be the main thrust of my sermon which will communicate the main point of this passage?* Now this may seem so obvious as to be hardly worth stating, but my experience listening to many sermons has taught me that time and time again the preacher has failed to ask himself this question. Either the sermon did not seem to have any point to it at all or the main thrust of the sermon did not in any way match what the biblical text was about. Sadly, very often there is such a disconnection that, although people may feel that they have heard a good sermon by the pastor, they don't go away having heard what Isaiah or Paul really meant. They can understand what the pastor was saying but they do not know how to connect it with the text. Obviously that is not expository preaching. Expository preaching takes its main thrust from the text. Through the preaching the congregation feels the heartbeat of the text; they understand what they are being asked to believe or feel in their hearts, and understand the commitment they are being asked to make.

Having decided what the main thrust of the sermon should be, *we then need to put in place the skeleton or the bones of the outline of the sermon* and, of course, it makes sense to make use of the X-ray of the text that we have already formulated. Very probably, however, the skeleton we have will actually be more complicated than can be managed in one sermon. There may be five or six points, each with two or three further points. Although it is laid out very clearly on our sheet of A4 or piece of card, we must remember that the people listening to us preach will be assimilating all we are saying through their ears. Even if we are using an OHP or giving out notes, we must provide them with a skeleton they can easily recognise. It must be recognisable as a human skeleton, rather than that of a crab or some other creature.

With regard to building the outline of a sermon, I personally feel that there is some scope for creativity and imagination. For example, we may or may not stick fairly strictly to the precise order of the text. The important thing is that, at the end of the sermon, what people have heard is the text – not the preacher's brilliant imagination. Even if the preacher has chosen perhaps to start at the end rather than at the beginning, or take a point out of the middle and then work around it, the structure needs to be clear.

I find personally that discovering the heartbeat of the text and deciding on the basic outline of what I am going to say takes about 80 per cent of the effort. Once I know what the thrust of my sermon is going to be and once the structure is in place, the actual meat of the sermon – the words I am going to say, the illustrations I am going to use and the application of what I am going to say – seems to fall into place fairly quickly.

I mentioned earlier that exegesis is like having a personal telephone conversation with the author of the text. I have another little mental picture which I find helpful actually while I am preaching. I imagine Isaiah or Moses or Mark, or whoever it is, standing behind my shoulder, listening to me preaching what he wrote. My hope is that, as I am preaching, he is saying, 'Right. That's what I meant. It's not quite the way I would have put it, but it's good enough.' The sermon we are preaching to a modern audience should be having a comparable effect upon them as the original writer or prophet had on the people to whom he was speaking or writing. In a sense the wall between the ancient text and the contemporary world is becoming transparent. What they are seeing and hearing is not new: they are actually seeing and hearing what the original author wanted to say and, of course, through him they are hearing the word of the Lord Himself who caused these human words to be written in the first place. That, it seems to me, is the real test of our preaching.

NOTES

1. Acts 19:9.
2. I owe this phrase to John Stott, who uses it often in *The Contemporary Christian* (IVP, 1992). See also Chapter 2.
3. E.g. Nehemiah 8:1.
4. E.g. Nehemiah 8:8; 8:18; 9:3. Sometimes the two descriptions are combined in a phrase such as 'the Law of God which he gave through Moses' or 'the Law of Moses which the Lord His God commanded him'.
5. 1 Peter 4:11.
6. See Chapter 2 'The Paradoxes of Preaching'.
7. Nehemiah 8:10.
8. Leviticus 23 and Deuteronomy 16.
9. See also Deuteronomy 33:10.
10. Acts 8:26ff.
11. *Scripture Sculpture: A Do-It-Yourself Manual for Biblical Preaching* (Baker, 1995).
12. Matthew 10:19–20.
13. Matthew 22:34ff.

Chapter 26

Connecting with the Real World

Stuart Reid

'We are interested not in how much the preacher prays, not in how much he fasts, not in how much he reads the Bible, but in whether he lives on the same planet that we do.' So commented a church member to a friend of mine. As preachers we need to be asking ourselves: do we understand the world in which the people in our churches live out their daily lives? We need to get connected with the real world.

What is the Real World?

It is the place where raising children is very difficult these days. It is the place where our neighbours live with their second spouse and their children are living with their partners. They leave home at 7.16 a.m. and travel back late, after 7.00 or 8.00 p.m. each evening. It is the place where 20 per cent of people are in debt. When we asked our home group what was the most pressing issue they were facing in their lives, every single person gave the answer 'Money'.

At a church at which I was speaking recently I bumped into a lady I knew from a previous church. As I chatted to her and caught up on her news, she told me with eyes full of tears, 'My daughter has tried to commit suicide this week, twice.' In response to my enquiry about her other daughter, she said, 'Well, you know she is an alcoholic, and we have got the grandchildren.' A few moments later she confided that her third daughter was HIV-positive. And this is middle-class England! At least once a month I have lunch with a friend whose wife left him last year. He is now bringing up their three young children alone. This is the real world for many people.

We also live in the post-Christendom era and the nation is in free-fall morally. The man in the street has no idea about God. If we are honest we all know the depravity and sin that is in each of our hearts. There are now around 150,000 pornographic websites on the Internet, presenting a very real temptation and pressure to many in our congregations. With all its affluence our land, as we are all aware, is in an incredible moral mess.

TWO REALITIES

The following illustration is well known but nevertheless it makes its point powerfully. A play written by David Lodge was being staged in the United States in November 1963. During the course of the play the actor had to turn the radio on for a few seconds and then turn it off again. At the very moment when he did so, the announcement was made that President John F. Kennedy had been assassinated. Immediately the illusion created by the play was shattered. Everything was changed because reality had broken in, and it could never be the same again.

This is what happens when a person becomes a Christian. Reality breaks in, and life can never be the same again. Jesus said to Nicodemus, *'I tell you the truth, no one can see the kingdom of God unless he is born again.'*[1] When a person becomes a Christian he or she is given new eyes. For the first time he or she sees another world, which is equally real; they see the spiritual world through the eyes of faith. When, in Revelation 4:1, the apostle John says, *'there before me was a door standing open in heaven'* he is talking about a reality that was just as real as the world in which he lived. Elisha's servant had the same experience when, confronted by the threat from the army of the King of Aram, the veil was lifted from his eyes, so that he could see the hills full of the horses and chariots of the heavenly armies.[2] As Christians we are aware that there is an invisible world that is all around us. God is spirit;[3] in the spirit realm there are both the angelic forces of heaven and the malevolent forces of evil.[4] This spiritual world is just as real as the physical world. Tom Wright has said that heaven is 'God's dimension of present reality': it is this that the born-again person can see by faith.

There are then two realities: an earthly reality and a heavenly one. Both are God given; both are created and controlled by God; and He is present in both. We must be very careful we do not compartmentalise God's world: in Him we live and move and have our being. We are not Gnostics or Neo-Platonists: we live in a real world, but the unseen world is just as real. Our task is to bring the two together. Although I am emphasising the vital importance for us as preachers to understand the real world in which our hearers live, we must never forget the truth that the unseen world is just as real.

PREACHING THE GLORY OF THE GOSPEL

As the comment I quoted at the beginning suggests, we as preachers have lost much of our credibility. Those listening in the pews sometimes doubt whether we have much of an understanding of the world in which they live their lives. For our part we need to work hard to make sure that we do connect with the real world.

One of the ways in which we can do this is by being students of our culture. When Karl Barth was asked how he prepared his sermons, he famously replied that he did so with the Bible in one hand and a newspaper in the other. Anyone who wants to preach must read widely. I don't want to listen to any preacher who does not read. We need to be reading about politics, about economics, about science, about medicine. We read about these subjects not because we intend to preach on them necessarily but because we need to be aware of what is going on in the world in which our people live. By the way, if we do end up including any of the material we are reading in our preaching, it is vital that we get our facts right. Only the other week I made an off-the-cuff comment about classical music and, sure enough, at the end of the service there was someone waiting to put me right about my mistake. If we do not get our facts straight, we will lose our credibility with our audience. If we are wrong about the facts we include in our sermons, what else might we be wrong about?

It is only by reading widely that we will be able to fulfil our task of equipping our people to live the life of God in the community. In this country we are greatly blessed by the Christian literature that godly men and women have written over the last twenty-five years, as well as over the preceding centuries. As a pastor I value greatly the writings of skilled Bible scholars who do the hard exegetical work for me and who, with their knowledge of the source languages, have a greater understanding of the texts than I could ever achieve.

As well as reading widely, we as preachers need to learn to listen to the members of our congregations. An excellent way of learning about their lives is by visiting them at their workplaces. I do this three or four times a week, meeting people for breakfast or lunch and, whenever I can, I pray with them about their work. I believe it is my duty to understand the lives of those to whom I am preaching. I need to understand how difficult it is for them to get up in the morning and face the many pressures on their lives. In order to be able to relate to young people, I also try to watch at least three hours of MTV a week, which I do in the gym. I don't know which is more painful: the exercise machines or the MTV! We have to know the worlds in which our people live. We don't have to like them, but we do have to know them!

We also need to visit people in their homes – across the age-groups and across the spectrum of society: married, single, divorced, widows, the elderly. Job is, of course, the classic case of suffering in the Old Testament. For seven days and seven nights Job's three friends sat on the ground with him, being alongside him in his suffering. The sad thing is that they then became preachers, trotting out the old sermon they had ready prepared in their pocket. If only they had just listened! We visit people, not to find illustrations for our sermons, but to get alongside them.

Our task as preachers is to equip the saints for the work of ministry, and for most people that work will not be within the confines of the church but out in the world.[5]

I think it is so important for the members of our churches to know that the minister is interested in what they spend the greater part of their lives doing. When I was preaching a series on work, each Sunday I invited church members out to the front with the express purpose of finding out about their work.[6] I asked each person three questions:

1. What do you do for a living?
2. What is the greatest problem you face as a Christian in your work?
3. How can we as a fellowship help you to live the life of God in that location?

Having found out about their work, we laid hands on them and prayed for them, asking the Lord to anoint them to live His life in their workplace. It was much appreciated.

I was called by God from the veterinary profession into the ministry. I have to say that in many ways my work now is much easier than my work as a vet. As preachers we are just the catering corps. Our task is to feed the church to enable them to live in a hostile world, and we must make sure we feed our people well. It is our duty to ensure that we choose the right people to preach on a Sunday morning because those listening have been battling it out on the front line all week, and they need to be fed. We need to make sure that those who are preaching are called and gifted. There is no place for pandering to the desires of those who want a platform but, if truth be told, have no ability. Our people come in starving, and they need to be fed. I know they should feed themselves but they get battered in the world and they need building up again. Those who preach must be called and gifted of God.

I have already tried to give a sketch of the hurting and broken world in which we live. In spite of people's apparent affluence and coping exterior, they are in the main damaged goods. The gospel of Jesus Christ is all about grace. We preach to people from a heart of grace. In other words we give them the Word not because they deserve it but because we love them – and if we don't love them, we shouldn't be preaching! Graham Johnson tells a story about Norman Vincent Peale, the incredibly popular American clergyman and promoter of the power of positive thinking, which he heard from his tutor Haddon Robinson.[7] When Norman Vincent Peale established a centre to promote ministry, he somewhat strangely, as he himself was not an evangelical, chose an evangelical to be its director. One day, when the director was alone with Dr Peale, he asked him, 'Dr Peale, I was wondering, do you know what it means to be born again?' In an uncustomary show of anger Dr Peale's face grew red. He shot back, 'Yes, I do', before concluding the meeting very abruptly. About a week later, Dr Peale re-initiated the meeting with his director, saying, 'I would like to finish the conversation you began a little while ago. Your question upset me because you assumed I did not know what it meant to be born again.' He continued, 'I was brought up under the same teaching as you. I understand the need for salvation based on the cross of Christ, but it bothered me that evangelicals seem to love the Bible and care so little about people, so I determined that I wouldn't follow that course. I would love people more than the Bible. In retrospect I acknowledge that in loving people I have not always honoured God's Word as I should have. However, you evangelicals have erred on the other side. You love the Bible and have disregarded people. Maybe we have something to learn from each other.' Truth and love must go together. As preachers we must love the people to whom we are preaching as much as we love to preach. Preferably, more. A preacher who does not love people, who just wants a platform to exhibit his eloquence, should never bother to preach again.

While we are preaching, some will look bored, some will look angry, some will look fearful, some will be half asleep but, as Spurgeon said, 'If people fall asleep when I am preaching, don't wake them up, wake me up.' We must not get cross with people: we must just be thankful they have come, because actually it took quite a lot of effort on their part actually to make it to church. We need to remember that every person to whom we are speaking, has been affected profoundly, in every part of their being, by sin. Whether we are talking about marriage, work, the family, or any other aspect of their life, the basic problem is always sin. They may need the help of a psychotherapist, or a counsellor, or a doctor but, fundamentally, what they need most of all in this life, is to sit under the Word of God again and again and again. Only the Word of God will really change people. I am not wanting to disparage the ministry of these other caring professionals in any way but it is the Word of God that changes people, not only as it is preached but through all the ways in which it is propagated throughout the fellowship. Until they become Christians it is the devil that pulls people's strings and they are brainwashed by the powers of darkness. The world in which they live is constantly reinforcing their prejudices, their habits, their sin and their desires. Our task is to help them to live a life which honours Jesus every day.

In order to do that, it may be that some of our people may have to leave the job of work they are doing. Some former prostitutes may, for example, have to leave the town in which they worked in order to be able to make a fresh start. Some Muslims, too, will have to relocate for their own personal safety. I have heard of cases of Muslims in the north of England being subject to death threats when they became Christians. For others the issue is not as black and white. For example, one young man I met was working in a betting shop when he was converted and he felt he could not stay in the job. Such cases are the exception, rather than the rule. Most people should be guided by Paul's words in 1 Corinthians 7:17: *'each one should retain the place in life that the Lord assigned to him and to which God has called him.'*

As preachers we need to take seriously our task of equipping Christians not just for the 3,000 hours they will spend in church-related activities, but for the 88,000 hours they will spend over the course of their lives at the work they have been called and gifted to do. We must recognise that it is hard out there. People work long hours; they face difficult decisions; they encounter many temptations. In his first letter, John writes that the whole world is in the grip of the evil one.[8] Our church members are not going out into neutral ground: they are going out into enemy territory. As Paul says, their struggle is not against the foreman, or the neighbour, or the head teacher, or any other human figure, but is against the rulers and authorities and the powers of this dark world, the spiritual forces of evil in the heavenly places.[9] When people become Christians it is as if they have to turn their canoe around and start paddling upstream. As preachers we need to be feeding them with the Word of God, so that they have the strength to do this. Across the world 2,800 Christians are killed every four days for their faith, the same number that were killed in the Twin Towers' tragedy. At the end of last year, Zeman Muhammad Ishmael, a taxi driver in North Iraq, was shot twenty-eight times for giving out extracts of the Bible to his passengers. Of course, Christians in Britain will not face such danger, but they will be ridiculed and they will be unpopular. We need to strengthen believers so that they will be able to cope with the antagonism they will face.

The most important way in which we can encourage and strengthen our congregations is by making sure that every week we preach the gospel, the Good News. By this I do not mean that we should always preach on John 3:16 or Revelation 3:20! God's Word is always good news. It is always good and it is always big. If our preaching isn't good and it isn't big, we are missing the point. Even the hard bits in the Bible are good and even the little bits are huge! In his book *Preaching Like Paul*,[10] James Thompson makes the point that there is no separation in Paul's preaching between *paraklesis*, encouraging and strengthening the believers, and preaching the gospel. All his teaching is rooted in the saving event of the death and resurrection of Christ. It is interesting that in the opening chapter of his letter to the church in Rome he writes,

> *That is why I am so eager to preach the gospel also to you who are at Rome.*
> (Romans 1:15)

We need to hear the gospel again and again and again – not the simple gospel, although we do need to hear that again and again, but the comprehensive and cosmic gospel with its enormity and wonder. When people leave church on a Sunday morning, having heard the preaching of the Word of God, they should go out thinking how wonderful it is to be a Christian. Christianity is always good. Jesus is always good. It is well known that Bill Clinton used to have in his campaign offices signs that reminded him and his supporters of the main issue on which they needed to focus in the forthcoming election, 'It's the economy, stupid'. As preachers we need to have a sign in our vestries which says, 'It's the gospel, saint'. We must give our people hope.

There is no point in having a go at people. We all know how it is on a Sunday morning. There is every likelihood that some of those sitting in the pews will have had a massive row with their wife before coming to church and their children will have been at each other's throats. They probably feel they have been a bad witness at work that week and are aware that they have not read their Bible for days. Through our sermons we need to lift their spirits and encourage them. We need to remind them who they are in Christ

Jesus. This is exactly what Paul does in his epistles. He does not start by writing about the issues he wants to tackle, such as marriage, work and family. No, he begins with the gospel, telling his readers who they are in God. He tells them that they are God's children; that they belong to Christ; that they are significant, adopted, forgiven, justified; that God has great plans for their lives; and that He has good works prepared in advance for them to do. For Paul identity came before action. So often preaching can be used as an excuse to scold and nag the members of our congregation. You see their heads go down and discouragement set in. But people don't come to church to be browbeaten. They need to be blessed and uplifted. To put it in grammatical terminology, the indicative mood must come before the imperative mood.

I watched the film *The Lion King* with my grandchildren. It is a story which has such strong echoes of the Christian message. It is about a beautiful kingdom which was stolen from its true king by an evil usurper, and its glory has been badly marred. The young lion heir to the throne, Simba, who wrongly holds himself responsible for his father's death, struggles with accepting his true identity. He runs away and wastes his life with his two friends, a warthog and a meerkat. One night Simba's father, Mufasa, appears to him in a vision and says, 'You have forgotten me.' The young lion denies this, but Mufasa persists, encouraging his son with these words: 'You have forgotten who you are and so forgotten me. Look inside yourself, Simba. You are more than what you have become. Remember who you are. You are my son, and the one true king. Remember who you are.'[11] Although it is just a story, this scene provides us with a very vivid picture of the way we as preachers need to speak to God's people. We need to tell them to remember who they are; that they are not ordinary people but have been chosen by the living God for a purpose. Of course, we need to avoid false triumphalism, but equally we need to avoid preaching in a way that is moralistic and prescriptive, bringing death rather than life.

More than anything else, the members of our churches need to know who they are in Jesus Christ. More than anything else they need to know that God has a destiny and a purpose for their lives. It is this knowledge that will give them the strength to live their lives well in the real world. Like Esther they need to know that God has put them in the job they are doing *'for such a time as this'*.[12] They may be the only Christian in their office or their school or their factory, and God has put them there for a purpose. Nobody else will reach those people for Jesus. Nobody else will show the character of Christ in that office. That is why our task as preachers is to feed and encourage our people with the Word of God.

Above all, we need to pray for God's anointing both on us as we preach and on our hearers as they listen. As preachers we need to be overwhelmed by the greatness and the glory and the majesty and the wonder of the Living God, who has broken into time and space in His Son Jesus – it must impact us first of all. As a famous preacher once said, a preacher will be forgiven anything if he brings a sense of God. Although it is not great poetry, the following poem expresses an important truth:

Not merely in the words you say,

Nor only in your deeds confess,

But in the most unconscious way, is Christ expressed.

Is it a beatific smile, a holy light upon your brow?

No, I felt His presence when you laughed just now.

To me, 'twas not the truth you taught, to you so clear, to me so dim,

But when you came, you brought a sense of Him.

And from your eyes He beckons me,

And from your heart His love is shared

Till I lose sight of you and see the Christ instead.

Most people are Christians because somebody brought the presence of Christ into their life. They brought 'a sense' of Him.

One of my present-day heroes is the preacher and writer John Piper, Senior Pastor of Bethlehem Baptist Church, Minneapolis. In one of his books he tells this story which was prompted by a sermon he preached at his church in Minnesota on Isaiah 6:1–4, Isaiah's vision in the temple:

> I didn't realise that, not long before this Sunday, one of the young families in our church discovered that their child was being sexually abused by a close relative. It was incredibly traumatic. They were there that Sunday morning and sat under the message. I wonder how many advisors to us pastors today would have said, 'Pastor Piper, can't you see your people are hurting? Can't you come down out of your heavens and get practical? Don't you realise what kind of people sit in front of you on Sunday?' Some weeks later I learnt the story. The husband took me aside one Sunday after service. 'John,' he said, 'these have been the hardest months of our lives. Do you know what has gotten me through? The vision of the greatness of God's holiness that you gave me that first week of January. It has been the rock on which we stand upon.'[13]

It is the glory of the gospel that will keep people persevering in a desperately unhappy marriage. It is the glory of the gospel that will give parents the strength to care for a severely handicapped child or a family to cope with a debilitating long-term illness. It is knowing that God is with us and that He can be trusted. There is nothing greater in this life than the gospel of Jesus Christ. In the story of the birth of Moses there is a wonderful verse which says, *'The midwives, however, feared God and did not do what the king of Egypt had told them to do.'*[14] We want our churches to be full of people who fear the Lord more than any human authority and want to spend their lives doing what pleases Him. As preachers, we need to give our people such a vision of the glory of the gospel of Jesus Christ that they take something of Him with them when they go out into the real world of their daily lives.

NOTES

1. John 3:3.
2. 2 Kings 6:8ff.
3. John 4:24.
4. Ephesians 6:10–12.
5. See also Chapter 27 which deals with the subject of work.
6. An idea suggested by Paul Stevens from Vancouver from whom I have learnt a great deal in the area of work.
7. *Preaching to a Post-modern World* (IVP), p. 20.
8. 1 John 5:19.
9. Ephesians 6:12.
10. Westminster John Knox, 2000.
11. My paraphrase.
12. Esther 4:14.
13. *The Supremacy of God in Preaching* (Baker Books, 2004), p. 10.
14. Exodus 1:17.

Chapter 27

PREACHING LIFE ISSUES: WORK

Stuart Reid

Since the average person spends 88,000 hours of their life working, I believe that it is very important that we preach on the topic of work. Scripture deals with the whole of life. It is God's Word for every situation. As preachers we need to build a strong base from which our people can go out into the world, sustained and strengthened to face the very real pressures and difficulties that will encounter them in the workplace on Monday morning. They need to know that God cares about their work – as He does about every area of their lives. God is not just concerned about getting people to heaven: He wants to build a people on earth who will demonstrate His life, His power and His nature to the world.

GETTING WORK IN PERSPECTIVE[1]

Right at the beginning it is very important to set work in its proper context. Although it is not possible to look at the biblical exegesis in detail, it is very clear from Genesis chapters 1 to 3 that God intended each human being to have not one full-time job, but three. The first full-time job which each human being has is to enjoy communion with God. The reason why each and every human being is made is to have an intimate relationship with God: to walk with Him, to talk with Him and to have fellowship with Him. Each human being's second full-time job is to build a family. In other words, we spend time developing relationships horizontally with one another. I, for instance, am a father full time. Although my four children are in three different countries I never cease to be a father, praying for them, writing to them, phoning them. I am also a husband full time, whether I am abroad or at home. Drawing the circle wider I am a member of the church full time.

I think 'church' all the time, praying for people, visiting them, ringing them and seeking to build community. Each human being's third full-time job is to be God's regent on the earth. This is the realm of co-creativity with God, which mandates us to take responsibility in three main areas:

- nature/environment
- culture/society
- work.

People suffer from burn-out not, I would suggest, because they have too much work as such, but because they have too few jobs. In other words, burn-out comes because people are only doing one job, instead of the three we are all called to do. If we do all three jobs for which we were created, we will not suffer burn-out.

We are actually meant to work at these three God-ordained full-time jobs for the duration of our lives. There is no such thing as retirement. Through the cross these original callings are redeemed and renewed and can be fulfilled in the power of the Holy Spirit. This then is my starting point on the subject of work: our work is only one aspect of our calling as human beings.

All Work is 'Spiritual'

I was brought up to believe that the real Christians were the missionaries, and all the rest of us looked on in admiration and wonder at the way these extraordinary people served God. It was never said but, if you were a plumber or a shop assistant, you could never be as spiritual as a missionary. I want to contend, however, that this way of thinking was completely wrong. I want to contend that it is as spiritual to work on the deli counter at the local supermarket as it is to pray for the sick. That it is as spiritual to be a repairer of bodies as it is to be an evangelist winning souls.

In Ephesians 4:1 Paul writes,

As a prisoner for the Lord, then, I urge you to live a life worthy of the calling you have received.

In saying this he is not just addressing theology graduates! He is talking to ordinary people: housewives, ex-soldiers, slaves, bakers, farmers ... Every one of us has a calling. We are called first to be disciples of Jesus Christ, but we are also called to use the gifts and abilities which God has given us. In 1 Corinthians 7:17 Paul commands:

Nevertheless, each one should retain the place in life that the Lord assigned to him and to which God has called him. This is the rule I lay down in all the churches.

332

When a person tells me that he or she wants to work full time for the Lord, whatever his or her job I always respond, 'You already do!' – and I am not just playing with words! We are all full-time workers for the Lord, whether we are a pastor, an evangelist, a nurse, a car mechanic, or a bus driver. And this statement holds true even if we are doing a job which we feel doesn't particularly use our gifts. Think of Joseph. He had a number of careers during his lifetime: he was a shepherd; he was Potiphar's steward; and he was a politician/governor for the king of Egypt. Despite the fact that he never chose any of those jobs, in each one of them he worked out his calling to be a servant of Yahweh and a faithful son of the covenant. In each of them he lived a righteous life, and that can be true for us too. No job will fit us perfectly. There will always be some part of our personality or our skills that our work doesn't stretch or develop, but that actually is a good thing because it stops us becoming workaholics and living for work.

But surely some jobs are more important than others? Surely God is more concerned with a person's soul than his or her body? Surely preaching is more important than accountancy? And those in the caring professions are more important than lorry drivers or stockbrokers or entertainers or whatever? But actually I don't see that in the Bible. We used to have great debates about whether the human person was bipartite (body and soul) or tripartite (body and soul and spirit), but whichever of these is true, in the Hebrew view God created human beings as a unity. God created a physical universe, and *'God saw that it was good'*. And when God came to earth He took a real body. Anyone shaking hands with Jesus would have discovered that He had a carpenter's grip. We might think that the first thing Jesus would have done after His death, would have been to cast off his physical body, but not so: He was raised with a physical body. He was able to say to Thomas, *'Put your finger here; see my hands. Reach out your hand and put it into my side.'*[2] When we are resurrected, we too will have a real body. We need to be very careful that we call good what God has called good. In our role as God's regents God has called us to care for creation. That is why we need hairdressers, housewives, builders and PT instructors. We need to look after our bodies and the fabric of this world because they are good, and we need to honour the people who do these things. Their task is as spiritual as that of the pastor and the preacher.

The Bible teaches that what happens now in the temporal is as important as the eternal. In fact, according to my reading of the Bible, it teaches that what happens on the earth determines what will happen for the vast aeons of eternity. What we do now determines how we will spend eternity. We will receive praise or condemnation for what we have done in the body. Serving people as a shop assistant is of eternal value in God's eyes. There is more to Christianity than evangelism. We are called to glorify the Lord in everything we do. Our work should have such a distinct quality about it that it arouses questions. I have always said that New Testament evangelism comes about as a result of New Testament lifestyles. A customer in a Christian's shop comments, 'I come and shop here because I feel you are trustworthy', and the Christian replies, 'Perhaps that is because I am a Christian.'

Or a Christian's colleague at work says, 'How can you respond like that when the boss is so unreasonable?', prompting an answer such as, 'Well, I feel God has put me here, and God has given me grace to love him.' I am so glad that William Wilberforce did not go into the church, although he was asked to do so, but instead spent his life as a politician campaigning against the slave trade. Paul reminds us that one day each of us will have to give an account of our lives, and we will have to give an account of our work life just as much as every other area.

It is very important for us to remember that, when God said, *'This is my Son, whom I love; with him I am well pleased'*,[3] as far as we know He spoke those words before Jesus ever performed a miracle and before He ever preached a great sermon. He said it after Jesus had worked eighteen years in a carpenter's shop.

In his book *The Abolition of the Laity*,[4] Paul Stevens argues that in one sense we are all clergy because the word 'clergy' is derived from the Greek *kleros*, which means 'inheritance' and can have the sense 'appointed' or 'endowed'. We are all appointed and commissioned to be the people of God in the villages, towns or cities where we live. I am not anti-leadership, but I do want to plead that we understand that all Christians are of equal value and equal status in God's sight. We are not all leaders, but we are all called. The secret call of the preacher does not make him any more spiritual than anyone else, and in saying this I dare to disagree with the great John Calvin. I believe in the call to preach, and I don't think anyone should preach unless he has a call and gifting, but I passionately believe that each member of our congregation is equally called to the job which he or she is doing, and is a missionary in that situation. In a church at which I spoke in America, over the door through which people walked as they left the church there was a sign, 'The mission field starts here'. We don't have to go on a boat or a plane to be a missionary: we just have to go out from the church into the world.

Recently I met up with an acquaintance in Hong Kong whom I had not seen for a long time. For many years he had worked as a submariner but he was now working for a Chinese evangelistic society. During the course of our conversation he commented, 'The difference is when they send me out now they pray for me.' God spoke to me through that conversation. He challenged me with the question of why, during all those years when that man had worked in a very tough maritime environment, no one had ever prayed for him. That was much harder than working in a Christian office among fellow Christians. We should pray for our people as they go out to their jobs, not just for those on the traditional 'mission field'. In the course of their work some people have to face extremely difficult ethical, moral or financial dilemmas and carry huge responsibilities. They need to know that the church cares about what they are doing and prays for them. I have been in prayer meetings where we have prayed for doctors working in West Africa, which I am very happy to do, but I think we should also be praying for doctors in our own city who have difficult ethical and moral decisions to face every day. Furthermore, I believe we need to be equipping God's people to serve in an extraordinary way in their work situations. We should be providing teaching on time management, ethics and ethical issues, how to deal with money, and the very many other issues they face on a daily basis.

GOD IS A WORKER

Work is a gift from God. It is a blessing, not a curse, although like all of creation, as a result of the Fall it was *'subjected to frustration'*.[5] The Christian view of work is very different from the Greek view, which regarded it as a curse – the lot of slaves, who comprised up to fifty per cent of the population, and not of free men.

Jesus said,

> *'My Father is always at his work to this very day, and I, too, am working.'*
> (John 5:17)

Since work is an activity in which both God the Father and Jesus are actively involved, it is intrinsically good.

I have already alluded to the fact that when God made the world, the statement is repeated that *'God saw that it was good'*.[6] Since we are made in God's image, we too should be able to enjoy what we produce as a result of our work. For example, when we have finished painting a bedroom or digging the garden, we should be able to say, 'That's really good.' Or when we have finished a pile of ironing or made a spreadsheet balance at the end of the year, we should be able to feel really satisfied. I believe that this is part of what it means to be made in the image of God. It is not just artists who should be able to say that, but all of us. We should be able to feel pleased with the work we do. The writer of Ecclesiastes describes such satisfaction as the gift of God:

> *That everyone may eat and drink, and find satisfaction in all his toil – this is the gift of God.*
> (Ecclesiastes 3:13)

As church leaders we need to remember that some of those in our congregations are working in jobs which are very mundane. They need to hear us say that God values what they are doing, that in His eyes their work is significant. In fact, they need to be filled with the Holy Spirit in order to do their work well.

THE DANGER OF LOVING WORK TOO MUCH

Work can become an idol or an addiction. Some people live for their work: they become workaholics. At one veterinary practice at which I worked, just before I joined one of the partners, whose wife was pregnant at the time, collapsed and died. He had worked for eighteen months without a day off. I never knew the man personally but, if he was anything like the other partners of that practice, their work had become their idol. They weren't Christians, but Christians are not exempt from this danger.

Amos 8:5 gives us a vivid example of people who are consumed by the desire to get rich and will stop at nothing to achieve their goal, in their case using false measures and cheating their customers. They long for the Sabbath to be finished so that they can get back to work and make more money:

> 'When will the New Moon be over
>   that we may sell grain,
>   and the Sabbath be ended
>   that we may market wheat?'

As human beings we can get ourselves in all sorts of difficulties when we begin to think that work can meet our ultimate needs. This is a complete illusion. So many people seek their value and status in their work. They think they must be worth something because they are the senior partner, or the foreman, or the head teacher. If the next week, that individual is made redundant, he or she can feel totally worthless. We have to teach our people that their worth comes from belonging to Jesus – not from being the head woman in their company. Their worth comes from the fact that Jesus loved them enough to lay down His life for them.

Working for the Lord

While we will never find total fulfilment from our work, we can and should offer our work to God as worship. God deliver us from the thought that what we do on a Sunday for an hour and a half is the sum total of our worship. I love corporate worship, but it is only a small part of our lives. All our life must be worship – whether we are making a fruit pie, or whether we are trying to sell someone a new car. We should be asking the Holy Spirit to help us to conduct our business in a way that pleases Him. Everything we do can be worship.

Paul's words in 1 Thessalonians 1:3 are helpful in showing us how we can do our jobs in such a way that they can be our acceptable worship to God:

> We continually remember before our God and Father your work produced by faith,
> your labour prompted by love, and your endurance inspired by hope in our Lord
> Jesus Christ.

Paul speaks first of our 'work produced by faith'. We should be exercising faith in the area of our work as much as in every other area of our lives. God wants to be involved in all that we do. Each morning, we commit our day to the Lord and fix our eyes upon Him. We remember that we are children of the Lord who live by faith. We know that the Spirit of God is within us. We are faith people.

We don't work *for* God as much as we work *with* Him. When we go to work on a Monday morning, He is already there and He helps us in the work that we do. I remember talking to some research chemists once who told me that most scientists, if they are humble enough, will say that the breakthroughs they have somehow have a givenness about them. The Holy Spirit is the Spirit of Truth – not just religious truth but all truth. When we talk about God being with us in our work, we do not mean that He is standing with His arms folded waiting to see if we are going to break one of the Ten Commandments. No, He wants to help us, and guide us into the truth we need in our work. We can call on the Lord at work and He is willing to help us. I know that, when I was a practising vet, some animals were healed which I did not expect to be healed, because God in His grace intervened and my face was spared!

The second characteristic of our work is that it is 'prompted by love'. When our work is prompted by love it has a power over and above that which it would otherwise have. Paul instructed believers that whatever they do they should work at it with all their heart. Jesus commanded that we should go the second mile. We are called to be different, not just to clock in and clock out like everyone else.

I remember hearing some lectures by a man called Don Flow, of Flow Automotive Companies, who ran his business on Kingdom principles, 'prompted by love'. His father had given him half his business and he had developed it, so that it is now a multimillion-dollar enterprise, selling and repairing cars. According to its mission statement the company aims 'To deliver an extraordinary level of service at every point of contact with the customer in a personal and professional manner'. In his lectures Don Flow talked about four levels of service, from the very basic (the car is repaired adequately but the cost is too high) to the top level of service at which his company aims. He pitches at the 'surprise' level. He wants his customers to go away thinking, 'Wow! That was extraordinary service.' So they always aim to go beyond the level of service that would be expected, by, say, valeting the car. Flow maintains that, if a company satisfies its customers, it always pays in the long run.

Some of Flow's core principles are: our service must exceed our customer's greatest expectations; we earn the right to keep customers by treating them like friends; the first and foremost responsibility of every employee is to provide good service for customers. In order to provide an incentive for his staff, he ensures that employees who provide extraordinary service are recognised and rewarded. He also places great emphasis on people development, aiming to ensure that all his staff achieve their full potential. The company also organises the sales staff to work in teams, so that, rather than one employee shining out above the others and earning a bonus, there is a winning team and failing staff are encouraged and supported by their team to improve and meet their targets.

The whole company is based on grace. Grace is giving when the recipient is totally undeserving. The whole of Christianity should be grace. Isn't that how we want to live our lives, at work as well as at church and in our homes? We need to be teaching our people to be prompted by an attitude of grace in their work, so that they go beyond fulfilling their duties and make that extra step. They will not always achieve that level, but they can make it their aim.

I remember taking a friend with me to visit an old lady in a nursing home. The person we were visiting was very frail and was nearing the end of her life, and she had lost almost all ability to respond. The woman who accompanied me was a nurse in her fifties. The level of care she gave this woman was beyond anything I had ever seen before, and the results were astounding. We make an extraordinary impact when our work is prompted by love.

We also need to teach our people to avoid the temptations that are associated with the world of work. For example, in a welfare state, there is a temptation to laziness but, at a time when believers were giving up work because they were expecting Jesus to return at any moment, Paul taught, *'If a man will not work, he shall not eat.'*[7] Of course, at the other end of the spectrum there is the danger of workaholism which I have already touched upon. The workaholic is always a thief, because he steals love and he steals relationships, and he only gives money back. Everyone else has to adjust their lives to suit his passion for work. Eugene Peterson and C.S. Lewis are biting in their criticism of such people, saying respectively: 'Busy people are morally lazy' and 'Only lazy people work hard.'

As pastors we also need to teach people how to establish values and set goals for their lives, rather than letting others set them for them. As Eugene Petersen says in his book *The Contemplative Pastor*,[8] if we don't take the time to find out what God wants us to do each day, during the course of the day people ask for our help, and because we want to please them, we become incredibly busy, until eventually we give the impression that we are too busy to be available to people. Jesus was never too busy. He only did what He saw His Father doing. I am not saying I am through on this, but we each have to decide that we will live to please God and not try to satisfy people. If we try to please people we will always be busy. We need to ask God what He wants us to do each day. Of course, there will always be emergencies to which we have to respond, but we set the principle in place.

I am always amazed when I read the end of Mark 1. In verse 32 Mark writes,

> *That evening after sunset the people brought to Jesus all the sick and demon-possessed. The whole town gathered at the door, and Jesus healed many who had various diseases. He also drove out many demons...*

In the morning Jesus goes out to pray in a solitary place. Later He is disturbed by Simon and his companions who interrupt Him with the news that, *'Everyone is looking for you!'*

But rather than continuing to respond to the need, which He can only have scratched the surface of the previous evening, Jesus makes this staggering statement:

'Let us go somewhere else – to the nearby villages – so that I can preach there also.'

In prayer Jesus had heard from His Father. The desire to be popular and accepted tempts us all, but we have to teach our people how to find the will of God and do it, not to lose ourselves in our busyness. It is a wonderful thing to 'get a life' and not be busy.

We are not called to be addicted to our work but we are called to work with enthusiasm. The writer of Ecclesiastes says: *'Whatever your hand finds to do, do it with all your might'* (9:10). If we find we can't do our work enthusiastically we need perhaps to go back to the Lord and ask Him if He is in it. If we can't do our work with faith, we need to ask Him the same question because *'everything that does not come from faith is sin.'*[9]

In the culture of greed and covetousness in which we live, working in moderation can be a real witness. *'Give me neither poverty nor riches'*, says the author of Proverbs, *'but give me only my daily bread.'*[10] It is always so refreshing to hear of a couple who choose not to move to a bigger house, but to live in a way that frees up their finances for world mission. In his life, Abraham went not from house to house to house but from altar to altar to altar. We need to re-examine our values to see if the way we are living is truly a reflection of the Kingdom.

The third phrase Paul uses in 1 Thessalonians 1:3 is *'your endurance inspired by hope'*. Everything we do has eternal significance. In 1 Corinthians 3:13–14 Paul writes:

his work will be shown for what it is, because the Day will bring it to light. It will be revealed with fire, and the fire will test the quality of a man's work. If what he has built survives, he will receive his reward.

How much of the work we have done in our lifetime will survive the test of heavenly fire? I find this question immensely challenging. It is all our work that will be tested, not just our Christian work. Will my sermons survive? Will my veterinary work survive? Will my work as a father survive? I know that only those works which have been produced by faith, prompted by love and inspired by hope will survive. Paul continues:

If it is burned up, he will suffer loss; he himself will be saved, but only as one escaping through the flames.
(1 Corinthians 3:15)

At the end of my life I don't want to discover that, although I was very busy, what I spent my life doing was not in God's will. Since we will all have to give an account to the Lord, whatever we do must be done for Him. Everything that we do for Him will make a permanent mark on heaven. Revelation says:

> 'Write: Blessed are the dead who die in the Lord from now on.'
>   'Yes,' says the Spirit, 'they will rest from the labour, for their deeds will
> follow them.'
> (Revelation 14:13)

Our deeds will follow us, that is, *all of our deeds*. Our task as preachers is to equip the people in our congregations to work for Christ in the workshop, in the shop, in the farm, in the factory, in the school, in the hospital. We need to encourage one another, to pray for another, to rebuke one another and to motivate one other. I will conclude with one final word from Paul:

> Therefore, my dear brothers, stand firm. Let nothing move you. Always give yourself
> fully to the work of the Lord, because you know that your labour in the Lord is not
> in vain.'
> (1 Corinthians 15:58)

NOTES

1. Much of what I say in this section I owe to my friend and teacher on this subject, Paul Stevens.
2. John 20:27.
3. Matthew 3:17.
4. Paternoster Press, 2000.
5. Cf. Romans 8:20.
6. Genesis 1:10, 12, 18, 21, 25, 31.
7. 2 Thessalonians 3:10.
8. Eerdmans Publishing Co., 1995.
9. Romans 14:23.
10. Proverbs 30:8.

Chapter 28

PREACHING FROM NARRATIVE

Chris Wright

It is worth reminding ourselves that half the Bible is narrative and story. Since God chose to present His Word in this form, He clearly felt it was important. If, therefore, preachers neglect the narrative parts of the Bible, as occurs in far too many of our churches, they need to realise that they are depriving people of a substantial part of the truth that God wants to communicate, which is a very serious thing to do. As preachers we need to be committed to preaching the whole of the Bible.

PREACHING THE STORY OF THE BIBLE

Before we preach any of the stories of the Bible, we need to aim to preach *the* story of the Bible. I often explain the story of the Bible to people as a line with four points on it. When they begin to understand the shape of the Bible and how a particular story fits into that shape, they so often tell me how helpful they have found it.

▨ *Creation*
God gives us the canon of His Word in the form of an overarching story which runs from creation through to new creation. Thus we begin, in the opening chapters of Genesis, with the narrative of God's creation of the world and it is all 'very good'. The creation is, as it were, the first point on the line.

▨ *Fall*
The second main point on the line comes soon after in Genesis 3 when the reality of human evil becomes evident and sin, rebellion, wickedness and disobedience begin to take

their toll on God's creation. Not only is every human being seen to be a sinner, but it also becomes obvious that sin has entered into every dimension of human life: people's thinking; their spiritual relationship with God; the social relationships between men and women; and the physical relationship with the planet earth. The Fall has affected every dimension of life. In our handling of the biblical story, we need to have a radical, biblical understanding of sin.

■ Redemption

The third point on the line occurs at Genesis 12 with the call of Abram when the story of redemption begins, although there are indications of it even earlier. From the time of Abram onwards there is the 'grand narrative' of God's dealings with Israel, then through Israel the coming of the Messiah, and through the Messiah the coming of the multi-national community of those who are in the Messiah, and the mission of the Church.

■ New creation

The story of redemption all leads forward ultimately to the climax of the Bible, which is the return of the Lord Jesus Christ and the creation of the new heavens and the new earth, the establishment of the Kingdom of God. This is the fourth and final point on the line.

These four points can also be imagined as four great planks building the platform on which human history is built. As biblical preachers we need to have a strong sense of the universal story of the Bible.

It is also worth observing that out of this story emerges a sequence of systematic doctrine in almost the order in which it is traditionally presented:

- the doctrine of God: Creator, Redeemer
- the doctrine of humanity: what it means to be human, made in the image of God
- the doctrine of the Fall and of sin: hamartiology
- the doctrine of election: the election of Abram and the people of God
- the doctrine of salvation and redemption: flowing right through from the Exodus and the sacrificial system to the cross of Christ
- Christology: the person, identity, mission and work of Jesus of Nazareth
- the doctrine of the Holy Spirit: pneumatology, the Spirit given in power to the Church
- the doctrine of the Church: ecclesiology
- the doctrine of the future: eschatology.

I believe that one of our aims as preachers should be to help our congregations to get to know the whole of the Bible story and thus provide them with a good understanding of the shape and foundation of the Christian faith. In a sense the Bible is like a stick of rock. Wherever you cut into it, you discover that the story of the great God and His great gospel and His great mission is written all through it. Wherever we are preaching from the Bible, we cut into His grand story.

On a return visit to India last year, where I worked for a number of years, I saw first hand some of the wonderful things that are happening in the villages in the North. Many people are coming to Christ and many are then doing exactly what Jesus taught His disciples to do. They are going out to the villages two by two, receiving a welcome, praying with people, working miracles in the name of Jesus Christ, and forming small groups of believers. Since most people in the villages are illiterate, those sharing the gospel are being taught how to tell the Bible story in its simplest form. They call it 'the story of redemption', but by that they do not just mean the story of Easter and the cross but the whole Bible story. Raju Abraham, who works with the organisation South Asia Concern, seeking to reach Indians both in India and scattered across the world, told me that they had the specific objective of 'myth-replacement'. Realising that, broadly speaking, Hindus learn their theology from the stories of Ram and Krishna, he explained that they are seeking to teach the story of the Bible in its broadest outline form. In this way they are aiming to transform the world-view of the Indians with whom they come in contact. I think we need to do the same for the Christians in our congregations.

Having recognised the importance of preaching the big story of the Bible, I want now to look at some of the questions we need to ask ourselves as we prepare to preach, which will help us consistently to relate the small stories of the Bible to this one big one.

How Does This Story Fit into the Big Story of the Bible?

When we think about preaching on the narrative sections of the Bible it is helpful to imagine a series of concentric circles increasing in size. The preacher's task is to set the nugget of the story on which he is preaching within the larger stories, which ultimately of course include the story of Christ. The largest circle is the big story of the Bible, at which we have just looked. As well as locating a particular story within this big story, we need to explain its significance in the wider narrative of which it is a part.

For example, when earlier this year I preached on the opening chapter of the book of Joshua, I took a little time at the beginning of the sermon to try to locate it within the context of both what God had done for the people of Israel in the past and what He intended to do for the people of Israel in the future. I then looked beyond the Old Testament to set this in the context of God's purposes of salvation through the coming of Jesus. In this way I was seeking to help people to see this one episode in the life of Joshua in its context within the book of Joshua, and wider still, as part of the story of the Bible. Seeking to fit the small stories of the Bible into the larger stories of which they are a part is, I think, a helpful exercise for all preachers to carry out as part of their preparation for preaching. As well as helping us to understand how the story fits into the big story, it often produces interesting angles on ways in which it can be preached.

WHY IS THIS STORY IN THE BIBLE?

In addition to looking at a story's context, as preachers we need to ask why a story is included in the Bible. We need to look at the story from the author's perspective and ask, 'Why did he choose to tell me this story?' There must have been dozens of other stories he could have told: why did he choose this one in particular? At the end of the Gospel of John we are told:

> *Jesus did many other miraculous signs in the presence of his disciples, which are not*
> *recorded in this book. But these are written that you may believe that Jesus is the*
> *Christ, the Son of God, and that by believing you may have life in his name.*
> (John 20:30–32)

While John is explicit about the reasons why he has selected his stories of Jesus, the Old Testament writers are not normally as transparent about this, but we can still ask the question.

In seeking to discover why the story has been included in the Bible, there are three important considerations that we must keep in mind:

- Not all the stories are there for the same reason
- Not all the stories have the same weight
- Not all the stories should be handled in the same way.

I would suggest that there are three broad categories of stories in the Bible:

1. Foundational stories

Some of the stories in the narrative of the Bible are *foundational*. They speak about unique events in which God acted in history, whether in revelation or salvation, for a very clear purpose. These are the historic events on which our faith rests. One such story is the call of Abram, which is clearly significant throughout the whole of Scripture. It is referred to on numerous occasions throughout the Old Testament as well in the New Testament, for example by the apostle Paul. It is key to the biblical narrative.

Another foundational story is the Exodus. The whole theology of redemption in the Bible is grounded in the meaning of this story. It is the story above all the stories of the Old Testament which gave the people of Israel their sense of who they were and who their God was. The God of Israel is defined by the Exodus: He is the compassionate and gracious God of justice and love, who brings people out of slavery, who loves the alien, who rescues people from oppression, and so on. We need to preach the story of the Exodus.

The same could not be said of all the stories of the Bible, however. Take, for example, the story of Jephthah.[1] Not knowing his story would not threaten anyone's salvation. I am not saying that God made a mistake in including it, but it is certainly not one of the foundational stories of the Bible.

I believe that it is possible to draw out these key events to build up, as it were, an X-ray of the Bible story. This is a very similar process to that I described in Chapter 25 'Starting from Scratch' when I suggested building up a skeleton of the text. Such an X-ray would certainly include the following milestones in Israel's history:

- the call of Abraham
- the Exodus
- the covenant of Sinai
- the Conquest
- the gift of the Promised Land
- God's promise to David
- the loss of the land through exile
- the return to the land at the time of Cyrus
- the birth, life, death and resurrection of Jesus
- Pentecost.

This is something that happens in the Bible itself. Both the Old and the New Testaments contain speeches in which either the author himself or one of his prominent characters gives a rapid survey or overview of the key events of biblical history: for example, the psalmist (e.g. Psalm 105), Daniel (Daniel 9), Ezra (Ezra 9), and Stephen in his powerful speech to the Sanhedrin (Acts 7). These great figures clearly had a sense of what the most significant elements of the Bible story are. I think that preaching through these key events in Bible history makes an excellent series of sermons, helping to build a good understanding of the big picture of the Bible narrative.

2. Stories that point to God

Some of the stories in the Bible show us what it means *to be in relationship with God and to experience God acting in human life and history*. They show us what it means to trust and obey God. In many ways these are stories *about God* rather than stories about their human characters.

Taking the story of King Saul and David, for example, if we ask the question, 'Why did the author include this story?', it would be possible to come up with a sermon built on the answer, 'The author wanted us to see that we ought to be like David and not like Saul.' But I think the original author might say, 'I think I can see that, but that is not why I actually wrote the story. It is there because I wanted us to see how human beings experience the power, the love, the patience of God in spite of their sin and wickedness, and in relation to their faith and obedience.' The purpose of some of the stories in the Bible is, then, to point us to God and what He can do, rather than tell us what we must do. In our preaching on such stories it is better to focus on who God is and what He has done, and indeed His patience in His dealings with the human race, rather than to rush too hastily to seek to apply it to ourselves. Examples of the stories that fall into this category are the stories of the patriarchs in the wilderness, the stories of the judges and, of course, the stories of Jesus.

3. Stories of suffering and the cost of commitment

A third category comprises those stories which we often do not like to read because *they describe suffering and the cost of commitment that faith may demand*. We can think, for example, of the early stories in the book of Daniel which illustrate what it meant to be a believer in a community in which keeping faith carried the threat of death. As well as providing good entertainment, the purpose of these stories was also to *encourage faith and perseverance* in situations of persecution and difficulty, even if it must have been the case that for every Daniel who was rescued from the lions' den, there would have been thousands who did not make it, just as has been the case throughout history for persecuted Christians. This is the point that the writer of Hebrews makes, when in chapter 11 after his long list of the great heroes of the faith who have done wonderful exploits for God, he goes on to speak of those 'others' for whom faith resulted in great suffering and even death. 'But,' the writer concludes, *'these were all commended for their faith'* (v. 39). It is clear that it was not their faith that was the issue, and this is a good argument to put to those who promote the sort of prosperity gospel which makes faith the only definer of whether the Christian will face suffering or not.

There are other stories which we do not like to read because they are, quite frankly, about human wickedness. However, it is a great mistake to skirt over those stories, because they illustrate for us the depths to which human beings can stoop. People are still doing the things that the Bible describes – and worse! Sometimes people say to me as a teacher of the Old Testament, 'How can you possibly believe the Bible when it describes these kinds of awful things?' I reply that it makes me believe the Bible even more, because this is reality. We live in a world of horrendous cruelty and suffering, and the Bible tells it like it is.

It is important to add that some of the stories in the Bible may have more than one of these three dimensions. If we take the stories of Abraham, for example, some are foundational to the narrative of the Bible, such as his call by God, and others illustrate the quality of his faith and his obedience, which we should emulate. However, there are also some other stories which recount aspects of his life which were less than ideal, and for which he had to be rebuked by God and in one case by a pagan king. We need to be looking out for different levels of significance.

How Do Stories Actually Work?

Stories are quite clearly a very profound part of human culture universally. They form part of our everyday lives in ways of which we are not always conscious. Whenever friends meet on the streets of London they start telling each other stories. They are not fictional stories but stories about what their son is doing at university or about what happened to them yesterday. Human beings generate stories very quickly. Even the television news is often presented in terms of a story. After a headline and a brief explanation, the news reader will hand over to the reporter on the field who 'has the story'. Advertisements are mini-stories, because marketing gurus know that stories are persuasive. In the 30–45 seconds of the advertisement's duration very often a story will have been generated, with a beginning, a middle, a crisis, and an ending. Recognising that stories are powerful, the advertisers are seeking to engage their audience so that they will remember the product in question.

Stories express cultural world-views. Before the Enlightenment the world-view of the whole of western society was shaped to a large extent by the biblical narrative. This did not mean that everyone professed faith in Jesus Christ, but that the Christian story in its most basic form influenced everyone's thinking.[2] It was replaced by the storyline of the myth of modernity, which is the scientific, materialistic view that the world originated as a result of cosmic chance and is the way it is now as a result of evolution. In this view, science and progress ensure that the world is continually getting better. Although it is a powerfully motivating story for all kinds of human endeavour, it is a false god. It has been superseded in post-modernity because people realised that it failed to deliver what it claimed.

Stories are used to preserve people's identities. We are who we say we are in our stories. The reason why history is so important is because it generates a whole self-understanding of what it is to be a particular people. It is not until the events are presented through the eyes of a different nation that we realise it is possible to see the same situation very differently. So the stories that the Indians tell of the British in India will have a rather different perspective from those that are told by the British. Stories preserve identity and memory from one generation to another. We see this very clearly in relation to the nation of Israel. They are a community of memory: the nation of Israel understood its identity by looking back to what God had done for them in the past. It shaped its future by looking ahead to what God would do for them in the future, and thus they were a community of hope.

Stories also teach moral values and transmit group memories across the generations. Whether through Bible stories, fairy tales, or historical stories told in order to motivate certain types of behaviour, stories preserve the values which a particular culture regards as important. And stories can give hope, because they have endings. So many of the great myths and fantasy stories which have been preserved through history are stories of hope. I believe that the reason why such tales as *The Lion King* and J.R.R. Tolkien's epic *Lord of the Rings* are so emotively powerful is because, while recognising that there is something deeply wrong with the world, there is the belief that it can ultimately be put right and then everything will be happy again.

In more recent years a new brand of biblical critical study has emerged called Newer Literary Criticism which is concerned with how the Bible works as literature and the impact which the different genres contained in the Bible have on those who read it. I personally am very grateful to some of the scholars in this field, from whom I feel I have learnt a great deal. In particular, I have found it helpful to examine some of the different techniques which the story-tellers of the Bible use, for example, their skill and artistry. In saying this, I am not for one moment suggesting that they were making the story up, but that they used great craft in its telling. Actual factual history can be combined with art and skill to tell great stories, and that is what many of the story-tellers of the Bible have been able to achieve. Jesus was, of course, an amazing teller of stories and He Himself used the technique of presenting history through story.[3]

Let us then look at the way stories work:

Stories engage our imagination. If they don't, we won't listen to them. Stories invite us into another world in our imagination, to live in the story as if we were there. This is the reason why most of us enjoy relaxing with a novel or a thriller. It lifts us out of the real world for a while and engages us with another one in our imagination. I believe that this is one of the reasons why God included so many stories in the Bible, because imagination is one of the highest gifts that God has given to human beings, made in His own image. In fact, if we think about it, it is one of the things that makes us most like God. What is the creation if not the product of the imagination of the Almighty? Having made us in His image, God has given us the ability to imagine that which is not yet, or that which may once have been. Stories engage the imagination. But sadly, so much of our preaching does not.

Stories are dependent on having a well-constructed plot. There is no point in opening a telephone directory and looking for a good story: it has lots of characters but no plot. A good story always has a plot, interwoven with elements of surprise and suspense as it builds to a climax. There is usually some sort of resolution of the problem in either a happy or tragic ending, or perhaps even ambiguously. Many of the stories in the Bible follow this pattern.

It can be very helpful to try and read the stories of the Bible as if we have never read them before – perhaps reading them aloud, which is the way they would originally have been heard. We can be listening out for the way in which the story-teller builds the story, not telling his listeners everything at once, but building to a suspense with surprise twists along the way. Think, for example, about the story of Abraham sitting at the door of his tent, enjoying his siesta, when he sees three visitors arriving.[4] Although the narrator has told his audience that it is 'the Lord' arriving, at that point Abraham does not know this, and it is only as the story unfolds that the identity of the visitors becomes clear. So often the biblical narratives have well-constructed plots full of complexity, suspense and surprise. We need to try and recreate them in our imagination and communicate all these elements in our preaching.

Stories need good characters. Good novels are replete with good characters, whose words are just as important as their deeds. In a good story the dialogue is as important as the action, because it is from people's words that the reader is able to detect their motives, their priorities and their moral values.

There is a tendency in the Bible to characterise people either very positively or negatively, but, when it comes down to the accounts of their life, most of the major characters are clearly portrayed as a mixture of both good and bad. A prime example is David. When we take a good look at his life, his relationships, his political calculations, his apparent generosity in life, yet his commitment of his son Solomon to follow up some of his grudges after his death, a degree of ambiguity begins to emerge. Nevertheless, the Scriptures describe him as *'a man after God's heart'*.[5] Since the Hebrew word translated 'heart' actually means 'will', this phrase is more likely to mean that David was the man who would accomplish God's purpose than that he was one of God's favourite children.

Some stories have gaps in them. For example, the stories told about David have holes in them, by which I mean that the story-teller does not tell the reader everything he or she would like to know. The reader is left to fill the gaps in for him or herself. I think this is a deliberate ploy on the story-teller's part in order to engage his listeners and get them to ask questions. The story of David and Bathsheba is full of such gaps. As just one example, the story opens with David on the roof of the palace and the narrator comments without any sense of blame that it was the time when the kings went off to war. He presents his listeners with the facts, leaving them to wonder, 'Why wasn't he at war?' By not telling us everything the narrative sparks our interest. This is one of the techniques that Hebrew narrators often used. We need to be careful what conclusions we draw when we try to fill in the gaps from our twenty-first-century perspective.

Good stories invite the reader to be the judge. This follows on from my last point. Good story-tellers do not tell their listeners what they are supposed to think about the story they have been told, but allow people to draw their own conclusions. Jesus frequently used this technique in His parables, leaving His listeners to make up their own mind about their meaning.

The parable Nathan tells David about the landowner who steals his neighbour's pet lamb is a brilliant piece of story-telling, because it is a story within a story and works in a very clever way.[6] Nathan comes to David after his adultery with Bathsheba and his murder of Uriah, and relates the story as if he is presenting a legal case, which is what David, who as king was used to acting as judge in people's disputes, probably thought he was doing. As Nathan tells the story, David's imagination becomes engaged and, hearing how the lamb was stolen and slaughtered, he explodes with moral anger and indignation, and pronounces, 'The man deserves to die!' But since under the law a man could not be put to death for theft, he pronounces the legal punishment of paying back four times what he owed. Nathan comes straight back with the words, 'You are that man.' David's judgement has fallen on his own head. If he thinks that a sheep stealer deserves to die, what does he think a wife-stealer deserves? The power of this story lies in the fact that it has engaged David's imagination and elicited a strong response. This is what good stories do.

When we are preaching on the stories of the Bible we need to try and bring them to life by using some controlled imagination. I use the word 'controlled' because I do not think we are at liberty to play fast and loose with the Bible text. However, I do think it is legitimate to try and bring the story to life and try and help people to enter into it, for example by retelling it in the present tense and introducing some dialogue between the characters.

We can also try to bring out some of the tensions, some of the surprise, some of the dilemma.

What Mistakes Do We Need to Avoid Making?

1. Avoid reducing a story to the lessons we can learn

This is a very easy mistake to make, particularly with the more well-known stories. So a preacher might start his sermon by saying, 'We all know the story of the Good Samaritan, so here is what we learn from it.' If it is a story on which we are preaching, we need to tell it as a story. If God had wanted to give us a list of five points of good and bad behaviour, He could have done so, but He chose to give us a story and we should respect that. It is the story of Scripture which is inspired and authoritative. It is *the story* that has authority, not all the principles and explanations that we may derive from it. We must avoid reducing the stories to doctrine. Of course, they include doctrine and teaching but it is the narrative aspect which is of prime importance.

2. Avoid moralising

We must avoid the temptation of reducing the story to simplistic points about the characters, always having to decide who is the 'goody' and who is the 'baddy', and therefore which one we should be like. This is the way Bible stories are often taught to children. Sadly some people never get beyond this level. They never progress beyond this childish mentality into adult thinking, which is tragic. They get stuck at this level because they do not take the time to reflect on the stories and try to enter into them in their imaginations. We also need to remember that the stories are intended to tell us more about God than they do about human beings.

3. Avoid being too dogmatic
We need to remember that a story can have many levels of meaning and new meanings will often suggest themselves as we take to time to ponder and reflect upon them. Furthermore, other people will often see meanings that would never have occurred to us, and people from other cultures will often see a story in a totally different light, which can lead to a fascinating exchange of ideas. I think God gives us stories and says, 'Well, there you are. What do you make of that?' Since there is such a tremendous richness in the stories of the Bible we should avoid giving the impression that there is one solitary monochrome meaning and, once you have explored that, you can go on to the next one.

4. Avoid trying to justify everything
This is one of the oldest mistakes in the book. The Bible tells us what happened: it does not tell us what ought to have happened. Even the best characters in the Bible like David and Abraham are flawed; they are sinful and they are fallible. We don't have to try to justify what they did. In fact, if what they did was clearly wrong, shady, or untrustworthy, it is better if we do not even try. If there is a certain degree of ambiguity about the character in the story, we need to recognise that this is also true of real life, and that is the way God has given the story to us.

5. Avoid assuming we are meant to imitate the story's characters
It is a mistake to assume that if a Bible character did something, then we can do it too. The classic example of this is Gideon with his fleece.[7] Gideon's fleece has become a whole metaphor for finding God's guidance. But was it really to Gideon's credit that he responded to God's word by wanting confirmation and that he couldn't really believe what he was being told, but had to be persuaded twice before he was ready to go out and do what God was telling him? Should we be imitating him in his unbelief? Furthermore, if we feel we should imitate Gideon's fleece, then why do we not feel that we should imitate Samson's exploit with the three hundred foxes?[8]

6. Avoid fanciful typology
I believe that the Old Testament as a whole leads us to Christ. However, it is one thing to explain, as Jesus did on the road to Emmaus, *'what was said in all the Scriptures concerning himself'*,[9] and quite another to say that 'Every verse in the Old Testament is about Jesus'. Not every verse is about Jesus. Sometimes people can make Jesus appear out of very unexpected corners of Old Testament stories, like a magician bringing a rabbit out of a hat. Sometimes trying to find Jesus in a story can become a distraction

from what the original author was trying to help us to understand or do, and we can end up missing the real point he was trying to make.

NOTES

1. Judges 11.
2. I.e. there is a God who made the world; there is a heaven and a hell; there is a Christ who died on the cross; and that you had better become good by God's grace and salvation, or you might end up in hell.
3. E.g. the parable of the vineyard owner who left his vineyard to be tended by his workers, Matthew 21:33–41.
4. Genesis 18.
5. 1 Samuel 13:14.
6. See 2 Samuel 12.
7. Judges 6:36ff.
8. Judges 15:3–5.
9. Luke 24:27.

Chapter 29

PREACHING TO YOUTH

Mike Pilavachi

Whatever age group you are speaking to, the content of your talk will stay largely the same whereas the way you deliver it may vary dramatically. In this chapter I want to look at how we can engage young people through the presentation of the message, though it is important to remember we must get both the content and the presentation right. This was brought home to me quite forcibly at a recent mission to young people, at which I invited two friends of mine to communicate the gospel. Both of them are outstanding preachers with very different approaches. One had fantastic content and explained the gospel and the doctrine of the cross brilliantly. Unfortunately, his message went over the heads of all the thirteen- to fifteen-year-olds in his audience, who were not only completely unchurched but also from a non-academic background. It didn't engage them. The other friend was brilliant in a totally different way. She was able to hold their attention. She laughed with them, she cried and they cried; she showed movie clips; she told stories: it was an amazing performance, if you like – post-modern to a T. But if I am being really honest, I was left thinking, 'Do they have enough information to be able to make a decision?' As we reflected later as a team we realised how important it is to get both content and engagement right. It is a huge challenge to know how to proclaim the eternal, unchanging truths of the gospel in a way that this generation will listen to, will understand, and will know how to respond to.

In preaching to youth it is, of course, important to remember that there is not one but many youth subcultures and that therefore there is no one method, no one system, no one way to one unified, unitary group. Within the youth subculture there are self-evidently all sorts of different elements and different streams. I would also want to add that many of the following principles do not apply exclusively to young people, but I believe they are important keys in proclaiming the truth to young people effectively.

353

1. WE NEED TO PREACH IN THE CONTEXT OF RELATIONSHIP

Working with young people is all about relationship. We must genuinely love the people that we are talking to. Young people smell authenticity – and they smell the opposite. Somehow they know if someone genuinely loves them. So often in my prayer before events I cry out to God, 'Oh God, break my heart again for them. Oh God, give me in the depths of who I am something of Your love for them, and Your grace towards them.' They need to know we love them. In one sense, in the context of a small youth group it is obvious whether the preacher loves them or not, but how does it work in a large gathering? One way in which the preacher can show his love is by expressing his own vulnerability, by being open-hearted, honest and sincere. This obviously does not just apply to speaking to young people but it is particularly true in their case. Young people are not interested in listening to disembodied thoughts; they are not interested in listening to theories.

In 1 Corinthians 4:15 Paul says: *'Even though you have ten thousand guardians in Christ, you do not have many fathers.'* In communicating with young people we need to pray that, whether we are men or women, God would give us something of His Father heart. Around fathers people grow; around fathers there is new life; around fathers confidence is imparted. Around good fathers children are willing to take risks, as the father urges, 'Go on, one more step, go on . . . ' When we have something of God's heart it begins to show through.

2. WE NEED TO PREACH WITH PLANNED SPONTANEITY

There's a very interesting, observable trend taking place in our culture today. One evidence of it is that pre-planned, pre-scripted soaps are becoming less popular and reality TV is taking over, whether it is out in the jungle with minor or former celebrities, or whether it is talent-scouting prime-time TV spectaculars like *Pop Idol* or *The X-Factor*. With these types of programmes that are not scripted in advance, young people have a sense that they can be involved – in some way they can shape what is going on. They can vote and say what they think. The same trend is also evident on the twenty-four-hour news channels. The viewers are encouraged to let the broadcaster know what they think or to vote in a viewer pole. It is an unscientific method and it won't make any difference, but it is feeding into the desire to be involved in what is going on, not just to sit on the receiving end. People want to be involved in shaping what is happening. How, then, does that relate to preaching? With our traditional preaching format everything from the joke at the beginning right through to the end is thoroughly planned and prepared. In a sense even any interaction is set up. If we want to engage with young people, we will need to learn to make space for spontaneity.

One way of doing this is being able to go off on a tangent, where the preacher is not in control, and then to bring the focus back again. A good example, which will certainly not work with adults but does work with young people, is joking with a latecomer, for example: stop what you are saying, look straight at the person and ask, *'You're late, where have you been?'* Although it may seem bizarre, young people find such interaction affirming. They understand that it is part of a game. It communicates to them that the person at the front is not a machine which will do its stuff irrespective of what it is happening around it. Preacher and congregation are engaging in what is happening together. Occasionally it backfires in a wonderful way. Once when I was in the middle of a talk and someone got up to go to the toilet, I said, 'Where are you going?' Without a moment's hesitation, she turned round, said, 'I've heard this talk before, I'm bored', and walked out to a chorus of cheers. If I had lost them before that moment, after it they were right back with me. Of course there were a few minutes of everyone whispering to each other, but after that I had their total concentration. Making space for spontaneity keeps everyone together. It provokes engagement because it says that the people listening are valued. That is why in our meetings we make space for banter and other types of interaction. Whether it is in a group of 11 or 11,000 we need to create a sense of family, a sense of community, a sense that we are going on a journey together towards Jesus Christ and into His Word.

3. We Need to Tell Our Story as it Relates to His Story

It is important to be vulnerable and self-disclosing. Now there is a caveat to this, which is that our story needs to be told in relation to His story and the Bible story, and not simply for the sake of telling our story. A little while ago I actually went too far on this, and a couple of close friends had to come to me and say, 'Mike, I just want to say to you, because I love you, that we are just hearing a little bit more about you than we are about Jesus.' We all need people who will do this for us and I was so grateful because they were right: it showed me that they really loved me. I was able to repent and seek to address the problem. The danger in telling our story is that we can end up pointing to ourselves and not to Jesus, and we must do our best to avoid making that mistake. The emphasis needs to be on looking at Christ, on following Him. If we get in the way, then I think we as preachers are sinning. In a valid way we need to tell our story – or it can be other people's stories – as it relates to His story because it is part of building relationship and giving examples that people can understand. It earths the truths of the gospel in human lives today.

4. We Need to Model Our Journey to Discovering the Truth of Scripture

My aim is not simply to teach Scripture. I am desperate to get the young people themselves to read the Scriptures and not to be afraid of the Bible. So many of them are afraid of the Bible because they don't know where to begin and they don't know how to engage with

God's Word. We need to explain not only the truth but also how we came across the truth, and later on I will give a couple of tangible examples of how we can try to do that.

5. We Need to Speak Their Language

In order to speak young people's language we need to understand their culture, and our model for this is Jesus Christ. I am just amazed by the way Jesus did this. Jesus did not speak in Hebrew, the language of the elite; He spoke in Aramaic, the language of the common people. And He spoke about sheep to shepherds, about fish to fishermen, about growing grapes to vineyard owners, about sowing seed to farmers. We need to find ways of doing the same.

But even more important than speaking young people's language is being authentic. As I have already said, young people can smell a fraud a mile off. Sometimes people put a great deal of effort into being relevant, but the young people realise that they are not being who they truly are. I am forty-five years old, still into Simon and Garfunkel, and there are aspects of youth culture that I just don't get! If we are truly 'us' and we love them, they will receive and accept that. We must not try to be something we are not.

It is much more important that we love young people enough to really listen to them. A little while ago I heard this story about a father and son. When the son was about eight or nine years old, he became interested in architecture, and he and his father would sit down and chat about architecture and design. The son's interest continued and eventually he went to university to study architecture. Whenever he came home he and his father would chat endlessly about the latest theories, the latest designs, the latest developments in architecture, and this continued when he left home and married. Whenever he visited, he and his father would sit down and chat about what he was doing. Then one day his father died, and the son had to go home and sort out the estate. When he went to his father's bedroom and opened one of the wardrobes, instead of finding clothes, he found it stacked full of magazines and other literature from top to bottom – and it was all about architecture. As he pulled out the one at the bottom, the date on it showed that it was from the time when that man, as an eight-year-old boy, had first expressed an interest in architecture. That father loved his son so much that he did his homework so that they could talk together and he could reach out to him. It is our job to reach out to young people. It is our job to build bridges to where they are, and walk across the bridges so that we might walk back together.

6. We Need to Provide an Answer to the Question 'So What?'

There is a danger that as preachers to young people we can always be looking for the big response. We give them the big vision of how they can change the world, and then we ask everyone who wants to change the world to come forward. However, if we make that sort of call too often, it demeans it. There are only so many times that a person can make a response to change the whole world. Sometimes the response young people need to make is a really practical one. Perhaps they need to make an offering of themselves in a particular area of their life and to be prayed for to receive, by the Holy Spirit, the power that they need to do so. Perhaps they simply need to sit quietly and ponder about what they are going to do every day for the rest of their life. We need to be showing or modelling that there has to be a practical response.

What models, by the way, do we have in secular society for one person speaking to a whole group of people for forty minutes? I can think of three, although I am sure there are more: (i) the college lecturer; (ii) the politician; and (iii) the stand-up comedian. From a human perspective, I think nearly all preachers can be slotted into one of those three categories. He can be like a college lecturer, standing up with his worked-out research notes imparting information as a lecture; or a politician rousing the audience with his oratory and eloquence; or a stand-up comedian who holds an audience for forty minutes with humour and a commentary on life. I am not saying this in any way to degrade the forty-minute sermon because I believe in preaching and, it may seem very old-fashioned, but that is what I do. But, actually, just recognising those three different styles helps us to work out whether what we are doing is working. I am not going to say that any one of these styles is better than the others and actually we need to use all three. I do, obviously, want to commend the stand-up comedian routine, in part because stand-up comedians with their commentary on society seem to have more influence than politicians with their speeches in our contemporary society. I believe we need to incorporate an element of all three styles in our preaching – we need to find every way we can to communicate. Neither am I saying that we all have to be comedians to communicate with young people. More than anything we need to be authentic, passionate about what we are talking about and excited about the truth we have found. If we want our young people to get into the Word, we have to let them see that we passionately love this Book, and we do that by the way we teach it.

Some Examples

In order to earth the theory I would like to give some examples of how I might communicate with young people. I will speak as I would to the young people and interpolate some comments of explanation.

1. Taking one verse

> Today I'm just going to look at one verse. Just one verse – I mean, who could go wrong with one verse? It can't take that long, if it's one verse. [*This makes everyone feel relaxed, except those that have heard me speak before!*] One of my favourite verses is in the book of Zephaniah. Hands up, who's read the book of Zephaniah?

[*Guaranteed, 75–80 per cent don't even know there is a book in the Bible called Zephaniah.*] What, hold on, hands up those of you who have never read the book of Zephaniah. [*Lots of people put their hands up. I continue in a very serious voice.*] I need to say to those of you who have never read Zephaniah, you need to read the book of Zephaniah … [*By now some of them are thinking, 'Are we being told off here?'*] … because one day you will die and when you die, if you know Jesus, you will go to heaven and somewhere in heaven you will meet Zephaniah. And he will ask you, 'Have you read my book?' [*Just saying this will probably make them go away and read it.*]

Halfway through chapter 3 of this book there is this amazing verse:

'The LORD your God is with you,
  he is mighty to save.
He will take great delight in you,
  he will quiet you with his love,
  he will rejoice over you with singing.'
(Zephaniah 3:17)

'The LORD *your God is with you* …' What does it mean that God is with us? [*At this point it is becoming evident that I have stretched the truth slightly by saying it's only one verse as I begin to unpack what it means by looking at other verses.*]

You can read that verse about 'The Lord your God is with you' and you can think, 'Yeah, big deal'. But wait a minute. It is a *big* deal. He is mighty to save. What does it mean He is mighty to save? [*Then I tell this story.*] I'm walking down a dark alley, late at night with Greg Haslam [*I substitute the name of any well-known local leader*]. And walking up the other way is a gang of gangsters. And the leader of the gang of gangsters comes up, stands in front of me and says, 'What you staring at, uh, uh, uh?' And then he says, 'You wanna make summink of this, uh? You wanna start summink?' I look at me, I look at them, I look at Greg … and I run for my life cos we're in trouble. But imagine if I am walking down that dark alley late at night and this time it's not Greg but Mike Tyson in his prime who is by my side. And this same gang of gangsters comes up, and the leader of the gang says, 'Come on then. You wanna make summink of this, uh? You wanna start summink?' Then I might say, 'Yeah, maybe I do. Maybe I do wanna start summink.' And I say to Mike, 'Mike, bite their ears off.' In this context, *and this context alone*, the Lord our God is more like Mike Tyson than He is like Greg. Because God is mighty to save. He is the Saviour of the world. Because in His vulnerability and His weakness, without biting any one's ear off, but by dying on the cross in humility and in brokenness, *He saved me and He saves you*. He's mighty. He can save anyone and everyone, and that includes you. But also He's mighty to save in the midst of your circumstances, not necessarily by taking all your circumstances away from you but by giving you the power to live through the circumstances.

[*Then I would go through the verse line by line. In the context of the line 'he will quiet you with his love' I might tell the following story.*] I am standing by the ice cream section in Sainsbury's, which is where I do all my food shopping, when I see down by the frozen peas this little boy sobbing his heart out. I am just thinking, 'There is something wrong here...' when two ladies come up to him and say, 'Hello, little boy. Are you lost?' At that point the little boy begins to wail even more loudly. [*Here I would elaborate, but to cut a long story short...*] When the mother eventually comes, she picks up her little boy who is still screaming and says, 'It's all right. I've got you. Mummy's here. I've got you. I'm not going to let you go. I'm here.' After a while he calms down until at last he is at peace. And there are some of you here, you're all right on the outside, you're smiling, but inside you are crying like that little boy because life is hard and you feel lost. Well, God wants to come and quiet you with His love, and I believe that, if you want Him to, He can do it, now. He can do it today. He will rejoice over you with singing.

By taking that one verse and unpacking it, I am not simply teaching the truth contained in it, but I am modelling to them that understanding the Bible is not difficult. They begin to think to themselves that they don't have to know Greek and Hebrew to understand the Bible, they could actually get what I have said out of the verse for themselves.

2. Acting out the Bible passage

E.g. Luke 15, the Parable of the Prodigal Son

Today I am going to read you the Parable of the Prodigal Son. But when Jesus told a story He used picture language and everyone could see it – it was a bit like theatre. So that is what we are going to do. We need a father [*for the father I always pick a girl for a reason that will become evident later*]; an older son; a younger son; some revellers, some party-goers; and a servant. Guys, as a Manchester United supporter, I have in the past said some dreadful things about Arsenal fans and Arsenal. But I have been convicted, and I want to repent, so I want to honour you because you are my brothers and sisters. So that I can honour you, if you support Arsenal, would you please stand up? When they stand up, I say, 'Guys, I ask that you forgive me for saying all those terrible things about your team, and, because I just want you to know I love you as my brothers and sisters, could you come forward – *you are the pigs*!' And they obey – it's amazing.

Then I read the story with my volunteers miming the story, and it always works really well. The best bit is where the son comes back home to the father, which we do in slow motion. Because I choose a girl to act the father, it's always hilarious, especially the line *'he put his arms around him and kissed him'*, which everyone knows is coming. Then I go through the story, and explain it. Acting out the Bible story is a great way of getting everyone engaged.

3. Larger portions of Scripture

E.g. Luke 5; John 21

[I begin by reading Luke 5.] *'One day as Jesus was standing by the Lake of Gennesaret ...'* Let's just pause there by the Lake of Gennesaret. In my Bible, the NIV, where it says 'Lake of Gennesaret' there is a little 'x'. Do you know I used to think that that little 'x' was God's way of saying 'I love you'. But it's not, because at the bottom of the page there is another little 'x' and by it it says, 'That is the Sea of Galilee.' So what have we learnt already? That the Lake of Gennesaret is actually the Sea of Galilee. If the Lake of Gennesaret is the Sea of Galilee, why don't they call it the Sea of Galilee in the first place? Interesting. *[I don't give an answer. I continue to read through Luke 5 teaching as I go. Then I read John 21.]* *'Afterwards Jesus appeared again to his disciples, by the Sea of Tiberias.'* Now in my Bible where it says 'Sea of Tiberias' there is a little 'g'. *[By this stage they are saying, 'Has anyone got an NIV ... ?', and they are thinking, 'I must remember to bring my Bible next time' because they all want to find out what the little 'g' stands for. This kind of approach is much better than going on at them to bring their Bibles with them.]* And at the bottom there is another little 'g' which says, 'That is the Sea of Galilee.' So the Lake of Galilee and the Sea of Tiberias are actually the Sea of Galilee.

I don't explain the fact that one is the Jewish name while the other is the Roman name, because it is not vital that they know that piece of information, and actually some of them will come up afterwards and ask me about it, which gives me an opportunity to talk to them. It is also saying that you don't have to understand everything immediately in order to read the Bible.

4. The big picture

Has anyone ever read Romans 1? You wouldn't want to read that, would you – that list of everything we have done wrong. I mean, it doesn't give you a warm fuzzy feeling like Ephesians or Philippians, does it? But do you know that in the middle of that list of all the things we have done wrong it says, *'They exchanged the glory of the immortal God for images made to look like mortal man and birds and animals and reptiles.'* These words are at the heart of that list. People stopped worshipping

God, and because of that He gave them over to the things on that list. Doesn't that tell us what the root of sin is? [*Then I go back to Genesis and explain how idolatry came in when the first human beings exchanged the worship of the Creator for the worship of creation and how, in Israel's later history, sacrifice was at the heart of Israel's worship.*] By offering their sacrifices the Israelites were saying that God the Creator is more important than creation. So why didn't that save people? Because there was no perfect worshipper to offer perfect worship. [*Then I look at what Hebrews says about that.*] God was looking for a perfect worshipper but He couldn't find one until He found Jesus. The cross was the one perfect sacrifice, the one perfect act of worship from the One who lived a perfect life and died a perfect death of worship. When Jesus was on the cross, He actually sang a worship song. You can't find it in *The Survivor's Songbook* or *Spring Harvest Praise*. It's no. 22 in *Hymns Ancient and Modern of Israel*. It starts 'My God, my God, why have You forsaken Me?', and it ends with 'It is finished'. [*Young people understand that I am not saying that Jesus started singing while He was on the cross.*]

Using this approach we can teach a huge amount of doctrine in a way that is understandable and accessible.

RETHINKING OUR APPROACH

In conclusion I want to say that I believe that as a Church we need to rethink the way we approach teaching apologetics to young people because, particularly on the issue of sex and relationships, it ain't working. They don't understand our apologetic for abstinence in sex; they don't understand why we are so hung up on the gay issue. Frankly, I would say that 50 per cent of Christian young people, who love Jesus and are committed to following Him, don't understand why we have such a problem with these issues. Why, they ask, aren't we much more bothered about the really important issues, such as feeding the poor? The culture in which they live has so encroached on their thinking that they do not view these issues in the same way as we do. We have got to change the way we approach our teaching on them.

One way in which we can do this is by majoring on the positive rather than on the negative. We need to model and proclaim the glorious gifts that God has given human beings, namely the gift of marriage and the gift of celibacy. In the context of understanding how wonderful they are and what high callings they are, everything else will fit in in a new way. Many of the young people to whom we speak, or their friends, are the victims of broken homes. They know the pain broken marriages cause. Therefore, when we give them a wonderful picture of something to work and to pray for – such as a happy marriage in which their children can be brought up in safety and security – they will want to go for it. They will see it as something worth working for. Then they will understand why there should be celibacy until marriage and why marriage should be between one man and one woman for life.

My final reflection is that I believe that, particularly for this generation, preaching and worship are linked. One of the things I love about working with young worship leaders is that, when God speaks to us through His Word, so often it ends up in a worship song. To my disgust young people do not sing my sermons in the shower, but they do sing songs from the likes of Redman and Hughes. Let's encourage our young musicians and worship leaders to take the doctrines we are learning together as a church and turn them into music in order to sing it back to God, and in this way to complete the circle of the Word returning to the Father as a sacrifice of worship to Him.

Chapter 30

PREACHING OLD TESTAMENT LAW

Chris Wright

Before we can look at *how* we should preach the Law, it is important to establish *why* we should preach the Law. In other words, we need a theological foundation for why we continue to preach and teach the Old Testament Law. I want to explain my own theological assumptions in preaching the Law, before looking more practically at how we set about it.

1. 'ALL SCRIPTURE IS GOD-BREATHED'

This is a truth which we all believe, but believing it is one thing and actually acting upon it is another. We need to remember that, when Paul wrote the words of 2 Timothy 3:16–17,[1] most of the New Testament had not yet been written. He was referring to the Old Testament Scriptures and, since he specifically says 'All Scripture', this must include the Torah and the Pentateuch. It is important, therefore, that we preach Old Testament Law as a part of God's Word, and do not simply abandon or ignore it.

2. THE LAW WAS FOUNDED ON GRACE

This truth is for me equally foundational. While we tend to think of 'the Law' as the Ten Commandments plus the other laws set down in Exodus, Leviticus and Deuteronomy, when an Israelite referred to the Torah he meant the five books of Genesis, Exodus, Leviticus, Numbers and Deuteronomy. There is therefore a whole book and a half of narrative before even one law is included, and this narrative context is very important.

Of particular significance is the context of the crucial moment in Exodus 19 when God through Moses explains to the people of God why He has brought them out of Egypt and what He has in store for them in the future. Before He speaks about the covenant, the Law, the tabernacle or the sacrificial system that are about to be introduced, He says:

> *'You yourselves have seen what I did to Egypt, and how I carried you on eagles'*
> *wings and brought you to myself. Now if you obey me fully and keep my covenant,*
> *then out of all nations you will be my treasured possession . . .'*
> (Exodus 19:4–5)

God places the giving of the Law in the context of what He has already done for the nation of Israel. There are eighteen chapters of salvation and God's grace and faithfulness before there is a single chapter of law. In my view this is not only structurally important for the book of Exodus but also theologically important for the whole of our understanding of the relationship between grace and law in the Bible. It is a fundamental mistake, in my view, to argue that the Old Testament is all about 'salvation by works' and the New Testament is all about 'salvation by grace'. It is a distortion both of the teaching of the Old Testament and of the apostle Paul. Paul makes it very clear that salvation came through faith in God's promise, which was motivated by His faithfulness and love. The Law is given in order to enable Israel to live appropriately as a response to God's love. God did not send Moses down to Israel with the message that, if they kept His laws, He would save them from their oppressors. Rather God, in His great mercy, saved His people, and then spoke to them about a way of life that was pleasing to Him. I think the order is very significant.

This same order is also seen in Deuteronomy 6:20–25 when Moses is teaching the people how to pass God's ways on to the next generation. He tells them how to respond if their son asks the question, *'What is the meaning of the stipulations, decrees and laws that the LORD our God has commanded you?'* It would have been very easy for Moses to tell them to give verse 24 as their answer: *'The LORD commanded us to obey all these decrees and fear the LORD'* – in other words, 'Son, stop asking questions. Just do it because God says so!' – and that would have been a legitimate response. But in actual fact Moses answers:

> *tell him: 'We were slaves of Pharaoh in Egypt, but the LORD brought us out of Egypt*
> *with a mighty hand. Before our eyes the LORD sent miraculous signs and wonders –*
> *great and terrible – upon Egypt and Pharaoh and his whole household. But he*
> *brought us out from there to bring us in and give us the land that he promised on*
> *oath to our forefathers. The LORD commanded us to obey all these decrees and to*
> *fear the LORD our God, so that we might always prosper and be kept alive, as is the*
> *case today. And if we are careful to obey all this law before the LORD our God, as he*
> *has commanded us, that will be our righteousness.'*

The answer to the question about the meaning of the Law is given within the context of the story of redemption. Or, to put it in more holistic biblical terms, the meaning of the

Law is to be found within the gospel. God asks His people to respond to His grace and salvation by living lives of obedience to Him.

The father is to tell his son that *'that will be our righteousness'*. Since God has already redeemed them out of Egypt, Moses cannot be referring to a righteousness of works by which they can earn God's salvation. On the contrary, he is talking about how they can make a right response to what God has already done for them. Their gratitude to Him can find expression in righteous living.

The Law constantly harks back to the grace of God and the Exodus as a motivation for obedience. For example, the Israelites are commanded, *'you are to love those who are aliens, for you yourselves were aliens in Egypt.'*[2] The fact that they know what it is like to be an alien should mean that they treat the aliens among them well.

There is so much more that could be said on this subject but let me add just one further point. When Moses asks the Lord God on Mount Sinai to show him His face, God tells him that no one can see His face and live, but He will permit him to see His back. When this extraordinary meeting takes place, the Lord passes by, declaring:

> *'The LORD, the LORD, the compassionate and gracious God, slow to anger,*
> *abounding in love and faithfulness, maintaining love to thousands, and forgiving*
> *wickedness, rebellion and sin.'*
> (Exodus 34:6–7)

God chooses to reveal Himself as the God of Grace. Yes, there is justice and there is punishment, but it is within the context of God's grace and mercy and salvation.

We must preach Old Testament Law on the foundation of God's grace. The Law was never intended to be a means of salvation or a means of earning salvation, but was intended to be a response to salvation. It is the same dynamic as for Christian obedience.

3. THE LAW WAS MOTIVATED BY THE MISSION OF GOD

In addition to being founded on the grace of God, the Law was also motivated by the mission of God. Here I am using the word 'mission' in a much wider sense than the sending out of missionaries or other Christians in order to evangelise. In biblical theology it has the fundamental sense that the God who is revealed to us in the Bible is a God of purpose, a God who has a goal, a God who is on a mission.

That mission goes right back to the Garden of Eden when God declares that the seed of the woman will crush the head of the serpent, but historically it is first proclaimed in Genesis 12 where God promises Abram:

> *'I will make you into a great nation*
> *and I will bless you;*

> *I will make your name great,*
>   *and you will be a blessing.*
> *I will bless those who bless you,*
>   *and whoever curses you I will curse;*
> *and* **all peoples on earth**
>   **will be blessed through you.'**
> (Genesis 12:2–3, my emphasis)

Right from the beginning of Scripture we see that God's mission is to bless the nations through Israel, i.e., through the descendants of Abraham. God's promise to Abraham is so foundational to the rest of the Bible that in Galatians 3:8 Paul actually calls it 'the gospel':

> *The Scripture foresaw that God would justify the Gentiles by faith, and announced*
> *the gospel in advance to Abraham: 'All nations will be blessed through you.'*

The gospel is about the incredible determination of God, in spite of all the wickedness that had occurred in Genesis 1–11, to bless the nations!

Some people seem to treat Scripture as a series of disconnected events. God chose Abraham; a few thousand years later He sent Jesus; and at the end of time He will bring human history to a close. It is a mistake to view Scripture in this way. God's original choice of Abraham is linked with His long-term mission for His creation. This is made clear when, in Genesis 18:19, while God is on His way to pronounce judgement on Sodom and Gomorrah, He says concerning Abraham:

> *'For I have chosen him, so that he will direct his children and his household after him*
> *to keep the way of the* LORD *by doing what is right and just, so that the* LORD *will*
> *bring about for Abraham what he has promised him.'*

This is a fascinating verse because it is God talking to God about God. In it God makes a link between mission (*'I have chosen him'*) and election (*'so that the* LORD *will bring about for Abraham what he has promised him'*). That link is ethics: walking in the way of the Lord; living a life of righteousness and justice. God called Abraham because He wanted him to be the starting point of a different kind of community. He wanted a people who would walk in obedience to Him, a community whose life together would display His character. In the context of a world of rebellion, disobedience, perversion and pain, God's mission was to create a community that would be different.

If we look back at Exodus 19, we will notice that here too the nations are in view: *'Although the whole earth is mine, you will be for me a kingdom of priests and a holy nation'* (vv. 5–6). In the same way that the priests of Israel stood as mediators between

God and the people, so the nation of Israel would have that same role towards the nations of the earth. The priests' work of mediation operated in two directions:

1. they taught the Law to the people; and
2. through their sacrificial work they brought people into fellowship with God.

This was also the purpose of the nation of Israel. The reason that it had a unique relationship with God was so that it could be a blessing to all the nations of the earth and so that the whole earth could learn about God and His ways through them. It is a wonderful analogy. Ultimately, of course, both these purposes are achieved through the Lord Jesus Christ who as our great High Priest brings God to the world and brings the world to God.

In Deuteronomy 4 Moses picks up on the destiny of the nation of Israel to be a blessing to the whole earth when he gives this motivation as one among many for obeying God's laws:[3]

> *Observe them carefully, for this will show your wisdom and understanding to the*
> *nations, who will hear about all these decrees and say, 'Surely this great nation is*
> *a wise and understanding people.'*
> (Deuteronomy 4:6)

Up until this point in Moses' exposition of the Law there has been no mention of the nations, but suddenly Moses clicks, as it were, on to a wide-angle lens. Keeping God's laws will give Israel visibility among the nations. She will become a model for other nations. In the language of Isaiah, she will be *'a light to the nations'*, or in the language of Jesus, *'the light of the world'* and *'the salt of the earth'*.[4] The nation of Israel is not to live in vacuum-sealed isolation from the world but is to live a life that is different in the midst of the world. God wants them to be different not only because of what He has done for them in the past but because of the ultimate purpose He has for them in the future, which is to be a blessing to the nations. I like to think that this point and my previous point are like two poles from which a hammock is suspended. On the one hand, the Law looks back to the grace of God towards Israel in the past and so is based on God's past action but, on the other hand, the Law is motivated by God's future purpose to bring blessing to the world.

Applying this now to our present context, we can see that we need to preach the Law not only to remind Christians of the grace of God to which they ought to respond, but also to remind them of their mission to live responsibly and distinctively as God's people among the nations. The Law has much to say to us about how we as God's people can live distinctive lives.[5]

4. THE LAW ITSELF IS BASED ON THE CHARACTER OF GOD

By obeying the Law, therefore, the people of Israel were imitating God, although the word 'imitate' does not express fully what I mean. More than imitate what He did, God wanted His people to reflect His character, which is seen in what He did.

This understanding is implicit in Deuteronomy 10, where Moses summarises the Law in the following statement:

> And now, O Israel, what does the LORD your God ask of you but to fear the LORD
> your God, to walk in all his ways, to love him, to serve the LORD your God with all
> your heart and with all your soul, and to observe the LORD's commands and decrees...
> (Deuteronomy 10:12–13)

All the nation needs to do is to obey those five stipulations and God will be satisfied. But I can almost imagine some of those listening to him wanting to jump in and ask what it means to 'walk in all his ways'? Moses does not immediately explain, launching instead into a doxology:

> To the LORD your God belong the heavens, even the highest heavens, the earth and
> everything in it.
> (Deuteronomy 10:14)

Moses makes the astonishing claim that Yahweh, the God of Israel, owns the whole universe. He then continues:

> Yet the LORD set his affection on your forefathers and loved them, and he chose you,
> their descendants, above all the nations, as it is today.
> (Deuteronomy 10:15)

Since the God of the whole universe has shown such mercy by choosing them as His people, they should respond in the following way:

> Circumcise your hearts, therefore, and do not be stiff-necked any longer.
> (Deuteronomy 10:16)

Then he breaks into praise again: 'For the LORD your God is God of gods and Lord of lords, the great God, mighty and awesome...' He is emphasising how awesome it is that the God who reigns supreme over all the world should show such mercy and grace towards the people of Israel. It is only at this point that Moses then begins to speak of the ways of this great God:

who shows no partiality and accepts no bribes. He defends the cause of the fatherless
and the widow, and loves the alien, giving him food and clothing.
(Deuteronomy 10:17–18)

When this superlative God, the God of the universe, acts on behalf of His people, He works counter-culturally on behalf of the weak and the poor. In the ancient world God's might was normally associated with the powerful, with those who ran society such as kings and their armies. They needed to have God on their side in order to keep society under control. The God of Israel, however, chooses to show mercy, care and justice to the weak and powerless, those who are without homes, without families and without land. Since this is how God acts, says Moses,

you are to love those who are aliens, for you yourselves were aliens in Egypt.
(Deuteronomy 10:19)

In other words, they are to replicate for others the love that they have experienced from God. What God has done for them in loving them, saving them, delivering them, leading them through the wilderness and feeding and clothing them, they must do for the foreigners in their midst.

The imitative walking in the ways of the Lord flows through Old Testament Law and is seen either explicitly or implicitly in the behaviour of Israel socially, judicially and economically. And, of course, it is encapsulated in the famous verse,

'You shall be holy, for I the Lord your God am holy.'
(Leviticus 19:2, NKJV)

They are to be a different kind of people because their God is a different kind of God. He is the living Lord God of the universe and He wants His people to reflect His character.[6]

I am aware that it may seem rather shocking to some people to preach the Law as a reflection of the character of God because all they see of God's character in the Old Testament is His wrath and anger, and the demand for vengeance and justice. I want to suggest very humbly that if that is all people see of God in the Old Testament, they need to look again, because there is actually so much revelation of God's grace, mercy, compassion and, above all, His patience.

5. The Law of Israel Was Intended to Be a Model or Paradigm for the Nations

Seeking now to draw together and build upon the first four points I have made, I want to look at the reality in which we live from a biblical world-view with reference to a simple

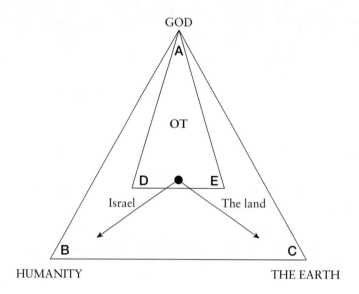

diagram. Consider first the outer triangle: the Bible tells us that there is one true Creator God who is both personal and moral (A). In the beginning He created the heavens and the earth (one corner of the triangle: C) and He put human beings, made in His own image, to live within it (another corner of the triangle: B). This triangle of relationships – God, the earth, and humanity – constitutes the basic pattern of relationships in the created order. We are God's creatures and we relate to Him in worship; the earth belongs to God but it has been given to human beings; human beings are part of the earth and yet we are given rule over the earth. Despite the fact that God's world has been twisted and fractured by sin and evil and each of these relational lines has been spoiled,[7] nevertheless the triangle is still basically intact.

Confronted with the marring of His creation, how does God respond? Rather than choosing to destroy it, which would have been one option, God decides to redeem it. He instigates a plan of salvation which will occupy the whole of human history and ultimately the whole of creation. He begins his project with one man, Abraham. Only God would have thought of a beginning as small as this. You can almost imagine the sharp intake of breath among the angels when they begin to realise what He is proposing. Out of all the nations of the earth, God chooses one man, then one family, then one nation. But it doesn't stop there, because He makes it very clear that His purpose through Abraham, through the family of Abraham, through the nation of Israel, is the multi-national community of all nations redeemed through Christ who will be the children of Abraham. As Paul says in Galatians 3:7, *'Understand, then, that those who believe are children of Abraham.'* There is therefore a theological link between Israel and the rest of humanity. The choice of Abraham and the calling of Israel is for the sake of the nations. It is not a rejection of the nations; it is for their blessing.

370

Out of all the earth God gives this people the land of Israel to live in, although more often it is called the 'land of Yahweh' because He is still the owner of it. It is the land of God's own blessing, but it is also described in eschatological terms with a bearing on the future. The land of Israel was intended to be a microcosm of God's ultimate intention for the whole of the creation: it was God's plan that the whole earth would be filled with the glory of God and filled with His love and justice.

Referring back to the diagram on page 370, there is then a second (inner) triangle which mirrors the relationships of the first. Whereas in the first (outer triangle) the relationships are between God (A), human beings (B) and the earth (C), in this second triangle they are between God (A), Israel (D) and the land (E). All that God did in and for and through Israel is intended to be relevant to the nations. God intended the nation of Israel to be a paradigm and model. It is this understanding that I believe provides us with the rationale for preaching and teaching the Law in our churches. We know that what we are doing is fundamentally in line with His purposes from the start. The connection between the second triangle and the first, which is the one in which we, so to speak, are standing, means that it is legitimate for us as preachers and teachers to preach Old Testament Law in a way that brings a challenge to the Church and a challenge to society on a range of social, ethical and justice issues. We are not trying to say that Britain is the covenant people and therefore should be keeping the Law of Moses. No, the Messiah has come and things have changed. But we are able to say that, if that was how God wanted those people in their cultural and historical context to live, then that provides us with a paradigm for the requirements of God in our own day, always bearing in mind that we need to take cultural changes into account.

6. The Law is Good for Us

So many people regard the Law as a great burden. I think this is because they read about the abuse of the Law by the scribes and Pharisees in the Gospels and how their behaviour angered Jesus, and transfer their perception of the Law as a great burden back into the Old Testament. But it is wrong to think that the Israelites perceived the Law in this way. On the contrary, they regarded it as an incredible gift of God's blessing and goodness. In Deuteronomy the Law is repeatedly said to be given 'for our own good' or 'for your own good' (expressed in Hebrew in the two words, *letov leah*: 'for good, for you'). 'The Law is good for us' was almost the nation's motto. For the people of Israel obeying God's Law was the way to experience blessing; it was the way that life worked best.

The Psalms are filled with praise to God for the gift of the Law, for example:

The law of the LORD is perfect,
  reviving the soul.

> *The statutes of the* LORD *are trustworthy,*
>> *making wise the simple.*
> (Psalm 19:7)

'Oh, how I love your law!' says the writer of Psalm 119 on more than one occasion. This is not the language of a legalist, and in fact the psalm emphasises the Law as a source of light and truth and grace. The reason the writer of Psalm 119 gives for how he knows that God is merciful and God is gracious and will forgive him is because he has read the Law! So he says, *'be gracious to me through your law'* (v. 29) and *'preserve my life according to your laws'* (v. 156).

As we study the Law it seems that human need was very often put before legal right, in the way that Jesus also often did. For example, runaway slaves were not to be sent back to their masters, which was extraordinary by the standards of the day. And not only were they not to be sent back, but they were to be given the right to choose where they lived. The rather obscure law relating to the treatment of prisoners in war is another interesting example (Deuteronomy 21:10–14). This is one of those passages that we may wish were not in the Bible, but in my opinion it actually goes far beyond the expectations of societies of that time, according to the common laws of war, in protecting the rights of vulnerable women. Several times it is stressed that any woman that is taken must be afforded the dignity of being made the soldier's wife, and in addition she must be given a full month of adjustment, during which she could undertake the rituals of mourning, before the husband was permitted to exercise normal sexual rights. These stipulations were designed to make men think twice before they acted recklessly in the euphoria of victory.

The Law, it seems, was constantly looking for what would benefit people as distinct to what would limit and oppress them, and I think that is why Jesus became so angry when He saw the purpose of the Law being turned upside down. The Sabbath is a good example. The Pharisees had turned the Sabbath into a burden for the people but Jesus said, *'The Sabbath was made for man, not man for the Sabbath.'*[8] The Sabbath was made for human good, and that is why He chose deliberately to heal people on that day. Again and again Jesus pointed people back to the roots of the Law, which were mercy, compassion and justice. Indeed, He said to the Pharisees:

> *'Woe to you, teachers of the law and Pharisees, you hypocrites! You give a tenth of*
> *your spices – mint, dill and cumin. But you have neglected the more important*
> *matters of the law – justice, mercy and faithfulness.'*
> (Matthew 23:23)

When we preach the Law, we too need to preach according to these same priorities of justice, mercy and faithfulness and emphasise its benefits, rather than placing a burden of legalism upon people's shoulders.

7. How Can We Find the Message of the Law Today?

Here I am following an important principle of good exegesis and hermeneutics, which is that it is always dangerous to ask the question 'What does this mean for us now?' until we have asked, 'What did this mean for them then?' The trouble is that as good evangelicals we often jump to this second question much too quickly. Then we get ourselves into all sorts of difficulties, because if we read a verse about not muzzling an ox while it is treading out the grain[9] and we haven't got an ox, we very quickly assume that it is irrelevant to us.

We would do much better to ask ourselves the following set of questions about particular laws or passages within the Law:

- What is the objective of the law?
- What kind of situation was the law trying to prevent or promote?
- What type of people would have benefited from the law or would have been protected by it?
- What kind of people would have been restrained by the law?
- Why should people obey the law?
- What are the values or the norms or the principles of which the law is an embodiment or an instance?

It has been said that the particular laws of the Old Testament are 'instantiations of moral principles', which is also the basis in British law. The judgement which is given in a particular case provides a precedent for a moral principle which is then applied to another similar case. Although the people are different and many other aspects of the case are different, the lawyer recognises the continuity between the cases through a principle or a precedent. Many of the laws in the Old Testament function in this way, providing judges with a principle or precedent to guide them in how they should operate.

I am not suggesting either that this is an easy process or that we will find immediate answers to some of these questions. In fact, sometimes there are no clear answers. For example, I have no idea why a kid should not be boiled in its mother's milk,[10] although I am quite sure that some laws have a purely symbolic value. The laws relating to clean and unclean foods were, for example, obviously intended to be symbolic of Israel's distinctiveness from the nations. The symbolic significance to these laws is, of course, no longer relevant since Christ has abolished the distinction between the ethnic Jewish people and the nations, which is why the story of Peter and Cornelius in the book of Acts is so significant.[11] We do need to remember, however, that 'clean' and 'unclean' is a ritual distinction, not a moral distinction. Just because something was unclean in the Old Testament does not mean that it was sinful. This is particularly true in connection with the bodily processes which caused men and women to be unclean for a period of days.

It did not mean that such individuals were sinners: they simply needed to undertake ritual washing before they could participate in worship again.

Having worked our way through the set of questions I suggested above, the next step is to evaluate what we have discovered and, to do this, we need quite deliberately to step *out of* the Old Testament context *into* our contemporary context. We now need to ask what our world and the world of the Old Testament have in common. The context is different but the living God is the same. Assuming that He is morally consistent and that He is the same yesterday, today and forever, we need to ask the same questions that we asked of the Old Testament context of our current context to try and establish what links there are between then and now. So we ask:

- What kinds of situations in our society do we want to promote or to prevent?
- What kinds of people in our society are in similar positions to the people in ancient society who were in need?
- Who today are the equivalent of the orphans, the widows, the aliens?
- What would be a comparable objective to the objective of the Old Testament law today?
- Who are the people who have power in our society?
- What clue does the Old Testament give us as to the kind of legislation that we might need to control them?
- How can the principles, the values, the priorities, that we have observed in Old Testament law be applied in my life and in the Church and in society?
- What kind of motivation can I have to obey the law?

All the time we are trying to move from there to here, from then to now. Generally speaking we will not be able to transfer the law's application literally, because obviously we are not ethnic Israelis living in a simple rural farming economy, but often we can still preserve its intended objectives and principles. We need to make careful and sensitive correlations between the ancient world of Israel and the contemporary world of today.

Notes

1. *'All Scripture is God-breathed and is useful for teaching, rebuking, correcting and training in righteousness, so that the man of God may be thoroughly equipped for every good work.'*
2. Deuteronomy 10:19.
3. E.g. Other motivations are: because obeying them is good for you; because you will live long in the land; because of what God has done for you in the past.
4. Isaiah 51:4; Matthew 5:14; 5:13.
5. See my *Old Testament Ethics for the People of God* (IVP, 2004).

6. This carries through into the New Testament where the behaviour of God is made the model of Christian behaviour. For one example in Jesus' teaching see Matthew 5:44–45.

7. The relationship between God and human beings has been spoiled by sin and rebellion; the relationship between the earth and human beings has been spoiled because the earth is subject to God's curse; and the earth is subject to frustration because as the result of the sin of human beings it is unable to praise and glorify God in the way it was intended to do.

8. Mark 2:27.

9. Deuteronomy 25:4.

10. Exodus 23:19.

11. Acts 10.

Chapter 31

Preparing Talks:
the Building Analogy

Greg Haslam

Both in the world and in the Church there is a wide spectrum of perspectives and assessments of the value of preaching. Typical of the world's perspective might perhaps be the Chambers Dictionary definition of 'to preach' as 'to give advice or exhort in an offensive, tedious or obtrusive manner'. At the other end of the spectrum is the definition which John Stott gives in his fine book on preaching: 'To preach is to open up the inspired text with such faithfulness and sensitivity that God's voice is heard and God's people obey him.'[1] It is interesting for each of us as preachers occasionally to ask ourselves where on the spectrum outside observers might place us. We know that as preachers we can lose our cutting edge. Like the man who, in the time of Elisha, lost the axe-head from his borrowed axe,[2] many of us, somewhere along the way, have lost our cutting edge in terms of effective ministry. Often it is due to jaded tiredness; at times it is due to busyness with other things, that has left us slothful over the 'one thing needed' as the priority investment of our lives. The prophet Elisha asked the man where he had lost the axe-head, and sometimes we have to go back to where we lost the effectiveness in ministry that used to characterise us.

Shortly after he had preached to the Queen, Billy Graham was asked what the experience had been like. He replied, 'It was a great, great privilege, but you must remember that every time I preach, I do so before the King of kings himself.' In the same way that we preach before the King of kings, so too should we prepare our talks before Him.

Good preaching is hard work, and that is why those of us who do a lot of it often look and feel quite weary. The British preacher Stuart Briscoe, who spent over thirty years in

Elm Brook Church, Milwaukee, Wisconsin, was given the following advice by a friend when he was going through a very difficult time: 'Stuart, the pastorate is a position in which you can get away with being bone idle or you can work your way into an early grave. Try to avoid both extremes.' Preachers should neither fade out nor burn out. Having said that, there can be no denying that a good talk or message requires very careful and often strenuous preparation. Mark Twain said, 'It takes me three weeks to prepare a good impromptu speech.' Through the course of the preaching school at Westminster Chapel it was interesting to hear some of the personal comments from the speakers which revealed just how much time they spend in preparation and never more so when they are giving an 'extemporaneous' talk.[3]

BUILDING THE HOUSE

In talking about the preparation of a sermon, I want to use the analogy of building a house. It is a good analogy in the sense that a house should be made from high-quality natural materials, it should be environmentally fitted to its location and it should be well designed. In the same way every sermon should literally be a 'show-home' for the Holy Spirit. The moment people enter it and begin to look around, they should feel His presence within it.

1. Select the site

The first and most elementary task in the building project of preparing a sermon is, of course, to select the site. This must be more than a frantic search for a text for next Sunday and more than a cold selection of topics planned six or twelve months ahead, with no flexibility to change according to redirection by the Holy Spirit. We must co-operate and move with the Holy Spirit, catch a burden, go where He shows us. If the ground of the Bible as a whole is the field in which we are going to build our sermon, then the site will be a particular passage or verse. *More often than not our sermon must arise out of the text of the Bible.* In saying this I do not want to imply that the preacher's own thoughts are not important. I strongly believe with Phillips Brooks that, 'Preaching is truth coming through human personality.'[4] God the Holy Spirit is glad to use our approach, our imaginations, our personalities. He never discounts us in the way we have been made and it is very important that in our preaching we are ourselves. We become artificial when we try to be someone else. Nevertheless, while our own thoughts are important, God's Word is *vital*. It is God's Word above all that must be heard in our preaching. If we are looking for somewhere to locate our sermon, it will be somewhere in the Book. In the sixteenth century John Calvin said, 'We owe to Scripture the same reverence we owe to God, since it has its only source in Him and has nothing of human origin mixed with it.' To our eyes these words seem almost exaggerated, but this is what those of us who believe in the full inspiration of Scripture adhere to. The Scripture is *all* God breathed. Calvin is right. We know that the only erroneous statements it contains are those it reports as the statements of others, and these God has chosen to report in a context in which the truth can be revealed.

If, then, all Scripture is indeed of God, then preaching finally must be expository preaching. This is a point I will emphasise several times. J. Alec Motyer has defined expository preaching in this way, 'Expository preaching is the proper response to a God-breathed Scripture. Central to it all is that concern which the word "exposition" itself enshrines: it is a display of what is there.' The site on which our sermonic building is to be erected will be found within the text of the Bible. The only question is, which part of Scripture are we next going to address? And this is true whether we are preparing to preach the following Sunday, or looking ahead to our turn once every month or six weeks, or whether we are preparing for a mid-week Bible study, or looking ahead to a conference at which we have been asked to preach.

As we come to choose the site for our sermon, I would suggest first of all that we need to use our common sense. Common sense tells me that it is not wise for a nineteen-year-old 'rookie', just starting out on a preaching ministry, to attempt to preach through the whole epistle to the Romans. The result will probably be far from satisfactory. It takes time to mature enough to tackle some books of the Bible – even the great Dr Martyn Lloyd-Jones did not feel ready to preach through the epistle to the Romans until he was fifty-four years of age. Nor is it a good idea for a preacher to begin his first pastorate fresh from Bible college with an exposition of the book of Job that will take him five years. Some of the books of the Bible require a great deal of familiarity with them, and a great deal of spiritual maturity, before we attempt to preach on them. Sometimes we need to have achieved a certain level of learning and experience, and sometimes, too, we need to know the audience to whom we are preaching before we preach certain texts to them.

My second suggestion is that as preachers we should keep a notebook of the thoughts, outlines and striking passages that come to us. When we are using the Scriptures devotionally, for example, we will find very often that certain texts leap out of the page to us. It is wise to note them down. We may not have an opportunity to use them at the time but we can keep them ready for the appropriate moment. Referring again to Dr Martyn Lloyd-Jones, his famous best-seller *Spiritual Depression*, which is an unfortunately named book for what is actually a manual on the living of the Christian life, brought together a series of sermon outlines he had composed in his daily devotional reading of Scripture. He realised that he had thirty messages that would make a preaching series, and these were later made into a book, which is still in print today, some forty years later, and has blessed countless thousands of people. This all came about because he saved what the Holy Spirit quickened to him.

Third, the preacher needs to know the needs of his hearers. The choice of the site of our sermon will not just come as a result of a divine moving of the Holy Spirit upon us, out of the blue, as it were. It will also come because we have interacted with people. Because we have been stirred by something we have heard or seen in the people of God, we will know that we need to address it and the Holy Spirit will flag up to us whole books or portions of Scripture that will enable us to do so. If this is to happen, we will need to keep in touch with where people are at, by our visitation of them, by our counselling with them and by our general interaction with them. In a preaching-centred church like Westminster Chapel, it has been a big temptation for me to withdraw to the study, but I know it would be a very unhealthy thing to do. It is only in interaction with people that we find out where they actually are and, therefore, what issues need to be addressed in the preaching ministry. It is also important to interact with those we are training in a special way, whether it be in our role in discipling others as a church leader or as leader of a small cell group. These are the sparks that point us to the site where we are to locate our next sermon.

Finally, we need to pray before we begin our specific preparation. One of the threads that has run through these lectures on preaching is our dependence as preachers on the Holy Spirit. We need to pray, asking God the Holy Spirit to open the Scriptures to us in ways that are fresh and new. It is the Holy Spirit who brings revelation of truths we have never seen before. Indeed, throughout a long ministry, it is possible to preach on the same passage four, five or six times without ever saying the same thing twice. The Holy Spirit also stirs our imaginations, so that we discover creative ways of connecting with people or illustrating what we want to say. The Holy Spirit also brings stimulation of how to apply the Scriptures in practical ways in people's lives.

I strongly recommend that, as background to their sermon preparation, preachers maintain regular habits of extensive reading. Primarily, we need to read the Scriptures very regularly and spend time studying them and meditating upon them. But we also need to be in the habit of reading good theological books and reading across a wide range of subjects. Buy lots of books then. Renaissance scholar Erasmus gave this advice: 'If I have a little money I buy books. If there's any left over I buy a little food and clothing.' Like a squirrel gathering nuts through the seasons of spring and summer because winter is coming, so preachers need to be gathering material because spontaneous inspiration will not always be there. We need to keep gathering, gathering, gathering. This requires that we develop patterns of study as a discipline in our lives. I urge young pastors newly embarking on their ministry to keep their mornings inviolable every day of the week, and some whole days, for study and for the direct preparation of sermons. Let this be the habit of a lifetime, not just the first few years, despite the fact that there will be huge forces at work mitigating against this practice.

Preaching is hard work. It usually takes an hour of preparation for every five minutes of public speaking – and that is only *direct* preparation. Behind the direct preparation is the hidden iceberg of nine-tenths of our time spent in indirect preparation that is not immediately related to the actual message. Dan Bauman put it like this, 'Quality preaching does not happen by accident. It is the result of hard work, creative thinking, careful research and dependence on the Holy Spirit. In other words, there is no short cut to homiletical excellence.'

2. Lay the foundations

As yet we have only found the location. The bulk of the hard work is still to come. We now need to begin to lay the foundations of what we trust will be a beautiful structure. The first step in laying the foundations is to measure out the ground and start digging out the earth. In order to discover what lies beneath the surface we will need to get our spiritual spades out and real effort will be required. In the words of the apostle Paul,

> *Do your best to present yourself to God as one approved, a workman who does not need to be ashamed and who correctly handles the word of truth.*
> (2 Timothy 2:15)

We are digging out ditches to lay a support on which to build our house. We are going to be laying a concrete base, allowing the concrete to set and making sure the angles of the foundations are right. What I am trying to convey through this metaphor is that we need to study the verse, the passage, or the theme as thoroughly as we possibly can. Whether it is a single verse, a paragraph or a chapter, or even the book as a whole, we need to look carefully at the context. If we are ignorant of the context, the likelihood of us misunderstanding and misinterpreting this text is far, far greater. Wider than the book and its author, we need to be examining the genre of literature with which we are dealing, and even the Testament within which the book or passage is found. Our understanding of what it means to lay the foundation will mature over a lifetime of handling the Scriptures and of imbibing the wealth of material that is available to us.

Until we really know what God is saying in this particular passage of His Word, we are not yet in a position to make a sermon out of it. This foundation of study gives power and conviction to our message. It undergirds it with authority so that all we say from that point onwards is built on the divinely revealed truth which we have brought to light. Without it the building may collapse. As in every other area of our lives, the laying of foundations is absolutely essential. Here again I want to underline the fact that I am convinced that all true preaching is finally expository preaching, because we are seeking to draw people's attention not to ourselves, not to our thoughts, but to the message of Scripture itself. John R.W. Stott said,

> To expound Scripture is to bring out of the text what is there, and to expose it to view. The expositor prises open what appears to be closed, makes plain what is obscure, unravels what is knotted and unfolds what is tightly packed. The opposite of exposition is imposition, which is to impose upon the text what is not there.[5]

The preacher is trying to lift the cover that has obscured the meaning of Scripture, at least to himself and perhaps to many others. He is trying to bring out what is actually there. In the same way that a warm pie might be carried to a neighbour's house wrapped in a thick cloth to retain the heat, and only once the cloth is removed are the aromas released and fully savoured, so the preacher attempts to bring out of the text what might otherwise remain obscured.

3. Study the plan

Most buildings are designed on paper before they become a reality on a building site. There is order and structure in the design, and it will be evident from the design what the final product will be, whether a garage, a house or perhaps an office block. In the same way we as preachers usually know what we are going to preach on from very early on in the preparation process. We formulate a plan and we try to put as much structure and form into it as we possible can.

I can recall buying sets of Lego bricks for my children. On the cover of the box or in a booklet inside there are always pictures of possible designs that can be made from the bricks. While the set may only have a hundred pieces in it, the suggested designs could have as many as 600 or 700 in them. The more bricks you have, the more options are available to you. But, whatever you have in mind to build, it is no good simply tipping the bricks out onto a table and saying, 'This is a helicopter. Isn't it magnificent?' It will not be a helicopter until all the bricks have been assembled according to the plan. It is the same with the materials we are gathering for a sermon. We need to formulate one single aim for what we are going to preach from our chosen passage. This we should be able to sum up in one single sentence, and there should be very little, if any, discrepancy between the message we intend to preach and the content of the Scripture. Recently I preached a sermon on the final paragraph of Colossians 2 which I entitled 'Christ and His Rivals'. I was able to sum up my message quite succinctly in the sentence 'I want to show the supremacy of Christ over all religious traditions, mysticism and legalism'. My whole talk related to that one theme. All preachers need to develop the skill of being able to sum up their message in one short sentence, and relate the whole sermon to that one theme. There should be nothing extraneous, nothing irrelevant. We need to be ruthless with all superfluous material. In our preparation we will come across all kinds of excellent stories, quotations and illustrations and all sorts of brilliant ideas will occur to us, which have nothing to do with our theme. We must resist the temptation to include them, because they will not serve our purpose: they will only distract. We must be ruthless with ourselves. We are assembling materials for this one building and this one building alone. We do not want a cluttered site. We need to keep asking God to show us what His message is for this particular occasion. W.E. Sangster, who preached at the Westminster Methodist Central Hall in the mid-twentieth century, said,

The preacher will be that rarest of men: a thinker. After his devotions, the best hour of his day will be the hour of sheer thinking, assembling the facts, facing the apparent contradictions, reaching for the help of God and then driving his brain like a bulldozer through the apparent chaos to order and understanding at the last.[6]

We are attempting to bridge two worlds. We are asking two essential questions. First, what did these words mean to readers in the first century AD? Second, what do they mean to readers in the twenty-first century AD? Don't begrudge the hard work involved in answering these questions.

4. Erect the scaffolding

The next stage in our building process is to formulate a simple plan or outline for what we are going to say. In our post-modern culture this is regarded by many as 'old-hat' and irrelevant, but I still maintain the view that people's minds move linearly, and that they are greatly helped in following any spoken discourse when it has a beginning, a middle and an end. People read novels and choose to watch films with a beginning, a middle and an end. They generally do not like confused narratives that go nowhere and leave them hanging in mid-air. This is, as far as I am concerned, the way God has designed the human mind and it is not just a western approach, as any who have preached in other parts of the world will know. We need, then, to develop a simple plan and divide what we are going to say into sections with headings. These divisions and headings can become pegs on which we hang our thoughts and which can help our listeners to remember what we have said. To change the metaphor, they are route markers for the journey, signposts to where we are going and where we have been, so that we know at any point of the journey where we actually are. Then, if we are prompted by the Holy Spirit to turn off down a side road for any reason, we can always find our way back to the planned route. Without a road map, if we turn down a side road, the likelihood is that we will soon get lost.

Here are some suggestions for how to choose the headings for our outline:

(a) Use the very words of the verse itself

The writer has assembled his material into units of thought. As we study these units, headings may suggest themselves to us. Unfortunately, we are not always helped in this task by the verse numbers and chapter divisions devised by the compilers of the Bible, which in some cases are insensitive to the flow of the author's argument. We are in essence looking to see the points the inspired authors themselves are making. This is a bit like eating a Terry's Chocolate Orange! The manufacturers have assembled the chocolate orange in such a way that if you lay it down and just tap it hard at one end, it falls into segments quite easily. In the same way it should be quite easy for us to see how Scripture falls into segments whether we are dealing with a verse, a paragraph, a chapter, or a book.

Some will find this process harder than others, but finding out what the segments are enables us to work with the flow of the text according to the maker's design.

(b) Ask some questions, such as who? what? why?
These questions then become the sequential development of thoughts and ideas in our sermon.

(c) Use 'Alliteration's artful aid'
Stephen Alford, the famous British preacher who for many years ministered in America, was an inveterate and unrepentant alliterative preacher. The use of this kind of verbal dexterity is sometimes really helpful, but at other times it can appear contrived. We need to keep in mind that we are not lecturers but preachers and our task is to try and make the ancient text speak to people today. A powerful technique in this regard is the use of the second person pronoun in our headings, which Jay Adams also advocates. The frequent use of the pronoun 'you' gives a directness and an immediacy to what we are saying. Try to avoid lecturing and keep to the preaching format: live words to live people.

As we erect each piece of our scaffolding, it is important to announce each major heading clearly. Our task is then to *explain* what that text heading means, to *illustrate* it wherever we can, and above all to *apply* that explanation to our listeners' lives. Speaking of the expository sermon, Bryan Chapell says, 'Expository preaching requires that we expound Scripture by deriving from a specific text main points and sub-points that expose the thoughts of the author, cover the scope of the passage and are applied to the lives of the listener.'[7] In doing just this, we are seeking to help people confront or be confronted with the Bible itself.

5. Build the walls
Having erected the scaffolding we now need to build the walls. For this we need to use the very best of materials. We do not want a jerry-built house which will not stand the test of time. As Paul put it in 1 Corinthians 3:12, we do not want to be building with '*wood, hay and straw*', but with '*gold, silver, and costly stones*'. The latter will last. The former will all be burned up. It is for this reason that we cannot afford to skimp on our preparation. It is not enough to rely on the few superficial thoughts that come to us in the twenty-five minutes or so we have allotted on Saturday evening for the next morning's message. We need to spend the time and work hard at gathering the very best materials. We do not want our life's work to be burnt up at the Last Judgement, which is what we are told will happen if we build with wood, hay and straw. Much preaching today, in an attempt to be relevant, is little more than a chat or talk-show babble, reminiscent of the light and ephemeral entertainment that is provided for the most part on daytime television to amuse those who are confined to the home. It is pleasant but it is easily forgotten. I heard

recently from a friend about a new church that has started in the south of England that is called 'a café church'. Reacting against models of church life that centre upon corporate worship and the preaching of the Word of God, this church has ripped out all the pews in the auditorium and installed small coffee tables, which seat up to six people. They have a band playing background music on the stage, which includes music from contemporary albums interspersed with worship songs. The congregation does not sing the songs but just listens to them as they sit drinking coffee, eating pastries and chatting. The teaching material is like a pub quiz with prizes awarded to the people who get the most points for the most correct answers. Now if that is the future of the church, then God help us all! The likelihood of anyone ever confronting the awesome presence and majesty of God in such a context is remote indeed.

In our sermons we need to build solid walls. Our talks need to be full of solid substance. We are to feed, instruct and inform our people, as well as stimulate, stir and move them. In order to do that, our sermons must contain plenty of doctrine and teaching, not just exhortations such as 'Put your trust in Jesus', or 'Maintain your prayer life', or 'Be a keener Christian'. In order to promote understanding of what we are talking about and provide motivation for our listeners to put God's Word into action, we have to balance indicatives and actives. 'Indicatives' are information from God about who we are in Christ, which must come before any 'active' exhortations of how to live out the Christian life. In the epistle to the Ephesians, Paul sets out three chapters of the most profound and majestic doctrine before he moves on to the practical sections of chapters 4 to 5. To gauge the importance of preaching in the New Testament we need only to consider the wide range of vocabulary used in connection with the preaching task. It includes the verbs 'preach', 'teach', 'reason', 'dialogue', 'argue', 'persuade', 'convince' and 'announce'. I do not think it will be possible to provide such sustained verbal utterance, addressed not only to the heart and emotions but primarily to the mind, in the context of something akin to a pub quiz.

We know that we live in a generation that loves amusement. The word 'amusement' is a compilation of three components: a-muse-ment. The word 'muse' means to think, but because it has an alpha privative (the 'a' at the beginning), the word is actually negated, so that 'a-muse' means 'not to think'. 'Ment' means to be in a state or condition of being. So 'a-muse-ment' means to be a state or condition of not thinking. Our sermons are not for people's amusement but for the very opposite. We are to help them think, and therefore we have to gather materials that are substantial. Once we have done our own thinking on the text, we need to draw from the very best commentaries and read a wide variety of published sermons from the greatest preachers of the past and present, as well as look at alternative translations of the passage we are studying. To repeat Erasmus' advice: never begrudge spending money on good books. Our purpose, above all, is to help people encounter God within these walls. Our preaching should not be purely academic but very practical and directed to people's lives, so that they can understand and implement what they are hearing. In Nehemiah 8:8, Bible-teacher Ezra 'gave the meaning' of the text in such a way that it was more than an academic exercise. It impacted minds, emotions, consciences and wills. People wept. That is the work of the Holy Spirit.

6. Install the windows

Spurgeon often used to quote the delightful dictum, 'Pleasantly profitable let all our sermons be.' The chief reason for windows in a house is, of course, to let the light in. It is for this reason that illustrations are so invaluable because they throw light upon what has been said. We must not rely on them alone to convey truth: they are there to illuminate what we have already declared. In the same way that houses do not normally just consist of windows, our sermons should not just be made up of illustrations alone. Who wants to live in a greenhouse? However, at the opposite extreme, neither does anyone want to live in a dungeon consisting of plain walls into which the light never penetrates.

Like a builder's merchant, we have to gather the material to illustrate our sermons in advance, collecting stories, quotations, topical news and so on as we come across them. People like stories and tend to remember good ones. Dr Martyn Lloyd-Jones said, 'The preacher must never be dull. He must never be boring. He should never be what is called heavy. I would say that a dull preacher is a contradiction in terms. If he's dull he's not a preacher.'[8] In his later years, however, Dr Lloyd-Jones expressed a sense of regret that in his thirty-year ministry at Westminster Chapel he had not used more illustrative material in his sermons. Let us not repeat his confessed mistake.

7. Make it fit for living

Spurgeon said, 'Preaching is a bit like throwing a bucket of water at a row of bottles. Some of the water goes into the bottles, but personal application ensures that all the bottles get filled up.' We need to ask the Holy Spirit to show us how to connect with the real people in front of us, so that they are also able to connect with what we are saying. This house we are building through our preaching is not an antiquarian museum, or a theatre for entertainment, or a reference library for obscure information. It is a house to be lived in. Our sermons should invite people in. As soon as they enter, they should know immediately that this is a wonderful place to be. Some preachers are totally predictable in the way they go about their sermons and are, therefore, boring. While others are alarmingly unpredictable which can often lead to discomfort. There is a balance that straddles both extremes where the preaching is predictably unpredictable and startling in its applications.

8. Install the front and back doors

As our sermon preparation is coming to a completion, we need to install the doors for entrance and exit. A good beginning invites people into the sermon, and a clear ending launches them out from it and into the task of living for Christ in the world. Some examples of good beginnings might be: questions; startling statements; interesting stories; an advert that has interested us; or a puzzle that we want to raise in people's minds that we can then answer through the course of the sermon. Here are two striking beginnings which I found in a book of radio sermons by an Assemblies of God pastor published in 1987:

> Nothing can quite command the fullest attention as much as a summons from the Inland Revenue Audit Service. A call for the audit of your books will strike terror into the heart of a cheat, and make even the most honest person mumble in his beard about bureaucracy and inconvenience. But a much more severe audit is scheduled for every Christian believer that frankly most church people know little about. It's called the judgement seat of Christ.
> (From a sermon entitled 'Audit')

> The boy on the hospital bed was not moving: he could not. He lay in traction with two holes in his skull, pins there connect to the chain and wait to pull on his body, because his back was broken in four places. He was paralysed from his shoulders down. A tracheotomy had been done and the pump was enabling him to draw air. Pathetic. Shortly before, he and a friend were hitting the drugs and booze and they climbed into the late model car and drove like crazy men. They hit the curb at seventy miles an hour and centrifugal force took over from the driver. The car careered off the trees like a little ball in a pin ball machine and the other guy was killed instantly. And this boy, if he lived, faced a life of incapacity and self-incrimination.[9]

Such beginnings draw people in. People stay with the preacher because they want to find out how the sermon will develop. W.E. Sangster put it like this,

> The preacher has the awful task of making the Word of God live to men and women who have been busy all the week seeking the bread of this life, and who even in the sanctuary find it hard to keep their minds on God and holy things. He must help them in every wholesome way he can. If he can get an arresting beginning he may have their awed attention the whole time and be able to hide the truth of God deep in their hearts, and I add, send them out thrilled, stirred up, and eager to implement what they have heard.[10]

As to the exit, we should aim for a nice, decisive touch-down, like most passengers want to experience as their flight on a Jumbo-jet lands at Heathrow Airport. No one wants to be kept hanging in the air indefinitely. Get that sermon down!

One black Pentecostal lay-preacher summed up his whole approach to preaching in this way: 'I reads myself full, I thinks myself clear, I prays myself hot, and then I lets myself go!' Building a house in the way I have tried to describe the process of sermon preparation here, should help us all to do just that. The sermon may well then become a 'show-home' for God and His people to meet together in. And who knows? Some may come to have their lives transformed there.

NOTES

1. *I Believe in Preaching* (Hodder & Stoughton, 1982, repr. 1998).
2. 2 Kings 6:1–6. See also Epilogue.
3. See, for example, Chapter 39 by J. John.
4. *Lectures on Preaching* (1877).
5. Stott, *I Believe in Preaching.*
6. W.E. Sangster, *The Craft of the Sermon* (Epworth Press, 1954), p. 150.
7. Bryan Chapell, *Christ-centred Preaching: Redeeming the Expository Sermon* (Baker Academic, 1994).
8. D.M. Lloyd-Jones, *Preaching and Preachers* (Hodder & Stoughton, 1971), p. 87.
9. Dan Betzer, *Revival Radio Sermons 1987* (General Council of the Assemblies of God).
10. Sangster, *The Craft of the Sermon.*

Chapter 32

THIRTEEN THINGS I WISHED
I HAD KNOWN ABOUT PREACHING

Jeff Lucas

In this very practical session I want to try and save my fellow preachers from some of the embarrassing moments which I have encountered in my own preaching ministry. By sharing some of my failures I hope that others will avoid making the same mistakes.

I felt called to preach at the age of seventeen having been a Christian for about three weeks, and very quickly I found myself studying the Bible. By the age of nineteen I was at Bible school and by the age of twenty-one, before I had left Bible school, I had planted a church. I think I preached my first sermon when I was about nineteen to a congregation of five or six people, four of whom were actually dead at the time, so I don't think too much damage was done. A couple of years ago I found my notes for that first sermon. It was a fantastic outline:

- *Point 1*: Christians don't have problems
- *Point 2*: If you have got any problems, Jesus will take them away
- *Point 3*: If Jesus hasn't taken your problems away, then you are probably not a Christian anyway.

I had the copyright on this sermon for years but I felt now was the right time to release it!

1. THE PULPIT IS A HIGHLY DANGEROUS ZONE

The first thing I wish I had known about preaching is that the pulpit is a highly dangerous zone. I now know it is really important for the preacher, particularly if he is speaking in a new venue, as a guest speaker, for example, to take the opportunity to familiarise himself with the pulpit area. From years of experience I know it can hold hidden dangers, and I know that, once I am up there ready to preach, it will be too late!

Take the microphone, for example. There is a spiritual principle throughout the Christian world that whenever you think microphones are on, they are actually off, and whenever you think they are off, they are actually on. I can remember the first time I spoke at Spring Harvest twenty years ago. I was so terrified that I threw up backstage before speaking. I had never preached to more than twenty-five people before, and now I was speaking to over a thousand young people. My conviction is still that the best communicators at these large events are normally not to be found in the adult programme, but in the youth programme. Anyone who can hold the attention of a thousand eighteen-year-olds, who are wrestling with hormonal overload, can really call himself a preacher because young people do not suffer fools gladly and the preacher needs to be able to connect. For some reason I had written the notes for my sermon in red felt-tip pen – not a good idea – and I had not yet learnt to check this danger zone that is the pulpit. I picked up the microphone, the microphone was on. I switched it off. I started talking into the microphone. I started tapping the microphone. I started breathing into the microphone. By this time the sound person, who was being forced to watch me destroy a very nice micro-phone, was tearing his hair out. Having finally turned the microphone on I looked down at my notes, but to my horror, due to the massive spotlight that was now shining down on me, the red-tip felt had become invisible. At that point I prayed that great prayer of St Francis of Assisi, 'Beam me up, Jesus.' Why, oh why hadn't I checked that zone?

Another important point that every preacher needs to check is at what point on the programme he is due to appear, because that will very definitely influence how he begins his sermon. First of all, it is very helpful to know whether he is being introduced, or whether he should expect a nod to indicate that it is time for him to step up to the microphone. It can be very disconcerting to try and follow a moving solo about Jesus' suffering on the cross with a hilariously funny story. My worst experience of this, in the days before I had learnt to check the programme, took place in a church in America. I had prepared a funny story to introduce my topic, not realising that I was following a drama presentation by the church's youth group who had performed what can only be described as a horrendous sketch on hell, which ended with four people being dragged off to hell, screaming, 'Oh my God, I am burning.' It was truly awful.

On another occasion in Oklahoma, just before I was due to preach the pastor introduced a soloist and then added, 'Sister, when you sing the third verse, the anointing of God is going to come on you.' I sat there with a sinking feeling, wondering how I would cope if, when I stood up to preach, nothing had happened. Helpfully during the third verse the young woman started to cry and then others in the congregation followed suit. When you add into the equation that under the anointing people had begun to run around the building at speed, like an accelerated march for Jesus without balloons, it did not seem the most appropriate moment to launch into a funny story.

To return for a moment to microphones, it is amazing what some preachers do with microphone leads. I once saw a preacher who throughout the time he was preaching was whipping his leg with the microphone lead. Then at another point he picked up the microphone lead and, throwing it over his shoulder, started marching around the platform. It was completely bizarre and totally distracting, so that no one listened to a word of what he was saying.

Take my advice and check out the pulpit zone. It can be a dangerous area, and if something goes wrong, everyone will notice.

2. At Least 25 per cent of the Preparation Time Should Be Spent on the First Three Minutes and the Last Three Minutes of the Sermon

Many preachers do understand how important it is to get the introduction of their sermon right, realising that if they don't work hard on that part of the sermon, they will probably struggle for the next ten minutes at least. In the introduction we need to try and establish some kind of relationship with the congregation because preaching is surely a relational experience. People should not feel they are being talked at. Very simple things such as saying, 'Good morning, how are you?', smiling, engaging in friendly banter and telling a joke can all help to establish a good rapport.

I am always interested in what people notice. Sometimes it is very little things. For example, I tend these days always to say, 'Please stand if you are able.' I say that because I have discovered that people with disabilities feel immediately excluded the moment the suggestion is made from the front that normality equals the ability to stand, which, of course, it does not. People have come up to me and wept in appreciation because of that one simple phrase. Others thank me for talking about both women and men when I am preaching. It is very interesting the way a phrase or an emphasis can suddenly empower people.

Although many preachers take great care with the introduction to their sermons, I believe most preachers need to work much harder on their conclusions because, quite frankly, there is a real problem with laziness. A Puritan preacher said, 'Thou art a preacher of the Word. Mind thy business.' In other words, the preacher should work hard on his message and carry out his craft well. It is all too easy to work hard on the message, and then end with a throwaway statement, such as, 'Well, we'll see what the Lord does at the end.' Of course, we do need to see what the Lord wants to do, and I believe that preaching should be a Holy Spirit prophetic experience. For example, while I am preaching I often find that the Holy Spirit inspires me with plays on words or analogies which people listening frequently pick up on. Perhaps He does not give me these things in advance so that I will remain dependent on Him. I believe in making room for the Holy Spirit, but it must not become an excuse for laziness. We need to know where our message is going, and we should not be fumbling around in the dark at the end. I believe we need to spend time in our preparation planning how we will conclude our sermon. Personally I actually need to write down in broad terms where I sense the Holy Spirit wants it to go.

I want to suggest, in particular, that we should not always feel that we need to end every sermon with a crisis and with an appeal. Sometimes as preachers we seem to resort to an appeal simply because we can't think of anything better to do. Why, sometimes, can't we preach and pray and go home? Perhaps it is because we are looking for something visible to happen, and we are not content to invest in the invisible.

3. DISINTERESTED PEOPLE ARE NOT FISH TO HOOK

Let me explain what I mean when I say that disinterested people are not fish to hook. In a congregation there will always be some people who naturally have an encouraging face, others who appear mildly interested, and at the other end of the spectrum those who look as if they are wrestling with an abdominal problem. The danger for the preacher is that he fails to notice the encouraging faces and begins to focus on those who are looking utterly disinterested. As a preacher I want people to like me; I want to win people over. If I am not careful I can begin to put all my effort into trying to draw these disinterested people in and can find myself preaching to them. However, here is what my experience has taught me. First, people's response is God's business, and not something for me to worry about. And, second, appearances can be deceptive. Those who are looking encouragingly at me may in their heart be harbouring me ill will, while those with a vacant expression may actually be receiving from God. It is impossible for the preacher to know what is going on in people's hearts and, anyway, it is a waste of time and effort to spend the rest of the sermon trying to hook them in. We need to do our job and stop being so insecure.

At one conference at which I spoke there was a married couple sitting on the front row, who were sending me bored signals, which began to play on my mind. Then he wrote her a note. I started thinking, 'That note's about me.' So, as I was preaching I was reading the note upside down. What I discovered was that the communication between husband and wife had nothing to do with me whatsoever, but was about their plans for that evening!

4. THE VOICE IS DESIGNED FOR VARIETY

Some preachers seem to think that shouting equals anointing. Others seem to think that when they are preaching they need to speak in a monotone. Twenty years or so ago it was quite common for preachers to employ 'the monotone of anointing' and add 'er' on to the end of every other word, so, for example, 'And the Word of the Lord...' became 'The Worder of the Lorder...'. Sometimes we Christians worry me, because we do such stupid things! On one occasion I went with a friend of mine, who is from the East End of London, to one of his preaching engagements. He preached very well, but on the way home I said to him, 'Who was that bloke preaching tonight?' He said, 'Me.' I replied,

'I don't know who it was but it wasn't you.' His preaching voice, on that occasion at least, was completely different from his normal speaking voice.

Over the years I have learnt that the variety of the voice can be a powerful tool in preaching: we can speak loudly; we can speak softly; we can speak slowly; we can speak quickly. We can even pause – silence can be devastating. Failing to use this variety can be very detrimental to the impact of our preaching. Many years ago, at the Albert Hall, I heard a large gentleman from Texas preach. His preaching was either loud or very loud. He told a story about his four-year-old grandchild, who had come running into his room just before he left to fly to England. Rather than try and modulate his voice to represent a child's voice, he simply shouted even louder, with the result that he lost his audience's attention very quickly.

5. PREACHERS WHO CONSTANTLY SCAN THE AUDIENCE WITH THEIR EYES CREATE THE WRONG IMPRESSION

In fact, they give the impression that they are an illegal drug user! At Bible school I was taught that I should scan my audience with my eyes as I was preaching. This, I was told, would help me connect with the people who were listening to me. However, I have since discovered that doing this actually makes people feel giddy and makes them think that the preacher is hallucinating because he never actually looks at them. I have since learnt that what we need to do is to focus on certain individuals for two or three seconds before moving on to the next person. If we allow our gaze to rest on a person for too long he or she will begin to feel very uncomfortable. Personally I tend to focus on the encouraging ones, which is probably a bit naughty of me.

As preachers we must never forget that our job is *not* to preach a good sermon: we must get away from the idea that preaching is about delivering a good sermon. Preaching is about connecting with people.

6. PEOPLE DON'T NORMALLY ENJOY THE PREACHING IF THE PREACHER DOESN'T SEEM TO BE

If the preacher does not look as if he is enjoying the experience, the congregation certainly won't. I have experimented with this and have discovered that if I tell an amusing story with a relatively deadpan expression on my face, people don't laugh. They do not feel they have permission to laugh, even to smile. Because I am looking so uptight, they empathise with my appearance. On the other hand, if I smile while I am telling a story, even if I have told it a hundred times before, they soon begin to laugh.

I am actually quite self-conscious about my smile. This is probably because a lady came up to me once after I'd preached and asked me, 'Have you ever had a stroke?' I said, 'No, why do you say that?' She said, 'Well, when you smile, only one side of your face goes up.'

Since then I have felt very self-conscious about my smile, but I know that if I want people to relax and enjoy the preaching event, I had better enjoy it myself. Otherwise I will communicate my tension to them. As preachers, we need to enjoy the preaching experience.

7. Mixed Metaphors Can Be the Death of a Good Sermon

We need to be careful with our use of metaphors. I heard about a preacher who said, 'Sometimes my friend, we are filled with the Holy Spirit, but we are like buckets with a hole in the bottom, and we leak. We need to be filled afresh. Let me ask you this evening, my friend, do you have a hole in your bottom?'

As we are preparing our sermons, we need to work through the metaphors we are planning to use to make sure we do not land ourselves in a big hole. It is also a good idea to put a large circle around any words which we might tend to confuse with another word. I want to save all preachers the pain that a friend of mine experienced when he had a slip of the tongue. He had intended to refer to the Church as 'a cosmic organism'!

8. Bad Habits and Reflex Words Are Irritating

Bad habits and reflex words can destroy a message. A preacher to whom I listened recently ended every sentence with the word 'yeah': 'The Bible is the Word of God, yeah? This book is completely inspired, yeah?' After twenty minutes I was thinking, 'If he says "yeah" one more time, I am going to...' Other preachers interpolate such words as 'hallelujah' or 'Amen' or 'hmmm'. This use of what I term 'filler' words is the sign of a vacant brain. My plea to all preachers is: 'Please engage your brain.'

In the pulpit both filler words and bad habits are magnified a hundredfold. I used to wear glasses that slipped down my nose when I preached, with the result that with the Bible in one hand and a microphone in the other I somehow needed to push my glasses back up my nose again. Apparently the action that I developed made me look as if I was having a fit. In the days when I had hair that used to fall over my face, I am told I also looked very strange when I tried to push it back. If we are preachers, we need to ask good friends to tell us what repetitive habits and reflex words we have and take efforts to eradicate them.

9. Relevance is Vital

Relevance is vital. Let me say immediately that by this I do not mean that we must be driven by a compulsion always to be topical. There are some things that we will need to teach that don't seem to have an immediate Monday-morning application. Sometimes we just need to say things about God which are true; we should not always be driven by felt needs.

Having said this by way of a disclaimer, I do believe that our preaching should be relevant. Just this morning I read an article that made the point that nobody goes to church to find out what actually happened to the Jebusites and nobody really cares about the history of the Amalekites. We need to preach about things that people do care about, and that includes some of the difficult issues that people face in their everyday lives.

One of the hardest subjects to talk about in the pulpit is sex, but we need to talk about it much more. The Christian Church still hangs on to mediaeval inhibitions about sexuality. I am convinced that we need more biblical teaching about human sexuality, and for this reason I want to speak about it bluntly for a few moments. The mediaeval Church had a belief that the Holy Spirit left the marital bedroom during sexual intercourse and came back in again when it was all over. As bizarre as that theology sounds, it governed my life as a brand new Christian. As a single young man I did not feel able even to discuss the issue of sex, and when Kay and I married, it influenced the way we began our married life together. All I am about to share, I do with Kay's permission and I do not do it lightly. When we got to our honeymoon cottage about one in the morning, after a long drive, I felt we had to have a Bible reading and a prayer before we could make love. And then the next morning we went to church for the 10.00 a.m. service. Somebody there knew me, and I ended up being asked to share a word of testimony – on the first day of my married life! We then had lunch and tea with the minister, and during the week we went to the prayer meeting and the Bible study. Our honeymoon was loaded with passionate, zealous, aggressive, exhilarating … hymn singing. Why was that? I am embarrassed to say it was because we genuinely thought our faltering steps into the land of Eros had to be sanctified by attending as many Bible studies as possible. A Baptist minister friend of mine got into serious trouble with his church because he preached on the subject of sex. We need to face up to the challenges of these issues.

Another article I read recently included the following story. A professor who was talking about sexuality was challenged by someone present as to why he was addressing it. The professor asked, 'What do you want me to speak about?' He received the reply, 'Why don't you speak about prophecy?' The professor said, 'How often do you entertain thoughts about prophecy?' One student answered, 'About twice a year, once around Christmas and then again some time around Good Friday when I hear Isaiah 53.' 'All right,' the professor continued. 'And how many times in a given day do you think about sex?' Silence. The professor had accomplished his purpose. We need to have more biblically relevant preaching on human sexuality, which is something people are thinking about all the time.

Number Your Points

Number 10 – no more needs to be said!

11. The Pulpit is Not a Bunker

The pulpit is not the place for the preacher to vent his spleen upon that painful person in the congregation whom he is scared to confront face to face. We must not use the pulpit as a bunker from which we can launch our missiles at individuals who have upset us. Even if that has not been our intention, there will inevitably be some people, full of their own self-importance, who will come up to us after our sermon and ask whether we were getting at them. Nevertheless, we should not intentionally dump something on an entire congregation that should have been shared with an individual personally.

12. Enjoy the Journey of Ministry

Gary Northrup, who is my colleague at Timberline in Colorado, tells a story about flying into Denver airport in the middle of winter and realising that his car has not got any petrol in its tank for the journey home. It is one o'clock in the morning, the petrol stations are closed, and his in-car computer tells him that he has twelve miles' worth of petrol left and there are eighteen miles to the nearest petrol station. He goes on to describe very simply how he drives those eighteen miles, gripping the steering wheel, with furrowed brow, perspiring, agitated and fearful, praying desperately, 'God, please help, help, help.' He makes it to the petrol station, fills the tank and, as he puts the petrol cap back on, he looks up. At that moment he says, 'I saw the most beautiful moon that I had not noticed before, because I was so concentrating on the journey.' Some Christian leaders are always on to the next thing. Paul Tournier says that most people spend their whole lives indefinitely preparing to live. As preachers we can do the same thing in our ministry. We can live our whole lives, promising ourselves that 'Someday I'll be happy'. 'Someday when I've preached in that situation...' 'Someday when I've had that ministry opportunity...' 'Someday when I get married ... when we have children ... when the children go to school ... when the children leave school ... when the children get married ... when I've got grandchildren ... when I retire...' Then when people retire, they relocate to memory lane. I am hugely grateful for the privilege and the opportunity of ministry, but I don't want to live a life that is not satisfied until the next opportunity, or the big breakthrough comes. I don't want to postpone living. I want to make the most of today. I don't just want to get through it. I want to enjoy the journey. I actually want to stop once in a while, look up and realise the moon is still shining.

13. Where the Setting is Appropriate, Always Leave Time for Questions[1]

Note _____

1. The session at Westminster Chapel ended with a question and answer session.

Section Six

Unity and Maturity

... speaking the truth in love,
we will in all things grow up into him
who is the Head, that is, Christ.
From him the whole body,
joined and held together
by every supporting ligament,
grows and builds itself up in love,
as each part does its work.

(Ephesians 4:15–16)

Chapter 33

PREACHING THAT UNITES
THE STREAMS

Joel Edwards

*Peter stood up with the Eleven, raised his voice and addressed the crowd:
'Fellow Jews and all of you who live in Jerusalem, let me explain...'*
(Acts 2:14)

The first sermon that was ever preached in the fledgling New Testament Church was a sermon that united. Acts 2:14–36 is both the first expression of Christian orthodoxy and the first expression of unity. Peter stood up with the eleven or, to put it another way, Peter spoke up 'with' or 'for' the eleven. Nevertheless, within a very brief period of time the diversity of the early Church would throw up huge conflicts in its message, its method and even its mission. I am very grateful for the fact that the New Testament is painfully transparent in its history. In the midst of some extraordinary acts of God Luke paid attention to the problems as much as to the power of the Church: personality conflicts, tactical variations and prejudice sit alongside miracles, signs and wonders. We do well to remember that. Right from the beginning we are given the clear message that disputes, differences and even, dare I say, temper tantrums are features of progressive sanctification in the Church. They don't put God off, which is just as well. Therefore, perhaps the problem isn't really the problem. Maybe we just need to learn how to handle our diversity.

The growing collection of disciples argued about tradition, law, the nature of Christ and forms of worship, and they tried to make sense of the role of women and of qualifications for leaders. And when the 120 descended from the upper room to infiltrate Jerusalem, Judaea and Samaria, they walked onto a rollercoaster of controversies, not an Utopian dream. In a word, the Christian Church was alive and well. These were real people doing Kingdom business and, in this regard, I think we can probably consider ourselves as no better than the early Church but – and here's the good news – probably no worse either. Unity like peace is more than the absence of war.

The fault lines in the Church of today are not exactly the same as those of the early Church, but I think they remain quite similar. Like the early Church we are also concerned about how truth works in worship and how truth works in our mission to the world: effectively we battle with the same issues in different cultural contexts. The irony of orthodoxy is that we are actually likely to agree on everything only at the point at which we become indifferent to truth. As long as we are keen about truth we are likely to have differences among us. Over my period of office at the Evangelical Alliance I have noticed that those sections of the Christian community which used to give us a very hard time for all kinds of reasons, in more recent times do not seem to be bothering so much. I wonder whether this is because they have become tired or because there is a growing indifference to argument. Maybe we have become far more deeply entrenched in our camps than we used to be, but I find myself asking if one of the reasons why there are less theological disputes with any heat or intensity happens to be the fact that increasingly our view and commitment to truth has become dissipated by other factors. We want to be tolerant; we are building strong relationships; the walls of demarcation are coming down; we are being touched by the culture. All of these things are positive, but sometimes I question whether or not biblical and theological indifference is good news and whether we are paying a price which we will reap at a later stage.

Before I begin to look at some of the current issues with which the Church is struggling, I want to say a word about the 'streams' which our preaching is to unite. I will be talking primarily about the range of evangelicalism, which my predecessor Clive Calver at the Evangelical Alliance used to talk about as the 'twelve tribes of evangelicalism'. Many other delineations are also possible. As evangelicals the fact that we are prone to the defence of the truth as we understand it from the Scriptures makes our task of uniting in preaching a very, very important task, albeit a formidable one. Our very self-identity is inextricably bound up with the concept of truth, and this makes us even more susceptible to fractious behaviour. Because we like to think of ourselves as 'good evangelicals', as the true children of the Reformation, we are sometimes more inclined towards protest than reform. Rob Warner, who has given so much to the Church in recent times, puts it this way: 'The history of evangelicalism tells us that among those with strong convictions a recurring pattern of debate and disagreement is inevitable.'[1] Our preaching has a very important role to play in our witness to the world but also in understanding how we work together.

As Peter stood up to preach on the Day of Pentecost, he addressed the crowds with the words, 'let me explain...'. This is a sobering reminder that preaching which explains things may serve to harmonise differences. But, of course, that is a lot easier said than done. There are still a good many issues on which we differ, and because preaching is invariably an explanation of our understanding of revealed truth which we have received, this will always be the case. In very broad terms I want to offer you *some* of the fault lines against which preaching is attempting to make a difference.

THE CURRENT LANDSCAPE

In broad, rather crude categories the fault lines, as I see them, are:

- a Word culture versus very heavy emphasis on the Spirit
- Bible-centred church/Bible-centred ministry versus story-telling
- exposition versus celebratory preaching, and
- proclamation versus action – whether the church needs to go out and tell the world or whether it incarnates the Word and simply seeks to act it out.

The diversity of the Church's approaches to the ministry of the Word is influenced by a variety of factors ranging from theological bias to cultural disposition or even just our individual temperament. We don't always take as seriously as we ought to the extent to which our cultural disposition, for example, influences our view of truth. This is something that we need to recognise and address. However, there is also an increasing trend for the variety of our approaches to the preaching task to be influenced by our understanding of our mission or the degree to which we engage with the world beyond the walls of the church. In my view, the argument has moved on from the insularity of how we worship differently to how we do mission differently and, therefore, how the Word of God provides us with a tool to handle those tasks and tensions.

In relation to that, I suspect there has been a subtle shift in the Word/Spirit debate, which resulted in some measure from the tensions between the Charismatic and non-Charismatic streams from the 1970s through to the 1990s, so that it has now become much more a debate about what I term the 'Word versus Jesus'. I wonder if the reason why a relative passivity has arisen between the two camps has to do with our experiences together as we came to terms with the 'Toronto' phenomena. It seems to me that, as a result of the intense debate of that period, we so exhausted our approach to Scripture and phenomena that we almost agreed to divide into separate camps, which has served in some ways to confirm people's differences and the a priori positions from which they came, including their starting point in assessing the preaching task. For me this was exemplified by a conversation I had a couple of years ago after hearing Terry Virgo, the leader of Newfrontiers, speaking at Stoneleigh Bible Week, I thought very powerfully, on the subject of the Toronto phenomena. When I told another evangelical leader about Terry's masterly exposition of the Scriptures on this issue, he set about dismantling everything Terry had said step by step. Why? Because the two men, coming out of very different theological cultures, started from a very different presupposition about how the Scriptures should be handled.

One of the reasons why the debate has, to a very large degree, now moved on is because the new worship culture has allowed the Charismatic flow to 'seep under' the door of even many conservative churches. This struck me quite forcibly at a recent visit to a very conservative Bible college. I would not have been able to tell from the songs being sung what the theological ethos and bias of the college was! Similarly some years ago at Keswick – a place of such history and pedigree – I was bemused to be singing one of David Fellingham's songs and was struck by the thought that, although David would never ever be allowed to lead worship at the conference, we were singing one of his compositions.

Do we, I sometimes wonder, approach our diversity with the wrong preconceptions? Take, for example, the Charismatic/non-Reformed and the non-Charismatic/Reformed wings of the Church which have historically been at variance. Today, with one or two notable exceptions, they either ignore each other or distantly co-exist. The first time I saw Keswick's motto 'All One in Christ Jesus' it really made an impression on me. When I made an enthusiastic comment along those lines to the person I was with, who knew I was soon to speak at the Keswick convention, he looked me up and down quizzically and then said, 'Good luck to you.' To my response, 'What do you mean?' he replied, 'Well, you are Pentecostal, aren't you?' His reaction motivated me even more to want to go to Keswick and give expression to that unity in diversity. What I in fact found when I went there was a tremendous amount of resonance with my own tradition, since at Keswick as in Pentecostalism, great emphasis is placed on the centrality of preaching.

On another occasion, during a conversation with an eminent Christian leader from a more Reformed church background, in which we were discussing the wide spectrum of churchmanship, he leant across to me and said, 'You know, Pentecostals I can understand, it's those Charismatics I can't cope with.' I think I understand what he meant – in both the Reformed and Pentecostal traditions great importance is placed on the centrality of the Word, with much teaching on sanctification and morality (although this is not to say that Charismatics do not also embrace those distinctives, but it is often sadly neglected). I believe we need to work with our diversity, yet labour to recover the biblical priorities that truly unite us.

In my view the 'Word versus Jesus' debate is now influenced more by mission than by worship, and reflects two sides of a very important conflict. I believe that the tension between these two may be viewed as the differing assessments of those who have a higher regard for proclamation of the Word and those who are more concerned to engage with culture, in what they would call the incarnation of the Word.

The tensions between exposition and story-telling or Bible-centred ministry and celebratory preaching remain very live issues for us. It is my impression, however, that God has shown a surprising flexibility and an interesting ability to change people's lives through either approach, and that, therefore, neither should be dismissive of the other. Instead, both should seek to affirm and challenge each other's particular excellence. I recently heard T.D. Jakes, pastor of the 30,000-strong Potter's House in Dallas, USA, comment that Christian TV has actually been doing an incredible service to the Church by enabling Christians, from the comfort of their armchairs, to imbibe the Word across a range of cultures. I had never thought about this before, but I think he is right. Christian television is actually getting us to listen to each other's sermons across the divides, which is something many of us have not been in the habit of doing. What does this say about our approach to unity and diversity? We should be looking for the things which unite. We absolutely must not get caught up in the issue of whether or not exposition is a superior approach to preaching than a celebratory, story-telling approach. I say, 'Both/and, please.' Dr David Hilborn, theological advisor to the Evangelical Alliance, has said: 'It is hard to get away from the fact that, when Jesus declared the good news of God, he relied a great deal more on stories than on abstract propositions.'[2] I believe that increasingly we need to have a growing appreciation for many varied types of preaching, provided they are biblical.

THE BEDROCK OF UNITY

Having looked at just some of the issues with which the Church is wrestling at the current time, I want now to turn my attention to the things which unite us. In doing so, I will draw on some helpful distinctives of the evangelical movement identified by the historian David Bebbington, which can, I believe, help to unite us in our preaching today across the whole spectrum of evangelicalism, and may perhaps even include representatives of the wider orthodox Christian community that would not necessarily call itself 'evangelical'.[3] In Bebbington's view evangelical identity has been defined by (i) a Bible-centred approach; (ii) a Christ-centred approach; (iii) the centrality of the cross; and (iv) transformation. To these four, I would want to add missions. It is important to make it clear that the very nature of our diversity means that not everyone is convinced by Bebbington's distinctions. The esteemed Bible expositor Dr John Stott, for example, is unhappy with these categories, proposing instead that the Trinity be used as a model, since it provides the same elements in a more efficient way.[4] I think both are right. Any approach to a succinct summary of our distinctives will I think be found wanting in some regard, but I believe Bebbington's still has much to offer.

1. Bible centred

Protestant Christianity was born out of its commitment to the Word of God, and this I believe remains our cardinal commitment in the task of preaching. Even as I say this, I am aware that we have very different views about the vitally important and related theological issues of inspiration and interpretation. At a special meeting organised to unify Evangelical Anglicans in 1996 Dr Tom Wright offered the following word of caution: 'What then does it mean to use a Scripture and to do so with full loyalty? It certainly does not mean ever-decreasing circles of doctrinal definitions whose main purpose is to exclude other people.'[5] It is very easy to use the Word as an offensive weapon in the name of truth: to speak truth without grace. Whilst recognising this danger, I think we have to agree together that any preaching which is aiming to unite people across the streams must take as its primary conviction the fact that God's Word is inspired, authoritative and authentic, and given to us to proclaim and pass on to others. Across our cultural and denominational lines we are still committed to the idea that God has spoken fully and conclusively through His Word. It still remains the final bedrock for preaching which can truly unite us. It is the metronome from which we set the pace in the pulpit, irrespective of our styles or cultures in preaching. No serious preaching can claim diplomatic immunity from the requirement to give primacy to the Word. All of our preaching must submit to the authority of Scripture and to what we understand the Word to be saying to us and to the people to whom we are called to speak. No one can put the Bible to one side, propound their own thoughts and still claim to be a Christian preacher. We hold to the great theme of the Reformation: *sola Scriptura*. This is the preaching that unites us.

2. Christ centred

It was John Calvin who said, 'Christ the Saviour is the beating heart of Scripture.' Preaching committed to Scripture must turn out to be an encounter with Jesus Christ. It is perfectly possible to have a sermon which is well crafted, exegetically correct and intellectually coherent, but few of us would agree that this is enough. One of the things that I have found, particularly in middle-class Anglo-Christianity, is that very often what is described as a 'good sermon' is something which is intellectually coherent, hangs together beautifully, and has great illustrations – and God certainly honours and uses it – but it is not necessarily the whole story in terms of preaching. In our preaching the person of Jesus must be central. The preaching that unites the streams presents us with a living Christ who emerges from orthodox faith into a living relationship with us. At the heart of the message about Jesus is Jesus Himself. People will be united not just by good exposition but by good exposition which brings Jesus alive to our hearers. Good exposition alone may appeal to people with a university background or a certain intellectual predisposition but its influence will not extend right across the streams. When the preaching exposes Jesus as well as the text, when it exposes Jesus as well as its literary faithfulness, then we are into the kind of preaching that brings the Word alive in people's lives across the streams. This is why Jesus prayed for those who would come to believe in Him through the message the disciples would give. Preaching that unites takes us to the heart of Jesus, and He draws us closer to each other. Dostoevsky once said that, if it could be proved beyond all shadow of a doubt that truth could be separated from Jesus, and he had to make a choice, he would go for Jesus. Although he could be accused of dangerous existentialism I think he was saying that the Word is authenticated only through an encounter with Jesus. There is an existential requirement in the preaching of the Word, so that people are confronted with Jesus, the living Christ, in the communication of the gospel.

I come from a New Testament Church of God background. Our sister denomination is the Church of God of Prophecy. Both movements were founded in the nineteenth century by the same person. It just depends whose history book you read as to which one you believe was founded first! Despite the fact that the two Churches are actually variations on the same theme, for a long time they didn't talk to each other. At a meeting at the headquarters of the Church of God of Prophecy in the USA to talk over their differences with their sister denomination, that Church's overall leader, Bishop Murray, talked about a way of looking at issues which I find extremely helpful. He took the picture of a triangle, with Jesus at the top and the two Churches at each corner of the base. 'As we try to talk to each other from the base line it is very hard,' he said. 'But the closer we come to Jesus, the easier it might be first to hear each other and then to understand one another, whether we are talking from the pulpit or from the pew. As we get closer to Jesus we both hear and understand one another more clearly as well as begin to speak the same things.' Jesus-centred preaching not only unites us, but also puts everything else in its proper perspective. Dr Martyn Lloyd-Jones said,

> I can forgive a man for a bad sermon. I can forgive the preacher almost anything if
> he gives me a sense of God, if he gives me something for my soul, if he gives me the
> sense that, though he is inadequate in himself, he is handling something which is very
> grave and very glorious. If he gives me some dim glimpse of the majesty of the glory
> of God, the love of Christ my Saviour and the magnificence of the gospel, I can
> forgive him anything.[6]

Preaching with Jesus at the centre unites.

The growing emphasis on covering the full story of Jesus in our preaching is, I believe, very important. Preaching which explores the life of Christ as a critical prelude to His death draws us together because it reminds us that, as a real person and a real leader, Jesus – except for the fact that He was without sin – really was like one of us in every other way. Here is something I wrote in a little book I put together a couple of years ago: 'The programme of redemption was well under way before they hammered the first nail into His body. All those who related to Him pulling love and healing from Him were making perfect sense of the cross. His life was the only intelligent prelude to His death because He was a real person.'[7] The preaching of Jesus in His vulnerability, as fully man as much as fully God, provides a powerful bridge across our streams, across our denominations, and helps us in our task of mission.

3. The centrality of the cross

There has never been a period in church history when the cross was neither misunderstood nor misrepresented. Making sense of what I call the 'mechanics of the mystery' has always been a very hazardous task for preachers and theologians. But authentic Christian faith is inconceivable without the cross. The cross dominates the Synoptic Gospels and the early letters of the apostles. To quote John Stott,

> The fact that the cross became the Christian symbol and the Christians stubbornly refused in spite of the ridicule to discard it in favour of something else less offensive can only have one explanation. It means that the centrality of the cross originated in the mind of Jesus Himself. What precisely happened when Jesus died and how precisely we understand the nature of that awful, incredible and redemptive death is always going to be a subject of debate and theological discourse. But the reality of His death and its central place in the programme of redemption is the given which draws us together.[8]

As Leon Morris reminds us, 'The New Testament consistently bases our redemption on the payment of the price in the death on Calvary.'[9] This story of the centrality of the cross unites us.

In a culture which does not readily accept the idea of sin and sinfulness, preaching the cross will increasingly be a challenge for us. In the light of the post-Freudian analysis which suggests that there is no such thing as guilt but only 'a sense of guilt', the preaching of the cross can be rather out of tune with our culture. But we must be persistent in saying that there is a thing called sin and that the cross is given in order that we may respond to it.

4. Transformation

The Bible, it has been said, was not given to inform us but actually to transform us. Authentic preaching is shaped by the mandate of the Great Commission to make disciples of all people (Matthew 28:16–20), to lead all people into obedience to the gospel (Romans 16:26). I want to suggest that there is only one thing worse than opposition to the gospel, and that is indifference to the gospel. Transformation is the cornerstone of what it means to have a transformed society – for through it a new world-view comes into being. Our insistence on the transformation of the individual – 'If anyone is in Christ, he is a new creation . . .'[10] – will unite us in our preaching across the streams. We must hold on to it for dear life.

There are a number of reasons why we might be tempted to abandon it – it feels rather individualistic, rather pietistic, rather 'otherworldly', rather deprecating, even 'old hat'; it leaves us open to ridicule and connects us with those people who talk about 'being born again'. But we must not abandon it. The starting point to a transformed world is transformed people. It begins with people who acknowledge their guilt, their sin and, through the work of the cross, the possibility of change. The truth that God through Christ wants to do a work of transformation must continue to unite us in our preaching. It has been a distinctive throughout our tradition, although it has at times aroused very different expectations in terms of a response. We believe that God's Word is like a hammer, which breaks up resistance. We believe that through the Spirit people are changed from sinners to those who by God's grace are adopted into the family of God. We believe that the Word engenders a changed world-view and behaviour, which we call discipleship, and generally this has significant implications for us in terms of moral issues which flow from that lifestyle. And we believe that this transformation leads to the renewal of our communities – perhaps even their revival.

The concept of 'revival' can be a divisive one. I often think of it as God replenishing or refurbishing society – it is never going to be about achieving an Utopian ideal. I remember on one occasion at Spring Harvest bumping into a man who asked me if I remembered him. I apologised because I didn't, but he reminded me, 'You met me when you were on tour. You came to my town and you prayed for me . . .' As he was saying the words, in my mind I was finishing off the sentence '. . . and I was healed', but his actual words were, 'And I got taken to the hospital . . .' OK, I thought, 'Fair enough, you win some, you lose some.' The story didn't end there, however, because I met up with him again a couple of days later. This time he was with some people from his local church. He introduced me by saying, 'This is Joel. He prayed for me and I had to go to the hospital', and they all fell about laughing. 'Listen,' I said, 'I know I prayed for you and you had to go to hospital. But can you imagine what would have happened if I hadn't prayed? You would be a dead man!' I wonder if revival is a little like that. It comes to wipe the mark of sin off our society through the Church. This is one of the aspirations of preaching that unites. We all have the desire that, through the preaching of His Word, God would bring about the transformation of individuals so that society would be brought to a place of renewal, and that the forces of death and decay will be pushed back and rendered powerless – at least for a while.

5. Missions

The good news about Jesus is inevitably news about God's mission in the world and, quite frankly, even where all of us are fully agreed about this, not all of us are fully involved. Mission is the natural overflow of a message married to future hope, and future hope imposes on all of us a mindset of global proportions. Nobody can think or preach about a Kingdom that will ultimately subdue all kingdoms and cultures, which does not in and of itself have a global outreach in this present world. We may express it differently and it may resonate more powerfully in some places than in others, but I find increasingly that this emphasis on the global dimension of our preaching is something which the Holy Spirit is stirring up and is therefore attracting increasing attention. Preaching which sets our relationship with Christ in a global context has a way of drawing us into a consciousness that we are more than church attenders: we are people of an expanding Kingdom. Preaching which unites sets us free from our denominational traps and boxes in order to allow us to think in truly Kingdom proportions. I love Christ's story of the mustard seed, which we sometimes conflate with the story of the yeast which follows it.[11]

It is the yeast which spreads, the mustard seed grows. And it grows into a tree on which the birds of the air come and perch. This liberal, expansive and inclusive nature of the Kingdom has increasingly to become a major component of the message we preach.

The privilege of mission poses huge challenges for us – on this we are all agreed. Even those of us who are not actively involved in mission at home or abroad, will agree that we are implicated in the mission. We may feel guilty that we are not doing it, but we know that God will not settle for what is happening within the four walls of our churches. Preaching which evokes that kind of challenge continues to be a unifying Kingdom-building exercise. We can claim no exemption from involvement in the world. Missions for an increasing number of churches, therefore, now involves some element of social engagement, as was true of many of the prominent preachers of the last 300 years. Today more and more preachers are coming to realise that there is a significant difference between practising merely a social gospel and preaching a gospel with social implications. And this difference is something we ignore at our peril. In his great book about the conversion of Europe, Richard Fletcher identifies the factors that enabled the Christian Church to grow so phenomenally in its first 300 years, leading up to Constantine, in a pagan community which had no Christian vernacular.[12] His thesis on how they managed to transform Europe so substantially in such a short period of time with the message of the cross and the message of redemption is that they displayed visible signs of the God of the Bible to help people to take God seriously. They involved themselves in the world in practical ways. Missions for an increasing amount of churches, therefore, must pull in this kind of distinctive.

The passion we as evangelical Christians have for truth and the gospel is the stuff of which diversity is made. Our diversity will mean that the task of preaching will always walk a narrow path between passion and partnership. Preaching that unites will never be the kind of preaching that goes for lowest common denominators in an attempt to stifle differences, and often the preaching that attempts to heal our differences will find itself battling with subjective attitudes rather than theological distinctives. Some of what we talk about as 'theology' is actually just bad attitudes. Listen to Francis Schaeffer: 'What divides and severs Christian groups and Christians, what leaves bitterness that can last twenty, thirty, forty years is not the issue of doctrine or belief that causes the differences in the first place. Invariably it's a lack of love.'[13] This is a challenge to us as we consider preaching that unites. Thus, preaching that unites the streams is ministry that touches our hearts and attitudes as much as our minds and spirits. And more than that: it is preaching which also implicates us with all our imperfections in a story which is ever unfolding and in which we by the grace of God are also included. Whatever brand of church I go to, I never cease to be touched when I hear a preacher who is obviously speaking of the passion of Jesus with an authority drawn from God's Word and who places himself with all of his inadequacies, weaknesses and flaws within the grace of God and the slipstream of this great story of redemption. I can resonate with him because I sense something happening which is real and authentic because it is Word based and Christ honouring. Such preaching helps us to recognise that we are part of a great unfolding story and draws us into the awareness that only on this basis alone can we truly be united.

NOTES

1. Rob Warner, *21st Century Church* (Kingsway, 1999).
2. David Hilborn, *Picking Up the Pieces: Evangelicals in a Postmodern World* (Hodder & Stoughton Religious, 1997).
3. David Bebbington, *History of Evangelicalism* (IVP).
4. John Stott, *Evangelical Truth* (IVP, 1999).
5. At the Anglican Evangelical Conference at Westminster Chapel, 1996.
6. *The Best of Martyn Lloyd-Jones*, compiled by Christopher Catherwood (Baker Book Group, 1993).
7. *The Candle, the Cross and the Empty Tomb: Sharing Your Faith with Confidence* (Hodder & Stoughton Religious, 2000).
8. John R.W. Stott, *The Cross of Christ* (IVP, 1986).
9. Leon Morris, *Apostolic Preaching of the Cross* (IVP, 1964).
10. 2 Corinthians 5:17.
11. Matthew 13:31–33.
12. Richard Fletcher, *The Conversion of Europe* (HarperCollins, 1997).
13. Francis Schaeffer, *The Mark of a Christian* (IVP, 1984).

Chapter 34

CHANGING WHOLE CHURCHES AND WHOLE LIVES

Stuart Bell

When the Word of God comes into the life of an individual or into the life of a church it always brings change. Many of us can look back to times in our lives when God's Word has made a dramatic impact upon us. I was brought up in a Methodist home and my parents were determined to provide me with a good foundation for the Christian life, for which I am extremely grateful. As well as going to church five times on Sundays, from about the age of eight or nine I would accompany my father, who was a local preacher, to a weekly Bible study he ran. In those days we used to listen to reel-to-reel tapes and I can particularly remember being very impressed by the sermons of a Baptist pastor called Francis Dixon. As I listened to those taped sermons I developed a love for the Word of God and I can think of a number of occasions where a message that was preached changed the very direction of my life.

THE WORD OF GOD BRINGS CHANGE

As I begin to look at my subject of 'Changing Whole Churches and Whole Lives' I want first to give a very brief overview of how, right through Scripture, when the Word of God is proclaimed or pronounced or read, change take place.

(i) The Word of God creates
For example:

> And God said, 'Let there be light,' and there was light.
> (Genesis 1:3)

411

The Word of God brings something out of nothing.

(ii) The Word of God sustains
For example:

> *Sustain me according to your promise, and I will live ...*
> (Psalm 119:116)

When the Word of God comes into our lives and into our churches, there is a sustaining power.

(iii) The Word of God directs
For example:

> *Your word is a lamp to my feet*
>   *and a light for my path.*
> (Psalm 119:105)

The Word of God brings clarity and direction, even if it is just for the next few steps ahead.

There is a great deal of pressure upon church leaders today to find the latest formula which will bring the growth and maturity we long to see in our churches. We see the deficiencies in our particular set-up and we hear of amazing things happening in other parts of the world – such as the success of the cell church movement in Singapore or the move of the Spirit in Toronto – and we think to ourselves that if only we could just find that one key, we too would succeed in moving forward. I want to declare that, although it is important to learn and to receive from the things God is doing in other parts of our country and other parts of the world, it is the Word of God coming to us as local churches that will light the way for us. We need to feel the gentle pressure of the Spirit encouraging us to follow after Him and His Word.

(iv) The Word of God moves mountains
For example:

> '*What are you, O mighty mountain? Before Zerubbabel you will become level*
> *ground. Then he will bring out the capstone to shouts of "God bless it!*
> *God bless it!"*'
> (Zechariah 4:7)

When the Word of God comes, the problems and difficulties that seem insurmountable, begin to diminish in size.

(v) The Word of God brings healing

For example, the Roman centurion said to Jesus:

> '...*just say the word, and my servant will be healed.*'
> (Matthew 8:8)

The gospel meets the needs of the whole person.

In speaking about the power of the Word of God to bring healing into people's lives, I am very aware that in our present-day experience there is often a gap between what the Word of God declares and what we actually see. My wife Irene and I have, over the last three or four years, had to face a number of struggles in which we have agreed together that we had no alternative but to stand on God's Word. By doing so we have learnt a great deal about what it means to be a man and a woman of faith. I thought that to be a man of faith it was necessary to speak to the mountain and it would be moved automatically, and that it was necessary to speak to the sickness and it would go. We know this does happen in the Body of Christ in various parts of the world. But having spoken and not seen things shift, Irene and I have had to ask ourselves what it really does mean to be people of faith. Through my experiences I have come to believe that a man of faith is someone who starts the journey believing in God and every day he moves forward until he overcomes the obstacles that are before him; he presses through by daily trusting in God's grace.

(vi) The Word of God stills storms

For example:

> [Jesus] *got up, rebuked the wind and said to the waves, 'Quiet! Be still!'*
> *Then the wind died down and it was completely calm.*
> (Mark 4:39)

The storms that we face both as individuals and in our churches can be stilled as the Word of God comes into the situation.

(vii) The Word of God restores sight

For example:

> '*Go,*' *said Jesus,* '*your faith has healed you.*' *Immediately he received his sight*
> *and followed Jesus along the road.*
> (Mark 10:52)

When the Word of God is spoken, revelation begins to flow again.

(viii) The Word of God makes the barren fruitful

For example:

> Then the LORD said, 'I will surely return to you about this time next year, and Sarah
> your wife will have a son.'
> (Genesis 18:10)

When the Word of God comes into those areas of barrenness in our lives or in the life of
the church, our emptiness is filled, our sense of hopelessness is met.

When the Word of God comes, churches are changed, redirected, moved on and taken
into a whole new dynamic by the power of the Spirit. Rather than constantly hearing
about a Church that is haemorrhaging members and in danger of becoming extinct, I for
one am looking for a vibrant Church, a Church that is moving forward and impacting
society, a Church with answers to the questions people are asking. Across the world there
are some wonderful examples of churches that are experiencing dynamic growth. Sadly
from our perspective, they are often in places like Brazil or Korea, but my prayer is that
the Word of God will stir a similar passion in the churches of our land.

Hebrews 4:12 declares:

> For the word of God is living and active. Sharper than any double-edged sword, it
> penetrates even to dividing soul and spirit, joints and marrow; it judges the thoughts
> and attitudes of the heart.

I believe that we need to contend for the Word. For example, there is a lie out there – which I
think I swallowed for a while – that our young people can only take a few soundbites,
perhaps ten minutes of preaching interspersed with video clips. I can remember being
scared to death the first time I was invited to speak to the youth at Stoneleigh Bible Week.
Before I spoke, I asked the leaders what they were expecting and, to my great surprise, they
said, 'Give them an hour. Give them your best.' As I looked over the thousand young people
in my audience, to be honest I felt quite daunted and I was expecting it to be difficult to
communicate, but as I saw them taking notes and seeming to be enjoying what I was saying,
I found myself opening up under their responsiveness. I am not saying that we should not
use much more visual methods in order to communicate well with young people, but I do
want to say that I believe in the Word of God. I believe that it is powerful, sharper than a
double-edged sword, that it penetrates even to dividing soul and spirit, joints and marrow,
and that it judges the thoughts and attitudes of our hearts. I want to go on record as saying
that I believe the Bible is an incredibly powerful Book! It is life. Sometimes I find I have to
retrace the attitudes of my boyhood days when, in simple faith, it was as though the Word
was alive to me. I want to get back to the refreshing clarity of God's Word.

I believe that God's Word brings change. Through the Word of God things are created and sustained; direction is found; mountains are moved; sicknesses are healed; storms are stilled; eyes are opened; the barren become fruitful; and whole churches are changed and blessed.

LOOKING FOR CHANGE

It is one thing to declare that the Word of God brings change but, if we really are to make a difference, it is important, particularly at leadership level, to begin to focus on the specifics of what needs to be changed. We are looking for momentum and change in all areas of the church, and we are also looking to see a maturing of every believer, which can be a difficult goal to achieve. Sometimes we get into a maintenance mentality, where we are content simply to hold our own, but as leaders we have a responsibility to ensure that we are moving forward.

I believe we need to be looking for change in the following five areas:

1. Looking to see a greater sense of unity

So often our churches have been scarred by division, schism and broken relationships. For twenty years in Lincoln I have been seeking to walk in unity with all those who love the Lord and, although it has not always been easy, I do believe that the investment has been worth it. In our local churches I believe that through our preaching and teaching we can at least begin to develop an environment in which unity becomes possible. We do this by determining on a regular basis to bring the main themes of Scripture to our people which build a sense of who we are in Christ, and that may mean not allowing ourselves to be side-tracked by our own personal hobby horses or personal 'soapboxes'.[1] Through our preaching we need to build a greater sense of unity.

2. Looking to see a greater measure of maturity

If we look closely at Paul's letters to the churches, we see very clearly that there were two sides to his teaching: there was both the doctrine and the practice. If we are to see a greater maturity among our people, we too must ensure that our teaching is not just theoretical but is earthed in its practical outworking.

In Ephesians 4:15 Paul writes:

> *Instead, speaking the truth in love, we will in all things grow up into him who is the Head, that is, Christ.*

Reflecting on the picture of the Body of Christ, so often there is a breakdown of communication between the head and the body, which, as we know, is caused by sin. We need to make sure that, both as individuals and as churches, we keep connected to Christ who is the Head. In our physical bodies it is so often where the parts of the body join that pain occurs – perhaps through a disease like arthritis or through dislocation – and this is also true of the Body of Christ. So often there is disunity at the places where the parts of the Body join together. As we bring the full counsel of God to the Body through our preaching and teaching, I believe we will bring healing to those places of dislocation. Although it is sometimes a painful business, the Word of God brings order back into the Body.

In this issue of seeing a greater maturity among the Body of Christ, I believe that our attitudes as leaders are so important. If we are looking for maturity in the church, it has to begin with maturity at leadership level.

I remember having a really bad Monday some years ago, when within minutes of arriving at the church office I had set the tone for the day and everybody was enjoying my depression. By midday I knew that we weren't really getting anywhere and so, trying to find a way out, I suggested we all go for a pizza. The problem was compounded by the fact that the service at the restaurant was bad, the food was late in coming, the coffee was tepid, and now I was moaning about British restaurants and service. What I had already brought into the church life, I had now brought into the pizza place. Eventually we returned to the office, a pretty miserable group.

It wasn't long before I felt God putting His spotlight on my attitude and on the way that as a leader I had not set the right agenda, and I became convicted that, as well as saying sorry to the Lord, which is sometimes a relatively easy thing to do, I needed to apologise to the staff members individually. At the time Chris Bowater was leading worship at the church and, as he is always nice, I thought I would start with him! As expected, he was very gracious, responding to my apology with some comment like, 'We all have our off days.' I gradually made my way down the list, leaving one person to the end because I guessed what his response would be. After explaining that I was sorry for the way I had behaved, there was a short silence before he said, 'Well, you should be.' Although a number of retorts came swiftly to mind with regard to his attitude I realised I had a choice to make. Was I really sorry? Or was I just trying to salve my guilty conscience? Knowing I was really sorry, I accepted his rebuke. Later, as I reflected further, I said to the Lord, 'Lord, I am genuinely sorry because if I am looking for maturity in the church, then how I conduct myself on a Monday morning and throughout the week with staff and others with whom I deal, is so vitally important.' I cannot be on a platform talking about who we are in Christ, if I cannot bring a leadership team into a positive place in our working life together. Now I am not saying that we shouldn't be able to act normally with our fellow leaders, but I am saying that we have a responsibility to set the tone for our dealings together. We are looking for change, we are looking for growth, we are looking for maturity.

I am not always convinced that as preachers we always understand the power of the preaching we bring to transform life. Recently I read the following statement by W.E. Sangster:

Preaching is a constant agent of the divine power by which the greatest miracle God ever works is wrought and wrought again. God uses it to change lives. It is hard for any mortal to tell either of himself or of others what forces have worked upon him to issue in some dramatic change of life but many affirm that the occasion and no small part of the cause was one sermon.[2]

Doesn't that cast a different light on the sermons we preach each Sunday? What we proclaim can bring change: it can redirect a person; it can cause a mountain in a person's life to be moved; through it a family can be saved; someone bent on a course of destruction can be diverted. What an incredible honour it is to be able to preach the Word of God! I never cease to be amazed when people come and tell me remarkable stories of how their lives have been impacted through sermons I have preached. Isn't it great that such life-change is not dependent on our words or our illustrations but on the dynamic of the Word and the impartation of the Holy Spirit!

3. Looking for greater growth numerically

There seems to be something in the British mentality that says 'small is good'. We think that big churches are OK in other parts of the world but we tell ourselves that it is more important for us in the UK to see purity and maturity in our congregations than have an emphasis on numbers. However, I actually genuinely believe that quality control is not to do with size. I believe that God intends that there should be large and influential churches in our land, and that going for quantity does not mean giving up on quality.

Sometimes I think we forget that in the New Testament numerical growth is often linked to the power of the Word of God. Taking the example of Antioch there are a number of verses which refer to strong numerical growth:

- *…and a great number of people believed and turned to the Lord* (Acts 11:21)
- [Barnabas] *was a good man, full of the Holy Spirit and faith, and a great number of people were brought to the Lord* (Acts 11:24)
- *So for a whole year Barnabas and Saul met with the church and taught great numbers of people* (Acts 11:26).

Later, in Acts 13:49, a link is made between numerical growth and the spread of the Word, '*The word of the Lord spread through the whole region.*' I believe that as we preach and teach the Word of God, we can expect that our churches will begin to grow numerically.

There are some thrilling things happening in our country. I know of a little church in Peterborough, for example, that currently has over 300 people on an Alpha course. I believe that it is very important that, when we are thinking of maturity, unity and growth, we should not make the mistake of concluding that it is only possible in small groups or small fellowships. Although I understand the value of breaking down into small groups, at the same time I believe the Church is intended to grow. I believe that God intends the Church to be influential in our land again.

4. Looking for the Church to have a greater impact on society

Sadly in the history of the Church, although there are some notable exceptions, there has often been a separation between the biblical exposition of the Word and involvement in social issues. I believe that the two need to come together. Our preaching and teaching should consistently be preparing people to be witnesses and to make a difference in the world. In every sphere of society Christian witness is essential. As preachers, we must set ourselves to discover what the Bible has to say about our work and our involvement in caring for the communities in which we live.

In this regard I can highly recommend a book by Martin Robinson and Dwight Smith called *Invading Secular Space*.[3] Speaking about individuals like William Wilberforce, one of the notable exceptions to which I just referred, they make this very interesting statement: 'They formed part of a comprehensive view of society that essentially flowed from a biblical vision of society.' For this reason it is not surprising that Wilberforce was also a founding father of the British and Foreign Bible Society. In the thinking of such activists there was a link between the proclaimed Word and invading secular space, which I believe we should be promoting today. In *Faithworks Unpacked*, Steve Chalke writes, 'Too often in our eagerness to preach the gospel we have forgotten to look back and see the model Jesus left us, a model of compassionate involvement in the needs of communities and individuals at every level.'[4] This is one of the issues that I believe will need to be resolved if we are to see whole churches changed.

5. Looking for every individual to reach his or her full potential

For the Christian leader it is one of the greatest possible joys to see people reaching their full potential.

Very early on in my leadership experience a number of young people were converted at an evangelistic meeting we held. Very naively, on Sunday mornings I tried to take them to the Methodist church in which I was involved at the time, but they simply could not connect with it. So, with the full permission of the church, we began to meet for a discipleship group in the minister's vestry each Monday evening. What a joy it was to teach the Scriptures to this group of young people who basically knew nothing. On one occasion a small delegation of them came to me with the suggestion that they would give up their half-term break, Monday to Friday 10.00 a.m. till 4.00 p.m., if I would teach them everything I knew. That sounded a great idea until I ran out of material by Tuesday afternoon – and then we were in it together. Through that group I began to see the way in which individuals can be changed and transformed by the Word of God.

The discipleship group continued in the minister's vestry for a time, but it was not all that conducive an environment, so eventually, again with the full permission of the church, we moved to our living room. The problem was that these young people had not been told that we were just meant to maintain things, and the group grew and grew as they brought along their friends. The twenty became thirty and then fifty and then up to seventy and eighty. First we knocked down a wall in our house to make space but eventually a new church came into existence. The beauty was that years later the Methodist church came and blessed us, and very generously recognised that this had been a genuine move of the Spirit. It was such a joy to see people coming to know Christ and seeing their attitudes change, and then to accompany them through the milestones of their lives. I can remember thinking to myself that I could do this for the rest of my life! I didn't know that ministry was meant to be hard.

In those days 120 was considered to be about the right size for a church, and so I was very happy with my 120! But, reading the Acts of the Apostles during that time, I saw my 120 in the upper room, and my whole thinking had to change with regard to church size. What I am saying is that I believe in the discipling element – seeking to bring everyone to maturity – but I also believe that the church must grow. Our preaching must involve equipping the saints for the work of ministry – it will involve both instructing them and releasing them to do the work. Our preaching and teaching should not just be information but formation: it should result in something being formed in people's hearts and lives. Surely that was what Jesus did in His ministry: He would give information to the disciples, who would then go out and implement it, returning stirred and excited by what they had seen God do; then Jesus would bring redirection.

We need to be aware that many of the people who come to church nowadays are in need of the 'lift factor'. By that I mean that they need the gospel to bring hope and transformation to their lives. In addition, we need to realise that the issues people are dealing with today are very different from the ones they were dealing with twenty years ago. Young people, in particular, have no knowledge at all of the Bible and have no basic foundation in morality. They have been brought up to believe that anything goes, which poses a real challenge for us as preachers and teachers. We have to achieve the difficult balance of bringing the Word of God into their context, without being judgemental and without being restrictive. I believe we will be able to do this by teaching them about God's grace. Increasingly we need to understand that it is not just about the message we bring: post-modern people will also be reading the book of our lives. The challenge is to live in our daily lives what we preach from the pulpit, and that is not always an easy thing to do.

HANDING THE FAITH ON

In thinking about 'Changing Whole Churches and Whole Lives' I believe we have a responsibility to the generations yet to come. The ongoing preaching of the Word of God is dependent upon the next generation receiving it. There is currently much discussion about how we reach the youth of our nation and, I believe, rightly so. But I want to suggest that it would be wise for us to go back still further and consider how we address the issue of the Word of God for our children. In the Old Testament there is a very strong tradition of handing the faith on to the children, and I would like to ask the question, what are we going to hand on to our children? How are we going to ensure that they understand the importance of God's Word and that they are actually equipped to read it in an effective way? In this connection I believe we face two challenges.

The first is the challenge of our culture. The church is meant to impact culture, and not the culture impact the church. The reality is that, in so many areas, we see the reverse occurring. For example, our culture is telling the church that our young people are only able to engage with subjects for a short period of time. It is telling us that we must not be dogmatic on issues of truth. The culture is so often against us. In preaching a series on Corinthians recently I have been struck by how similar our situation today is to the one the Corinthian church faced. The church of Corinth had been impacted by the culture of its day, and to that church Paul consistently says, 'You are meant to make a difference.' The church has got to become counter-cultural; it has got to make a difference. We have got to have different values and different ways of doing things. G. Campbell Morgan said, 'What the church supremely needs is to correct the spirit of the age.'[5] Having imbibed the spirit of Corinth, the Corinthian church became anaemic and weak, and failed to deliver the message of God to the city. We need to heed the warning.

I think there is a particular challenge concerning the Word of God. In some places where I go to preach, I almost feel I am being looked down on because I have opened the Bible. But preaching from the Bible is the only way I know. I can't do it any other way. Sometimes I put on Saul's armour and try another method, but it always ends in disaster. The only way I know is to let this Book speak. That is the call of God on my life. And I believe it is the Word of God that has the power to change lives and churches: it has got nothing to do with me. In the face of the challenge being presented by our culture, I believe we need to be bold and preach the Word of God.

The second challenge with which the church is being faced is the challenge of how to hand the faith on to our children. Today we need to think carefully about how the Word of God can connect with all the departments of our churches, with all ages and with all cultures. I want to contend for the fact that our children need the Word of God as much as every other age group does. Of course, we need to communicate it in a way they can relate to, but our children need the Bible. I believe it is time to tell our children what the Lord has done.

In Deuteronomy chapters 6 and 11 there are two almost parallel passages in which the importance of passing on God's commands to our children is emphasised. After reminding the people of Israel of the great command to *'Love the LORD your God with all your heart and with all your soul and with all your strength'*, Moses says regarding God's commands:

Impress them on your children. Talk about them when you sit at home and when you walk along the road, when you lie down and when you get up. Tie them as symbols on your hands and bind them on your foreheads. Write them on the doorframes of your houses and on your gates.
(Deuteronomy 6:7–9; cf. 11:18–21)

There was a persistent burden that the message should be passed on, and I believe we should take up this burden in our generation. I want to see the children rise up. I was impressed by the Word of God at the age of about eight or nine; in some parts of the world there are child preachers proclaiming the gospel. Let us use every opportunity we can to impress our children with the Word of God so that they do not repeat the mistakes of the past. Let us echo the words of the psalmist, who proclaimed:

. . . I will utter hidden things, things from of old –
what we have heard and known,
* what our fathers have told us.*
We will not hide them from their children;
* we will tell the next generation*
the praiseworthy deeds of the LORD,
* his power, and the wonders he has done.*
(Psalm 78:2–4)

May the Lord help us all as we are on this journey together to see a maturation take place in our churches, and in every believer whom we serve.

NOTES

1. See also Chapter 33 'Preaching that Unites the Streams' by Joel Edwards.
2. W.E. Sangster, *The Craft of the Sermon* (Epworth Press, 1954).
3. Monarch Books, 2003.
4. Kingsway Publications, 2002.
5. *Messages from the Books of the Bible* (Hodder & Stoughton Religious).

Chapter 35

PROPHETIC PREACHING

Greg Haslam

IS THERE A PROPHET IN THE HOUSE?

Old Testament scholar and preacher J. Alec Motyer said, 'In their own day the prophets were headline makers and pacesetters in the national news, so if we find their ways tedious, unclear, less than exciting the fault does not lie with them.'[1] In their own generation the prophets invited considerable hostility. For example, Elijah was forced to go into hiding for two whole years to escape the wrath of King Ahab; Elisha was subject to assassination attempts from a hit squad; Amos had a deportation order served upon him; Jeremiah was buried up to his waist in a cesspit; and, according to tradition and history, the prophet Isaiah was sawn in two. Rather than being thought of merely as eccentric cranks or bearded poets, as some would like to think, these men must have been regarded as dangerous. Because the texts of the Old Testament prophets are hard to grasp as we read them in condensed form, many of us don't realise just what a mighty impact these men had. They were considered traitors and subversives in their time.

Many prefer to believe that the only prophets they are ever likely to hear are dead ones – safely locked away in history. However, God wants us to know that prophetic ministry is for today. He is still sending prophets to His Church. But the Church will only hear this prophetic voice when men and women seek God for this dimension to their ministry. I believe the all-important question each church, denomination and network of churches must ask is this: 'Is there a prophet in the house?' It is a question the Church needs to ask from time to time for, by and large, she has become a 'non-prophet' organisation!

I am also convinced that the major work of prophetic ministry is the removal of the blockages to a move of God's Spirit in our day and hour. It seems to me that the Church is always standing poised between backsliding and progress and that, therefore, there is always need for a mighty move of God to give us momentum and drive us into the future that He has for us. Certainly, we in the West, and in Britain particularly, have lost so much ground to the forces of secularism, materialism and compromise. The one-time leader of the African nation of Zambia, Dr Kenneth Kaunda, declared his conviction that: 'What a nation needs is not so much a Christian king on the throne, but a Christian prophet in the palace.' Even more vital, I believe, is that we welcome this ministry into the Church, for the greatest witness a Church can be to a nation is to receive, respond to, and become renewed by prophetic ministry in her midst.

I want to illustrate this neglected emphasis from the well-known prophetic messages of Revelation 2 and 3. The Letters to the Seven Churches are, of course, instances of Christ Himself speaking prophetically to His people through human agency, and they vividly illustrate the elements of this ministry in every age until Christ's second coming.

First, the backdrop of each of these messages was the commissioning and inspiration of none other than the mighty risen and ascended Lord Himself. This is Christ's voice to His people; He is the One who actively intervenes in His Church today, as He did then. He knows the life of each congregation intimately, walks among the candlesticks in every city and town, and therefore speaks authoritatively to His church. In Revelation 19:10 it says: *'Worship God! For the testimony of Jesus is the spirit of prophecy.'* This phrase 'the testimony of Jesus' is a description of what prophecy really is. It has been disputed whether the Greek uses an objective or subjective genitive, i.e., whether Jesus is the source of prophecy (the subjective genitive), or the terminus of prophecy (the objective genitive). Actually, we do not need to choose. Jesus is both the source of all prophetic utterance in the life of His Church and the One to whom it all returns in terms of worship and obedient response.

Second, we notice that each message or letter is addressed to a concrete situation in a real place and time, and therefore becomes God's 'now' word to a particular people, in that place and time.

Third, the Lord speaks in these letters in terms of both commendation and condemnation. This is the double-edged sword that is characteristic of all genuine prophetic ministry. It is both positive and negative. It removes obstacles and steers us in the right direction. It delivers us *from* hindrances in order to free us *for* victory. In the words addressed to Jeremiah, at the beginning of his decades-long ministry in the final years of Judah's existence, it *'uproots and tears down'* before it can *'plant and build'*.[2]

Fourth, the message is addressed to 'the angel' at each of the seven churches. Much ink has been spilt over the identity of this nomenclature 'the angel of the church'. One suggestion worth noting is that, since the word can mean 'messenger', it is a description of the senior leader of the church. Another is that it refers to some kind of invisible guardian angel of the congregation. Others prefer a more abstract interpretation and regard the 'angel of the church' as being the corporate spirit or identity of the church. Certainly every congregation has a different feel to it. God does not clone churches any more than He clones individuals. I find this final explanation very persuasive indeed, because what these messages do is literally unmask the present character and essence of the churches. The Lord knows each church's characteristic features and, more notably perhaps, He knows their besetting sins. He commends their redemptive strengths while admonishing them for tolerating destructive blockages to blessing. So, for example, at Ephesus there was a loss of first love and therefore cooled zeal in their lives. In Smyrna, seduction by false teachers was threatening the very life of the congregation. At Thyatira there was illicit sexual uncleanness that had caused many of God's servants to lose their purity and become compromised. At Sardis, there was spiritual deadness in spite of a superficial reputation for being alive. And the sickening lukewarmness of Laodicea made Jesus want to vomit. Thus, when prophetic ministry operates in church life, it is able to cut through camouflage and surface appearances to the reality of what is really happening, both positively and negatively.

Fifth, and perhaps most notably, these messages confront the spirit of Jezebel, that ubiquitous stronghold in Christ's Church. Many believe that this is the same heresy as that of the Nicolaitans, which is named in connection with the church at Thyatira. It is anti-authority – particularly the authority of God; self-appointed (*'that woman Jezebel, who calls herself a prophetess'*, 2:18); arrogant, and often strongly feminist and anti-male. It is always anti-Christ, because it is not only opposed to Christ but also supplants His place in the life of His people. Since, in essence, it is lawless and immoral, it manifests itself in excessive control, manipulation, intimidation and sexual corruption.

The chief role of prophetic ministry in the Church today is to confront the 'spirit of Jezebel', and anything else that sets itself up against the knowledge of God. This includes the spirit of witchcraft that literally controls many, many local churches, preventing anointed leadership from leading churches in the way they should go. Prophetic ministry is spiritual warfare of the most intense kind.

Sixth, specific direction and counsel is given: Christ calls the church to repent. He calls for lasting change. We are left in no doubt as to exactly what He finds wrong, and what He wants done about it. The church is to become a company of overcomers, in a potentially adversarial and defeatist situation. Through such prophetic ministry, Christ will not let His church remain, as it so often is, defeated and compromised.

Finally, the whole emphasis is repeatedly summarised: 'He who has an ear let him hear what the Spirit says to the churches' (2:7, 11, 17, 29; 3:6, 13, 22). Hence, prophecy is the living voice of the Spirit to His people living now. Our summons is to hear what the Spirit *is saying* (present tense) to the churches. This introduces us to the 'feel' of what prophetic preaching might look like in practice.

PROPHETIC MINISTRY IN THE NEW TESTAMENT

Some introductory comments on this will help clear the ground a little.

First, the gift of prophecy was obviously a fairly normative experience in the New Testament Church. I instance Agabus' prediction of a coming famine.[3] Prophecy is as practical as a special offering for the poor, because that was the action taken in the light of it. Later, Agabus warned Paul of forthcoming danger awaiting him in Jerusalem, a warning others took so seriously that they urged Paul not to go. Paul, however, inferred from this prophecy that it was an endorsement for him to do that very thing: *'I am ready not only to be bound, but also to die in Jerusalem for the name of the Lord Jesus.'*[4] It was also prophets and teachers who were used by God in the church at Antioch to set apart Saul and Barnabas, key leaders throughout its formative years, to be launched on the first apostolic church-planting mission.[5] Later, as a result of the findings of the Council of Jerusalem on the subject of circumcision, two leaders of the Jerusalem church, Judas and Silas, were sent back to Antioch with Paul and Barnabas to minister prophetically in Antioch.[6] In Acts 21 we are told, almost casually, that Philip the Evangelist had four daughters with a recognised prophetic gifting (v. 9). According to 1 Timothy 1:18 and 4:14 Timothy discovered or received a gift for his ministry at Ephesus, through the prophetic words of the body of elders who had laid hands on him. These hints are scattered through the New Testament to show us that prophecy was used to prepare God's people for the future; guide chosen individuals into the next phase of their ministry for the Lord; instruct the Church on the burning controversies of the day; and to impart spiritual gifting to the servants of God so that they might be competent and adequate to their task. This is its normative function, and all of these things are happening on a wide scale in God's Church today.

Second, unlike the writings of the Old Testament prophets and the apostles of the New Testament, the gift of prophecy is not infallible. The importance of this is underlined, for example, by Paul's words in 1 Corinthians 13:9: *'we prophesy in part'* where *ek merous*, 'in part', means 'partially' or 'imperfectly'. When we speak prophetic words today we are not laying claim to full-blown verbal inspiration. We prophesy 'in part', but we thank God for that 'part'. Furthermore, in 1 Thessalonians 5:19–22, Paul commands, *'do not treat prophecies with contempt'*, and instead, we are told to weigh them, rejecting 'what is evil' and 'holding fast to what is good'. In 1 Corinthians 14 the apostle provides a number of criteria for the testing of prophecy. We test prophecy as to its accuracy in terms of scriptural content and substance. We test its source of inspiration: is it human, demonic or divine? We test its edificational value. We test prophecy not to demolish or eradicate it, but with the positive aim of finding out what is encouraging, instructive and profitable in it.

The New Testament occasionally records examples of slightly inaccurate but still genuine and helpful prophecies, e.g. Agabus' interpretation and application of his revelation of Paul's forthcoming journey to Jerusalem. He prophesied that Paul would be seized by the Jews and handed over to the Romans. Visually, what he was seeing was perfectly accurate, but in practice what eventually happened was that the Jews who had seized Paul began to riot and the Romans rescued him *from* their hands – not quite the spin that Agabus placed upon it. Although this word could not be described as complete and accurate verbal inspiration, nevertheless it was substantially right and therefore helpful (see Acts 21:10–14).

Finally, we note that Paul insisted that his apostolic authority in writing Scripture took precedence over the gift of prophecy. Having encouraged the use of the gift of prophecy throughout 1 Corinthians 12–14, he still concludes in verses 37–38 of chapter 14:

> *If anybody thinks he is a prophet or spiritually gifted, let him acknowledge that what I am writing is the Lord's command. If he ignores this, he himself will be ignored.*

Prophecy is always sublimated to the authority of the written Word of God, the apostolic Word of Scripture, and teaching content of that canon. Nevertheless, it is still seen as operative, then and now, as an adjunct and supplement to scriptural revelation. It helps keep churches 'up to date' in the Holy Spirit.

The New Testament, therefore, teaches not only the *priesthood* of all believers – the watchword of the sixteenth-century European Reformation – but, as we might put it: the *prophethood* of all believers. In accordance with the prediction of the prophet Joel that in the last days '*I will pour out my Spirit on all flesh; and your sons and daughters shall prophesy*',[7] there is an extension of the franchise of prophetic gifts, so that their distribution crosses ageist, sexist, ethnic and social divides. The Holy Spirit is an 'equal opportunity empowerer', and the prophet Joel saw in advance this increase of the prophetic in the 'last days', which competent New Testament scholarship affirms as a description of the whole era from the first to the second coming of Christ.

WHY IS THIS GIFT SO VITAL TO THE CHURCH?

I have seven suggestions:

1. *Prophecy exposes us to a vital dimension of Christ's own ministry to His Church.* In Ephesians 4 we read:

> *This is why it says:*
>
> '*When he ascended on high,
> he led captives in his train
> and gave gifts to men.*' ...
>
> *It was he who gave some to be apostles, some to be prophets, some to be evangelists, and some to be pastors and teachers, to prepare God's people for works of service ...*
> (Ephesians 4:8, 11–12)

427

Historically, since the time of the Reformation onwards, there has been a line drawn under the first two ministries of apostles and prophets by many denominations, but that line cannot be successfully supported by the data of the text. All five ministries are being donated by the Ascended Christ to perform particular functions in the life of His Church throughout all time. We cannot omit any of these dimensions of ministry of the Word without suffering loss. If we delete apostolic and prophetic ministry, we are missing two-fifths of Christ's Word-ministry to His Church. If they are operating and being received well, all five of these ministries *'prepare God's people for works of service'*: they are equippers of the saints. They stimulate activity and productivity and, according to verses 12–13, they also promote unity among the people of God, *'so that the body of Christ may be built up until we all reach unity in the faith'*. In Ephesians 4:3 we are told that there is a unity to be *maintained*, but in Ephesians 4:13 we discover that there is also a unity to be *attained*. Before the Lord returns, a Church will emerge across the whole world that is characterised by incredible beauty and unity, but this is contingent upon these ministries being donated and properly received: to do what they are meant to do. Furthermore, the reception of these five-fold ministries will bring maturity to the Church, *'until we … become mature attaining to the whole measure of the fullness of Christ'* (v. 13). They help the church to grow.

2. *Prophecy conveys vision and purpose to the people of God*. Amos 3:7 expresses this succinctly,

> Surely the Sovereign LORD does nothing
>   without revealing his plan
>   to his servants the prophets.

Prophecy helps keep us up to date with God's plans and purposes. In the Old Testament, prophets are called 'seers': they are people who 'see'. Prophetic men and women are, in effect, the eyes and ears of the church. They see regularly what others don't regularly see. They help convey vision and direction to the church because the sovereign Lord does nothing without revealing His plans to His servants the prophets.

3. *Prophecy prepares and fortifies the Church for things yet to come*. We see this in the book of Ezra in connection with the rebuilding of the temple. Not only did the Jews face enormous resistance and hostility from their Samaritan neighbours, but there was also the danger that the empires to the East, that still held sway over Israel, might view their spiritual building project as a threat. In the midst of great uncertainty, this is what God arranged:

> Now Haggai the prophet and Zechariah the prophet, a descendant of Iddo,
> prophesied to the Jews in Judah and Jerusalem in the name of the God of Israel who
> was over them. Then Zerubbabel son of Shealtiel and Joshua son of Jozadak set to

work to rebuild the house of God in Jerusalem. And the prophets of God were with them, helping them.
(Ezra 5:1–2)

Zechariah and Haggai represented two very different styles of prophetic ministry: the one extremely poetic and colourful, the other very earthy, succinct and basic, in speaking what the people needed to hear. Together, both of these men helped orientate the lives of God's people towards the future: they reassured them that God was with them and was aware of their situation and able to help them. Though the building may not have looked much in comparison with Solomon's temple, nevertheless *'The glory of this present house will be greater than the glory of the former house'*.[8] Prophetic ministry helps us persevere in the face of danger and threat. In Ezra 6:14 we learn that the people of God finished the job. In contrast, perhaps the reason we often give up so easily is because we ignore the inspiration and hope that prophetic ministry can give us.

4. *Prophecy confirms and focuses the leadings that God's servants have already received.* In Acts 13:1–2, we saw the apostles Saul and Barnabas being launched into their ministry as church planters as a result of the prophetic word, and in Acts 21 Paul's ministry as an apostle being further directed through the prophet Agabus. From informal surveys that Rick Joyner has carried out at major Christian conferences asking delegates about their discernment of the Lord's will for their lives, it appears that even in the most vibrant Charismatic and evangelical congregations, only 10 per cent can affirm that God has spoken to them clearly, and of those 10 per cent, only 10 per cent can say they are actually now walking in the guidance God gave them. Rick Joyner concludes, this is an alarming statistic because it means that only one per cent of the Body of Christ know what they are on earth for! We need to heed the fact that the prophetic can help unlock the meandering cluelessness of many churches and individuals.

5. *Prophecy strengthens, encourages and comforts the Body of Christ.* In 1 Corinthians 14, verbs are piled up that relate to the functions of prophecy. We are told that prophecy 'edifies' (v. 3). The Greek verb *oikodomeo* was used in connection with the completion of a building, when every piece of masonry, stone and wood was in place. Prophecy completes and 'finishes' the church, so that it becomes, as it were, a show-home in the Holy Spirit. People should be able to walk into our churches and, as they experience the dynamic life of the congregation, say, 'Wow, this is what church *should* be like!'

Another verb is *parakaleo*, to 'exhort' (v. 3). Prophecy comes alongside us, so that we hear God's counsel and encouragement at this particular time in our personal history.

Then we're told it 'encourages' (*paramuthia*) (v. 3). It calms fears and brings peace to the disturbed and troubled, speaking closely to them with great tenderness.

According to verse 24 it also 'convicts' (*elenchetai*),

> But if all prophesy, and an unbeliever or an uninformed person comes in,
> he is convinced by all, he is convicted by all.
> (NKJV)

Prophecy marshalls the evidence and convinces the unbeliever, so that God's assessment or verdict on his or her life becomes irrefutable. We need this dimension in our preaching.

Furthermore, according to verse 31 'it instructs', from the Greek *manthano*, which means 'to convey knowledge' so that lives are changed. This is not just cognitive knowledge – facts and information – but experiential and revelatory knowledge, the disclosure of things that one could not have known. There is an intuitive dimension to prophetic speech that ensures that it builds up, stirs up, cheers up, cuts up, and 'gens' up the Church of Jesus Christ.

6. *Prophecy makes ordinary teaching and preaching extraordinary*. It helps the *logos* word to become *rhema* word; the *timeless* Scriptures to become the *timely* Word of God to specific people in a specific situation, imparting boldness and relevance to the ministry of the Word.

7. *Prophecy lifts every believer into the possibility of becoming a voice and not merely an echo*. Much of the Church and its leadership today merely echoes the current consensus of opinions in the world. 'Political correctness' has robbed the Church of her voice. But when we think of Joseph in Egypt, or Solomon before Sheba, of Daniel in Babylon or Jesus before Pilate, then we know there is a challenge to our generation to recover that voice again, and not merely to echo the status quo. Robert Brow has said, 'Prophecy is not just a question of a little word of building up or a few consoling thoughts. The building up is lifting men and women up out of the humdrum into the great movement of God in history and the *paraclesis* is the application of the Holy Spirit, the Paraclete Himself, to shake a man to the very core and stand him on his feet again to do exploits for God.'[9] That's why the prophetic ministry is utterly indispensable in the life of the Church. In short, prophetic ministry helps make whole churches truly prophetic in everything they do: their preaching, their teaching, their evangelism, their social action, their leadership style, their community life, their small groups, their worship.

THE DISTINGUISHING MARKS OF PROPHETIC PREACHERS AND MINISTRIES

I want now to ask what distinguishes prophetic preachers and ministries from other types of teaching and preaching ministry, for these are the marks that those who seek to be prophetic in their preaching need to covet.

1. *Prophetic preachers spend time with the Scriptures but what they receive is not just a result of study and reflection*. In nearly all the examples that I know of, the preaching of

prophetic preachers has substantial biblical content. However, what they receive from God often goes beyond the discoveries of the teacher. Whenever they stand up and speak, even during a regular expository preaching series, their preaching carries a revelatory note, in that they have overheard something from God, either in the preparation of their sermon or its actual delivery. It is more the case that the Word of the Lord has found them, than that they have found something in the Word, although in common with all preachers that is also their experience. As I said earlier, *logos*, the inscripturated, inspired canon of Scripture now becomes *rhema* word in the ears of the people. Everybody knows the Shepherd is speaking to His sheep (cf. John 10:4). It speaks directly to the needs of the moment. It sets things in relation to God's purposes, past, present and future. Prophetic preaching is marked by hindsight, insight and foresight so that people constantly feel themselves anchored in sacred history while at the same moment being made alive to both the present and the future. It leads people to encounter God in new ways. As Paul expressed it in 1 Corinthians 14:24–25,

> *But if an unbeliever . . . comes in while everybody is prophesying, he will be convinced by all that he is a sinner . . . So he will fall down and worship God, exclaiming, 'God is really among you!'*

God meets with people through such preaching. Prophetic preachers don't often announce that what they are saying is a prophetic word, but when people hear it, they know that it is. If preachers are truly prophetic, then their preaching nearly always comes out as prophetic in some way. Just as cows moo, sheep bleat and dogs bark, prophets prophesy: they cannot help it.

2. *Prophetic preachers have supernatural access to both God and to His people.* As those whom God calls and anoints to stand in His presence and hear His voice, prophetic people share both God's concerns and God's dreams for His people, and accurately report both. They are the eyes and ears of the church, and God opens doors of opportunity for them to minister what they have received. God opens doors that are seemingly shut to other people. They hear what others cannot hear, and they dare to speak what others dare not say. They are not, nor ever could be, mere 'yes-men', either by temperament or by calling. They have a large measure of emotional independence from the institutions and prominent people around them. They may be on the payroll, but they will not roll over like a lap dog for pay. Jeremiah 23:18 challenges, *'which of them has stood in the council of the LORD to see or to hear his word?'*, implying the possibility of access to a kind of cabinet meeting in heaven, to which the prophet is privy (cf. v. 22). There is therefore an intensity to prophetic preaching. The Spirit always attends it. It cuts to the heart with a sense of urgency because of its penetrating power and relevance. It fosters a sense of expectancy among God's people. These are the preachers people queue to listen to; these are the messengers who sometimes fill auditoriums; these are the men and women who

never leave their hearers unblessed. There is penetrating enquiry into the deepest recesses of their lives. It might be unpleasant at the time, but if the enquirer is God, it will ultimately bring great blessing.

3. *Prophetic preachers are people of strong passions and emotions, as well as strong convictions and insights.* They really *feel* the truth of God's Word. They are not mere lecturers, reporters or detached delivery boys. They care about the content. It has become a 'burden'. It is in Jeremiah's words a *'fire in my bones'*.[10] Like Hosea they feel the pain of God over His unfaithful people. It is not possible to be a clown and a prophet at the same time. Neither can a prophetic preacher be everybody's friend, in the sense of easy affability. But he is the best friend a person ever had, because *'faithful are the wounds of a friend'*.[11] Everything prophetic preachers say and do grows out of the soil of their own lives. They often have a history of rejection, pain and insecurity, as well as regular encounters with God and deep experiences with Him, as others do, but they are not mere recorders or secretaries: their personalities are caught up in their task and they have found that the nearer they get to God, the more truly human they become and the more truly themselves they can be. This is why a black preacher gave this advice to some seminary students about to embark on their life's ministry, 'Be who you is because if you ain't who you is, you is who you ain't.' Prophetic preachers are authentic people – not slick, creepy or sycophantic.

Prophetic people are thus bold with God in prayer: it is there that they learn to dialogue with God over great matters, as Abraham did before doomed Sodom and Gomorrah, and Jonah did regarding his commission to go and preach to the city of Nineveh. They dialogue honestly and earnestly with God about the commission He gives them, but they realise that in hearing from God they have a responsibility to people, and they will not shirk that responsibility. Prophets are likely to be unbalanced in their emphasis for a period of time, until the paint dries on that issue and the people have really understood what the Lord wants; then they can move on. Consequently, prophets are often quite 'difficult' people. They are commonly not easy to live with; there is nothing casual, trivial or petty-minded about them. They take God, His Word and His world very seriously indeed. They see the big issues and, as a result, they often set in motion huge movements of men and of God. Things happen around prophetic people; they do not remain the same. Prophets bring the fear of God and arrest the attention of men. They are not afraid to offend because the offence is in the message that they carry, not necessarily in them. Prophets tell both the Church and the world what neither of them wants to hear.

4. *Prophets carry enormous responsibility from Christ for His wider Church.* Prophetic preachers carry burdens. They feel uncomfortable about the very things everybody else feels at ease about. Their burden has to be discharged even if it means interrupting their current preaching series, or indeed, never finishing it at all! Often, they simply await God's timing for a particular message. God may not be in a hurry. He may, perhaps, want

the preacher to prepare for it by extensive reading and prayerful incubation of what He is saying, knowing that when it is time, some are not going to like it. For the prophet, that is always the risk. John Goldingay says, 'Prophets may bring good news, or bad news, but if it is good news they are probably not telling the truth.'

Sometimes like Jeremiah they complain to God about this and try to give up this ministry, but they cannot. They are honest with God in prayer and honest with men and women in their speaking. They hate plastic piety and sham, falsehood and lies, in the Body of Christ. They help us all to truly see God again, a God who cannot be safely domesticated as our local pet tribal deity, club mascot or denominational emblem, but who is still the Lion of Judah, before whom nations tremble at His roar. Prophets are scary people because they represent a truly scary God. They are called 'man of God' in the Bible, a term denoting someone who utters words of fearful significance, often followed by 'signs' that put the fear of God into people. They expect results. Life doesn't become less complicated with prophets around, but it does become more exciting. Prophetic preachers re-kindle our otherwise jaded imaginations because that is what God sends them to do.

5. *The role of the prophet and preacher is by definition a gutsy and courageous one.* It is the twofold call of afflicting the comfortable and comforting the afflicted. It may prove dangerous and it will certainly not be universally popular. But such men and women tread on their own fears, and help others to tread on theirs. The prophet is a rooted person. In common with all Christians, his roots are in the past and also in the future. It is as though we have roots that extend up to heaven itself, to the final glorification that awaits us there, and this makes it impossible for us to settle for the 'status quo', which is Latin for 'the mess we are in'. Prophetic ministry prevents the Church from bedding down with 'the spirit of the age'. Why? Because this is the 'age of the Spirit', and the Church needs to be constantly reminded of that fact.

6. *Prophetic preachers are usually more truly themselves than most other preachers are.* Why? Because they have been liberated from the fear of man and have found their true identity in the Lord. Consequently, they shun pretence, time-serving and insincerity, and minister in a way that is true to their own personality, place and time. They know what they are supposed to be, and this conviction colours all of their ministry. They cannot be scared off or shooed away – they are not here at man's request in the first place. Since they are here by God's appointment and sending, everything they do and say is conveyed with authenticity and rings true to men and women of good heart and good will who know the voice of God when they hear it.

Walter Brueggemann writes, 'The task of prophetic ministry is to nurture, nourish and evoke a consciousness and perception alternative to the consciousness and perception of the dominant culture around us.'[12] We are to clear the ground of refuse and rubbish so that a new reality may be built in its place. Furthermore, prophetic preaching ministers hope. Somebody once complained in my hearing, 'You know, the trouble with these prophets is that they just go around building everybody's hopes up.' Yes. That's their job! And if there is one commodity the Church in the West needs most at this particular time, it is hope.

7. *Finally, prophecy sharpens the edge of proclamation so that it truly cuts deeply.* A mere series of Bible studies is not enough. There must be the powerful impress of God's voice. What God wants cut (Hebrews 4:12–13). It is possible for a preacher to make the Bible his God, and for the God of the Bible rarely to be heard. Prophetic anointing makes preachers bold and uncompromising. On the Day of Pentecost the one hundred and twenty disciples ceased being the slaves of public opinion and became instead the shapers of public opinion. They did not fearfully follow the trend, instead, they set the trend, until *'all Jerusalem was filled with their doctrine'*, as the Sanhedrin complained.[13] The prophetic enables us to illustrate and apply the Word with such pinpoint accuracy that our hearers are literally nailed to the pew. The prophetic brings the disturbing elements of Scripture into the predictable religious routines of church life, and grips people with a sense of urgency at the power and relevance of the Scriptures. The prophetic enables us to see the whole and not just the parts, so that we can at last see the 'Big Picture'. John Calvin said, 'Prophesying does not consist in the simple or bare interpretation of Scripture but also includes the knowledge for making it apply to the needs of the hour and that can only be obtained by revelation and the special influence of God.'

In his book *Leadership: Reflections on Biblical Leadership Today* Philip Greenslade gives this striking summary of the five-fold ministries of Ephesians 4:

> Without the prophet the church becomes a spiritless organization in which even apostolic work hardens into a new form of religious bureaucracy, and without the prophetic thrust the teaching ministry perpetuates cycles of timeless truth but is deaf to what the Spirit is now saying to the churches. Without a prophetic voice challenging God's people to lay down their lives for the world, pastoral nurture can easily degenerate. Evangelism, too, desperately needs to hear the prophet if its methods are to be as godly as its message, and if it is to avoid giving stereotyped answers to questions people are not asking.[14]

Therefore earnestly desire spiritual gifts, and especially that you may prophesy.[15]

Notes

1. J. Alec Motyer, *A Scenic Route Through the Old Testament* (IVP, 1994), p. 79.
2. Jeremiah 1:10.
3. Acts 11:27ff.
4. Acts 21:12.
5. Acts 13:1–2.

6. Acts 14:22, 32.

7. Joel 2:28 KJV.

8. Haggai 2:9.

9. Robert Brow, *Twenty Century Church* (Victory Press, 1970).

10. Jeremiah 20:9.

11. Proverbs 27:6 NKJV.

12. Walter Brueggemann, *The Prophetic Imagination* (Augsburg Fortress, 2001).

13. Acts 5:28.

14. CWR, 2002.

15. 1 Corinthians 14:1.

Chapter 36

PENTECOSTAL AND BLACK PREACHING

Doug Williams

The title for this chapter may be somewhat misleading as not all Pentecostals are black, and not all Pentecostals can preach! In many ways the actual style and approach of both black and white Pentecostals share a number of dynamics, but they are also very diverse – as diverse as the individuals they represent. As a Pentecostal preacher my best understanding of preaching came from a Baptist. Charles Haddon Spurgeon said,

> However learned, godly and eloquent a minister may be, he is nothing without the
> Holy Spirit. The bell in the steeple may be well hung, fairly fashioned, and of
> soundest metal, but it is dumb until the ringer makes it speak. And in like manner the
> preacher has no voice of quickening for the dead in sin, or of comfort for living
> saints, until the divine spirit gives him a gracious pull, and bids him speak with
> power. Hence the need of prayer from both preacher and hearers.

In my background research I tried to find out as much as I could about preaching in both Africa and the Caribbean but, despite the fact that there have been great preachers in both these contexts, it is an area that has clearly not been subject to much research. For that reason I will be drawing mostly on the African-American context which is well documented. Inevitably the following account will be a somewhat myopic view of Pentecostal and Black Preaching from my own experience and personal encounters.

THE HISTORICAL BACKDROP

In his excellent little book called *History of the Church in Africa*[1] Jonathan Hildebrandt has collected an intriguing amount of information about the emergence of Christianity in

Africa. It is his contention that, despite the commonly held belief that the gospel's introduction to Africa is a recent one, this perception is built on a limited understanding. He points out that 'Christians in Africa in 1875 could be counted in their tens of thousands', which casts a new light on the idea that the nineteenth-century missionaries were introducing the gospel to Africa for the first time.

In terms of the biblical history of black preaching I could find very little concrete information, but there are a few hints. The first of these is in Acts 8:26ff. which records the Ethiopian eunuch's powerful encounter with the gospel and his subsequent return home. Since it is generally agreed by scholars that he was a governor in Nubia, this was almost certainly the first introduction of the gospel into Africa.

There are two other references in the New Testament which may shed light on black preaching. We are told about church planters from Cyrene in North Africa[2] and about Apollos. Although Apollos is clearly identified as a Jew, he is described as a 'native of Alexandria'. If Apollos' North African roots are accepted, then comments about his preaching skills may be of real interest, especially for this study.

> Meanwhile a Jew named Apollos, a native of Alexandria, came to Ephesus. He was a
> learned man, with a thorough knowledge of the Scriptures. He had been instructed in
> the way of the Lord, and he spoke with great fervour...
> (Acts 18:24–25)

Although there is nothing to suggest that the African context for his study and development influenced his style and delivery, there is no doubting that the man could preach!

Church tradition also provides us with a few interesting details which may suggest evidence of black preaching. According to tradition the Church in Egypt was started through the missionary activity of John Mark and the Coptic historians even claim to be able to cite his first convert as Anianus the cobbler. Furthermore, we know that significant numbers of Christian believers gathered at the church of Baucalia in Alexandria, and there are records of a Christian gathering to celebrate Easter on 26 April 68 where, as a result of a riot instigated by the pagans but fuelled by the Roman prefect, John Mark was actually martyred.

We also know that during the second and third centuries a very important school developed at Alexandria. Called the Catechetical School of Alexandria, it was a theological training centre – in fact, Africa should probably be credited as having the first Bible Institute in the history of the Church! Unfortunately, I could find no information about the preaching classes that were held there, but the college did have some very significant principals – among them the great church fathers Clement (d.c. 215) and Origen (185–254). During this era there were also other important African church leaders, including Tertullian (c. 155–230) and Cyprian (d. 258), men with considerable theological insight and influential communication skills. By AD 300 there were eighty bishops in Egypt and an estimated 250 bishops across the North African provinces, all responsible for whole districts of churches. In its first 300 years the Church made incredible advances in Africa. Unfortunately this information does not tell us much about the preaching process, but it does tell us there was a great deal of preaching going on.

Another factor which we must take into account in our understanding of black preaching is the influence of African folklore. From the earliest times, in every land and in every culture people have told each other stories, and some of these stories or folktales have been passed on from generation to generation, until they have come down to us today. They have survived for centuries because they are both entertaining and incredibly instructive. Henry H. Mitchell, who is the founder and director of the ecumenical Centre for Black Church Studies in Los Angeles, is convinced that it is significant that such stories as Aesop's fables and the tales of Uncle Remus have been handed down within the African and African-American traditions. These collections of stories are classical examples of the customary method used for the teaching and transference of community skills, moral values, and the insights and practices of traditional African religion. It is very important that these stories are part of our thinking when we are looking at the development of black preaching. The African rhetorical style which developed in the telling of these stories was very musical and was characterised by considerable audience participation. This is, I believe, extremely relevant as we look at the development of black preaching as it emerges in the American context.

Before going any further, I want to say a few words about the horror of the history of the black experience, because I believe it is impossible to understand black preaching without understanding what it came out of. The white theologian Ron Rhodes, who has undertaken in-depth study of black theology, black power and the black experience, has made the following very disturbing historical observations:

> Between 1517 and 1840 it is estimated that some twenty million blacks were
> captured in Africa, transported to America and brutally enslaved. The experience
> of these blacks – and descendants – serves as the backdrop for understanding
> contemporary black liberation theology.
>
> During slave-trading days, blacks were crammed into ships like sardines into a
> can, and brought across the Atlantic. Many died at sea from dysentery, smallpox,
> and other diseases. Some starved themselves to death, refusing to eat. To prevent this
> form of suicide, hot coals were applied to the lips to force the slaves to open their
> mouths to eat . . .
>
> The brutality shown to the slaves is among the saddest chapters in American
> history . . . black women were raped at will by their masters at the threat of death
> whilst their husbands could only look on. Families were separated as they were
> bought and sold like cattle.

For tax purposes slaves were counted as property – like domestic animals. Eventually, however, a question arose as to how to count slaves in the nation's population. The Congress solved the problem by passing a bill that authorized the U.S. Census Bureau to count each slave as three-fifths of a person. This congressional compromise resulted in what one Negro writer in 1890 called 'The Inferior Race Theory', thus placing the Negro somewhere between the barnyard animals and human beings.[3]

Because of the political and economic implications of slavery many of the Christian leaders of the time were reluctant to challenge the system. Some were even reluctant to evangelise the blacks, although there were a small number who broke through their reticence and tried to reach out to the slaves on the plantations. In the course of my research I discovered the following baptismal vow which was offered to black baptismal candidates:

> You declare in the presence of God and before this congregation that you do not ask for holy baptism out of any design to free yourself from the duty and obedience that you owe to your master while you live, but merely for the good of your soul, and to partake of the graces and blessings promised to the members of the church of Jesus Christ.[4]

The ambivalence of the Church over the issue of preaching to the blacks and baptising them had the unsurprising consequence that not many embraced the message.

The situation changed with the arrival of Revival evangelicalism in the 1800s. Henry Mitchell is convinced that the Revival preaching of George Whitefield, Jonathan Edwards, and William and Gilbert Tennents had a huge impact on the black slave community. He even goes so far as to say that he considers Whitefield to be the bridge between black religious sentiment and white colonial faith. He describes white religion before the Great Awakening as formal, cold and unattractive, but in the wake of the Revivalists 'the response to preaching became very fervent and dramatic, with extreme physical manifestations ... the instant attraction of Africans in the North and the South to Whitefield's preaching can be readily seen.'[5] Mitchell's view is confirmed by the following extract from the autobiography of an ex-slave called Gustavus Vassa:

> I saw this pious man exhorting the people with the greatest fervour and earnestness, sweating as much as I ever did while in slavery ... I was very much struck and impressed with this; I thought it strange I had never seen divines exert themselves in this manner before, and was no longer at a loss to account for the thin congregations they preached to.[6]

The fact that the Revivalist style of preaching became attractive to blacks, whose oratorical tradition, as we have seen, was rich in story-telling and emotional expression, should not really be of surprise to us. As well as responding to this enthusiastic style of preaching, some of the black converts took it up themselves, even preaching in the white churches, and often came to be regarded as some of the best preachers in their locality.

However, it was not long before the racialisation of American culture, in the period in American history known as 'Jim Crowism', resulted in the segregation of the blacks and the whites, which led to blacks developing their own church culture with a unique style of worship and preaching at the very heart of it. Ronald L.F. Davis says,

> In general the Jim Crow era in American history dates from the late 1890s, when southern states began systematically to codify (or strengthen), in law and state constitutional provisions, the subordinate position of African Americans in society. Most of these legal steps were aimed at separating the races in public spaces (public schools, parks, accommodations, and transportation) and preventing adult black males from exercising the right to vote. In every state of the former Confederacy, the system of legalized segregation and disfranchisement was fully in place by 1910. This system of white supremacy cut across class boundaries and re-enforced a cult of 'whiteness' that predated the Civil War.[7]

Theologian and pastor Leonard Lovett explains:

> New black churches were formed as black leaders sought to exercise their powers of leadership and to control their own affairs and destiny ... These native and original black churches emerged for several reasons. Some were initiated because blacks were encouraged to form separate congregations often under white supervision, due to the vast size of the mixed congregations. Several congregations were formed as a direct result of missionary activity. Frequent cases of blatant discrimination, and the desire of black Christians for equal privileges within mixed congregations also became the basis for separation. The disapproval by whites of black worship and lifestyle also played a major role in the separation of blacks from mixed fellowships, and in the founding of independent black churches.[8]

It is salutary to note that even some of the most prominent preachers of the time, including Charles Finney, struggled in this area of equality between the blacks and whites in their congregations. The disapproval of the whites of black worship and lifestyle also played a major role in the separation of blacks from mixed fellowships and in the founding of independent black churches.

This did not have to happen. Blacks and whites were enjoying each other's preaching and ministry. When Jim Crowism forced the issue of legal separation, 11.00 a.m. on

Sunday morning became the most segregated hour of the week – a legacy which remains in America to this day. These new congregations did mean, however, that black Christians developed a unique expression of their faith, and that is where we find some of the most interesting dynamics of black preaching emerging.

Common Methods and Dynamics of Black Preaching

Most students of black preaching are quick to note that the term does not denote an exclusive methodology. One of the professors of preaching at Harvard, Cleophus J. LaRue, says, 'Few, if any African-Americans, would claim that there is a single style of preaching that is faithful to all that it means to be African American, and that is appropriate for all its churches.'[9]

Having made this disclaimer, he then outlines the following methods and dynamics, which he believes to be common to black preaching.

1. Strong biblical content and the approach of Narrative Theology

Narrative Theology seems to be an attempt to reclaim the centrality of Scripture in modern theology. Borrowing Karl Marx's description of Scripture as 'the story of God', it focuses on drawing out the story from the narrative sections of the Bible. Outlining some of the positive contributions that such an approach offers modern theological debate and discussion, Alistair McGrath says that narrative is the main, but not the only, literary type in Scripture and to approach the text with this in mind is to be faithful to Scripture and to be less theoretical.[10] I believe that this theological method has some real correlation with the black approach to biblical hermeneutics and application. Because of their history and because of the rhetorical training and method that they have had, black preachers find this unashamedly text-centred approach extremely attractive.

The story-telling aspect of black preaching is very strong and very important. But it is not story-telling for story-telling's sake. It is story-telling on the basis of the secure biblical narrative: we are telling the story that God tells us. The preacher looks for the real story of the text and encourages an experiential approach.

One of the reasons, I believe, why there is such powerful audience participation when a black preacher speaks is because he sets the scene in the context of where people live. His preaching is not about theological abstraction; it is not an excursion into intellectual debate. It is saying, 'This is real life, and we have a God who stepped into the time-space continuum and has faced real issues. He knows what it is like to be flesh and blood; He knows what it is like to feel human pain.' The preacher makes the story of the Bible so real to his congregation that they can often actually see the application before the preacher articulates it. Preaching to a black congregation can be a little disconcerting because, if the preacher is doing well, they will say, 'Hallelujah! Praise God!', but if he is not doing well they will say, 'Bless him, help him, Jesus' or 'Come, Holy Spirit'! It can be a wonderful lesson in humility for the preacher. However, it is a great environment in which to preach.

Narrative Theology also affirms that God meets us in history. The story creates the opportunity for the listener to watch the outworking of God's sovereignty in the context of human limitation. Through the story of Job, for example, we are given a front-row seat on the story of his life. We see the limitations of human thinking; we see him trying to grapple with making sense of his experience. But his very real struggles are set against the backdrop of a God who knows that Job is a good and righteous man. This is an important dynamic for black preaching.

2. The creative use of language and the art of story-telling

Another very important aspect is the emphasis black preachers place on the creative use of language. They aim to paint such a vivid picture with words that their listeners are able to see themselves in the frame.

I have often asked black preachers how they have managed to preach so fluently and how they are able to get their illustrations to live in the way they do. They usually tell me that they have preached their stories to themselves first – in the shower or driving along in the car – so that they can find the best words to use. Black preachers are very aware that they only have one shot at their sermon and therefore it has to be memorable. It has to hook into the minds of those listening; it has to grab their soul and release enthusiasm in their hearts. The art of story-telling is very much a part of what black preachers do.

Many of the illustrations that are used in black preaching are very anecdotal. A preacher will talk about his home life scenario, or his upbringing, or tell stories about his grandmother. It may appear a little quaint, but people can relate to it. It resonates with their own story, engages their own emotions and expresses their own sense of reality.

3. The sense of prophetic conviction and divine encounter

Of course, this third aspect is shared with non-black preaching too, but it is a key dynamic of black preaching. The black preacher preaches with the conviction that what he is about to share is a word from God. There is the strong sense that he is preaching out of the overflow of what he has heard from God, what he has been meditating on in the privacy of his own devotions, what has been transforming his own thinking, what has absolutely changed his own family's circumstances. The black preacher believes he is bringing something from the heart of God. Out of all that is of so much value in black preaching, this is the one aspect that I wish all preachers would take from it. As preachers we must preach with a sense of prophetic conviction. We must not stand up in the pulpit and apologise for what we are about to say, nor must we content ourselves with giving a dazzling display of our eloquence and erudition. What we really need to hear and what we really need to sense is the heartbeat of God that speaks right into our current situations. That is what will make the difference.

Added to that there is in black preaching a strong sense of divine encounter, the fact that the preacher is working in partnership with God. People articulate this sense of partnership in a number of different ways, for example: 'being filled with the Spirit'; 'having an impartation of the Spirit'; 'feeling the anointing of God'. Many talk about 'the unction' and 'the anointing'. But what is meant is that there is an awareness that God is assisting the preacher not only in the preparation of his sermon but also in the actual process of delivery. While he is speaking he is receiving flashes of inspiration. There is a sense of divine deposit in what is being preached, so that the hearts and lives of those listening are impacted. Often, after I have preached, people come up and tell me that they were blessed by something in particular that I said. When they go on to tell me what it was, I can't remember having said it. The Spirit was at work so that there was a dual conversation going on. The Spirit of God was at work in the hearts of those who were listening.

In addition to these elements which Cleophus J. Larue has identified, I also see the following as key:

4. The immense pulpit authority of black preachers

In black churches an immense authority is afforded to those who have the honour of preaching God's Word. In some of the churches in which I have preached, they would not even allow me to carry my own Bible to the pulpit: there is the sense of being honoured and appreciated as a carrier of the Word of God. The preacher speaks as a prophet. He also speaks as a pastor, as one who cares.

For black pastors the role of care is not a professional exercise. It is not something they have learnt in books but through years of being in and out of people's lives, working through issues with them, listening to their pain and helping them to learn how to make their own decisions and take responsibility for their lives. I believe that the level of care that black pastors give their people is one of the reasons why they are afforded such respect in the pulpit. I can't be professional about what I do. It hurts too much when people hurt. It bothers me when their marriages are falling apart, when their children go off the rails, when there is economic hardship in their homes. Sharing our lives with our people provides preaching with a gravity that nothing else can give it.

5. The sense of family

In the black churches it seems as if the pastors and leaders of the church are everybody's father, grandfather or uncle. This sense of family is a very important part of the community security that encourages people to flow together. It has its roots in the tradition of extended family life which has been handed down through the generations from its origins in Africa and the Caribbean, and it is part of the survival technique of a group of people who in a very oppressive culture at large have had to find their strength in that kind of connection because it could be found nowhere else. Their willingness to fulfil the role of a parent is another reason why black pastors are held in such respect by their congregations.

6. Their willingness to pioneer

Many of our leaders have had to be pioneers. They have started independent churches and from very small beginnings have seen them grow into thriving churches in sometimes very difficult situations. We honour our leaders for their pioneering endeavours, as of course white Christians also do in their own context.

7. The context of life experience

Black preaching is informed by the black theological conviction that the oppressed condition of the waiting congregation cannot be ignored. If the Bible has the power to emancipate humanity, then what could be achieved if that power was unleashed against racism or slavery? It became the job of the community elders, the medicine men – the clergy – to make this connection and to make it plain. Although there were many issues of inequality and hardship facing blacks, the key element was fundamentally racial oppression. While it was true that there were also white people who shared some of the same hardships, at least they were free – they were not subject to laws that marginalised them to the periphery of society. Given the struggles of everyday life, when the blacks went to church, the preacher had better make sure that his preaching made some sense!

In the 1960s when black power issues broke out on the streets of America, liberal theologian James Cone was teaching theology to a class of mixed students and found himself faced with a huge challenge. Here he was teaching theology using the terminology, language and framework worked out by white theologians. Having heard his lectures, his black students were having to go back out onto the streets and were having to face burning estates and police violence, with people being herded into corners by dogs and the use of high pressure water jets. When they came back into class, they wanted to know how what they were being taught related to this experience, which forced Cone to address these issues in his own thinking.

At the time many black church leaders felt that those who were espousing a black power rhetoric had some very important things to say, but they were uncomfortable about some of the methods that were being suggested and about the use of violence. They wanted to say something positive about the equal worth of human beings, but they wanted to do it from a secure theological framework. It was really Cone's books on black power and black theology that gave church leaders the theological framework from which to express this solidarity while also affording them enough critical distance from the black power movement to be able to speak prophetically into it. Cone thus played an extremely important role in giving the black Church the language to express its affirmation of what was right in black power from a theological point of view.

445

As black church leaders began to explore the Bible afresh to see what Christianity had to say about the black experience of oppression, the Exodus story became incredibly powerful for them. The story of the Israelites became their story, expressing as it does the deep groaning of a people in oppression. There is always a danger when the truth of the Bible becomes too localised, because if the truth does not belong to everybody, it is not Christian truth. Some of the books I read on black theology can sometimes seem a little too focused on the black truth only. However, it is important to recognise that at the time it provided a very strategic way of understanding life at a particular situation in a particular time, and I think it should be honoured and recognised for that.

The context of life experience continues to be an important consideration for black preachers. Very rarely will a black preacher preach without undertaking some kind of cultural exegesis which examines the pressures and difficulties currently facing the members of his congregation. He will paint his reading of a Bible story in such a way that the people can see their own life mirrored in it. Although an important dynamic, it should be balanced against the fact that black preaching is, as I have already explained, very committed to biblical truth and a secure exegesis of the text.

8. Community building and corporate concern

Life in a community under pressure makes individualism a nonsense: we are in this together. In black preaching the gospel's call to a new humanity modelled through the church is a theme which is never far away. It provides the language of fellowship that is needed for group security and group support. I believe that it is this sense of solidarity that fuels the building of churches and wide-ranging community regeneration projects amongst the black community. But as I said in connection with my previous point, the flip side of this is the danger of projecting the idea that Christian community is exclusively a black issue, and we need to take care to avoid giving this wrong impression.

THE BLACK SERMON

The actual organisation of a black sermon is not too dissimilar to the homiletical methods employed by white preachers, although, as Henry Mitchell explains, it is less likely to follow the traditional structure: 'More black sermons are apt to consist of one single Bible narrative (with or without extended comments on the side). Thus the percentage of classical or traditional sermons – with text, exposition, and the inevitable trinity of points or applications, and climax – would be somewhat lower in the black total.'[11] In other words, the listener to a black sermon will not very often be able to understand it by identifying the introduction, points 1, 2, and 3, followed by a poem and the conclusion! This is not to say that black sermons are anti-intellectual, but they are different in intention. In black preaching we want people *to feel* as well as to think.

As black preachers we do believe that people should love God with their mind. We do believe that we should bring every rational and intellectual capacity we have to bear on the whole hermeneutical process – from the preparation of a sermon right through to its delivery and application – and that we should work as hard as we can in loving God with our minds. However, we believe we are supposed to love Him with our soul and our heart as well! We want the truth to be on fire! Not only do we want our people to receive instruction from our sermon, but we want them to *experience* what we are preaching about.

As well as being instructional, we want our sermons to be *motivational*. We want them to result in action and change. We want our listeners to be transformed by hearing the Word of God. While those who preach in the white context may set out with the same intention, perhaps the way this intention is expressed in the black context is rather different. The black preacher sets out to stir people so that their hearts are open and there is a free flow of unashamed emotion. This is not hype or emotionalism. It is an attempt to say that the experience that is being talked about can also be felt and responded to.

It is also helpful to understand that black sermons are often climactic and celebratory. Where in other contexts, the preacher might close with a review of his points and an application for the people to put into practice, in black preaching the conclusion can be explosive. Having preached up a storm, it is not uncommon for the preacher to just walk off the stage and leave the people to it. It can be quite an experience. This celebratory style is currently enjoying a resurgence among young black preachers in America. The sense of climax, as the sermon draws to its end, is often heightened by the traditional response of 'whooping' or 'moaning' or 'tuning' or 'whining', as it is variously termed. There is even evidence that some white preachers are now beginning to enjoy the powerful impact that whooping can have on their congregations and are seeing an increase in the diversity of their congregations as a result.[12] In my view it should be appreciated for the dynamic that it gives to the people who understand it and appreciate it, without others feeling that it should be incorporated into their own context.

When this celebratory style is combined with relevant content and good theological understanding, it is tremendously powerful. If it is not, it can be superficial. I always feel embarrassed when I go to a meeting at which there is very little content in the preaching. The preacher has used the black style, without having understood all the background that I have been seeking to explain, which is exegeting the rich heritage of black culture. We really do need to make sure that what we are doing is based in real life and has real substance to it and is not just an extraction, whether a black extraction or a white extraction. There can be no reneging on the hard work which is required if our preaching is to achieve its desired goal.

I like the idea that black preaching is celebratory. I think it is a valid expression of hope despite the negative circumstances in which many people have found themselves to be living. Despite their soul-destroying circumstances domestically or economically they can still access the anticipated blessings of eschatological reality. They can sense themselves living in 'the presence of the future', to borrow a phrase from Laing. Black preachers seem to be masterful at injecting that celebration and that sense of hope into often very dark and difficult situations. They are able to do this because they understand that the God who steps out of eternity into history is their God. They understand that He is also the Redeemer who has come to liberate us, to bring us our individual and corporate exodus experience. This is what the preaching of the Christian gospel should be all about. When people hear the message of the God who has come to liberate them, they are incredibly stirred and motivated to live in a way that honours Jesus in all they do, even in the midst of difficult situations, even while they are waiting for the social and political environment to change.

NOTES

1. Intl. Academic Pub., 2001.
2. Acts 11:20.
3. From an article by R. Rhodes, 'Black Theology, Black Power, Black Experience', posted on the Internet.
4. Quoted in *Divided by Faith* by Michael Emerson and Christian Smith (Oxford University Press, 2001), p. 24.
5. Henry Mitchell, *Black Preaching* (Abingdon Press, 1990), p. 32.
6. *Ibid.*, p. 9.
7. From an article entitled 'Creating Jim Crow', posted on the Internet.
8. From an article entitled 'Black Holiness-Pentecostalism' in *Dictionary of Pentecostal and Charismatic Movements* (Regency/Zondervan, 1989), p. 79.
9. Cleophus LaRue, *The Heart of Black Preaching* (Westminster John Knox Press, 2000), p. 9.
10. See Alister McGrath, *Christian Theology* (Blackwell Publishers 1994), pp. 170–174.
11. Mitchell, *Black Preaching*, p. 114.
12. E.g. Linda Jones, 'Whoop it up', *The Dallas Morning News*, Saturday 29 August, 1998.

Chapter 37

PASTORAL PREACHING AND TEACHING

Stuart Bell

The picture of the shepherd with his flock is a helpful one for us as we look at the subject of pastoral preaching and teaching. Pastor and people are on a journey together. It is not enough for us as pastors to confine our role to speaking or sharing at meetings: we must connect with people on their journey. Just as the need of the shepherd is both to lead and feed, so our task as pastors is to help our people on their journey through life – through the good times and through the hard times – being available not only through our speaking but through our very lives.

In our pastoral preaching and teaching we have three major tasks. First, as good shepherds we must set in good foundations that will equip and help people through their entire lives. Second, we must understand that as we preach and teach week by week people are at various points in their journey – for some in the meeting it is a moment of challenge, for others a moment of crisis, for still others a moment of change. It is not an easy thing to be able to identify with all the needs of the people and for this reason it is essential that we have a breadth of teaching and that we are very sensitive to the Holy Spirit. Third, we must bring people to a place of maturity by continually pointing them to Christ. We must equip the saints for the work of ministry and see people develop so that they are not trusting in us but are trusting in Christ. So many people start their journey with us feeling a measure of rejection, or feeling failures, or feeling that they have nothing much to contribute. Thankfully we are in days when there is a renewed emphasis on the Body of Christ in which every person is gifted and has a contribution: every person is a minister. Through the preaching and teaching of the Word we can see people come into their destiny, as they understand who they are in Christ and that they are unique and special in His service.

I want to look at four vital dimensions of our preaching and teaching of God's Word which will help us to fulfil these three important tasks. The pastor needs to know how to bring:

1. words of life,
2. words of freedom,
3. words of comfort, and
4. words of challenge.

1. WORDS OF LIFE

As preachers and teachers we need to have a growing understanding that the Word of God carries with it life. Every time we teach, every time we preach, our intention is that the life which is found in Christ should permeate through every individual member of the Church so that they begin to believe in who they are. It is the pastor's task to bring life. Hebrews 4:12 speaks about this dimension of the Word of God: *'For the word of God is living and active'*. Here again there are three aspects:

(i) The power of the word

All words have power – there is power in the tongue. The Scriptures teach that words can bring life or they can bring death. Of course this is true in terms of the natural world in which we live but it is even more so in terms of the way we handle the Word of God. Even if we are speaking words that are full of life, by our very demeanour we can actually be stating something different. As a family, in recent years we have discovered something of the power of words. As we have faced serious illness, we have received a great deal of advice – some of it helpful, some of it not – and have been the recipients of many people's opinions about why things happen as they do. We have discovered that the spoken word has incredible power, especially if the person is speaking in an official capacity. It is one thing for an ordinary person to voice his or her opinion but quite another for a hospital consultant to do so. In his or her mouth even an 'mmm' can have the power of death. The words that have been spoken over our family have not always been words of life. In part, this is a characteristic of our British culture. We Brits do tend to see things as half empty rather than half full; we do tend to see the darker side of life. But as Christians, and even more so as Christian leaders, it is important for us to recognise that when we lay our opinions on people we can sometimes bring death rather than life. As we preach and teach, we need to understand the life-power in the Word of God. It has the power to encourage, the power to build up. All of us can see what's wrong; all of us can talk about what isn't happening; all of us can point out other people's sins and weaknesses. Indeed, there are times when we need to do that, but I believe that what the Church in Britain needs at this present time is a good dose of encouragement and of life. People need to hear the words: 'you can do it', 'you will make it'. As preachers and teachers we need to realise the great responsibility we carry: every time we speak and teach we can be ministers of life because in the Word is life. We need to be agents of life. We need to give space in our preaching and teaching for the bringing of words of life. What a good thing it is when people of faith speak words of life: 'you will get through it'; 'God is with you'. People need words of encouragement – not just nice words but words that are full of potential and hope. Psalm 119:28 says, *'strengthen me according to your word'*. When Jesus was tempted and tested, He countered the attack of Satan with the words, *'It is written . . .'* (see Matthew 4:1–11). There is power in the Word of God.

(ii) The prophetic nature of the word

Our preaching and teaching should give room for a relationship between the Holy Spirit and the word. When the Holy Spirit takes hold of the word and applies it into someone's heart and life, it has the power to bring amazing change. The dynamic of the prophetic word has both the element of *forthtelling* and the element of *foretelling*. Forthtelling brings encouragement and strength, sowing into people's lives, while foretelling brings direction, challenge and destiny. People's lives are shaped by the prophetic word. We all, I am sure, experience times when the Word of God lights up to us – whether through another person or simply as we read the Scripture – and there is a prophetic dimension that gives our lives direction. This is, I believe, what our people need. Our preaching and teaching must have that prophetic dynamic of bringing direction and purpose, encouragement and strength.

(iii) The preserving word

The Word of God has the ability to assure our people that they are being preserved, being held, being kept safe and secure. In the same way that the Israelites in the wilderness received fresh manna each day, so there is a freshness about the Word of God which we preach and teach. This is a dynamic that is evident right through Psalm 119. For example:

> *How I long for your precepts!*
> *Preserve my life in your righteousness.*
> (v. 40)

> *My comfort in my suffering is this:*
> *Your promise preserves my life.*
> (v. 50)

> *Hear my voice in accordance with your love;*
> *preserve my life, O LORD, according to your laws.*
> (v. 149)

> *Your compassion is great, O Lord,*
>   *preserve my life according to your laws.*
> (v. 156)

Through the bringing of the Word people's lives are preserved, strengthened and blessed.

In my reflection on pastoral preaching and teaching I so often turn to Psalm 23. I like to think of this psalm as a day in the life of a sheep. Right at the beginning of the day there's a sense of starting it with the Lord, in relationship with Him:

> *The Lord is my Shepherd, I shall not be in want.*
>   *He makes me lie down in green pastures,*
> *he leads me beside quiet waters.*
> (Psalm 23:1–3)

We know times when we start the day relaxing in His presence, 'beside quiet waters', and it is good to be alive. But then there are the noon-day experiences when the sun has been hot and we are plain tired. *'He restores my soul.'* In the heat of the day the Word of the Lord brings refreshment to our lives. Finally there is the picture of those night-time experiences:

> *Even though I walk*
>   *through the valley of the shadow of death,*
> *I will fear no evil,*
>   *for you are with me;*
> *your rod and your staff*
>   *they comfort me.*
> (Psalm 23:4)

These are the times on our journey when we are confronted by the issues of pressure and of death. The pastor as the shepherd accompanies the flock through all the seasons of their lives bringing the words that give life. The Word of God is relevant to all seasons of our life. Sometimes the same word that is refreshing one person is challenging another. Sometimes as the Holy Spirit applies the teaching, some people are finding that it is giving direction or clarity about an issue that needs to be addressed in their life. Often the preacher and teacher is unaware of the stories that are taking place, and I find that highly exciting.

2. Words of Freedom

As preachers and teachers it is our task is to make sure that people are brought into freedom and continue to walk in freedom – to see people set free to become who they were designed to be. Again, depending on where they start their journey, the issues that bind people will be very different. Some need to be brought out of legalism or out of religious systems and brought into the life of Christ; others face the stark reality of being set free from all manner of things that have gripped their heart. What a joy it is to see people find freedom! My church relates quite closely with a group of churches called Betel, which originated in Spain and are largely made up of people that were once caught up in addiction particularly to drink and drugs. There are three of these churches now in England and they are seeing astonishing results in people being set free.

In the book of Galatians Paul writes about freedom in Christ. He challenges the Galatian church about changes that have crept into their beliefs and attitudes: they had come to faith in Christ and found true freedom but now they were making additions to the original message they had received. They were beginning to trust again in human endeavour and works. Paul has to speak very directly:

> *It is for freedom that Christ has set us free. Stand firm, then, and do not let*
> *yourselves be burdened again by a yoke of slavery.*
> (Galatians 5:1)

His heart is really stirred. They started the race well but they have been diverted from the pattern that was originally established. In chapter 1:6 Paul says,

> *I am astonished that you are so quickly deserting the one who called you by the grace*
> *of Christ and are turning to a different gospel.*

These people were turning away from trusting in Christ alone and lapsing back into the realms of the Law. Paul feels so strongly that in Galatians 3:1 he says, '*You foolish Galatians! Who has bewitched you?*' They have been robbed of the freedom that was theirs in Christ.

In these passages I see three marks of legalism, from which churches consistently need to be freed so that they remain in the freedom of trusting in Christ.

The first, which is found in chapter 1:6–10, is *heresy*. The Galatians fell into the heresy of believing that they were saved by human effort. In verse 6 Paul exclaims, '*I am astonished that you are so quickly deserting the one who called you by the grace of Christ...*', and then in verse 10 he goes on to ask, '*Am I now trying to win the approval of men or of God?*' They began by trusting in God, but now heresy has crept in and they have begun to trust in man-made rules and regulations in addition to the gospel, with the result that the traits of legalism have begun to grip the Galatian church.

The second is *harassment*, which is found in chapter 2:1–7. The Galatian church is under pressure, probably from the circumcision party, to fulfil obligations that were once required by the Law. Paul writes,

This matter arose because some false brothers had infiltrated our ranks to spy on the freedom we have in Christ Jesus and to make us slaves. We did not give into them for a moment, so that the truth of the gospel might remain with you.
(Galatians 2:4–5)

Outsiders are trying to rob the church of freedom. Most churches will have stories of how pressure has come to try and enforce the keeping of this rule or that rule. We need to resist this kind of harassment. Pastoral ministry will be on the watch to ensure that, having found true freedom in Christ, people continue to walk in it.

The third mark is *hypocrisy*, and even the apostles were guilty of it. Paul recalls how he opposed Peter very strongly on this issue:

When Peter came to Antioch, I opposed him to his face, because he was clearly in the wrong. Before certain men came from James, he used to eat with the Gentiles. But when they arrived, he began to draw back and separate himself from the Gentiles because he was afraid of those who belonged to the circumcision group. The other Jews joined him in his hypocrisy, so that by their hypocrisy even Barnabas was led astray.
(Galatians 2:11–13)

Ralph Keiper has written a paraphrase of this passage that encapsulates the hypocrisy that was going on: 'Now when the no-ham-eaters have come from Jerusalem you have gone back to your kosher ways, but the smell of ham still lingers on your breath. You are most inconsistent, you are compelling Gentile believers to observe Jewish law which can never justify anyone.' The challenge is to remain in the grace of Christ and ensure that we do not fall into this type of hypocrisy.

It is interesting to look at Paul's journey into life, for this was a journey out of legalism into freedom, which he wanted all people to enjoy. In Galatians 1 Paul says,

For you have heard of my previous way of life in Judaism, how intensely I persecuted the church of God and tried to destroy it. I was advancing in Judaism beyond many Jews of my own age and was extremely zealous for the traditions of my fathers.
(Galatians 1:13–14)

There are some key words here which can help us to discern the presence of legalism in our fellowships and churches. The first one points to an intensity of action. Paul says, '*how **intensely** I persecuted the church of God*'. I am always a little suspicious when there is a drivenness, an intensity to change things. The second word indicates a desire for 'advancement': '*I was **advancing in Judaism**'*. There is a sense of wanting to be the best, a competitiveness, a need to advance *'beyond many Jews of my own age'*. Another indication is the word 'zealous': Paul describes himself as being *'extremely **zealous** for the traditions of my fathers'*. It is not a bad thing to be zealous, nor it is not a bad thing to have tradition, but, put the two together, and it is a short step from being zealous to being 'a zealot'. Paul knew what it was to strive and to push, but he says, *'you have heard of my previous way of life'*. All these things characterised his previous life: now he has changed.

> *But when God, who set me apart from birth and called me by his grace, was pleased to reveal his Son in me, so that I might preach him among the Gentiles, I did not consult any man . . .*
> (Galatians 1:15–16)

He has moved away from that compulsion, that intensity, that desire for advancement. He is a changed man. From verse 15 onwards there is a noticeable shift in the way Paul writes, which highlights the freedom he now knows. There is now a relational aspect (v. 16). Up until he met with the Lord Paul was a self-made man, and although on the surface it looks as if he is still non-relational (verse 16: *'I did not consult any man'*), yet in verse 18 he says,

> *Then after three years, I went up to Jerusalem to get acquainted with Peter and stayed with him fifteen days.*

The self-made man now needs others. He has moved on in his journey and the new freedom he has found requires relationships to be built. He has moved into a relational dimension.

Secondly, he begins to make himself accountable. In chapter 2 he says,

> *I went in response to a revelation and set before them the gospel that I preach among the Gentiles. But I did this privately to those who seemed to be leaders, for fear that I was running or had run my race in vain.*
> (Galatians 2:2)

He became accountable to others in the things that he spoke and in the things that he did.

Thirdly, he became dependent. He says,

> *For God, who was at work in the ministry of Peter as an apostle to the Jews, was also at work in my ministry as an apostle to the Gentiles.*
> (Galatians 2:8)

No longer is he boasting about himself as the 'Pharisee of Pharisees' but he is boasting that his dependence is totally upon the Lord. It is from Him that he gets his strength and his sustenance.

The fourth word that indicates a shift in his attitudes is 'recognised' in verse 9:

> *James, Peter and John, those reputed to be pillars, gave me and Barnabas*
> *the right hand of fellowship when they recognised the grace given*
> *to me.*

Godly men have recognised the grace in his life.

In our churches we want people to be relational; we want them to be accountable; we want them to be dependent upon the Lord; and we want the grace upon their lives to be recognised and endorsed by godly people. In the Galatian church, where there was once the freedom of the grace of God, there was now heresy, harassment and hypocrisy. And Paul challenged it. I believe the pastor's task is from time to time to ask the question: are we as a church moving in the freedom that Christ bought for us on the cross? Or have we drifted away from that freedom? A few very simple supplementary questions can help us discover the truth, such as: are our people free to laugh? I have found that legalistic people so often don't have a sense of humour. There is a hardness about them and it is difficult to get to the real person. They deliver words, but they don't share their heart. I strongly believe there is a need for our people to be free to laugh. I also believe that they need to be free to cry. I heard Rob Parsons say that he cries much more now as an adult than he ever did as a child. The freedom that Christ brings liberates us in every area of our lives – physically, spiritually, emotionally – so that we are free to be ourselves. There were times in my life when I didn't feel I could be free and happy to be who I am, but it is important for each of us to get to that place. But what about the people in our churches? Are they free? Are they free to laugh? Are they free to cry? Are they free to befriend and to relate? Are they free to be themselves? Are they free to explore – and here's the big question in our churches – are they free to fail? Of course, all these things apply to ourselves as well. The Word of God and the Spirit of the Lord bring us into freedom.

3. WORDS OF COMFORT

There is a great need today for preachers and teachers to be able to bring life and help to people who are in need of comfort. As preachers and teachers we need to make room consistently to bring words of comfort. Our task is to bring God's Word into every area of people's lives. In the book of Isaiah there are a number of times when it was appropriate for the prophet to speak tenderly and bring words of comfort to God's people Israel. Isaiah 40 opens with these words:

Comfort, comfort, my people,
  says your God.
Speak tenderly to Jerusalem . . .
(Isaiah 40:1)

It is so important for us as pastors and teachers to get hold of this little phrase 'Speak tenderly'. There are times when there needs to be a tender handling of the Word of God. Just by connecting with a children's cancer unit, my wife and I have suddenly become aware of how much pain and hurt there is in our world. I think of a mother who has been in hospital for perhaps six months, just occasionally going out, not knowing whether her child will live. There is such a need for the tender word of the Lord, because He does understand and He does care. When people are going through the mill, harsh teaching can be such a painful experience.

In Isaiah we see a number of different types of words of comfort:

(a) Comfort for the tired, for the weary

. . . and proclaim to her
that her hard service has been completed,
  that her sin has been paid for,
that she has received from the LORD's hand
  double for all her sins.
(Isaiah 40:1–2)

(b) Comfort for the overwhelmed

When you pass through the waters,
  I will be with you;
and when you pass through the rivers,
  they will not sweep over you.
When you walk through the fire,
  you will not be burned;
  the flames will not set you ablaze.
(Isaiah 43:2)

(c) Comfort for the barren

'But now listen, O Jacob, my servant,
  Israel, whom I have chosen.

457

This is what the LORD says –
  he who made you, who formed you in the womb
  and who will help you:
Do not be afraid, O Jacob, my servant . . .
For I will pour water on the thirsty land,
  and streams on the dry ground;
I will pour out my spirit on your offspring,
  and my blessing on your descendants.'
(Isaiah 44:1–3)

(d) Comfort for the confined

'I will go before you
  and will level the mountains;
I will bring down gates of bronze
  and cut through bars of iron.
I will give you the treasures of darkness,
  riches stored in secret places,
so that you may know that I am the LORD,
  the God of Israel, who summons you by name.'
(Isaiah 45:2–3)

(e) Comfort for the burdened

'Listen to me, O house of Jacob,
  all you who remain in the house of Israel,
you whom I have upheld since you were conceived
  and have carried since your birth.
Even to your old age and grey hairs
  I am he, I am he who will sustain you.
I have made you and I will carry you;
  I will sustain you and I will rescue you.'
(Isaiah 46:3–4)

As pastors and teachers we need to understand that every time we speak there are people listening who feel they are ready to give up, who are carrying so many burdens it is a wonder that they even made it to church that day. It is so important to reach a place of understanding. In my own congregation there was a lady who I assumed didn't like me at all. Every time I preached her body language seemed to catch my eye. She always had her arms folded and she looked miserable and bored. Although I always teach that preachers should concentrate their focus on those who they sense are with them, I know in practice that it is hard to do. I couldn't stop my gaze coming to rest on this unhappy lady. I knew I had to do something about it, so after one Sunday morning service I went and sat at her side, and started to have a little chat with her. After a while, I asked her how she was doing. She replied that she was not doing very well, so I invited her to tell me her story. I was horrified by what I heard. She told me about a horrendous catalogue of health issues which caused her to be in so much pain that it made it very difficult for her to sit through a sermon. I felt terrible. I had made judgements that were based on a complete lack of understanding.

Every time we preach and teach there are people listening to us who need something from God's Word that will take them through the next week. Sometimes pastors can fall into the trap of thinking that when we have delivered the word, we have done our job, but we need to understand that the word needs to be received. We won't always get it right, that's for sure, but it is such a wonderful thing to know that on a regular basis we are helping people by allowing God's Word access into their lives, and of course pointing them to Jesus.

4. Words of Challenge

At other times it is right to be direct in our preaching and teaching because the Word of God is direct. Sometimes it is right to challenge behaviour, attitude and lifestyle. In his book *The Practice of Biblical Meditation* Campbell McAlpine says about the Bible, 'Because this book is God-breathed it has the power to convict and convert, to sanctify and to edify.'[1] The Word of God contains a challenge for every area of life. Here are just a few that I believe are important:

(a) Morality

It is not easy to address issues of morality without pulling people back into rules and regulations and we must be very careful not to expect people to conform to things that are actually not pronounced in Scripture, but the Word clearly states:

> *How can a young man keep his way pure?*
> *By living according to your word.*
> (Psalm 119:9)

The Word of God challenges us in our morality.

(b) Lifestyle

We live in a day when in church life so often the issue of counselling seems very strong. However, in Psalm 119:24 we read:

Your statutes are my delight:
  they are my counsellors.

It is above all the Word of God that brings counsel in terms of lifestyle and behaviour.

(c) Family issues

The Word has a lot to say about our families. Speaking of his heritage in Christ Paul wrote to Timothy of:

> *how from infancy you have known the holy Scriptures, which are able to make you*
> *wise for salvation through faith in Christ Jesus.*
> (2 Timothy 3:15)

The Word instructs husbands and wives, and parents and children on how they should relate to each other, and this must be a part of our preaching and teaching as we seek to be good leaders and carers of the flock.

(d) Finances

This is a key area for our churches. Dr R.T. Kendall said, 'The big problem with the British churches is that they just don't tithe.' So many can quote what the Bible has to say about tithes and offerings and hilarious generosity, but only a minority enters into it. As preachers and teachers we need to bring the challenge of obedience in the area of our finances.

(e) The future

The Word of God speaks into our future bringing direction to our lives. For example, in Psalm 119:

> *Your word is a lamp to my feet*
>   *and a light for my path.*
> (Psalm 119:105)

> *Direct my footsteps according to your word;*
>   *let no sin rule over me.*
> (Psalm 119:133)

The Scriptures deal with every aspect of our lives. As we bring words of challenge about these and many other areas of daily living we bring our people into maturity in Christ. It is not enough for us to be *'hearers of the word'*: we must be *'doers of the word'*.[2]

  Our preaching and teaching should continually impart life, freedom, comfort and challenge to the people of God. As we walk with our people in their journey through life, seeking to apply these four vital dimensions of the dynamic of the Word of God, we will encourage and strengthen the flock and see them built into the mature people God intends them to be.

NOTES

1. Sovereign World, 2002.
2. James 1:22.

Chapter 38

PREACHING AS SPIRITUAL WARFARE

Doug Williams

The term 'spiritual warfare' has been given a new lease of life in recent years. Although the motif of the Christian being involved in military warfare is not new but is seen throughout Christian history, it has been given fresh impetus through the emerging prayer movement around the globe, led among others by such people as Peter Wagner, Ed Silvoso and Cindy Jacobs, and also by the popular novels of Frank Peretti. Whether generated by excitement, intrigue, or fear, spiritual warfare is being talked about again. In my exploration of the subject, however, I have been unable to find a comprehensive definition of what 'spiritual warfare' means, which is, in my view, a quite inexcusable omission. If we are to engage in the activity of spiritual warfare we need a secure understanding of the biblical framework for doing so.

Spiritual warfare means different things to different people across a wide spectrum. It can mean aggressive Christian discipleship; addressing socio-political issues by lobbying and delivering petitions for social change; a specialised form of prayer and intercession; the ministry of personal exorcism, sometimes both to 'sinners' and 'saints'; and the authority to 'name and shame' spiritual powers over communities and break their territorial grip. I have even met people who anoint the window frames of their houses with olive oil to keep out evil spirits and wear certain types of clothing or jewellery to obtain spiritual protection.

In all of this sometimes weird and bizarre behaviour I want to look for a biblical balance. It is my understanding that, broadly speaking, spiritual warfare is a description of the common struggles in which all Christians are engaged as we seek to live out our lives as faithful and fruitful Christians. Everything we do, in terms of living for Jesus and in terms of responsible discipleship and a sense of spiritual formation and maturity, will inevitably bring with it a number of struggles and challenges that will affect our families, our relationships, our workplace, our church, our neighbourhood, our communities and our cities. Living out our Christian faith is never going to be easy.

THE FLESH, THE WORLD AND THE DEVIL

It is possible to bring further clarity to this quite general definition by looking at three main areas of negative spiritual influence over our lives which the Bible tells us are intent on drawing us away from obedience to God's Word: the flesh, the world and the devil.

The *flesh* seems to be mentioned so rarely nowadays. In Romans 6:4–6, Paul writes,

> *Therefore we are buried with him by baptism into death: that like as Christ was raised up from the dead by the glory of the Father, even so we also should walk in newness of life. For if we have been planted together in the likeness of his death, we shall be also in the likeness of his resurrection: Knowing this, that our old man is crucified with him, that the body of sin might be destroyed, that henceforth we should not serve sin.*
> (KJV)

There is in all human beings a principle that causes us to have a bias to do that which is outside the purposes and will of God and consequently estranges us from Him. Our humanity is dysfunctional. We delight in sinning. For this reason, *the flesh* has to be dealt with. Coming to Christ should result in a change in our essential humanity. If there is anything that is a fruit of genuine Christian conversion, it is change!

However, it is my experience that whenever preachers seek to address the issue of the flesh in their hearers' lives – and, indeed, the two areas of the world and the devil which I will shortly move on to – there is conflict. Perhaps this should not come as a surprise to us since it was also the experience of Jesus, even with some of the religious leaders of His day! When Jesus spoke about certain topics, something was stirred up within His hearers, making them want to undermine Him or come into conflict with Him. It was, of course, their unrepentant and rebellious hearts. We as preachers will also find that when we seek to address issues in people's lives that are not submitted to the Lordship of Christ we will encounter conflict.

I can well remember one occasion, when at the age of only eighteen I tried to bring a biblical sense of balance to a church meeting at which an ugly discussion had arisen and the deacons had turned on the pastor. That church really was 'deacon-possessed'! I stood up and said, 'Can we just stay focused on what is biblical and not get lost in personal opinion or temperamental expressions that are not helpful at this point?' Even at that young age I understood the need to go back to the Bible and seek to look at the matter in question from a biblical perspective. Of course, it created a stir because I had touched into the area of the flesh in people's lives. In fact, one of the elders was so upset with me that, after the meeting, he came up to me and grabbed me by my tie. What he didn't realise was that, neither then nor now, I am not frightened by angry elders! And I have the scars to prove it. As preachers we must be prepared for the fact that, if our hearers have not submitted their dysfunctional humanity to God's redemptive transformation, the flesh will begin to manifest itself, and it can become ugly. Such conflict is all part of spiritual warfare.

The second area of negative spiritual activity over our lives is *the world*. In Galatians 6:14 we read:

> *But God forbid that I should glory, save in the cross of our Lord Jesus Christ,*
> *by whom the world is crucified unto me, and I unto the world.*
> (KJV)

By 'the world' Paul means the God-denying world-system or matrix of values and ideas through which people see life and which makes them function in the way they do in society. This world-system needs to be challenged. The thinking of each one of us has been affected by the environment and social context in which we have been raised and in which we have been trained and developed, namely our family, our neighbourhood, our ethical context and our corporate community. We need to look again at all our areas of thinking through the lens of Scripture.

In some of the churches in which I preach, particularly the black churches, there is a very strong, sometimes extreme emphasis on holiness, with very definite ideas being preached about what constitutes being worldly. This usually includes the wearing of earrings and perfume and the perming of hair. They used to have to preach on such issues to the women, but now they have to preach them to the men as well! As far as these churches are concerned, a worldly attitude is expressed by what is happening on the outside, and no one really penetrates to the heart of understanding the deeper implications of having a worldly mindset. They never go beyond the externals to confront the mindset that is dominated by the prevailing attitudes of the culture and is not only outside the purposes of God but also solidly resistant to any intrusion of godly light. This lack of understanding needs to be challenged, but anyone who does so must expect to encounter conflict.

As preachers we must understand that our preaching of God's Word will cause us to come into opposition not only with people's personal dysfunction in terms of their own flesh, but also with their worldly mindset and way of looking at life. Part of our responsibility as preachers is not to renege on the prophetic and confrontational nature of our preaching. We must not apologise for the message God has given us to preach from His Word, but we need to preach it with every ounce of energy and passion we have, regardless of the reaction we fear we may receive. Our culture needs to be challenged and reshaped by a fresh understanding of the Word of God.

The third area is, of course, *the devil*. On the cross Jesus gloriously defeated the spiritual principalities and powers:

> *And having spoiled principalities and powers, he made a shew of them openly,*
> *triumphing over them in it.*
> (Colossians 2:15 KJV)

As a result of His victory, these fallen spiritual beings are doomed to eternal destruction. In some contexts it is very difficult to speak about the spiritual beings to which the Bible clearly refers without appearing weird or strange, because such talk is often completely outside people's experience. They have never been in a situation where they have seen somebody's body contort horribly under the power and influence of a demonic spirit, or where the voice coming out of an individual's mouth has struck terror in their heart. Encountering the demonic can be very frightening. I have had too much experience of it for anyone to try and tell me that it is not a very real issue. But thank God for the power of His Word that sets people free. Jesus is the Lord of both the seen and the unseen, and He has absolute sovereignty and mastery over demonic powers.

We need have no fear about dealing with any of these areas, with confronting the flesh, or the prevailing mindsets of our culture, or the influence of spiritual evil. The fact of the matter is that the cross of Christ has dealt a death blow to every one of these areas and their power has been dissipated through the redemptive work of God. It is my conviction, however, that when we talk about spiritual warfare, we need to consider all three of these areas of negative influence, and that our thinking can become unbalanced if we focus on any one of them and neglect either of the others. Preaching on any one of these areas will produce spiritual conflict and we must be ready to face it.

SPIRITUAL STRONGHOLDS

Another aspect of spiritual warfare which is often raised in my discussions with Charismatic Christians concerns the concept of spiritual strongholds and the responsibility of prophetic preaching to speak into them. However, here again, if our preaching is to have an impact on spiritual strongholds, we need to understand what the term means and, as with 'spiritual warfare', the definitions of 'stronghold' are wide ranging.

Peter Wagner, for example, sets his definition of a spiritual stronghold within a multilevel strategy for spiritual warfare. He identifies three levels of warfare: ground-level warfare of deliverance ministry in which the demonic is encountered; occult-level warfare in which battle is raged against witchcraft and sorcery; and strategic-level warfare which seeks to disarm community or area-wide powers or principalities which hold sway over a particular group of people. In Wagner's view it is at this third strategic level that spiritual warfare needs to be directed at the prevailing local mindsets or strongholds over which spiritual powers are said to have jurisdiction. This is done by prophetic preaching and declaration. On the other hand, Ed Silvoso, whose understanding is disseminated widely through his countrywide seminars on prayer, bases his definition on 2 Corinthians 10:3–5 (see below) and defines a stronghold as 'a mindset impregnated with hopelessness that causes us to accept as unchangeable situations that we know are contrary to God's will'.[1] Liberty Savard, whose books are becoming increasingly popular, proposes this definition: 'Most minds come into the state of salvation stubbornly filled with old attitudes, wrong patterns of thinking and some pretty strange ideas. Self-erected strongholds will protect many of these old ideas and attitudes.'[2]

Each of these three definitions, of the many I could have quoted, is articulating truth in some measure, but I am not convinced that any one of them is a comprehensive and biblically defined understanding of the word 'stronghold'. Do they, for example, line up with what Paul writes in 2 Corinthians 10:3–5:

> For though we walk in the flesh, we do not war according to the flesh. For the
> weapons of our warfare are not carnal but mighty in God for pulling down
> strongholds, casting down arguments and every high thing that exalts itself against the
> knowledge of God, bringing every thought into captivity to the obedience of Christ...
> (NKJV)

As I began to consider the context of this passage, which biblical hermeneutics surely requires us to do, I was forced to reach the conclusion that they do not. From my reading of chapters 10 and 11 (particularly 11:4) I became convinced that the chief concern that Paul was articulating was that the believers would accept false doctrines about Jesus, that they would, as it were, accept another Jesus. He also makes reference to 'another spirit' and 'another gospel'. Later, in chapter 11 verse 13 he refers again to the existence of false teachers or false apostles within the church. This understanding leads me to believe that it is Clinton Arnold, Professor of New Testament at Talbot School of Theology, USA, who correctly defines a stronghold as 'a demonically distorted concept of Jesus, a Christological error'.[3] This seems to be one of Satan's key strategies. If Satan cannot prevent a person's conversion, he seeks to corrupt the new believer's faith and tries to create diversions, disruptions and divisions, as 1 Timothy 4:1 warns will be the case,

> The Spirit expressly says that in the latter times some will depart from the faith
> giving heed to seducing spirits and the doctrines of devils.
> (NKJV)

Paul is concerned that the truth of who Christ is – His centrality, His power, His person, and His work – is being corrupted and it is this that he seeks to address in his preaching. I believe that we as preachers are engaging in spiritual warfare when we are bold enough to confront people's wrong understandings of who Jesus is. We need to be willing to stand up against such strongholds. If they are being promoted in the public arena by well-known figures, I believe it is right to ask our congregations to assess their teaching in the light of Scripture, but it is certainly not right to make any negative comment about an individual's ministry or person. We need to make sure that our congregations are listening to truth because, as well as being subject to all kinds of temptations and intimidations in their daily lives, they also face the danger of slipping into false teaching and false understandings of Christ.

Understanding some of the heretical teachings that have arisen concerning Jesus Christ throughout church history, can help us to be on the lookout for present dangers. Three of the more well-known false teachings are:

- *Doceticism*: the belief that Jesus was not a real man, but only appeared to be human. The apostle John addressed this false teaching in some of his writings (e.g. 1 John 4:2–3; 2 John 7).
- *Ebionism*: the belief that Jesus was not fully God; He was not divine and His mother was not a virgin. Jesus was a good man adopted by God at His baptism by John the Baptist, on which occasion He was also filled with the Spirit.
- *Gnosticism*: the belief that Jesus is a spiritual intermediary who helps people on their journey to spiritual enlightenment (countered by Paul in the book of Colossians).

Another group which was in Christological error were the Judaizers, who accepted Jesus as the Messiah but demanded conformity to the Jewish purity regulations and festivals, and also required that male believers should be circumcised. They wanted to add something to Jesus. It is faith in Christ and faith in Christ alone that brings people into redemptive relationship with God.

Throughout history these false teachings have been overcome by the tenacious preaching of the truth of who Jesus really is. These preachers knew that they were engaged in a spiritual battle. They combated error with a secure understanding of the text and a willingness to engage in protracted discussion and theological deliberation so that the truth could be preserved. By their endeavours they have preserved spiritual purity for those who would come after them, and for that we should be profoundly grateful.

We need too to be aware of the Christological errors of our own day. I have found the books of Clinton Arnold very helpful in this regard since he has done a great deal of work on what contemporary Christological errors will mean for the Church. Here are some of the Christological errors which can be identified in our day:

- *Academic confusion over the identity of Christ.* In some university courses on Christian theology there is a denial of Scripture as a true record of the words of

Jesus and many academics regard Scripture as inspired literature on the same level as the holy books of any other religious tradition. We must never compromise either on the eternal truth of the Word of God or on the historical Jesus as portrayed in its pages.

- *The denial of the virgin birth and the physical resurrection.* Because we have worked these important doctrines through in our private study or in the course of our theological education, it is a mistake to think that everyone in our congregation has done the same. Increasingly, we are going to find people in our churches who are basically illiterate where the Bible is concerned and have never been exposed to Christian truth at all. It is the preacher's task to explain to them the fundamentals of Christian belief. In our preaching we need to combat the mindset of unbelief that permeates our age, and it will require spiritual warfare.

- *The pluralistic agenda of our society* which does not allow for the exclusivity of salvation in Christ alone. We are constantly being told that, in a multiracial and multifaith country like the United Kingdom, we can only preach that Jesus is 'a way' to God, not 'the Way'. Those who continue to preach that Jesus is the Way to God find themselves in conflict with society, because although pluralism prides itself on being tolerant we can be sure it is only tolerant of pluralists!

- *The body-less Jesus.* Many Christians nowadays seem to believe in what I jokingly call a 'body-less Jesus', preferring to hop from conference to conference and church to church, rather than locate themselves in a Christian community where there is an expression of life and a context in which they can live out their discipleship. Such people say they belong to the universal Church and that they do not need the local church. I am committed to the truth that each Christian needs to have a local context for accountability, ongoing development in Christian maturity and spiritual expressions of service.

- *The 'Jesus angel'.* There are a great many people who are looking for mystical experiences, and in many cases it seems the wilder the better. It is almost as if the truth of the Christian faith has been synchronised with a sort of New Age agenda. Those who are seeking such experiences usually espouse very strange ideas about who Jesus is and what He has come to do, so that their 'Jesus angel' bears no resemblance to the Jesus of the Bible. Consequently, whenever I am talking to a person who claims to be a follower of Jesus, I always dig a little bit deeper to make sure that we are talking about the same Jesus.

- *The 'no-discipline' Jesus.* Some people purport to follow Jesus but are unwilling to submit their lives to His Lordship. I believe that Jesus has very clear expectations of those who call Him 'Lord' and their lives should express their allegiance to Him.

- *The 'buddy' Jesus.* There seems to have been a whole spate of books appearing in Christian bookshops recently which include accounts of visionary experiences in which people have encountered Jesus. It is not the visions that bother me but the way

469

in which people talk about Jesus, as if He is their 'buddy' in the sky. There is no sense of awe and transcendence, of falling flat on their faces before Him. God is not the Great Sugar-daddy in the sky; He is not an indulgent Dutch uncle. We also need to understand that if we really did come face to face with an angel, we would be terrified.

- *The 'financial adviser' Jesus.* Some people seem to believe that meeting Jesus will mean that their bank account will suddenly become much healthier. I do believe that there is such a thing as 'redemptive lift', that when people come to Christ they become more focused and industrious, and more responsible with their lives and their use of their resources and, as a result, their situation improves economically and materially. But I am concerned when 'a prosperity gospel' is preached. It is my understanding that Jesus came to die for our sins, not to make us financially rich. A prosperity gospel does not represent the Jesus that I serve. As Christians we need to be responsible stewards of all the resources which God gives us, and that involves taking care of the poor with a generous and magnanimous spirit. In some circles our preaching into this issue will provoke a violent reaction!

As preachers we cannot avoid the confrontational task of addressing the Christological errors in this list, which, I might add, is not exhaustive. To quote Clinton Arnold again, 'Evangelism represents a frontal assault on the kingdom of Satan, yet the Lord has called us to this task. It is an integral part of our mission and we can expect spiritual warfare to occur quite intensely and in a variety of ways on this battle front.'[4] The purpose and the power of preaching is to address understandings, imaginations, speculations and thoughts that are outside Christian truth and to force them into obedience to Christ. It is a difficult and challenging task, and we must not take it lightly.

THE PREPARATION OF THE PREACHER

The other side of the coin, in terms of the spiritual warfare of our preaching, is the preparation of ourselves as preachers. It is time for leaders to pay more attention to their own spiritual health than to techniques, Charismatic trends and growth plans. God has so designed His creation that what is healthy will grow. Thus, the real challenge for preachers is to make sure that they are healthy in the unseen hidden realm.

The most powerful sermons we will ever preach will come out of the overflow of who we are as people and what God is doing in our lives. There will be an authenticity and transparency about it because it is coming out of own experience. That is not to say that preachers should only preach what they are living out in their lives but, like the apostle Paul, we need to admit honestly our own struggles and the areas on which we are still working.

As preachers we also need to share our humanity so that the people in our congregations can recognise God's grace at work in our lives. Not so long ago I shared

470

a story with my congregation about an incident that had occurred with a neighbour over parking some years earlier. My wife had parked her car quite legitimately but for some reason my neighbour, who even had his own garage, took the view that she should not have parked where she did and left a dirty old milk crate on top of her car. It created quite a stir in the street, and all the neighbours were urging me not to let him get away with it. I calmed everybody else down and sent them away, but inside I was steaming mad. I was surprised at how angry I had become. In the middle of the night I went to his garage and filled the lock with some cement-type paste, which went rock solid, so that he could not open it. At the time I could feel the Holy Spirit saying, 'What are you doing, Doug?', but I thought to myself that I would repent later. Several days later I met my neighbour in the supermarket. It felt like a shoot-out at the OK Corral. As we approached each other, he said, 'I just want to say I'm sorry about your wife's car', and I ungraciously replied, 'Yes, you should be!' Then he said, 'Well, fair enough, but you did my garage in, didn't you?!' I too apologised and, shame-faced, admitted that it was even worse because I was a preacher. To my deep embarrassment, he replied, 'Yeah, I had heard that.' I was so ashamed and repentant.

The reason I told my congregation that story was because I wanted them to realise that it is possible for people to change. That had happened a long time ago and even I could now hardly recognise the man who had on that occasion become so angry. I had changed. I had been transformed by the grace of God. People need to know that the preacher in the pulpit is just as human as they are and that the grace of God can work in all our lives.

Rick Warren has said, 'Only healthy leaders can build healthy churches.'[5] It is an interesting comment, because he allows for the fact that gifted leaders can build, but what they build will not be healthy. I have seen this in my own experience. I know some church leaders whose work is growing despite the fact that they are rascals, but in the long-term the growth will not be healthy. We reproduce after our kind. The personal disciplines we develop in our own hearts will sooner or later be mirrored in the lives of those whom we serve.

As the following men of God were well aware, we need to renew our commitment to the devotional disciplines:

A prepared messenger is more important than a prepared message.
(Robert Boyd Munger)

Nothing can happen through you until it has first happened in you.
(Lloyd Ogilvy)

The first building blocks to church growth are the inner disciplines of the pastor.
(Dan Ryland)

I often say that people do not practise what you preach, they practise what you practise. I have to *be* my message before I deliver it. When it comes to the renewal of devotional disciplines, private prayer and worship are non-negotiable. John Maxwell, a man whose leadership has influenced me a great deal, has said, 'My message, my vision, my heart for the people begin with my time with God.' There can be no negotiation on this issue. It will take far more than our learning and eloquence to break the spiritual strongholds we are called to address in our preaching. We will need the assistance of the grace and power of the Holy Spirit to enable us to come to the pulpit with a real sense of prophetic conviction, knowing that we are not just bringing a word about God but a word from His heart. For such an important task I need to pray; I need to be spending time in the presence of God; I need to take time out for personal retreat.

Each year I spend time on retreat with a friend of mine who is a Baptist pastor. We spend our time together praying over our families and over our churches and we challenge one another about our regular devotional habit. At least once a month I try to spend a day on retreat on my own. I book myself into a local hotel, so that no one knows where I am, and spend time just waiting on God. It is very important to spend time with God over and above the hours that are required by our service of Him. We need protracted periods of waiting on God for own spiritual renewal and refreshing.

We also need to be constantly aware of how dependent we are on God. We need to humble ourselves in His presence and remind ourselves of how much we need Him. It is very easy for the work of ministry to become just a job, in which we work hard to meet the needs of those in our congregations. We need to be crying out to God that He will give us servant hearts willing to be dependent on Him and free from arrogance and pride. It was the Puritan pastor Richard Baxter who said, 'One proud, surly, lordly word, one needless contention, one covetous act, may cut the throat of many a sermon and blast the fruit of all that you have been doing.' What a powerful word!

If I am going to preach with any degree of reality and connectedness, the people I serve need to know they have my heart. I must never let paperwork take precedence over people-work. I cannot afford to do a 'professional job' without letting what I am doing affect me. My heart must be in what I am doing. If my people hurt, I hurt. Sometimes my tears are the most eloquent sermon I could ever give.

As preachers we need to practise accountability. I have mentioned that my friend and I make each other accountable about our personal times of devotion with God. We all need to have someone who will ask questions of us about our private time with God; about whether we pay our bills on time and are honest about our tax accounts; about whether we struggle with impure and morally compromising thoughts; about whether we are trapped in any issues of sexual compromise. I have found that having someone to ask me such questions is vital if my preaching is to be sharp and pure. I am as human as everybody else. We all have the same struggles and the same temptations. We need to be honest. The reason I am saying this is because I have had too many great, gifted friends, whose words and insights were penetrating into culture and bringing social change and transformation into the hearts and lives of people, who did not heed this kind of warning, and I have seen their lives fall apart. They were doing so well in the public arena, but in the private arena things were going wrong, and then one day the private became public. And it needn't have happened.

In addition to having at least one friend with whom he can develop such accountability I would encourage every preacher to find someone who would be willing to act as a mentor to him. By coming alongside him, a mentor will encourage him to think more sharply about the task in hand and will also hold him to account in every area of his life, thus ensuring that he makes progress in his development. I believe that if the preacher's life is appropriate, his life-message will have grace and will be expressed in power and authenticity.

Our dedication to the devotional habit must not lessen our commitment to such motivational disciplines as focusing on our priorities. If we are to preach well, we need to make sure that we allow ourselves sufficient time to prepare well. In the light of the gravity of the task and the spiritual warfare it will necessitate, we need to learn to manage our time wisely. But I believe there is an even more important reason why we need to learn to manage our time wisely, and that is so that we save enough time and energy for the ones that we love the most. I have discovered that my most eloquent sermon will probably be the nature of my home life, so that if I haven't got time to discipline my own children and to care for the spiritual formation of my spouse, there is something very wrong. People who enter our home will probably begin to think, 'Why should I believe what he is expounding from the pulpit if it doesn't work at home?' That is a great challenge to each one of us as preachers.

In conclusion, I want to urge all preachers not to underestimate the importance of preaching in the task of spiritual warfare. Our task is not an easy one. There will inevitably be difficulty and conflict, and sadly there will be some casualties along the way. However, I believe that when we preach the revealed Word faithfully and consistently, it has the power to transform men and women's lives so that their flesh is overcome, their mindsets are transformed and the devil is expelled from their lives. If we as preachers will make sure that our inner lives are kept pure and focused and that we keep growing in our faith, we can be confident that what we preach is the overflow of a life that is nurtured by waiting and dwelling in the presence of God.

Notes

1. Ed Silvoso, *That None Should Perish* (Regal Books, 1994), p. 154.
2. Liberty Savard, *Shattering Your Strongholds* (Bridge-Logos Publishers, 1998), p. 5.
3. Clinton Arnold, *Spiritual Warfare* (Marshall Pickering, 1997), p. 63.
4. *Ibid.*, p. 46.
5. In a radio interview.

Preaching into the Culture

Jesus spoke all these things to the crowd in parables;
he did not say anything to them without using a parable.
So was fulfilled what was spoken through the prophet:

'I will open my mouth in parables,
I will utter things hidden
since the creation of the world.'

(Matthew 13:34–35)

Chapter 39

EVANGELISTIC PREACHING

J. John

Preaching is an audience participation event. If it weren't, it would be private preaching. We proclaim, preach, teach. The Greek word for 'proclaim' *kerussō*, which is used sixty times in the New Testament, literally means 'to make a public announcement from a king'. This reminds us that our message is from God the King and therefore we should not be diffident in our speaking. We don't preach because we want to say something. We preach because we have something to say. The Greek word for 'preach' *euaggelizo*, from which we get the English word 'evangelise', is used fifty times in the New Testament. It is usually translated 'preach the gospel' or 'preach good news'. This reminds us that our preaching should contain good news. Our message, especially to the unchurched, has to be good news.

As an evangelist I do not want to try and persuade preachers and teachers that they should instead become evangelists. The apostle Paul's words to Timothy, *'do the work of an evangelist'*,[1] have often been misinterpreted. So often he has been misinterpreted as saying, 'Timothy, you're a pastor. Don't be a pastor any more. Do the work of an evangelist.' But he didn't mean that. Paul was saying: 'Timothy, you're a pastor. Do it as if you were an evangelist.' To others he might have said: You're a teacher, do it as if you were an evangelist. You're a secretary, do it as if you were an evangelist. You're a cleaner, do it as if you were an evangelist. I want to say to preachers: preach as if you were an evangelist. It is a mindset.

As part of a survey[2] one thousand churches were asked the question: 'In the last five years have you ever undertaken to do a course to teach your church how to evangelise?' Only thirty-six churches, i.e. 3.6 per cent, answered yes. The Church in this country does not think about evangelism: it does not have a heart for evangelism. Without a heart for evangelism, whatever I might try to teach preachers about the skills of evangelistic preaching would simply be clinical. Without a passion for the lost, our efforts to be effective in our evangelistic preaching will not work. There is no short cut to having the fire in our belly.

Imagine that my wife and I and our three children decide to go to the forest, have a barbecue and play games. We have great fun. When it is time to go home, once we have packed everything up, we discover that only one son, Benjamin, is still with us. The other two, Simeon and Michael, are lost. We search for them in the forest and after a while we find Simeon. We can't find Michael. Would we say, 'Oh, never mind. Let's just go home. At least we've got two of the boys'? No, of course not. We would search for Michael until we found him alive or dead. This is the kind of analogy that is used in Scripture to inspire us in our search for those who do not know Jesus. A missionary is not someone who crosses the seas. A missionary is someone who sees the cross. That is why the apostle Paul said, *the love of Christ compels me*.[3] This love must come from the heart. If, as an individual, a preacher does not have a passion to seek and save the lost, then there is very little anyone can teach him about evangelistic preaching. He can learn some techniques, but in reality it is not going to do very much. We have got to revisit the cross, because it is the love of Christ that compels us.

This is such an important point. The other day I had a meeting in Canary Wharf, London. Not wanting to be late I set off in good time. In fact, I was half an hour early so I decided to get a cup of coffee. As I was walking through the shopping centre I saw a man cleaning shoes, and I thought I would get mine cleaned. Looking down and realising my shoes were clean I was having second thoughts when I felt God prompt me to go ahead. Discovering it cost £4, once again I hesitated but God was still urging me on, telling me that the cause was worth the cost. Sitting down on the chair I asked the man cleaning shoes, 'Why do you look so sad?' He said, 'How do you know?' I said, 'I can see it in your eyes.' He responded, 'I have cleaned many people's shoes. Hundreds. You are the first person who has ever said that to me.' As I invited him to tell me his story, he started crying. He spent the next twenty-five minutes telling me his story. When he had finished, I said to him, 'I know someone who can help you.' I gave him some of the resources I had with me and then dashed off to make my meeting.

Afterwards, since I was feeling a little bit peckish, I decided to have a quick sandwich before getting the train. I walked into a café and bought a sandwich, but I could not find anywhere to sit because all the tables were taken. I saw a table with only one man sitting at it, so I asked him if he would mind if I joined him. 'Oh no,' he said, 'that's fine', and we exchanged a few pleasantries. After a while I asked him, 'Are you married?' He replied, 'That is such an interesting question. I've been engaged to the same woman for seven years and I just can't get my act together to marry her.' I said, 'Do you know, I've written a book on marriage. I haven't got it with me, but here's my business card. Here's the deal. I am going back to my office now. If you email me, I will send you the book.' I thought I would leave the ball in his court. By the time I got back to my office an hour later, he had already emailed me. He wrote, 'This has been one of the most intriguing conversations I have had in a long time. Yes, please, send me the book.' Both he and his fiancée are reading the book. I tell these stories to make the point that, unless conversations like these are the normal practice of our daily lives, we are not going to be passionate in our preaching of the gospel. It is so important.

The Parable of the Sower is a two-edged sword (see Matthew 13). With one edge it cuts through the discouragement we are tempted to feel when people do not respond to the message or when they fall away. It is reassuring to know that even Jesus felt the same. With the other edge, however, it slays us for the carelessness with which we sometimes approach our task. The task of communication is not an easy one. Often our attempts at communication are distorted by misunderstanding. We speak out of one set of assumptions and our hearers hear through their own grid of past experience, personal prejudice and misinformation. The Parable of the Sower, like many of the stories Jesus told, gives us an insight into communicating the gospel. I want now to give five pointers or principles on how to preach evangelistically.

1. It's Not What We Say, It's What They Hear

Jesus concluded the Parable of the Sower with the words: *'He who has ears, let him hear'* (v. 9). There is as much emphasis in the Bible on hearing as on speaking. We have a great urge, even a need, to speak. Some of us speak because we are full. Others of us speak because we are empty. When our need to speak is more important to us than people's need to hear, there is a problem. One man pleaded with the leader of his church for opportunities to preach. But he was not a good communicator. He said to his pastor, 'Woe is me, if I do not preach the gospel.' The pastor replied, 'And woe is the people if you do.' The people to whom we are communicating are of primary importance. A fascinating verse in the Gospels is Matthew 13:12:

> *'Whoever has will be given more, and he will have an abundance. Whoever does not have, even what he has will be taken from him.'*

In Matthew 25 and Luke 19 Jesus applies this truth to the issue of the use of talents, but here He applies it to knowledge and its acquisition. New knowledge has to be linked to existing knowledge, and if we do not keep adding to our knowledge we lose it. This concept has great importance for those of us who preach. We need to get the attention of the people by building on what they already know. This is why Jesus used parables to tell people things that have been unknown since the creation of the world. He built on what the people already knew by using parables about familiar things. Jesus understood the people because He *'knew their thoughts'*.[4] In order to build on existing references we need to know as much as we can about people. What kinds of things do we need to know? The range of Jesus' parables and sayings provides a good guide. It shows He was quick at observational people research – at noticing what made the world go around in people's lives. He kept His eyes open. Since home and family are the greater part of any person's life, He noticed what went on in people's houses. He knew a lot about kitchens where the leaven made the dough rise. He saw children ask for the bread when it came out of the grass-fired ovens. He knew that they liked fish and eggs, but not without salt. He knew how exciting weddings were and how heart-breaking funerals were. He knew about hostility between brothers. Jesus was familiar with the work situations of His hearers. He knew about farms, ploughing, sowing, weeding, harvesting. Sheep, oxen, dogs all came into His examples. He knew about vines, figs, mustard trees. He was familiar with the market-place with its pearl merchants and traders. He was at ease with fishermen, builders and soldiers. He observed social conditions: crime, the courts, the prisons, the banquets of the rich and the misery of the poor. He knew about sickness and doctors' bills. He sensed impatience with neighbours and antipathy to strangers, and He noticed the commonplaces of conversation. The world of nature made its impression on Him: the wind in the trees and flowers, sparrows, foxes, camels, wolves, serpents and their ways. Why do all these things appear in His parables and sayings? Because that is what people knew about, and He had to build upon it if He was to introduce them to the unknown love and grace of the Father who sent Him. This was vital if He was to capture their attention and hold their interest.

Some other features about the parables worked to draw the hearers' interest. They were used in an unpredictable way. The easiest way to lose attention is to be predictable. With Jesus there was always the unexpected turn to the way He took the familiar and used it. His parables were stories, and everyone likes a good story. Good story-telling heightens interest. And what is very interesting with Jesus is that He left a lot to His hearers, often leaving them thinking – and causing His disciples to ask Him later what He meant. In this way the people ended up saying things to themselves that they would have resented if He had said them directly. Jesus didn't have the urge that most preachers have to say it *all* every time. Listeners are like a radio: they have an off-switch. They can totally switch the preacher off. It was this type of people that Jesus was referring to when He spoke of the seed falling on the hard-trodden path. The truth did not even get a hearing. It was screened out. Knowledge of our audience and the skill to build on what they already know in a way that captures their curiosity are essential factors in getting their attention. Sometimes the fact that the truth does not get a hearing is the responsibility of the listener. Often, however, preachers harden their hearers by being irrelevant, insensitive and skilled only in activating the off-button in their minds. We need to understand the audience that we are endeavouring to communicate to.

2. It's Not Just What They Hear, It's What They See

Just before Jesus tells the Parable of the Sower he quotes Isaiah 6:9–10. He repeats the words 'seeing', 'hearing', 'understanding' (or 'eyes', 'ears' and 'minds'/'hearts') four times. It is not accidental that every time He says 'see' as well as 'hear'. It has a natural as well as a spiritual significance. We imagine that what we say is all important, but we are mistaken. People hear our words but they see our body language. They notice how close we stand to people or how far away. Sometimes one distance is appropriate, sometimes another. When He was preaching to a large crowd on the seashore Jesus – knowing they needed to see Him – got into a boat which was pushed a little distance off-shore. He sat as other teachers did, because in those days sitting communicated authority. When we go up into a high pulpit, six feet above contradiction, it says something. Sometimes this is good, sometimes it is not. The Gospels often describe the body language of Jesus: He stretched out His hand and touched a leper; He showed surprise at the Roman officer; He touched the eyes of the blind; His heart was filled with compassion; He took the five loaves and two fishes, looked up to heaven and gave thanks. When they brought to Him the woman taken in adultery they made her stand before them, but He bent over and wrote on the ground with His finger; He straightened up and spoke to them about throwing the first stone; He bent over again and wrote on the ground, and with only the woman still standing He straightened up and asked her, *'Where are they?'* Jesus' body language spoke volumes. He turned His back on Peter; He placed His hands on the children; He wept at the grave of Lazarus; He washed and dried His disciples' feet with a towel. If we are part of the community where we preach, people see us not only when we are speaking, but at other times too. It is very important that we understand this.

3. It's Not Just the Message, It's the Meaning

After seeing with the eyes and hearing with the ears must come an understanding of the message in the minds of the hearers. The preacher can deliver a message but his hearers must be able to fit the message into all that they already know. They live in their own world with a set of beliefs, ideas and values, which all colour what they hear. If the truths being preached do not fit well with the world-view of the hearers several results can occur. Firstly, it can make no sense at all. Having heard an explanation of the Trinity, a prospective Japanese convert from Shintoism remarked, 'Most High Person of Honourable Father, Him I understand. Honourable Son, Him also I understand. But please tell me who is that Honourable Bird?' The idea of the dove as a symbol of the Holy Spirit was totally incomprehensible. Secondly, it can lead to a distorted version of the gospel. This is the situation with the seed that fell on shallow ground. The hearers accepted a gospel that they thought promised them a prosperous and easy life. When, contrary to their expectation, trouble and persecution arose, they gave up following. When Paul preached at Antioch, he used many references to the Old Testament because his hearers were Jews and they knew the Scriptures (see Acts 13). When he preached in Athens, he did not quote the Bible at all (Acts 17). Instead, he quoted the Greeks' own poets to confirm what he was saying and he let their context give meaning to his message. It is not just the message, it is the meaning that matters. As preachers let us do all we can to help our listeners understand the meaning. I like what Paul says in 1 Corinthians 2:1, *'when I first came to you I didn't use lofty words and brilliant ideas to tell you God's message'* (NLT). Jesus taught profound truths in very simple ways. Sadly today we do the exact opposite. We teach simple truths in profound ways, and a lot of the time we think we are being deep but we are just being muddy. Spurgeon wrote, 'A sermon is like a well. If there is anything in it, it appears bright and reflecting and luminous. But if there is nothing to it, it's deep and dark and mysterious. A lot of preachers are just empty wells with a dead cat or two and some leaves in it.' Simple does not mean shallow; simple does not mean superficial. The Christian message is very simple. But Satan loves to complicate it. And sometimes Satan doesn't have to complicate it, we do it for him. I am not a theological teacher in the same league as my vicar Mark Stibbe, but I really love to teach theology. I love to do it at a very simple level, without using theological terms and without people knowing that I am teaching them theology. Nowadays people don't talk in theological terms, they talk in psychological terms: I am ready to throw in the towel; I'm at the end of my tether; I am just a bundle of nerves; I'm falling apart; I'm at my wits' end; I feel like resigning from the human race. They do not say, as I heard someone say in a church, 'I'm experiencing moral depravity.' I know ministers who speak in an unknown tongue every week, and they aren't Charismatics! Our preaching of the message must be simple. My last Easter Sunday message was: If you want to have forgiveness from the past, if you want to have new life today, if you want to go to heaven and have a hope for the future, you have got to go via King's Cross. That was my whole message. My whole teaching backed up that statement. The handful of non-Christians present were converted and the rest of the congregation was inspired and encouraged. We have got to keep the message simple.

4. It's Not Just the Truth but the Relevance of What We Say

Everyone wants something. Sometimes, as in the case of blind Bartimaeus, Jesus asked, 'What do you want me to do for you?' Sometimes He detected it without their saying anything as in the case of the woman of Samaria or Zacchaeus. Sometimes they said it before He asked, like the rich young ruler who wanted eternal life. This young man did not want eternal life enough to let his wealth go so he went away unchanged. Zacchaeus and the woman of Samaria saw that Jesus could meet their needs, and they believed in Him. Unless the new pearl is seen to be worth more than all the old ones, there will be no response. Unless the treasure is worth selling everything for in order to buy both the field and the treasure, there will be no transaction. Unless people are ready to give up all they have, they will not become disciples of Jesus. The relevance of the gospel to the individual is as important as its objective truth, and we need to take this into account when we preach. As we present Jesus we need to speak to what people are hungry for. We need to realise that people's most pressing need may not be for forgiveness first. They may want acceptance first like Zacchaeus. They may want to be healed first like the man at the pool of Bethesda. They may want a new identity first like Simon who had the prospects of becoming Peter. They may want a purpose in life first like James and John who wanted to be fishers of men. They may want physical safety first like the Philippian jailer. They all came to need and want forgiveness, but that was not the need they first felt. We need to recognise the needs that people themselves feel and not act as though we know their needs better than they do. Some evangelistic preaching tries to generate an artificial conviction of sin because the preacher feels that repentance and forgiveness are the needs that must be faced first. Of course they must be faced, but sometimes they come a little later. In an old fable the sun and the wind had a contest to see which of them could get a man to take off his coat. As the wind blew harder and harder, the man only drew his coat closer around him. Then the sun sent out its warmth and in a short time the man willingly took off his coat. Some preaching is like a cold wind to the hearers: it makes them more defensive. Preaching that is warm, that meets people's needs, adds motive to understanding and makes communication effective. We don't have to make the Bible relevant, it already is. But we do have to show its relevance by applying it to people's needs.

5. It's Not What People Like About Our Talks and Sermons That Matters, but What They Do

When all has been said and done, a lot more has been said than done. The object of preaching the gospel is that people might turn to Christ and be healed (Matthew 13:15). A key verse for every preacher is James 1:22:

Do not merely listen to the word, and so deceive yourselves. Do what it says.

Several times Jesus concluded His preaching with the words, *'Now go and do likewise.'* We need to make sure our preaching is not long on diagnosis and short on remedy. When I go to the GP, I don't just want diagnosis, I want remedy. Christianity is more than a belief, it is a behaviour. It is more than a creed, it is character and conduct. The active response that should follow preaching can be temporary or permanent: the seed that fell in good soil bore lasting fruit; the seed sown in the rocks and among thorns did not last. Jesus calls us to bear fruit that remains (cf. John 15:16). Whether we get a life-changing response from preaching, of course, depends on the work of the Holy Spirit. The Parable of the

Sower, however, shows that the hearers' response is affected by how well they understand the message, and that hangs on effective communication. It is not what people like about our talks and sermons that matters but what they do. If we as preachers desire our seed to fall on good soil and produce a harvest of life-changing results, we need to be aware of the needs and perceptions of our hearers. Telling the gospel story is not enough. We must communicate it in a way that reaches our listeners at their point of need and brings the good news into focus for their lives.

Rather than being inspired to give the occasional evangelistic sermon, I would much prefer preachers always to preach and teach as if they were evangelists. Then hundreds of churches would be changed. In my own church, St Andrew's Chorleywood, most of the talks that I give are evangelistic – throwing out the net to pull in the fish. However, our vicar Mark Stibbe teaches as if he were an evangelist. What he teaches is relevant to believers, but it is also relevant to unbelievers. In our church we want our services to be open to unbelievers every Sunday; we don't want to rely on tailor-made occasions when we can invite those who do not know Jesus. The five principles I have outlined can be used by preachers in any sermon – whether or not it is specifically evangelistic – so that they preach as if they were evangelists. In addition, they can set aside seasons, such as the Sundays surrounding Easter, when they preach evangelistically.

In conclusion I would just like to add a few words on the way we communicate. We must communicate with confidence. I think the key to preaching is to be yourself. Trying to be like someone else simply doesn't work. When we get to meet Jesus I think He is going to ask many of us, 'Why weren't you more like you?' Being ourselves gives us confidence. We can be relaxed and confident in who we are. We must also communicate with credibility and with clarity. These qualities are so important. Many people who hear me preach totally unscripted, totally extempore, think that when I do that, I simply walk on the stage and make it up. On the contrary, speaking totally extempore requires even more preparation than speaking from a script. On those occasions I have spent more time preparing myself and preparing what I am going to say than when I preach from a script. Even then, whenever I give a new talk, I always write out the text completely and ask my wife and various people to read it through and comment on it. I even ask my children to read it and tell me what they don't understand. It is a fascinating exercise. Sometimes I think we could all do a lot more of that, so that when we get up and preach, we can do so with more confidence, with more credibility and with clarity.

Preaching evangelistically is not about clever ideas and clever techniques. I believe that, if a preacher will take the five principles I have given, and will put himself and what he already knows into them, and if he will preach as if he is an evangelist, God will honour him and he will see people won to Christ. May the gospel be preached not simply with words, but also with power, with the Holy Spirit and with deep conviction (1 Thessalonians 1:5)!

NOTES

1. 2 Timothy 4:5.
2. Carried out by The Philo Trust in 2000.
3. 2 Corinthians 5:14 NKJV.
4. Luke 11:17.

Chapter 40

APOLOGETICS AND PREACHING

Michael Ramsden[1]

I am an apologist and an evangelist. Although 'apologetics' is a biblical word which is used in a positive sense in the Scriptures, I am always nervous about it because of the image it conjures up in many people's minds. Apologetics is not about introducing a dose of confusion into the gospel in order to make it sound more profound. It is about communicating the profundity of the gospel so as to remove the confusion surrounding it. The goal of preaching is not to ask people to accept the apologetic offered by the preacher, but instead to offer an apologetic through which Christ Himself can be accepted.

In his first letter Peter writes,

> *But in your hearts set apart Christ as Lord. Always be prepared to give an answer*
> *to everyone who asks you to give the reason for the hope that you have. But do this*
> *with gentleness and respect...*
> (1 Peter 3:15)

The Greek word translated 'answer' in this verse is *apologia*, from which the word 'apologetic' is derived. As Christians, the only reason we can give for the hope we have is Jesus Christ. All apologetics must flow to or from the person of Jesus Christ. It is His life, death and resurrection that is the basis for our hope.

Having stated that the apologetic we offer is fundamentally about Jesus, I would like to take one biblical model to expound and sum up what I consider to be the goal of apologetic preaching. In Acts 17:1–4 we read,

> *When they had passed through Amphipolis and Apollonia, they came to*
> *Thessalonica, where there was a Jewish synagogue. As his custom was, Paul went*

into the synagogue, and on three Sabbath days he reasoned with them from the Scriptures, explaining and proving that the Christ had to suffer and rise from the dead. 'This Jesus I am proclaiming to you is the Christ,' he said. Some of the Jews were persuaded and joined Paul and Silas, as did a large number of God-fearing Greeks and not a few prominent women.

Luke tells us that *'as his custom was'* Paul went to the synagogue on three consecutive Sabbaths. It was not a one-off event. The apostle made many missionary journeys, during the course of which, like most preachers, he probably repeated himself many times. He developed customs or habits in the way he approached what he was doing, changing the emphasis or content as he felt appropriate to the individual setting. Since this is a description of Paul's customary habit when preaching, I want to focus on four verbs from this passage which will help us to gain a deeper understanding of preaching that is thoroughly apologetic in its nature and style. These four verbs are: 'reasoned', 'explaining', 'proving' and 'persuaded'.

1. TO REASON

Paul *'reasoned with them from the Scriptures'*. The very first person in the New Testament to do this was Christ Himself (see Luke 24:13ff.). After the crucifixion, two of the disciples are on their way out of Jerusalem when Jesus joins them as they are walking along, although they do not recognise Him. When He asks them what they are discussing, they reply, *'Are you only a visitor to Jerusalem and do not know the things that have happened there in these days?'* Of course, the truth is that He is the only one who *does* know what has happened. When Jesus probes further, they begin to explain to Him the events of recent days. They lift the facts, they describe the events, and the result in their hearts is despair. *'He was a prophet,'* they say, *'powerful in word and in deed'*.

First rebuking them for being foolish, Jesus then takes their 'what' and turns it into a 'why'. Where they have lifted facts, He interprets; where they have described, He explains. As He does so, their despair begins to turn to hope and their hearts begin to beat within their breast. By the time He sits down and breaks bread with them, their eyes are opened and, all of a sudden, their whole understanding of who Jesus is changes. Instead of thinking that He is a prophet, they now understand He is the Lord. Rushing back to Jerusalem where they burst into the upper room, they inform the other disciples, *'The Lord has risen'*. Their understanding has shifted from a human perspective to a divine perspective. This, we are told, Jesus achieved by 'reasoning' with them out of the Scriptures (v. 27).

There are two ways of understanding the phrase 'reasoning from the Scriptures', both of which are legitimate, depending on the context. It can either mean that a passage of Scripture is explained so that it makes sense to those seeking to understand it, or that a person who is 'reasoning' with others is doing so in a way that is thoroughly biblical, even if the Bible itself is not expressly used. Both are implied and I think both are intended in this passage in Luke. Now the word translated 'to reason with' literally means 'to say something thoroughly'. What was Christ trying to say thoroughly when He modelled this for us on the road to Emmaus? He was trying to speak thoroughly about His identity. Today we live in a culture which is confused as to the nature of its identity. Not only are we not sure who we are but we are not even sure *if* we are – if there is even an identity to be questioned. Yet, understanding who someone is is profoundly important.

One of my brothers works in accountancy. He told me about the following incident that happened when he was doing some audit work for a firm. When the audit was finished he asked the client, as was their standard practice, if there was anything else he could help him with. The man admitted he had some personal taxation problems but was very reluctant to ask for help since, following the previous audit, he had taken up a similar offer of help only to be invoiced for the sum of £2,500 for half a paragraph of advice via email. Although personal taxation does not fall within my brother's expertise, he promised the client that he would find out the information he needed from the personal taxation department at his company and that there would be no charge. When my brother got back to the office, he rang up the taxation department, explained the situation and received the information he wanted within thirty seconds. But then the person on the other end of the phone asked for the job number. 'What do you mean?' my brother asked. 'Well,' he replied, 'I have to bill for my time. Every call is logged; every enquiry goes down on the sheet. I need a job number.' 'How much will this cost?' 'About £3,500.' Then my brother simply said, 'Do you know whom you are talking to?' The voice at the other end fell silent, before admitting, 'I haven't a clue.' With the retort, 'Well, neither have I' my brother hung up the phone!

This story illustrates that answering the question about who someone is can be awfully important. Answering the question 'Who is Jesus?' is pivotal. Jesus reasoned with the two disciples on the road to open up to them who He was; to explain His identity. Beforehand their minds were simply closed to who He was.

We live in a culture of confusion. We don't know who we are any more. We no longer know how to define ourselves. We used to buy clothes with the labels sewn onto the inside of our clothes; now we wear clothes with the labels sewn on the outside to tell people something of who we are. We're so confused about our identity that we also think everybody else is equally confused about theirs. And so when we talk about someone like Jesus, we don't think He really knew who He was. In the film *The Matrix*, the key figure, a young man called Neo, is the saviour of the world but he doesn't even know it himself. He's confused about his own identity. Similarly, many often assume that Jesus must have been confused. This is not true.

Chris Walley and J. John's book on the person of Jesus, *The Life*, does a brilliant job of opening up who Jesus is.[2] In Acts 17 we hear how Paul thoroughly opened up to the

Thessalonians who Jesus is. In this age of cultural confusion, when we don't even know who we are, we have to be very clear in our minds who Jesus Christ is. Paul reasoned with them from the Scriptures. He reasoned with them in a completely biblical way, whether he was quoting Scripture or using Scripture as his starting point. He said it thoroughly.

2. To Explain

Paul **explained** the gospel. The verb translated here 'explain' literally means 'to open something thoroughly'. Whereas the word translated 'to reason with' means 'to say something thoroughly', 'to explain' means 'to *open* something thoroughly'. What are we doing when we explain something to somebody? Surely we open it up, so that he or she can understand it. However, the problem that we have in our post-modern culture is that most of the words we use no longer mean what we want them to. In fact, most of them don't mean anything at all.

Ten years ago, on a visit to London, I took a cab to get to my destination. The driver was a woman who was capable of sustaining a one-way conversation. She talked, I listened. She talked about politics and the weather, this and that, and then she said, 'I had a guy in my cab yesterday who worked for Goldman Sachs.' My ears pricked up because that was where my brother was working at the time. She relayed to me the conversation she had had with this man: 'I said to him, "Are you married?" and he said, "No." And I said, "Why aren't you married?" and he said, "Because I have so much money. If someone marries me, eventually they'll divorce me and when they divorce me, they'll take half of my money. I don't want to lose half my money, so I've resolved never to get married." ' Then I said the first words I'd uttered since getting into the cab, 'That's sad.'

She looked in the mirror and caught my eye, and said, 'You know, I used to be married myself.' She then told me the story of her marriage, how she and her husband were both black cab drivers and had worked night-shifts to earn as much money as they could. They bought a run-down old house and worked hard to do it up, gradually refurbishing it, until finally she had the house she had always wanted. 'But,' she admitted, 'I still wasn't happy. Then I fell in love with a guy who sold fruit and veg in my local market and I've been living with him for the last five years.'

I asked, 'Well, are you happy now?' She said, 'You know, I used to think there was something wrong with my husband, but now I'm beginning to wonder if there's something wrong with me.' I asked myself what I could possibly say to this lady. So I did what we Greeks do – we talk about words. This is how the conversation proceeded:

'When you went to school, did you do Religious Education?'
'Yeah.'

'Do you remember reading the Sermon on the Mount, "Blessed are those ... Blessed are those ... Blessed are those ... "?'

'Yeah.'

'Do you know what the word "Blessed" means?'

'I haven't got a clue.'

'Well, look, it's hard to explain, but it literally means "life-joy". It means the happiness that goes beyond the superficial into the centre of our existence.'

'Have you known that kind of happiness in your life?'

'You know, there was a guy called G.K. Chesterton who once said that before he became a Christian there was happiness on the edge of his life and a misery at the centre of it, but ever since becoming a Christian, even though there had been a misery and a pain around the edge of his existence, there had been a fundamental happiness at the centre of it. That's what happened to me when I became a Christian: something central changed even though I went through a lot of other pain and suffering.'

'I've been looking for this all of my life.'

Just opening up that one word which before meant nothing to her, now meant everything to her. When we arrived at my destination she asked if we could keep talking and she plied me with questions, 'What is this blessedness? Where does it come from? How can I enter into it?'

In his commentary on Galatians, John Stott says that 'Although "grace" and "peace" are common monosyllables, they are pregnant with theological substance.'[3] While this should be true for the Christian, for the non-Christian these, and many other richly significant words, mean nothing. Another word for which this is also the case is 'love'. Before living in Oxford my wife and I used to live in Worksop, North Nottinghamshire. When we moved to the church, we inherited a youth group of thirteen girls aged between thirteen and eighteen. Those were the most terrifying meetings I have ever had in my whole life. I can say without hesitation that I spent more time praying and fasting every time I had to meet with those teenagers than I have ever done since. Preaching in the White House was a cinch compared to trying to communicate with thirteen teenagers.

On one occasion I gave them each a blank piece of paper and a pen and asked them to write down the issues that were important to them. It was the most foolish thing I have ever done. Every single one of them wrote down a question along the lines of: What is love and why get married? Berating myself for my stupidity in ever undertaking the exercise, I did what everyone does when they are scared and promised the girls that we would talk about this issue at our next meeting!

The next week when everyone came back together, this is what I did. Asking everyone to close their eyes, I said, 'I want you to imagine the following scenario with me: imagine tomorrow that when you go to school the boy you like most comes up to you and says, "I love you." How do you feel?' Never have I seen so many smiling faces in my whole life.

'And now I want you to imagine that the day after that you go back to school and you hear the same boy telling a different girl, "I love you." Now how do you feel?' All the smiles disappeared. 'You see, the words "I love you" only mean something because they are directed exclusively and committedly to you.'

I was trying to help the girls to understand that outside of a moral framework of exclusivity and commitment the words 'I love you' mean nothing. If the word 'love' does not mean anything to those with whom we are trying to communicate, our talk of a God of love will not make sense. As we try to communicate the gospel, we as preachers need to ask ourselves how we can open up the words we use so that those listening to us can understand what they actually mean.

Why is passion in the preacher so important? It is important because it convinces people that this person really believes what he is saying. It seems to have actually changed him. But our passion must not stop at our words; it must also be evident in our lives. Our lives need to open up our words. In Matthew 5 Jesus tells His followers, *'You are the salt of the earth . . . You are the light of the world'* (vv. 13, 14). While light can illuminate an object from a great distance away, salt can be brought very close to a piece of meat without changing its flavour in the slightest. Salt can only enhance the flavour of meat if it comes into contact with it.

Part of the gospel can operate at a distance: it can and indeed must be proclaimed and preached out into the world; but there is another part of it that has no effect whatsoever unless the lives of believers make contact with the people around them. Without this contact people will only hear Christians speaking about love: they will not experience it – the salt will not do its work.

Of course Jesus had something else to say about salt. He said, *'If the salt loses its saltiness, how can it be made salty again?'* It is very interesting to consider the question, 'How can salt lose its saltiness?' It can be ground into a fine powder, it can be heated in water, it can be dissolved in water and the water evaporated: all to no effect. Salt is the most stable compound known to humankind. How, then, can it lose its saltiness? The salt we buy and use today in the twenty-first century has been highly purified, but in the first century it contained impurities. If those impurities reached a certain level, it became unstable and it was worthless to anyone.

It used to be true that if you flew into Larnaca airport in Cyprus, you would see the great salt lakes nearby (they have now been removed). The salt harvested from those lakes would be stored in huge pyramids. One year they overharvested and allowed too many impurities into the salt with the result that the whole lot was ruined and became useless. The phrase 'loses its saltiness' is translated from the Greek *moranthe*, which comes from the Greek root *moros*. It is the word from which 'moron' in English is derived and means 'to become stupid'. Translated literally, Jesus is saying, 'If the salt becomes foolish (stupid), it is worthless and has to be thrown away; it is good for nothing.' So if we then as Christians are living our lives in a foolish way, our salt, even though it may come into contact with society, is utterly useless. That is why the Bible says, *'Be very careful, then, how you live, not as unwise but as wise.'*[4] In other words, 'Don't live life like a moral moron.'

Paul reasoned with people and explained the truth of the Scriptures but at the same time every ounce of his energy, everything about his life, was also opening up the gospel to them. That is why he was able to write back to them and say, 'How did I live when I was with you? Was I a burden to you?' He appealed to the moral quality of his own life, and we also need to be able to do this. Our lives and our words need to open up the truths of the gospel thoroughly.

3. To Prove

The third verb is '**proving**', which is a very good translation of the literal Greek. It doesn't mean that at this point Paul produced a flip chart with diagrams and mathematical equations, which at the end said 'equals God'. The word translated 'proving' literally means 'laying alongside'. What does good apologetic preaching do? It lays one thing alongside another, alongside another, alongside another . . . It takes those listening along the tracks of a train of thought until eventually they are surprised at the destination at which they have arrived. It brings them to the point where they have to ask themselves the question, 'What am I going to say to Jesus? Yes or No?' But it is vital that the tracks get laid in two directions. In our lives we are all wrestling with issues – with poverty, injustice, suffering, meaninglessness, just to name a few. If a person struggling with poverty is saved, the assumption might be that since Jesus is the answer, he or she will now become rich. But we know that this is not the answer Jesus offers. No, the tracks are laid in two directions. One line of tracks goes back to the fact that the world was created to be different from the way it is – it is fallen. The other set of tracks goes forwards to the cross, and this is the fantastic news: Christ is the answer to the fundamental problem of the fallen world in which we live. The preacher has to lay both those tracks down, and it takes time and it is difficult.

I love listening to people. I love hearing how people chatting in a pub with a group of friends answer the question, 'So, why are you a Christian then?' Nine times out of ten in response the Christian will tell them how he or she became a Christian. He or she might say, 'I went to a meeting, where a guy was speaking and it was very interesting. Then I was invited to go on a course, and at the end of it I thought, "Yeah, I want to become a Christian."' Now, *how* a person became a Christian is very interesting but it doesn't answer the question, '*Why* are you a Christian?' The explanation given may sound very random to a non-Christian who may wonder, 'So what would have happened if you met a Buddhist and went to an interesting talk and course on Buddhism? Would you have become a Buddhist?' How a person may have become a Christian doesn't answer the question, 'Why?' As Christians we need to be able to answer the question 'Why did I become a Christian?' We need to be able to lay the tracks one alongside another and answer the question when we are asked it by non-Christians.

4. To Persuade

Finally, *'Some of the Jews were **persuaded**'*. Anyone who makes a study of the words translated 'belief', 'persuaded' and 'faith' in the Bible will make an astounding discovery. They will discover that the verb 'to believe' and the verb and noun 'to have faith' are both derived from the same root verb *peitho*, which means 'to be persuaded'. There are two words for 'faith' in the New Testament. One is the word *pistis*, which is derived from the verb *peitho*; it is always used in a positive sense. Every time the word 'faith' appears in the New Testament it is actually that noun, and every time the verb 'believe' occurs it is the verb form of that noun. The other word for 'faith', *nomizo*, has the connotation of speculation, and it is only ever used in the Bible in a negative sense. When Jesus says to the crowds, 'Why do you think this in your hearts against me?',[5] the Greek word used is *nomizo*. It is a faith-based decision, but there is no firm ground for it.

Sometimes people say to us as Christians, 'I wish I could believe what you believe, but I can't.' What do they mean when they say this? I think they are saying: 'Look, if I am honest, there is a desperation in my life that hasn't been met, but you seem to have found a peace, a joy, a completeness that I am looking for and that is very attractive. I wish I could believe what you believe, but what you believe isn't real.' Now, people who believe in things that are not real are usually regarded as mad. So by making this statement people are inferring that in order to come to faith they have to be willing to step out of the realms of sanity. But this is too great a step for them to make. The Bible says, however, that faith is a gift – and it is not the gift of insanity. This is why the best linguistic alternative to the word 'faith' as it is used in the Bible would be the word 'trust'. When people say, 'I trust that person', they are saying two things. Firstly, that the person actually exists. If he or she doesn't exist, then the person who trusts really should be playing with the fairies at the bottom of the garden. And, secondly, that there is an integrity about the person which means they feel they can trust him or her. They can trust his or her moral character; they can trust his or her promises. Trust means that when we hear something bad about a person, we don't leap immediately to the wrong conclusion, but take the trouble to find out whether the slur or accusation has any basis to it. One of the reasons the Church is in such a mess is that we actually seem to have lost that kind of trust. We never even bother to pick up the phone when we hear stories about other people; we just believe them because it makes us feel better about ourselves.

The reason why Acts 17:4 says, *'some of the Jews were persuaded'* is because the verb here describes the action of their coming to faith. They came to believe that Jesus Christ was real and that they could lean on Him. They were persuaded that they could put their trust in Him. As Christians we need to be careful when we describe ourselves as 'people of faith'. The world defines faith as that which people need in order to believe something which they are not sure is true. Strong faith, therefore, is that which they need in order to believe something they actually suspect is not true, but want to continue believing. And the strongest possible kind of faith is that which people need in order to continue believing something they definitely know is not true. But these Thessalonians *were persuaded*. The word 'faith' itself needs to be rescued if for no other reason than that the doctrine of salvation by faith is very important. It is crucial that these two concepts of faith should not be confused. Faith that comes through persuasion must be differentiated from speculation. If people's faith is just speculation, their trust is not in Christ: they are trusting in their speculation. The great danger of apologetic preaching is that the people listening put their trust in the preacher and his ability to explain rather than in the person of Jesus Christ. It will only be avoided if the preacher is filled with the Holy Spirit and presents a very clear reasoned explanation of who Jesus is.

Some people think that because I describe myself as an apologist, I must have everything sorted out in my mind. I wish that were true. No one gets to that place, and if they think they have then there is a great danger that they have fallen into self-deception. So, why am I a Christian? Is it because I can answer every question put to me? No. It is because I am sure of the person I trust. That's why the apostle Paul says, *'I know whom I have believed and am convinced…'*.[6] In our apologetic preaching we must always remember that it is the 'whom' and not the 'what', that it is the 'why' and not just the facts, that are important. So long as we rely on the Spirit every time we stand up to proclaim the gospel, we will not go far wrong. We need to say it thoroughly and in a way that makes sense; we need to open it thoroughly so that the people can understand what we are saying; we need to lay one track alongside another so that people realise that they need to make a response; and then we need to pray and cry out to God that people will be persuaded, not by our eloquent speech, but by the person of Christ and put their trust in Him. Paul writing to the Corinthians said,

> *When I came to you, brothers, I did not come with eloquence or superior wisdom as I proclaimed to you the testimony about God. For I resolved to know nothing while I was with you except Jesus Christ and him crucified.*
> (1 Corinthians 2:1–2)

This is an incredible passage, and it is also Paul's most poetical preaching. So often people say to me, 'Isn't eloquent preaching a stumbling block?' Yes, it is a stumbling block if we put our trust in our eloquent preaching and not in the Spirit of God. We preach Christ crucified as powerfully and eloquently as the Lord has enabled us, not trusting in ourselves but trusting in Him, that the apologetic preaching we bring may truly proclaim what He has done for us, so that lives can be changed and so that this nation can be transformed.

NOTES

1. Further material from Michael Ramsden, and other members of the Zacharias Trust, is available in a family of new books published by IVP (see www.ivpbooks.com/zachariastrust).
2. *Authentic Lifestyle*, 2003.
3. *The Message of Galatians*, The Bible Speaks Today series (IVP, 1988).
4. Ephesians 5:15.
5. Mark 2:8.
6. 2 Timothy 1:12.

J. John

Nathan was the guest speaker, King David the audience. Nathan had a message from the Lord to deliver to David and, being the excellent communicator that he was, he opened with a story: 'There were two men in a certain town, one rich and the other poor. The rich man had a very large number of sheep, but the poor man had only one little lamb that he had bought. He raised it and it grew up with him and his children. It shared his food, drank from his cup, and even slept in his arms. It was like a daughter to him. Now a traveller came to the rich man but the rich man refrained from taking one of his own sheep to prepare for him. Instead he took his neighbour's young lamb and prepared it.' The story, of course, had King David on the edge of his seat. He took it seriously and responded with gut-wrenching emotion, 'As surely as the Lord lives, the rich scoundrel who took that little lamb deserves to die.' Bingo. The rest of Nathan's message required few words. All he had to do was apply the story to his audience. 'You, sir, are that man.'[1] Nathan knew what every good speaker and teacher knows: a picture is worth a thousand words.

Jesus appreciated a good story. Scripture records that Jesus never spoke without using a parable (see Matthew 13:34). In other words, Jesus never spoke without telling a story, and He was the master communicator. I want to be like Jesus. Jesus consistently sprinkled His teaching with stories and real-life situations to drive home His points. He drew His illustrations from everyday life in the Middle East, describing farmers and families, sheep and goats, barns and wheatfields, and people were *'amazed at his teaching'*.[2] Now, 'amazing' is not how most teenagers describe church preachers and teachers. I think we are wrong to assume that adults prefer dull and boring abstractions to interesting and colourful illustrations. In the twenty-four years that I have been preaching I have discovered that the best way to communicate with adults is to speak to them as if they are all about fourteen years of age – assuming of course you don't speak to fourteen-year-olds as if they were children. That way, our preaching will reach everybody.

What then have I learnt in my twenty-four years of preaching about the art of seasoning our sermons?

1. AIM TO HIT THE TARGET

A preacher must not build his talk around a story he is eager to use. I have made this mistake many times but we must not do it. We must begin with the point, the truth, that we want to communicate, and then find or create the illustration that supports it.

A young boy received a bow and arrow as a present from his father, and he immediately went outside to shoot it. A little while later his father went outside and saw that the boy had shot his arrows at several targets that had been drawn on the side of a fence. To his amazement each arrow had hit a bull's eye. The father was impressed and said to his son, 'I didn't realise you were such a good shot.' 'Oh, it was easy,' his son replied. 'I shot the arrows first, and then drew the targets around them.' When we use illustrations simply because they are good illustrations, we are drawing targets around our arrows. Right at the beginning of planning a talk we need to decide what the point, the target, is. Then we enhance the talk with seasoning in order to drive home the point effectively, keeping in mind that it takes different kinds of arrows to hit different kinds of targets. Changing the metaphor, we need to be selective in the seasoning that we choose. This is very important. I am bit like a squirrel when it comes to stories. I am continually collecting, collecting collecting ... banking, banking, banking. As preachers we are not going to be able to draw from the bank if there are no resources in our account. It is a mindset, an attitude, which all preachers need to develop.

2. CHOOSE THE CONCRETE, THE INTERESTING AND THE UNPREDICTABLE

An effective story uses concrete images, familiar to the hearer and drawn from everyday life. Even the most illiterate, uneducated peasant could identify with the situations, objects and people Jesus described in His parables. One reason why John Newton's hymn 'Amazing Grace' has remained popular over the years is because of its familiar, concrete language:

> Amazing grace, how sweet the sound,
> That saved a wretch like me.
> I once was lost, but now I'm found,
> Was blind but now I see.

As well as using concrete images, a good illustration is interesting. A story needs a plot that engages the listener all the way to its conclusion. Take, for example, the parables

Jesus told. As people became caught up in these stories, they lowered their defences, allowing Jesus to drop a 'truth bomb' on them. Finally, and perhaps most importantly, an effective illustration uses surprise. Surprise helps drive a message home. Surprises are remembered. More than once Jesus' illustrations captivated listeners who were comfortable in the certainty that the point was meant for some other group of people: they got caught out when the ending pointed the finger straight back at them. As we have seen, the Old Testament prophet Nathan used the element of surprise to change King David's opinion about his adultery and murder. When the King heard Nathan's story of the rich man with many sheep who confiscated the poor man's one sheep, he became incensed. He angrily demanded that the evil rich man be brought to justice. What a surprise when Nathan enlightened David that he had just pronounced judgement on himself! Choose the concrete, the interesting, the unpredictable.

3. When the Point is Obvious, Don't Illustrate it

If I stand up in front of a group and say, 'God is good', the truth of the claim may not be clear to some people. I will need to illustrate the statement with a story or an example or an analogy that describes what I mean. If, however, my group is meeting in a room registering sub-zero temperatures and I say, 'This room is cold', then an illustration would labour the point. My group doesn't need to be enlightened by a story about someone freezing. Many of the things we say are actually quite obvious and don't need illustrating.

4. Leave an Audience Room to Think for Themselves

An audience can feel put off if the preacher is too explicit in his application of the point he is trying to make. At times it is appropriate to make sure that the audience gets the point quickly by explaining it in detail. In the parable of the sower Jesus explained to His disciples the meaning of the symbols He was using, but most of the time He simply told a story and then allowed His audience to think about it for a while and to discuss its meaning among themselves. Sometimes the listeners came to different conclusions. That is all right. When Jesus' disciples asked Him why He used parables, He explained that the stories allowed those with an open heart to hear what God wanted them to hear while those with hardened hearts were kept in the dark (Matthew 13:10ff.). Jesus stimulated His disciples to learn by allowing them to ponder the meaning of His parables for themselves.

5. Use Illustrations Strategically

The primary reason for using illustrations is to drive home a point but they can be used for other purposes as well. An illustration may be used for the purpose of holding a group's attention, or to provide a change of pace to make a talk more interesting. If I speak to a congregation for even ten minutes without including a story or illustration I soon notice people becoming bored. They begin to look around, the atmosphere begins to change: they are enjoying the roast beef and Yorkshire pudding, but they are longing for some gravy. It is so important to give people the gravy; it is so important to add the seasoning. A properly chosen illustration causes the audience to stay tuned, to discover the point that the preacher is trying to make.

Illustrations can also be used to set up a point the speaker is about to make. In other words the illustration may not communicate much truth on its own but because it is interesting, or funny, or serves as an ice breaker, it helps the speaker transition towards his point. I might, for instance, tell the story of the Zirka bird.

> Two wealthy brothers set out one Christmas to purchase the very best present they could find for their mother. The search for this present became so fierce that the two brothers turned it into a contest to see who could find the most unique and extraordinary present that was available. One brother thought he had done it when he discovered the Zirka bird. The Zirka bird was no ordinary bird: it was very rare and special, and had to be flown in at great cost from overseas. It could speak five languages; it could recite poetry and sing opera. It was an amazing bird. So this one brother paid dearly for the Zirka bird and had it sent to his mother for Christmas. Finally he could wait no longer. He called his mother and, when she picked up the telephone, he almost shouted into the phone, 'Mother, Mother, what did you think about the beautiful, intelligent Zirka bird that I sent you?' She replied, 'Oh son, it was delicious.'

Of course, it is a silly story, but people will remember it. Its application is that God has given us some wonderfully unique gifts. Unfortunately we sometimes don't realise how wonderful they are and we end up misusing them or doing great damage to them.

Although illustrations may be used to hold a group's attention, or to get laughs, if those are the only reasons they are used, the audience becomes frustrated and bored. Like the boy who shouted 'Wolf' when there was no wolf, audiences eventually tire of speakers who have no content to their messages.

6. Choose the Right Illustration

It goes without saying that no preacher should use an illustration or story that is not right for him. A person who has a difficult time being dramatic or funny may have to avoid those types of illustrations. When we are considering choosing an illustration, we need to ask ourselves how comfortable we will feel using it. Once selected, we need to rehearse the illustration until we can present it fluently and convincingly. There is nothing worse than giving an illustration that makes no sense because a key element has been omitted.

I have myself sometimes come to the punchline and been unable to remember what exactly it was.

The following illustration can be used to great effect. Holding up a brand new £50 note I say:

> 'I've got a brand new £50 note. Who would like this £50 note? Please put your hand up if you would like it. Listen, I am going to give this to somebody. But at the moment I think it's too clean and nice. So what I am going to do is crease it up [I make a show of creasing up the note]. Now, who wants a creased £50 note? Hands up. Oh, isn't it interesting? It was worth £50 when it was nice and clean, but now that it is all creased up, it's still worth £50. It hasn't lost its value ... But I still think it's too clean – it needs some dirt. [I make a show of making the note dirty.] Who wants a dirty, creased £50 note? Oh, you do still want it? It was worth £50 when it was nice and clean and then, when I creased it, it didn't lose its value. It was still worth £50. Then I dirtied it, but it still didn't lose its value. It's still worth £50. It doesn't matter how creased you and I feel, it doesn't matter how dirty you and I feel our lives are, you and I have never lost our value in God's eyes.'

The application of the illustration hits home. Then I continue:

> 'Right, now I am going to come and give this to somebody. And do you know, the strange thing is that some of you are going to be thinking, "Oh, I hope he doesn't give it to me", because you would feel embarrassed and as though you are not worthy to receive a £50 note. And afterwards that person will probably come up to me and say, "Here's your £50 note back. It was a great illustration." But I will say, "No, no. I don't want it back. It was more than an illustration. I want to give it to you."'

Then I go out into the audience and, after searching round, I go up to somebody and say,

> 'I'd like to give the £50 note to you. You can do whatever you want with it.'

Isn't that the message of Christianity? We may feel we have lost our value but the gospel shows us that in God's eyes we are still as valuable as ever.

Although I am in danger of contradicting what I said earlier, occasionally we do come across such a powerful illustration that it is worth focusing a message around it. But that is the exception to the rule. The principle is that, whatever truth we are trying to drive home, we teach it, apply it, and illustrate it. As we do so, the more of ourselves we can put into it, the better. Therefore we need to find illustrations or stories that will enable us to do this.

7. CONSIDER YOUR AUDIENCE

Not all illustrations are appropriate for every audience. Teenagers love stories; they enjoy making the connection between a concrete illustration and an abstract idea. Little children love stories too, but they have not yet developed the intellectual ability to understand metaphoric or symbolic language and it is hard for them to figure out the meaning of an allegory or a parable. Take, for example, the story of Jimmy and the Genie:

> Once upon a time there was a boy named Jimmy who, as he was walking in the desert, found a magic lantern on a pile of rocks. Jimmy thought to himself, 'Maybe if I rub this lantern, a genie will come out and grant me three wishes.' He tried it and, sure enough, a genie appeared. Jimmy was really excited and asked the genie for three wishes, but the genie replied, 'I am not that kind of genie. I give advice.' [Note: good element of surprise.] 'Oh,' said Jimmy, 'then give me some advice.' 'Pick up as many rocks as you can and take them home with you,' said the genie just before he disappeared. 'This is stupid,' said Jimmy, 'I have a long way to go and these rocks are heavy. I am not going to pick up any rocks.' He did pick up one small rock, however, and stuck it in his pocket.
>
> When he finally got home Jimmy took off his dirty clothes to be washed. His mother went through his pockets and found the rock. After examining it closely she asked Jimmy where he had got it. Jimmy replied, 'Oh, some stupid genie told me to pick up a bunch of them but I only picked that one up.' 'Jimmy,' his mother cried, 'this isn't a rock. This is a huge diamond. It is worth thousands of pounds.' Unfortunately, Jimmy was never able to find the pile of rocks again.
>
> *Application*: There are many things in life that seem like rocks, but in reality are diamonds.

Little children, for example, will undoubtedly be captivated by the story simply because of the subject matter, but they will miss the point of the application entirely. If they are asked what they learnt from the story, they will probably say, 'You should always pick up rocks when a genie tells you to'! We need to evaluate the stories we use from the perspective of the different age groups that will hear them. What will children make of it? What will adults make of it? People will differ in their capacity to apply the principle.

I find that the situations in which we are communicating to all ages, for example family services, are the most difficult. As I said earlier, I have learnt to aim for the fourteen-year-old, but we do need to take special care with the application. The following simple Christmas message is an example of an approach that can be used in an all-age setting. Having made a giant Christmas cracker, which is quite easy to do, I say:

'I have got a cracker here and I need somebody to help me pull it. Who wants to come and help me? [Pull the cracker with the volunteer.] When we pull a cracker, what comes out? Three things: a hat, a message and a present. [Put the hat on.] Later today, at Christmas dinner when you put your hat on, I want you to remember it isn't a hat, it's a crown. The reason it's a crown is because a King has been born. The second thing you get is a little message. Normally you get a stupid little message, but today when you read your message I want you to remember that the message of Christmas is: A Saviour has been born to us today. And when you receive your little gift, I want you to remember that the gift of Christmas is Christ. So I want you to remember those three things – see if you can remember them at Christmas lunch today.'

No matter whether the person hearing this message is a senior citizen, an adult in their forties, a teenager or a four-year-old, they will take something home with them about the message of Christmas.

It must have been great to have been one of the crowd who heard Jesus preaching. Imagine them chatting among themselves as they are waiting for Him to speak. 'I love Jesus' stories.' 'Yeah, I like the gardening ones.' 'No, I don't like the gardening ones, I like the political ones.' 'No, I like the ones where the parents tell the sons what to do but they don't do it.' 'Well, let's see what Jesus is going to tell us today.' Jesus tells a story:[3]

[Jesus]: *A certain man was going down from Jerusalem to Jericho...*

[Crowd]: Well, that's not surprising. A lot of people travel on that road...

[Jesus]: *...and he got attacked...*

[Crowd]: Well, that's not surprising either: there are a lot of robbers hiding out in those bushes on that road.

[Jesus]: *They attacked him and left him for dead.*

[Crowd]: What, this is going to be a sad story today. He has not told us a really sad one for a while.

[Jesus]: *But a priest came that way...*

[Crowd]: Oh, good, our brother is going to live after all ... The priest will look after him. That's part of his job, isn't it?

[Jesus]: *...and he stopped...*

[Crowd]: Yeah, of course he would stop, wouldn't he?

[Jesus]: *...and he looked. Then he walked by on the other side.*

[Crowd]: Uh, what kind of a story is this? What do you mean? Our brother is dying, the priest has stopped and looked ... But the priest is busy, isn't he? He's got lots of things to do.

[Jesus]: *But a Levite came along...*

[Crowd]: Good, a Levite ... A Levite doesn't have to do all those weddings and funerals. He's got more time ... Our brother's going to be fine, after all.

[Jesus]: *...and the Levite stopped...*

[Crowd]: Yeah, we knew he would stop...

[Jesus]: *...and he looked, but then he walked by...*

[Crowd]: Uh, what kind of story is this? The priest comes, he looks, he goes. The Levite comes, he looks, he goes. Ah, we know what kind of a story this is. It's the kind of story where the person you didn't think would help comes and helps. The underdog, yes, it's that kind of a story. The priest fails, the Levite fails, but an ordinary Jewish man comes out on top.

[Jesus]: *A Samaritan comes along...*

[Crowd, spitting on the floor]: If our brother isn't dead already, he will be now. And if the robbers have left anything behind, it will go now.

[Jesus]: *...and the Samaritan stopped and he picked the man up. He put him on his donkey, he looked after him, poured oil on his wounds, fed him and gave him accommodation.*

[Crowd]: We never heard of a story like that before.

The priest looks and walks away – surprise. The Levite looks and walks away – surprise. The Samaritan stops and shows compassion – intense surprise. Jesus is the Good Samaritan: whoever else might ignore us in our time of greatest need, Jesus always stops and cares for us. In this retelling of the parable I am seeking to demonstrate the principle of trying to connect and engage with people in the same way that Jesus knew how to. In His telling of stories there must always have been this kind of connection and interaction.

Our goal in our preaching is to communicate the truth.

> A cartoon depicts a dog sitting next to its owner with the caption 'What we say to dogs'. The owner is reprimanding the dog for its bad behaviour with phrases like, 'Bad dog, Ginger. I have had it with you. From now on, you stay out of the dustbin. Do you understand me, Ginger. Do you?' The next scene has the caption 'What dogs hear'. What the dog is actually hearing is, 'Blah, blah, blah, Ginger. Blah, blah, blah, blah. Blah, blah, blah, blah, Ginger.'

We need to keep in mind that our goal is to communicate the truth in such a way that what we say matches up accurately with what people hear, understand and apply.

As preachers who are endeavouring to season our sermons I believe that we need to access the resources that are becoming increasingly available, which can provide us with good stories and illustrations to enable us to make our point, or can be used to change the atmosphere or set the scene for what we want to say. We can take the story or illustration and make it our own by putting ourselves into it. One such resource is a set of three books which Mark Stibbe and I have compiled called *Barrel of Fun, Bucket of Surprises* and *Box of Delights*.[4]

PUT THE CHERRY ON THE CAKE

It is my perception that as preachers we are often very good at the presentation of the message, but we are not very good at pulling in the net and helping people to make the step of becoming a Christian. Recently, on an occasion when I was speaking evangelistically, I used this illustration before making an appeal:

> A man and woman were making their vows during their marriage ceremony. The minister asked the groom, 'Will you take this woman to be your lawful wedded wife?' He replied, 'Well, I've been thinking actually . . . ' The minister responded, 'Well, it's good that you have been thinking but actually I have asked you a question, "Will you?" ' The groom said, 'Well, I get very excited when I think about her.' And the minister persisted, 'I'm very glad you get excited when you think about her, but the question I am asking you is, "Will you?" ' And the man said, 'I will.' The minister then turned to the bride and asked, 'Will you take this idiot to be your lawful wedded husband?'

This little anecdote was like the cherry on top of a cake. I followed on by saying, 'Look. You may be thinking about what you have heard and your heart may have been stirred, but it is a question of the will. *Will* you?' Somebody came up to me afterwards and said, 'Mr John, Mr John, I've got to speak to you.' He told me that he had become a Christian and that it was that final addition that had spurred him on to come straight through to commitment to Christ. The cherry helped that man to receive the cake. I believe we need to become better equipped in knowing how to explain the gospel in such a way that we will see people come through to faith. After my message on last Easter Sunday a lady came up to me and told me with great excitement, 'I saw it for the first time. I hadn't seen it before'. The aspect of my sermon that had sparked off the revelation about which she was speaking, was simply this:

> People will often ask, why Jesus? There are many other religions, many other philosophies, so why Jesus?
>
> There are only four major world religions that are based on personalities. Every other major religion could be termed a 'philosophy'. The four major world religions that are based on personalities are: Judaism, Buddhism, Islam, Christianity. The father of Judaism, Abraham, died in 1500 BC. The founder of Buddhism, Buddha, died of dysentery. The founder of Islam, Muhammad, died of a fever. The founder of Christianity, Jesus Christ, died by crucifixion. You can go all over the world, but you will not find one Jewish person who will say, 'Father Abraham lived and died but he is alive now and I talk to him.' You can go all over the world, but you will not find one Buddhist who will say, 'Buddha lived and died but he is alive and I actually

communicate with him.' You can go all over the world but you will not find one Muslim who will say to you, 'Muhammad lived and died but he is alive now and I communicate with him.' But you can go to every country in the whole world (bar fifteen), and you will find people who will say to you, 'Jesus Christ lived and died, but He is alive now and I actually communicate with Him.'

You are walking down a street which branches into two and you don't know which way to go, left or right. You are really confused, you just don't know which way to go. There are two men lying there, one's dead, one's alive. Which one would you ask for directions?

It was this simple explanation that enabled the woman to see the truth for the first time. The Holy Spirit takes our illustrations and illuminates them. I believe that, if God can speak through a donkey He can speak through anything! But He has chosen to speak through us, and I believe that we need to pray, 'Lord, thank You for giving us the recipe to put the cake together, please help us now to put on the icing with the cherry on top. Thank You, Lord, that You have showed us how to cook the meal. Please help us to put some gravy and seasoning on it.' In order to do this we need to access all the resources that are available and ask the Lord to help us to be like squirrels, so that we can see and hear things and store them up for the appropriate moment. Sometimes people say to me, 'Where do you find all these stories?' I think I find them because I am constantly on the lookout for them. We all need to develop the mindset, the perspective, of learning to look out for resources and then to bank them.

NOTES

1. See 2 Samuel 12.
2. Matthew 7:28.
3. Luke 10:30ff.
4. Published by Monarch Books.

Chapter 42

Using Movies in Preaching

Mark Stibbe[1]

Graham Cray, Bishop of Maidstone, has said that if Christianity cannot be inculturated successfully within the post-modern context, there will be no western Church. The Church needs to face up to the challenge of how to present the truth of God's Word in this generation; of how to bridge the gap between Church and culture. I believe that faith and film give us as a Church a great opportunity to speak into our post-modern generation, for never before has there been a time when faith and film have come so closely together.

The transition from modernity to post-modernity has been well documented. One of my favourite books on the subject is Stanley Grenz's *A Primer on Postmodernism*.[2] In it he compares two characters in different *Star Trek* series. While the original *Star Trek* series features Mr Spock, the archetypal enlightenment man, full of rationality and priding himself on logic, *Star Trek: The Next Generation* has as his equivalent an Android robot called Data who desires to experience emotions and wants an emotion chip. As Grenz eloquently says in his book, this development encapsulates the change from modernity to post-modernity. We now live in a much more integrated culture, where reason and emotion, truth and experience, can be held together. I believe that we need to take this cultural transition into account in our preaching: it is no good our continuing to use a style of preaching that worked in modernity but will not be as effective today. In terms of evangelistic preaching, in particular, we need to recognise that a purely cognitive, verbal, rational appeal is of limited value. We must adjust our preaching style to our culture: without watering down the message we must adapt the medium so that we can bridge the gap and connect in a relevant and persuasive way.

Jesus and Paul did this the whole time in their communication with their listeners. With a water carrier Jesus talked about water; with a tax man He talked about money;

with fishermen He talked about fishing. The message was the same, but the style, the idiom, the medium varied in order to enable Him to connect with the need of the listener. Paul did the same. In 1 Corinthians 9:20–23 he writes,

> *When I am with the Jews, I become one of them so that I can bring them to Christ.*
> *When I am with those who follow the Jewish laws, I do the same, even though I am*
> *not subject to the law, so that I can bring them to Christ. When I am with the*
> *Gentiles who do not have the Jewish law, I fit in with them as much as I can. In this*
> *way, I gain their confidence and bring them to Christ. But I do not discard the law of*
> *God; I obey the law of Christ. I do all this to spread the Good News, and in doing so*
> *I enjoy its blessings.* [3]

In Acts 17 Paul takes a very different approach in his presentation of the gospel message to the Athenians from the one he uses when speaking to Jews, opting, for example, to quote from their local poets (v. 28). I am convinced that, if Paul were ministering today, he would use the movies and that in particular he would make the most of the unprecedented opportunity afforded the Church by Mel Gibson's movie *The Passion of the Christ*.[4] I base my view on the following five good reasons:

1. Movies are one of society's most popular art forms

Watching movies is now as routine as eating or sleeping. Film has been called the medium of the masses. At dinner parties, at the pub, whenever people interact, film is one of the most common topics of conversation and acts as a connector between people who have not met before. Particularly significant is the fact that films have a potent impact on the 15–34 age category. For the past three years J. John and I have been running a movie series at St Andrew's Chorleywood, from January through to March every year, tackling about eight films each time. Large numbers come to these meetings, particularly in the 15–34 age group, which the church has not been good at reaching in recent years. For this series the church is packed with young people. It has been very interesting seeing how my own son has responded. Over the last series he invited between five and ten friends from his local comprehensive school each week, and they came faithfully to a showing of the movie in the vicarage, from about 3.00 till about 5.30, with pizza of course and other allurements, and then to the service in the evening, when there is a talk on the movie. At least two of his friends have come to Christ. The use of movies to illustrate biblical truth connects particularly well with this age group.

Young people certainly watch films, as the statistics demonstrate. During the year 2000, cinema attendance in the UK topped 142 million, approaching 3 million a week. Over 2 million 7–14 year olds, 4 million 15–24 year olds, and 3 million 25–34 year olds visited the cinema at least once a month. Between 1989 and 1999 the number of cinema screens rose by almost 1,200 to 2,758. Over the same period video retail transactions rose from 38 million to 96 million, plus 4 million DVDs in 1999. The figure for DVD sales continues to soar. There can be no doubting film's popularity.

2. Movies are a very powerful communicative medium

I remember watching the film *Schindler's List*, directed by Steven Spielberg (1993), in the Warner Bros. cinema in Meadowhall, when I was a vicar in Sheffield. I used to go to the cinema frequently, but seeing that movie was an extraordinary experience. Everybody was riveted to their seats; when the credits rolled at the end of the film nobody moved. More recently I was invited to go to an early showing of *The Passion of the Christ* at the Odeon, Leicester Square, with a thousand journalists. This was in preparation for twelve BBC radio programmes on which I spoke about the movie. Beforehand I wondered what it would be like seeing the film with an auditorium full of cynical journalists, many of whom employ a secular humanistic world-view, and for whom anything Christian is certainly not trendy or cool intellectually. But, to my surprise, the same dynamic occurred: as the credits rolled at the end, although there were some who walked out angrily, the majority remained sitting quietly and reflectively in their seats. As in the case of *Schindler's List*, it is not appropriate to talk about 'enjoying' *The Passion of the Christ*; it is more a case of 'experiencing' it. Films are a very powerful communicative medium.

Movies at their best offer moments of transcendence. We need to ask the question, do our churches? As I have said many times before in many places, people often say to me that they get more of an experience of God on a Saturday night in Warner Bros. than they do on a Sunday night in the local church. It is not how it should be, but it is how it is. Movies appeal to the primary organ of receptivity in our culture which is the eye. Again, we need to ask ourselves, how much of our worship of God is visual? Furthermore, movies affect our values, attitudes and behaviour for good and for evil. Although the jury is still out on this issue, there is compelling evidence that there is some cause and effect relationship between movies and values.

3. Movies are a window onto contemporary culture

It is my perception that a sea change occurred in our society at around the time when the first movie of the Star Wars Trilogy was released. Contemporary culture was affected in a noticeable way with everyone talking about 'the Force being with you', for example. Since that time films have become increasingly spiritual in an overt way. That is not to say that they have become increasingly Christian, although some have, but mainstream contemporary cinema definitely reflects a search for spirituality.

One of my favourite films is *Signs* which was written and directed by M. Night Shyamalan, who also wrote *Sixth Sense* (1999) and *Unbreakable* (2000). The film stars Mel Gibson and tells the story of an Episcopalian priest in rural Pennsylvania who loses his faith and stops exercising his ordained ministry. Let me just interpolate here that one of the reasons why I believe movies are so successful is because our post-modern culture embraces suffering and ambiguity right at the very centre of its values. A priest, Graham Hess, loses his faith because his wife Colleen is tragically killed while she is out taking an evening walk. Graham, left alone with two children to bring up (a boy Morgan, acted brilliantly by Rory Culkin, and his younger sister Bo), regards his wife's death as proof that God does not exist and that there is no one watching over them. But during the course of the film things happen that indicate that maybe there really is someone or something out there after all. *Signs*, like many contemporary movies, overtly explores spiritual themes. It is a brilliant movie. Others unconsciously reflect spiritual, even Christian, truths, and a number of recent academic books have explored how both unconsciously and consciously movie directors are putting Christ figures into their movies.[5] The movie *The Matrix* is an interesting case in point. What is particularly fascinating about *The Matrix* is that, even though a Christian perspective can be employed in understanding it, and names like 'Trinity' actually invite that, it can also be interpreted from a number of other spiritual or religious interpretations, including Buddhist and Jewish. In many ways it is a classic representation of the religious pluralism of post-modernity.

4. Movies are conducting conversations about God

We have already seen this in relationship to *Signs* but, as far back now as 1997, in the film *Contact*, based on a novel by Carl Sagan and directed by Robert Zemeckis, there is a very unashamed exploration of the relationship between science and religion, reason and faith. All the way through this movie Palmer Joss, acted by Matthew McConaughey, and scientist Dr Eleanor Arroway, acted by Jodie Foster, discuss how far science can take us and how far faith can. In one conversation, talking about when he became a Christian, Joss says: 'I had an experience of belonging, of unconditional love, and for the first time in my life I wasn't terrified and I wasn't alone.' It continues:

> [Ellie]: 'And there's no chance you had this experience simply because some part of you needed to have it?'
> [Joss]: 'Look, I'm a reasonable person and reasonably intelligent, but this experience went beyond both. For the first time I had to consider the possibility that intellect, as wonderful as it is, is not the only way of comprehending the universe, that it was too small and inadequate a tool to deal with what it was faced with.'

By the end of the movie Dr Ellie has an experience herself and, in front of a tribunal, she says:

> 'I had an experience I can't prove. I can't even explain it, but everything that I know as a human being, everything that I am tells me that it was real. I was part of something wonderful, something that changed me forever, a vision of the universe that tells us how undeniably tiny and insignificant, and how rare and precious we all

are, a vision that tells us that we belong to something that is greater than ourselves, that we are not, that none of us are alone. I wish I could share that, I wish that everyone, even for a moment, could feel that awe and humility and the hope for that continues to my wish.'

The movie theologian Barry Taylor has said, 'There is a very, very serious conversation going on in western culture at the end of the twentieth century about God, and the Church is not a part of it.'[6] We are not invited to the conversation and most of the time we are not even aware it is going on.

And not only is this conversation being conducted in the movies, it is also taking place in popular music. Many contemporary songs overtly express spiritual hunger. When I have had the opportunity to meet some of the key people in the music industry, I have asked them, 'Have you noticed popular music becoming more spiritual?' Without exception their answer has been 'yes', and some have also commented that this has been a particular trend since 9/11. One example is the song 'Where Is the Love?', released by the Black Eyed Peas in 2003, which ended with the appeal, 'Father, Father, Father, where is the love?' Another is a song by Anastacia, 'Left Outside Alone' (2004), which actually finishes with the prayer, 'Heavenly Father, please save me'. In his excellent book *Reel Spirituality* Rob Johnston says: 'With attendance at church stagnating and with movie viewing at theatres and through video stores at an all-time high, Christians find themselves wanting to get back into the conversation, but often we are not able to do so effectively.'[7] This is a conversation that we should be a part of. Using movies can help to bridge the huge gap between Church and culture.

5. Movies are preoccupied with tales of redemption

We must understand that the Holy Spirit's activity is not just confined to the Church's stories. The world's stories so often retell His story, and some of the most unlikely people are telling stories of redemption with an obviously Christian resonance. This is even true of someone like Stephen King, the mere mention of whose name causes some Christians to freak out because they associate him exclusively with the horror genre. Two great movies which echo with redemption themes, *The Shawshank Redemption* (1994) and *The Green Mile* (1999), were adapted from his stories. Both were directed by Frank Darabont. The story of *The Green Mile* centres around a prisoner who is able to perform healing miracles, and in the end dies even though he is innocent. Stephen King originally called him 'Luke Coffey' but later changed his name to John Coffey – JC – in order to draw out the fact that the character is intended to be a Christ figure.[8] You can't make it more obvious than that. 'Movies may be about stories,' says Brian Godawa, 'but these stories are finally, centrally, crucially, primarily, mostly about redemption.'[9] The word 'Saving' even appears in the title of *Saving Private Ryan*, which, like many of Spielberg's movies, has as its central theme the value of one solitary life.

One of my favourite movies with a redemption theme, certainly my favourite animation movie, is *Finding Nemo*, which is a great movie to use in church. It is about a little clownfish called 'Nemo', which in Latin means, of course, 'nobody', who rebels against his father, Marlin. Marlin is overprotective towards his son because at the beginning of the film his wife Coral and all their other children are completely wiped out by a barracuda, in what seemed like the perfect world of the Great Barrier Reef in Australia. However, when Nemo rebels and is captured by a cruel dentist, the father, who is rather timid by nature, faces unbelievable dangers as he crosses the ocean in order to pursue and rescue his son. As a tale of rescue from the consequences of rebellion and redemption, it provides a great way of talking about sin in terms our culture can understand.

At St Andrew's we recently heard a testimony from a teenage girl who was one of a group of young people taking part in our Sunday evening meeting. I felt nudged by the Holy Spirit to ask her how and when she came to the Lord. She told the congregation that she had come to the Lord the previous October in the foyer of the Warner Bros. cinema after watching the movie *Finding Nemo*. Through it she had been impacted by the love of God so strongly that she wanted to give her life to Him then and there. We must not confine our understanding of the work of the Spirit to the four walls of our churches.

How to Use Movies in Presenting the Gospel

In choosing movies to use in preaching,[10] it is good to choose ones that we feel passionate about, because that will ensure that our preaching will be passionate. It is also good to choose movies that are widely known because they will draw more people. Here are some practical suggestions:

1. Develop a philosophy of critical appropriation

Over the last hundred or so years there has been a wide spectrum in the Christian response to film, as Rob Johnston has pointed out.[11] These responses include: avoidance; caution; dialogue; appropriation; divine encounter. I am fascinated by the fact that people in our culture who are not Christian nevertheless want to hear from the Church about film. Just before Christmas I was invited to do some radio programmes for the BBC about the relationship between the movies that were in the cinemas at Christmas time and the Christmas message. In order to do the necessary research, the week before Christmas I went to see six movies, which even by my standards was a bit much. However, believing as I do that there are traces of God's story everywhere, the task provided me with an invaluable opportunity.

It is really important not to be ignorant or negative about films. I always find it a little bit difficult when I am talking to Christians who are so spiritual that they never go to movies and in fact actively dislike them. I encourage Christians to enjoy films and to inform themselves of what is going on in our culture. I want Christians to learn to think Christianly about the things we are watching at the cinema or on TV, or hearing over the radio. Yes, films can be used for dark purposes but that isn't the whole story.

2. Cultivate the skill of prophetic movie watching

Whether we are watching a movie or listening to music or viewing TV, all of these things can give us revelatory moments. W.H. Auden said, 'Even the most commonplace things are tinged with glory', and I love this quote which I found in a letter from J.R.R. Tolkien, 'We have come from God, and inevitably the myths woven by us, though they contain error, will also reflect a splintered fragment of the true light, the eternal truth that is with God.'[12] There is no doubt that God speaks to seekers through films and television programmes. At St Andrew's we have preached a series on 'What We Can Learn about Prayer from *The Simpsons*'. One of the sermons was based on a great episode called 'Bart Gets an F', in which Bart in desperation gets down on his knees in his bedroom and prays. Bill Dark has commented that, 'Statistically speaking there is more prayer on *The Simpsons* than on any sitcom in broadcast history.'[13] It's true – we have got a whole series out of it. A couple of years ago J. John was sharing the gospel in a church in London. After the service a young man came up to tell him that he had given his life to Christ in the service. J. John asked him what had brought him to church that evening, and the young man replied that it was an episode of *The Simpsons*, in fact the very same one I have just mentioned. This was a young man in his twenties who had no experience of church, but when he saw Bart Simpson in this episode kneeling and praying, it prompted him to say to his friend, who was watching the programme with him, 'I never pray. I need to learn about how to connect with God.' The two young men decided to visit a church one of them passed on his journey to work each day. The night they attended happened to be the occasion on which J. John was preaching. That young man is still worshipping God and attending church. I believe that God uses all sorts of means to speak to seekers. I believe that He will speak to us too if we employ double listening, as it has been called: listening to what is going on in a film or television programme and at the same time listening to what the Holy Spirit is saying.

3. Use movies and movie scenes as visual parables

There is great potential for using movie clips in preaching to illustrate biblical truths and Bible passages, particularly in evangelistic or seeker-orientated services. Movie clips can be used as illustrations and the stories of films as visual parables. Some films actually are already visual parables, such as, for example, the film *Bruce Almighty*, directed by Tom Shadyac, who is a Christian, and starring the magnificent Jim Carrey. Tom Shadyac and Jim Carrey have teamed up before for the comedies *Ace Ventura* (1994) and *Liar Liar* (1997). *Bruce Almighty* tells the story of a news reporter called Bruce Nolan who has been typecast as someone able to capture trivial human interest stories on camera. He blames God for his mundane and boring life. On a day in which one mishap after another occurs, Bruce takes issue with God. 'God,' he shouts to his girlfriend, significantly called 'Grace', acted by the superb Jennifer Aniston, 'is a mean kid sitting on an anthill with a magnifying glass and I am the ant. He could fix my life in five minutes if he wanted to.' On Grace's recommendation Bruce tries praying to God for help with very unexpected results.

I believe the core of a movie message should always be the gospel and an actual Bible passage. We are not preaching on the film, we are preaching on Scripture, but film clips can be used very successfully to highlight the good news. It is most effective, I think, if one film is used per sermon. As an example, I have used the character of Gollum from *The Lord of the Rings: The Two Towers*, in a message centred around Romans 7. The character of Gollum is, in my view, director Peter Jackson's finest achievement in this movie. Gollum, having been polluted and corrupted by the power of the ring, has become a monster but the Hobbit Frodo is still able to see something of humanity in him. The scene in which Gollum is having a conversation with his alter ego Sméagol about whether to kill Frodo or whether to go with him to Mordor echoes Paul's own struggles within himself (see especially vv. 16–17). Extracts from this film can be used to great effect.

In using clips from movies a very important practical consideration is achieving a high-quality picture. One of the reasons why we run our movie sermon series from January through to March is because at that time of year it is very dark in the evenings, and there is no problem at all with colour and light definition on big screens. I would recommend that any church that is serious in its desire to explore the medium of film should if at all possible invest in a state-of-the-art video projection system.

4. Create an appropriate environment

The following practical suggestions have been tried and tested in our movie series at St Andrew's. When putting on a movie sermon series, it is important for the church building to have a different atmosphere from the one it normally has. To create this, we play movie music over the loud speakers as people are coming in. We also lower the lights and display movie posters in the entrance foyer.

We start the service with an interactive welcome, which someone like J. John is really good at. One idea is to take the microphone and ask people in the congregation what their favourite movie is. On a *Finding Nemo* evening we had a quiz for all the children present, with prizes purchased from the Warner Bros. store. After the warm welcome we often use the theatrical trailer or special features from the DVD of the movie as a 'taster'. Then we pray for the presence of God because these meetings are not just entertainment: they need to be an encounter with the living God; we want these meetings to be presence-shaped as well as purpose-driven. This is followed by a time of worship through song, which we aim to make both seeker-sensitive and inspirational and Jesus-focused. After a Bible reading there is a thirty-forty-minute presentation using clips that have been professionally edited.

It is very important to iron out anything that is not appropriate for use in a church setting, particularly bad language. One of the movies J. John has spoken on is *Phone Booth* (2002) with Colin Farrell, in which just about every third or fourth word is an expletive that couldn't possibly be used in church, but it is an amazing movie. The message can be followed by a testimony or interview that serves the theme. Other art forms can also be used to great effect.

Again, on the *Finding Nemo* evening, we invited Steve Murray to perform a six-minute mime to music called *The Father's Chair*, which was extraordinarily powerful for all age groups. We need to think outside the box. In post-modernity we are going to find that the Arts in the wider sense are one of our greatest allies in terms of presentation. We end the evening with an appeal to the congregation to respond. We don't normally make a call for people to come to the front, but on the evening just mentioned J. John felt that this was the right thing to do. After having explained the gospel and the cost of following Christ, he called people to come forward and the whole of the front of the church was filled with people who wanted to make first-time commitments or rededications to Christ. It was a most remarkable evening, and we certainly hadn't seen a response like that before. We then have a final rousing hymn or song that relates to the theme.

For about the past two years I have been training a small group of people in the prophetic and this group meets before the service to listen to the Lord and ask Him what He wants to minister into on that evening. At this point in the evening I simply read out a selection of the words given, which takes about three or four minutes. The environment remains very controlled, but it is very much the prophetic at work in a way that seekers find very attractive and unthreatening. It has provoked a great deal of response and has resulted in both emotional and physical healing as well as salvation during the course of the series. The evening concludes with the blessing, an invitation to the next service and the offer of prayer ministry.

After the service we offer not coffee and biscuits but Coca Cola, popcorn and other refreshments that relate to a movie environment, which people really seem to like. Some of our congregation in their twenties don specially designed Big Picture T-shirts and caps and walk around with trays, offering sweets and other treats that particularly relate to the evening's presentation.

After the evening has taken place it is important to debrief so that there is the opportunity to learn from any mistakes.

In conclusion I want to say that I am really sold out on this idea of using movies in presenting the gospel. Once again I would stress that it is the gospel that is the central focus: the movie must serve the sharing of the gospel in a relevant post-modern way. As the Church we dare not miss out on the conversation which, as we have seen, is already taking place in our culture. Just as theologians are exploring the significance of film, so film-makers are exploring the significance of theology. Martin Scorsese has said:

When I was a little younger I wanted to be a priest. However, I soon realised that my real vocation, my real calling, was the movies. I don't really see a conflict between the Church and the movies, the sacred and the profane. Obviously there are major differences, but I can also see some great similarities between a church and a movie house. Both are places for people to come together and share a common experience, and I believe there is a spirituality in films, even if it is not one which can supplant faith: it's as if movies answer an ancient quest for the common unconscious. They fulfil a spiritual need that people have to share a common memory.[14]

Although we might have questions about how successfully Martin Scorsese as an individual director is fulfilling some of those aims in his own movies, one thing I know for sure: I love Jesus and I love films. And I love being part of a church that is prepared to take some risks and explore the interface between the two. And especially for the young people in our church and in community, using movies in preaching has made such fun of going to church – and for that and for all the conversions we have seen I praise God!

NOTES

1. When this seminar was given at the Preach the Word conference it was illustrated by movie clips from *Signs, Finding Nemo, Bruce Almighty* and *Lord of the Rings: The Two Towers*.
2. William B. Eerdmans (1996).
3. Scriptures in this chapter are taken from the New Living Translation.
4. See *Saint Paul at the Movies: The Apostle's Dialogue with American Culture* (Westminster/John Knox, 1993), and *Saint Paul Returns to the Movies: Triumph over Shame* (Eerdmans, 1999), in which Robert Jewett explores this subject.
5. See further, Lloyd Baugh, *Imaging the Divine: Jesus and Christ Figures in Film* (Sheed and Ward, 1997) and C. Deacy (ed.), *Screen Christologies* (University of Wales Press, 2001).
6. Unpublished address at Fuller Theological Seminary, 1999.
7. Baker Academic, 2000, p. 14.
8. He speaks about this in the Introduction to his novel *The Green Mile* (Orion, 1999).
9. Brian Godawa, *Hollywood Worldviews: Watching Films with Wisdom and Discernment* (IVP, 2002), pp. 50ff.
10. For more help on this, see Mark Stibbe and J. John, *A Passion for the Movies: Spiritual Insights from Contemporary Films* (with Study Guide) (Authentic, 2005).
11. Johnston, *Reel Spirituality*, p. 41.
12. *J.R.R. Tolkien: A Biography* (Humphrey Carpenter, 1977), Ch. IV.
13. Quoted in the excellent book by Mark Pinsky, *The Gospel According to the Simpsons* (John Knox Press, 2001). See also Mark Pinsky's article at http://www.snpp.com/other/articles/gospelhomer.html.
14. Quoted in *Faith and Film* by Ian Maher (Grove Booklets, 2002).

Chapter 43

ENGAGING WITH
THE POST-MODERN GENERATION

Michael Ramsden

'You are the salt of the earth. But if the salt loses its saltiness, how can it be made salty again? It is no longer good for anything, except to be thrown out and trampled by men. You are the light of the world. A city on a hill cannot be hidden. Neither do people light a lamp and put it under a bowl. Instead they put it on its stand, and it gives light to everyone in the house.'
(Matthew 5:13–15)

I want to take a very practical approach to the subject of 'Engaging with the Post-modern Generation' by concentrating on Jesus' teaching on salt and light from Matthew 5:13–15, which comes straight after the Beatitudes.[1] The most obvious way to tackle this passage is to come up with a two-part sermon, each with three points. The preacher begins by asking the question: what does salt do? The three-part answer is that salt purifies, adds flavour and preserves. Asking the same question of light, we discover that it illuminates, shines out into the distance and attracts. This is a very valid approach. However, there are at least thirteen other points which come out of these three mini-parables. I intend to concentrate on six of these to draw out what I believe we can learn from the Scriptures about engaging with our post-modern world, all of them coming out of the contrast between salt and light.[2]

I am choosing on this occasion not to be global in my remarks because many preachers will already have received a great deal of teaching and heard a great deal of theorising and analysis on post-modernism. I have to say I find it strange that we live in an age in church history where never before has there been so much analysis on how to reach a culture and yet never before has our evangelism been so ineffective. That is not to say that the picture is completely bleak. There is hope, but we urgently need to get refocused. There comes a point where endless analysis leads to paralysis. We end up not knowing what to do with what we know and we feel de-skilled by it. So aware are we of everything that we cannot do, that we are not sure any more of what we can do. It is for this reason that I want to take a practical approach by looking at the Scriptures which are our most useful guide on all these issues. I believe Jesus' teaching on salt and light has some very important lessons for us.

1. Visibility/Invisibility

Light works visibly, salt works invisibly. I know it is a statement of the obvious but when we turn on a light, we can see what light does and is by its very nature. However, it is not possible to see salt preserving food, cleansing a wound, or adding taste to a particular ingredient. It works secretly; it works invisibly. It is generally recognised that in these verses Jesus is teaching about the nature of mission. Therefore, part of what He is saying is that while some Christian mission is highly visible, other expressions of it will not be seen. Both are vital. This, I believe, is an important point for us as we engage with a post-modern generation.

I often work at the visible end of the evangelism spectrum. I travel a great deal and receive invitations to speak in many different countries and in many high-profile situations. This can give the impression that somehow what I am doing is more significant for the sake of the gospel – because it is so visible – than all the invisible things which happen around me. But that simply is not true. It is very easy to nod our heads in agreement and acknowledge the truth of this fact, but the time must also come when we in the Church begin to teach about its importance. One of the things a post-modern generation struggles with is the empty promises that have been offered to it by other world-views or alternative answers to life's big questions, where it is all talk and there is no real difference. For many Christians a significant factor in their conversion was a friendship with someone, perhaps a family member or friend or neighbour, whose life impressed them deeply. Those who were changed as a result may not even have been aware of the salt and the saltiness of that individual's life rubbing off on them – they just knew it began to change the flavour of life for them. Even though it cannot be seen, this 'saltiness' must be encouraged in every single church.

I have had the privilege of being invited to speak in the White House and to deliver a lecture on Capitol Hill. These opportunities sound very impressive, but it was only possible for me to receive these invitations because there are nameless, faceless people who are working as salt and light in both of those communities and are taking the risk to invite their friends in order to expose them to something different. Salt works invisibly. As a matter of fact, some Christian ministry, such as counselling and certain types of prayer ministry, can actually be damaged when its visibility is seen. Invisibility is an essential part of the nature of mission, and we need to recapture this truth.

We preach a life-changing gospel. It is then not surprising that people want to see lives changed. Where is the saltiness that works invisibly? How do we empower the people in our churches, in our homegroups, the people we know, to get hold of the fact that they are the salt of the earth? They are the ones who can make a difference. We need to tell them that, although some of what they do has to be kept in secret, we want to honour them. We need to recapture and understand that there is a part of the gospel which is invisible.

2. EXPOSED/HIDDEN

The second contrast concerns two types of light. It is very hard to hide a city on a hill – in fact it is not even worth the attempt. However, it is possible – though quite stupid – to light a candle and hide it under the bed. There are some parts of the gospel which can never be hidden. For example, people will notice us walking in and out of the church on Sunday and at other points in the week. But the personal light of the testimony of our lives can be hidden by us: at work, in our family, from our neighbours. There is a danger of hiddenness. Post-modernism was not born out of disagreement with modernity, but out of disillusionment. Whereas to disagree with something is to reject it rationally, to be disillusioned with something is to experience it and find it wanting, which is why we talk about 'a culture of disillusionment'. We experience something and find it wanting. If, at the same time, we have told everyone how great we think it is, we normally end up feeling embarrassed about the fact that it hasn't worked out. How then do non-Christians feel when they meet embarrassed Christians?

Right from the very beginning of my Christian life I had a great passion for evangelism. I have always wanted to be an evangelist. I can remember, two days after having made a commitment to Christ, my youth leader saying to me, 'Michael, if I can pray one thing for you what would it be?' I said, 'I want to be an evangelist. I want to preach the gospel.' Does that mean, therefore, that when my family and close friends ask me about Jesus I never feel embarrassed? I wish I could say that I never am. Or that when I am on a plane and I am talking to someone, I never want to pretend I am someone who I am not? Sadly, I am tempted! It is possible for all of us in every walk of life to hide the light of our personal witness. Light-bearing has to be encouraged. Like everyone else, I need people around me to encourage me to share my faith.

On one occasion when I was flying to India, I really needed to write a talk I was scheduled to give on how to witness to people we meet. I had just been so busy I had not had the time to prepare it. So I pulled out my Bible and a notebook, and started reading and making notes. A man sitting next to me said, 'Is that a Bible?' I said, 'Yeah.' He said, 'Do you often read the Bible?' I said, 'Yeah.' He said, 'I used to read the Bible but I stopped some time ago.' I said, 'Oh.' He said, 'Do I take it you're a Christian?' I said, 'Yes.' After that he fell silent. A few moments later it hit me – this man wanted to talk to me. I wanted to write a talk about how to witness to people about the gospel. I just closed my notebook and my Bible and asked, 'So why did you stop reading the Bible?' He told me that he had lost his faith as a result of undertaking ordination training for the Church of England. How often we remain silent when we should speak because we are scared of losing relationships either in business, or with friends, or with family.

Another reason why we hide our light is because often we haven't thought through what we believe and consequently, when a question comes up, we end up saying something inappropriate; we get burned by it and in the future decide to remain silent. There are a number of courses available, such as J. John's *Calling Out* course or *The Alpha Course*, which can provide Christians with the confidence they need to be able to speak about their faith. Post-moderns are normally not ashamed of what they believe because they don't feel they have to justify it. However, they find it strange when they meet a church that seems embarrassed to advocate what it believes and won't stand by it. I was most bemused by the editorials I read about Pope John Paul II on the occasion of his eightieth birthday. I have never read such contradictory editorials. All the broadsheets said much the same thing: this man is a moral dinosaur, he is against abortion, he is against homosexual relationships, he is against all kinds of moral things which we believe are right. Next paragraph: you have to respect and admire a person who has stood so solidly and firmly for what he believes. Isn't that the case? No one respects people who just capitulate in the face of opposition to what they believe. The post-modern generation isn't any different. Where are the lights that are *not* being hidden under a bushel but rather have been put on the lampstand so that they shine out?

Now this is not an excuse for rudeness. Some people seem to think that the goal of evangelism is to help you lose your friends, and they have turned rudeness into a spiritual gift! In some cases a reaction will occur that the Christian sharing their faith had no control over, and they have done nothing wrong. In other cases, the individual is most definitely at fault. On a trip to Cyprus, for example, I met a man who was pleased because he had been persecuted for the gospel. This man worked for a Christian missionary organisation. Soon after his arrival, he had gone to a Greek butcher and tried to explain to him that he had been sent from America to tell him about Jesus Christ. The butcher couldn't speak English; the evangelist couldn't speak Greek. All the Greek butcher could understand was the words 'American' and 'Christ', and therefore he concluded that this man was trying to tell him that Christ was an American, so he picked up his meat cleaver and chased him down the street with it. That is not persecution for the cause of the gospel; that is persecution for being stupid, insensitive and rude. Sometimes we may simply have to admit that we have not handled a situation sensitively.

We may have to recognise the fact that our past failures in sharing the gospel have caused us to put our light under the bushel and we have stopped shining our light before the world so that people can see our good works and praise our Father in heaven. We need to recapture this vision so that the Church can reach a post-modern generation.

3. HOME AND AWAY

While the light is the 'light of the *world*', the salt is 'the salt of the *earth*'. The Jewish readers of the Gospel of Matthew would have understood the 'earth' to refer to the 'land of Israel', to their immediate communities, and the 'light of the world' to be universal, shining throughout the cosmos. Here we have the home and away vision of mission. As J. John expressed it, 'A missionary is not someone who crosses the sea. A missionary is someone who sees the cross.'[3]

The truth is that most of us prefer to do our mission away, rather than at home. This is the opposite to most football teams who prefer to play at home rather than away, since it is on their home turf that they receive the greatest amount of support and the greatest amount of respect. Why is it that we as Christians feel the reverse? Why is it that most Christians instinctively feel that it would be easier to go on a mission trip to evangelise than to do it on their doorstep?

I have a vision for where I live. I call it 'Eat the Street'. My goal is to eat my way through everyone who lives on my street, not literally but by means of barbecues, dinner parties, cheese and wine evenings – everything I can possibly do to get my neighbours around to my house to eat with me. What is the point of my travelling halfway round the world to go and evangelise someone else's street if I am not prepared to evangelise my own? Where am I going to be most effective as salt? Obviously, in my local area: that's where I live, that's where people know me. It takes time to get to know people. For me this means in my Christian ministry that I cannot fill my calendar up so much that I am too busy to spend time with my neighbours and friends. It is very important to me that I know if the person who is living a few doors down from me isn't feeling well or is struggling with life. I have a responsibility for my street. We must not be so busy thinking about the 'world' that we forget about the 'earth', the community in which we live.

Nevertheless, the gospel is also the light of the world and it has to shine out into the world: it has to be preached. Professor Isaiah Berlin was one of the giant figures of British intellectual history in the twentieth century. He was at Oxford University for all of his academic tenure, and wrote many books and addressed many different issues. However, the single most important issue for Isaiah Berlin was freedom. He wrote and spoke about freedom more than any other issue. He maintained that freedom must be pluralistic. By 'pluralism' he did not mean 'relativism'. He meant a kind of peaceful co-existence or social tolerance, where we must allow many different opinions to be held in the same way at the same time even though they might contradict each other. He believed this because he had lived through Nazism and Stalinism. As a matter of fact, in one of his most famous essays he listed all of the 'isms' and schisms he could think of, adding in Christian religious fundamentalism just to round it all up. He then drew the conclusion that history shows that whenever people are monists – by which he meant those who believe that their understanding of the world is the only true and correct one, that they have the 'truth' – they believe they can justify doing anything they want to anyone who disagrees with them.[4] Consequently, a Stalinist leader has no qualms about torturing or murdering his own people or perpetrating wars, because he believes he has the one correct path. This is equally true of all groups who believe they have the truth. Not many people read Isaiah Berlin, but almost everyone we meet will be scared of people who think they have 'the truth'.

Now as Christians we do have the truth, but we also have been given grace and we worship a gracious God. The reason why a proper understanding of grace is so important is that truth without grace becomes tyranny. This does not at all mean that I am a relativist on the issue of truth, or that I don't believe there is such a thing as truth, or that I don't regard the gospel as the truth. I believe all of those things and I have preached on them many times. But truth *without grace* results in tyranny. The light is the light of the world: it has to go out into the world; it has to be preached into the world. However, if we are to reach a post-modern generation we must realise that they are instinctively suspicious of people who believe they have 'the truth'. This does not mean that we should not proclaim 'the truth', but it does mean that we must make sure that, both in our preaching and in our lives, the proclamation of the truth is accompanied by grace.

Let us take the issue of judgement as one example. I believe preaching about judgement is important, but it can be approached in two ways. We could say something like this:

> 'Your life is completely messed up; it is an offence before God; one day God will
> judge you and He will throw you into hell, where you will be tortured for ever; but
> since God is a God of love, He would also like to forgive you and therefore He
> commands you to repent.'

Or alternatively we could say:

> 'Have you ever done something wrong to somebody that you shouldn't have done?
> Have you ever bumped into them a few days later? How did you feel? Answer:
> ashamed.
>
> Or maybe your car has been vandalised. How would you feel if the person who
> vandalised your car was arrested? Answer: good.
>
> But supposing you vandalised someone else's car because that person had annoyed
> you, and you got caught. How would you feel then? Answer: ashamed, and even
> angry.
>
> If you feel angry at the prospect of someone judging you, what is that normally
> indicative of? Answer: that I have done something wrong, and I didn't want to get
> caught.

> If I were to talk to you about God's judgement right now and you were to feel angry, what might that be indicative of? Answer: maybe that I have done something wrong, and that I feel ashamed.'

By using the second approach, we are not shying away from the issue, but we are thinking about the best way in which to communicate the central concepts of the Christian gospel. We need to reflect on what it means to cast the light out into the world so that it truly appeals and does not repel.

4. WITHIN/WITHOUT

There are two lights. There is one light which shines out into the world and another light whose purpose is to shed light within the room. There are two forces of mission: one that reaches out beyond the community and one that provides the warmth of light within it. There needs to be a warmth in our communities. There is no point in attracting people in if they are then not going to be fed and cared for. Many people only experience the chill of 'God's frozen chosen'! Somehow the light radiates little warmth or heat, just the cold of a sodium or neon streetlight in winter.

5. IN TOUCH/OUT OF TOUCH

As I have already mentioned, while the light spreads out into the distance, salt must make contact in order to effect change. So many of us as Christians are like ships passing in the night when it comes to our non-Christian friends and family. As we go out of our front door and see everyone going off to work, we smile and say, 'Hi, nice to see you', and that's it. We could just as well smile and say, 'Nice to see you, go to hell', because that is all there is to our relationship with them. There is no contact. Salt must make contact if it is to do its work. It must be rubbed in by friendly relationships if it is to do its work and arrest the decay.

6. RELEVANT/IRRELEVANT

Some time ago I was asked by a colleague to speak on 'The Contemporaneity of the Gospel'. This is the only title I have ever been given in the last seven years which has made me reach for a dictionary. The man who chose it is very good with languages – he can speak seventeen different languages, seven of them fluently – so I knew there was a reason why he had phrased it in this way, and it therefore deserved careful thought. I needed to discover why, rather than asking me to speak about 'The Contemporary Gospel', he had asked me to speak about the gospel's 'Contemporaneity'. I discovered that the word 'contemporary' has several possible meanings. (1) It can mean 'approximately equal in age' as, for example, when we speak about 'a contemporary'. This definition evidently does not apply to the gospel. (2) It can mean 'occurring at the same time as something else' which, since we live two thousand years after Christ died on the cross, also does not apply. (3) It can mean 'fitting in with modern fashion, ideas or design'. Although some people might think that this is what apologetics sets out to do – to take the gospel and repackage it to make it fit with modern fashion, ideas and design – that is not its goal. It is much more what liberal theology sets out to do.

Having considered these definitions, we can see that it is not appropriate to speak about a 'contemporary' gospel. However, the word 'contemporaneity' means to talk about 'a living thing active at the time of someone or something else'.[5] So, since we worship a living God who is active at the same time as us, it is possible to speak about the 'contemporaneity' of the gospel. As always, my colleague was right in his choice of titles! What I am trying to say is that our goal is not to try to make the gospel relevant to post-moderns. Attempting to do so assumes that it isn't already relevant and that something has to be done to it in order to make it relevant. The gospel is *perceived* by post-modern people to be irrelevant to their lives, and it is that faulty perception which we have to tackle, dismantle and remove by demonstrating that it is relevant.

Salt, which obviously refers partly to the gospel, can lose its saltiness in a variety of ways. If the gospel is tampered with, it loses that which makes it salty; it is worthless to everybody. If we seek to change it in any way, it will lose its saltiness and it will become useless.

Salt also refers partly to us; we personally are 'the salt of the earth'. If we lose our saltiness, we also become worthless. Many will be familiar with an eighteenth-century Middle-Eastern story about a merchant who tries to corner the salt market. He buys up all the salt he can lay his hands on, the idea being that if he is the only one who has any salt, everyone will be forced to buy it from him and he can drive up the price. However, the salt he buys contains impurities and goes bad, so then he is faced with the problem of how he can dispose of the bad salt. If he puts the salt on his fields, the cattle will eat it and it will be bad for their health. If he throws it in the river, the fish will be poisoned. If he throws it down a well, he will pollute the water supply. So what solution does he eventually come up with? He takes the sacks of salt, punches holes in the bottom of the bags and has them dragged up and down the streets of the city, where it is trampled underfoot.

In the Middle East, the rudest thing a person can do is to show someone the sole of his foot. In the iconic pictures of the bronze statue of Saddam Hussein coming down during the Iraq war, people were taking off their shoes and throwing them at the statue. I even saw one film clip of a man holding a portrait of Saddam Hussein which he was repeatedly slapping with his sandal. Rubbing his shoe in the dictator's face was the strongest gesture he could possibly make in his culture to express his hatred. In Scripture, the worst thing that can happen to human beings, in terms of God's judgement, is to fall under His shoe. This is why when God is expressing His outrage at Edom, the only thing He has to say is, '*over Edom will I cast out my shoe*'.[6] So the idea that salt is to be trampled underfoot is the most degrading and awful thing that could possibly happen. If salt loses its saltiness, it is good for nothing but to be thrown out and trampled underfoot. If the impurity of our lives reaches such a level that, like the salt, we become useless, then we are worthless to everyone and everything. This is a serious teaching. The good news is that when a candle goes out, it can be relit. So there is a warning, and there is hope.

How we live our lives before a post-modern generation is absolutely vital. We are in the life transformation business. There should be something about the fruit of our lives that causes the world to say, 'There is something different about you. What is it?' People sometimes say to me, 'Michael, no one asks me about the Christian faith.' In some ways this should not come as a surprise to us since, as I have already indicated, we live in a culture which believes that there are no answers to life's big questions, and therefore people begin to wonder whether it's worth asking the questions in the first place. Having said that, if we are not being asked any questions, we should ask ourselves: Why not? What does my life look like? How does it read? Am I the salt of the earth?

I said earlier that there is hope for the Church as we seek to reach out to a post-modern generation. Our hope lies in the fact that society has actually not changed that much since Jesus gave us His teaching about the nature and role of mission, and the way to change any society has not actually changed that much. In order to reach the post-modern generation we need to understand again what it means to be salt and light in our society; to understand that we need to be visible and that our lives need to proclaim the gospel clearly. It is being the salt of the earth that will make the difference, and here every single Christian has a role to play.

I will finish with a story about three grains of salt. The three grains of salt in a salt cellar are having a conversation about the merits of being a grain of salt. The first grain of salt, who is an optimist, looks around and says, 'Isn't it fantastic to be a grain of salt! Look at this glorious crystal cathedral we were placed in when we were taken out of that dark cardboard container and poured into here. Do you see how the light is reflected through the windows and the wonderful spectrum of colours we can behold? Isn't it amazing to be a live grain of salt?' Then the second grain, who is more of a realist, says, 'My friend, I don't want to disturb your poetical flow but have you seen that pot of boiling water on the stove over there? Has it never occurred to you that every time that water is boiling someone comes and picks up this glorious cathedral of light, turns it upside down and some of our brothers are irretrievably lost through those holes, disappear into the water and we never hear from them or see them again. Think about that and then tell me how wonderful it is to be a grain of salt.' Then the third grain of salt says, 'My friends, it is wonderful to be here. And it is also true that one day we will be poured out through one of those holes, but one thing I know for certain, when I disappear through that hole and plummet into the steaming water, it will never taste the same again.' As the salt of the world, we are meant to make sure that life itself never tastes the same again; that as we make contact, we change the flavour of our world. When it stops tasting the same, people will start asking us questions: Why are you a Christian? Why do you believe what you do? How has it changed your life? Then in answering those questions we will make Christ known, with the result that life itself will be changed.

NOTES

1. I am indebted to the scholarship of Dr Kenneth Bailey, who has guided and inspired through his teaching insight into these passages.
2. There are also similarities, but there is not enough time to look at these.
3. See Chapter 39.
4. *The Power of Ideas* (Chatto & Windus, 2000).
5. Oxford English Dictionary
6. Psalm 60:8 KJV.

Chapter 44

THE PROPHETIC DIMENSION

Mark Stibbe

In any one of the preaching genres, whether it be evangelistic preaching, pastoral preaching, expository preaching, doctrinal preaching or topical preaching, we can be listening to what God the Holy Spirit is saying as we preach, but prophetic preaching is distinctive. Through it the preacher brings about a fusion between what the Holy Spirit is saying *now* through prophecy and what the Holy Spirit said *then* through Scripture. Of course, in a sense all preaching does this, but prophetic preaching takes this tendency to a higher degree.

Prophetic preaching involves a combination of two spiritual gifts. The first of these is the gift of teaching, which I define as the special God-given ability to provide new insights into an old Word, the Scriptures.[1] The second is prophecy, which is the special God-given ability to know and declare what the Holy Spirit is revealing today. Sometimes it is mistakenly seen exclusively as *fore*telling but in my experience it is more ordinarily *forth*telling.[2] With its combination of the two spiritual gifts of teaching and prophecy, prophetic preaching is a potent form of communication. Prophetic preaching is not an excuse for the bypassing of good sound biblical exegesis or exposition: that is the path to gnosticism. Prophetic preaching requires the teaching gift to be exercised, but it also requires the prophetic gift. If handled responsibly, the marriage of these two gifts in the preacher's life can bridge the gap between our present context and the past text in remarkable and startling ways.

THE 'THIS IS THAT' DYNAMIC

Prophetic preaching involves a 'this is that' dynamic. The 'this' is what the Holy Spirit is saying and doing right now – and, of course, we require the gift of prophecy to be able to sense and understand that. The 'that' is what is recorded in Scripture for all time. In fact, it is this 'this is that' way of speaking in which we see Peter engaging in Acts 2:14, the first sermon after Pentecost. In doing so he was drawing on a common Jewish form of exposition known as *peschar*, which would have been very familiar to him. In the New Living Testament Acts 2:16 reads: '*No, what you see this morning was predicted centuries ago by the prophet Joel*'. The King James Version renders this verse: '*But **this is that** which was spoken by the prophet Joel*' (my emphasis). In the Greek *touto estin to*. 'This' is what the Holy Spirit is saying and doing now; 'that' is what the Scriptures described then in the book of Joel. We see this dynamic again in Acts 2:33 when Peter says:

> *Now he sits on the throne of highest honour in heaven, at God's right hand. And the Father, as he had promised, gave him the Holy Spirit to pour out upon us, just as you see and hear today.*[3]

There is an almost electric connection between the two horizons of present work and past Word. It is this revelatory nature of prophetic preaching that I want to emphasise. As Luke redescribes the Pentecost event in Acts 2:14, he says 'Peter declared', employing the Greek word *apophtheggomai*, which in the Septuagint is used of the utterances of the prophets. Clearly in Luke's mind and heart, what Peter is doing is prophetic. It is prophetic preaching: it is preaching that is prophecy, and prophecy that is preaching. I would stress again that all preaching is prophetic, but with prophetic preaching there is a difference of degree. It majors on the 'this is that' dynamic. In prophetic preaching a spark of revelation is fired up by the surprising connection between our present contexts and the past text. When we sense what the Holy Spirit is saying and in our study of Scripture we see it already there in the Word of God, the two come together and there is a Eureka moment.

Having explained the theory, I would now like to give an example.[4] Just before Christmas a couple of years ago I was faced with the challenge that most preachers face at times in their ministry of trying to find something fresh to preach about in the very familiar texts of the Christmas narrative. I was preaching a series on the various characters in the Gospel accounts, and on that particular Sunday it was the turn of the shepherds. As I studied Luke 2, I began to see an amazing fusion between what I sensed the Holy Spirit was saying prophetically and what the past text has always said. That night, like every other night, the shepherds were out on the hills, most of the time sitting around watching out for bears and wolves, playing their flutes, singing their songs. But that night their hearts were captured in the most extraordinary way by a vision of the glory of God. As first one angel appeared, and then a whole choir of angels, singing, 'Glory to God in the Highest...', they were told about the Saviour's birth. Straightaway they left their flock of sheep and ran into Bethlehem for an encounter with the baby Jesus that absolutely transformed them. They went from being shepherds to being heralds because Luke says that they *'told everyone what had happened'*. How long it was before they went back to the sheep that they had abandoned, we do not know, but clearly for a while they were going around spreading the good news of the Saviour's birth. Something had really grabbed hold of their spirits, not just their minds, and these shepherds became evangelists. 'Everyone was amazed' because these weren't the likely people to be engaged in this task.

As I reflected on these events, the Lord really spoke to me. I felt Him say that what He had done to the shepherds those many years ago, He was doing now among pastors in churches up and down the country. When many of us first came to Christ, we were absolutely apprehended by Jesus. Our hearts were captured by Jesus and for a while at least we went around gossiping the gospel. We couldn't get enough of Jesus. Our whole lives were 'a magnificent obsession', if I may quote the phrase, with the person of Jesus Christ, and it was as if we were naturally supernatural about evangelism. We couldn't stop sharing Jesus because we were so in love with Him. Then we were called into the Church, and before long we found ourselves immersed in maintenance, administration, watching the flock – the same old thing week in, week out, patching up the wounded, playing the same old songs. But in our hearts we felt, 'There has to be more than this. We were born again for more than this.' Even though we found ourselves providing pastoral oversight, 'supervision' as it were, what we ourselves have needed most is a super-vision. We have needed a new vision of Jesus Christ.

As God spoke to me from this passage, I believe He told me that He is giving pastors a new revelation of the wonderful, matchless person of Jesus Christ. This new vision will turn us from being merely watchers of the sheep in the same old field of limited influence, to being men and women who run with an enthusiasm we haven't had for years to share Jesus. We may be said to be the unlikeliest of people to be doing it. People may question why we aren't with the sheep in the fold. But the reason will be because something has grabbed hold of our hearts that compels us to get out of this limited field of 'Christians only' and moves us from consumerism back to evangelism, from merely supervision to a super-vision that will transform us. We will go from being merely pastors to being heralds. Heralding the good news of Jesus Christ outside of the flock and the fields will again become the greatest passion of our lives. This country will only be won by people who rediscover that passion. It won't be won by anything else. It will only be won by people who are radically in love with Jesus and can't stop sharing Him.

This is the journey that I am on. When I had this word, I questioned how I might manage this process. I knew it was what the Lord was saying and it really excited me, but I have a really large church to run and already the pastoral needs were not all being met. In a way that I could not have imagined possible, the Lord brought two new members of staff into our team. One is the church manager who is now running all the administration, and the other is a fabulous pastor who has a strategy for meeting everyone's pastoral needs through small groups and mid-sized communities, so that already the level of belonging has shot up. Now, with those posts in place and the flock being supervised properly, I am able to be involved in evangelism. I love being with non-Christians and I love sharing Jesus with them in relevant ways. I love moving in the prophetic with non-Christians. I love daring to pray for healing for non-Christians and seeing the Holy Spirit move in their lives. And I think I've been too long away from it managing and supervising churches. I want to get stuck back into the harvest.

For me there is something poetic about the experience of prophetic preaching and the key to this is, I am convinced, metaphor. Metaphor will certainly be very familiar to those like me who have a background in the study of literature, but there is much metaphorical thinking in science too. Metaphor is a particular use of language in which a person finds similarities in two apparently dissimilar things. For example, one of my favourite poets, Ted Hughes, uses the metaphor of a thistle as 'a grasped fistful of splintered weapons'.[5] In this metaphor he brings disparate things into a surprising unity. As well as the apparent connection in terms of sight, there is also a connection in terms of sound: 'thistle' and 'fistful' are almost a half-rhyme. In addition, in terms of touch there is a similarity between the pain of grasping a thistle and the pain of grasping a fistful of splintered weapons. The use of language in this way is extremely clever. I think prophetic preaching employs the same synthesising function. It involves an anointed and imaginative or metaphorical synthesis of present context and past texts. 'This is that.' This synthesis has great synergy. Not only does it create a greater range of meanings than each could do separately, but it works to evoke a sense of revelation. It is the marriage of apparently dissimilar things which produces the sense of surprise and disclosure in prophetic preaching. Such unlikely accord succeeds in defamiliarising the familiar.

This potential to defamiliarise the familiar is very important. When I was looking at the shepherd story in Luke 2 it was as if I had never read it before. The familiar was suddenly gloriously defamiliarised by the prophetic anointing of the Holy Spirit! This has always been a feature of Pentecostal preaching at its best, which is often both lyrical and poetic. Black Pentecostal preachers, in particular, frequently have the extraordinary ability of being able to see the connections even in the most familiar texts between what the Holy Spirit is saying right now and what the past text has always said, and to make it all feel as if it was brand new to us. It is obvious, and yet it is a surprise – in the same way that good poetry is. I would love an academic to do some work on the lyrical poetic metaphorical nature of black Pentecostal preaching because I think there are some real lessons to learn about inspirational preaching under that anointing. This type of preaching does not just address the head: it addresses the heart and it goes even deeper than that to touch the soul and the Spirit, in a way that merely dry cerebral preaching often and in fact almost always won't.

DEVELOPING PROPHETIC PREACHING

There are two points I would like to make:

1. Develop the discipline of rigorous exegesis

Prophetic preaching has got to start with Scripture and end with Scripture. The more disciplined the study of Scripture, the more prophetic the preaching. Without the rigorous exegesis of the Word of God it is impossible to preach in a prophetic way. None of the greatest revivalists in history – men and women filled with the Holy Spirit and living in the most extraordinary times – has ever said that we should despise learning or the study of the Word of God. Indeed, revivals have always brought a new hunger and delight for the Word of God. In the First Great Awakening in the 1730s, in Northampton, USA, it was said that some Christians burst into tears at the mere sight of a Bible. Nothing of what I am saying should take us away from the systematic study of the Scriptures. I know, in fact, that if we depart from the Bible we will not be able to preach prophetically. We need to be constantly filling up our well of biblical knowledge.

The reason why this is so important is because in prophetic preaching, in the preparation process and sometimes as we are preaching, the Holy Spirit pulls, as it were, a bucket out of the well of the preacher's biblical knowledge and offers living water to the people in the congregation to drink. But if, as a result of our laziness over many years, there is no water in the well, we will not preach prophetically. We have to keep filling the well. We have to keep investing, investing, investing, working, working, working: otherwise we will never preach prophetically. The best prophetic preachers have an extraordinarily rich understanding and love of Scripture. I am making this point so emphatically because I know that in this whole area of prophetic preaching sometimes I can be just as guilty as others of implying that it is all just up to the spontaneous work of the Holy Spirit, and we have no part to play. In prophetic preaching we have to start with the meaning of the text under study. That means the original meaning intended by the original author in an act of communication with the original audience in the author's original context.

I have not bought into the deconstructionism which says that, since the author has died, authorial intention has no relevance. In a preaching series I undertook on John 18 and 19 last Good Friday I looked at every single verse in those two chapters of the Passion narrative. I not only had a section entitled 'Historical Record' but also one called 'Evangelist's Interpretation'. I do believe that authorial intention can be interpreted meaningfully and responsibly. It can be discovered by the standard tools of biblical scholarship, such as grammatical and historical criticism, redaction criticism and especially narrative criticism.

The more we study God's Word, the better equipped we will be for prophetic preaching. Only through knowing the Word will we be able to spot the 'this is that' dynamic. We must actually have spent a lot of time in the 'that' to be able to make a connection under the anointing of the Holy Spirit with the 'this'. Immersion in God's Word is the foundation for this ministry.

In around 1994/5, sitting in a vestry in the east end of Oslo, the Lord began to speak to me out of John 4, a passage I have lived in for many years. This story of Jesus at the well with the woman of Samaria is, I believe, very relevant for our age. For the first time I began to notice that in this story everything happens on the edge. Jesus is on the edge of town. He is with a woman who is literally marginalised. In that context, on the edge, Jesus prophesies into the woman's life:

> 'You're right! You don't have a husband – for you have had five husbands, and you aren't even married to the man you're living with now.'
> (John 4:17–18)

Jesus, Son of God, Saviour of the world, Second Person of the Trinity, but also prophet, teacher and all the rest, had the gift of prophecy par excellence. He saw right into her life. She responds, *'you must be a prophet'*, because that is what prophets were supposed to do: they were meant to be able to see in a way that was not possible by purely natural means. After further conversation, in which Jesus speaks to her about worship and the fact that He is the Messiah, at least by implication, she runs into town with a new enthusiasm – reminiscent of the shepherds who became heralds – and says, *'Come and meet a man who told me everything I ever did!'* This is an extraordinary statement – and one which not every man in town would have been pleased to hear! The result, we are told, is that most of the townspeople go out to meet Jesus on the edge of town. A well has been opened up spiritually, and they come and drink. By the end of the story they too are confessing that Jesus is the Saviour of the world.

Although, as I say, I had lived in that Scripture, I had never before noticed this extra-ordinary dynamic of the margins and the mainstream in the story. It starts on the margins but at the end the mainstream catches up. Everything happens on the circumference, but God's amazing grace works through to the centre. And it was prophecy that was the catalyst. I felt the Holy Spirit saying that there was coming in the days, months and years ahead a move of God on the margins of society, and many people on the margins would come to know Jesus. However, it would eventually come to the mainstream. I also felt the Lord saying that prophecy was going to be a very key tool in the harvest, as it was for Jesus.

At the time I kept quiet about this revelation, sensing that I needed to watch and pray. Later I started to preach it everywhere, and within about two years I was getting reports of amazing things happening in the prisons, among gypsies and in other places where God was clearly at work on the margins revealing Jesus. A current staff member at St Andrew's was, in the late 1990s, the senior chaplain at a prison in Bristol for young offenders, and in two years his team saw between 400 and 500 prisoners come to Christ. A major factor in this move of God was the gifts of the Spirit, including prophecy, being exercised by ordinary people. More recently I am starting to see it in the mainstream! I am telling the story not to claim that I had a great word from the Lord, but to make the point that I would never have sensed this 'this is that' dynamic if I had not spent years in John's Gospel. I believe God uses what we *have* studied, not what we have *not*. We need to develop the discipline of rigorous exegesis and expect God to speak to us through it.

2. *Develop the discipline of prophetic listening*

Just before his death, the great Smith Wigglesworth, the radical, reckless Bradford plumber who preached the gospel with extraordinary passion and did many signs and wonders by the grace of God, gave a prophecy concerning future moves of the Holy Spirit in the Church. In 1947 he prophesied: 'During the next few decades there will be two distinct moves of the Holy Spirit across the Church in Great Britain. The first move will affect every church that is open to receive it and will be characterised by restoration of the baptism and gifts of the Holy Spirit. The second move of the Holy Spirit will result in people getting back into the Word of God.'

Wigglesworth also speaks of 'a coming together of something that has not been seen before: a coming together of those with an emphasis on the Word and those with an emphasis on the Spirit.' When the Word and the Spirit come together, there will be the biggest move of the Holy Spirit that the nation, and indeed, the world has ever seen. It will mark the beginning of a revival that will eclipse anything that has been witnessed within these shores, even the Wesleyan and Welsh revivals of former years.

When I heard that prophecy for the first time something inside of me leapt in recognition that it was the word of the Lord. In the decades since Wigglesworth died we have certainly seen an amazing new move of God's Holy Spirit amongst Bible teachers, with outstanding men like John Stott and many others with extraordinary ability to interpret and expound the Bible being raised up. Since the Second World War, particularly in Great Britain, the number of evangelical Bible scholars and preachers has been quite phenomenal, and I believe we need somebody to undertake the very important task of charting that historically.

In those decades, particularly in the early 1960s, we have also seen the Holy Spirit move in the historic denominations, with the result that what the Pentecostals had already been enjoying came to them too. The New Churches were also birthed in that timeframe. Baptism in the Holy Spirit started to be talked about again, the charismata were rediscovered and the old cessationist and dispensationalist argument was actually intelligently critiqued not just on the basis of experience but on the basis of Scripture. Now I am praying for the Word and the Spirit to come together, so that we have a whole generation of people preaching in the pulpits and evangelists evangelising on the streets who love the Word of God and are really rooted in the gospel but are also moving in the power of the Spirit and are actually daring to pray for the sick, prophesy over the lost, and all the rest.

The Word and the Spirit need to come together, as R.T. Kendall so frequently emphasised. In order for this to happen, in addition to disciplined, rigorous exegesis with the best of the skills and tools that biblical criticism has given us, in our prophetic preaching we need always to be open to the Holy Spirit. Like Jesus, who only ever said what He heard the Father saying, who only ever did what He saw the Father doing, we need to know such intimate communion with the Father by the power of the Holy Spirit that we can say confidently what the Holy Spirit is doing. Like the apostle Peter in Acts 2, we can see it, we can hear it. The world is waiting for this kind of living encounter with God, Father, Son and Holy Spirit. They are not waiting for more information, they are waiting for more reality.

Bible interpretation involves significance as well as meaning. The meaning is fixed: it is what the original author intended to say. But the significance is fluid. It is how the passage speaks to people in each new situation. We even find this in Scripture itself. In Acts 15, for example, when the Church is confronted with the interesting problem of Gentiles becoming Christians and being filled with the Holy Spirit, James interprets the book of Amos in a way that draws out its significance for the situation they are currently facing. It is an application of Amos that goes beyond what the prophet originally intended but is continuous with it and is anointed by the Holy Spirit. In prophetic preaching the significance of a biblical text arises out of our knowledge of what the Holy Spirit is saying and doing right now, and we must be alert to this dimension. The devil wants to kill the prophetic in preachers. He comes to steal and destroy. Each preacher who is filled with the Holy Spirit has this prophetic dimension, but the devil, who knows that dry boring preaching will not save anyone, wants to root it out and destroy it. If, however, the prophetic is alive in us, as we read and study the Scriptures and as we preach the Word of God, then life-change will happen. Even if we can't see it, it will be happening.

We cannot make the connection between present context and past text without the use of prophetic phenomena. For about the last two and a half years my daily prayer has been: 'Lord, would You increase the prophetic in me and in my church. I welcome the prophetic in Jesus' name. I recognise my responsibility to weigh the prophetic, to test and evaluate everything, but Jesus You say, "Ask and you will receive", and I am asking.' I also pray daily for higher levels of authority and accuracy in the prophetic. I believe that the Lord loves that kind of praying. Whether we see ourselves as a pastor or a teacher or in any other role in our service of Jesus Christ, the Bible says that thanks to Pentecost anyone can now prophesy. In the glorious democracy of the Holy Spirit the gift of prophecy is no longer confined to a few as it was in the Old Testament, but is available for anyone who calls on the name of the Lord. I pray every day that the Lord will give me visions, open visions, pictures, dreams, impressions, thoughts, puns, riddles and messages from God. Why puns and riddles? Because God speaks through puns and riddles in the Scriptures.

Ever since I started praying in this way God has begun to speak to me through puns. At New Wine last year I nearly ran into a juggernaut with 'M.E. Heal' on the cab. The next day I was going to be preaching on healing, and immediately I wondered if God wanted to heal people of ME, although I was really not sure whether God would speak through this really rather unconventional means. So I asked Him, if it was indeed Him, to remind me of the incident the next day when it was time to pray for the sick. The next morning, when I had finished teaching on blind Bartimaeus in Mark 10, it came back to me with full force, so I said, 'I believe that the Lord Jesus has spoken about ME. If you suffer from ME I want to pray for you now.' Even before I had finished speaking the words, somebody was healed totally, and so far I have received twelve letters from people completely healed of ME during those few minutes of praying. Some people were actually healed in the meeting; some were listening to the talk on the radio in their caravans; one teenage girl was lying on a mattress outside the tent. All through a pun! Some of those healed have come to St Andrew's and given their testimony. I believe God speaks today. We need to be open to it and pray for it. Prophetic preaching involves attending both to the meaning of a passage and alertness to what the Spirit is saying now. We need to listen to what God is saying through whatever prophetic means He chooses.

In conclusion, I would like to give some words of warning and some words of encouragement. First, some words of warning. Prophetic preaching must not be the only kind of preaching we do. I reserve this kind of preaching for what I refer to as *kairos* moments in the life of the local church. On a week by week basis at St Andrew's we have sermon series, because I believe it is helpful for people to know what is being preached on in the life of the church. From time to time, however, when we sense that there is a new season in God or there is a gap between series, God will give a 'this is that' message to excite the church, mobilise or equip the saints, or move us on to the next phase. I am not talking about the next fad, but about the next stage of its mission to reach the lost, which should be the mission of every church. In any case we can only preach prophetically if we feel we have something from the Lord to say, which should be submitted to a proper process of testing. If the Lord gives something to me, I always share it with my staff team first and ask them to weigh it. I won't necessarily ask for an immediate answer and I won't preach the message straightaway. It might take weeks or even some months before it is actually brought into the public domain. In Acts 2 when Peter delivered his 'this is that' sermon he stood up with the eleven: he was part of a community, a team. I really believe in team, especially in this whole area of prophetic preaching. It is so important not to be individualists.

This leads me on to my second word of warning, which is that we do have a responsibility to weigh and test what we sense the Holy Spirit might be saying. In my book *Know Your Spiritual Gifts* I list a number of criteria which can be used for this purpose.[6] It is so important to be able to discern what is of the Lord, what is of our human flesh, and what may even be of the devil, because even the elect can be deceived. We must never allow ourselves to be tipped over into exegetical gnosticism. Some of the silliest things I have ever heard have been said in the name of prophetic preaching or prophetic exegesis. I met one Christian woman in Sheffield who divorced her husband for, as it seemed, no apparent reason – she was just rather fed up with him. When I asked her to explain the rationale for her decision, she said that, reading Ephesians 4:22 in an old translation, she had come across the phrase 'Put off the old man', which she had taken as a word from the Lord. If it hadn't been tragic and utterly foolish, it would have been hilarious, because it was so unbelievable. There was no continuity with the original meaning of the passage, which has to be one of the tests of the validity of a prophetic word. Prophetic preaching involves responsible interpretation.

Second, and finally, some words of encouragement. Prophetic preaching can be the most inspirational kind of preaching. '*Where there is no vision the people perish*' (Proverbs 29:18 KJV), or as Rick Warren has put it, 'Where there is no vision the people leave the parish.' The people of God really need vision, and this kind of preaching excites people and gives them a new impetus for serving God and getting stuck into the harvest.

Prophetic preaching can also warn God's people. While I was worshipping in a church in Stratford, Ontario, God began speaking to me, through a vision and a Scripture, about the fact that two Churches are going to arise, one a confessing Church and one a compromising Church. Whenever God speaks to me prophetically about the Church there is always Scripture alongside the prophecy: the prophecy is never given in isolation. The Lord warned me that a time was coming when there would be a real polarisation between these two Churches, and in my own diocese in this very week an issue has arisen which will force St Andrew's as a church to take its stand. I have also felt the Lord warning me that a time of testing is coming to the nations. As I was preaching about this in a church in St Alban's, I felt the Lord say, 'And within five days people will see this testing, and it's coming to Europe.' The following Friday the Madrid bombing which killed 200 people took place. In that instance I didn't speak the word I had been given because I feel that accountability is very important – I just shared it privately afterwards. Prophetic preaching can encourage, comfort, strengthen and warn the Church.

I will finish with two Scriptures:

> *Do not stifle the Holy Spirit. Do not scoff at prophecies, but test everything that is said. Hold on to what is good. Keep away from every kind of evil.*
> (1 Thessalonians 5:19–22)

> *Let love be your highest goal, but also desire the special abilities the Spirit gives, especially the gift of prophecy.*
> (1 Corinthians 14:1)

NOTES

1. See my book *The Teachers' Notebook* (Kingsway, 2003), which is part of a series edited by Barry Kissel, with other titles including: *The Apostles' Notebook*, *The Prophets' Notebook*, *The Evangelists' Notebook*, *The Pastors' Notebook*.
2. I have a whole chapter on this topic in my book *Know Your Spiritual Gifts* (Zondervan, 1997).
3. The Scriptures in this chapter are taken from the New Living Translation.
4. This example is also recorded in the conclusion of *Prophetic Evangelism* (Authentic Lifestyle, 2004).
5. From 'Thistles', published in *Wodwo* (Faber, 1967).
6. See chapter on 'Discernment' (Zondervan, 1997).

Section Eight

THE MAKING OF
A PREACHER

But if I say, 'I will not mention him
or speak any more in his name,'
his word is in my heart like a fire,
a fire shut up in my bones.
I am weary of holding it in;
indeed, I cannot.

(Jeremiah 20:9)

Chapter 45

THE CALL TO PREACH

Steve Brady

In the year that King Uzziah died, I saw the Lord seated on a throne, high and exalted, and the train of his robe filled the temple. Above him were seraphs, each with six wings: With two wings they covered their faces, with two they covered their feet, and with two they were flying. And they were calling to one another:

> *'Holy, holy, holy is the LORD Almighty;*
> *the whole earth is full of his glory.'*

At the sound of their voices the doorposts and thresholds shook and the temple was filled with smoke.

'Woe to me!' I cried. 'I am ruined! For I am a man of unclean lips, and I live among a people of unclean lips, and my eyes have seen the King, the LORD Almighty.'

Then one of the seraphs flew to me with a live coal in his hand, which he had taken with tongs from the altar. With it he touched my mouth and said, 'See, this has touched your lips; your guilt is taken away and your sin atoned for.'

Then I heard the voice of the Lord saying, 'Whom shall I send? And who will go for us?'

And I said, 'Here am I. Send me!'

(Isaiah 6:1–8)

Almost thirty years go, in the first year of our marriage and of our ministry, my young wife and I made our first ever visit to the Keswick Convention. Amid the good teaching and much else that was on offer, one sentence was spoken that went deep into my heart and has remained with me to this very day. Although I had completed less than one year of ministry, I was physically exhausted and losing vision, even wondering whether I had made a mistake in entering the ministry. Listening to the outstanding Old Testament scholar J. Alec Motyer, who was preaching through the book of Nehemiah, one statement, made simply as an aside, burned its way into my heart and has remained with me. It was, 'I'll tell you what your problem is, you've lost your vision of God.' The great problem with many of us is that we so easily lose our vision of God. Amidst all the busyness and pressure of ministry, we lose our vision of God and the work of the Lord becomes more important than the Lord Himself. We lose focus. We lose direction. We lose sight of the big calling which first captured our heart. Our greatest need is a vision of God.

When we lose our vision of God, everything in our life gets out of kilter. The difficulties with which we struggle, the setbacks we endure, the heartbreak we suffer, all come between us and God. We become almost paralysed. The well-known chorus tells us that 'In His presence, our problems disappear'. In my own personal experience I have not found that my problems disappear, but in His presence I do find perspective, I do find encouragement, and I do find the resources to deal with my problems and difficulties. We all need to have our vision recalibrated in the presence of our glorious God, so that we can discover a new vision of how great and how marvellous He is. Only if our call to ministry springs from a vision of God upon the throne – as Isaiah's did in the passage I want to look at – will it lead us in the right direction. Any other motivation for ministry will lead us astray.

The Divine, Impelling, Constraining Call

I am aware that in the Evangelical Church at the current time there is debate about what constitutes a call to the ministry and whether it is appropriate for us to compare our call with that of the prophets and apostles. For example, is it right exegetically for us to draw an analogy between ourselves and the prophet Jeremiah who complains,

> But if I say, 'I will not mention him
>   or speak any more in his name,'
> his word is in my heart like a fire,
>   a fire shut up in my bones.
> I am weary of holding it in;
>   indeed I cannot.
> (Jeremiah 20:9)

or the apostle Paul who says, *'Woe to me if I do not preach the gospel'*?[1]

Quite recently I was looking through a book published about forty years ago, entitled *My Call to Preach*, in which some of the great preachers of the era – men such as Alan Redpath, Stephen Olford, Dr Paul S. Rees, Leighton Ford, R.P. Martin and Derek Prime – told the story of their own call to preach. Among the accounts was one written by my great predecessor at Lansdowne Baptist Church in Bournemouth, Francis Dixon. I found his account very moving. Francis had come to the church in 1946 and, by the time he left in 1975, he had a worldwide Bible school with 40,000 people on his mailing list. Every free country in the world received his tapes and his Bible school material. Just a couple of years ago, on a visit to China I met a pastor who had been in a Communist prison for twenty years. Very recently he had been given 15,000 copies of Francis Dixon's Bible school notes translated into Mandarin. Francis Dixon had only been a Christian for about three days when he felt burdened to preach. Opening his Bible almost at random, he read those wonderful words from Luke 4:18ff., *'The Spirit of the Lord is on me, because he has anointed me . . . '*. Although he was a very young Christian he realised that he could not assume that he could apply these words to himself but needed to consider their context. Then from nowhere another verse came to him. He looked it up in a concordance and discovered it was John 20:21: *'As the Father has sent me, I am sending you.'* I made a note of what he said next: 'I want to say that this divine impelling, constraining call has come to me every day since. This is no exaggeration.' It was this divine, impelling, constraining call that motivated Francis Dixon to preach with great fruitfulness over a whole lifetime.

I take it as axiomatic that Jesus sends His people to preach His Word. He sends all of us. In Romans 10 Paul poses the question, *'how can they hear without someone preaching to them?'* We are all sent to tell the good news of Jesus, but for some of us that burden – the burden of the Word – becomes so overwhelming, so irresistible, so inevitable, that we can do none other than preach the unsearchable riches of Christ.

ISAIAH 6

A young schoolboy wrote in his essay, 'The skeleton is what is left after the insides have been taken out and the outsides have been taken off. The purpose of a skeleton is something to hitch meat to'! This is a rather graphic description of what I would like to do now with reference to Isaiah 6. As we look at Isaiah's vision of God in relation to the call to preach, we will see that we need to look up; we need to look in; we need to look to; we need to look out; and we need to look forward.

1. Look up!

> *In the year that King Uzziah died, I saw the Lord seated on a throne, high and exalted, and the train of his robe filled the temple . . .*
> (Isaiah 6:1)

We need to look up to the awesome face of God. Comparatively speaking, during his fifty-two-year reign, Uzziah had been a good king, but towards the end of his life he made some serious mistakes and ended his life badly. In 2 Chronicles 26 we are told about how he tried to involve himself in the priesthood, which was forbidden, and how he ended his life as a leper, alienated and excluded, almost a living metaphor of what was happening in Judah in the eighth century. The Chinese saint Wang MingDoh was right when he said, 'Many young men start well; few finish well.' The purpose of gospel ministry is not to start out like a hare but fail to last the distance, but to be faithful throughout a whole lifetime. There are many extremely talented men and women who have ended their lives stranded down blind alleys because, somewhere along the line, they blew it. Charisma without character will lead to catastrophe. Ability without integrity becomes a liability. Like Uzziah we too can end our lives badly, if at some point we begin to make the wrong choices.

Although there is not time to look at the background to the passage in depth, it is worth noting that the story of Uzziah reminds us that no man lives to himself and, although he was a comparatively good king, his areas of failure had infected the nation. Earlier in the book of Isaiah reference is made to some of the nation's failings:

> 'They are full of superstitions from the East;
>   they practise divination like the Philistines
>   and clasp hands with pagans.'
> (Isaiah 2:6)

> ...'The women of Zion are haughty,
> walking along with outstretched necks,
>   flirting with their eyes,
> tripping along with mincing steps,
>   with ornaments jingling on their ankles.'
> (Isaiah 3:16)

> Woe to those who call evil good
>   and good evil...
> (Isaiah 5:20)

There is incredible hedonism and materialism as well as the influence of eastern religions and a total confusion of good and evil. Isn't that the world in which we are living today? In fact,

> From the sole of your foot to the top of your head
>   there is no soundness –

only wounds and bruises
and open sores,
not cleansed or bandaged
or soothed with oil.
(Isaiah 1:6)

The people of God are in disarray and turmoil and, with the death of Uzziah, yet another plank in the nation's life has been removed. It is against this background that Isaiah has his vision of the glory of God.

Commentators have differed about how much Isaiah depended on the ambivalent and ambiguous though generally good king Uzziah. However, there is a consensus about the fact that something monumental happened to Isaiah in the year that King Uzziah died. *Something* was knocked out of his life which enabled him to become *someone* for God. There are times when God has to knock something or someone out of our lives and bring us into some form of crisis that becomes the process for God's call and challenge to go to the nations for Him. Perhaps it is our job or our health. Perhaps it is somebody we relied upon, somebody we respected and looked up to, somebody who was an example to us. Perhaps he or she was taken away by death, or perhaps he or she suffered a moral lapse. A friend of mine, who is a preacher living in the United States, said to me recently, 'Steve, don't you get worried that all the worthies that we used to look up to, who were there as our captains and helping us to move forward, are disappearing, and we're being invited up on to the plinth and we're not ready for it?' Whatever the thing or whoever the person that is taken away, God uses the situation to give us a wake-up call.

About three or four weeks ago I was driving home late at night. As I was driving I was talking to the Lord about all sorts of things, but there were two particular things on my mind. I was worried about a check-up I was due to have the following day for the bladder cancer that I suffered last year, and I was also wondering whether I should change my very old car which my son, who is a mechanic, had managed to keep on the road. I was saying, 'Lord, do You think it's time I changed this car? Perhaps You could give me a sign.' Anyway, a few minutes later, having driven a hundred miles and with only three miles to go until I reached home, I suddenly saw a dim light and, to cut a long story short, I realised, coming down a motorway class road into Bournemouth, that I was about to hit a moped which was doing about twenty miles an hour with no reflectors on it. I hit my brakes and disappeared into the trees at between fifty and sixty miles an hour, ending up with the car upside down. The car was written off, and I almost was. One of my friends really encouraged me by commenting, 'Eee, lad. The Lord's a Yorkshire man. He gave you two for the price of one. He gave you your wake-up call and the irrevocable sign you needed to change your car.' Thank you very much! As I extricated myself from the wreckage, the woman driver of the moped came up and exclaimed, 'Jesus Christ!' I said, 'Excuse me. It's because of Him I'm still here. I was speaking to Him about a minute or two ago and it's He who has just saved my life.' She was surprised. It is often in these critical situations when something has been knocked out of us that we receive fresh vision and a fresh revelation of the glory and splendour of God.

'In the year that King Uzziah died, I *saw* the Lord...'[2] To Moses God declares, 'you cannot see my face, for no one may see me and live'[3] and in John 1:18 we read:

> No one has ever seen God, but God the One and Only, who is at the Father's side, has made him known.

So, in our language of accommodation, Isaiah sees the Lord, and, in fact, he says, he sees Him 'high and exalted, and the train of his robe filled the temple'. It was not even the robe itself that filled the temple but just the train of the robe. In the year that the good though ambivalent king died, Isaiah tells us that he saw the deathless God, the immortal King, the eternal Ruler, the everlasting Lord on His throne. Even the pagan king Nebuchadnezzar knew that God was upon His throne and does whatever He will:

> His dominion is an eternal dominion;
>> his kingdom endures from generation to generation...
> He does as he pleases
>> with the powers of heaven
>> and the peoples of the earth.
> No one can hold back his hand
>> or say to him: 'What have you done?'
> (Daniel 4:34–35)

This God is the King of the ages. There is nothing small or domesticated about Him. Isaiah is being reminded that the Lord is on His throne. He is the Lord of the universe and, although his own personal world may seem very shaky, God is still in charge.

He is also the God of absolute purity. The word 'seraph' means 'burning one', and even these burning ones, who are before the throne of God, cover themselves with modesty in the presence of the one who is 'Holy, holy, holy'. In the Hebrew language, in order to express a superlative, a word is repeated, so, for example, if you wanted to express that a song is the best of all the songs, you would say 'the song of songs'. The fact that the word 'holy' occurs three times indicates that the holiness of God goes beyond a superlative: 'He is the holiest of the holiest.' Although there is some debate about the Hebrew root of the word translated 'holy', it seems to derive from the word meaning 'to cut', 'to make a difference', 'to be separate from'. This is at the heart of what Christians believe about our God. He is different from; He is separated from; in theological terminology He is transcendent. God is separated from His creation, while remaining involved in it. He is Other. Holiness is part of His nature.

In the time in which we live the Church is losing transcendence. We have lost a sense of the otherness of God. We like to see God as our friend, as our therapist and in other ways which are true. But if He isn't totally other, then He isn't the Lord God Almighty. This, I believe, is the reason why some Christians are turning back to High Anglican, Roman Catholic and Orthodox Churches, because they are looking for that otherness, that transcendence, that glory, that majesty of God, which is so little found amongst us. We have made God into our errand boy. He just turns up to satisfy our desires. But, in Isaiah 6, the prophet catches a glimpse of God's holiness and he is reminded that the whole earth is full of His glory.

The word translated 'glory' is another interesting Hebrew word. It is the word *kabod* which means 'weight'. In relation to God this does not have the sense of 'heavy', but the sense that He has 'substance' or 'gravitas'. He is who He is. The problem is that sin makes human beings insubstantial. It makes us lightweight. It makes us other than God. We become lighter than a feather; we become like chaff. Our lightness is in stark contrast to the weight of God's glory.

The whole earth is full of His glory. Let me give just one example from the many in the realm of nature. On Christmas Island, every year around December, a hundred and twenty million female land crabs make their way down to the coral reef and each of them lays about a hundred thousand or more eggs into the sea. If only five out of a million make it back every five years, the indigenous land crab population of Christmas Island is maintained. Nobody knows why this phenomenon of nature occurs – not even David Attenborough! But I believe that God makes these land crabs for His own glory.

On his face before God, Isaiah is made to feel something of his weakness and his smallness. He sees the abject failure of himself and of the whole human race, and he cries out:

> 'Woe to me! I am ruined! For I am a man of unclean lips, and I live among a people of unclean lips, and my eyes have seen the King, the LORD Almighty.'

Isaiah feels himself to be on the raw edge of terror.

2. Look in!

In the early twentieth century a theologian called Rudolph Otto wrote what has become a very celebrated book *The Idea of the Holy*, in which he coined the word 'numinous'. In it he explained his thesis that when human beings encounter the otherness of God – the greatness, the majesty, the raw terror of the holiness of God – they feel both overwhelmed by it and attracted to it. We see this in Isaiah's reaction to his vision of God. He is not only aware of his smallness and his own personal angst but, deeper than that, when he comes face to face with the glory of God, he is also confronted by his own sinfulness. His mouth is shut. It is grace teaching his heart to fear.

How vastly different is our contemporary notion of God as a Father Christmas in the sky to our forebears' understanding. Listen, for example, to the words of Thomas Binney's great hymn:

> Eternal Light! eternal Light!
> How pure the soul must be
> When, placed within Thy searching sight,
> It shrinks not, but with calm delight
> Can live, and look on Thee!

> The spirits that surround Thy throne
> May bear the burning bliss;
> But that is surely theirs alone,
> Since they have never, never known
> A fallen world like this.

> O how shall I, whose native sphere
> Is dark, whose mind is dim,
> Before the Ineffable appear,
> And on my naked spirit bear
> That uncreated beam?[4]

God is not only the God of love, He is the God of holy love. If we do not have a true vision of God, we run the danger of presenting a distorted gospel. We may tell people about the benefits of having Jesus in their lives, because He can sort out their marriage or help them with their depression, all of which are true as spin-offs, but this is not the heart of the gospel. The heart of the gospel is finding peace with God by getting right with Him. As Isaiah sees God, he becomes aware of his own desperate need. He becomes aware of how much there is in his life still to be overcome. As those who have heard God's call to preach the gospel, preachers need to have the same experience that Isaiah had. Being a minister of the gospel is not just a job that a person can do regardless of what is happening on the inside. It is deeply connected to the experience of the individual. Colin Morris said, 'It is not from a pulpit but from a cross that power-filled words are spoken. Sermons need to be seen as well as heard to be effectual. Eloquence, homiletical skills, biblical knowledge are not enough. Anguish, pain, engagement, sweat and blood punctuate the stated truths to which men will listen.'[5] The preacher himself must be affected in his inner being.

3. Look to!

I once heard a preacher give the following illustration. On a nice bright but cold day he was travelling by car to the Midlands. Although there was snow still lying on the ground outside, the passengers in the car were getting very hot. When he put his finger on the windscreen, which was refracting the sunlight on to them and making them very uncomfortable, to see how hot it was, he was very surprised to discover it was icy cold. God is not interested in preachers exercising a ministry that may warm others up, but leaves them as cold as ice. It is as important for the messenger to be prepared, as it is for the message to be prepared. That is the part I find hard in my preparation, and I think that is true for most preachers. It is at the point when Isaiah realises how desperate his own need is, that he is encouraged to look to the amazing fullness of God's grace as the live coal is taken from the altar, the place of sacrifice, the place of blood offering, the place where holiness and justice is satisfied. As this live coal from the altar touches his lips, it cleanses him.

On a recent trip to Liverpool, I had half an hour to kill so I popped into the Walker Art Gallery, which I had not visited for a long time. As I walked round, I was confronted by a painting by Rubens, which he completed between 1632 and 1634 in Antwerp. The painting is called 'The Virgin and Child with St Elizabeth and John the Baptist'. Despite the fact that the Virgin dominates the scene somewhat, it is a wonderful painting. Alongside the painting there was a brief commentary supplied by the gallery which talked about the continuous movement of human and divine love and drew attention to the glances between the Virgin and St Elizabeth and their respective sons. While Jesus is depicted at Mary's breast, St John is portrayed as a young boy with a lamb at his side. The commentary goes on to explain that the lamb, which looks at the viewer, encourages our thought and contemplation. I was struck by the image of the lamb which did seem to be looking at me and by the thought that in essence this is what the whole of the Old Testament does. It encourages us to contemplate our need for a Saviour.

I don't come from a Christian home. When I was fourteen, somebody bought a Bible for me and I struck a bargain with God that I would read three chapters of it every day, and double it at weekends, if God would help me and help Everton Football Club. It worked a treat because we won the cup that year – it was fantastic! I read right through the Bible in about six or seven months, and then I started again, because I knew I was on to a winner! As I went through it a second time, reading about all the sacrifices in the Old Testament, lying on my bed in inner-city Liverpool, I found myself thinking, 'Where can I find a lamb to sacrifice for my sins?' Isn't that what the Old Testament is supposed to impress upon those who read it? A very old hymn has the following verse:

> We look back through the ages,
> Where the saints and sages trod,
> And we see the altars reeking with the sacrifice and blood.
> But these were merely pointers to the pascal Lamb of God.

Isaiah's vision of God confronts him with his need for atonement. The Old Testament reveals to us our need for atonement and points forward to the incredible story of Christ, the Lord Himself, who will come as a real Saviour, to offer real forgiveness, to real sinners, who have blown it with a real and holy God. The Old Testament exposes the need for a substitutionary death.

Another of the current debates in theological circles is the whole question of whether Christ's substitutionary death was in fact necessary, with some even going so far as to suggest that Christ's death on the cross constitutes a form of 'cosmic child abuse', with a vengeful Father punishing His Son for an offence He did not commit. But I want to say that this truth is at the very heart of the gospel, and without it the gospel makes no sense whatsoever. At the heart of the gospel is not the truth that God punished an innocent victim in our place: at the heart of the gospel is the profound truth that it was against God that we sinned and God Himself has come to pay the price. If I owe my friend a hundred pounds, and he tells me that I do not have to pay it back to him, I am in his debt. He has taken my debt. It is the one who forgives the debt that pays it. This is the message at the heart of the gospel. James Denney was right when he somewhere said, 'I would not say that God died on the cross, but the One who died on the cross was God.' At the heart of our gospel is the cross that brings grace from this holy righteous God.

4. Look out!
As he receives this amazing grace, Isaiah is encouraged to look out:

> Then I heard the voice of the Lord saying, 'Whom shall I send? And who will go for us?'
> And I said, 'Here am I. Send me!'

It is really important to understand what is happening here. This is not a call to ministry that is motivated by a sense of debt or guilt, that says, 'Since God has done all this for me, I ought to respond by serving Him.' This is not a call to ministry which is responding to a sense that God needs him, and without him His plan for the redemption of humanity will fail. Although there is some truth in these motivations, this is not what causes Isaiah to respond. His motivation is very, very different. Here is a man who is forgiven; here is a man who is cleansed; here is a man who is changed. Here is a man who is so excited that God has put him right and is so full of joy that he is saying something like, 'Will I do? Could You count me in? Could I be a possibility? Would You please, Lord, consider me?' I am sick of hearing ministers moaning about the hard lot they have been given in life. If that is how they feel, they should go and do something else! The greatest privilege this side of heaven is to serve the Lord. Isaiah is so full of joy and gratitude that he counts it a privilege to be able to serve the Lord.

Isaiah's ministry would not be an easy one, as God reveals a little later in Isaiah 6:

He said, 'Go and tell this people:

"Be ever hearing, but never understanding;
be ever seeing, but never perceiving."
Make the heart of this people calloused;
make their ears dull
and close their eyes.
Otherwise they might see with their eyes,
hear with their ears,
understand with their hearts,
and turn and be healed.'

Then I said, 'For how long, O Lord?' And he answered:

'Until the cities lie ruined
and without inhabitant,
until the houses are left deserted
and the fields ruined and ravaged,
until the LORD *has sent everyone far away*
and the land is utterly forsaken.
And though a tenth remains in the land,
it will again be laid waste.
But as the terebinth and oak
leave stumps when they are cut down,
so the holy seed will be the stump in the land.'
(Isaiah 6:9–13)

We may feel we are facing a very similar situation to the one Isaiah faced. While the Church is growing phenomenally in other parts of the world, we in Europe seem under a cloud of judgement and as preachers we often seem to be hitting a brick wall.

On 22 October 1996 a memorial service was held at St Martin's in the Fields for Sir Kingsley Amis. Summarising his life, Amis's son Martin recalled a conversation his father had had with the Russian novelist and poet Yevgeny Yevtuschenko. The Russian had asked Amis whether he was a Christian, which he strongly denied. 'So, you're an atheist?' Yevtuschenko persisted. 'I am,' Amis replied, but a moment later continued, 'No, no, it's more than that. I hate Him.' Amis could not even see that he was shooting himself in the foot by admitting hatred of a God he did not believe in. There is a battle going on for the soul and the heart of the nation in which we are living and in which we are called to preach.

5. Look forward!

It is, however, not all doom and gloom for Isaiah. God promises him that, *'But as the terebinth and oak leave stumps when they are cut down, so the holy seed will be the stump in the land.'* It is, of course, clear from other verses in Isaiah such as chapter 11 verse 1, which talks about a shoot coming up from the stump of Jesse, and verse 10, which refers to *'the Root of Jesse'*, and the critical passage in Isaiah 53, which talks about the Suffering Servant, that God is referring here to the promised Messiah. He is talking about the seed of a woman, who will come and bring transformation. Isaiah is being told to look forward to the astonishing future which Christ will bring.

Even though it will not come for another 700 or so years, God tells Isaiah to look forward to the Messiah's coming. We do not know the times or the seasons for they are in the Father's hands, but whatever our situation, whatever our circumstance, whatever we are going through, we need to be able to look forward. The message of the Bible is, 'Hallelujah! We win in the end!' Isaiah is going through an incredibly difficult time, and he is told that he is not going to see immediate results from his ministry. In fact, it is going to be very hard, but there is One coming who will put it all right and He will be well worth waiting for. That one is Jesus.

On the visit to the Walker Art Gallery to which I referred earlier, I went to see perhaps its most famous painting which is by the Victorian artist W.F. Yeames. It is a country house scene set in the heady days of Puritan England. The Roundheads are interrogating a boy of undoubted truthfulness and innocence, who is standing on a little box, about the whereabouts of his father, while his mother and two sisters look on anxiously. It is a scene that is charged with all sorts of meanings and metaphors, but it is the title of the painting that is most illustrative. The title is the question the boy is being asked, 'And when did you last see your father?' We each need to ask ourselves the same question. When did we last see our Father seated on His throne and when did we last hear a word from Him? And when did we last say, 'Count me in, Lord. I don't care how tough it is or how seemingly futile and fruitless it is: if this is what You are calling me to, then here am I, send me.'

NOTES

1. 1 Corinthians 9:16.
2. My emphasis.
3. Exodus 33:20.
4. Written *c.* 1826.
5. Colin Morris, *Wrestling with an Angel: Reflections on Christian Communication* (Collins, 1990).

Chapter 46

THE MAKING OF A PREACHER

Jeff Lucas

I want to begin by saying that I believe in preaching. I feel very privileged to be one of the teaching pastors at Timberline Church in Fort Collins, Colorado, where I have been working for about twelve years as part of an itinerant ministry and where we have now made our home. In the relatively small town of Timberline with its 140,000 inhabitants, the church has grown from about 300 to around 9,500, having doubled in the last year. We have five services every weekend. I preach the same message – exactly twenty-six minutes in length – five times. I even include the same spontaneous humour each time. Preaching has played a major part in the growth of Timberline Church.

I believe in the power and the validity of preaching, and I am very pleased to be addressing the topic of 'The Making of a Preacher'. Preaching the Word of God is not just about the creation of sermons but about the moulding of women and men who are the deliverers of that message, both by word and by life. I would like to suggest that the following six factors will be key in determining whether we as preachers will be 'made'.

1. WILLING TO BE SHAPED

My involvement with Timberline Church means that I cross the Atlantic approximately once every fifteen days, which is much too often. I often tell the story of one landing I experienced in Chicago. I was on American Airlines flying into Chicago when the pilot made the following announcement: 'Ladies and gentlemen, this is your pilot speaking. We have a slight problem. [Now I never believe pilots when they say there is a "slight problem".] We are losing hydraulic fluid from the left-hand side of the airplane. If those of you seated on the left-hand side look out of the window, you will see it shooting out of the wing.' I did. It was. The 'slight problem' of the loss of hydraulic fluid means three things: (1) that the wing flaps don't work, making descent impossible; (2) that the landing gear doesn't work, so, even if it were possible to descend, it would be impossible to land; (3) that the brakes don't work, so, even if it were possible to land, it would be impossible to stop. This is known in the aeronautical industry as a 'slight problem'. Nonetheless, unlike my travelling companion, who was in the overhead baggage compartment screaming for his mother, I was brave and courageous in this situation. As a good Charismatic I was engaging in the Vienna Boys' Choir glossolalia, which is not as bad as it sounds. We did get down, we did land, but we couldn't stop and the pilot threw the plane into reverse thrust. The pilot, who had actually done a good job of encouraging us through the trauma, just said, 'Don't worry, they've closed the rest of the airport down and we do have fire trucks and paramedics standing by' – which made us feel warm all over. We went shooting down the runway pursued by the fire trucks and finally, with about ten feet to go until the end of the runway, we came to a stop, and great relief broke out across the plane. The men were giving each other high-fives and pretending to be very brave. The ladies were exchanging Body Shop products and three nuns were singing 'Kumbaya' in the back. As my friend climbed out of the overhead baggage compartment, suddenly Nigel – for all pilots are known as Nigel – said, 'I have another announcement for you, ladies and gentlemen.' What, I wondered, was he about to say? Would he thank God, perhaps quote the Lord's Prayer or make some other meaningful comment? No. What he, in fact, said was, 'Ladies and gentlemen, this is your pilot speaking: on behalf of American Airlines I'd like to be the first to welcome you to Chicago. Have a nice day.' This was a man who read a script every day of his life. After a moment of tension, panic, dare I say, even excitement, he reverted back to his normal habit.

As we think about the making of a preacher, I want to suggest to you that one of the great challenges for us as preachers is not to let preaching become a habit. Bergman says, 'The gospel can simply become an old habit among us, neither valued nor questioned. Our technical way of thinking reduces mystery to problem, transforms assurance into certitude, quality into quantity and so takes the categories of biblical faith and represents them in manageable shapes.' This is a theologian's way of saying, 'We can get really boring.' We can do what we do. In the vestry of Westminster Chapel there is a stereographic report of a sermon delivered by Spurgeon on 4 September 1881, in which he makes this statement: 'I dread getting to be a mere preaching machine, without my heart and soul being exercised in this solemn duty lest it should merely be a piece of clockwork.' In Robert Munger's words, 'A prepared messenger is more important than a prepared message.'

As preachers we need to be shaped, and it is a lifelong process. We matter: not just as mouthpieces but as people. One of the most scary times for me as someone who travels the world preaching, is the prayer meeting before the service. I may be feeling fairly good about life but attending the pre-service prayer meeting sometimes makes me want to have a conference call with the Samaritans. The intercessors – whom I thank God for most of the time – gather around me; they rub my chest, they spit in my ear, and then they pray their great expectations: 'Oh God, we just want Jeff to be himself, but may six million people come to Christ tonight. May the dead be raised, the blind see, the deaf hear. And may Auntie Mabel, the Satanist, who's coming this evening and will probably never come to church again for the rest of her life, come to Christ tonight.'

Having survived the pre-service prayer meeting I then discover whether or not I am supposed to exist. At one extreme are those churches where there is a huge personality cult around the preacher and there is a sense that 'the man of God is in the house', and he is one step short of being the Messiah. But at the other extreme are those churches where the preacher's presence is not really required and they articulate their hope that the preacher will fade into the background or be 'hidden behind the cross'. Neither of these positions reflects the truth. The truth is neither that the 'man of God is in the house' nor that somehow God wants to annihilate the preacher's life and personality, but 'Preaching is the bringing of truth through personality.'[1] The very reality of the incarnate Christ speaks to us not of a God with a megaphone but of a God who expresses himself through life and through the episodes of our lives, from Monday to Saturday as well as on Sunday. As C.S. Lewis demonstrated in his writings, the church is a community of people, each of whom is gifted to be able to see a different aspect of God's beauty, which no one else can see in the same way, and blesses other worshippers by sharing it with them. Of course, we have to be careful that we do not take this to an extreme and so drift into some form of Gnosticism, but the truth is that we all have something to bring. In his brilliant book *Grief, Grace and Glory* Phillips Brooks speaks about personality as a prism, through which the light of God can shine. However, this can only happen if as Christians we are continually moving on with Jesus.

As preachers we can get stuck. We can gather enough information to survive; we can become professional Christians. As Roger Forster says, 'The trouble with us is that they pay us to be Christians.' Like Popeye the Sailor Man, we sing that hopeless song 'I am what I am', and on his more depressed days, he would say, 'And that's all I am.' Jesus did not command His followers to invite Him into our hearts, end of story. He said:

> '*Come, follow me, and I will make you fishers of men.*'
> (Mark 1:17)

Being a disciple of Jesus is not a static experience: it is a mobile experience. The *ecclesia*, the Church, the called-out people of God, go with God where He is going. I love the call of Abraham:

> '*Leave your country, your people and your father's household and go to the land I will show you.*'
> (Genesis 12:1)

God has got things He wants to show us. The danger for us as leaders is that we stop being fellow travellers, and instead we become travel agents, who know the details of what the vacation could look like but we are always booking other people on the trip and never go ourselves.

As preachers we need to be shaped. I know I can become stuck in predictability. Because I am flying so much I often feel weary, and if anyone asks me how I am doing, my default mechanism is to say, 'Fine, but I'm a bit weary.' Recently Kay and I went on holiday with the children's evangelist Ishmael and his wife Irene, and we had a great holiday and came back feeling very alive and invigorated. However, when someone came up to me and asked me how I was doing, I automatically said, 'Fine but weary.' I realised that actually I was not weary but was feeling happy, but the moment had passed and the person to whom I was talking was saying, 'Yeah, you do look a bit tired.' If we are going to be shaped as preachers, we have got to be fellow travellers.

2. PREPARED TO SUFFER PAIN

The call to preach is the call to the crucible as well as the pulpit. Martin Luther said that prayer, meditation and suffering are what make a preacher. Helen Keller said, 'Character cannot be developed in ease and quiet. Only through experience of trial and suffering can the soul be strengthened, ambition inspired, and success achieved.' I want to be honest and admit that when I hear about the possible cost of being a better preacher I feel very scared. I begin to fear that God will take my children away from me, or I will suffer some other calamity. Whether or not our preaching will involve suffering, it will certainly involve pain.

▪ *There is the pain of rejection*
For seven years of my ministry planting and pastoring a church I had a board member who was also a bored member, and he let me know it. Whenever I preached, he would turn his chair around to face the wall. That hurt. It also hurt when a man came up to me in a church in America and told me he saw a mark on my head, which he thought was the mark of the Beast and then told me that he loved me – which was surprising since Christians are not really supposed to love the Beast! Anonymous letters can also hurt.

▪ *There is the pain of doubt*
In evangelical circles admitting doubt is like admitting you are suffering from herpes. I remember one year speaking at an event which I shall not name, but it happens at springtime and they bring in the harvest. Sitting on the platform about to speak to four and a half thousand people, I suddenly had one of those crises that as Christians we don't like to talk about. I sat on the platform thinking, 'I really hope there's a God.' Of course, I know there's a God, but there are times when I'm jet-lagged or fed up or bored with

Christians when I find myself plagued with doubts. We need to be much more honest about our doubts. Although we are agents of assurance for others we are still on the journey ourselves. We need to understand that it is normal to doubt and we should not get upset about it. One day we will see Jesus face to face, and then all doubts will be gone, but until that time we will experience doubt. It is part of the pain of preaching.

■ There is the pain of criticism

Recently I gave an interview to a magazine in which I talked about the fact that my life is full of little calamities and stories and I compared myself to an evangelical Mr Bean. As part of that interview I made the throwaway comment that I was a 'gifted idiot'. When I saw the article in print, guess what the title was: 'Gifted Idiot?' Thank goodness for the question mark, but I didn't like that. I don't like it when, because I use humour, people think I'm superficial and don't have a theological brain. But in the end I get over it because I know that those who preach will face criticism. It is a sad truth that as Christian leaders we can be the most insecure people in the universe, with a drivenness to try and use our ministry to fill the black hole within us. We will never do it, no matter how big the platform on which we stand. We need to be willing to be criticised. The editor of my books is so helpful to me. In a big red pen she writes 'So what?' over a page of text that I have written. It is painful but I need that.

When Richard Branson started Virgin Airlines, he wanted to do away with the traditional airline classifications of 'first class', 'business' and 'economy' and he had baggage stickers printed with the words 'upper class', 'middle class' and 'riff raff'. Now there was a winner of an idea! Fortunately, he was eventually persuaded against introducing it. Richard Branson was open to others evaluating his ideas. As preachers and teachers, we too need to be open to critique, evaluation and development. It is so easy for leaders to be blinded by their own vision. It is so easy for leaders to be threatened by people in their congregation who think for themselves, branding them as 'divisive' or even 'rebellious'. One of the most helpful people in my ministry and development as a preacher was a lady who, twenty-five years ago when I did not believe in women in ministry, relentlessly pursued me, irritated me and goaded me on the subject. At the time she drove me to distraction, but eventually I realised she was right, and I am now committed to a full release of women in ministry.

One response to people who differ from us on any of the major issues of the Christian faith, is to say, 'You serve God in your way and I'll serve Him in His.' This may evoke a laugh in the person on the other side of the argument, but actually it betrays our hearts. So often as leaders we refuse to enter into dialogue. We refuse to listen to the other side of the story. If we want to be people who are formed in the crucible, we must be willing to be those who enter into dialogue and interaction. Iron sharpens iron. In the process it may wound and hurt us, but that is part of the pain of preaching.

3. ABLE TO EXERCISE FAITH

Preaching is a faith activity. The preacher must begin and continue in faith. If we fail to realise this, we will become driven people. Five times in Ephesians Paul talks about the heavenly places. Along with many commentators, I have come to believe that 'the heavenly places' are not some distant nirvana, but refer to the air immediately surrounding our bodies: it is the invisible realm in which angels and demons tussle. We are people of the invisible.

We need to recover a healthy sense of the invisible. As preachers we need to face up to the fact that, when we are preaching, we will not have a clue about what our efforts are achieving. I would suggest that 99.9 per cent of the time we are throwing out seeds and most of what the Holy Spirit is doing will remain unknown to us. The danger is that as preachers we want to be able to be like factory workers who can come home at the end of the day and say, 'I made ten spanners today.' But we are people who are casting seeds into the invisible and it will not be possible for us to know what is achieved. Sometimes we get obsessed with results. I love to preach for a decision, and of course there is a right time to lay challenges before people which arise from our preaching. But we must not do it if what we are really looking for are signs that our preaching has hit the target. We have all been in meetings where the appeal gets broadened wider and wider to try and make sure that there will be an adequate line-up at the front of the meeting. What can be happening is that the preacher is trying to fill the black hole which is inside him by seeing tangible results for his ministry. If we are going to allow ourselves to be 'made' as preachers, we need to understand that most of what we do is an investment into the invisible as God builds His Kingdom, and that is a faith activity. I have heard Paul Yonggi Cho say to himself before speaking, 'Let's go, Holy Spirit. Let's go, Holy Spirit', and I love that. It is a recognition that what is about to happen is a faith activity, the full results of which will not be known on earth.

4. READY TO REMEMBER AND CELEBRATE OUR CALLING

If we compare Luke 5 and John 21 we will see that in the later incident Jesus is rebuilding the scenery of the earlier one, which is the occasion on which Peter originally received his calling. It is as if Jesus is saying to Peter, 'Do you remember?' It is very important for all of us as preachers to recall our own calling and celebrate it, however it came. Very often, just as I am about to speak, I will spend two or three minutes rehearsing in my mind some of the things that God has said to me in calling me to the preaching task. I will wrap myself in those statements and then I will say to myself, 'All right, let's go.'

My calling to preach was surprising. Very briefly, I became a Christian at the age of seventeen with no Christian background at all. I got kicked out of Sunday school, having attended three times, for stealing the gold stars, so that was not really much of a background. I got healed of a physical problem and I ended up going to a little Pentecostal church in Barking where I met some wonderful people who loved me and cared for me. Within two weeks of becoming a Christian, not knowing the difference between the Old Testament and the New Testament, I began to feel a bizarre calling to preach.

Around that time I went on a youth weekend at which the guest speaker was a very remarkable man with a strong prophetic gift by the name of Johnny Barr, for whom I thank God. He is now in heaven. On the opening night, not knowing any of us, he said, 'On my way here today, God spoke to me about three of you whom He has called into ministry. God has given me your first and last names. I will chat with you over the course of the weekend.' Now that was what I call a word of knowledge! I remember sitting there, thinking 'whoa'. On the Saturday evening, I was filled with the Holy Spirit, and this was long before the Charismatic Renewal began. As I started to go down under the Spirit I wanted to speak something out. At that very moment Johnny Barr stood up and said, 'Someone here's been filled with the Holy Spirit and you want to speak out.' And I thought, 'I really hate you, you know everything.' At the end of the meeting I went up to him and, without introducing myself, I said, 'Mr Barr, that was me tonight having that experience of the Holy Spirit, I'm sorry I didn't respond.' He said, 'Don't worry, son. Next time obey God.' And I said, 'Thank you, sir.' As I turned to walk away, he tapped me on the shoulder and said, 'Hold on, your name is Jeff Lucas, isn't it?' At that moment I wasn't actually sure. I said, 'Yes, it is.' He said, 'God has called you to preach, hasn't He?' And I said, 'Yes, He has.' Then he said, 'Get on with it.'

He was an amazing prophet, but a terrible pastor. That night I cried myself to sleep because the Almighty God, who said, 'Let there be light', knew my name and address. Three weeks later I went to another conference. Hearing that Johnny Barr was there, I thought, 'I'd better go and find him.' I ran up to him and said, 'Mr Barr, Mr Barr, do you remember me – Jeff Lucas? I've been looking for you.' He turned around and said, 'No, son, I've been looking for you.' And right there and then he placed his hands on my head and said, 'You will be like a hammer that breaks men's hearts and you will preach.'

Sometimes I have to remember the way that God called me to preach. Perhaps others might wish that God had called them in an equally dramatic way. This is something I have thought about quite a lot, and the reason I believe God called me in such a dramatic way is because He knows that I am more stupid than most people. I am utterly serious. God knows that I'm more likely than the average person to drive down the road saying, 'I hope there's a God.' He knew that I needed a calling I would not be able to forget. Others may not have had a memorable calling but can recall other significant times in their lives. We need to remember and to celebrate.

I spent a lot of my life as a teenager going to a youth club on the Isle of Wight. I went forward for everything, every night. I repented for everything. I even went forward one night and repented for being happy. A few years ago, I was speaking on the Isle of Wight for a couple of days. On an afternoon off I borrowed a bike and cycled to a field, where an annual camp would be held. I worked out where they used to have the marquee and, within five or ten feet, where as a virginal seventeen-year-old I used to kneel. In those days I didn't know about church politics or evangelical feuding or boring churches. With some bemused cattle standing around me, I knelt in that field and prayed, 'God, twenty years ago I knelt here. I still want to do this thing.' If as preachers we are going to be made, we need to remember and celebrate our calling.

5. Able to Deal with Success and Failure

Failure and success are part of the road that we have to navigate if we are going to be shaped as preachers. Can God trust us with success? I remember one year at Spring Harvest I preached in the Big Top, and it went really well. I felt good about the message and there was a very positive response. The next morning I felt happy and grateful to God. I went over to the bookshop and there was a healthy line of discerning people at the tape desk waiting to buy the tapes of the meeting and my books were also being snapped up. As I walked through Butlins, people were nudging each other and saying, 'That's him', and I smiled back beatifically. Someone even rushed over and asked me to autograph a copy of one of my books. Of course, I engaged in 'Vicar of Dibley' humility, 'No, no, no, no, no, no, yeees', signing the book with a flourish and a text. 'There's nothing wrong with signing a book,' I thought. 'It's a nice relational thing to do.' But then, as I was walking through the site with my pen at the ready, God spoke to me with a question, as He often does. He said, 'Famous in Butlins for a day, are we?' We need to be careful with success. It can challenge our character just as much as failure can.

While we should be careful not to let our success go to our heads, we should also beware of being one of those freaky evangelicals who can never be encouraged. There are some preachers who, if you go up to them and say, 'Thanks for your message', will respond with something like, 'Oh no. Look up, look up. Give Him the glory.' It is much better just to say, 'Thank you very much.' A woman went up to her pastor at the end of the service and said, 'That was a wonderful sermon, Pastor. Absolutely wonderful.' Rather embarrassed about her gushing praise, he responded, 'Well, it wasn't me, it was the Lord.' 'Oh,' she said, 'it wasn't that good.'

6. Able to Maintain Our Membership of the Human Race

As preachers we need to remember that there is only a short step between dignity and pomposity. We need to chill out and lighten up. I wish there was a verse in the Bible that said, 'Lighten up, my people' or 'Chill out, sayeth the Lord'. So many of us are much too uptight and serious. I was at a conference two weeks ago and one of the speakers said, 'Every Sunday needs to be a powerful encounter with the Holy Ghost, with anointing and power and blessing.' I stood up and said, 'Please grow up.' Why do we have to have a seismic encounter every time we have a church service? Why do the rafters have to shake every time? This is Charismatic immaturity. We are human, and there will be times when life is simply boring. Jesus cleansed my sins, but I still have to wash the car.

Forgive another Spring Harvest illustration, but a couple of years ago I was on my way to speak at a Bible Reading at Spring Harvest when a seagull from Satan pooed straight on my head. I thought, 'Great, I am just about to speak to 4,000 people and I have got bird poo on my head.' So I had to head straight to the bathroom to sort myself out. Of course, when I stood up to speak, the first thing I did was to tell everyone that I had been 'pooed' on. A couple of weeks later I was preaching at a United Reformed Conference and the man who was introducing me had been at that Spring Harvest meeting. Having been really amused by what had happened, he introduced me by relating the story. What he liked was the fact that here was a Christian leader talking about something so down to earth. As preachers we need to rejoin the human race, get vulnerable, lighten up and tell the truth.

A couple of months ago I was speaking in Canada at a conference attended by 4,000 Christian leaders from around the world. Shortly before I was due to speak I was in the loo. It comes as a surprise to some people to discover that preachers have to go to the toilet. I was in the toilet recently in a church and a man came in and said, 'Oh Jeff, nice to see you. I'm surprised to see you in here.' I thought, 'What do you think we do? Pray about it?' Anyway, back in Canada I am in the toilet when I hear them introducing me – they even have speakers in the loo at these conferences, which is really helpful for multitasking. Hearing the speaker announcing me, I realise I had better hurry. But I can't get out of the toilet. I'm pushing the door; I'm rebuking the door; I'm demanding that the door open. But it won't. As I turn round, I suddenly realise that I am trying to break into the broom cupboard. And the irony of it hit me. Here I was about to try and communicate to these leaders about what God is doing around the world and I can't even get out of the toilet. As preachers we need to get real. We need to be redemptive in our vulnerability. People don't want our dirty laundry but they do want the truth about our perhaps weak and struggling attempts to pursue the things of God. They don't want to hear, 'I'm a load of rubbish, and so are you', but they do want to hear, 'I fail sometimes but I am pressing on.' They want to hear about the grace of God in our lives.

As preachers we are on a journey. We are on a journey of being made into a vessel that communicates the grace and awesomeness of God, which is such a great privilege. Let us allow the Holy Spirit to mould and shape us so that we are better able to deliver the amazing truth of our God and His Word.

NOTE

1. *Lectures on Preaching* (1877; Baker, 1969).

Chapter 47

GROWING AND MATURING
AS A PREACHER

Steve Brady

One of the fantastic wonders of God's grace (Greek *charis*) is that when it touches our lives it blesses us with *charisma* or, in the more familiar plural form, *charismata*. Grace graces us so that we are gifted in the world. The only trouble is that it takes a while for some of us to work out not only what our spiritual gifts are but also the fact that these spiritual gifts need developing. At the church of a friend of mine they filled in one of those questionnaires which are designed to help people discover what their spiritual gift is. Through ticking the boxes my friend discovered that he had a spiritual gift that most people do not want, namely the gift of celibacy. It came as a bit of a shock, particularly to his wife and four kids!

The great temptation with spiritual gifts is to think that all we have to do as the recipient is to unwrap the gift and use it. Recently, after having had an accident in my car, I have had to lease a brand new car which I have really been enjoying. In fact, I have done something remarkable with this car. Two nights ago I washed it, which I never did with my old car! I just wanted to keep it looking nice. But I know that in about another week's time the novelty will have worn off and I will leave the car to the mercy of the elements. We tend to treat spiritual gifts in the same way. We think that all we need to do is keep them looking nice. However, the truth is that spiritual gifts are meant to be developed and strengthened.

To some it can come as a relief to discover this fact, because as preachers, for example, it helps us to realise that we do not immediately have to sound like Martyn Lloyd-Jones or Billy Graham! They too had to start somewhere. I often tell people that I have been preaching for more than thirty-five years, and if they think I am bad now, they should have heard me when I first began! The only way a preacher can develop his preaching gift is by practising what he preaches, both in the sense of actually engaging in the preaching task and of ensuring that his life backs up the words he is speaking. As preachers we need to be constantly growing and maturing.

THE SPAR TREATMENT

For a number of weeks a little boy, a deacon's son, would come out of church with a very furtive look, and would go up to the pastor and give him a 10p coin. After this had gone on for half a dozen or so weeks the pastor said to him, 'Well, Johnny, it's very good of you to have given me this money for the last few weeks, but you don't have to do it, you know.' 'Oh no, I want to give it to you, Pastor,' the boy replied, 'I want you to have it.' 'Why is that?' the pastor asked. 'Well, my dad said you're the poorest preacher that we've ever had.'

We are all aware that there is a great deal of bad preaching around. Some years ago *The Times* was so appalled at the standard of preaching in Great Britain that it introduced The Preacher of the Year competition, although anyone who has read some of the sermons that have won will probably be wondering how positive a contribution it is making.

We are all concerned about what kind of preachers we are. Before we explore how we can grow and develop in our preaching skills, I want to give a caveat to what I intend to say on this subject. John Piper has written a book with the provocative title *Brothers, We Are Not Professionals*.[1] His thesis in the book is that the ministry is being killed by a professionalism in which love for the people is being squeezed out. Some time ago I read a remarkable chapter in a book with the very clever title *The DMin-isation of the Ministry* (DMin is the abbreviation for the Doctor of Ministry degree), which had a very similar message. It is very easy for ministers, pastors and Christian leaders to develop such a professionalism in their ministry that people in their care are kept at arm's length. If that is what we mean by 'being professional' and developing in our gifting, I want nothing to do with it, and I want to emphasise that I am not talking about how we can become slicker, more objective and more detached for God. What I am talking about is how we can become better at what we are doing as red-hot, passionate followers of Jesus Christ.

At the Bible college of which I am the Principal, we summarise what we regard as our mission in the acronym 'SPAR'. We say we want to give our students the 'SPAR' treatment:

Spiritually on fire for Christ
Practically trained
Academically credible
Relationally skilled.

On a trip to Ireland recently, I was explaining this acronym to a group of people over lunch and one man seemed particular impressed. 'I really like that,' he said. 'I'm head of Spar shops here in Northern Ireland.' I encouraged him to support our college!

As a college we are committed to helping our students to become men and women who are both passionate about Christ and excel in the gifts and abilities that God has given them. So often we applaud incompetence in the Church, under the guise of relying 'on the strength of the Lord' and not wanting to promote ourselves. But imagine sitting waiting for a plane to take off and hearing a voice coming over the intercom which says, 'Hello. It's your captain speaking. I want you to know that, although I've never flown a plane before, I am looking forward to the trip.' I would be off that plane in a flash! Why is it then that we applaud competence and ability in every sphere, but when it comes to preaching the Word, the most exhilarating and demanding task in the world, we act as if the more incompetent a person is, the more room there is for God. While I want to warn against professionalism, I want to emphasise the necessity of growing in our gifting as preachers and teachers.

Instructions to a Young Minister (1 Timothy 4)

In 1 Timothy 4 Paul is, of course, talking to the young minister, Timothy. We know he is young because in verse 12 Paul says, *'Don't let anyone look down on you because you are young . . . '* Commentators tend to think that Timothy was probably in his thirties, but it is not possible to be certain. It is comforting to some of us to know that in the Graeco-Roman world anyone under the age of forty was regarded as young.

There are two additional bits of information that we can glean from Paul's letters about Timothy. We know that he was subject to various illnesses, or 'infirmities', as the Authorised Version puts it.[2] Paul's reference to the fact that *'God did not give us a spirit of timidity'*[3] also suggests that he tended to be rather timid, but again we cannot be sure. Thus, we have a picture of a young man who was a little bit introverted, sometimes quite vulnerable to physical problems and, as someone has put it, 'more inclined to lean than to lead'. Through his letters Paul encourages this young minister serving the Lord to be a man of strength and fervour.

There are clearly various problems facing the church. At the beginning of chapter 4, Paul refers to the fact that 'deceiving spirits' are at work (v. 1) and in verse 2 he talks about 'hypocritical liars', whose *'consciences have been seared with a hot iron'*. The issues about which these people have cauterised their consciences are sex and food, two of the most basic human instincts. They are promoting celibacy and vegetarianism. In passing, it is helpful to notice the importance which the writers of the pastoral letters place on having a 'good conscience'. We must realise that, as men and women of God, if we deliberately go against our conscience, we are really playing with fire. We all know what would happen if we got so fed up with the oil light coming on in our car that we just pulled out the wires. It would not be very long before the engine blew up! It is equally dangerous if we ignore the warning sign of our conscience.

After instructing Timothy on how he can deal with these pressures on the church, Paul says,

> *If you point these things out to the brothers, you will be a good minister of Christ Jesus, brought up in the truths of the faith and of the good teaching that you have followed.*
> (1 Timothy 4:6)

I think it is very important to notice that Paul does not say that if Timothy points the truth out to his brothers, he will be a 'brilliant' or an 'excellent' minister of Christ'. He contents himself with saying that he will be 'a good minister' who will be giving 'good teaching'. I like that. Timothy was not immediately being called to be an excellent minister, a brilliant minister, a superbly gifted minister. It was enough in Paul's eyes to be a 'good minister', or literally 'a good deacon' or 'servant' of Jesus Christ. Being good is good enough. Some of us tend towards perfectionism and strive to be excellent at everything. Then we become depressed when we fail to achieve our goal. Paul is happy to set realistic goals for the young Timothy. The first point I want to make about the biblical basis for growing and maturing as a preacher is that we are to be good ministers.

Later in the chapter Paul reinforces this biblical basis when he says:

> *Be diligent in these matters; give yourself wholly to them, so that everyone may see your progress.*
> (1 Timothy 4:15)

Through the consistency of our lips and our lives people are to see progress. To me it is so liberating to realise that people do not have to see perfection in my life, but they do have to see *projection.* That it does not matter where I have come from, but it does matter where I am going, what I am striving for. A good minister is one who makes progress.

This is also the reason why in verse 12 Paul commands, '*set an example for the believers in speech, in life, in love, in faith and in purity.*' The Greek word which is translated 'example' here is the same word as that from which the English word 'type' (in the sense of model or paradigm) is derived. Timothy is to be a model for others. His life is to be an encouragement. So often we feel very reticent about the thought that other people should model their lives on us. We say, 'No, no! You mustn't follow me, you must follow Jesus!' Yes, of course they must follow Jesus, but the apostle Paul was able to say, 'Follow me as I follow Christ.'

A lady I knew used to introduce her husband to everyone as 'a model husband', which he found very encouraging until he discovered that one of the dictionary definitions of 'model' is 'a small imitation of the real thing'! God does not want us to be a small imitation of the real thing, He wants us to be *the real thing*. By chance recently, in the TV magazine which accompanies *The Times*, I happened to read an article about Bruce Forsyth who at the age of seventy-six was just embarking on a new television series. You either love him or hate him, but there is no doubt that Bruce Forsyth is a brilliant entertainer. I was fascinated by the following comment he made in the article:

> There comes a point at which sheer professional skill, raised to the highest degree by the refining drudgery of constant practice, evolves into something different in kind, conferring on its possessors an assurance that enables them to take off, to ignite, to achieve outrageous feats of timing and audience control that would, even a few years before, have been beyond them.

Exactly the same comment could be made of a preacher who has mastered his art. No one starts out as a great preacher. A great preacher has practised his skills and perfected his craft. Why can we not applaud such skill as we do in every other area of life?

A Model of Ministerial Excellence

So much of our preaching can become humdrum and predictable. Some of our preaching is not much better than this sermon outline based on the nursery rhyme 'Old Mother Hubbard went to the Cupboard':

- the *person* she was: old Mother Hubbard
- the *pet* she owned: the dog
- the *place* she went: the cupboard
- the *purpose* she had: to get her poor dog a bone
- the *poverty* she expressed: it was empty
- so the *pain* she knew: the dog got nothing.

We need to get beyond this type of preaching. Acts 18:23–28 provides us with a model of ministerial excellence, in which we are shown the importance of *developing our biblical faith*.

In Acts 18:24 we are introduced for the first time to Apollos who, we are told, is 'from Alexandria'. To anyone who is a biblical scholar this piece of information immediately sets a few bells ringing. In the history of the Bible, Alexandria is a significant place because it was there that, two hundred years before the coming of Jesus, the Old Testament had been translated from Hebrew into Greek in the version called the Septuagint. Alexandria was also the home of the scholar Philo the Jew, a contemporary of Jesus, who worked on synthesising Hebraic and Greek philosophy. Alexandria was, therefore, noteworthy as a place of great scholarly, biblical activity, and it is significant that it is the place from which Apollos comes and that he is *a learned man, with a thorough knowledge of the Scriptures*' (v. 23). It was John Calvin who said, 'If a man is not a scholar he is not called to be a preacher.' It is not necessary to be a rocket scientist to be a preacher, but it does require some intellectual ability and the willingness to be prepared to apply one's mind. People are prepared to put their minds to learning about all sorts of complex subjects, whether it be the intricacies of the human genome, astrophysics, computers or all sorts of general knowledge trivia for pub quizzes. Those who aspire to be preachers should not fight shy of applying their minds to studying the Word of God. Developing a thorough knowledge of the Bible is essential for the preacher. It is to govern everything they do. That is why Paul says to Timothy,

> *Do your best to present yourself to God as one approved, a workman who does not*
> *need to be ashamed and who correctly handles the word of truth.*
> (2 Timothy 2:15)

We learn, then, that Apollos is a man with a robustly biblical faith. Furthermore, we learn that,

> *He had been instructed in the way of the Lord, and he spoke with great fervour and*
> *taught about Jesus accurately, though he knew only the baptism of John.*
> (Acts 18:25)

It is important for us to understand that he had a thorough knowledge of the Scriptures, but that this knowledge also needed to develop. I have a five-year-old grandson whom I call 'my living, loving theologian' because he keeps me sane in all sorts of different areas of life. A few weeks ago, while I was telling him the parable of the Good Samaritan and was introducing the story by saying, 'This guy came to Jesus and said, "What must I do to go to heaven?"', without batting an eyelid he said, 'Well, you'd have to die first, Granddad'! Now, my little grandson understands the meaning of John 3:16 but he doesn't understand it to the same depth that I, with my knowledge of the original Greek, understand it. Nevertheless, he still has a true knowledge of it. I have understood John 3:16 from the moment I was saved, but, now, thirty-five years on, I understand it much better. Does that mean that, when I have been in heaven for a million years, I will understand it totally and exhaustively? According to Ephesians 3:8, not necessarily, since Paul speaks of *'the unsearchable riches of Christ'*, which are inexhaustible. We see, then, that I can know something truly and accurately, without knowing it exhaustively. Relating this to Apollos, we understand that he had a certain amount of knowledge but he did not know everything, and therefore he needed Aquila and Priscilla to take him under their wing and teach him all that they knew. But notice how they went about it:

When Priscilla and Aquila heard him, they invited him to their home and explained to him the way of God more adequately.
(Acts 18:26)

Priscilla and Aquila did not confront him publicly. They did not hijack him after the service and 'sort him out', as happens so often to the preacher in some of our churches – sometimes in quite disgraceful ways – but they took him home and explained to him what he needed to know. Apollos went on to become a great teacher and preacher, and it has even been suggested by some biblical scholars, including Martin Luther, that Apollos wrote the Epistle to the Hebrews.

If we are to mature as preachers, we must continue to grow and develop in the Word of God. There is the danger for every preacher that as we become familiar with the Bible and read the texts again and again, we miss what they are really saying. Apollos was a man who was open to further instruction, and God provided the right people to give him the help that he needed. No matter who we are, we all need help and we all need further training. No matter how good we are as preachers, we can always get better.

I always recommend to preachers that, if at all possible, they should try and get even a basic facility in the languages in which the Bible was written, not as an end in itself, not to be clever or smart, but so that they can hear the original words, not just the translation. One of the purposes of Bible college is to help people to read between the lines of the Bible, but with many of our students at college we discover all too often that they have not even read most of the lines that they are now supposed to be reading between! Becoming an excellent preacher requires the hard work of studying the Bible, as well as the delight of allowing the Word of God to 'dwell in us richly'.[4] And, unlike the 1960s when I started out, nowadays there is no shortage of material written by excellent scholars to aid the person who is serious about studying the Bible. One book that it is worth selling one's shirt to buy is Graeme Goldsworthy's *Preaching the Whole Bible as Christian Scripture*.[5]

THREE CARDINAL RULES FOR PREACHERS

I want now to be very practical and talk about a code of practice in approaching the Word of God that can help us to grow and mature as preachers. I have followed these three cardinal rules ever since I heard Leith Samuel, a man who had a formative influence on my life, preach on them about thirty years ago. When I heard him speak about them, I thought, 'How very simple. How utterly profound', and I have used them ever since.

1. Think yourself empty

When we come to the text of Scripture, before we make use of any other resources, we need to do some of the hard work for ourselves. We need to spend time meditating on the Scripture and trying to discover its meaning for ourselves.

2. Read yourself full

Having thought ourselves empty, we then need to read ourselves full by exploring what scholars and commentators have written on the text. In doing so, we need to be sensible. It is very easy to become so overloaded with what we read in commentaries that we don't really know what we think ourselves any more. I remember in my early days as a young assistant minister, I would read ten or more commentaries and spend between ten and fifteen hours preparing my sermon. At the end I was so overloaded with information that I did not have a clue what to preach on. I felt as if I had been around the supermarket five times and still did not have a clue what to cook for Sunday lunch.

A practical solution is to equip ourselves with a good exegetical commentary, i.e. one that tells us what the text says, and one or two commentaries that will help us apply the text to our situation today. I have found the New International Version's Application Bible and *The Bible Speaks Today* series published by InterVarsity Press very helpful. The books of men like John Stott and Warren Wiersbe[6] are, of course, excellent but, after reading them, the preacher can be left feeling that there is nothing else he could possibly add on the subject!

3. Write yourself clear

If we are going to develop as preachers, we need to be able to see the big idea in the text on which we are preaching. If we can't see a big idea emerging, then perhaps we need to make the passage wider. If there are too many big ideas, then perhaps we need to make the text smaller. *Working on the big idea* is the first step in writing our sermon.

Let us ask, for example, what is the central idea in the well-known verse John 3:16:

> *For God so loved the world that he gave his one and only Son, that whoever believes in him shall not perish but have eternal life.*

Here we have a number of choices:

- For God – the person of God
- so loved – the love of God
- the world – the world's brokenness
- that He gave – the heart of deity – giving love
- His one and only Son – the Christology of John.

Whichever way we decide to go – and because we are all different, we will make different choices – we have got to decide on one big, controlling idea. I personally look for what Jay Adams has called the 'telic' purpose of the passage or, as he puts it, 'where you are driving for'.[7] We do not want to be like the Duke of Wellington who said about his addresses, 'I just jump in and splash about.' Or like the explorer Christopher Columbus who set off not knowing where he was going, when he got there he didn't know where he was, and when he came back he didn't know where he had been. But he was a great explorer! Once we have established the central idea of the passage, it is helpful to choose a title for our sermon. This may change in the course of our preparation, but it helps us to know in which direction we are ultimately heading. If we disappear down a rabbit hole or two along the way, it helps us to reappear on the main route and arrive at our final destination.

The next step is to *work out an outline* for our sermon. A friend of mine who is a farmer told me something about ploughing which I had never understood before and which I think can be helpful for us as preachers too. He told me that it is impossible to plough a straight furrow simply by putting up one marker post. At least two and preferably three marker posts are required. In preaching we need to let people know where we are going by setting up marker posts. This enables them to see that there is a logical progression in what we are saying, that we are going from one marker post to the next.

Thankfully, when we are preaching there is the sheer sovereignty of the Holy Spirit, and how well or how poorly we have prepared is not the end of the story. There will be times when the preacher steps into the pulpit with a sinking feeling that his sermon is not as clear in his mind as he thought it was, and yet it really flies, because the Holy Spirit has taken hold of it. There will be other times when he thinks he has really got it together, but it turns out to be a disaster. A while ago I preached at Cambridge University Christian Union. I was well prepared, in fact far more prepared than I usually am, but when I came to preach, the sermon just did not take off. It did not even leave the hangar, let alone get as far as the runway. This story has encouraged my students at college more than anything else I could have told them! Even experienced preachers have their off days.

We also need to *fill in the blanks* by explaining and illustrating the points that we are trying to communicate. Choosing illustrations requires care. Some illustrations need illustrations to illustrate them. This is especially true if we have a particular interest in a specialist area, such as computers, which we understand but is gobbledegook to everyone else. Our illustrations need to communicate, and therefore it is best to draw them from everyday life.

Finally, we need to learn how to *introduce wisely* and *withdraw graciously*. Both the introduction and the conclusion are important. If we do not know how we are going to conclude our sermon, we will be like a man going down a hole on a bicycle, who would like to get off, but is not quite sure how!

'PRAY YOURSELF HOT'

There was an old West Indian preacher, who in addition to the three cardinal rules I have outlined, had two more. He used to say, 'I prays myself hot and then I lets myself go!'

If we go back to Acts 18, we can see that, as well as having a thorough knowledge of the Scriptures, Apollos was a man with a passion,

He had been instructed in the way of the Lord, and he spoke with great fervour and taught about Jesus accurately, though he knew only the baptism of John. He began to speak boldly in the synagogue.
(Acts 18:25–26)

Apollos not only developed a biblical faith but he maintained his biblical fervour. As preachers we need to maintain our spiritual fervour. We need to pray ourselves hot. The Greek root of the word 'fervour' means 'to boil'. This was not 'theology on ice'. Preaching is not a lecture. Preaching is not simply the dissemination of information. It is possible to preach the Bible and miss out on God. Apollos spoke with great fervour. He boiled. He enthused. I believe that one of the ways in which we can get hold of such fervour is by spending time on our knees before God. His presence sets our spirits on fire.

I believe we need to preach each sermon as if it were the last sermon of our lives, as if it were the last opportunity we might ever have to preach God's Word. When I came off the road in my car just a few weeks ago, that very thought was in my head. As I was sailing off the road and calling on the Lord's name, I was thinking, 'This could be goodbye. I may have just preached my last sermon.' When we come to preach, there needs to be passion and fire. I can forgive a preacher almost anything, if he preaches with a holy passion. One of the privileges of my job is to listen to would-be young preachers beginning to exercise their skills. It is immediately evident when somebody has a Holy Ghost passion in their heart – even in the artificial setting of a sermon class. You know when they have heard a word from the Lord.

For those of us who are preaching regularly, maintaining our fervour is one of the hardest things. In my first charge as a young minister, between 1975 and 1977, I was blessed to work in Leicester as the assistant of a godly and gracious man called Sidney Lawrence, who was nearing the end of his ministry. What was remarkable about Sidney was that, although he was approaching sixty years of age, he still preached with such passion that it was as if he was just starting out. When he died in his eighties he was still preaching like that. One of my great predecessors at East London Tabernacle was a man called Geoffrey King who was a brilliant Bible teacher. In 1984, realising that it was the fiftieth anniversary of his ordination, I invited him back to the Tabernacle for a celebration, at which he preached on the subject 'I am not ashamed of the gospel'. I was so blessed when I heard the passion with which that man in his late seventies was still preaching. We must never let our fire go out. We must stir up the gift that is within us.

There will be times for all of us when we feel as if our fire is going out, and then we need to take whatever steps are necessary to stir it up again. Perhaps we are overtired and need to take a week off. Perhaps we have let ourselves get too busy. Whatever it takes, we need to maintain our spiritual passion. I am not talking about emotionalism, but if our own hearts are not being touched by God's words, why should anyone else's heart be touched? I like the comment made by the well-known eighteenth-century sceptic David

Hulme about the great evangelist George Whitefield. When one of his friends asked him, 'You don't believe what Whitefield does, do you?' he replied, 'No. But he certainly does!' When we preach, we need to make sure that, even if nobody believes it, at least they know that we believe it! When Whitefield preached there was a boil-factor, an enthusiasm factor, a passion-factor in his heart. God deliver us from the professionalism that leaves us untouched and unmoved. When we have the most incredible message in the world, our preaching should never be dull and boring.

STIR UP YOUR EVANGELISTIC FIRE

> *When Apollos wanted to go to Achaia, the brothers encouraged him and wrote to the disciples there to welcome him. On arriving, he was a great help to those who by grace had believed. For he vigorously refuted the Jews in public debate, proving from the Scriptures that Jesus was the Christ.*
> (Acts 18:27–28)

Apollos was no ivory-tower academic. He was at the sharp end of evangelism, involving himself in public debate and seeking to prove to people that Jesus is the Christ. One of my friends who started out as an evangelist decided to go into pastoral ministry, but after some years he returned to full-time evangelism. When I asked him why, he said, 'Because I believe Jesus called me to be a fisher of men and not the keeper of an aquarium!' Neither has the Lord called us to be the keeper of an aquarium. We are those who have been sent out with the gospel for the whole world. Apollos used all his great skills, all his apologetic ability and all his knowledge of the Scriptures for the purpose of making Jesus known. Isn't that the purpose of all preaching, whether it is preaching the gospel to one person or to a thousand people? More than anything else, in Great Britain today we desperately need growing and maturing preachers with evangelistic passion and fire, who want to win the nations for Christ! At Moorlands Bible College we are not seeking to train pastors to minister the word of life to maintain congregations. No, we train pastors so that the world might come to know Jesus. We need a rebaptism of fire and a passion for the lost. We need the boldness and fervour that motivated Apollos to preach to the Jews in Achaia. He honed and sharpened his gifts so that others might come to know Jesus. The purpose of all our growing and maturing in our preaching is so that the world might know that the Father sent the Son to be the Saviour of the world.

NOTES

1. John Piper, *Brothers, We Are Not Professionals: A Plea to Pastors for Radical Ministry* (Mentor, 2003).
2. 1 Timothy 5:23.

3. 2 Timothy 1:7.
4. Colossians 3:16.
5. Eerdmans, 2000.
6. He has written a series of commentaries on the books of Bible e.g. *Be Complete; Be Restored; Be Committed; Be Right; Be Rich*, published by Victor Books.
7. *Preaching with Purpose: The Urgent Task of Homiletics* (Zondervan, 1986). For more on the telic purpose, see Chapter 21, 'Preaching for a Verdict and Response' by Colin Dye.

Chapter 48

NARRATIVE PREACHING

Jeff Lucas

I was once at a meeting at which the preacher spoke on Rudolf Bultmann's theology for fifty-five minutes – in a morning family communion service! It was mind-numbing. When he had eventually finished I turned to my minister friend who was sitting next to me and asked, 'What did you think of the preaching then?' And he said, 'I didn't understand a word of it but it was really deep.' That, for me, was a typical 'evangelical' response. It didn't seem to matter that those who were listening had no idea what the preacher was talking about.

As preachers we need to get away from the idea that our job is to give a good sermon. Our job is never to give a good sermon. When the sermon becomes the focus of our agenda we have missed the point completely. Our job is to connect with people. It is not to deliver the material we have prepared – however 'deep' it may be – but to communicate with people. I am embarrassed to admit that there have been too many times in my ministry when I have delivered my talk but I didn't see people. I saw fodder in a pew.

The Jewish theologian Martin Buber has recognised that in our technological age we tend to objectify people because we are so used to going into a high-street store and buying a piece of technology that will serve our needs. We are so interested as consumers in getting what we want to solve our problem that we are treating our relationships in the same way. We no longer see beyond the brief horizon of our selfhood. In the Spring Harvest Leadership Team we have an unwritten rule that we will not refer to the visitors to Spring Harvest as 'punters' but as our guests. They are women and men and children with stories. As we consider the subject of narrative preaching, I want to make this the umbrella for our thinking: that the preacher's task is to connect with people.

I also want to emphasise that we must not set different styles of preaching against each other. There is always the danger of saying that one style of preaching is the only valid approach. We either go for thematic, narrative-based preaching or we go for exegesis. Those who favour exegesis are only happy if the preacher zooms in with a microscope, as it were, and dissects, examines and opens up the text, while I, as someone who favours the narrative approach, could insist that in today's post-modern culture, which is without a meta-narrative, there is a desperate need for story and therefore only story-based preaching is valid. But, as my friend Pete Broadbent says, 'Why does it have to be either/or? Most of the time it's both/and.' We need to be more mature in our thinking.

Whether our approach is exegesis or a story-based, thematic approach, I strongly believe that there is a need today for a refreshing genre of preaching that doesn't just fill in all the blanks. Too much preaching is simplistically catechismic. By this I mean that we let the preacher tell us what we believe from the pulpit. When the preacher has finished, we close our Bibles. The preaching, rather than activating a search, ends the search. This is in stark contrast to Jesus' approach: the whole basis of His telling of story and parable was to provoke a search, not end it. He didn't just fill in all the blanks and give all the answers. By the time He had finished speaking, people were scratching their heads and asking, 'What was that all about?' His preaching was the green light that birthed the search rather than the red light that ended it. I believe that both narrative-based preaching and exegetical preaching can be used just as effectively to this end.

In the 1989 Lyman Beecher Lecture at Yale University Walter Brueggemann called for the Church to be 'a space for grace'; he called for the Church to be a 'people who create poetry in a prose-flattened world', to use language to 'surprise, to enquire, to relieve rather than to batter and to compete'; he called for 'danger, newness and dialogue' to characterise the Church. Although in my church we call ourselves 'seeker aware' or 'seeker sensitive', I find myself less and less happy with that designation. This is because the phrase 'seeker sensitive' seems to imply that when people become Christians they stop seeking: they now belong to the 'found' and have it all figured out. When, some years ago, Bono from U2 sang 'I still haven't found what I'm looking for', Christians were outraged that he would dare to suggest that, having found Jesus, there could still be something missing. As Christians we have got Jesus but I hope we still haven't found what we are looking for, because actually the Kingdom of God is about discovery and investigation – it is an unfolding story.

Thirty years after becoming a Christian I realise that I have got a whole lot less now than I thought I had back then. When I first became a Christian, I had the answer to every question – I even knew when Jesus was coming back. These days I am not so sure. I believe in healing, but do I know definitively why some people don't get healed? No, I do not have a clue. These days I am far happier with mystery. Far happier to say I don't know. The fact that I don't know doesn't matter. I'm overstating it to make the point, but what is it about us preachers that makes us want to be the ones that know it all? There are times when I tell people that I simply don't know the answers to their questions.

For me narrative preaching gives us the opportunity to take, if you like, a widescreen approach – a projector approach – to episodes of Scripture, rather than immediately rushing in forensically with a microscope. When the Ephesians received a letter from Paul, they didn't immediately rip it up into little bits and stick it on their fridges. They read it widescreen. It was a letter. Narrative preaching gives us an opportunity to look at the story, and actually there is something beautiful about it because it allows the story to tell itself. The stories of the Bible tell themselves. Exegesis can be wonderful but on occasion it can also lead to utterly unbiblical preaching because the preacher zooms into the text so closely that it is no longer the wood that is seen but the trees. The weakness of narrative preaching is that the preacher can so let his imagination run away with him that the end-result is eisegesis, reading into the text something that is not actually there, where the Scriptures are portrayed as saying something that was never intended. There are dangers in both.

Four Reasons Why Narrative Preaching is Powerful

Narrative preaching is an important art

It was an art practised by Jesus who told lovely, sometimes mildly confusing and provocative, sometimes quite funny stories. Some people raise their eyebrows at the idea that Jesus told funny stories. When, for example, they are referred to the one about the camel and the eye of the needle, they can't see anything vaguely amusing about it. The story is not funny to us because we are separated by two thousand years from the cultural humour of the day. I have actually had Christians come up to me and say, 'There's no record in the Bible of Jesus ever laughing.' That may be true theoretically, but why, then, did children rush to Him? Children love rounded, healthy, fun people.

The Jews have a long tradition of story-telling, *midrashim*. As the people sat around the campfire, the rabbis would tell their stories. Each would have a different approach and a different hermeneutical interpretation. The Jews have passed this powerful heritage on to us. In his book *A Community of Character* the American theologian Stanley Hauerwas calls on the Church to rediscover itself as 'a story-formed community'.[1] The autobiography *A Long Walk to Freedom*[2] tells of how as a boy Nelson Mandela was profoundly impacted by stories which sustained him through his long years of imprisonment. I have read of an Auschwitz survivor who was similarly upheld through his mistreatment at the hands of the Nazis by recalling the Hasidic stories of his tradition. There is power in story. I can preach you a sermon about loneliness but that dear lady who has just walked through a horrendous divorce six months ago and is on her way back to a sense of emotional stability may have a lot more to say about loneliness than I can ever say.

Recently I preached at my church, Timberline in Colorado, on unconditional forgiveness, the same message that R.T. Kendall is carrying around the world at the present time.

As part of my sermon I invited a man from the congregation to tell his story. In 1999 this man's lovely daughter was strangled to death. With trembling voice he told of the night he got the phone call – *the phone call* – from the police telling him that his daughter was dead. It took nine months for the police to find the killer. He wanted to kill that man – of course he did – but he spoke of the journey he has taken to come to a place of forgiveness. He told of how he started to pray for the law enforcement officials, for the judicial system, and eventually for the murderer himself, that justice would be done. He prayed his way through the whole nightmare. Such grace was upon that man. As he stood there weeping, a few thousand people in the congregation wept with him. Whatever I preached about forgiveness that day, this man's story drove home the point beyond anything that I could have shared. This is what I would call community hermeneutics.

The story of God must be danced and sculpted and spoken and painted and mimed and sung and rhymed, so that people are provoked and arrested and confronted. Narrative preaching is powerful because it makes us think. If preaching doesn't make people think, what is the point? In evangelical circles it has become blasphemous ever to offend anyone. I do not want to offend people by being inappropriate, thoughtless or unkind, but I do want to offend if it stirs people up and provokes them. I believe narrative preaching can do that.

■ *Narrative preaching demands an empathetic approach to the text*

It demands that the preacher delve into the text with all sorts of questions: 'What did it feel like?' 'What did it taste like?' 'What did it smell like?' When I am approaching narrative preaching I imagine myself as a BBC producer with six cameras. I organise the cameras around the text. Take, as an example, the story of the woman caught in adultery. In John's Gospel it seems clear that the woman was brought straight into the temple area from the bed of immorality (8:1–11). According to Jewish law, in order for any accusation to stand up in court, two witnesses were required, and so two men must actually have witnessed the act of adultery. John also notes for us that the incident occurred early in the morning. As I probe the text, my mind says, 'This is really seedy, it's gross. She's been caught in the act. These Pharisaic voyeurs have watched her having sex with a man and have dragged her out of that bed of immorality. Her hair is tussled and she is sweaty, and she is shamed. Her eyes are wild. They make her stand before everybody and she trembles as she stands there. She daren't look into their eyes, but they glare at her.' It is fairly obvious that, although those onlookers are exhibiting a sheen of outraged piety, in their minds they are rerunning what she has just been doing, and there is an unhealthy delight in what they have witnessed. Or you could just say, 'There was a woman caught in adultery.'

As we explore the text, we need to allow it to have a period of gestation in us. Whatever approach to preaching we take, this is a very important thing to learn: we must let the story live in us. Out of the vast and rich heritage that John Stott has given us, one of the most helpful principles for me has been his simple statement: isolate the dominant thought. John Henry Jowlett says this: 'I have a conviction that no sermon is ready for preaching until we can express its theme in a short pregnant sentence as clear as crystal.' If someone asks, 'So what are you preaching on Sunday?', we need to be able to crystallise our message in one sentence. If we can't, then our message has not yet reached gestation. This isn't dumbing down the message, it's letting the text live in us.

◼ *Narrative preaching demands an eyes-wide-open approach to life*

Preachers who use story or illustration need to have their eyes wide open. People sometimes say to me, 'How come all these things happen to you?' Pete Broadbent, whom I mentioned earlier, said to me recently, 'Jeff, you live in Technicolor.' Why do all these things happen to me? It may be because I'm stupid, but there is also another reason. *I notice.* I have committed myself to being a deliberate observer of life, both my own and other people's. I make it my aim to connect with people and to listen to their story, not because I'm on the look-out for more sermon fodder, but because I genuinely enjoy it. I believe that we need to open our eyes. I love what Annie Dillard says: 'We are here to abet creation and to witness it and to notice each thing so that each thing gets noticed. Together we notice not only the mountain shadow and each stone on the beach but we notice each other's beautiful face and complex nature, so that creation need not play to an empty house.'

It is a particular failing of Charismatic Christians that we only notice the extraordinary. In his fabulous book, which won Book of the Year in Australia a couple of years ago, *Seeing God in the Ordinary*, Michael Frost writes, 'We have locked God into the so-called sacred realms of church and healings and miracles and marvels. We seem to be trying so hard to bring down fire from heaven in our worship services while all along God's favour is to be found in sunshine on our faces, the sea lapping at our toes, picking our children up at school, or a note from a caring friend.'[3] We fail to notice what God is doing. While we cry out for God to work in mighty ways, He is saying: 'I was at work when your son handed you that painting from his class today. Didn't you notice?'

Anyone who wants to be a narrative story-based preacher, needs to open their eyes. The great story-teller Garrison Keillor says this:

> What keeps our face cheerful is the extreme persistence of gentleness and humour.
> Gentleness is everywhere in daily life, the sign that faith rules through ordinary
> things, through cooking and small talk, through story-telling, through making love,
> fishing, tending animals and sweetcorn and flowers, through sports, music and
> books, raising kids. All the places where the gravy soaks in, grace shines through.

We need to have our eyes open to life. About six months ago I spent all one morning writing about *Paying It Forward*, a film about random acts of kindness, 'mugging people with grace'. Then my wife Kay and I decided to go out for a walk and managed to get ourselves lost – in our own neighbourhood! So we are hot and tired and lost. Suddenly an ice-cream van pulls up, driven by Bert who is singing an Elvis song tunelessly. He says, 'Hello. How are you?' and, being British, we reply, 'We're fine, thank you. Nice weather, we're having!' He says, 'Do you want some ice cream?' Neither of us has any money, but for some reason I ask, 'How much?' 'Oh don't worry about that,' he answers, jumping out and offering us the full choice of his ice creams and lollies. As we take the ice cream I thank him and say, 'I really feel bad that I can't pay.' With the words, 'Don't you worry, have a great day', he jumps back in the truck and drives off again, resuming his rendering of 'Crying in the chapel'. As we stand there gratefully eating our ice creams, I suddenly realise that what I have written about all morning, God has organised for me to experience in the afternoon. We need to notice the things that God does in the ordinary of our daily lives.

■ *Narrative preaching requires a textured approach to the message using illustrations as windows*

Story gives us the opportunity to connect with those who are listening. Some preachers don't even bother to connect with the congregation by saying hello to them. They launch straight into their message. Stories can be a tremendous hook enabling the preacher to take the people with him. I have experimented with the way I begin my sermons. I have tried beginning my message with the words: 'Let us turn to Romans 4:11 which says this...', and within forty-five seconds people's eyes have begun to glaze over. On the other hand, when I begin what I am saying by telling a story, I find I connect with people immediately; their imaginations fire up and they pay attention. Then I can read what Romans 4:11 says. The power of story enables the preacher to connect relationally with those who are listening.

There are a few points to make about the stories we use. We need to make sure they are true. I embellish stories all the time, but I never embellish the core facts and I will never imply that God did something that He did not do. Moreover, I never take somebody else's story and say it happened to me. There are four preachers going around the UK at the moment telling the same story. One of them is me: it's my story. People keep coming up to me and saying, 'That didn't happen to you. It happened to Joe Bloggs.' I make it very clear that it did actually happen to me. Why can't preachers just say, 'This happened to a friend of mine' and tell the story?

As story-tellers we need to be informed. Every week Bill Hybels reads *Time* magazine, *Newsweek*, *US News and World Report*, *Business Week* and *Forbes* magazine. He normally has his radio on in his car, switching between two News channels, and he watches the News channel on TV when he gets home in the evening. Why? He explains that he wants the people in his church to know that he is connected to their reality, and the only way he can do that is by staying absolutely informed.

Another important point is that we must not allow our illustrations to become legislations. For example, I might tell a story about the fact – which hasn't happened to me yet but I think I am open to it – that I felt the Lord wanted me to give up drinking wine for forty days. It is then a very short step from this illustration to the implication that everybody in the congregation needs to give up drinking wine for forty days. My revelation – my illustration – can so quickly become your legislation. We have to be very careful about the way we use our illustrations.

Generally speaking books full of illustrations should be avoided, unless there is absolutely no other alternative. Most of the stories are way out of date and they have more than likely been thrashed to death. I would suggest that people strive to be original.

HUMOUR IN NARRATIVE PREACHING

Having given four reasons why I believe narrative preaching is a powerful approach, I now want to say a few words about the use of humour in preaching. Humour is a powerful gift from God; it has a rhythm which can be very effective in story-based preaching. However, it can also be dangerous, for this reason: any preacher who uses humour in his preaching will more than likely be tagged as a clown. It is a sad fact, but it needs to be faced. A lot of Christians seem to think that if a person enjoys what he or she is doing, it doesn't quite count. Nobody wants to be written off as a joker; we all have an innate desire to be taken seriously. I was at a conference a couple of years ago when a man whom I hadn't seen for twenty years came up to me and said, 'Jeff, I never realised that you were theologically astute.' His comment was unthinking and it was unkind. Spurgeon said, 'I must confess I would rather hear people laugh than I would see them asleep in the house of God.'

This is an area with which I have struggled over the years, but God broke me out of it. A few years ago I said to God, 'God, I tell these stories, most of my preaching is narrative. Am I a fool for Christ?' And God said to me, 'Yes.' I thought, 'Thanks a lot.' Soon after I went off to a conference where I met Gerald Coates. Not knowing anything about my recent conversation with God, Gerald said, 'I've got a prophecy for you that I need to share at the meeting tonight.' That evening, he called me up in front of a thousand leaders in order to prophesy over me. As he began he pulled out a multicoloured jester's hat complete with bells – the hat of a fool – and stuck it on my head. I stood there trying to look religious and spiritual, my heart sinking by the second. People were giggling and laughing and I felt so stupid. Then he began to prophesy, 'You have been willing to be a fool for Christ' and went on to prophesy a number of amazing things, which included the encouragement that the fool often says words to the king that no one else can say. There is a dignity in the fool and in the use of story, but there is also a cost.

On a more practical level, preachers should be careful about punchlines. The reason why I don't tell jokes when I am preaching is because punchlines are too dangerous. They can so easily be forgotten. A friend of mine was once preaching before thousands of people in Trafalgar Square. He tried to tell a joke but he forgot the punchline. Something like that is difficult to live down. Punchlines can also be dangerous because, if they don't get the reaction the preacher was hoping for, a wall comes up between him and his audience. Preachers should only use jokes if they know they can pull it off.

Humour should never be used to pick on people. Preachers who use humour or story in this kind of vindictive way will be hated by their congregations, and rightly so. It is one thing to engage in banter with close friends and associates where there is a prior relationship and mutual understanding, but quite another to make congregation members the butt of a joke or the victim in a story. It can be deeply mortifying. It is always best for the preacher to make himself the victim in the story and to put himself down.

Multimedia in Narrative Preaching

In conclusion I would like to highlight the dangers of the use of multimedia such as PowerPoint, film and music in preaching. Narrative preaching, in particular, can be greatly helped by the inclusion of these kinds of media, but only if the preacher bears this warning in mind: the use of media can be a powerful servant but a tyrannical master. The misuse of PowerPoint, for example, can be very counterproductive if people become overwhelmed by the excessive use of subheadings and bullet points. Technology must be harnessed. Recently I was at a publishers' convention and had twelve minutes to address a group. Some bullet points of the book I was promoting were being displayed on a screen, but it was sited away from where I was speaking. As a result my listeners' eyes were glued in a totally different direction from me, which was very disconcerting when I had flown six thousand miles to be there. Clips from films can be great, so long as the preacher is aware that he will need a verbal stun grenade to get everyone's attention back on to what he is saying. One minute the congregation is gazing at a Hollywood great, then the lights come up, everyone is blinking, everyone is distracted – the preacher has to have a dramatic way of grabbing their attention again. Too many preachers think it is trendy to use technology. They should only use it if it supports their communication: it must not be allowed to take it over.

Notes

1. University of Notre Dame Press, 1981.
2. Abacus, 1995.
3. Hendrickson, 2000.

Chapter 49

PREACHING APOCALYPTICS

Steve Brady

A young undergraduate at Cambridge who had never read the Bible before was given a New Testament to read. When he had done so, he commented, 'It was a bit repetitious at the beginning, but I did enjoy the science-fiction at the end!' He was trying to fit the book of Revelation into some kind of category he could identify. This was, in fact, a very sensible thing to do and, indeed, something which many Christians fail to do. So many people approach the Bible with a flat-footed literalness that attempts to explain all the books in the same way. It is, however, a mistake to approach the Bible as if it were all doctrinal epistles. The Bible is made up of different kinds of genres or types of literature. Some of it is poetry and some of it is prose; some of it is history and some of it is prophecy. Failing to recognise a book's literary genre can land the reader in all sorts of trouble.

For example, I remember hearing a tape by somebody who was trying to prove that our soul is different from our spirit, which may or may not be true. However, in order to prove his point he turned to Luke 1:46–47 where as part of the Magnificat Mary says,

> 'My soul glorifies the Lord
> and my spirit rejoices in God my Saviour...'

This preacher had failed to take account of the text's literary genre. It is poetry and has a great affinity to the Hebrew poetry of the Old Testament, which makes frequent use of the technique of parallelism. Understanding the text's literary genre helps the biblical interpreter to understand that the reference to 'soul' and 'spirit' is actually expressing one reality.

Let's take as another example the book of Proverbs. Some Christian parents torture themselves because of a wrong understanding of the well-known proverb:

> *Train a child in the way he should go,*
> *and when he is old he will not turn from it.*
> (Proverbs 22:6)

They beat themselves up with the thought that if they had trained their child properly, he would not have gone off the rails. In order to understand the book of Proverbs, it is important to realise that although it does contain some promises,[1] it generally contains principles. Moreover, some of the principles which the book promotes stand in direct contradiction to one another, such as:

> *Do not answer a fool according to his folly,*
> *or you will be like him yourself.*
> *Answer a fool according to his folly,*
> *or he will be wise in his own eyes.*
> (Proverbs 26:4–5)

But in this they are not so different from our British proverbs, where we have the seemingly contradictory 'Many hands make light work' and 'Too many cooks spoil the broth'. On one occasion when I was questioning my students about the contradiction posed by Proverbs 26:4–5 ('Do not answer a fool'/'Answer a fool'), one bright spark piped up, 'We're not answering you!' I retorted, 'Hey, what a way to fail your term paper! He who laughs last is always the marker.' We will run into serious problems if we try to turn all the proverbs into promises.

When we come to Revelation, we discover that it is made up of several literary genres. Some of it takes the form of an epistle. In fact there are seven epistles: seven letters to seven specific churches with very specific messages. Many years ago the scholar Colin Hemer wrote an excellent commentary which contained a great deal of research into how these letters relate to the historical background and culture of the seven churches.[2] However, Revelation is also prophecy. In the opening verses of the book we are told:

> *The revelation of Jesus Christ, which God gave him to show his servants what*
> *must soon take place. He made it known by sending his angel to his servant John,*
> *who testifies to everything he saw – that is, the word of God and the testimony of*
> *Jesus Christ. Blessed is the one who reads the words of this prophecy, and blessed*
> *are those who hear it and take to heart what is written in it, because the time*
> *is near.*
> (Revelation 1:1–3)

What is about to be written is also described as 'the revelation of Jesus Christ'. The word translated 'revelation' is *apokalupsis*, from which our word 'apocalyptic' is derived and from which the literary genre 'apocalyptic' gets its name.

Apocalyptic has been defined as 'a literary form which developed firstly under the influence of the highly symbolic, prophetic apocalyptic'. Into this category falls such passages as Isaiah 24–27, which was written in the eighth century BC, Ezekiel 38–48, which was written in the sixth century BC, and Daniel, which the liberals and some evangelicals would like to locate in the second century BC, though I am quite happy to leave it in the sixth century BC. Although Daniel has many apocalyptic features, Revelation is the only fully apocalyptic book in the Bible. Without some knowledge of the apocalyptic genre we will spiritualise the literal and literalise the spiritual, thus making nonsense of the book.

I once belonged to a brand of the Church that loves to spiritualise the literal. Take the parable of the Good Samaritan, for example. This is what it is really about: the second coming. The fact is that humanity has gone down from Jerusalem to Jericho, from the city of God to the city on the plain of destruction. There we have fallen amongst thieves; the devil has robbed us. Religion came along but it could not help us. Then the Good Samaritan came, who is obviously Jesus. Jesus poured His blood and His Spirit (oil and wine) into our wounds to make us clean and to renew us, and then He brought us into the Church (the inn) where the Holy Spirit (the innkeeper) looks after us. Of course, the two coins represent payment for two working days, and since *'With the Lord a day is like a thousand years, and a thousand years are like a day'*,[3] this means that the Lord is going to return in two thousand years' time. And anyone who believes a word of that is the last remaining character in the parable – the donkey! The parable of the Good Samaritan is, of course, intended to answer the question 'Who is my neighbour?'

It is fatuous and highly dangerous to try and spiritualise the Bible in this way. Take the catch of 153 fish in John's Gospel,[4] which has been given all sorts of interpretations. For example, it means: 12×12 (the complete number of the elect) equals 144; the square root of the remaining 9 is 3, which is the triune God in the fullness of His being redeeming His elect! Hey presto! If I preached that, people would come out saying, 'Oh! It was very deep.' But it is not deep, it is wide of the mark. Although there may be other reasons why John chose the number 153, I believe that he recorded it because it was the size of the catch, and just as real as its presence was that of the Lord Jesus, who was there on the beach with them.

Since we need to be very careful how we interpret the apocalyptic of Revelation, I now want to explain some basic principles which will help us.

BASIC PRINCIPLES OF THE APOCALYPTIC

1. Apocalyptic generally claims to reveal truths that readers could not arrive at by themselves

It professes to be, as it suggests, a revelation from God usually delivered via an angel or some other intermediary, telling the readers something they would not already know.

It is important to understand that apocalyptic is not exclusively a Christian genre. This kind of literature, which is now becoming increasingly available in English translation, flourished between the second century BC and the second century AD. Jewish apocalyptic literature includes such books as 1 Enoch and the three books of Maccabees. The latter was written against the backcloth of second-century BC Judaism, when the famous Antiochus Epiphanes tried to impose paganism on Jewish worship, even sacrificing pigs in the temple, and there was a massive revolt under the leadership of Judas Maccabeus, whose name literally means Judas the Hammer. This revolt is the first guerrilla warfare ever recorded in history, and I understand that at the West Point Military Academy in the United States Josephus' account of the Maccabean revolt is included in the curriculum, because it is regarded as still having things to teach soldiers about guerrilla warfare today.

There were also other Christian apocalypses, for example, the Apocalypse of Peter. As a literary movement, it would have been within the sphere of understanding of the people of its day. Because it is not familiar to us, it does not mean that it was not familiar to them.

2. The language of apocalyptic is often highly esoteric and symbolic
For example:

- frequent use of certain significant numbers: 3; 4; 7; 10; 12
- references to wild animals, which usually mean foreign armies
- references to horns, e.g. 'the horn' and 'the great horn', which always mean kings, kingly authority, power
- stars, which often but not always refer to angels.

Apocalyptic literature is laden with symbolism because it was a kind of code, addressed to people who were going through very hard times and whose future was very uncertain.

3. It is often deterministic, bordering on dualism
Apocalyptic literature is written in such a way that it seems as if nothing can change what is about to happen. There is an inevitability about it. It is a very black and white view.

Some Christians are like this about the will of God. In experience they are more Muslim than Christian, seeming to believe that God's will is so determinative that *que sera sera*, 'whatever will be will be'. But the Bible in general is not deterministic. It emphasises God's sovereignty and our human responsibility and accountability – simultaneously. However, there is in the apocalyptic the suggestion that this is the way it will be and nothing will change it.

WAYS OF INTERPRETING THE BOOK OF REVELATION

There are no short cuts to understanding the book of Revelation but there are some traditional routes into it, which it can be very helpful for us to understand. One scholar has said: 'Once the symbolism of the book of Revelation is understood it is easier to interpret than the epistle of Romans.'

1. The preterist route

Since 'preterist' means 'to do with the past', this line of interpretation recognises the value of understanding the historical and cultural background at the time the book was written. Now this is always a good, sound principle for understanding any part of the Bible. We ask, what did the book mean to its original hearers? What did they make of it? Presumably they did not regard it as gibberish and nonsense. If it had not communicated to them, surely they would not have kept it as part of the canon of Scripture. We need, therefore, to understand how it made sense to them.

By way of illustration let us look at Revelation 3:16, addressed to the church at Laodicea, from a preterist interpretation:

> 'So, because you are lukewarm – neither hot nor cold – I am about to spit you out of my mouth.'

A standard interpretation, which I am sure I have preached in the past, is that Jesus wants His followers either to be totally for Him or totally against Him. The last thing He wants is for people to sit on the fence. People should nail their colours to the mast and, taken to its logical extreme, if they are against Him, they should go out and start killing some Christians. This interpretation has to be weighed against other scriptures such as, '*A bruised reed he will not break, and a smouldering wick he will not snuff out*',[5] which seem to suggest that even a little faith in a great God is better than a lot of faith in a small God. Is Jesus saying that He wants nothing to do with those of weak faith? No, He isn't, and this is where a preterist interpretation can help us as we begin to understand more about the city of Laodicea.

Laodicea was situated in the Lycus valley. Not far away at Hierapolis there were hot, refreshing springs and at Colossae there were cold, refreshing waters. Due to the fact that it was built on sandstone, Laodicea had the reputation of having the worst water in the empire. The water there was vile. It was lukewarm and it tasted horrible. If you drank it, you wanted to spit it out immediately. The Laodicean Church thought that they had achieved mega-church status; they thought they had made it:

> 'You say, "I am rich; I have acquired wealth and do not need a thing."'
> (Revelation 3:17a)

They were very proud of their achievements as a church, but Jesus has a very different view:

'*But you do not realize that you are wretched, pitiful, poor, blind and naked.*'
(Revelation 3:17b)

His reference to being blind is again very topical because there was a famous eye centre in Laodicea. Jesus is not saying that He wishes that the Laodicean Christians were either for Him or against Him, but that they would either refresh Him like a hot, refreshing spring on a cold day or slate His thirst like a cool drink on a hot day. We see, then, that understanding the background of the text can be very helpful in interpretation.

2. The 'historicist' route

This has also been called the Protestant view, because it stems from the sixteenth-century Reformation understanding that the beast in Revelation 13 whose number was 666, was the pope and the city set on seven hills was Rome.[6] It is still held by some Protestants. Inherent in this view is the idea that the unfolding drama of God's redemption is actually taking place in Western Europe, i.e. we are the centre of the universe!

John Calvin wrote on every New Testament book except the book of Revelation. John Calvin was an outstanding theologian for two reasons: he was a brilliant exegete of the Bible, but he also was a brilliant 'big picture' man – what theologians would call a 'systematician'. He could see both the big picture and the detailed picture: it is very unusual for one individual to have both these skills. Why then did Calvin not write on the book of Revelation? The well-known D.A. Carson reports having heard F.F. Bruce express the view that Calvin was too good a theologian to try and make the text of Revelation apply to the Roman Catholic Church in sixteenth-century Europe and therefore, not wanting to let his own side down, he did not even try. I don't know whether this is true, but it is an interesting thought.

3. The symbolical idealist route

This approach acknowledges that the book of Revelation is full of symbols, which are intended to be illustrations of the truth and not necessarily the truth themselves. We can draw an analogy with the characters Gandalf and Frodo in Tolkien's immensely popular *Lord of the Rings*, who, although they themselves are not real, illustrate important aspects of truth.

Imagine for a moment that someone who has never been to the cinema before, let alone to a science fiction film, is taken to see the film *Star Wars* and asked to write down everything that happens. When he comes out, he has to find ways of expressing all the unusual characters he has seen such as Chewbacca and Darth Vadar and all the imaginary worlds, as well as all the details of the plot. Then imagine what somebody reading his account two hundred years later, who is also not familiar with science fiction, might make of it. This is precisely what is happening in the book of Revelation. John is seeing a revelation played out before him in a vision and is told to write down what he is seeing.[7] He is faced with the very real challenge of having to find images and symbols to express what he is seeing.

4. The Dispensationalist route

The Dispensationalists believe that the Church will be whisked away to be with Jesus before the Tribulation and, therefore, that from chapter 6 onwards Revelation does not apply to Christians. While it is interesting from a theoretical point of view, it will not affect us as Christians directly. It is the view propounded by the Scofield Reference Bible and the Left Behind series of books written by Tim LaHaye. It is widely held in America and, since it has huge implications for the Middle East, has a huge influence on American policy in the Middle East.

5. The moderate futurist route

This approach emphasises the fact that the future is still unfolding; the events of Revelation have not already happened in the past. As we approach the end of time we will see more and more of the events prophesied in Revelation coming into being, including the rise of the Anti-Christ, great apostasy and a period of intense tribulation on the earth.

These, then, are five major ways in which the book of Revelation is interpreted. Let me sum up this section by looking briefly at how four prominent biblical scholars approach the book.

Warren Wiersbe, who uses a Dispensational framework, suggests a very simple outline. In his view the book has three sections: what has been (chapters 1–3), what is (4–5), and what shall be (5–22).

Michael Wilcock breaks from tradition and makes the interesting assertion that the book of Revelation has eight scenes.[8] Since a Jewish boy was circumcised when he was eight days old and Jesus rose from the dead on the eighth day (having died on the sixth day and been buried on the seventh day), he sees eight as a number signifying a new beginning. In his interpretation of Revelation, the eighth scene is chapters 21 and 22 of Revelation, which is ultimately about the new beginning of a New Heaven and a New Earth.

From a former generation, William Hendricksen said that the book of Revelation is based on the contrapuntal principle and that there are actually seven parallel sections. In music contrapuntalism, I understand, is the building of successive layers of music into a harmonious whole. In Hendricksen's view, in Revelation John is describing scenes of the same event from different angles to present the complete picture. Thus, in his view the book should not be seen as sequential (as a chronological account starting at the beginning), but as thematic (it keeps coming back to the same event again and again).

George Beasley-Murray emphasises the big picture of Revelation. He says, 'It was not written to hold threats of damnation before sinners but to encourage saints to press on despite all opposition, and to win the inheritance. The Revelation was written that men might enter the city of God, and the vision of the city is the true climax of the book.'[9]

As we seek to decide for ourselves what is the best way to approach the book of Revelation, I think it is important to remember what I said earlier about literary genres. Different literary genres are appropriate to different types of subject matter. When it comes to handling an account of an individual's life, for example, the narrative style is most appropriate. As we read the story of David's life, we are able to come to an understanding of him as a complex character, who was both 'a man after God's heart' and also capable of adultery and murder. This can be strangely encouraging for many of us who see similar ambiguities in our own lives. However, the apocalyptic genre works in black and white, although in Revelation there is a great deal of Technicolor in the detail. It does not deal with ambiguities and this is, I believe, because the subject matter with which it is dealing is extremely serious and requires that people should make up their mind one way or the other – either for Jesus or for Satan.

In the Bible, the apocalyptic genre also has the important attribute that it is able to convey the transcendent. It is able to communicate the otherness of God. In chapter 4, for example, we are given a glimpse into the throne room of God:

> And the one who sat there had the appearance of jasper and carnelian. A rainbow, resembling an emerald, encircled the throne. Surrounding the throne were twenty-four other thrones, and seated on them were twenty-four elders. They were dressed in white and had crowns of gold on their heads. From the throne came flashes of lightning, rumblings and peals of thunder.
> (Revelation 4:3–5)

It is an incredible and awesome scene. A few verses later John describes how the four living creatures are constantly calling out 'Holy, holy, holy!' which takes us straight back to Isaiah 6 and reminds us that it is still the same God who is being worshipped. John weeps and weeps as he observes the angel holding the scroll, which signifies the redemptive purposes of God, but finding no one who is worthy to open it. The elders comfort him with the words, 'Do not weep! See, the Lion of the tribe of Judah, the Root of David, has triumphed', but as he looks up expecting to see a lion, he sees 'a Lamb, looking as if it had been slain'.[10] I often ask those who like to take the Bible literally, whether they are expecting to see a lamb when they get to heaven? Of course they aren't. This is not a picture that is meant to be drawn, but a picture that is meant to be imagined. Its colourful language is meant to fire the imagination. The Old Testament is our grammar and phrasebook for the New Testament. The Lion is the 'Lion of the tribe *of Judah'*, who turns aside for no one. The lamb is, of course, a picture of sacrifice. When we come to the book of Revelation we need to let our imagination take controlled flight.

A Case Study: Revelation 12

At first sight, due to our ignorance of the apocalyptic, this is a most obscure passage.

> *A great and wondrous sign appeared in heaven: a woman clothed with the sun, with the moon under her feet and a crown of twelve stars on her head. She was pregnant and cried out in pain as she was about to give birth. Then another sign appeared in heaven: an enormous red dragon with seven heads and ten horns and seven crowns on his heads. His tail swept a third of the stars out of the sky and flung them to the earth. The dragon stood in front of the woman who was about to give birth, so that he might devour her child the moment it was born. She gave birth to a son, a male child, who will rule all the nations with an iron sceptre. And her child was snatched up to God and to his throne.*
> (Revelation 12:1–5)

The first decision we have to make is whether it is a flash-back or a follow-on. Then we have to decide who the cast of players are in this scene:

- *the woman giving birth*: at first sight it may seem obvious that the woman is the Virgin Mary but, since later in the chapter there is a reference to 'her seed',[11] it seems that she is intended to be a picture of the people of God. The Messiah came through a nation. Jesus Himself said, *'salvation is from the Jews.'*[12]
- *the dragon*: this is made easy for us because we are given the code in verse 9:

  > *The great dragon was hurled down – that ancient serpent called the devil, or Satan, who leads the whole world astray. He was hurled to the earth, and his angels with him.*

  Sometimes in apocalyptic literature we just have to read on a bit to discover what a particular symbol means.
- *the child*: the horrific picture of the dragon waiting to devour the child as soon as he is born is an allusion to attempts by Satan to destroy Jesus, e.g. Herod's murder of all infant boys under the age of two, as well as at other times in His life. The child then refers to Jesus. In the scene the child is snatched straight up to heaven, without any mention of His saving life, His death or His resurrection, but this is because John has already spoken about these things.

591

In verses 7–12 the drama unfolds and we are told the immediate consequences in the heavenlies of Christ's ascension, namely that there is war in this invisible realm, and the devil and his angels are hurled down to the earth. We then read:

Then I heard a loud voice in heaven say:

'Now have come the salvation and the power and the kingdom of our God,
and the authority of his Christ.
For the accuser of our brothers,
who accuses them before our God day and night,
has been hurled down.'
(Revelation 12:10)

Through the birth of the child things have changed dramatically in the heavenly realm, and this change will have momentous consequences for the earth:

'But woe to the earth and the sea,
because the devil has gone down to you!
He is filled with fury,
because he knows that his time is short.'
(Revelation 12:12)

As a consequence of the spiritual warfare in the heavenlies, there is a spiritual chain reaction which results in the devil coming down to earth in great wrath because he knows his time is short.

There are some Christians who all the time seem to be focused on demonic activity, but since the text makes it clear that a third of the angels were expelled from heaven with him (v. 4), it is evident that two-thirds of the angels remain in God's service. So, since the 'goodies' outnumber the 'baddies' two to one, and since the almighty God is on our side, we Christians have nothing to worry about! We need to keep our focus on God and not on the devil. There are some things that we do not know and that we are not meant to know. The curtain is drawn back far enough for us to know that there is spiritual warfare going on in the heavens. That battle is not ours to fight: we have to be engaged in the battle that is being waged on earth.

Over sixty years ago now, on 6 June 1944 the Allied Forces began their liberation of Europe with the D-day landings, sustaining huge casualties in the battle for Normandy. Within just a few days, over a million men and thousands of tons of equipment had poured into Europe. It was the decisive battle of the Second World War. Meanwhile, of course, the Russians were also beginning to fight back and the Americans were starting to make their way up the 'boot' of Italy. Although D-Day marked the beginning of the end, it was not yet the end. It would be almost a year before victory would be declared. With his days clearly numbered, did Adolf Hitler simply lay down his arms and surrender? No! Quite the contrary, all hell broke loose! Thousands more would have to die before his tyranny was finally defeated.

A theologian called Oscar Cullmann has used this period between the beginnings of victory and actual victory in the Second World War as a way of explaining the phase in cosmic history in which we as Christians are living out our lives. Cullmann explained that on the cross Jesus has won the decisive battle and we are now headed towards VE-Day, but we have not arrived at it yet. The Christian is someone who lives between the times. We are still involved in a raging and even intensifying battle, but by the grace of God it is one we are going to win.

Some Advice on Preaching on the Book of Revelation

In conclusion I would like to give some advice to any preachers who are thinking about tackling Revelation.

First, I would strongly advise that a young preacher does not start a new pastorate by preaching on the book of Revelation. There is a temptation to want to start with a bang, but although the first few chapters may go quite well, by about chapter 6 he will probably wish he had never started. The book of Revelation can humble even the most experienced of preachers, so my advice to any preacher at the beginning of his preaching career would be to start on some of the more straightforward books.

Second, before preaching on the book of Revelation, a preacher needs to have a good understanding of the apocalyptic genre. He also needs to have familiarised himself with the books of Daniel, Ezekiel and Isaiah, the writers of which use similar timeframes and symbolism, and to have developed his own ideas about the patterns and symbolism in the book, which requires a certain amount of background reading and research. I have preached and lectured on this book more times than I can remember and, every time I do so, I still come across something new and I wonder how I could have missed that before. Before tackling the whole book of Revelation it is perfectly acceptable to start with small sections of it, perhaps with the letters to the churches or some of the themes which run through it.

Third, a preacher needs to make sure that he spends some time trying to work out the big picture of the book, before getting into the details because, as the saying goes, the devil is in the detail. To some people having to put in hours of study will be very boring, but it is impossible to get to grips with the book of Revelation without it.

It is possible to read the book of Revelation and see only bowls, beasts, scarlet women and all the other vivid images and symbols that John describes. It is possible to read the book of Revelation and miss the point of it all, which is to see Jesus. Jesus is the big story of Revelation. In chapter 1 we are given a revelation of the risen Lord. In chapters 2 and 3 we see Him walking among the churches. In chapters 4 and 5 He is in the very centre of the throne room of God. And when we reach the end of the book we read:

> *I did not see a temple in the city, because the Lord God Almighty and the Lamb are its temple. The city does not need the sun or the moon to shine on it, for the glory of God gives it light, and the Lamb is its lamp.*
> (Revelation 21:22–23)

There is one message which this 'Jesus-book' tells us over again and again. The word *pantocrator* means 'God rules over everything'. It is used ten times in the Greek New Testament, and nine of those ten occur in the book of Revelation. It tells us that no matter what is happening, Jesus is Lord over planet earth. The devil may keep winning battles, but God is going to win the war. God in Christ will overcome and, by the blood of the Lamb and the word of our testimony – if we do no not love our lives so much as to shrink from death[13] – we shall too!

NOTES

1. E.g. Proverbs 3:5–6.
2. Colin J. Hemer, *The Letters to the Seven Churches of Asia in Their Local Setting* (JSOT, 1986).
3. 2 Peter 3:8.
4. John 21:11.
5. Isaiah 42:3.
6. See Revelation 17:9.
7. Revelation 4:2; Revelation 1:19.
8. M. Wilcock, *The Message of Revelation: I Saw Heaven Opened*, The Bible Speaks Today series (IVP, 1975).
9. G.R. Beasley-Murray, *The Book of Revelation* (Marshall, Morgan & Scott, 1974).
10. Revelation 5:5, 6.
11. Verse 17 KJV; 'offspring' NIV.
12. John 4:22.
13. Revelation 12:11.

RECOVERING YOUR CUTTING EDGE

Greg Haslam

*The company of the prophets said to Elisha, 'Look, the place where we meet with
you is too small for us. Let us go to the Jordan, where each of us can get a pole;
and let us build a place there for us to live.'*

   And he said, 'Go.'

   Then one of them said, 'Won't you please come with your servants?'

   'I will,' Elisha replied. And he went with them.

   *They went to the Jordan and began to cut down trees. As one of them was cutting
down a tree, the iron axe-head fell into the water. 'Oh, my Lord,' he cried out,
'it was borrowed!'*

   *The man of God asked, 'Where did it fall?' When he showed him the place, Elijah
cut a stick and threw it there, and made the iron float. 'Lift it out,' he said. Then the
man reached out his hand and took it.*

(2 Kings 6:1–7)

In many ways the story of Elisha and the company of prophets sums up the reasons why
the preaching school at Westminster Chapel, London, at which each of the talks in this
book was originally preached, came into being and what we sought to achieve through it,
and what we are now seeking to further through the publication of this book. The
inclusion of the story of the floating axe-head at this point in Israel's history is significant.
It is sandwiched between the account of the personal and domestic tragedy of the death of
a child and the national tragedy of the siege of Samaria which was threatening to bring
devastating famine. We are all too aware that we are living at a time in our nation when
hope is dying. In particular, it is a time of deep gloom for the Church. We know, too, that

political upheaval and spiritual decline are giving rise to a great deal of fear in people's hearts. The story of the lost axe-head carried lessons for the nation of Israel, and I believe that it carries lessons for us today.

We note, first of all, *that the incident occurs in the context of a 'company of prophets' who had outgrown their current accommodation and were anticipating further growth.* Throughout the Westminster conference there was a very real sense that we were a company of people brought together by the Holy Spirit with a common burden for our nation, and for the gospel and the churches we represent. And this fact meant that it was a matter of little importance which denomination we came from. We all came in faith for future growth. I believe that many of us who preach and teach in Great Britain have a feeling that we must prepare ourselves for what God is going to do in our land. We want to be instruments in His hands because growth is coming to the Church once again. Believing we are going to experience blessing as never before – in our lifetimes we trust – we are willing to prepare for it. That is what the company of prophets in Elisha's time were doing: they were chopping down trees and getting the raw materials ready for growth.

Similarly, we all came together with the sense that we had been 'fetched' for something bigger than ourselves and our own local settings. We felt a divine 'pull' to be together, like the animals drawn to Noah's ark. God had in mind new beginnings and expansive multiplication for us all.

Fifty hours of teaching is no mean task. It is impossible to calculate how many hours of preparation went into the preaching school – not only in terms of the speakers' preparation for their talks, but also in the hours spent by the delegates in travelling and the sacrifices they made in order to attend. In doing so, we were preparing for growth. We were all saying in effect that the place where we meet is too small for us, and that is a big thing for the minister of Westminster Chapel to say, since we can hold 2,000 people! But I am saying that by faith, and I hope you, the reader, are beginning to believe for that also.

Second, *the company of prophets did not want to set about their building project on their own: they wanted Elisha's presence.* Elisha was God's representative, the most prominent prophetic figure in Israel's life at that time, a man clothed in the mantel that had been worn by Elijah, with the Holy Spirit's presence oozing from every pore of his body and every word that he said. The prophets wanted the presence of God in their project. Isn't that what we all want as preachers? Then we must long for it, ask for it, and consciously depend on God for it.

Third, and perhaps most importantly, *the story speaks of the loss of cutting edge.* Speaking more broadly about the Church in this nation, despite our evident strengthening in some areas of activity such as worship, small group life, ministry to the poor, etc., there is a real awareness that we have lost our cutting edge, particularly in our spoken ministry of God's Word. The prophet's axe-head fell off in the midst of sustained hard work and busyness, and, God knows, for decades we have diligently tried all kinds of means to turn our nation around. But in that very busyness and feverish activity we seem to have lost our cutting edge. As the axe-head fell into the water, the axe was rendered useless for any further effective work. It was impossible to gather resources of timber for building, or to assemble them properly, without the recovery of the fallen and lost axe-head. In the same way, we have often become blunted and rendered useless in this ministry of preaching.

The distressed prophet who had lost his axe-head cried out, *'Oh, my Lord, it was borrowed!'* As preachers our ministry is not ours, it is borrowed; it is on loan to us. It was not ours to lose. We are compelled to ask ourselves, where on earth did we lose the effectiveness that former generations of believers came to expect and experience in this business of preaching? If our cutting edge is lost, then it must be retrieved. Since this task has been entrusted to us and we will be held accountable for what we do with it, it must be returned and sharpened to good order for further effective use.

For me personally, a major theme of this preaching school was loss and recovery. Some things have to be lost before they can properly be recovered again. I think most of us arrived at this conference knowing that whatever we had been enabled to do so far, it had not been good enough. We needed something more. We need resurrection power. We not only need to die to what we have been, but also to rise to something fresh and new, to something more effective than we have ever experienced before. It is noteworthy that the axe-head was lost in the River Jordan which, in the Bible, often speaks of death, or at least of transition to something better. Objects and people do not emerge from a plunge into the Jordan the same as they went in. It is a crossover point. Some things have to be lost before we get them back again.

Fourth, *the happiest outcome of our exposure to this material would be the recovery of our 'cutting edge'*. For the prophet in question there was an amazing recovery of his 'cutting edge'. We are told that Elisha the man of God asked him, *'Where did it fall?'* and, when he was shown the place, he cut a stick and threw it into the river at that point. Miraculously, the iron floated and Elisha instructed that it should be retrieved. In order for the axe-head to be recovered, we see that there was something the prophet needed to do, and something that God alone could do. I believe this is also the case both for us and for the Church, as we seek to recover our cutting edge.

What *we* need to do is to cry out and admit our loss. In response to the prophet's cry Elisha asked, *'Where did it fall?'*, and in the same way each one of us needs to go back to the place where we lost our cutting edge. There are many possible places where this could have occurred. We may have lost it through discouragement and criticism, or the climate of unfaith in which we live, not only in Britain as a whole, but in the Church in this nation. We may have faced put-downs so often that we have lost our confidence. Perhaps we have lost faith in the act of preaching itself, having been told so many times that this is a Word-resistant age, and that nobody is interested in preaching any more, and that it can't be done effectively nowadays. Perhaps our motives have been spoiled by greed, pride and competitiveness with other leaders and churches, so that actually, God Himself has withheld blessing from us. Perhaps we have become angry and bitter – angry with God and angry with God's people – or nursed wounds we have received as a result of people's reactions to our faithful preaching, vowing never again to put our head above the parapet and risk having it shot off. Perhaps we have become angry with God at the lack of success in our ministry. Or maybe we have lost confidence in the Bible, or simply become lazy and negligent about the preaching task, merely throwing some 'blessed thoughts' together a few hours before we are to preach. Worst of all, we have allowed ourselves to be intimidated by the fear of man, because this axe cuts and hurts if it is wielded properly, and people react to that. We need to go back, mentally and emotionally, to the place where we lost our cutting edge.

However, we must also realise that there is something that only *God* can do. God is able to fix even the most impossible of situations. Humanly speaking, it was impossible to recover an axe-head from the mud at the bottom of the River Jordan, but the prophet of God was there. Elisha was good at doing things that made no sense, like throwing salt into a bitter spring and making it fresh and drinkable again, and on this occasion throwing a stick into the river to retrieve an axe-head. The stick was the catalyst for God to go to work. It acted in almost the same way as a sacrament, in which God empowers a physical action to effect spiritual change. Elisha's throwing of the stick into the water reminds us that, dead sticks as we are, God is able to relaunch us and then do something that only He can do – give us back our cutting edge. 'Bad luck' for this young prophet was then turned into 'bad news' for the devil. The axe-head was recovered, and a ministry that seemed sunk was now afloat again. Dead sticks can recover their edge again!

God wants to give back to each one of us our cutting edge. God is in the salvage business. Whatever it is we have lost, and however we lost it, with God we can receive it back again and we can become very effective men and women in the years ahead. God wants to restore our cutting edge so that we will take more risks than we have ever taken before, become bolder and more outspoken than we have ever been before, and sharper and more hard-hitting than ever. God wants to restore us to that place where we will promise Him that we will faithfully relay everything that He has given us to speak and everything He has put on our hearts to say. But if this is to happen, like the prophet, we will need to lift it out, and once again take hold of what has been miraculously restored to us, never allowing it to sink and become lost again. Take hold of that for which God took hold of you (Philippians 3:12).

Only in this way can we 'build God a house', accommodate the growth He wants to give us, and form a 'school of the prophets' in the shape of a renewed Church that will once again become a prophetic voice to our nation. God is in the salvage or recycling business. He can put us all back into circulation.

'BE FILLED WITH THE SPIRIT'

(EPHESIANS 5:1–21; ACTS 2:38–41)

Greg Haslam

One of the most important things we have sought to address throughout this volume of lectures on preaching is that preaching is an act of speaking unlike any other, in that it is dependent on the power of the Holy Spirit for its effectiveness. In many ways we come to the heart of the issue with the exhortation of the Apostle Paul in Ephesians 5:18. Here the Apostle Paul commands us to *'be filled with the Spirit'*, the Lord's expressed intention for all believers (v. 17a), and especially those charged with the task of preaching His Word. It would be the height of folly to ignore or despise such a directive as this.

BUT WHAT DOES IT MEAN TO BE FILLED WITH THE SPIRIT?

At the very least it has implications related to our joy and satisfaction in this work and our effectiveness in enhancing God's praise and glory through this ministry, for in Ephesians 5:19–20 Paul indicates that such praise is the result and first overflow of being filled with the Spirit, as worship is outpoured toward God through a wide variety of musical and poetic expressions. A man once said to me, 'I would rather spend eternity in silence in hell, than in eternal sing-song in heaven with you Christians!' I concluded that his idea of hell was my idea of heaven, and my idea of heaven was his idea of hell! But the Holy Spirit can make worshippers of us all. It's difficult to have joyful worship in a church unless people are filled with the Spirit. With the Spirit we are caught up in deep joy in the knowledge and adoration of the three Persons of the Trinity, and the delight they have in each other. We feel the Father's delight in Christ the Son, and the Son's rapturous love for the Father too. So the Holy Spirit's great priority is first to make worshippers of us all – the primary end of all preaching.

In explaining this matter of being filled with the Spirit, we are sometimes urged to seek a 'second blessing'. But this might imply that we could end our spiritual quest right there, on the grounds that we have now 'had it'. The New Testament never urges us to settle for the first time we were baptised in the Holy Spirit, as if that was the sum total of His power and presence that we would ever need. The truth is, we need the Lord to pour out on us a continual effulgence of the Spirit's life and power so that we will be filled with joy, victorious over temptation, bold in witness, and maturing in all our relationships. By these four criteria alone it is obvious that some Christians are not yet filled with the Spirit.

- If He comes to glorify Jesus (John 15:26–27), not all Christians seem to live consistently towards that end.
- If He comes to give power in witness (Acts 1:8), why do so many believers remain low-profile and in hiding?
- If He comes to prompt us to service, using our grace-gifts (1 Corinthians 12:4–5), why are so many apparently inactive and idle, like 'sleepers' still awaiting their wake-up call?
- If He comes to elevate corporate praise and worship (Ephesians 5:19–20), why do so many people remain silent, joyless and miserable?

The answer must be that many are not yet filled with the Holy Spirit, even if they resent the suggestion that this may be so. A.W. Tozer once wrote, 'There are many people in our churches who would like to think they are filled with the Holy Ghost, even though they do not know it.' If there really are many 'have nots' and 'are nots', then the explanation for this may be that there are so many who are still 'know nots', 'want nots', 'will nots' and 'ask nots'. It is obvious also that many others are simply too afraid to ask for more of the Holy Spirit, and resist all attempts to teach and persuade them to experience otherwise. But we must regard this apostolic exhortation in Ephesians 5:18 more seriously than that.

THE NEED FOR THE HOLY SPIRIT'S POWER TODAY

This apostolic directive and command here in Ephesians 5:18 is the fulcrum or centre point of the doctrinal and practical sections of this epistle. This is the reason why Paul introduced the empowering and assuring work of the Holy Spirit in the first chapter (1:12–13). And as we read on, we are meant to note that the fullness of the Holy Spirit is not just evident in terms of the 'tingly' feelings, exquisite ecstasy or emotional highs that some believers experience from time to time. He comes to do a lot more than this in our lives.

■ *The Spirit comes to make Christ and His work more real to me* (1:1–2:10)
This is why Paul prays,

> *I keep asking that the God of our Lord Jesus Christ, the glorious Father,*
> *may give you the Spirit of wisdom and revelation, so that you may know*
> *him better.*
> (1:17)

The Spirit helps us to see something more of the wonders of God's sovereign choice of us, the efficacy of Christ's saving blood shed for us, and the profound assurance of the Spirit's inner witness within us. He makes real to us the objective event of the resurrection of Christ and the subjective spiritual resurrection of once-dead unbelievers (1:19–23; 2:1–4).

■ *The Spirit comes to make our fellow Christians more important to us*
(2:11–22; 4:1–16)
The American Founding Father Thomas Jefferson once declared concerning his religious convictions, 'I am a sect unto myself'. By contrast the Puritans claimed that outside the Church 'there is no ordinary possibility of salvation'. Some Christians have never had a revelation of the glory of the Church. It is God's new people, God's 'new citizenship', God's own 'family household', and God's 'Temple' in which God lives and does powerful things. The Spirit will not allow us to remain critical or contemptuous of it, nor to speak pessimistically of 'the end of the Church by the mid twenty-first century'. Some speak of God's Church as a 'bag of dried bones', just as rotten and just as dead. They have no desire to join one or to be there. They have given up on the Church. But the fullness of the Spirit will change all that and help make us agents of change within it, assisting the task of building God's Church as Christ wants it to be.

■ *The Spirit makes my witness to the world more powerful* (3:1–21)
Here Paul alludes to the astonishing privilege he felt in having been called to preach these revealed mysteries of the gospel, which was the greatest message the world could or ever would hear (3:2–9). The famous eighteenth-century London stage actor David Garrick once responded to a clergyman who had asked him how he kept his crowded audiences spellbound for an hour, whilst the cleric could only bore his dwindling congregations in just ten minutes of sermonising. Garrick replied, 'The answer is simple. I declare fiction as though it were fact, and you declare fact as though it were fiction.' Often, there isn't enough power in our hymns, prayers and sermons to convert a gnat! The Spirit is ignored and His fire is quenched. The Holy Spirit was sent to glorify Christ and when He is honoured in this role, supernatural power attends even our feeblest efforts to do this.

■ *The Spirit progressively transforms our once godless character, making it more godly* (4:17–5:16)

So when we ask questions like 'Are you attractive to look at and good to be with?' 'Do you work hard at your job, and have you ceased living dependently on others?' 'Are you patient with irritations and with difficult people, or do you have a volatile temper or deep-seated roots of bitterness and resentment?' 'Is your mouth a polluted sewer of bad language or a spring of clean water?' 'Does your life appear to be directed and on course within the will of God, or are you drifting and directionless?', then the Spirit is the one who sanctifies us in all these varied ways and more. Martin Luther once said, 'I would rather obey than work miracles.' But I've sometimes observed that some Christians would rather work miracles than obey! The Holy Spirit wants to produce a holy life in us, as well as a life marked by 'signs and wonders'.

■ *The Spirit enhances all my relationships and makes me a threat and danger to the devil* (5:21–6:20)

We live at a time of relational breakdown and disintegration. Men have ceased to be men, and become abusers. Women have become resentful and mistrustful towards men and sought power through manipulation and illicit control. Divorce is at an all-time high. Children roam the streets in violent gangs. The workplace is often an oppressive prison for so many. But here, Paul spells out the dramatic changes the Holy Spirit makes in our marriage, home and work. He brings divine order to the super-ordinate and subordinate parties in each relationship, and eliminates oppression, cruelty and abuse. He fosters true respect for one another, the ability to resolve conflict, the release of our full personal potential and economic prosperity, and much fun and laughter in all our social contacts, especially within the church. Marriages can last and be filled with love. Children can be secure and mature under the Lord's discipline and wisdom, so that they come to know God and live enthusiastically for Him. The workplace can become an environment where Christ is present and operative through His people whether they are management or employees, and He can impart to all a sense of dignity and purpose in their work, reforming ugly and tense situations for the better. And all of this, when we are filled with the Spirit.

All of these concrete and specific expressions of the Spirit's fullness are not simply the prelude to spiritual warfare – they are spiritual warfare! Confronting the demonic and donning the whole armour of God are concurrent with, not subsequent to, engaging in these vital activities.

BE FILLED WITH THE HOLY SPIRIT!

It is notable that Paul compares and contrasts this with drunkenness. Drunkenness is a life-dominating problem. It 'fills' every area of a person's life, and manifests itself in erosive, destructive and terrifying effects. It affects all areas of life, determining how the drunkard spends his money, loves his wife, raises his children, chooses his friends, behaves in his leisure times, accomplishes his work and fares in all his relationships. The Holy Spirit wants similar access to all areas, but with precisely the opposite effects. He does not lead us to ruin but to redemption.

Things can only get better when we are filled with the Holy Spirit for only then are we under an entirely different influence. Jay Adams helpfully comments,

> When the Bible talks of being filled with amazement, with fear, with jealousy, with joy ... the idea of domination is in view. A person who is filled with fear is dominated by fear, everything he does or says in that condition is coloured by *FEAR*. His voice, his actions, his decisions, everything is under the influence and domination of that emotion. The same is true of one who is 'filled' with jealousy, joy, or amazement.[1]

This is what the Bible means by being 'filled' or 'dominated' by the Holy Spirit. All of our lives are meant to be dominated by the all-pervasive influence of God's Holy Spirit. He will make hypocrisy and inconsistency no longer tolerable. Instead, every area of daily life will become more spiritually real and authentically human.

A.W. Tozer once affirmed that, 'We're all just about as filled with the Holy Spirit as we want to be.' And this can be true of Christian leaders also. Jay Adams said, 'Preachers today believe they do not need the filling of the Spirit, or have a distorted view of what that filling is, or do not think it is possible. It is time to re-examine the biblical teaching on the subject, then perhaps we would begin to experience power in our lives and in our preaching.' We need to listen carefully to Paul's directions here. Paul is telling us that with all the pressures on our lives and ministries, the answer is not to turn to drink, but to turn to the Holy Spirit. Four things are worthy of note in this connection:

1. This is a command in the imperative mood: 'Be filled.'
Therefore it is not an optional extra in the Christian life. Your car can still function properly without a multi-disc CD player, alloy wheels, sun-roof and under-seat electric heating, but you cannot live the Christian life effectively without being filled with the Spirit. Most of us heed Paul's command 'do not get drunk with wine', but in my experience it is not drunken Christians who give us the most problems, it is those who have not been filled with the Spirit. Think of the rivalry, slander, gossip, meanness, rebellion, 'do-your-own thing' individualism and lazy apathy that are ruining so many churches – and all because such people refuse to be filled with the Spirit.

2. This is a command in the passive voice
It carries the force of urging us to drop all resistance and argument against this experience, and instead, 'let yourself be filled with the Spirit'. To do this we should try

to avoid liquid analogies at this point, and think more in terms of letting a person come into your life and make a big difference to it. When we think of the contribution a person can make in this way, we can think of illustrations like an unmarried bachelor, a church building or a holiday-makers' hotel:

- If a bachelor finally lets down his defences and falls in love with his girlfriend, all his waking thoughts are occupied with her
- If a place of worship is open to new visitors and members it may well be filled with people before long, and full of life as a result
- If a hotel suddenly becomes popular in a certain holiday resort, it will soon be crowded with guests, so that every room is filled and all the facilities are fully functioning. The place comes alive!

So you can only obey a command to be filled with a Person by surrendering to that Person and allowing Him in, to change and influence your life. Yet many have treated God's Holy Spirit in a resentful, negligent and defiant way. No wonder they are struggling.

3. This is a command in the present tense
The force of this is 'keep on being filled' with the Spirit. Rid yourself of ideas of a sudden crisis like a dangerous fall or a car crash, after which you say, 'Phew! I'm glad that's over.' We are not meant to ever get over being filled with the Spirit. We don't use the language of 'I've got it' or 'I've had it'. We don't settle for the first and last time we were filled with the Spirit. Instead, we seek to be filled with His presence and power every day.

4. This is a command in the plural form: 'All of you be filled'
So rid yourself of elitist ideas or of some 'special forces' like the SAS in the Body of Christ! It's true that in the Old Testament era only select individuals or groups were Spirit-empowered, like priests, prophets, kings and judges. But since Christ's resurrection and ascension, this is now the 'era of the Holy Spirit' and this fullness is available to all believers everywhere. The Holy Spirit is an equal opportunity empowerer! Whole churches need to be filled with the Spirit, and every member of them, if they are to become effective for Christ.

This is why the great nineteenth-century Baptist preacher C.H. Spurgeon once said, 'We need to learn once again what it means to be baptised in the Holy Spirit.' And commenting on the elements of 'wind' and 'fire' on the Day of Pentecost, Charismatic theologian J. Rodman Williams wrote,

> To be filled with the Spirit is not so much to have something 'more' as it is to be in a new, wonderful and at times fearful situation of having the Spirit of God break into

the whole round of existence and pervade it all. As a result of this – yes, 'explosion' – what may be violent at the beginning, a crisis experience, can become the steady and driving power of a mighty dynamo – the Spirit of the Living God.[2]

THE DAY OF PENTECOST

This is why, in the account of the coming of the Spirit on the early Church on the Day of Pentecost in Acts 2, the Apostle Peter was at pains to launch all of his potential converts on the best possible start (vv. 38–41). We all need to experience a safe and thorough launch to our new life with Christ. We dare not inadvertently miss out anything that truly represents a vital component of apostolic teaching, and which is also considered to be absolutely necessary for a long, safe and effective pilgrimage through this world. And this is the point of this pregnant passage here:

> *Peter replied, 'Repent and be baptized, every one of you, in the name of Jesus Christ for the forgiveness of your sins. And you will receive the gift of the Holy Spirit. The promise is for you and your children and for all who are far off – for all whom the Lord our God will call.'*
>
> *With many other words he warned them; and he pleaded with them, 'Save yourselves from this corrupt generation.' Those who accepted his message were baptized, and about three thousand were added to their number that day.*
> (Acts 2:38–41)

What Peter directed and told his converts to do that day has often been called 'The Peter Package' of salvation. Every item in it has been the subject of argument, debate and controversy, and the devil has thrown a great deal of dust in the eyes of confused Christians concerning it. But lively churches are made up of lively Christians. When churches are so frequently full of carnality, factions, disunity, disaffection and dis-illusionment, before real progress proves possible, perhaps it would be wise to check out the apostolic foundations of that church again. And each of the remaining members needs to check their own personal foundations again. Did this church and its members get off to a good start? We dare not 'inadvertently' overlook anything that the Lord has told us would be essential and important for our mission together with Christ, however much others try to tell us it doesn't really matter.

And among the essential ingredients in a list that included repentance, faith, baptism in water and being added to the church, Peter promised his hearers, *'And you will receive the gift of the Holy Spirit'* (v. 38). This cannot be a reference to regeneration and the indwelling of the Spirit that accompanies God's sovereign activity in initiating new life within us by our experience of being 'born from above', for that is assumed. Regeneration is what leads and enables us to repent and believe in the first place. Peter is offering something more, as a subsequent experience to that – namely, 'Receiving the Holy Spirit'. This is distinct from the sovereign, passively encountered, involuntarily invasion by the Spirit, or His regenerating work that initiated our conversion. This is a subsequent, actively sought, voluntary reception of the Spirit that new converts are now qualified to receive when they have already come to Christ.

REGENERATION AND DYNAMIFICATION

Regeneration is our 'vivification' in Christ; receiving the Spirit is our 'electrification' or 'dynamification'. One is essential for making us alive to God; the other is essential for empowering that life for God. Dr D. Martyn Lloyd-Jones once affirmed, 'There is nothing, I am convinced, that so quenches the Spirit as the teaching which identifies the baptism of the Holy Spirit with regeneration or new birth.' So we need to be very clear on this issue. And if someone asks, 'Surely we got it all automatically when we believed?' Dr Lloyd-Jones replied, 'If you have got it all why are you so unlike the New Testament Christians? Got it all? Got it all at your conversion? Well, where is it I ask?'

All of the apostles taught the necessity of this 'filling', 'sealing' or 'baptism' of the Spirit. And speaking at Holy Trinity Brompton Anglican church, London, in 1996, New Testament scholar Gordon Fee said, 'For Paul, the Spirit was an experienced empowering reality. Paul would not have understood most historic Protestantism. I know that sounds unkind, but it is true. The reason he would not have understood it is because he would not have understood a Christian faith in which the experienced life of the Spirit was not the key to every dimension of that life.'

We can affirm from Peter's words here that baptism in water and baptism in the Spirit are meant to settle forever the question of the new convert's assurance of salvation. At our water baptism, we put on, as it were, the uniform of a soldier of Jesus Christ. We have defected governments, changed sides and joined up, and both men and devils now know it. It's now public knowledge to whom we belong and whom we intend to serve. But it is baptism in the Spirit that gives us the weapons to fight with, *'But you will receive power when the Holy Spirit comes upon you'* (Acts 1:8). The word *dunamis* – translated 'power' here – is not directly related to justification or to sudden sanctification, but to *dynamification*. You cannot be a Christian without the Holy Spirit *indwelling* you (Romans 8:9), but you can be a Christian without Him *empowering* you.

THE SPIRIT'S FIRE

Peter is inviting the crowds who heard him that day to receive immediately what he and his friends had waited ten days to receive that very morning – the power of the Holy Spirit. John the Baptist had said of Christ, *'He will baptize you with the Holy Spirit and with fire'* (Matthew 3:11). That is what happened to the 120 on the Day of Pentecost.

Now in the programme of the historical outworking of God's work of redemption, at Pentecost the privilege of receiving the Spirit in fullness became the birthright of every believer. There is no question what Peter's hearers would have understood by this, for they were seeing it unfold before their very eyes among 120 joyous, bold and excited believers in the risen Christ.

The reference to fire was not just metaphorical but literal that day, as tongues of fire arced and settled on the heads of each of them in a visible sign as the Spirit came upon them. The great need for the *entire* church – ministers, deacons, members, Sunday-School teachers, youth leaders, evangelists, missionaries, preachers and prophets – is for the fire to fall! It is not just *a* need for the church today, it is surely *the* need. It marks us out from both mad fanatics on the one hand, and cold formalists on the other. It is more than fervour for a temporary fad that changes from one day to the next. It is not mere human enthusiasm or excitement that varies according to our emotions and moods. No, this is God on a man or a woman, setting them on fire. And this is vital for several reasons:

1. Fire burns

It is a threat to anything contrary to its own nature. It has the power to burn up decay, rottenness, darkness and cold. You've probably had the experience of staring into the window of an electricity showroom and noticing the electric coal-effect fires. One man, new to the city, was fascinated with the technology and thought the fire effect was so convincing that he was sure it was real. He wondered why the heat didn't crack the shop window. The sales manager allowed him to see it close up. There was no heat but a very convincing flame – fire with no heat. The manager said, 'I'm not surprised you were fooled. Many others have been too. Actually, this "heater" gives out no heat at all. It is what we call a *"cheerer-upper"*. It's for people with central heating who want to see what appears to be a fire, but with no cost and no effort. As it simply glows with the flick of a switch, it's just something they can see alight even on a warm afternoon or evening as they sit and relax. It cheers them up. They don't want a real fire; they just want something that looks like one.'

Many Christians are like that. They want the appearance of fire, the cosy pleasure, the make-believe and the warm glow, but without the cost and without ever having to leave the room. They won't surrender to anything that will really burn. It's just a *cheerer-upper*. But God wants us to have the real thing.

2. Fire spreads

Given the freedom, fire will lay hold of everything in reach that is combustible, and set it ablaze. The Spirit's fire is the source of all revival. It burns up and burns out everything God wants changed or removed. The Spirit will help us all recover our nerve. Major W.F. Batt once spoke of what he called 'filleted Christians' – they have no back-bone! They can neither stand up for what they believe in nor swim against the tide of popular opinion. They are evan-jellyfish. We all need to recover our nerve again.

3. Fire lights

It spreads a luminance and makes a radiant glow. It once completely enveloped a common dried-up bush in the desert without consuming it, and drew Moses aside in that wilderness, in order to encounter God and his earthly destiny. It subsequently so transformed him that Moses had the boldness and power to confront and expose the darkness and powerlessness of all the Egyptian demon gods, and then light the way to hope and deliverance for three million Hebrew slaves at the Exodus.

4. Fire empowers

When it burns inside the engine of a truck, a car, or a railway locomotive engine it releases such force and driving power that it throbs, snorts and moves the immoveable, speeding and spreading an influence over great distances at a fantastic pace. Similarly, God's Spirit can make the gospel work and mobilise static and inert people into action.

We all need this fire! This is the great need of the Church today – the energising flame of God's Holy Spirit. The two indisputable indicators of the Spirit's power in someone's life are a *cry* (Romans 8:15–16) and a *confession* (1 Corinthians 12:3) – 'Abba, Father' and 'Jesus is Lord'. The one deepens and assures our relationship with God the Father, the other intensifies and confirms our relationship with God the Son. The one gives us confidence with God; the other emboldens us before men. The first makes us liberated worshippers of God; the other makes us powerful witnesses for Christ to the world. So power for worship and boldness for witness are the essentials of the Spirit's work within us. Along with these, therefore, comes access to all the gifts or manifestations of the Spirit (spoken of in Romans 12; 1 Corinthians 12; Ephesians 4; 1 Peter 4, etc.), designed to help us complete the Son's mission through His Church. These are all the tools necessary to get the job done.

The *baptism of the Spirit* imparts to us the spiritual weaponry necessary to become Christ's co-belligerents in spiritual warfare, and to reinforce and extend Satan's defeat and the victory already won for us at the cross of Calvary. No wonder the devil wants God's people to remain ignorant or totally confused about these matters. And no wonder the Church in so many places has for so long hung on like grim death for mere survival with little or no hope of success, and without the remotest expectation of advance and victory. The baptism in Spirit changes all that!

The baptism of the Spirit is a movement of the Spirit both within us and upon us. It is, as we have seen, both a 'baptism' and a 'filling'. It is a movement of God's Spirit from the outside in, so that He descends upon us and penetrates our very life. It is a movement of God's Spirit from the inside out, so that He pervades every part of our redeemed humanity and personality. This is both a deluge from above, and a flooding from within. Either way, you are then said to be 'filled with the Spirit' (Acts 2:4; Ephesians 5:18), and the overflow looks for the nearest exit from us – usually our mouths – in praise, prayer and proclamation!

RECEIVING THE HOLY SPIRIT

The risen Christ is Himself completely devoid of fear, and He wants you to be also. He has unlimited authority over the powers of darkness and wants to impart some of that authority to you. He wants to give you a mouth that none of your adversaries can successfully resist. The way He does this is by baptising us in His Spirit. And this power is freely available to all believers until the end of history. It has never, and could never be withdrawn, until the task is complete. It's been ignored, feared and neglected, yes, but it still remains available to us until Jesus returns.

> *For in him you have been enriched in every way – in all your speaking and in all your knowledge because our testimony about Christ was confirmed in you. Therefore you do not lack any spiritual gift as you eagerly wait for our Lord Jesus Christ to be revealed.*
> (1 Corinthians 1:5–7)

C.H. Spurgeon once said, 'Only out of a *full* church shall the world receive salvation, never out of an empty one. The first thing we want as a church is to be filled with the Holy Ghost.'

So how do we participate in His energising power? How do we receive the Spirit? Acts 2 gives us all the clues we need. It is clear here that Peter was offering the gift of the Spirit to people who wanted to be rightly orientated towards God. You can't hold on to sin *and* take hold of the fullness of the Holy Spirit at the same time!

1. Confess any known sin

This is not a plea for perfectionism, simply a summons to 'get real' and to 'come clean'. God gives the Spirit to the repentant. Peter said later, '*We are witnesses of these things, and so also is the Holy Spirit whom God has given to those who obey him*' (Acts 5:32), i.e. to those who are determined to please God, without excuses or qualification, for the rest of their lives. We are not to become morbidly introspective here, but rather to respond to what the Word shows us about ourselves, so that we will not grieve the Holy Spirit by deliberately indulging in some vice or unholy activity and pretending it is unimportant or irrelevant. Are there any well-defined wrongs and clear offences to God that I am being convicted of or made conscious of by the Spirit? For example, is there any history of involvement with the occult, sexual immorality, covetousness, envy, broken relationships, or carnal ambition? Then repent of them and let them go from your life.

2. *Yield yourself to God*

Saving faith includes submission to the Lordship of Christ. You don't want to quench the Spirit, so settle this matter now by sincerely telling Him, 'I will do whatever you tell me. I will yield to Your revealed will for my life at every stage, and act on the directions and promptings of the Spirit as He fills me.' You simply decide that you are not going to 'resist' or 'say no' to God again. You want to 'walk in the Spirit' from now on and no longer gratify the desires of the flesh (Galatians 5:16) So, are you willing to *be* whatever God wants, willing to *go* wherever God sends, and willing to *do* whatever God commands? Then 'be filled'!

3. *Come to Christ Himself, the Source of the Spirit*

In water baptism, our total immersion signifies our spiritual union with Christ, and here the Spirit is the Baptizer and the medium into which we are baptised is not only water, but Christ Himself (1 Corinthians 12:13; Romans 6:3). But with baptism in the Spirit, the Baptizer is Christ Himself and the medium into which we are baptised is the Holy Spirit (Matthew 3:11; Acts 1:8). So if you want to be baptised in the Spirit don't come primarily to a minister or a friend, or to a sacred building or ceremony. Instead, come to Christ. Sometimes, as for example on several occasions in Acts, someone may lay hands on you to receive the Spirit (e.g. Acts 9:17; 19:6), but it is always Christ Himself who gives us His Spirit; the human agent is just one of Christ's means to bless us.

4. *'Ask for' and 'drink of' His Spirit*

Jesus said, '*If anyone is thirsty, let him come unto me and drink*' (John 7:37). We only ever ask for what we really want. We only drink that which we know we need and are convinced will really do us good and quench our thirst. But it is a simple thing to 'ask' and 'drink', and both are done by faith in God's promises to His children:

> '*If you then, though you are evil, know how to give good gifts to your children,*
> *how much more will your Father in heaven give the Holy Spirit to those who*
> *ask him!*'
> (Luke 11:13)

Christ went on to add,

> '*So I say to you: Ask and it will be given to you; seek and you will find; knock and*
> *the door will be opened to you. For everyone who asks receives; he who seeks finds;*
> *and to him who knocks, the door will be opened. Which of you fathers, if your son*
> *asks for a fish, will give him a snake instead? Or if he asks for an egg, will give him*
> *a scorpion? Or for bread, will give him a stone?*'
> (Luke 11:9–11)

Three great incentives then:

1. *The gift of the Spirit is only for God's 'children'.* You have to be a Christian to receive the Spirit – it is for God's children only. If you're His child, then you qualify.
2. *When we think of receiving the Spirit, we often think we're at risk and in terms of imminent danger* – scorpions, snakes and stones. But Christ assures us that God will not give us something *other* than what we ask for, nor something *less* than what we want. And certainly not something that could *harm or kill us*. He cannot frighten, hurt or disappoint His children. Instead He gives an 'egg', a 'fish' and 'bread', i.e. everything we need for our spiritual health, and gifts and operations that are all only ever good for us and for others too. So if you believe, you will receive.
3. *This is not 'A' level Christianity; it is our basic need* – the children's bread! Christ assures us that we cannot live without this. This is the beginning. You have not completely arrived when you receive the Spirit. You have just begun in the way Christ intended. It is not the terminus; it is the gateway to more, so much more.

So 'ask and you will receive!'

NOTES

1. *Preaching to the Heart* (Timeless Texts, 2004), p. 10.
2. *Renewal Theology* (Zondervan, 1996).

Appendix 2

EPHESIANS 4 MINISTRIES AND CHURCH UNITY

Greg Haslam

One of the remarkable features of the Preach the Word! conference was the number and diversity of delegates in attendance. They represented nearly every sector of the Church in the UK, with its diverse denominational profile and spread of creeds and convictions. In turn, each of the speakers modelled diverse church backgrounds and various ministries and this was reflected in the many allusions to the ministry gifts listed in Ephesians 4:1–11 in their papers. It may be helpful to offer some further biblical reflection upon how such ministries can foster spiritual formation and church unity in the Body of Christ today.

Spiritual formation is nothing more nor less than the reversal of the Fall and the process that leads to the restoration of the ruined image of God in man. God is in the business of re-creating and renewing people's lives, imparting saving knowledge to them and, over time, dramatically transforming their thinking, character and lifestyle. We are all interdependent upon others for the successful outcome of this process. God uses the direct power of His own Word and Spirit to effect these changes, but He rarely bypasses human agency in this transformation, for Christian leaders and mentors play a vital role also. Jesus said,

> *'A student is not above his teacher, but everyone who is fully trained will be like his teacher.'*
> (Luke 6:40)

We eventually become like our mentors in every way. This is a process that involves information, impartation and imitation, i.e. personal growth in knowledge, skills and character.

I want to suggest that as we tackle this key question of assisting God's people grow towards unity and maturity, and equipping them to do the works He has ordained in advance for them to do, then the five-fold ministries of Ephesians 4 are crucial. Indeed, I want to suggest that one of the greatest single factors that could unite and accelerate the maturity of the Church today would be the emergence, influence and spiritual authority of many such teams, in which the diverse gifts of apostles, prophets, evangelists, pastors and teachers genuinely work together towards the goal of completing the Body of Christ on earth as an effective agent of God in the planned *'restoration of all things'* (Acts 3:21 NKJV). These five-fold ministries are Christ's gifts to His entire Church throughout the 'last days' until the *parousia*; they are not just the monopoly of one sector of that Church, or merely for one temporary period of time – the first century AD for example.

THE CONTEXT OF CHRISTIAN UNITY

Any detailed discussion of the definition, calling and functioning of the ministries delineated in Ephesians 4:11–16 profitably begins with the discussion of the context in which these ministries are listed. A fresh consideration of the flow of these verses will help us to see that the ministries of Ephesians 4 are Christ's ascension gifts to the universal Church throughout the inter-adventual period. They therefore function as Christ's human instruments or 'hands' to help govern, guide, gather, guard and ground His people in the truth, and so foster their growth in ministry (v. 12), unity (v. 13a), maturity (v. 13b), stability (v. 14) and Kingdom activity (vv. 15–16). But to understand this fully we must look at these 'Ephesians 4 ministries' in context, allowing the whole of the Apostle Paul's letter to the Ephesians to shape our understanding of how God intends these ministries to function effectively. Most importantly, we should note Paul's understanding of Christian unity, the theme uppermost in the apostle's mind following his exploration of God's sovereign grace and purpose in chapters 1–3, for this governs his thinking about their overall function. Sin has fragmented and disintegrated God's cosmos. The gospel re-orders and re-integrates it, and the prototype model of the gospel's success is to be seen in the Church. This is the governing idea of this epistle.

But first, we must clarify terms. The unity Paul speaks of in this letter is not organisational or institutional, it is *organic*. It is a *'unity of the Spirit'* (v. 3). This is not 'union' – as someone once remarked about merely human organised 'unity', 'Putting two coffins side by side will not produce a resurrection.' Nor is it 'uniformity', the cloned and often politicised 'unity' that marks some expressions of modern ecumenism – a mass of icebergs assembled into one huge continent of ice – just as cold, and just as dead. Instead, unity is really the 'unanimity' or heart agreement and common witness, that God alone can achieve by His Spirit (Romans 15:5–7). This requires a mentoring process, in order to facilitate this transformation, and Paul is modelling that process even as he writes. He is discipling his readers in attitudinal change, fresh understanding and action.

EPHESIANS 4 MINISTRIES AND NEW CHARACTER (VV. 2–3)

Paul knows that there are genuine believers to whom we feel both *drawn* and *distant* at the same time. So we're first summoned to desire and work hard for unity, knowing it will not be easily achieved; *'Make every effort...,'* he says (v. 3). Paul calls us to cultivate four attitudinal changes to make this possible (vv. 2–3).

1. *Instead of pride let there be humility* (v. 2a)
An air of superiority over doctrinal purity (Reformed evangelicals), historic ancestry ('Catholic' groupings), spiritual vitality (Charismatics and Pentecostals) or 'anointed' leadership authority ('Restoration' streams) is *pride*; it results in a refusal to network with those we consider 'inferior'. Humility helps us acknowledge our deficiencies and to be genuinely grateful for the complementary strengths of others within the Church, e.g. their theological legacy, ethical purity, social action, faith expectancy or church-planting success.

2. *Instead of harshness let there be gentleness* (v. 2b)
Harshness springs from either a defensive 'fortress' mentality or the selfish ambition to build 'our own little empire'. This must give way to a restraint and self-control that believes and speaks well of fellow-Christians.

3. *Instead of frustration let there be patience* (v. 2c)
Other Christians may intensely irritate us sometimes. They're often slow to believe what we clearly see, and we become impatient. The Elizabethan Puritans had a slogan 'Reformation without tarrying for anybody', but we have to tarry! Christ will bring the whole fragmented Body into His end-time purposes, so that as with Israel at the Exodus, *'not a hoof shall be left behind'* (Exodus 10:26). God hasn't finished with us yet. We can afford to be patient as stragglers catch up with what others have seen well in advance of them.

4. *Instead of contempt let there be love* (v. 2d)
Love is *the* identifying mark of the true Church of Christ (John 13:34–35). It is the Spirit's primary work (1 Corinthians 13).

Ecclesiastical exclusiveness from others is ultimately self-defeating. We need each other. A passion for unity necessarily entails a larger-heartedness that gives expression to the familial love that the Father has implanted in all of our hearts by His Spirit.

EPHESIANS 4 MINISTRIES AND NEW UNDERSTANDING (VV. 4–6)

The prophet complained, *'my people are destroyed from lack of knowledge'* (Hosea 4:6). And so Paul also models the art of giving cognitive instruction as he develops his readers' knowledge and understanding, in order to persuade and motivate them to pursue unity. Though differences exist between believers, there is also a profound common-ground that is more fundamental than the issues that divide us. The great essentials that Paul lists here (vv. 4–6) express the complete seven-fold foundation for unity. All Christians share these in common. That is why each component is prefaced by the number 'one' – each undergirds our *unity*.

- *'One body'* – The whole Church is congenitally joined together like a human body. Geographical, cultural and even minor doctrinal differences cannot affect this reality. So, 'what God has joined together, let no man put asunder'!
- *'One Spirit'* – Every believer has experienced the same spiritual power, since we're all 'born from above' (cf. John 3:2–7) and possessors of Christ's Spirit (Romans 8:9), with access to the same supply of more, and entitled to 'drink of one Spirit' (1 Corinthians 12:13). If the Holy Spirit seals someone as His own (Ephesians 1:13), then we're obliged to own them as ours also.

And Paul's list goes on:

- *'One hope'* – we will all unite at the same eschatological future destiny, so why not start practising now!
- *'One Lord'* – a fact that explains the serendipity we feel when we encounter other genuine believers. The Christ in me will not quarrel with the Christ in you.
- *'One faith'* – our common saving faith in God's saving Son is the focus of profound union for us all by His powerful grace.
- *'One baptism'* – dramatically depicting our death to sin and resurrection to unfragmented new creation in Christ.
- *'One God and Father'* – initiated and experienced by regeneration and adoption, which makes us all siblings in the same family of God whether we like it or not!

Doctrine matters. Once we know these things we cannot un-know them. Once we have seen this, we cannot turn a blind eye to its implications. Louis Berkhof summarises the thrust of this passage:

> The Reformers argued that the body (referring to the invisible church) was controlled by one head, Jesus Christ, animated by one Spirit, the Spirit of Christ. This unity meant that all those who belong to the church share in the same faith, are cemented together by the common bond of love, and have the same glorious outlook upon the future.[1]

There are no valid rivals to these seven essential components of true unity. Indeed, it is the false belief that there are rival alternatives that has fragmented mankind in the first place, and continues to do so.

In short, Christian people, no matter how diverse in ethnicity, social status, speech, style, dress, culture or age, all share a unity in Christ that is more fundamental than any lesser issues which may attempt to divide them. The Ephesians 4 ministries help us to *grasp and know* this. Facts are facts, and facts are stubborn things.

EPHESIANS 4 MINISTRIES AND NEW SKILLS (vv. 7–13)

In the light of this, it is obvious that the true unity of the Church is as indestructible as the Godhead itself. We can no more split the Church than we can split the Trinity. Yet the reality remains that our historic and existential situation appears very different. There are 30,000 Christian denominations worldwide and the fragmentation continues. There are widespread manifestations of selfish ambition, protectionism, exclusivism, rivalry, mutual recrimination, ignorance, fear and strife.

The Apostle therefore adds to his exhortation to grasp the right attitude and understanding about unity, the practical and existential processes by which unity is attained. He underscores the crucial role that the ministry gifts of the Ascended Lord play in this. They each possess the vital skills necessary to promote and advance true interdependence and unity. Their very diversity underlines the fact that in Paul's thought, unity does not equal uniformity. The Church will ultimately display a diversity-in-unity like that of the Trinity itself, reflective of the kaleidoscopic grace of God (1 Peter 4:10), and this involves the dynamic co-operation of three agencies in the perfecting and maturing process leading to one great and glorious outcome:

1. The Ascended Lord
2. The anointed ministry gifts of the Ascended Christ
3. Issuing in the every-member ministry of the whole Body of Christ. And the final outcome?
4. An end-time glorious Church on earth.

1. The Ascended Lord – the Donor of ministry (vv. 7–11)

As authoritative ruler at the right hand of God, it is Christ who calls, commissions and equips His followers. He alone is *the* Apostle (Hebrews 3:1), Prophet (Luke 24:19; John 4:19), Evangelist (Mark 1:15), Pastor (John 10:14) and Teacher (Matthew 7:28; John 13:13). Yet in these anointed and appointed ministries also, we encounter the same powerful expressions of Christ's own words, works and wonders as He deploys them to extend His Kingdom and build His Church. Their appearance challenges both existing leaders and whole churches to recognise and receive them as Christ's ascension gifts to help advance our progress towards His eschatological goals. This is why Christ sends them.

2. The anointed ministry gifts of the Ascended Christ – existing in a wide diversity (v. 11)

Please note the time reference in verse 13, '*until...*'. This indicates Christ's continuous donation of them to His Church until the climax of history, and not their cessation at a much earlier time, as some have maintained was the case. These goals have not been attained yet, so the means must still be available. Christ's own ministry skills are in effect divided among the individuals listed. Perhaps the most controversial are the apostles and prophets.

▪ *Apostles*

The word 'apostle' (from the noun *apostolos*, 'sent one', and its related verb *apostello*, 'to send') means one who is sent to represent and exercise authority on behalf of another, carrying a kind of ambassadorial status for a superior who cannot personally be present. It carries different senses in different contexts in the New Testament. The early Church fully understood that certain individuals were commissioned by Christ to spread the gospel and found healthy churches, in order to ensure its preservation and expansion in a geographical area. There are five kinds of apostle in the New Testament:

(a) *Jesus the Chief Apostle* – there is no one like Him ('*the Apostle and High Priest of our confession*' [Hebrews 3:1 NKJV]). All other ministries only share a small measure of His gifting and ability, by the Spirit.

(b) *the foundational twelve apostles of the Lamb* (Revelation 21:14) – these accompanied Christ for three years during His earthly ministry and became eye-witnesses of His resurrection, and in some cases wrote Scripture. There are none like them today (Acts 1:22; Revelation 21:14). Interestingly, Matthias joined this select company as a replacement for Judas Iscariot (Acts 1:25).

(c) *Paul, the thirteenth apostle* – the '*last of all ... born out of due time*' (1 Corinthians 15:8 NKJV). Yet he shared equal authority with the Twelve (1 Corinthians 15:9; Galatians 1:15–17; 2:9; Ephesians 3:8), and also wrote inspired Scripture as the definitive standard of teaching for the Church. No apostle today has this stature or function. Yet Paul also acted as a 'bridge' apostle and model for later individuals who became 'apostolic' missionary church planters, since he was distinctly called by the Ascended Lord to model this task among the Gentiles, and for all time (Galatians 2:7–9; 2 Timothy 2:2).

(d) *pioneer church planters* – who, like Paul, make new converts, plant churches, lay foundations of life and doctrine, decide matters of controversy or conduct, and generally set things in order (see Paul's procedure throughout 1 Corinthians 11, for example, in dealing with such matters as they arose at Corinth. And note also 1 Corinthians 3:10; Acts 15:1, 2, 23; 2 Thessalonians 3:6–8; Titus 1:5, etc.). Paul did this personally of course, but he also taught others to do the same, and so he not only belatedly completed the small circle of 'apostles of the resurrected Lord' as eye-witnesses of His resurrection, he also launched a new series of 'apostles of the *ascended* Christ', many of whom are named in the New Testament and who were not part of the Twelve. These often travelled together, usually in teams, and included individuals like Barnabas, Silas, Timothy, Titus, James the Lord's brother, and possibly Junias and Andronicus (Romans 16:7). Lastly,

(e) *any Christian sent anywhere to do anything, as an envoy of the church* – e.g. Epaphroditus who was 'sent' to represent the Philippians as Paul's servant in Rome (Philippians 2:25). Many are sent on special errands like this by churches today, e.g. linguists, school teachers and medical 'missionaries'. The context alone determines the meaning and use of the term 'apostle'.

Prophets

The prophet is also a word-based ministry, one that builds people's hopes up, and brings revelation, insight, exhortation and transcendent guidance to the church that is not available by ordinary, natural means. Agabus, Judas and Silas are fine examples (Acts 11:27–28; 21:10–11). The Holy Spirit imparts verbal and visual information to their spirits in words, warnings, visions, dreams, impressions and symbolic actions that stir hope and movement in God's people. The Apostle Paul instructs us on how to covet, practise and pastor this ministry and also to esteem their utterances if genuine and properly tested by Scripture. Prophetic words stand under the authority of scriptural revelation not over it, and should only be honoured if truly beneficial (1 Corinthians 14:3, 37–38; 1 Thessalonians 5:19–22). Walter Brueggemann writes, 'The task of prophetic ministry is to nurture, nourish and evoke a consciousness and perception alternative to the consciousness and perception of the dominant culture around us.'[2]

And Hans Küng believes, 'A Church in which prophets have to keep silent declines and becomes a spiritless organisation.' It's good for churches to ask, *'Is there a prophet in the house?'* Mostly, the Church has become a non-prophet organisation!

Evangelists

Evangelists spearhead the church's outreach into the unbelieving community, and equip others to do the same. They broadcast the evangel and persuade others to embrace faith in Christ, by proclamation and demonstration of His Kingdom power in both words and deeds. We should expect social change and signs and wonders to accompany their ministry (Mark 16:15–20; Acts 8:4–8). And finally,

■ Pastors and Teachers

It is unclear whether Paul refers to one or two distinct ministries here. Both have special abilities to influence people's lives by their counsel, care and teaching of the Word of God in the power of the Spirit, privately and in public. They feed, guide, mature, protect and lead new converts by their ability to patiently expound and wisely apply Scripture, as they instruct, admonish, discipline and train whole churches to become healthy and influential.

We can summarise the contribution of this wide range of word-ministries delineated here, in this way: *apostles govern, prophets guide, evangelists gather, pastors guard and teachers ground* the Church in the whole of God's revealed Truth. In Acts, all five ministries travelled and worked together in flexible *mix 'n' match* teams, launching churches and helping develop them also (Acts 13:1–2; 15:22–34; 16:1–10; 16:40–17:1; 18:5, 27, etc.). Since this is the model for all time, it is entirely appropriate that we should look towards the formation of varied 'apostolic teams' of gifted individuals operating among denominations worldwide today. We should honour them whenever and wherever they appear. We ignore them to our loss or even peril.

The greatest single factor that could unite and accelerate the maturity of the Church today, would be to recognise and benefit from the influence and spiritual authority of these trans-local ministries. God authorises and empowers them to disciple and equip others, giving them both the necessary permission and power to command change in people's beliefs and behaviour in line with the will of God. Without their influence people's lives will remain deficient, endangered and under-developed.

Their function is clearly not to promote themselves or even to form an organisation or 'ministry' centred on one individual alone. It is to take their place within flexible networks or teams of similarly gifted servants, for much higher ends. The Bible says, *'Two are better than one'* (Ecclesiastes 4:9), and Jesus sent the first apostles out 'two by two', and later did the same with the Seventy-two (Luke 9:1–6; 10:1ff.). Paul rarely chose to work alone, and travelled with many individuals like Barnabas, Mark, Silas, Timothy, Luke, Priscilla and Aquila and scores of others. *In the New Testament, 'leadership' is clearly a collective noun.*

Individualism, independence and isolation are, therefore, quick routes to error or imbalance in belief and behaviour. *They also hamper the discipling of the church.* Without this diversity of mentoring influence, the full development of the Body is impaired. Teachers functioning alone tend to produce passive lovers of doctrine; lone-ranger evangelists may gather large numbers of spiritual babies who forever remain immature. Lone prophets may only fire up a handful of fanatical and visionary enthusiasts, whilst isolated pastors may simply cultivate only a flock of well-taught but inward-looking, bloated and smugly contented sheep! Exposure to the diversity of Christ's word-ministries, however, brings balance and fresh perspectives to individuals and whole congregations.

3. Issuing in the every-member ministry of the whole Body of Christ (vv. 12–13)

Their complementary giftings ensure that Jesus, in the totality of His five-fold ministry, is free to address His life-changing word to the totality of His Body upon earth. No one person possesses all that is necessary to bring the Church to maturity. No single stream or team does either. To ignore or silence such ministries is to defraud the Church of some aspect of Christ's ministry to her. Vital emphases will be excluded. Welcomed, these dynamic ministries will advance us toward God-ordained goals. They are *'to prepare God's people for works of service'* (v. 12a), as Christians labour in dual roles, both in the Church and also for the benefit of our needy world – for there is nothing 'secular' except sin!

The effects of exposure to these five-fold ministries will be that apostles will make us more 'apostolic' and mission-minded; prophets impart ability to prophesy and become future-oriented and filled with hopeful optimism; evangelists not only win the lost themselves, they also stir and train us to become more evangelistic and skilled in that task ourselves; pastors cause us to become caring and familial in our community life together – the 'wow' factor that outsiders quickly notice; and teachers awaken our appetite for truth, deepening our faith theologically so that we are characterised by an informed Biblicism and doctrinal accuracy. These effects are wonderful and highly desirable – especially at this present time of fragmentation, immaturity and weakness in much of the Church.

4. The result – an end-time glorious Church! (vv. 13–16)

We are to become nothing less than the vanguard display of God's ultimate plan for the whole cosmos! As trans-local ministries ignore denominational boundaries and cross-fertilise diverse congregations, they will help break up the lonely, isolated and, in some cases, fiercely independent ethos of many Christian groups. It is because such ministries have hitherto been comparatively scarce, barely recognised, and frequently unwelcome, that the Church has remained ill-taught, ill-equipped, numerically small, immature and vulnerable to deception. It is futile to long and pray for unity and expanding mission whilst at the same time disparaging the instruments God uses to effect this.

Ephesians tells us that we are headed towards four divinely appointed ends within the purposes of God:

(a) Unity: in the Faith and in the knowledge of the Son of God (v. 13a)

That is, unanimity and commitment to the essentials of the Apostolic Faith revealed in the Bible (Romans 15:5–7).

(b) Maturity: attaining to the whole measure of the fullness of Christ (vv. 13b, 15)

Infancy is a condition of vulnerability, waywardness and untapped, under-developed potential. To grow up is to move towards a full expression of all that Jesus has in mind for us by reason of our union with Him. On earth He had power to preach with authority, heal and deliver with dramatic effects, bring radical groups and new converts together in community, and then launch them to speak prophetically to the 'principalities and powers' of His day. A mature Church will do the same today.

(c) Stability: no longer easily unsettled by false teaching (vv. 14–15)

Infancy is a time when convictions are held lightly and there is vulnerability to deception. Children are fooled by trickery and charm, ostentation and show. The present-day kindergarten of 'baby' Christians still learning their ABCs, could yield to a vast company of biblically well-informed men and women who know what they believe, and are able to defend it.

(d) Ministry: the whole Body functioning together as each part does its work (v. 16)

Isolated and maverick ministry will give way to a fresh understanding of our interdependence upon one another. At present the Body of Christ is not healthy. Muscles are paralysed, limbs hang useless and vital organs malfunction. In some quarters we appear to be in critical condition. But the Church can indeed fully function again. When will this happen?

The answer depends to a large extent upon our individual and corporate response to the overall challenges presented above. What might this mean?

- Are you willing to pay any price, as Paul himself was, to see the goal of Christian unity come to closer realisation through your own influence and personal sacrifice?
- Do you need to repent of any past or present pride, harshness, impatience and contempt displayed towards other members of the Body of Christ?
- Will you resolve to honour the impact and witness of *every* genuine Christian congregation and effective leader you know, and be willing to demolish some of the barriers to fellowship with them?
- Will you permit your own life and ministry to be mentored by good relationships with any genuine apostolic, prophetic, evangelistic, pastoral and teaching ministries Christ sends you?
- In effective partnership with others, will you make it your goal to use whatever gifts Christ has given you to equip Christians for their works of service, wherever God has called them?

Until such ministries are again heard and seen in action among us, we shall remain somewhat handicapped and stunted indefinitely, and never reach our full potential. God help us if that should prove to be the case.

Notes

1. Louis Berkhof, *Systematic Theology* (Banner of Truth Trust), p. 577.
2. Walter Brueggemann, *The Prophetic Imagination* (Fortress Press, 1978), p. 13.

Recommended reading

Conner, Kevin J. *The Church in the New Testament* (Bible Temple Publishing, 1982).

Conner, Mark. *Transforming Your Church* (Sovereign World, 2000).

Eaton, Michael. *How to Enjoy God's Worldwide Church* (Sovereign World, 1995).

Greenslade, Philip. *Leadership – Reflections on Biblical Leadership Today* (CWR, 2002).

Virgo, Terry. *A People Prepared* (Kingsway, 1996).

————— *Does the Future Have a Church?* (Kingsway, 2003).

Wagner, C. Peter. *Churchquake* (Regal, 1999).